TO KNOW OUR MANY SELVES

Dirk Hoerder

TO KNOW OUR MANY SELVES

{ FROM THE STUDY OF CANADA TO CANADIAN STUDIES }

AU PRESS
Athabasca University

© **2010 DIRK HOERDER**

Published by AU Press, Athabasca University
1200, 10011 – 109 Street
Edmonton, AB T5J 3S8

Library and Archives Canada Cataloguing in Publication

Hoerder, Dirk
    To know our many selves : from the study of Canada
to Canadian studies / Dirk Hoerder.

Originally published in: Beiträge zur Kanadistik, Vol. 13, by
    Wissner-Verlag, Augsburg, 2005.

Includes bibliographical references and index.
Also available in electronic format (ISBN 978-1-897425-73-2).
ISBN 978-1-897425-72-5

1. Canada--Civilization.
2. National characteristics, Canadian.
3. Canada--Study and teaching.
I. Title. II.°Title:°Beiträgezur Kanadistik.

FC95.H6413 2010   306.0971   C2010-902356-0

Cover and book design by Sergio Serrano.
Printed and bound in Canada by Marquis Book Printing.

This book was originally published in 2005 as Volume 13 of *"Beiträge zur Kanadistik. Schriftenreihe der Gesellschaft für Kanada-Studien [in deutschsprachigen Ländern]"* by Wißner-Verlag, Augsburg. Permission of the publisher for this revised edition is gratefully acknowledged.

Changes to the AU Press edition comprise a few minor additions and edits, and changes per Canadian and North American publishing conventions in spelling, punctuation, and editorial style. Please see the Bibliographic Notes for some further explanations.

CONTENTS

Bibliographic Notes — x
Preface — xiii
Acknowledgements — xvii

INTRODUCTION — 1

    1. TRADITIONS AND PRACTICES: FROM COLONIAL AND
    AREA TO CULTURAL OR SOCIETAL STUDIES — 6

        · Area Studies: Its long history as Colonial and Country Studies — 9
        · From the social psychology of lesser others to the quest for
         self-knowledge — 15

**I. FRAMING RESEARCH ON CANADA: BURDENS AND
ACHIEVEMENTS OF THE PAST** — 20

    2. THE ATLANTIC WORLD: CREATING SOCIETIES IN IMPERIAL
    HINTERLANDS — 21

        · "Discovery" and the production of knowledge — 21
        · Imperial interests and intellectual changes in the
         hegemonic Atlantic World — 28
        · Canadian specifics: Regions, boundaries, incomplete
         nation-state — 32

    3. CANADA'S PEOPLES: INCLUSIONS & EXCLUSIONS — 37

        · First Peoples: Teachers, equals, subalterns — 38
        · Second Peoples: Interactions, solitudes, hegemonic pieces
         of the mosaic — 43
        · Early African and Asian Canadians: Presences and exclusions — 52
        · Immigrant Ethnics of European backgrounds: Subalterns
         creating societies — 56
        · Discourses about belonging and sentiments of citizenship — 59
        · Creating social spaces in everyday lives — 62

4. SELF-CONSTRUCTIONS: FROM REGIONAL
CONSCIOUSNESSES TO NATIONAL BILLBOARDS — 65

· Regional specifics, generic folklorization, few First Peoples — 65
· Canada's West: New settlers, few national symbols, the rise of a
world of consumption — 71
· Canada's East: Multiple literatures and hierarchies after
Confederation — 77
· Billboards of self-advertising: Canadian firsters, English Canada's
British imperialists, French Canada's advocates of race — 83
· The billboards' small print — 90

II. FROM PRIVILEGED DISCOURSES TO RESEARCH ON SOCIAL SPACES — 93

5. PRIVILEGED DISCOURSES UP TO 1920: SCHOLARSHIP IN
THE MAKING — 94

· Religion as guide for research: The establishment of universities
up to the 1920s — 94
· Folklorists to ethnologists: Grave-robbing, appropriating,
researching — 99
· Historians' promotional, compilatory, nostalgic, and
constitutional narratives — 104
· Hegemonic scholarship and subalterns' lesser discourses — 114
· Outside perspectives: Observers' interpretations of Canada — 118

6. SUBSTANTIAL RESEARCH: THE SOCIAL SPACES
OF THE GEOLOGICAL SURVEY OF CANADA — 121

· The making of maps: Physical, social, and mental — 121
· Exploring the territorial and economic basis for
nation-building — 124
· The human implications of surveying a territory — 129

7. LEARNING AND SOCIETY: SOCIAL RESPONSIBILITY,
EDUCATIONAL INSTITUTIONS, ELITE FORMATION — 132

· An informed society: Nineteenth-century movements for
self-instruction — 132
· Schools: Dissemination of whose identity-providing
narratives? — 136
· Applied Scholarship I: The training of social workers — 143
· Applied Scholarship II: Transforming researchers into the
federal elite — 148

III. THE STUDY OF CANADA: THE SOCIAL SCIENCES, THE ARTS, NEW MEDIA, 1920s–1950s — 154

8. DATA-BASED STUDIES OF SOCIETY: POLITICAL ECONOMY, HISTORY, SOCIOLOGY — 158

- · Canadian universities and U.S. foundations, 1920s–50s — 161
- · From social reform to sociology: The city and the West — 164
- · Political economy: Staples, markets, consumption, and cultural change — 174
- · Political history and political science: Institutions, revolt of the West, Cold War — 181
- · As yet marginal: Immigrants in scholarship — 191
- · Twice marginalized: "Indians" and folk and the emergence of anthropology and ethnohistory — 200

9. DISCOURSE-BASED REFLECTIONS ABOUT SOCIETY: WHERE WERE THE HUMANITIES? — 205

- · One, two, many literatures—or none? — 208
- · Images large and small: The nationalization of the arts — 221
- · Communication as a resource and as a tool of power: From common people's telecommunication to global communication theory — 226
- · New nationwide media: Whose investments, power, and contents? — 232
- · Gendered cultural elites: Nationalists, reformers, radicals — 239
- · The study of Canada: Problems and perspectives at the turn to the sixties — 243

IV. THE THIRD PHASE: MULTIPLE DISCOURSES ABOUT INTERLINKED SOCIETIES — 246

10. DECOLONIZATION: THE CHANGES OF THE 1960s — 248

- · Nationalizing the material and the cultural: The Marsh and Massey recommendations — 251
- · The centennial's new climate of opinion — 258
- · A different centennial: The weight of the past in the socialization of new generations — 264
- · Academia: From decolonization to recolonization? — 267

11. VISIONS AND BORDERLINES: CANADIAN STUDIES SINCE THE 1960S — 273

· Frames of meaning: The simultaneous centering and decentering of Canada — 274

· An institutionalized quest "to know our many selves" or disdain for Canadian Studies? — 278

· Creating national and pluralist Canadian and Canadian Studies institutions — 284

12. VIEWS FROM THE OUTSIDE: THE SURGE OF INTERNATIONAL CANADIAN STUDIES — 289

· Canadian foreign policy and Canadian Studies outside of Canada — 292

· Perspectives from the outside: Topics and questions — 299

· Multicultural diversity in the Atlantic World . . . and beyond — 304

13. AGENCY IN A MULTICULTURAL SOCIETY: INTERDISCIPLINARY RESEARCH ACHIEVEMENTS — 311

· Past-oriented societal sciences: A gendered history of the people — 314

· Present-oriented societal sciences: From Cold-War camp to social spaces — 322

· Self-articulation of women and mainstreaming gender — 329

· From First Peoples in a fourth world to participants in an open society — 334

· Redefining ethnocultural belonging and transcultural identities — 341

· Decentering hegemonies: The humanities as discourse-centered societal sciences — 348

V. PERSPECTIVES — 360

14. FROM INTEREST-DRIVEN NATIONAL DISCOURSE TO TRANSCULTURAL SOCIETAL STUDIES — 361

· The natural and the social: Discourse in the production of knowledges and identities — 361

· Transcultural Societal Studies: An integrative approach — 373

· Education: Intergenerational transfer and transcultural embeddedness — 386

Interviews with the author — 392

Index — 394

BIBLIOGRAPHIC NOTES

In view of the large number and variety of titles cited in the notes, a structured, alphabetical bibliography would not reflect the author's particular way of organization. Thus no separate bibliography concludes this volume, but in the index, all first citations in the notes are included under the author's name. Short title forms are used if more than one work of an author has been cited in a note, and when a work has been previously cited.

In the annotation to the text, works from the nineteenth and first half of the twentieth centuries are cited only by author, title, and year. In the case of Canada-related publications, place of publication is provided if outside of Canada since some authors preferred to publish in London or Paris; some had to publish there because Canadian publishers could or would not publish their works, which they considered either marginal or too controversial. In the case of post-1945 publications, literary works with many printings have been cited by first date of publication only and, when social science studies are cited to indicate a new trend, the publication data have also been limited for reasons of space.

Footnote numbers are usually placed only at the end of a paragraph, although the footnote itself may contain source information for quotes anywhere within the paragraph.

Some abbreviations have been used in the citations:

Éd.	*Éditions* or *Éditeur*
ACS	Association for Canadian Studies
ACSUS	Association for Canadian Studies in the United States
AUCC	Association of Universities and Colleges of Canada
CCS	Commission on Canadian Studies
CHA	Canadian Historical Association
CJEPS	*Canadian Journal of Economic and Political Science*
CPSA	Canadian Political Science Association
DEA	Department of External Affairs
ENCS	European Network for Canadian Studies
ICCS–CIEC	International Council for Canadian Studies – Conseil international d'études canadiennes
MHSO	Multicultural History Society of Ontario

MQUP	McGill-Queen's University Press
NYUP	New York University Press
OUP	Oxford University Press
PU	*Presses Universitaires*
PUL	Presses Universitaires de Laval
PUQ	Presses Universitaires de l'Université de Quebec
RHAF	Revue d'histoire de l'Amérique française
SSFC–FCSS	Social Science Federation of Canada – Fédération canadienne des sciences sociales
SSRCC	Social Science Research Council of Canada
UBC	University of British Columbia
UTP	University of Toronto Press
WLU	Wilfrid Laurier University

PREFACE — "A BEAUTIFUL AND COMPLICATED COUNTRY"

For many years I have taught a course on the linkages between society and scholarship, to introduce my students to the concept that academic research and teaching is not an independent, objective activity of disinterested scholars. The U.S. "American Studies" and German *Amerikastudien* serve as examples. Developing in the 1930s, American Studies reflected society and reflected on its history and literary production. *Amerikastudien* originated in the era of friendship between Theodore Roosevelt and Emperor William II, both rough riders aware of their powerful states' second place to the empires of France and Great Britain. *Amerikastudien* changed when, during World War I, the United States was an enemy nation; changed again when the United States financed some of the rebuilding of war-devastated democratic Germany; changed again in 1933 with the coming of fascism; and then when the United States was an enemy nation again. There came further changes when the United States was the main liberator from fascism, when it financed another rebuilding of, this time Western, Germany and when it turned into big brother and cultural hegemon.

To counter my students' impression that the United States *was* North America, I intended to devote a few sessions of the course to Canadian Studies. But no history of Canadian Studies suitable for teaching was available, a considerable number of essays on specific aspects and thoughtful reflections since the 1960s notwithstanding. Thus I set out to develop my own text. Canadian scholarship as well as Canadian literatures and arts, proceeding partly in frames of reference of multiple colonization, helped me to take another look at the long history of Country or Area Studies and to place more emphasis on their relations with Colonial Studies. Their sophistication and trans- or interdisciplinarity led me to fuse the many concepts into an approach I call Transcultural Societal Studies.

Even the best-intentioned Transcultural Societal Studies cannot transcend the limitations of the respective author. Vijay Agnew, in *Where I Come From* (2003) self-critically described how she had been socialized into a middle-class family in India, in both New Delhi and Bombay, the dislocations of the partition of 1947 notwithstanding. All scholarship could improve vastly if academics laid open their own socializations as honestly as Vijay Agnew, now a professor at York University, Toronto. My own socialization was perhaps unusual as it forced me to live many contradictory discourses. Raised in the immediate post-World War II years in a Germany in ruins, I am German by birth and nationality but the regimes moved over me: born into Nazi Germany; childhood in the British zone of occupation to some, liberation to others; first school years in the new Federal Republic. We were taught democracy and openness but lived the thought-control of the Cold War. In my three-generation, middle-class family, two men were missing: both grandfathers had perished in World War I. The young war widows and their children—my parents—kept the aspiration to become middle class, but with the Depression and another German expansionist war intervening, had their means to support the aspiration reduced; I lived in a post-war, port-town, proletarian neighbourhood (I avoid the term *community*) with fathers missing through war or abroad as sailors. I had no way to escape awareness that the discourse and the habitus I was supposed to talk, live, and act changed between school, neighbourhood, and family, and within the latter by generation. My perspective broadened when I left the staid and unchanged authoritarian German university system to study for a year in the far more intellectually open United States in 1967/68. My perspective broadened further when, much later, my family and I lived in multicultural Toronto for a year.

Diversity, like all social phenomena, has many sides to it. The diversity of discourses taught me never to believe any one storyline. This impacts in two important ways on the text that follows. First, since scholarly discourses in Canada always offered divers options, I judge those that became hegemonic. I try to do so in the frame of options available at the time, but I do have preferences. Second, when writing this survey of the Study of Canada, I was uncomfortably aware of the diversity of potential audiences and their particular discourses and socializations. This diversity created problems. Who is the audience and what might I expect them to know? Canadianists, such as myself coming from outside of Canada, may have less background information than those having gone through the Canadian schools and universities, though it is being debated to what degree Canadian schools provide information about Canada. Then, English-language and Quebec's French-language researchers have different backgrounds. On the basis that fewer English-language than French-language Canadian scholars are bilingual, I have included more background on Quebec literary writing but do quote in French, which is my third language, without translation. As regards students as an audience, my German students whom I confronted with a draft version wanted much more background; Canadian students from parents of pre-1945 immigration may have some of the background through socialization; and students from the post-early-1960s changes in immigration may lack background information, consider it irrelevant and, perhaps, justly so, do consider their different pre-migration traditions more important. To include those who have lived in Canada only for part of their lives or for a generation or two, Canadian Studies will have to include Culture-of-Origin Studies beyond Britain, France, and other European cultures. It will also have to include the study of transculturation emerging from the many interactions. I hope to have found a balance.

Another balance was difficult to achieve. In his *Five-Part Invention: A History of Literary History in Canada* (2003), Edward D. Blodgett engages other interpretations and can draw on some five dozen literary histories. For the many disciplines I cover, I had some critical and thoughtful histories of the fields but no historically and theoretically grounded discourse on social sciences scholarship in Canada provided a frame to argue with. Thus, in some respects this study is more additive, though, as said above, I evaluate and voice opinions. To paraphrase theoreticians of knowledge production, a history of scholarship has the task to construct a convincing and readable whole of the functioning of the many given disciplines and their approaches in each period's societal, economic, discursive, and normative context. W.H. New concluded the first edition of his *A History of Canadian Literature* (1989) with: "the entire book is a history-in-process." So is this history of the Study of Canada.

ACKNOWLEDGEMENTS — "A LAND OF OPEN DOORS"

My outside view as someone not socialized into Canadian culture in child-hood permits a distance to received Canadian discourses, but also exposes me to the threat of errors and misunderstandings. Jean Burnet and Richard Cavell kindly agreed to read parts of the manuscript both for errors and for stringency of argument. I am deeply indebted to them. I discussed the revised draft in a research seminar in spring term of 2003 with my German students, and their thoughtful comments permitted me to make the book more readable to non-specialists. Like many researchers, I was often impressed by vivid detail; Annegret Kuhlmann, as assistant, helped me to pare down the text. When my own institution drowned me in work, the Deutsche Forschungsgemeinschaft provided a sabbatical during which I could complete the final version.

I have incurred many debts in the process of coming to terms with the development of Canadian Studies. As for many newcomers and observers, Canada was a society of "open doors" for me. While doing research in Toronto, the home of Franca Iacovetta and Ian Radforth provided an agreeable space to work and to discuss ideas in. Many other colleagues from York University and the University of Toronto need to be named: Wsevolod Isajiw, Valerie Preston, Wenona Giles, Michael Lanphier, and Yves Frenette among them. My friends in Quebec, Danielle Juteau and Anne Laperrière among many others, provided a running critique when they felt that my views became Anglo-centric. Friends at universities in the Prairie provinces—Jim Frideres, Tamara Seiler, Tony Rasporich, Yvonne Hébert, Gerald Friesen—helped to overcome the Central-Canada bias or, more exactly, a Montreal- and Toronto-centeredness. They also pointed to Quebec-centredness in some of my perspectives on francophone Canada. To counter the "old metropolitan" bias, I lived for a couple of months in Vancouver where Richard Cavell, Allan Smith, Veronica Strong-Boag, Julie Cruikshank, and many others were accommodating and stimulating hosts. I am also most grateful to the colleagues who provided advice and possibilities to visit in all other Canadian provinces and I have come to cherish regional distinctiveness. Those whom I interviewed are listed in the Bibliographic Note. Annegret Kuhlmann, Bremen, meticulously proofed the manuscript. My "home" organization, the Association for Canadian Studies in German-language Countries, does its best to treat English, French, First Peoples, and immigrant Canadian cultures equally. I made an effort to do so.

While writing this preface in Winnipeg at the turn from 2004 to 2005, I heard a radio announcer in the background call Canada a "beautiful and complicated country." For me, the beauty includes skaters from many cultures in the bright sunshine on the Assiniboine River at 20 degrees below. Elegant (feminine?) skating is an image different from a frozen North and hardy masculine explorers. Complications arise when I—a non-skater—pass by wanting to greet them: "Season's greetings" or "happy holidays" have replaced the once common but now excluding "Merry Christmas."

To redirect this greeting to the potential audience of this study: "Happy reading" (provided the cultural background and the language fits) or, to paraphrase "as Canadian as possible under the circumstances": "happy reading of a text as informative as possible under the circumstances."

DHo.
January 2005

INTRODUCTION

In the early 1970s, the Commission on Canadian Studies prepared its report under the title "To Know Ourselves." From a perspective from outside of Canada and a perspective of diversity of the 1990s—"our many selves"— the present study argues that rather than place the beginning of Canadian Studies in the 1960s and '70s, the Study of Canada evolved in three major phases of innovation: (1) the study of natural resources by the Geological Survey since the 1840s, which encompassed complex notions of both social spaces inhabited by First Peoples knowledgeable about the terrain and the future arrival of immigrant farming families, labouring people, and investors; (2) research on urban as well as prairie societies by social scientists and political economists since the 1920s; and (3) from the 1960s on, "Canadian Studies" with emphasis on literatures.

In a comparative perspective, the study of Canada is one of several nationally bounded studies of whole societies, whether the United States, Great Britain, France, or other countries. These so-called "Area Studies" or "Country Studies" were concerned with and limited to either one assumedly monocultural society or with a "foreign" country as part of a process of making that society accessible for cultural exchange or economic penetration. Around 1900, Country Studies in Europe began from self-images propagated by "high culture." Canadian Studies in the 1960s, in contrast, began as self-study at the end of a colonial context but neglected Canada's own colonized Native peoples. Thus decolonization approaches and nationhood perspectives clashed or engaged each other.

It has become commonplace that scholars write from particular positions and assumptions, but in the Study of Society they are part of what is being studied in a double sense: they are part of it in the sense of having no distance to their enquiry, and they are a part, only one specific part of it. Being part, or "part-isan" or "part-icular," regardless of society, implies that scholars are inextricably involved in a country's discourse while scientific approaches claim universalist approaches. Within their country they are embedded in a discourse specific to their social group. Thus scholarship, even when attempting to be open to all questions, theories, approaches, and methods, is in fact bounded, first, by the mental frame of each author as developed in childhood socialization, and second, by the received discourses imbued during adolescence of his or her social class or group, cultural background, gender, and skin colour—and white is also a skin colour—as well as, third, by the current preconceptions, paradigms, methods, and theories of the field.

Thus, in the study of Canada, the vast body of writing on the British and French Canadians (most of it written by British and French Canadian men) offers a detailed perspective on these two particular if sizable segments of society. At the same time, such publications rest as historical dead weight on those of different cultural, class, and gender backgrounds. Scholars with innovative approaches even had to clear a space for their new positions and research agendas. The early partisan academic publications, as in any society, leave a legacy of problems. Not only has much of Canadian experience started in women's spheres and in rural as well as urban lower-class cultures, input also came with migrants from African, Asian, Caribbean, and Latin American cultures. First Peoples lived in social spaces of their own or were relegated to them. All of these, as has been repeatedly stated, have been excluded from view and awareness by scholars of self-arrogated high status and hegemonic culture, keepers of the gate to historical memory, as not fitting their interests, their concepts of society, or their aesthetics. In this study, Ralph Ellison's theory of invisibility, Black Americans as "invisible men" and women, and Luise Pusch's discussion of the "symbolic annihilation" of women will serve as frame of reference and will be extended to other subalternized groups. To uncover their own experiences, everyman, everywoman, and everychild have to clear away the mountains of publications by educated White mainstream men as well as the hidden presuppositions of accepted discourses.[1]

In this analysis, the historical frame of Country Studies (chapter 1) will provide a background to assumptions and practices of the field of study. Discussion of the developments in Canada will serve to develop a concept of Transcultural Societal Studies in the conclusion (chapter 14). Since any study of a culture and a society conceptualized as Country Studies implies restrictions by political borders, it is necessary to place Canada's historic evolution and intellectual traditions in the Atlantic World (chapter 2). To question the narratives common to the early 1960s, and among some far beyond this date, the historical agency of the many people and groups in society will be discussed and, in the process, Canada's space will be expanded to include the cultures of Asia and Africa. Gendered cultures and First Peoples' impact on newcomers are part of this inclusive history (chapter 3). To bring

---

1 : Renée Hulan and Linda Warley, "Cultural Literacy, First Nations and the Future of Canadian Literary Studies," *Journal of Canadian Studies* 34.3 (1999): 59–86, esp. 61; Ralph Ellison, *Invisible Man* (New York: Random, 1952); Luise Pusch, *Das Deutsche als Männersprache: Aufsätze und Glossen zur feministischen Linguistik* (Frankfurt/M.: Suhrkamp, 1984, repr. 1996), 11.

the weight of excluding narratives of the past into the open, an outline of the development of regional perspectives as well as of national billboards will conclude the introductory section (chapter 4).

The development of scholarship from the 1840s to the 1920s and from the 1910s to the 1950s and the creation of collective memory or memories is the topic of Parts II and III. In the first phase, "scholarship" meant privileged discourses of White male scholars of British and French cultural background based on selected sources and emerging methodologies.[2] A positivist Country Studies approach described the two firstcoming groups of European background as creating institutions and ways of life rather than as colonizers. A critical approach would note that the early newcomers had well-considered reasons to leave their societies of birth and the respective institutions forever. It would note that new circumstances—the physical and climatic environment, the composition of the emigrant communities, and the institutions in the making—demanded new attitudes to civic society. It would also differentiate between permanent immigrants and the sojourning imperial administrators charged with replicating the old institutional frame. Interests of empires often stood in conflict with those of the respective colonists. Attachment to "roots," to childhood-socialized ways of life, might coexist with increasing alienation from the institutions and impositions of the old regimes (chapter 5). Substantial research about place and space in Canada emerged from a project called the Geological Survey, which encompassed the human implications of surveying and understanding inhabited territories (chapter 6). Scholars' roles in society acquired a new quality, while the dissemination of knowledge in the provinces' educational systems remained the realm of British or French-Catholic ideologues (chapter 7). The reform impulse, both Catholic and Protestant from the 1880s to the 1910s, and the changes in population composition and expansion of settlements to the prairies resulted in data-based studies of society in all of the social sciences including economics, in the second phase of the Study of Canada (chapter 8). Such Canadian distinctiveness was not to be found in discourse-based reflection about and communication in society, in the humanities and in studies in education though the literatures and

---

2 : "Origin" in this study refers to an evolving culture from which migrants depart at a certain point in time. It does not imply a static or essentialist culture. However, migrants often essentialize the respective society's stage of development at the time of their departure since they no longer experience the changes of their society of socialization but believe that they "know" the culture. See Dirk Hoerder, "From Migrants to Ethnics: Acculturation in a Societal Framework," in Hoerder and Leslie P. Moch, eds., *European Migrants: Global and Local Perspectives* (Boston: Northeastern Univ. Press, 1996), 211–262.

arts evidenced nationalizing tendencies (chapter 9). The innovations of the second phase involve (a) Harold Innis's comprehensive structural approach to Canadian development from a perspective of political economy that did, however, totally neglect human beings as actors in economic processes; (b) the settlement studies of the social sciences; (c) studies of immigrants' and urban ways of life; and, perhaps, (d) some attempts in the humanities to cut across disciplinary boundaries.

In the 1960s, the third phase, the intellectual ferment, the liberation from Britain- or France-centred colonial mentalities, and the breaking down of the hierarchies of culture was seminal. Parallel to but independent from the scholars from the Birmingham Centre for Contemporary Cultural Studies, scholars of Western Canada emphasized the multicultural character of the society. This phase was characterized by an initial 1960s/Centennial exuberance, but decolonization's duality—externally from Britain, France, and Rome, and internally of the "other ethnics," women, First Peoples, "coloured" or "visible" "minorities" from British- and French-Canadian hegemony—posed problems: those decolonizing themselves were challenged by those colonized internally (Part IV). Thus achievements of anglo- and francophone Canadian scholars, with gender inserted, received less recognition than expected because the many other Canadians came to the fore at the same time and demanded attention. In addition, old-style administrators in academia, a generation of university teachers socialized before the 1960s, a sponsored immigration of U.S. academics, and an immobile school system retarded the institutionalization of the vibrant new ideas (chapters 10 and 11).

From the 1970s on, the Study of Canada outside of Canada developed and added its many perspectives (chapter 12). From the 1980s on, however, memory and agency came to be accepted as multiple and diverse. Now scholarship incorporated the many experiences. Linguistic limitations of many scholars and the underdevelopment of a French- and English-Canadian intellectual exchange have resulted in separate developments with allophone Canada as part of neither and Native languages-speaking Canadians' lifeways as yet another separate field (chapter 13).

In none of the three phases did an explicit theory or a comprehensive methodology emerge, recent explorations of interdisciplinarity notwithstanding. This may explain the reluctance of scholars from highly theorized disciplines with sophisticated methodologies to engage in Canadian Studies. It may also explain the field's flexibility to accommodate multiple themes, multidisciplinary methodology, and multicultural backgrounds, presents, and outcomes. A new Transcultural Societal Studies (TSS) became possible (chapter 14). As an analytical field, TSS questions the assumptions on which a society bases its self-views, understands that societies consist of many components (Pluralist Studies), and dissolves clear borderlines into fuzzy borders or borderlands (Transcultural Studies). While Country Studies took an overarching "nation" for granted, TSS deals with societal institutions and the people; individual men, women, and children. Since every human action as well as established patterns and processes impact on structures, Societal and Cultural Studies deal with processional structures and structured processes. Rather than providing snapshots, research has to present a movie—a difficult undertaking for scholars and their categories. Dealing with societies as a whole or with individual lives in societal contexts, the field is comprehensive. Discerning between groups, it analyzes power relationships, in particular when a hegemonic group limits the access of others to the national myths and societal resources, when it disadvantages those slotted into special categories by gender, culture, religion, skin colour, stage in the life cycle, or other specializing characteristic. The resulting multiple perspectives deconstruct myths, the billboards of a society, and rediscover long-hidden historical signposts that indicate that national history was not a predetermined (or "natural") one-way street. Rather, those who directed society, its politics, economies, and ideologies, made conscious choices for a particular course of development and thereby relegated other options to invisibility.

Chapter 1

TRADITIONS AND PRACTICES: FROM COLONIAL AND AREA TO CULTURAL OR SOCIETAL STUDIES

Up to the 1990s, the twin approaches to the study of societies, discourse-centred "Cultural Studies" and data-centred Social and Cultural History, usually dealt with "national" cultures—British Studies, American Studies, Canadian Studies—though lived cultures are not necessarily contained within political borderlines or concepts of nationhood. "Culture," which in the past referred to middle-class culture or to those with secondary education, has come to include popular culture, sometimes called "trivial" or "folk-life." Material aspects of life became part of the term's connotations. Since Raymond Williams's pathbreaking work, the input of Clifford Geertz, and Pierre Bourdieu's conceptualizations, culture is taken to mean a habitus, the patterns and improvisations of a way of life that embraces the material, cognitive and emotional, as well as spiritual world as viewed, processed, and as acted upon, whether in re- or in pro-action.[3] Habitual ways of life as well as expectations for the future vary between local social spaces, from region to region and state to state. Within a society, ways of life vary by gender and class, between generations and life stages, according to assigned or self-assumed position in social, political, and economic hierarchies and relationships. "Cultural Studies" has concerned itself with representations and semantics of expressions. Some of its recent practitioners have used the "linguistic turn" to avoid time-consuming research on the material world, thus marginalizing social science research while floating in misty jargon. The designation "Societal Studies" avoids the narrow connotation of culture but, in turn, runs the danger of reducing the role of the humanities. Transcultural Societal Studies as term and concept includes both post-national approaches.

Culture as a term and concept has passed through many stages. In sixteenth-century texts, culture was material and comprised the basic labour to produce people's livelihood: agri-, horti-, and viticulture. The connection to family economies was made explicit in the English term *husbandry* and the French *culturer* as working the soil. A second usage referred to mental growth, the cultivation of the mind. Both usages implied a binary juxtaposition of cultivated versus wild. Within societies, only some individuals,

---

3 : Raymond Williams, *Keywords: A Vocabulary of Culture and Society* (London: Fontana, 1976; rev. ed., 1983); Clifford Geertz, *The Interpretation of Cultures: Selected Essays* (New York: Basic Books, 1973); Pierre Bourdieu, *The Fields of Cultural Production* (New York: Columbia, 1993).

groups, or classes were said to be cultivated; in inter-societal comparison, cultured peoples and, later, nations were juxtaposed to primitive ones. By the eighteenth century, "culture" had been deprived of its material content and its practice, the "arts" of artisans, artists, and scholars, was also re-interpreted. The triad of useful, liberal, and decorative arts became a new triad of craft and technology, scholarship, and "arts" in the new narrow sense. Cultural production had become a class-specific and Eurocentric term—noble and bourgeois classes' high culture of intellect, music, literature, sculpture, theatre, and painting. According to European views, high cultures outside of Europe were of the past, such as Mughal India, the Aztecs and Inca, and ancient Egypt. While some open-minded early twentieth-century scholars introduced more comprehensive meanings: "culture" as the process of development of humankind, whether European, Indian, or Chinese, European and American gatekeepers constructed "Occidental" culture as particularly advanced. In its quest for status in nineteenth-century nobility-dominated societies, the bourgeoisie changed its reference point; from search for ennoblement it turned to search for authentic people's cultures in a folk-to-nation quest. "Folk" or, more broadly, "people's cultures" became acceptable, usually in a hierarchical relationship. Definitions of culture involved positioning in society and claims to political power: the traditional nobility's ostentatious display of refined culture and luxury as a sign of its pre-eminence; a counter-hierarchization elevated folk culture to "pure" and original to middle-class nations. With the commercial-bourgeois transoceanic expansion, a further hierarchization emerged. Colonizers argued that they had to uplift colonial peoples—and devised work-as-education strategies from which they could profit. In contrast, some humanist thinkers considered the cultures of different peoples as equal, others included aspects of evolution from more simple to more complex ("higher") cultures. In the second half of the twentieth century, the restriction of culture to one class was breached by concepts of popular and mass culture. Production of culture (rather than the early modern production as culture) became part of Marxist analysis as in the term "cultural producers"; in Western discourse the common people produced or consumed mass or "canned" culture. In analysis, culture came to be seen as differentiated by social class and status—peasant, working-class, bourgeois or middle-class, or elite, ethnic or national—as well as by gender. When de-industrialization hit powerful economies in the 1980s, a retrospective concept of "industrial culture" emerged as an aestheticized version of production facilities, which made production processes and working people invisible. In contrast to the integrative approach of Transcultural Societal Studies, most scholarly disciplines are divisive: labour and working-class history versus middle-class or national history, ethnology of simple societies versus sociology, history, and humanities of complex societies.

A non-hierarchized and comprehensive approach may define culture as follows: In order to survive and to project life courses, human beings as individuals and in communities and societies must provide for their material, emotional, intellectual, and spiritual needs. These are satisfied by culture, a complex material and symbolic system that includes tools as well as productive and reproductive work; practices, values and norms; and arts and beliefs. Culture involves patterns of actions as well as processes of creating meaning, symbols, and signifying practices, whether oral or body language or other expressions. Culture encompasses "memory," social and historical categories which coalesce as societies' narratives. Such narratives are fluid and unstable complexes of social meanings varying from one social space to another, from one stage of material life to another. They are constantly being transformed by new material products, political conflict, published and private discourses, and by everyday practices of all. Thus, created culture is a frame from within which human beings determine their concept of reality and their life projects.[4]

Transcultural Societal Studies originate from country-specific scholarly discourses. "Area Studies," usually based in 1920s U.S. scholarship, have, in fact, a far longer history. In the eighteenth-century age of colonialism, Europe's colonizer states established research and teaching institutions to provide knowledge about recently acquired actual and about coveted potential colonies as well as to train administrators for service in these regions. In the age of imperialism and of competition between the states of the Atlantic World, these "Colonial Studies" were supplemented by a quest for information about neighbouring competing states, "Country Studies" or, perhaps, "Competitor Studies." In the 1920s United States, globally comparative "ethnological Area Studies" emerged as did, in the 1930s, under the name of "American Studies," a humanities- and history-centred quest for self-understanding. The role of other countries, as British, French, German, or Canadian Studies, is neglected in this genealogy. The outside-imposed hierarchy of such Colonial or Competitor Country Studies and of ethnological and anthropological research in general was exposed only toward the end of the twentieth century when the "gaze" of the keepers of colonizer knowledge onto Others was questioned, as was the appropriation of the voice of

---

4 : A first comprehensive definition was given by English anthropologist E.B. Tylor in 1871 who, however, excluded the material sphere. The best survey of the term's historical meanings still is Alfred L. Kroeber and Clyde Kluckhohn, *Culture: A Critical Review of Concepts and Definitions*, Papers of the Peabody Museum of American Archaeology and Ethnology 47.1 (Cambridge, MA: Harvard, 1952).

Others. In parallel, the narrative of the Self in Country Studies was deconstructed as an interest-driven narrative of spokespersons, mainly spokesmen. In analyzing the emergence of particular discourses, codes, or images that include some and exclude others, spokespersons with the power to define, who are part of the nation, are called "gatekeepers" or "custodians of discourse."[5] They could close the door or open it according to the class-specific thinking of the time and according to their own particular interests. While language is said to be an essential part of each culture, its unquestioned assumptions are misleading, patently false, or even intentional lies. Language is an instrument of power to appropriate things, places, and persons. Elites may codify exclusionist terminologies or accept the input of all social strata, genders, cultures, and age groups.

Area Studies: Its long history as Colonial and Country Studies

The study of areas is based on the assumption that they are delimited by boundaries said to be historically rooted or self-evident, or to date from times immemorial. The historicity of such construction in European thought, which still shapes twentieth-century minds, needs to be addressed first. In early modern times, the continent was divided into dynasties' family holdings. Such possessions could be partitioned among children (usually only the sons), combined through marriage alliances, lost to other dynasties when no children survived to adulthood, or taken over in warfare. At a cataclysmic but accidental conjuncture of warfare and political thought, the concept of sovereign rule over more permanent boundary-defined territories was introduced. In 1648, at the end of the first European (or Thirty Years') War, about one third of the war zones' population was dead. Dynasties, fighting over variants of the Christian faith, had killed producers and taxpayers at a rate that threatened the survival of their societies. To prevent such population and revenue loss in the future, the negotiators of the Peace of Westphalia agreed on the formula that the treaty-defined boundaries delimited the extent of sovereign rule and non-intervention. Sovereignty thus concerned territory; concepts of neither social space nor of culture were part of political thought. When such polities became republics or democratic states, the dynasties (but interestingly, not the concept) lost power. States are still organized according to the Westphalian System and territory and sovereignty are still associated, supplemented by a vague notion that sovereignty also resides in people. Since bounded territory remained the conceptual organizing principle, no "Social Space Studies" emerged.

Dynasties in co-operation with merchant elites had shifted expansion to

---

5 : Terry Eagleton, *Literary Theory: An Introduction* (London: Verso, 1983), 201.

territories on other continents since the sixteenth century. Acquisition of new spaces, called "territories" to avoid conceptual inclusion of those who lived there, implied sovereign rule over natural and population resources. The eighteenth-century dynastic states and empires of northwest and central Europe, when replacing those of the Iberian peninsula as predominant colonizer powers, needed personnel to cope with rule in culturally different or "alien" spaces, whether Canada, the Caribbean islands, India, Sumatra or others among the many. The populations acquired with the territory were constructed as "primitive" in order to justify why power had to be exerted over them.

Area Studies emerged as study of such acquired territories, as Colonial Studies: knowledge about languages and customs, natural resources, traditional economies, and, above all, about the imposition of rule in the colonized areas was imparted to the personnel of dynastic rulers and private investors, noble clans and bourgeois families, plantation owners and commercial houses, or corporations of merchants such as the various East India companies to rule, administer, and exploit. Since the best returns on investments were provided by colonies to the east of Europe, "oriental" academies[6] were established: the Orientalische (later Konsular-) Akademie in Vienna in 1754, the École Speciale (later Nationale) des Langues Orientales Vivantes in Paris in 1795, the Institute for Oriental Languages in Moscow in 1814, and similar institutions in England which merged into the School of Oriental Studies in 1906.[7] In the latecomer colonizer states of the 1880s, the United States and Germany, institutionalization of rule followed different patterns. U.S. churches sent missionaries, who, curious about customs and plants foreign to them, collected and transmitted information back home from spheres of interest. In Germany, a centre for oriental languages was established at the University of Berlin in 1887, an institute for research on tropical diseases in Hamburg in 1899, and an institute for marine research in Berlin in 1900.[8] All such academies combined language training with geographic information and the study of commerce, administration, law, and military subjects. The specialization of institutes in Germany reflected the shift from general Area Studies to research dealing with particular aspects of Europe's out-

---

6 : "The Orient" might begin in Greece, Palestine, Egypt, Persia or India depending on the territorial interests and viewpoint of the state involved. Thus the designations Near East and Middle East refer to different regions in British and U.S.-American usage.

7 : The institutions had been preceded by merchants', travellers', and administrators' clubs and associations, which collected, compiled, and systematized data and exchanged knowledge. Interest groups, like associations for the promotion of colonization, also had their say.

8 : German geographers were prominent in the study of Canada's northern regions.

reach to other continents rather than to other peoples—received language reflects the territorial aspect. Since scholarship and power were intricately related, Area Studies were *Herrschaftswissenschaften*, sciences of rule.[9]

Few scholars and teachers in Colonial Studies questioned their complicity in rule; most confirmed power by positing Europe as the "sovereign theoretical subject of all histories."[10] The concomitant paradigm of Europeans' or Euro-Canadians' "natural" or "innate" superiority carried two implications: (1) the political-geographic research emphasis on territory was supplemented by narratives about people and their (allegedly) superior or inferior use of resources and (2) a hierarchization into Christian and heathen at first and then, more lastingly, into white and dark. This white/brown/red/yellow/black scale was scientificized in the high imperialist phase into a system of biological descent and volume of brain. Those with the self-allocated superior skin colour or brain volume directed their gaze toward the Others and, in order to communicate what they (thought they) saw, resorted to naming. Since many of these scholars neither spoke nor understood the languages of the people studied, they translated their gaze through their own grids of meaning (Foucault 1966) into terms of their own languages. The relation between interest and knowledge (Habermas 1968) and the power of words is illustrated by geographers who "studied"/named colonized distant territories to indicate their state's presence on maps—a kind of affixing a corporate-imperial brand onto other people's societies. This process of penetration was supported by navies and private commercial companies. In large regions of the colonized world, the colonizers, rather than immersing themselves in existing thought, imposed a point zero, a new name unrelated to the historical-social space to be explored, and from there began their research or exploitation.[11] In the case of Canada, naming was triple-layered:

---

9 : Dirk Hoerder, "Bedingungsfaktoren der Auslandsstudien im Deutschen Reich: Imperialismus, Auslandsdeutsche, Wirtschaft," in *Gulliver: Deutsch-englische Jahrbücher* 11 (1982): 118–39, esp. 118–23; Günter Moltmann, "Die 'Übersee- und Kolonialkunde' als besondere Aufgabe der Universität," in Eckhart Krause, Ludwig Huber, Holger Fischer, eds., *Hochschulalltag im "Dritten Reich:" Die Hamburger Universität 1933–1945* (Berlin: Reimer, 1991), 149–78.

10 : Dipesh Chakrabarty, "Postcoloniality and the Artifice of History: Who Speaks for 'Indian Pasts'?" in Padmini Mongia, ed., *Contemporary Postcolonial Theory: A Reader* (Delhi: OUP, 1997), 223.

11 : Michel Foucault, *The Order of Things: An Archeology of the Human Sciences* (French orig.: *Les mots et les choses*, 1966; New York: Harper and Row, 1972); Jürgen Habermas, *Erkenntnis und Interesse*, Engl. *Knowledge and Human Interests: A General Perspective*, transl. by Jeremy J. Shapiro (Beacon Press, 1971; 2nd ed., London: Heinemann Educational, 1978); Ranajit Guha and Gayatri Spivak, eds., *Selected Subaltern Studies* (New York, Oxford: OUP, 1988).

Euro-Canadian settlers named Native peoples and were, in turn, labelled "colonials" by British and French gatekeepers.

Colonizer scholars faced a challenge when dealing with societies they had to acknowledge as complex hierarchically structured "high" cultures. While the Aztec and Inca cultures, labelled as "despotic," had been destroyed by Spanish conquistadores, the human and cultural resources of the South Asian and Chinese societies, with their sophisticated intellectual and artistic life, vibrant crafts, and multiple belief systems, were needed to produce goods and profits for the colonizers. "Academic orientalism," as Edward Saïd in his classic indictment of Western hegemonic thought argued, constructed "the East as a stereotyped Other to legitimize imperialist expansion." The British East India Company's officials and administrators pursued a dual strategy of rationalization of hegemony (sciences of rule) and of establishing informed interest-driven patterns of interaction with native people through intermediaries. Scholars who took a serious interest in South Asia's cultures restricted themselves to the records of the past; their interaction with living "Indians," whether traders, producers, or domestics, in contrast, was blatantly racist: skin pigmentation did matter. Domestic servants had to be interculturally competent to overcome the scholars' and other colonizers' intercultural incompetence.[12] The critique of the many internal contradictions as well as the exploitative and appropriative logic of Colonial Studies that served racialized power politics on a global scale has brought forth post-colonial empiricism and theory.

Colonial Studies, specialized in the region that was to become Canada, was characterized by overlapping and contradictory interests and involved multiple (mis-) translations. The economic nexus was clear: get fish—little or no help of resident peoples needed; get furs—impossible without the superior knowledge of the peoples resident along the river that was named St. Lawrence. The spiritual nexus was less clear: Christian missionaries saw their religion as superior and inflexible and could not even recognize other religions as valid belief systems. In contrast, the spirituality of Montagnais, Micmac, Huron, Abenaqui, and other peoples was flexible and could incorporate attractive elements of Christianity. The black-robed, "white"-skinned, often highly intelligent men from the Jesuit Order wrote *Relations* (1632–73) about people they deemed inferior but whose knowledge of con-

---

12 : Bernd-Peter Lange and Mala Pandurang, "Dialectics of Empire and Complexities of Culture: British Men in India, Indian Experiences of Britain," in Dirk Hoerder with Christiane Harzig and Adrian Shubert, eds., *The Historical Practice of Diversity: Transcultural Interactions from the Early Modern Mediterranean to the Postcolonial World* (New York: Berghahn, 2003), 177–200, quote p. 181; Edward W. Saïd, *Orientalism* (London: Routledge & Kegan Paul, 1978).

text and climate, of the social and physical spaces was superior and without whose co-operation neither fur trade nor the French dynasty's rule could function.[13] The post-colonial critique of Western scholarship and conceptualizations emerged out of India more than out of Canada, not only because the White Britishers had talked down to brown Indians more than to White British Canadians, but also because anglophone Canadians, having the same language, could talk back and challenge their "mother country's" impositions more easily, though at the same time they assented to hegemony as the mother country's "children." Language and hierarchies of communication play an important role in establishing or challenging hegemonies.

In the Atlantic World and beyond, the colonizer powers competed with each other but co-operated in establishing Europeaneity or Whiteness as superior to any other identity and pigmentation. Within Europe, transcultural exchange, teaching the language, literature, art, and music of neighbouring societies, the French one in particular, had been an unquestioned aspect of elite education. By the late nineteenth century imperialist age, "Transeuropean High Culture Studies" came to be replaced by "Country" or "Competitor Studies," or, in German, *Auslandskunde*, the study of foreign countries to help understand neighbours competing in the struggle for colonies, commerce, and power. Country Studies privileged political territories over larger economic regions such as the world of the North Sea, or smaller cultural regions such as the social space of the English Midlands or the French Atlantic ports. Positively, knowledge of trading partners was necessary for effective commercial exchange; more aggressively, it was necessary to out-manoeuvre competitors in international trade. Detailed knowledge of their goods, methods, and values was required. Thus, in Germany, for example, Country Studies began as applied *Realienkunde*, imparting knowledge of everyday practices and facts, the *real* things of life, and was designed to aid economic penetration of other societies. However, in a bourgeois world with concepts of human agency rather than of subject-status to a dynastic ruler, the people in the neighbouring countries could not simply be left out of the picture. Two opposing approaches to other cultures emerged: a humanist and a nationalist one.

The humanist *Kulturkunde* had first emerged at the critical conjuncture of the Enlightenment, Age of Revolution, and Age of Romanticism. When dynastic states were challenged by their subjects-turning-citizens, the Baltic-German bicultural Johann Gottfried Herder (1744–1803) advocated respect

---

13 : English translation with the original French, Latin, and Italian texts: Reuben Gold Thwaites, ed., *The Jesuit Relations and Allied Documents: Travels and Explorations of the Jesuit Missionaries in New France 1610-1791*, 73 vols. (1896-1901).

for diversity and cultural pluralism. He grew up in the multi-ethnic society of East Central Europe and later lived in one of many regional variants of German society. On the basis of experience and empirical observation he conceptualized the equality of languages and cultures of "peoples."[14] Some of his contemporaries, aware of the relation between culture and power, between hegemony and rule, pursued a different approach. A few decades after England had conquered and incorporated Scotland in 1708, the Scottish poet James Macpherson published *The Works of Ossian* (1765), a mythological Gaelic bard of the third century BCE, as *Fragments of Ancient Poetry Collected in the Highlands of Scotland and Translated from the Gaelic*. He committed to writing what conquered people elsewhere—the Beothuk, for example—could pass on only orally; writing permitted storage and accumulation of knowledge. When the authenticity of Macpherson's "collection" was questioned (Macpherson had merely translated Gaelic manuscripts of a Scottish dramatist) the most influential scholar of Scottish literature, Hugh Blair, certified their embeddedness in a great Scottish national poetic tradition. Thus the conquered Scots, culturally, stood at par with their colonizers, the English.[15] Ossianism was some intellectuals' reinvention of a culture in decline not only because of the conquest by the English but also because of the highland clans' new economic interests. Many of the latter's dispossessed tenants as well as artisans and traders from the lowland cities were to migrate to Canada. There, a century later, a writer of Scottish background would recommence the production of now Scottish-Canadian folklore.

On the continent, Herder's ideas were still gaining ground when Napoleon's imperial expansion wrought havoc in dynastic societies. Strategists used rhetoric of the "nation" to mobilize soldiers for the defense of old dynasties against the upstart "dynast-to-be." Among cultural rights lost in the transition from corporate and diverse dynastic polities to unified national ones was the right to one's own language—the several versions of Gaelic in Great Britain, for example. Language, as mother tongue spoken in a mother country (British usage) or a fatherland/*patrie* (German and French usages) is double-edged: it permits long-distance communication while silencing non-hegemonic voices, voices that might question hegemonic *langue et par-*

---

14 : See esp. Herder's *Die Stimmen der Völker in ihren Liedern* [Voices of the Peoples in Their Songs] (1778, definitive 2nd edition of 1807); *Ideen zur Philosophie der Geschichte der Menschheit* [Thoughts on the Philosophy of the History of Mankind] (incomplete, published 1784-91); Dirk Hoerder with Inge Blank, "Ethnic and National Consciousness from the Enlightenment to the 1880s," in Hoerder et al., eds., *Roots of the Transplanted*, 2 vols. (New York: Columbia Univ. Press & East European Monographs, 1994), 1:37-110.

15 : Hugh Blair, *Critical Dissertation on the Poems of Ossian, the Son of Fingal* (1765). This sentimental poetry received attention in literary and middle-class circles across Europe.

ole (Saussure). The humanist version of equality of cultures in a Euro-Atlantic World divided by rivalries lost out to nationalist hierarchization.

In the nationalist version, Country Studies and *Realienkunde* pursued approaches imposed by the respective state's education ministry on research and curricula. In Germany, mirror theory (*Spiegeltheorie*) or backdrop theory (*Folientheorie*) postulated the teaching of other cultures—French, English or British, (U.S.-) American—as a mirror or a backdrop before which the German nation's achievements appeared superior. Scholarship was partisan; whatever the empirical data, scholars were to increase the renown of their nation and help win the competition for territories and resources. European Country Studies differed from Colonial Studies since in the latter, hierarchies between "white" and "coloured" peoples could be invented and then be said to exist a priori. In contrast, among "white" European peoples hierarchies could not be "a prioritized." In Canada, those of "red" skin colour could be marginalized; the two "white" groups jockeyed for pre-eminence. The scale and rank of shades of skin colour is determined by those with the power of definition and the guns to support their labels.

From the social psychology of lesser others
to the quest for self-knowledge

At the end of the nineteenth century, the emphasis on territories receded. The physical geography was known, rule had been imposed, and territories had been divided among the colonizer powers (e.g. Europe's Africa Conference of 1884/85, or the U.S.'s war against Spain in 1898). At the same time, the study of peoples advanced—colonized ones as resources, neighbouring ones as competitors, "primitive" ones as objects of curiosity. European colonizer states provided scholars with access to colonized other peoples and the North American states to the "vanishing cultures" of colonized "Indians." Study of the Other proceeded from ethno*graphy* to ethno*logy* to anthropology, and developed increasingly sophisticated approaches to cultures. Franz Boas, who as a Jew in Germany and as German-Jewish emigrant in the United States had experienced cultural discrimination, bicultural life and transcultural research became the most renowned representative of the new scholarship, which, however, still used human beings as illustrative material for museums and other public displays.

At the transition from Colonial Studies to Studies of Lesser Peoples, George P. Murdock (1897–1985) and Margaret Mead (1901–78) began to pursue a broadly comparative approach with the Cross-Cultural Survey at Yale University's Institute of Human Relations during the interwar years. Still partly steeped in socio-biological concepts of linear timeline human development from simple to complex societies, the Carnegie Foundation-funded researchers established a cross-referenced index system of some 150 historic and contemporary cultures, the Human Relations Area Files (HRAF). While they considered the files a laboratory of world history, other Rockefeller and Carnegie Foundation-supported scholars considered Canada, as a young society, a laboratory of human self-organization and studied settlement in the West.[16] After the aggressions of the corporatist Japanese and the fascist German states, U.S. scholars began to use the HRAF to understand the social psychology of enemy peoples and of peoples in liberated/occupied territories. Just as German nationalists had called for a better knowledge of enemy mentality during World War I, advocating a vague, interest-driven *Wesenskunde*, so did U.S. nationalists during World War II and the Cold War intend to use knowledge of the spirit and the ways of behaviour of peoples for political intervention. In 1948, an essay in the *Yale Review* demanded a new "understanding of areas." The author noted that it had been a step ahead to study a different society's "economic structure, its industrial potential, natural resources, social organization, political myths, class structure, and so on." However, "[w]e are just beginning to recognize that we must forge ahead into the relatively little explored social psychology of other peoples. . . . No "hard-headed" assessment of economic and military resources can explain the behavior of the Japanese Kamikaze pilots or the fanatical Russian defense of Stalingrad. Such performances are rooted in the psychology of a people."

In a way, Area Studies became Enemy Sciences and sciences of rule. In the 1950s, HRAF-related research projects explored controlled social change in decolonizing societies in Latin America to avoid revolutionary upheaval considered detrimental to U.S. interests.[17] While a study by the State Department did express respect for cultures in India and Southeast Asia, ranking

---

16 : Marvin Harris, *The Rise of Anthropological Theory* (London: Routledge & Kegan Paul, 1969); Talal Asad, ed., *Anthropology and the Colonial Encounter* (London: Humanities Press, 1973); Jean Copans, ed., *Anthropologie et impérialisme* (Paris: Maspero, 1975); Donald Fisher, *Fundamental Development of the Social Sciences: Rockefeller Philanthropy and the United States Social Science Research Council* (Ann Arbor: Univ. of Michigan Press, 1993).

17 : John W. Gardner, "Are We Doing Our Homework in Foreign Affairs," *Yale Review* 37.3 (1948): 400–08, quote p. 407, cited in Thomas Zitelmann, "'Area Studies' in den USA: Strategie und Wissenschaft," *Gulliver: Deutsch-englische Jahrbücher* 11 (1982): 140–49; Nelson Fenton (for the Commission on Implications of Armed Services Educational Programs), *Area Studies in American Universities* (Washington, D.C.: American Council on Education, 1947); Christopher Simpson, ed., *Universities and Empire: Money and Politics in the Social Sciences during the Cold War* (New York: New Press, 1998).

military officers and employees "in the field" summarized, "these are naïve, emotional, vain people and simple logic and bare facts do not appeal." Gut-level *Wesenskunde* held sway over analysis.[18]

Parallel to the social psychology of lesser Others, a quest for self-knowledge emerged among U.S. scholars. History and the humanities, disciplined by disciplinary boundaries, separately studied particular aspects of society. In the 1930s, an interdisciplinary approach, American Studies, was developed to provide a more complex self-understanding. It included none of the control-driven aspects of the Area Studies or Files of other societies. Scholars explored the discourse about nation and identity in the myth-and-symbol approach and attempted to democratize "received culture" by adding popular and industrial culture to the canon. While thus exposing earlier research as a *pars pro toto* approach that uncritically assumed high culture to stand for the whole of national culture, they remained focused on one single idea in American culture, *e pluribus unum*. The model for the homogenized unum, never explicated, was implicitly White, of European background, and male. With the entry of women into academia, gender became a category while, in the tradition of, but without reference to Colonial Studies, people of non-"white" skin colour were left out. Studies of "Negro Americans," "ethnics," and First Peoples remained separate and under-funded fields practised by scholars from these groups. American Studies was White Studies until the 1960s civil rights and the 1970s new-ethnicity movements as well as multi-"racial" strategies diversified the field. Since social scientists left American Studies to the humanities and history, the program could not fulfill its interdisciplinary promise and avoided dealing with the economic sphere as well as issues of class, race, and social hierarchy. Conceived as early Cultural Studies, American Studies was often self-referential and thus provincial.[19] Only Women's, African American, Native, and Chicano Studies, jointly with the Social History and Cultural Studies of the 1970s and '80s brought forth an inclusive cultural history, theoretically and

18 : U.S. Department of State, Office of Intelligence Research, "Cultural Background Paper: Indonesia," Intelligence Report no. 5613, June 1952, 35. I am grateful to Marc Frey, Univ. of Cologne, for the citation.

19 : Robert Merideth, ed., *American Studies: Essays on Theory and Method* (Columbus, OH: Merrill, 1968); Linda K. Kerber, "Diversity and the Transformation of American Studies," *American Quarterly* 41 (1989): 415–31; Gary B. Nash, Charlotte Crabtree, and Ross E. Dunn, *History on Trial: Culture Wars and the Teaching of the Past* (New York: Knopf, 1997); James A. Henretta, "Social History as Lived and Written," *American Historical Review* 84 (1979): 1293–1333; Lynn Hunt, ed., *The New Cultural History [in the United States]* (Berkeley: Univ. of California Press, 1989); Lawrence Grossberg, Cary Nelson, Paula Treichler, eds., *Cultural Studies* (New York: Routledge, 1992).

methodologically sophisticated. Since the 1990s, innovative transnational approaches have emerged.[20]

British Studies began to develop later and started from a different intellectual context.[21] At the end of World War I, Great Britain lost its worldwide economic predominance to the United States and after World War II also its political role as a global power. Cultural self-perception, however, remained welded to the nation's grandeur though scholars and social thinkers on the Left had established a tradition of their own since the early 1900s. In the 1950s, a New Left scholarship challenged traditional views. Raymond Williams's *Culture and Society* (1958) became the founding text of materialist "Cultural Studies," which drew a distinction between the given material practice in society and among particular groups in it and the cultural traditions and practices through which material and immaterial (intellectual, emotional, and spiritual) resources are appropriated, reworked, reinvented, recycled in a process first of unconscious childhood socialization, then in youthful self-assertion and rebellion, and finally, often explicitly and narrowly interest-driven, in adulthood.[22] Since the 1960s, the work of the

---

20 : Attempts to internationalize American Studies and American historiography have gained increasing impact since the 1990s. Thomas Bender, ed., *The LaPietra Report: Project on Internationalizing the Study of American History* (New York: Organization of American Historians and New York Univ., 2000); Thomas Bender, "Wholes and Parts: The Need for a Synthesis in American History," *Journal of American History* 73 (1986): 120–36; David Thelen, "Of Audiences, Borderlands, and Comparisons: Toward the Internationalization of American History," *Journal of American History* 79 (1992): 432–62; Paul Giles, "Reconstructing American Studies: Transnational Paradoxes, Comparative Perspectives," *Journal of American Studies* 28 (1994): 335–58; Lora Romero, "Nationalism and Internationalism: Domestic Differences in a Postcolonial World," *American Literature* 67 (1995), 793–800; Jane C. Desmond and Virginia A. Dominguez, "Resituating American Studies in a Critical Internationalism," *American Quarterly* 48 (1996): 475–90; "Globalization, Transnationalism, and the End of the American Century," topical issue of *American Studies* 41.2/3 (Summer/Fall 2000); Thomas Bender, ed., *Rethinking American History in a Global Age* (Berkeley: Univ. of California Press., 2001); Ann Laura Stoler et al., "Tense and Tender Ties: The Politics of Comparison in North American History and (Post) Colonial Studies," *Journal of American History* 88 (2001): 829–65; Dirk Hoerder, ed., "Internationalizing U.S. History," *Amerikastudien/American Studies* 48.1 (Spring 2003).

21 : The British Studies approach had antecedents in a quest for self-knowledge, for example the documentary photography of English rural life in the second half of the nineteenth century, when urbanization and mechanization resulted in deep-going changes. While this approach included peasant folk, it excluded urban proletarians from the sphere of social documentation.

22 : Richard Hoggart, *The Uses of Literacy* (London: Chatto, 1957); Paul Willis, *Profane Culture* (London: Routledge, 1978); Stuart Hall, Dorothy Hobson, Andrew Lowe, and

Centre for Contemporary Cultural Studies, Birmingham, as well as the New Left reconceptualization of national and imperial history—by Christopher Hill, Eric Hobsbawm, E.P. Thompson, and others—have influenced scholars in the humanities and social sciences on the European continent (where popular culture was still often called "trivial culture") and in North America. British Studies are undertaken within the boundaries of one state (Country Studies) but concern three cultures—English, Scottish, and Welsh, and perhaps Cornish (Pluralist Studies). Often the Irish societies—Catholic, Protestant, and Ulster-Scottish Protestant—are also included.[23] British Studies include the contributions of Jewish, German, and other immigrants to the isles in the past, and, seminal for the development of post-colonial approaches, of men and women from the Caribbean or former British colonies in the present.[24] This group of scholars also turned to youth cultures, interpreting them in terms of resistance to the world of the adults. Youth cultures rather than merely being a stage in the life cycle often reflect an intergenerational cultural change and thus are future-oriented and society-wide.

In the present, traditional Country Studies—whether British, American, Canadian or other—as Societal or Cultural Studies are engaged in a process of shedding the respective national focus to accommodate several cultures within a historically evolved and changeable institutional and relational set-up. Cultural memory or memories play a shaping role in the process of self-understanding, of reading space and time, and of creating meanings.

Paul Willis, eds., *Culture, Media, Language: Working Papers in Cultural Studies, 1972-79* (Birmingham: Centre for Contemporary Cultural Studies, 1980); Raymond Williams, *Keywords: A Vocabulary of Culture and Society* (1983); Stuart Hall and Bram Gieben, eds., *Formations of Modernity* (London: Open Univ., 1992); Graeme Turner, *British Cultural Studies: An Introduction* (1990; 2nd ed., London: Routledge, 1996); Catherine Hall, ed., *Cultures of Empire: A Reader* (Manchester: Manchester Univ. Press, 2000).

23 : Linda Colley, *Britons: Forging the Nation, 1707-1837* (New Haven: Yale, 1992); Laurence Brockliss and David Eastwood, eds., *A Union of Multiple Identities: The British Isles, c.1750-c.1850* (Manchester: Manchester Univ. Press, 1997).

24 : Kenneth Lunn, ed., *Hosts, Immigrants and Minorities* (Folkestone: Dawson, 1980); Peter Fryer, *Staying Power: The History of Black People in Britain* (Atlantic Highlands: Humanities Press, 1984); Colin Holmes, *John Bull's Island: Immigration and British Society, 1871-1971* (London: Macmillan, 1988); Margaret Byron, *Post-War Caribbean Migration to Britain: The Unfinished Cycle* (Aldershot: Avebury, 1994).

I. FRAMING RESEARCH ON CANADA: BURDENS AND ACHIEVEMENTS OF THE PAST

Practitioners of Societal / Cultural Studies who have been reared within the intellectual framework of their society's educational institutions need to ask themselves whether they have been framed or are free to establish new frames. Parents and teachers socialize children into a particular regional society and nationhood. Convictions, often unquestioned, appear to be knowledge; the background "information" for them comes from seemingly reliable, even loved sources, such as parents, and appears self-evident to children. As adults, they pass it on to their children and grandchildren and thus the "wisdom" of ages emerges. Resulting convictions about the past shape attitudes and actions in the present. Narratives of nationhood, "Canadian" history among them, are part of such conviction to possess knowledge. The name of the country stems from the Huron-Iroquois *kanata*, village, which Jacques Cartier used to refer to the whole region of Chief Donnacona's influence. The country's name thus points both to the Native–White interconnections as well as to the misunderstandings and appropriations in the minds of the Europeans, as yet uninformed. To contextualize the societies that became Canada, they need to be placed in the Atlantic World and, less important at first, in the Pacific World (chapter 2). Second, the peoples involved in creating the many Canadian societies are discussed, as are biased terminologies and their recent revisions. In the process, the shortcomings of earlier colonial, White, and male historiography are criticized (chapter 3). Third, the cultural symbols, literary narratives, and billboard slogans are discussed, which writers and propagandists established and which have been part of the socialization of Canadians (chapter 4).

Chapter 2

THE ATLANTIC WORLD:
CREATING SOCIETIES IN IMPERIAL HINTERLANDS

The societies that were to become Canada emerged in the context of Europe's discovery that west of the Atlantic there was no "India" but a new continent and numerous peoples. The political, social, and economic thought of the Euro-Atlantic World was adapted to the establishment of colonies. "Knowledge" about the new spaces sent "home" was fraught with preconceived images. When the personnel of European rulers imposed their colonial polities on lived social spaces, they drew border*lines* across landscapes inhabited by First Peoples. Some lines separated patterns of interaction; others were shaped into cultural and economic border*lands* by people who lived there. First Peoples, Second Peoples, and immigrant ethnics struggled about belongings in colonial settings and under incomplete nationhood. Once British North America achieved Dominion status in 1867, a nation-building English-language "Canada First" movement and a French-language "conquest of Quebec" movement broadcast their slogans from nation-wide billboards. Parallel to that, the many-cultured common people created complex interacting societies and lived lives of many cultural variations.

"Discovery" and the production of knowledge

People's discoveries of or trajectories to new worlds, new knowledges, and new narratives or imageries occur within or start from their specific view of the world. In 1492, European seafarers, searching for a route to "the Indies" that would avoid the Portuguese-dominated South Atlantic, found their way blocked by a continent unknown to them and inhabited by many peoples.[25] Hoping that this "new" land was some part of the India they longed to reach, they misnamed the people "Indios" or "Indians." By another misunderstanding a cartographer misnamed the continent "America." For Europe's elites, meeting the peoples of the Americas implied the collapse of their worldview. According to the Bible, the basic "knowledge" text of the time, God's word had been spread to all peoples of the earth, although the people of the Americas evidently had not heard of the Christian

---

25 : The land had been reached more than five centuries earlier by Norse seafarers who had called a part of it "Vinland." The still enigmatic person called Columbus, according to the data available, had travelled to English ports and to Icelandic centres of learning to collect information for his contemplated trip across the Atlantic. The data from the defunct Norse migration system were part of the Icelandic sagas and of North European chronicles.

God. Was the Bible wrong or were they not human beings? Once lengthy debates among the "learned cultures" of the Iberian peninsula—conducted in the absence of the peoples of the Americas—determined that these un-Christian creatures were human beings, if primitive or depraved ones, they were viewed as potential labourers, preferably in bound condition, and as heathen savages in need of religious salvation.[26] However, the European newcomers, whether the equally self-righteous Catholic Spanish or Puritan English, had to rely on food from the Arawak and the Massachusetts peoples. They survived by Native peoples' generosity or, in the thinking of some present-day administrators, by "food handouts," which undercut a person's initiative and self-reliance. Food would become a central though little remembered element in the Atlantic exchange. Without potatoes and many other nutrients and stimulants from the Americas, European population history would have been different—and in consequence so too migration from Europe to the Americas.[27]

With the rise of territorial dynasties and merchant houses of Western Europe to a position to challenge the Iberian ones, they, too, aspired to gain influence in the Americas. In the name of the English Tudor dynasty, the Italian navigator Giovanni Caboto (anglicized as John Cabot) found an island unknown to him ("new found land") in 1497. In 1534 the French Valois dynasty sent a Breton from Saint-Malo, Jacques Cartier, who explored the as yet unnamed St. Lawrence River. As part of imperial strategies, these

---

26 : Anthony Pagden, *European Encounters with the New World* (New Haven: Yale, 1993), and Pagden, *The Fall of Natural Man: The American Indian and the Origins of Comparative Ethnology* (Cambridge: Cambridge, 1982); Lewis Hanke, *All Mankind Is One: A Study of the Disputation between Bartolomé de Las Casas and Juan Ginés de Sepúlveda in 1550 on the Intellectual and Religious Capacity of the American Indians* (DeKalb, IL: Northern Illinois Univ. Press, 1974); Peter Mason, "Classical Ethnography and Its Influence on the European Perception of the Peoples of the New World," in Wolfgang Haase and Reinhold Meyer, eds., *The Classical Tradition and the Americas*, 2 vols. (Berlin: deGruyter, 1994), 1:135–72; Helmut Reinicke, *Wilde Kälten 1492: Die Entdeckung Europas* (Frankfurt/M.: Iko, 1992); Peter Mason, *Deconstructing America: Representations of the Other* (London: Routledge, 1990); Karl-Heinz Kohl, ed., *Mythen der Neuen Welt: Zur Entdeckungsgeschichte Lateinamerikas* (Berlin: Frölich & Kaufmann, 1982); Tzvetan Todorov, *The Conquest of America: The Question of the Other*, translated from the French *La conquête de l'Amérique: la question de l'autre* by Richard Howard (Paris: Seuil, 1982, repr. 1991; New York: HarperPerennial, 1992, 1985); Fredi Chiappelli et al., eds., *First Images of America: The Impact of the New World on the Old*, 2 vols. (Berkeley: Univ. of California Press, 1976).

27 : Jonathan D. Sauer, "Changing Perception and Exploitation of New World Plants in Europe, 1492–1800," in Chiappelli, *First Images*, 2:813–32; Earl J. Hamilton, "What the New World Gave the Economy of the Old," ibid., 2:861–65; J. Sermet, "Acclimatation: Les jardins botaniques espagnols au XVIIIe siècle et la tropicalisation de l'Andalousie," in *Mélanges en l'honneur de Fernand Braudel*, 2 vols. (Toulouse: Privat Éd., 1973), 1:555–582.

"discoveries" were advertised to the world and, reprinted in history books, such publicity became the wisdom of the ages. However, Basque and Bristol fishermen probably had plied the routes to the abundant supplies of cod earlier. They had kept this knowledge a trade secret to safeguard their way of gaining a livelihood and, for historians, the White male "explorer" stories were far easier to reproduce than references to fishermen's voyages were to investigate.[28] Thus, the many-cultured composition of the fishermen and the explorers' sailors notwithstanding, an image of two exploring men emerged from the strategies of production of "knowledge" and their underlying gender and class concepts. No view of the European seafarers' arrival by resident First Peoples has come down to us; the Newfoundland Beothuk and most of the peoples living along the St. Lawrence River succumbed to the newcomers' diseases.[29] However, knowledge is never unitary. Among the intellectuals of French-Canadian society Père Lafitau's *Moeurs des Sauvages américains, comparées aux moeurs des premiers temps* (4 volumes, Paris, 1724) argued that the peoples living in the new continent from ancient times might be compared to the highly cultured ancient peoples of Europe, especially the Greeks.

Subsequent visitors to or intruders into existing First Peoples' societies left a multitude of accounts. They knew nothing and were interested in everything. Within their European frames of mind, they recorded details of geography, described the impact of the vast spaces, reflected on the men and women of the First Peoples, and calculated potential benefits from natural resources. Their reports ranged from descriptive to encyclopedic, from credulous to critical, and, since publication had to be profitable, they were often embellished into "a tangle of truths, half-truths, plagiarised adventures and wholesale fiction." Scholarly institutions such as the *Academie française* (founded 1635) and the Royal Society of London for Improving Natural Knowledge, founded in 1660 on the French model, by the mid-eighteenth century were instructing expeditions to become more scientific.

---

28 : Mark Kurlansky, *Cod: A Biography of the Fish that Changed the World* (London: Cape, 1998), 19–153.

29 : Olive P. Dickason, *The Myth of the Savage and the Beginnings of French Colonialism in the Americas* (Edmonton: Univ. of Alberta Press, 1984, repr. 1997), and Dickason, *Canada's First Nations: A History of Founding Peoples from Earliest Times* (Toronto: McClelland & Stewart, 1992), 86–135. For the other British colonies, subsequently the United States, see Robert F. Berkhofer, Jr., *The White Man's Indian: Images of the American Indian from Columbus to the Present* (New York: Random, 1978); Roy H. Pearce, "The Significance of the Captivity Narrative," *American Literature* 19 (1947–48): 1–20. For a Native person's view, see Daniel N. Paul, *We Were Not the Savages: A Mi'kmaq Perspective on the Collision between European and Native American Civilizations* (1st ed., 1993; new ed., Halifax: Fernwood, 2000).

But maps of the time exemplify "the continuing force of European perspective in governing the representation of Canadian wilderness." Explorers "named in order to claim" and "imposed a European style on the landscape by means of the verbal conventions" they employed.[30]

In this process of "possessive knowledge acquisition," new information was fitted into prior societally developed cognates by particular interest groups and diffused to whole societies. Given that European and Native American peoples had different concepts of property, the former believed that they physically owned the social spaces new to them, and, once independent from food handouts, began to impose their system of Crown or "private" ownership on the original residents. The verb *privare* at the time of the Roman *republic* (*res publica* or "the things of the public") meant "to rob someone." Processes of appropriation, based on power hierarchies in terms of weaponry and definitions, imply destruction of the previous users' mental worlds.

In a Euro-imperial perspective, plans for territorial-mental acquisitions occurred in a competitive framework: the tiny settlements in Acadia and Nouvelle-France were part of a struggle between France, England, Sweden, and the Netherlands to gain a foothold and establish their rule in the region from the St. Lawrence to the Delaware. Jean Talon, French *intendant* from 1665 to 1672, envisioned a profitable realm from the St. Lawrence River to Mexico (*Mémoire*, 1665)—an early North American Free Trade Agreement—based on France's metropolitan views, structures, images, and interests. Viewed in terms of access, northern entryways were the St. Lawrence Valley, the Hudson River, and Hudson Bay. Viewed in terms of a struggle between religions—and in the seventeenth century religion rather than ethnicity was the identity-providing factor—it was a Catholic-Puritan-Protestant struggle with Lord Baltimore's Maryland and William Penn's woods (Pennsylvania) as a refuge for those persecuted because of their religion. This section of the continent was part of a Dutch, British, and French strategy to encircle Spanish tropical America from the north and the south (the Guianas and Dutch Brazil). What came to count in the long run was not the fur trade but the plantation islands in the Caribbean: Guadeloupe, Martinique, and Saint-Domingue in the case of the French Empire, Jamaica and others in the case of the British Empire. The settlements of the early Acadian and St. Lawrence Valley immigrants as well as those of the Illinois and Louisiana territories were part of a transcontinental design; the settler families were pawns of Euro-imperial politics.[31]

---

30 : W.H. New, *A History of Canadian Literature* (London: Macmillan, 1989), quotes p. 40.

31 : D.W. Meinig, *The Shaping of America: A Geographical Perspective on 500 Years of History*, vol. 1: "Atlantic America, 1492–1800" (New Haven: Yale, 1986). See also Catherine

Subsequently, the struggle of European men against nature (the other family members were not mentioned) became a theme of North American discourse in general as heroic feats in a bitterly cold and inhospitable climate. This theme, perpetuated by writers in Quebec and Ontario, became an identity-defining topos in post-1867 Canada. It scared nineteenth- and twentieth-century potential immigrants from selecting Canada as their destination. "White" immigration bureaucrats instrumentalized it to exclude men and women of African or African-Caribbean background, who, they said, could not stand the climate. At the beginning of the Great Depression in 1929, one author still counselled, *Go North, Young Man!*, and in 1980 a first bibliography on women's history was entitled *True Daughters of the North.*[32] In the present, tongue-in-cheek book titles suggest that Canadians' lives include "sex in the snow" and that social policy is a sign of "warm hearts in a cold country."[33] The cliché has become a signifier of identification to a degree that in the year 2000 the 46-cent postage stamp showed the Maple Leaf flag in front of an iceberg. A picture of southern Ontario's vineyards would never have served the same purpose nor would, yet, the silhouette of a Canadian city. But what do frozen spaces mean to young people who have no experience of northern blizzards but live in Canadian metropoles from the time of their arrival? What does it mean for people growing up with central heating? Even for a Finnish immigrant family of the 1920s, moving from urban Helsinki with its good schools and centrally heated apartments, life in the cold of Timmins, Ontario, simply meant backwardness. In imagery and memory, the North is the product of writing, of representations, as Renée Hulan and Sherrill Grace emphasized, "The real north (or norths)

Collomp and Mario Menéndez, eds., *Amérique sans frontière: Les États-Unis dans l'espace nord-americaine* (Vincennes: Univ. Paris 8, 1995), and on a journalistic level, see Joel Garreau, *The Nine Nations of North America* (Boston: Houghton Mifflin, 1981).

32 : Horst Walter Blancke, "Reisen ins Ungewisse," *Zeitschrift für Kanadastudien* 38 (2000): 87–111; Joe Cherwinski, "The Rise and Incomplete Fall of a Contemporary Legend: Frozen Englishmen in the Canadian Prairies During the Winter of 1906–07," *Canadian Ethnic Studies* 31 (1999): 20–43; Courtney R. Cooper, *Go North, Young Man!* (Toronto: McClelland & Stewart, 1929), an adventurer-explorer account; Beth Light and Veronica Strong-Boag, *True Daughters of the North: Canadian Women's History; An Annotated Bibliography* (Toronto: OISE Press, 1980). The best survey and discussion of images of the North is Sherrill E. Grace, *Canada and the Idea of North* (Montreal: MQUP, 2002). For the impact on young Canadians' socialization see Konrad Groß, "North of Canada—Northern Canada: The North in 19th-Century Juvenile Fiction," *Zeitschrift für Kanada-Studien* 28 (1995): 19–32.

33 : Michael Adams, *Sex in the Snow: Canadian Values at the End of the Millennium* (Toronto: Viking, 1997); Daniel Drache and Andrew Ranachan, eds., *Warm Heart, Cold Country: Fiscal and Social Policy Reform in Canada* (Ottawa: Caledon Inst., 1995).

is not . . . the issue." For social and cultural historians, both the real or experienced North and its representations are the issue.[34]

The Helsinki immigrants' narrative, like First Peoples' oral transmission of culture and their versions of interaction with the Second Peoples, remained inaccessible to scholars restricting themselves to written sources and two Euro-Canadian languages. Fur traders and early farming families, who lived with "Indians" as trading partners and neighbours, often held differentiated and intimate views of their lives. But the Jesuit missionaries, from the frame of their militant evangelism, described the new world as "a theatre" where God, represented by themselves, and Satan, represented by the "Savages," fought "a bitter, unending battle." Again, thought was not uniform. The French Baron de Lahotan in his *Dialogues . . . avec un sauvage dans l'Amérique* maintained that First Peoples' social customs were preferable and, in the guise of a fictitious dialogue with a Huron, he attacked the five bastions of European civilization, "le christianisme, les lois, la propriété, la médecine, le mariage." The book, published in The Hague in 1708, or fifty years before Rousseau invented his "noble savage," went through thirteen editions in a decade and a half. Out of such initial contacts, New France's and New England's clerics consolidated narratives about themselves and "the Indians" and handed the imagery down to subsequent generations.[35]

A further step in the appropriation of Canadian space was the emphasis on particular landmarks: spectacular like Niagara Falls, alluring like the "great West," or majestic like the cordilleras. Travellers, in their printed accounts, generalized from their particular, often very limited experience. Some dramatized lives and created the "hardy backwoodsmen" without pointing out that many were part of families or, in customary language, "had" families. The newcomers, after consolidating their power over First Peoples, established internal hierarchies. Thus the British took possession of the image of St. Lawrence Valley French. The Dutch immigrant painter, Cornelius Krieghoff, in the 1840s and '50s earned his living by painting quaint habitant scenes. They sold well, mainly to educated British, and so he increased production. His colourfully dressed but simple French Canadian subsistence farmers, often depicted in the cold of winter, catered to British notions of superiority. The habitants' scraggy and often tired little horses were a signifier in the frame of British codes of racy steeds, a code embodied

---

34 : Dirk Hoerder, *Creating Societies: Immigrant Lives in Canada* (Montreal: MQUP, 1999), 99–105; Grace, *Canada and the Idea of North*, quote p. 21; Renée Hulan, *Northern Experience and the Myths of Canadian Culture* (Montreal: MQUP, 2002).

35 : Pierre Savard and R. Ouellet, "Exploration and Travel Literature in French," *Canadian Encyclopedia* 2:737.

in a genre of paintings, for example those by George Stubbs.[36] The newcomers from Europe migrated not only with their skills into fertile lands or to job-providing cities, but also with preconceived images into the social and mental spaces of people of other cognitive and affective conventions.[37]

This selective summary of "images," "myths," or "knowledges" associated with the region that became Canada reflects a perspective that is often considered "normal" or even "natural": that of the Atlantic-St. Lawrence River contact zone. Other contact zones have received far less attention. Through the Arctic Sea came the men of the London-based Hudson's Bay Company who, with their Native women consorts, created another of the many Canadian societies, that of the English-speaking Métis. A third perspective was the African-Atlantic one, current in the African community in Halifax and later among escaped slaves from the United States. Another perspective would begin at the Pacific Coast and include the impact of two more empires: from New Spain, Spanish-Creole and Mestizo entrepreneurs and ship captains explored opportunities for fishing or other profitable undertakings, perhaps as far as the Skeena River, and from Siberia, Russians with the help of Aleutian fishermen came and settled as far south as California. Even the British-Pacific imperial perspective has been buried by the mass of Atlanto-centric writing. When, in the late eighteenth century, the London-based East India Company planned to compete for the lucrative fur trade, controlled by the Northwest and Hudson's Bay Companies from the east of the continent, its directors decided on a western, trans-Pacific access route. From their possessions in Asia they sent Chinese sailors and craftsmen to establish a base on the southern tip of Vancouver Island. The continuing search for a Northwest Passage indicated that contemporaries were well aware of the economic potential of societies in Asia. Historians have provided stories of the exploring men in the Arctic but have rendered invisible the cultures of the Pacific.[38] Only in the late twentieth century did

36 : New, *History of Canadian Literature* (1989), 98. Exhibition of Krieghoff's paintings in the Vancouver Art Gallery, March 2001; Stubbs's paintings in Tate Gallery, London.

37 : James Clifford, "Traveling Cultures," in Lawrence Grossberg, Cary Nelson, Paula Treichler, eds., *Cultural Studies* (New York: Routledge, 1992), 96–116. See Carl F. Klinck et al., eds., *Literary History of Canada: Canadian Literature in English*, 4 vols. (second 2nd ed., Toronto: UTP, 1976, 1990), vol. 1; New, *History of Canadian Literature* (1989), 1–80; Pierre de Grandpré, *Histoire de la littérature française du Québec*, 4 vols. (Montreal: Beauchemin, 1967–69), vols. 1–2; Maurice Lemire, ed., *Dictionnaire des oeuvres littéraires du Québec*, 6 vols. to date (Montreal: Fides, 1980–94), vols. 1–2.

38 : Robin Fisher and Hugh Johnston, eds., *From Maps to Metaphors: The Pacific World of George Vancouver* (Vancouver: UBC Press, 1993), explore not only an approach from the World of the Pacific as perceived by George Vancouver, but also the perceptions

the new economic role of Canada's Pacific ports and the large-scale trans-Pacific migrations result in a re-admission of these early connections to collective memory.

Imperial interests and intellectual changes
in the hegemonic Atlantic World

The colonizing, military expansion of European states across the globe made resident peoples part of dynastic states' imperial and economic competition. Some resisted, others negotiated, and yet others were destroyed. Tracy N. Leavelle suggested a "two-way flow of information, power, and people" in the exchanges between French missionaries and Native peoples and analyzed the visit of a leader of the Illinois people to France, who described the many-cultured communities to French thinkers. Revolutionary developments need to be analyzed in a hemispheric perspective, as Lester Langley stressed. Donald J. Ratcliffe argued that the United States, too, "remained in a neo-colonial position to Britain even after 1815" as evidenced by the "public's continuing preference for British books and respect for British cultural judgments." Later, intellectual exchange in the Atlantic World moved both westward and eastward as Daniel T. Rodgers has recently reemphasized.[39]

Typologically, colonies of exploitation and colonies of agrarian settlement have been distinguished. What was to become Canada was both: its natural resources were exploited, though not with Native labour as in British India or with slave labour as in the French and British Caribbean. Its fertile lands, along the Atlantic coast and in the St. Lawrence Valley between Quebec City and Montreal were settled in the seventeenth and eighteenth centuries by emigrant peasant families, soldiers, as well as individual men and women from the cities of the two metropoles. These settlers remained in limbo—were they the advance guard of European civilization or were they instruments of imperial struggles? To the end of the nineteenth century and perhaps as late as the 1950s, neither of the two Second Peoples developed a coherent strategy for building a Canadian society. They operated in depend-

---

others had of him; Louis Miranda and Philip Joe, "How the Squamish Remember George Vancouver," 3–5.

39 : Lester D. Langley, *The Americas in the Age of Revolution, 1750–1850* (New Haven: Yale, 1996); Daniel T. Rodgers, *Atlantic Crossings: Social Politics in a Progressive Age* (Cambridge, MA: Harvard, 1998); Tracy N. Leavelle, research prospectus, p. 1, and Donald J. Ratcliffe, research prospectus (1999), p. 4, for the Project on Internationalizing the Study of American History of the Organization of American Historians and New York University.

ent positions and in an Atlantic World that underwent major changes as regards (1) relative positions of economic power; (2) political thought and emphasis on peoples' cultures; and (3) the shift from colonial expansion to imperialism.

The wars between the British and French dynasties about predominance in Europe and, over time, across the globe, turned the North American colonies into battlefields. French and British colonists had to fight each other and a collective memory of antagonism was one result. In the colonies that came to form the United States, settlers stood up for their rights as Englishmen (as well as their economic interests as English Americans), while those in the British colonies further north remained dependent on (or loyal to) the Hanoverian dynasty. When the Bourbon dynasty lost out to its British competitor in 1763, the French settlers in the Americas were in a double bind: they felt loyalty to a French culture and the Roman Catholic Church, but had achieved liberation from France's statism. The English-speakers, too, were in a bind: they felt the Anglican Church's claim to hegemony, but they had an option to accept the ever-present Scottish Protestantism. No blueprints for societies, whether Quebec, Upper and Lower Canada, union or federation, were available. The inhabitants had to merge their many experiences with political-intellectual imports from Europe, dependent minds in a pre-existing physical space.

In eighteenth- and nineteenth-century European political thought, the Enlightenment concept of human equality and natural rights and Romanticism's attachment to a cultural "nation" signalled a fundamental shift in the discourses of literati, scholars, political thinkers, and statesmen. Enlightenment thought and the revolutionary activities of people in thirteen of the British colonies in the Americas and in France changed the concept from dynastic to popular rule, but in Europe the practice of statehood did not change. The Central European German-language Enlightenment philosopher Immanuel Kant, a precursor of modern discourse theory, emphasized the limitations of language and thought and argued that laws could be virtuous only if free from personal interests. He thus juxtaposed the public and the private and recognized the connection between knowledge and human interests. Thus, alternatives to state and commercial-capital approaches were available in the marketplace of projects and ideas for social organization. It has long been clear that no story should ever be told as if there were only one outcome. However, these open, flexible, and egalitarian approaches lost out to institutional continuity, the state and its personnel as well as its intellectual corollary expressed in Georg W.F. Hegel's single-purpose statism. Hegel, who lived in a German-language dynastic world that had divided itself into political oblivion and observed its reorganization by a powerful outside ruler, Napoleon, developed his theories when the position of the middle classes had been secured. He started from the family as the basis of the state (*bürgerlicher Staat*), which thus constituted the highest moral principle (*sittliche Idee*) and, as such, became primordial to society and to the families on which it was based—a circular argument if ever there was one. Intellectuals in other European states concurred or, for example in Scottish pragmatism, demurred.[40] Among historians, stateside approaches won and no histories of peoples as agents of building societies emerged. A century later, the stateside ideologues of empire—whether Hanoverian-Windsor, Bourbon, Hohenzollern, Habsburg, or Romanov—appropriated the theory of a folk–people continuum to justify the political domination and cultural hegemony of powerful people, "nations," which they constructed as existing from times immemorial. In this climate of opinion, even a scholar as different from mainstream as Karl Marx could not but concur and call the subalternized "people without history."

The inventors of nationality turned to two newly emerging natural sciences, biology and studies of race, to develop a male bloodline version of nationhood, though, if "blood" lines were at all an analytical concept, the umbilical cord would suggest a feminine version of national myths. The scholar-ideologues' leap into a bloodline continuity was a prerequisite to gloss over the many-cultured present of the nineteenth century. Both the British and the French "nations" were plural societies with many regions, cultures, and dialects, held together only by unitary governmental institutions.[41]

Parallel to this, economic thought underwent a transformation from emphasis on urban producers to propagation of strong national economies and colonial-imperial expansion. In his pathbreaking *The Wealth of Nations* (1776), the Scottish moral philosopher Adam Smith discussed the economic aspects of human agency. In his world of small regional economies, each actor, whether small capitalist or skilled worker, could act according to his own best interests and select between multiple options. His free market was one of equal producers and perfect communication, presumably the visible market space of his hometown Glasgow. Such self-regulating socio-economic spaces interacted through commerce with other such spaces. The sum total of these self-interested and self-enlightened actions Smith named "the

---

40 : Jürgen Habermas, *Knowledge and Human Interests*, translated by Jeremy J. Shapiro (2nd ed., London: Heinemann Educational, 1978); Anthony Giddens, *Social Theory and Modern Society* (Cambridge: Polity Press, 1987); David Held, *Democracy and the Global Order: From the Modern State to Cosmopolitan Governance* (Stanford, CA: Stanford, 1995).

41 : See Chapter 3.

invisible hand of the market" since he wanted to unburden economic activities from the heavy hand of the eighteenth-century British "state," that is, the non-producing gentry. This class monopolized the state's offices, the power to rule, and lived off the revenues extracted from producers as taxes and duties. It eschewed work of any kind; its ostentatious consumption was based on an unproductive servant class. In an unfortunate turn, the critique of the non-productive servant class was taken to devalue reproductive work, that is, women's work, as a whole. In a second, interest-driven turn, imperial ideologues transformed the concept of "free commercial exchange" into a liberalist concept of market's freedom from moral constraints, thus turning mutual exchange and information relationships into imbalanced power relationships. "*Free* trade, if it was to be profitable, assumed the existence of an unchallengeable fleet and points of supply on all world routes," in Henri Brunschwig's concise assessment, or as Paul Kennedy has emphasized, comparative advantages accrue to great powers. The resulting globally unequal economic developments, among other causes, induced those nineteenth-century mass migrations from Europe outward that were to bring people to Canada and other parts of the world; and, with the twentieth-century unequal terms of trade, still induces the poverty migrations of the present. Markets are "created in and derived from social circumstances" and power relationships, to expand on Christopher Clark's term.[42]

The third major change after the nationalism–imperialism continuums and the fusion of state and commercial power was the liberation of the European working classes from the many types of bound labour. Since the reorganization of European societies under the impact of the French Revolution and the Napoleonic wars, bondage of agrarian labouring families was reduced. Through the early trade union movements, artisanal and industrial working classes achieved some measure of self-determination and mobility. Such mobility was in the interest of planters and other capitalists in the colonies of exploitation, since slavery was being abolished in the Atlantic World. It was also in the interest of the colonies of settlement, which needed White settlers and labourers.

---

42 : Adam Smith, *The Glasgow Edition of the Works and Correspondence of Adam Smith* (6 vols.), vol. 2; R.H. Campbell, A.S. Skinner, W.B. Todd, eds., *An Inquiry into the Nature and Causes of the Wealth of Nations* (1776), (Oxford: Oxford, 1976); Henri Brunschwig, *French Colonialism, 1871-1914: Myths and Realities*, translated from the French by William G. Brown (London: Praeger, 1966), quote p. 6 (emphasis added); Paul Kennedy, *The Rise and Fall of the Great Powers: Economic Change and Military Conflict from 1500 to 2000* (New York: Random, 1987); Christopher Clark, *The Roots of Rural Capitalism, 1780–1860* (Ithaca, NY: Cornell, 1990), quote p. 13; Anthony Richmond, *Global Apartheid: Refugees, Racism and the New World Order* (Toronto: Oxford Canada, 1994).

The intellectual, social, and economic changes in the Atlantic World produced new options. The imperial frame, with the British Empire dominant after the defeat of France, involved the Canadas in a market in which the strongest took the profits. Access to this economy was predicated on (1) knowledge of the English language, and thus it disadvantaged speakers of French and other languages, and (2) on capital and access to imperial political elites, which disadvantaged colonial elites even if of British background and culture. The mainstream of the intellectual elites did not pursue the egalitarian options of late eighteenth-century cultural and economic theory but recast Adam Smith as a proponent of the power of the market and Herder as founder of the power of nationalism, and adopted Hegel's praise of a strong state and heroic statesmen. Out of these fallacies emerged the basic contradiction of the "nation-state": the conflation of democratic states and populations equal before the law with a hegemonic nation and its special rights as well as the conflation of national cultural institutions with a particular class of office-holders. The "nationals" were elevated over others designated "minorities," "ethnics," or "allophones." They were hierarchically gendered, excluding women from political participation, and they were White, excluding all those designated "coloured." The Canadas of the mid-nineteenth century were part of this Atlantic intellectual and British imperial world. As colonials, its elites remained subservient.

Canadian specifics: Regions, boundaries, incomplete nation-state

Canada's economic development depended on imperial connections as well as on world markets. For almost three centuries, its many regions—Acadia and Nouvelle-France, Nova Scotia and Upper Canada—produced staples for imperial metropoles: fish, fur, lumber, and, finally, with the Prairies added, grain. While fishery was confined to the regional economic space of the Northern Atlantic's littoral zone, the fur economy encompassed a northern global space from Scandinavia via Siberia to northern North America. Its centres of capital procurement and of processing furs into fashion were the urban cores of a succession of empires: Swedish, Dutch, Russian, French, and English. Only the lumber economy, also in competition with Scandinavia, expanded to involve skilled shipbuilding work in the Maritimes. This North Atlantic economy with its marginal raw material-supplying spaces was disrupted since 1806 by the Napoleonic blockade of the trade between the British Isles and the European continent. Temporarily the North American colonies profited from the increased demand for lumber. But by the 1840s, with British supremacy restored since 1815, the "motherland" / economic core, moved to reduce the cost of governing and administering the colonies. It granted a degree of self-administration to the settler or so-called "white" colonies or, in the "national" discourse of the times, the societies of colonial Britain. Other cultural groups of colonial inhabitants—the French in the Canadas or the Dutch in South Africa—became minorities facing processes of subalternization.

At the same time, the imperial leaders set out to improve the profitability of the Empire. With no competitors to fear, they abolished the Navigation Laws and opted for free trade buttressed by the navy. In the process, the colonials, who proudly referred to their Britishness, lost the economic benefits of this affiliation. Social discontent in the Canadas, expressed in the "rebellions" or self-assertions of 1837/38, indicated inequalities in access to societal resources. In 1840, the Union of Upper and Lower Canada (renamed Canada West and Canada East) created an internal market that promised economic growth and improved political institutions. An attempt to further enlarge the economic space by free trade with the United States remained a brief phase, from 1854 to 1866, in this problem-laden relationship. The outside borders were fixed when the United States asserted its continental domination and incorporated about half of British-claimed Oregon territory in 1846 and half of the independent state of Mexico in 1848, as well as, in 1867, part of the Northwest Coast during the Alaska-British Columbia boundary dispute. Unification of the Canadas with Dominion status in 1867 was expected to permit both political and economic development according to the interests of Central Canada's economic bourgeoisies. Markets expanded by accession of the Maritime provinces in 1867, the purchase of Rupert's Land in 1869 from the privately owned Hudson's Bay Company, and the entry of British Columbia in 1871. The one exception to negotiation was the military intervention against the Manitoba Métis.[43] Building the "nation," in the view of the Dominion's policy-makers and powerful entrepreneurs, was primarily an economic task. The regions had to be tied together by steel—by rails—in distinction to European military statehood by "blood and iron." A mystique of "the end of the steel" emerged and, less mysteriously, huge amounts of capital were fed into the three companies that constructed the Great Trunk, the Intercolonial, and the Canadian Pacific Railways. Dominion status and the railways ended the separation of Canada's regions (*désenclavement*) and opened the way for their long-term unequal development by privileging the economically strong central Canadas.

Since achievement of Dominion status, Canada's history has been writ-

---

43 : Prince Edward Island joined in 1873; internal provincial boundaries changed repeatedly until fixed in 1912.

ten in terms of political units: federal, state, and provincial. This imposed a bureaucratic-administrative perspective on Canadian peoples' culture(s) and their economies. Provincial and national boundaries were but lines over rocks or in the grass. First Peoples' cultural spaces were different: Arctic, Western and Eastern Subarctic, Northwest Coast, Plateau, Great Plains, and Northeastern Woodlands, or, in more detail, Inuit, Dene, Tlingit, Haida, Cree, Ojibwa, Algonkin, Montagnais and many others. In the nineteenth century, however, none of these had the power to insert their voice into the political-national discourse. From among the hegemonic White cultures, the Acadians, the Nova Scotians, and the "foreign Protestants" of German dialects in the Maritimes lost political and economic clout. The new state-wide society consisted of seven cultural-economic regions, the Atlantic provinces, Quebec along the St. Lawrence River, southern Ontario, the southern Prairies, British Columbia with its triple subdivision into cordilleras, fertile valleys, coastal lands, and, sixth, the northern belt of logging and mining from Labrador to the Pacific. From this Euro-defined "North," a seventh remained separate: the Arctic region of the Inuit and, since the 1940s, of military installations. Administrative borderlines hamper rather than advance the understanding of socio-economic and cultural regions. William C. Wonders suggested to begin conceptualization of regions with the geographic determinants of human life, then add agricultural, demographic, and linguistic criteria. An isodemographic view of Canada, an "equal number of inhabitants" projection, does justice to human activity and yields a map almost unrecognizable in terms of "standard" geographic knowledge: the North, important in certain periods of the construction of (male) Canadian identities, shrinks almost to invisibility, and the urban agglomerations in the southern belt *are* Canada. All of these spaces, composed of smaller ensembles, were also part of the Atlantic World, the North American space, and of relations between micro-regions, as Guy Massicotte argued, and British Columbia was already a part of an emerging Pacific World.[44]

In the 1880s, the space on both sides of the boundary along the 49th parallel became a borderland of cultural and economic interaction. Earlier commercial relationships between Acadia–Nova Scotia and the New England colonies had been close; since the 1830s, Quebec's agrarian and New England's industrializing spaces were linked by the migrations of single men and women as well as of whole families to the textile factories. Later,

---

44 : William C. Wonders, "Canadian Regions and Regionalisms: National Enrichment or National Disintegration?" in William Westfall, ed., "Perspectives on Regions and Regionalism in Canada," topical issue of *Canadian Issues / Thèmes Canadiens* 5 (1983): 16-53; Guy Massicotte, "Les études régionales," *Recherches sociographiques* 26.1-2 (1985): 155-73, esp. 156.

French- and English-speaking Canadians moved to Michigan. For more than a decade after Confederation, the Canadian Prairies were connected by rail to Central Canada only via Windsor/Detroit, Chicago, and St. Paul.[45] U.S. citizens migrated to Central Canada's cities and to Prairie farms. Mid-nineteenth century migrants from Asia used California as a stopover before moving to the Fraser River Valley. Canada was a *pays d'escale* (Ramirez) for millions of European immigrants before moving on to the United States. While, from the 1920s, increasing border controls reduced the physical permeability of the line of political separation, and from the 1930s ever more "cultural content"-bearing airwaves were broadcast across it, mainly northward. Political borderlines neither conform to landscapes nor to cultural ways of living; they reflect divisions at arbitrary points in time cemented into particular institutional regimes. Over time, however, such institutional regimes and social discourses resulted in distinct national identities: one U.S.-American and one Canadian.

In Canada, as in the other countries of the Americas, the process of establishing institutions and of merging the many regional cultures into a single statewide or national one differed from Europe's "nations." Neither was a timeless cultural continuity extended into the past, since First Peoples were not claimed as ancestors, nor was a timeless state institutional continuity extended backward to dynastic Britain or France. The "first new Canadians," later styled British or French Canadians, had left the British and French monarchies in discontent. In polities labelled New France, Nova Scotia, New England, New Amsterdam, or New Sweden, settlers pursued utopian motifs while administrators attempted to duplicate the old institutional regimes. All faced new natural environments and created new social spaces. In contrast to the essentialist construction of "nationhood," which embodied unchangeable and genetically determined "Britons" and "French," the immigrants—even under the imperial authorities' watchful eyes—made decisions as to which aspects of their cultural and institutional background to develop, change, or abandon. The "home country" was no longer theirs, it was a memory, at best a good one. Migration into spaces without institutions turned subjects of rulers into political actors and freed many from bondage to the-past-forever constructs. This process of creating

---

45 : The St. Paul–Winnipeg line was completed in 1878, the Port Arthur–Winnipeg line in 1882. Bruno Ramirez, *Crossing the 49th Parallel: Migration from Canada to the United States, 1900–1930* (Ithaca: Cornell, 2001); Nora Faires, "Poor Women, Proximate Border: Migrants from Ontario to Detroit in the Late Nineteenth Century," *Journal of American Ethnic History* 20.3 (Spring 2001): 88–109; John J. Bukowczyk and David R. Smith, eds., "Canadian Migration in the Great Lakes Region," topical issue of *Mid-America: An Historical Review* 80.3 (Fall 1998).

societies implied the appropriation of social and cultural spheres of First Peoples through raw physical and mental power, through destruction and definition. In the new regional and national worlds, only cultural gatekeepers would not let go, remaining bound to imperial views of their world. Their decolonization, retarded by a whole century, came at the time of the Confederation's Centennial.

The Dominion did not, in the short term, become a Canadian nation-state. First, important political functions remained located in the imperial government in London. Second, territory, borders, and institutions of government were not congruent with a unified political space, regional patterns of settlement, or practices of civil society. Third, economic unification through railway tracks involved population re-composition of unforeseen cultural consequences: Chinese and East Europeans were needed as workers. Fourth, the railways, meant to be the basis of a unified transcontinental economy, did integrate small-town and rural producing and trading families to larger markets. This integration, however, did not only stimulate a region's economic potential, it also meant competition from mass-produced goods and of powerful capitalist corporations. From local people's perspectives, late nineteenth-century Canada was to be a co-operative or mutualist economy of small producers rather than one ruled by private corporations.[46] Fifth, as regards a national culture, no consensus had been achieved between the self-centred French-language and the expansive English-language segments of the new country's elites. Thus collective memory was to remain bifurcated, competitive, and combative; no master narrative ever achieved a hold over Canadian societies as a whole. If collective memory in Quebec was self-centred and that of Ontario and the rest of English-speaking Canada British imperial, where was Canada?

---

46 : Hoerder, *Creating Societies* (1999), Chapter 14, and Hoerder, "Towards a History of Canadians: Transcultural Human Agency as Seen through Economic Behaviour, Community Formation and Societal Institutions," *Histoire Sociale/Social History* 33, no. 76 (Nov. 2005): 433–59.

Chapter 3

CANADA'S PEOPLES: INCLUSIONS AND EXCLUSIONS

A comprehensive study of Canada's peoples, commonly undertaken since the 1990s, indicates the many blank areas and analytical shortcomings of institutional, firstcomer, national, or any other narrow master narrative.[47] Until the 1970s, First Peoples had been deprived of a place in collective memory. Contact with Second Peoples, whether French or British, changed the perceptions of both Native peoples and newcomers. Though post-contact history has often been reduced to the Eurocentric French-British dichotomy, First Peoples played a significant role and *métissage* created new societies. From the African-Atlantic world came sailors, rebels from the Caribbean islands ("maroons"), and self-liberated slaves from the United States. On the Pacific Coast, pioneer men came from Asian cultures. Furthermore, the Eurocentric approach locked the two "founding peoples" (*fondateurs et fondatrices* in gendered French language) into non-communicating slots, "two solitudes," though they did communicate with each other and were internally heterogeneous.[48] From the 1880s on, men, women, and children from other European cultures arrived and new discussions about "preferred

---

47 : J.M. Bumsted, *The Peoples of Canada, A Post-Confederation History* (Toronto: Oxford Canada, 1992); Margaret Conrad, Alvin Finkel, Cornelius Jaenen, *History of the Canadian Peoples*, 2 vols. (Toronto: Copp Clark, 1993). The TV series and book by Don Gillmor and Pierre Turgeon with Mark Starowicz, *Canada: A People's History*, 2 vols. (Toronto: CBC, 2000), unfortunately lacks depth and accuracy. Dirk Hoerder, in *Creating Societies* (1999), attempts a history of Canada viewed through the lifewritings of common people; Gerald Friesen, *Citizens and Nation: An Essay on History, Communication, and Canada* (Toronto: UTP, 2000), uses six personal narratives and "the media in which they were communicated" to discuss "the structure of human history" and "the character of Canada," 3. For francophone Canada see Paul-André Linteau, René Durocher, Jean-Claude Robert, and François Ricard, *Histoire du Québec contemporain*, 2 vols. (Montreal: Boréal, 1979, 1991), Engl. as *Quebec: A History, 1867-1929* and *Quebec Since 1930*, translated by Robert Chodos (Toronto: Lorimer, 1983, 1999).

48 : Contrary to the rigorous divisiveness implied in the image, Hugh MacLennan in *Two Solitudes* (Toronto: Collins, 1945) has an all-Canadian boy of both English *and* French background marry an American girl and thus not only resolves the national dualism but also the South-North cleavage. While MacLennan became the first Canadian writer of fiction who portrayed the nation as engaged in a struggle with separate identities, he was at ease with the status quo and accepted a mandatory strife within Canadian society for a unity in diversity. Wolfgang Klooss, "From Colonial Madness to Postcolonial Ex-Centricity: A Story about Stories of Identity Construction in Canadian Historiographic (Meta-)Fiction," in Bernd Engler and Kurt Müller, eds., *Historiographic Metafiction in Modern American and Canadian Literature* (Paderborn: Schöningh, 1994), 53-79, esp. 66-68.

races" and races to be excluded began. Historians, drawing their salaries from hegemonic institutions, accepted such racializations and preferred some groups to others in their narratives. While the newcomers from other than British cultures expected inclusion as Canadian citizens, they had to accept British citizenship. The gatekeepers, in limbo between colony and empire, did not come to terms with Canadian statehood and citizenship.

First Peoples: Teachers, equals, subalterns[49]

At the time of contact around 1500, people of many cultures inhabited the space that was to become Canada. They numbered some five hundred thousand according to the most widely accepted but probably conservative estimate, a figure that Europeans in the region were to reach only about three centuries later in the 1820s.[50] Except for the Pacific Coast societies, Aboriginals lived widely dispersed in an Inuit cultural region and six "Indian" ones with twelve language groups comprising some fifty different languages according to Edward Sapir's classification of 1921. These men and women had developed trading networks that crossed the vast spaces, used exchange protocols to reduce friction, and communicated across language differences. Their universe had been created by Sky Woman or a similar being. Living beings were related and some could slip into each others' personae; human beings had to deal with malign or benevolent tricksters who, in contrast to omnipotent Christian spirits or Saints, often tricked themselves. Relatedness of all beings, meant to imply unity, could neither prevent conflict between the various cultural groups nor depletion of resources under the fur trade.

To Native peoples in the early 1600s, most European newcomers must have appeared as deficient. They could not live off what the natural environment provided, they engaged in strange rituals such as raising a cross, and their magic transformed local social spaces into property of a ruler across the waters. The newcomers, who arrived with many-cultured ship crews from the Portuguese, French, Dutch, Swedish, English, Spanish, and Russian dynastic states, met hunting and gathering peoples along the

49 : The normally used term "First Nations" (in Canada) imposes a European concept of nation onto societies with different concepts of organization. Its advantage lies in the emphasis on political self-action. Since the designation "First Peoples" is often understood to refer to "Indians," the Royal Commission on Aboriginal Peoples decided to use "Aboriginal" to refer to "Indians," Inuit, and Métis.

50 : Helen H. Tanner et al., eds., *The Settling of North America: The Atlas of the Great Migrations into North America from the Ice Age to the Present* (New York: Macmillan, 1995), 30–43; New, *A History of Canadian Literature* (1989), 75.

Atlantic coast, agricultural peoples along the shores of the St. Lawrence, and highly organized societies along the Pacific Coast. On the upper Yukon River, residents named the strangers "K'och'èn, or 'cloud people,' because of their colorless skin." In their travelogues, the newcomers implied that absence of local people was the rule and the occasional sighting of an "Indian" noteworthy, but Aboriginal oral testimony provides "ample evidence that indigenous people observed the strangers."[51]

While the newcomers slowly learned basic survival techniques from First Peoples, the latter had no means of survival when the Europeans' germs undermined their health. The Beothuk succumbed; other peoples were decimated. Trade connected the two worlds. When a war between Sweden and Russia cut off Western Europe from the Russian fur supply in the 1580s, the French quickly intensified trading at Tadoussac, a traditional meeting place of northern hunting and southern agricultural First Peoples. Within a few decades, the existing infrastructure for trade expanded to reach as far as Hudson Bay and Lake Superior. First Peoples did value many European imports. Ironware such as metal knives and needles eased the work of women who had used brittle tools made of bone. Trade, which had functioned through protocols and to mutual advantage, was transformed to competition about access to resource regions and redirected to the Europeans' posts. Imperial European wars fought on the American continent provided First Peoples, acting as independent nations, with opportunities to form alliances according to their interests, but proved disastrous when a losing European empire simply abandoned the respective ally with neither protocols of fairness nor concepts of honour. Parallel to trade and war, the Rome-centred religious empire of the Catholic Church established a hierarchical cultural–religious relationship with the "heathens" that over time left the latter spiritually, emotionally, and materially impoverished. When the fur trade spread across the continent and the European-owned companies sent Iroquoian and other men west as far as the Rockies, cultures mingled and spiritual values changed. The spiritual connection between all living beings ended when Native and European hunters came to "harvest" furs and thus deplete stocks. Cultures, based on the balance between humans and nature, were depleted, too.

Life in these social spaces as well as Euro–Native contact involved neither exoticism nor fantastic imagery. Late seventeenth-century third-generation French Canadians, "nés au pays, instruits dans les écoles locales, influencés

---

51 : Julie Cruikshank, *The Social Life of Stories: Narrative and Knowledge in the Yukon Territory* (Vancouver: UBC Press, 1998), quote p. 9. Edmund S. Morgan has graphically described Virginia's first Whites and their incompetence in "The Labor Problem at Jamestown," *American Historical Review* 76 (1971): 595–611.

par le milieu, [étaient] souvent proches de l'Indien dont ils apprennent fa-
cilement les langues." In the late nineteenth-century West, many recently arrived settler families could distinguish between Native cultures and
communicated through Chinook, a Creole lingua franca combining Native
languages with Spanish, French, and English. Notions of superiority, on
the other hand, limited intercultural co-operation. When the prestigious
Royal Engineers, called to build the Cariboo Road, pursued costly patterns
of consumption but did not even finish a survey of the land, the governor
contrasted their ineptitude to the Native peoples' "remarkable cleverness
in sketching out a map of the route, marking the rivers, mountain valleys,
passes & buildings." Europeans named the living spaces of Micmac and
Abenaqui "Nouvelle-France," and those of the Salish, Nootka, and Kwakiutl
"British Columbia," and "Vancouver Island." Names misrepresent the cultural composition of the actors.[52]

Intimate relations have characterized the fur economy. Native families incorporated French Canadian and Scottish men through marriage, partnership, and commercial relations. Most men adopted their wives' ways of life.
First Nations' women had knowledge of the territory and were part of social
networks. They provided the European men, alien to local ways of hunting,
uninformed about the physical environment, and without social support,
with access to the existing societies. Children were born, the Métis cultures
developed: French Métis along the routes of the Northwest Company with
an early centre in the Red River Valley; Scottish-Métis along the routes of
the Hudson's Bay Company (HBC). The culture of the women, whether
Cree or Dene, Ojibwa or Saulteaux, has not become part of the hegemonic
naming or collective memory. The Northwest Coast, settled by some twenty
different societies, such as the Tlingit, the Haida, and the Salish, became
a shared as well as contested domain of the Spanish, Russian, and British
Empires. The first British forts were built by free Chinese craftsmen sent
by the East India Company (EIC) and Native peoples exchanged goods with
the eighteenth-century trans-Pacific vessels. From among the empires, the
British won out, and from among the companies, the HBC, a kind of early
multinational, won over the EIC. Just as Europeans had craved beaver pelts,
Chinese craved sea otter pelts, and Native suppliers hunted species to near-
extinction. Much of British Columbia's first "white" elite was of "mixed
race." The first governor, James Douglas (1803–77), had been born in British Guiana to a free "coloured" mother and a Scottish merchant father.
The English-speaking British Columbia Métis could use their status in the

---

52 : Pierre de Grandpré, *Histoire de la littérature française du Québec*, 4 vols. (Montreal:
Beauchemin, 1967–69), 1:65; Hoerder, *Creating Societies* (1999), 218–22.

power hierarchy and their access to the colonizer government in London to establish themselves as founders. In contrast, the French-Métis of the Red River Valley, *"la nation métisse-canadienne-française"* in Louis Riel's term, spoke the "wrong" language and could not easily insert themselves into political discourse. At the time of Confederation, land speculators and insensitive surveyors provoked an assertion of the right to self-government, then asked for the military to quell the "rebellion." Troops sent by Ottawa ended the Métis' attempt to define themselves as part of the new society and dispersed their culture—the one conquest in the making of Canada. The gatekeepers of the "Ontario orthodoxy" subsequently alienated almost all of the provinces' inhabitants.[53]

Hierarchical constructions replaced intimate relations when the number of "whites" grew, when missionaries imposed their belief systems, and when "white" women positioned themselves as superior to "red" women. Missionaries of the many Christian denominations undermined what they considered "heathen" and depraved cultures. The men of the Roman Catholic Church and of other all-male Orders, under imposed celibacy and denial of their sexuality, were fearful of temptation and constructed "Indians" as men, "their" women as "squaws," a heavily sexualized term.[54] Since the cleric-outsiders could and did write, while the inside Native peoples and Native-acculturated fur traders usually could not or did not write, the opinions of the former became the point of reference for collective memory, whether public opinion or scholars' analyses. However, common people of European background in the prairies and in British Columbia's valleys in the second half of the nineteenth century expressed little racism and few stereotypes about "Indians." To them, men and women from the many Aboriginal cultures appeared as friendly, capable, and helpful. Still, Euro-Canadian and Native Canadian cultures remained distant and distinct.[55]

---

53 : Marcel Giraud, *Le Métis canadien* (Paris: Institut d'ethnologie, 1945; repr. in 2 vols.: Saint-Boniface: Éd. du Blé, 1984); Auguste-Henri de Trémaudan, *Histoire de la nation métisse dans l'Ouest canadien* (Saint-Boniface: Éd. des Plaines, 1984). Margaret McWilliams, in her *Manitoba Milestones* (Toronto: Dent, 1928), 110–20, 129–48, provided an account of the numerous grievances of Manitobans against Ontario and federal policies.

54 : Sarah Carter, *Capturing Women: the Manipulation of Imagery in Canada's Prairie West* (Montreal: MQUP, 1997); Janice Acoose (Misko-Kìsikàwihkwè, Red Sky Woman), *Iskwewak - Kah' Ki Yaw Ni Wahkomakanak: Neither Indian Princesses nor Easy Squaws* (Toronto: Women's Press, 1995). In boarding schools, male clerics sexually assaulted Native children whom they had taken by force from their home communities. The U.S. American Indian Movement in 2002 demanded that place names containing the term "squaw" be changed (Manchester: *The Guardian*, 22 Feb. 2002).

55 : Dickason, *Canada's First Nations* (1992), 136–246. Regarding immigrants' views see Hoerder, *Creating Societies* (1999), 167.

After the end of the French-British imperial competition in 1763, the victorious British considered First Nations, recently their allies, as groups without rights. According to their view of law, lands of heathens and the usufruct was at the pleasure of the Crown. Major-General Darling's *Report on Indian Conditions* of 1828 became the founding document of a program to Euro-"civilize" ("re-program" in modern terms) these many civilizations. The project was cast into law in 1857 with the Gradual Civilization Act and, after Confederation, the Indian Act of 1876. From the 1870s, treaties rather than U.S.-style anti-"Indian" wars reduced the resident First Peoples' living space for the benefit of the newcomers. The lawless and reckless appropriation of power was graphically expressed by the ideologues and men of the law, Premier Oliver Mowat of Ontario and the courts, during the first Aboriginal rights case from 1885 to 1889: "As heathens and barbarians it was not thought that they had . . . any claim thereto as to interfere with the plantations, and the general prosecution of colonization." In other words, possessive Whiteness included the right to take away—from another perspective "to steal"—non-White peoples' properties.[56]

To understand, learn, and record Native peoples' cultures, European newcomers translated their spoken languages into writing. What was meant to permit intercultural exchange soon became random collecting of Aboriginal peoples' historic tales, legends, and spiritual myths. Since the observer-intruders spoke French, English, or other European languages, collection involved translation, publication, and making stories palatable to readers' Euro-Christian frames of reference. Thus the trickster Raven's sexuality was expunged from texts published for Victorian audiences.[57] Sky Woman, who came down to the earth on the turtle's back, might be misunderstood in terms of the Bible as a fallen angel, a devil. The complex spiritual, emotional, and intellectual worlds of the many Aboriginal peoples were turned into simple stories, so simple that they could be read to children, who, as adults unaware of the process, reflected the simplicity back onto the Native peoples: child-like, quaint, perhaps colourful men and women in need of guidance. Spiritual worlds of Native adults became amusements for White children. First Peoples' oral culture re-appeared as anecdotal or cautionary moral tales for Euro-North American readers. Men of an inimical belief system, whether the Christian missionaries or writers who made a living

---

56 : Dickason, *Canada's First Nations* (1992), 257–89, 319–54, quote pp. 340–41; Cheryl I. Harris, "Whiteness as Property," *Harvard Law Review* 106 (1993): 1707–91.

57 : T.M. McIlwraith's *The Bella Coola Indians* (1948) remained unpublished for two decades because he refused to purge "sexually explicit" segments of the texts. New, *History of Canadian Literature* (1989), 6.

from producing books, appropriated the cultures for their purposes. Only a few Euro-Canadian artists and writers took inspiration from First Peoples' artifacts in general and West Coast peoples' ceremonial "totem" poles in particular.

Second Peoples:
Interactions, solitudes, hegemonic pieces of the mosaic

Modern Québécois and British Canadian scholars as different in their positions as Marcel Rioux and Susan Mann Trofimenkoff agree that the histories of all Canadian regions, Quebec included, were one of interaction if in a hierarchical setting. Most of pre-1960s historiography deformed the plurality to the two self-designated founding nations without recognizing that these were internally heterogeneous and came from many regional cultures of origin in the frame of two competing empires. The "founding peoples," in the perspective of the European empires of origin, were but a marginal part of a Caribbean-North American colonial realm. The subtropical Caribbean plantation colonies based on African slave labour were much more profitable than the colonies of settlement in the temperate (or cold) zones further north.

The immigrants from the French territories and the British Isles arrived neither with feelings of national belonging nor with ethnocultural homogeneity. As regards France, a recent study noted the *métissage* of Gallo-Romans with Germanic Goths, Franks, Allemanic and Burgundian peoples, with Bretons from the Celtic islands, with Gascons from the Pyrénées, and with Normans from Scandinavia. In addition, there were Jews, a few Syrians and Greeks, and small groups from Saxony, Iberia, and Ireland. Strong regional cultures and allegiances emerged—Bourgogne, Normandie, Aquitaine, Gascogne, and Flanders, to name only a few. Dialects and languages remained heterogeneous.[58] As regards the English—not to mention the Scots, Welsh, Cornish, and Irish—Daniel Defoe sarcastically replied in "The True Born Englishman" (1701) to the labelling of Dutch-born King William III as a "foreigner": the English were a mixture of "Norwegian pirates, buccaneering Danes, Norman French, Dutch, Walloons, Flemings, Irishmen, and Scots, Vaudois, Valtolins, and Huguenots, French Cooks, Scotch Pedlars, and Italian Whores,"

---

58 : Robert-Henri Bautier, "Le 'Melting Pot' de la Gaule du Haut Moyen Age," in Jacques Dupâquier et al., *Histoire de la population française*, vol. 1 (Paris: PU de France, 1988), 123-70, 409-15; Gérard Noiriel, *The French Melting Pot: Immigration, Citizenship, and National Identity*, translated by Geoffroy de Laforcade (French orig., *Le Creuset français: Histoire de l'immigration XIXe–XXe siècles*, Paris, 1988; Minneapolis: Univ. of Minnesota Press, 1996).

> With neither name nor nation, speech or fame . . .
> A true-born Englishman's a contradiction,
> In speech an irony, in fact a fiction.[59]

National belongings were to be a nineteenth-century middle-class construction.

In the Atlantic's North American littoral zone, "the French" established two societies: L'Acadie (Acadia) and Nouvelle-France; "the English" a religiously dogmatic New England and the religiously tolerant Pennsylvania among others. Out of economic proximity, a New England-Acadian maritime trading space emerged while from Euro-imperial politics and geographic separation the St. Lawrence Valley and the New England-New York societies, as a "warring space," engaged in a sequence of resource-draining hostilities. Beyond this northern region, Bourbon France "owned," ruled, or claimed the Illinois and Louisiana territories, that is, the space from the Great Lakes along the Mississippi to Nouvelle Orléans, as well as the Caribbean islands of St. Domingue (later Haiti), Guadeloupe, and Martinique. In size, this realm far surpassed that of the British. The vast gap between profits accruing to the imperial cores from the Caribbean as compared to the northern mainland colonies was to play a decisive role in the future of Acadia and Nouvelle-France.

The two different physical, economic, and social environments along the Atlantic coast and in the St. Lawrence Valley explain the emergence of two new Frances since 1604 and 1608 respectively. The governors and *intendants*, even outstanding personalities like Jean Talon (1665–72), had to subordinate local colonial development to the perceived economic interests of distant metropolitan France, to blueprints of a society drawn up by men whose opinions were welded to social hierarchy, centralism, dynastic grandeur. Intent on mono-religious institutions, the Crown forbade the settlement of expelled Huguenots in the colonies. Their skills were welcomed in many Protestant societies in Europe, British North, and Dutch South America. Old France's mercantilist-statist blueprint stifled entrepreneurial or adventurous activities in a colony that once had been brought into existence by Tadoussac traders and Samuel de Champlain's explorations, as the perceptive historian François-Xavier Garneau noted as early as the 1840s. The peripheral position, in the context of empire, of Acadia and Nouvelle-France made both different from what had been planned in Paris.[60]

---

59 : First published in 1701, repr. in James T. Boulton, ed., *Selected Writings of Daniel Defoe* (Cambridge: Cambridge Univ. Press, 1975), 51–81.

60 : Fernand Dumont, *Genèse de la société québécoise* (1st ed., 1993, 2nd ed., Montreal:

French imperial policies often were detrimental to French colonials. The imposed societal hierarchy bound the settlers, *habitants*, to the landowners, the *seigneurs*. But many habitants quickly realized that they could do better in the fur economy and, without the required official permission, young men left as coureurs des bois from a colony in need of people since migration from France, in contrast to that from England and Scotland, ended early.[61] Though unintended, a major benefit from the restrictive policy accrued to the English Crown and merchants. When the governor deprived entrepreneur Pierre Esprit Radisson of the profits from an unauthorized but highly successful fur-trading trip to the interior, Radisson returned to Europe and published a travel account for England's mercantile-minded society in 1669.[62] Some merchants did raise "risk" or "venture capital" and organized themselves as the Hudson's Bay Company of Adventurers, which to the French St. Lawrence Valley society became a permanent British competitor from the north just as New York's Hudson River valley society was from the south. French Canadian traders, who clandestinely sold their furs down the Hudson River, avoided the 25 percent export duty imposed by Old France on New France. The competition and conflict that has been designated an ethnocultural French-British antagonism began as two different concepts of relations between state and private economies: the early commercial-capitalist model was to win over the mercantilist state-oriented one.

After costly military reversals in the wars with imperial Britain, imperial France lost interest in its colonial Acadian and St. Lawrence Valley settler families. It ceded the Acadian peninsula (1713), which was renamed Nova Scotia. London, which had never punished New England's merchants, who in the midst of imperial wars profited by supplying French first in Acadia, deported the majority of the Catholic Acadians to Louisiana and Massachusetts in 1755 on the assumption of disloyalty. It also imported "foreign Protestants" from the British Crown's European-continental realm to offset the Catholic factor. Returning Acadians, Protestants from the Germanies, and Scottish as well as Irish immigrants created a many-cultured society. Half a century after ceding Acadia and its people, imperial France in 1763 also abandoned the Catholic *colons* of Nouvelle-France in order to retain the profitable centrepiece of its holdings in the Americas, the Caribbean island

Boréal, 1996), 285, 299.

61 : In France, the population stabilized early since married couples practiced birth control. In England, as elsewhere in Europe, population growth exceeded expansion of agricultural land.

62 : As a captive, Radisson had spent two years with Native peoples and, adopted by them, learned their language and customs.

colonies with their Creole and African-Caribbean slave populations. Cost-benefit analysis won out over imperial belongings.[63]

British North America's position was equally precarious in the British Empire, whose imperial treasury also engaged in cost-benefit calculations. With France expelled from continental North America and a Catholic-French Quebec gained, it seemed inadvisable to commit British taxpayers' money to a military and administrative-institutional conquest of the latter's culture. The population was to be left sufficiently satisfied with British rule so as not to require expensive garrisoning. Thus the Quebec Act of 1774 recognized the tithes to the Roman Catholic Church, which thus accepted the seigneurial system, and reintroduced French civil law—a kind of early biculturalism and bi-institutionalism. At the same time, the British imperial authorities began to charge the cost of the colonial administration to the North American English colonists. Styling themselves "Englishmen" (and women) the colonists of thirteen colonies rebelled and achieved independence in 1776. For neither of the two empires, the attempt to subject its colonials to rule from the core had been successful and thus ended the first phase of conflictual or commercially co-operative interaction between colonists of the two hegemonial groups.

The second phase was played out mainly in Quebec, where the British victory in the battle of the Plains of Abraham in 1759 had liberated the population from a corrupt French regime that had little sympathy and where the Quebec Act of 1774 provided protection for the distinct culture. The departure of French administrators was welcomed, that of segments of the upper classes deprived the society of a part of its social, cultural, and commercial elites. Later ideologues would decry this as a "decapitation." Economically, the decline of the middle merchants was of great and lasting impact. As creditors of the public treasury, they were devastated by the French colonial government's bankruptcy. While, upon withdrawal, the French government left unpaid debts to the amount of eight million dollars, the British government, a few years later, supported the Loyalists with fifteen million dollars. Socially, the new order was co-established by the elites: the Roman Catholic Church kept its position by teaching submission to the new God-given secular government, the French Canadian nobility by marrying its daughters to British officers, the village notables by accommodation to the new rulers. Only the French Canadian mercantile bourgeoisie faced competition of in-migrating merchants of British background and credit restrictions from the

---

63 : Similarly, the Dutch Empire had ceded Nieuw Amsterdam (thereafter New York) to the British Empire to retain the profitable Suriname in the Guianas in the Peace of Breda, 1667.

new British-controlled banks. The French Canadian political-clerical elites remained content to transmit British colonial policies to the middling and rural lower classes, and the urban commercial elites and the artisanal producers, over time, recovered and established a place of their own, the British merchants' ascendancy notwithstanding.[64]

Two major migrations changed the interactive, if hierarchical, coexistence. First, connections between Quebec and France changed: the British rulers admitted few French of importance and, after 1789, the French Revolution discouraged *Canadiens* from departing, but sent French royalist clergy fleeing. Within a decade, Quebec's clerics increased by one third, the newcomers aligning themselves on the conservative side.[65] Second, from the mid-1770s some seventy thousand Loyalists or, from a U.S. perspective, counter-revolutionary Tories, fled from the American Revolution northward and increased the Anglo-Celtic cultural groups over the French-cultural one. They strengthened the British–imperial connection but demanded increased political participation. Though they consisted of Dutch and Germans, Blacks and Mohawks, Huguenots and Quakers in addition to the English and Scots, in a politically circumspect and profitable move they constructed themselves as "United Empire Loyalists," a quintessentially British ethno-political interest group that fit the frame of imperial discourse. As such they carved for themselves a prominent place in historiography.[66]

The second phase of interactive coexistence came to an end in the 1830s. The expectation that the French Canadian elite would assimilate to Britishness had proven a miscalculation. In Europe's stratified dynastic societies, elites of different cultures usually had more in common between themselves than any elite had with people of a lower social rank or class but of the same culture. In this frame of mind, the French Canadian elites had pursued *métissage* with the British upper classes. The interactive, if hierarchical biculturalism and bilingualism faced three challenges. One came from assimilationist British forces and another from rural French-Canadian

64 : Marcel Rioux, *La Question du Québec* (Paris: Seghers, 1969), translated by Hames Boake as *Quebec in Question* (Toronto: Lewis & Samuel, 1971), 28–44; Edmond de Nevers, *L'avenir du peuple canadien-français* (Paris, 1896), new ed. with preface by Claude Galarneau (Montreal: Fides, 1964), 43–117; Peter Moogk, *La Nouvelle France: The Making of French Canada: A Cultural History* (East Lansing: Michigan State Univ. Press, 2000).

65 : After 1815, no barriers existed and French-Canadians visited France or settled and plied their trades. In contrast, few French emigrated or visited the St. Lawrence Valley.

66 : Dennis Duffy, "Upper Canadian Loyalism: What the Textbooks Tell," in "Canadian Mythologies," topical issue of *Journal of Canadian Studies* 12.2 (Spring 1977): 17–26; Norman Knowles, *Inventing the Loyalists: The Ontario Loyalist Tradition and the Creation of Usable Pasts* (Toronto: UTP, 1997).

families' self-sufficient lives. In a process of ruralization, the urban share of francophones declined from 25 percent in 1760 to only 10 percent in 1825. The third challenge was Quebec's *elites définitrices* in historiography, literature, and poetry constructing a self-image of a noble but conquered people. They emphasized first arrival, before the English; reconstructed the military defeat of France in Canada in 1759 into a "conquest" of a French culture in Canada with no mention of the privileges of 1774 and the constitution of 1791; and juxtaposed British and British-Canadian arrogance to humble French Canadians' attachment to soil and faith. British Canada's elites, in turn, constructed an image of rule and French-Canadian inferiority. To reinvigorate the assimilation paradigm, to introduce the nation versus minority concept, and to achieve an integrated economic region in the interest of the urban commercial classes regardless of language, Lord Durham, in his *Report* of 1839, recommended a union of Lower and Upper Canada. He called the French Canadians "un peuple sans histoire et sans littérature" that would fare best by assimilating English-Canadian ways of life: "There can hardly be conceived a nationality more destitute of all that can invigorate and elevate a people."[67] The Union of 1840 gave French Canadians equal say in the legislative assembly but, in view of the massive immigration from the British Isles, made them a minority in the total population.

From the 1840s, the elites of the two warring rather than founding groups, set out to develop a master narrative of separate and unequal. In this third period, French Canadians, still a majority in their historic area of settlement, could pursue the options of the enlarged market and the transatlantic trade. But the gatekeeping intellectuals and clerics, except for the liberals of the *Parti rouge*, pursued a *repli sur soi-même* and were wary of new developments. The backward-oriented *survivance* period began. In this process, the *elites définitrices* reduced the far-ranging French North America to the St. Lawrence Valley. They excluded the Acadians, Ontario's French, and, later, Prairie French (whether migrants from Quebec, France, Belgium, or French Switzerland), but claimed to speak for a Franco-America just as the elite British Canadian imperialists claimed to speak for Canada as a whole. They overlooked the francophone settlers in Newfoundland, who had arrived a century before the St. Lawrence Valley settlers. A mythology of *vieille souche* or *pure laine* Québécois emerged at the time when railway building initiated a *desenclavement* of Canada's regions. The Roman Catholic clergy, whose

---

67 : Durham's *Report* quoted in Marine Leland, "Quebec Literature in its American Context," in David Staines, ed., *The Canadian Imagination: Dimensions of a Literary Culture* (Cambridge, MA: Harvard, 1977), 188–225, quote p. 212. Regarding historiographic reactions see Arsène Lauzière, "François-Xavier Garneau: L'éveil du romantisme libéral," in Grandpré, *Histoire de la littérature française*, 1:141–47.

utopian project of converting "the Indians" had ended with the decline of Huronia in the 1720s, now claimed a new religious mission in North America, a manifest destiny similar to U.S. Protestants' imperial continentalism. Quebec's re-catholicization began in the 1840s, when Ignace Bourget, Bishop of Montreal 1840–76, and subsequently Louis-François Laflèche, Bishop of Trois Rivières 1870–98, confronted all secular forces as well as dissenting opinions within the Church. They claimed the divine origin of three "human institutions—the church, the family, and the state" and, since the Church taught the law of God, it was entitled to pre-eminence.[68]

When France urbanized and industrialized and when in 1871 the Commune briefly reigned in Paris, Québécois intellectuals and bishops in a "theory of two Frances" juxtaposed a metropolitan France, "mondaine, sceptique, railleuse, impie et athée," to a purer, pious, and rural French Quebec, immune to innovation. Ironically, one of this myth's most eloquent spokesmen was an immigrant from Kentucky, the writer Jules-Paul Tardivel.[69] Differences did exist: Quebec French reflected usage of the time of immigration, a stage that was considered archaic in France; the government in France encouraged industrialization, the Quebec one ruralization. As regards relations between State and Church, France was a secular state, Quebec a Catholic one. As regards distinctiveness of culture, France never accorded Bretons, Basques, Corsicans, or Alsatians special status, while Quebec never doubted its special place in Canada. In a "clerical offensive," the bishops in 1871 instructed Catholics to vote only for candidates who demonstrated an unqualified obedience to the Church.

Like each of the regions of Canada, Quebec was unique in terms of population development, economics, and society. Due to a "natalité triomphante" (Blanchard 1991), the French-Canadian population increased tenfold in the century after 1760.[70] Around 1850, only one quarter of the Québécois was

68 : Susan Mann Trofimenkoff, *The Dream of a Nation: A Social and Intellectual History of Quebec* (Toronto: Gage, 1983), 118–19. When Pope Pius IX, who had to flee Rome from the revolutionary forces of 1848, condemned rationalism, liberalism, and socialism in his *Syllabus errorum*, the powerful conservative segment of the Quebec clergy made this document its guiding text.

69 : Tardivel cited in William Metcalfe, ed., *Understanding Canada: A Multidisciplinary Introduction to Canadian Studies* (New York: NYUP, 1982), 423. Pierre Savard, *Jules-Paul Tardivel, la France et les États-Unis*, 1851–1905 (Quebec: PU Laval, 1967).

70 : Chad Gaffield, in "The New Regional History: Rethinking the History of the Outaouais," *Journal of Canadian Studies* 26.1 (1991): 64–81, argued that as a French scholar of international importance, Raoul Blanchard brought to his work on Quebec an original perspective and methodology. Jean-Pierre Augustin and Vincent Berdoulay, *Modernité et tradition au Canada: Le regard des géographes français jusqu'aux années 1960* (Paris: Harmattan, 1997), 37–50.

of British background, a mere 1 percent was of other backgrounds including First Peoples and by 1911, French-speakers had increased to 80 percent or four fifths, those of British background had declined to 16 percent, the "Others" amounted to 3.5 percent, and First Peoples to 0.5 percent. For the expanding population, land was scarce and so were jobs, industrialization notwithstanding. Young people migrated to the river cities, the vast majority southward to New England's industries. Others, under the clergy's prodding, rather than migrating to the fertile and market-accessible land in the prairies, moved to marginal contiguous lands. Such colonization of regions of poor soil, difficult climatic conditions, and distant from markets— northward to the Témiscamingue and Abitibi as well as eastward to the Gaspésie—saved French Canadians from having "to exile themselves" to the West, 3,200 kilometres from Montreal.[71] In addition to spiritual control, the Church pursued its economic gain: it had invested heavily into land but rather than developing a profitable agriculture, it shaped a hinterland.

In a Canadian and Atlantic context, Quebec elites' economic and moral thought was a hinterland, too. In 1889, Benjamin-Antoine Testard de Montigny, highest judge of the city of Montreal, pontificated regarding the brutal exploitation of working children by employers, "I consider it in accordance with common sense, which is the natural law, and conforms with positive Divine law, and the civil law." In 1895, he declared, "l'agriculture est l'état de ce peuple, qui s'est implanté si mystérieusement dans nos quelques arpents de neige," on snow-covered hills, which, without explanation, he pronounced superior to Europe, "d'une fertilité prodigieuse." In fact, Quebec society was highly differentiated, urban and rural, industrial and intellectual, *grande bourgeoisie, petite bourgeoisie, notables* of different professions, in the small towns *rentiers, artisans, curés, fermiers, colons, journaliers.* Jean Hamelin, Yves Roby, Raoul Blanchard, and others have emphasized that agriculturalists near the urban agglomerations specialized and modernized. Lumber exports since the end of the British Empire's preferences for its colonies competed with Scandinavian ones. With the exception of 1891, Quebec had higher rates of economic growth than Canada as a whole; lower ones, however, when compared to Ontario only.[72] Quebec's past-oriented

---

71 : French-Catholic missionaries in the West, such as Adrien-Gabriel Morice, encouraged Quebecers' colonizing migration to the fertile prairies and emphasized French-Catholic rights. See in general the Church-centered but differentiated study by Robert Painchaud, *Un rêve français dans le peuplement de la Prairie* (Saint-Boniface: Éd. des Plaines, 1987).

72 : *Report of the Royal Commission on Relations of Labour and Capital*, 2 vols. of reports, 5 vols. of evidence (1889), abridged edition *Canada Investigates Industrialism*, ed. Gregory Kealey (Toronto: UTP, 1973), Quebec evidence: 211–313, quote p. 307; Linteau, Duro-

slogan "je me souviens," originally engraved in the Hôtel du Parlement du Québec in 1885, refers to a complex past. The architect Eugène Taché added on occasion of Quebec's tercentenary a reference to the Bourbon lily and the British rose, "née dans les lis, je grandis dans les roses." The version "Je me souviens / Que né sous le lys / J'ai fleuri sous la rose" refers to the interactive French and British past.[73]

British Canadians, too, were hampered by gatekeeper elites, whose mental backward orientation to imperial Britain is evidence of a dual culture, the cultural limbo often ascribed by these very ideologues to first-generation immigrants. The self-image contained as many fallacies as the Quebec one and placed the emergence of a Canadian identity *en retard*. First, "the British" consisted of several cultures of which the Scottish, Welsh and Irish had suffered English conquest involving loss of the respective Gaelic languages and, in Ireland in particular, loss of the basis of economic subsistence. After migration to Canada, the four ethnocultural groups lived in separate ethnic enclaves but had to learn to get along with each other. Ethnocentric Irish and Scots Canadian historians developed their own narratives in the 1870s and 1880s.[74] Second, while Ontarian, Maritime, and federal elites took Great Britain as point of reference the imperial centre never accepted this dependent elite as equal. Thus the anchor point of British Canada's hegemonic culture was a misconception. Third, nineteenth- and twentieth-century immigrants from Britain, though the largest newcomer group before 1914, did not buttress this elite's hegemonic position. Those Canadians who had developed a Canadian identity considered "British" newcomers as misfits. Two social groups from opposite ends of the class spectrum met with particular resentment: surplus sons of the English gentry, most of whom had never learnt to earn a living and depended on remittances from their families, and British trade union men, who came with a high craft consciousness but had difficulty in adapting to the demands for flexibility.[75] Thus,

---

cher, Robert, Ricard, *Histoire du Québec contemporain*, 1:83–234, quote p. 129; Dumont, *Genèse*.

73 : When, in 2000, the author (D.H.) attempted to research the origin of the shortened version, neither the *Canadian Encyclopedia* nor those Quebec academics approached could provide the full text. First leads came from a Dutch-French Canadianist. Recent research by Gaston Deschênes has been summarized by Ingo Kolboom, "L'invention de la nation canadienne-française," in Kolboom and Sabine A. Grzonka, eds., *Gedächtnisorte im anderen Amerika: Tradition und Moderne in Québec* (Heidelberg: Synchron, 2002), 55–81, esp. 71–72.

74 : See Chapter 5.

75 : Lloyd G. Reynolds in his research for *The British Immigrant* (Toronto: Oxford, 1935) found that British unskilled manual workers and farm labourers often ended up on public relief.

the institutionalized English-language hegemonic culture rested on fragmented auto-stereotyped Britishnesses. When, at the turn to the twentieth century, British Canadian imperialists pronounced Canada to be a constituent part of the White section of the Empire and when educators modelled the school curriculum for Canadian children on Great Britain and the Empire, Frank H. Underhill had admonished the anglophone elites, "Stop being British if you want to be nationalist." English-language gatekeepers "faced the dilemma of cultural dependence less successfully than Quebec." They ended with a *Lament for a Nation* by G.P. Grant as late as 1965.[76]

The many fault lines in the French-Canadian and British-Canadian self-constructions provided cracks in the hegemonic discourse through which a many-cultured Canadianness of common people could insert itself, which the many other cultural groups could use to undercut both the dichotomy and the hegemony. While lived Canadian identities were multicultural, the Europe-centred linkages to France and Great Britain retarded the emergence of a national culture: the school systems taught imperial and clerical feats of no meaning to children in Canada's many societies, and the Quebec-French idiom was useless for communication with speakers of standard or Caribbean or other French. Such in-betweenness may have helped prevent a state-proclaimed national chauvinism from emerging at a time when such chauvinisms became the hallmark of the White Atlantic World around 1900. With the two elites in limbo between European frame of origin and lived society, ensconced in self-enclaving ideologies, the emergence of a Canadian belonging is the achievement of common Canadians. While, in 1990, a critic of multiculturalism, Reginald Bibby, held "mosaic madness" responsible for what he considered shortcomings of identification with one Canada, the many agents in the mosaic provided the country's common ground despite the divisive, elite dualism.

Early African and Asian Canadians:
Presences and exclusions

Men and women of African background came as early as the French and British newcomers—the White and Black Atlantics were inseparably entwined. Men and women still lived remnants from specific West African cultures or had been culturally homogenized through life and procreation under slavery. Pioneer enslaved Africans came with Samuel de Champlain

---

76 : Veronica Strong-Boag, "Cousin Cinderella: A Guide to Historical Literature Pertaining to Canadian Women," in Marylee Stephenson, ed., *Women in Canada* (Toronto: New Press, 1973), 262–90, quote p. 263; George Grant, *Lament for a Nation: The Defeat of Canadian Nationalism* (Toronto: McClelland & Stewart, 1965; repr. Ottawa: Carleton, 1995).

and others around 1600. Free African sailors moving through transport connections of the British Empire settled in Halifax. From the Caribbean colonies, called the West Indies, with their self-organized "maroon" communities, imperial authorities deported "unruly" men and women to Halifax in the late 1730s. More than three thousand slaves and freed families came as part of the "Loyalist" migrations in the late 1770s and after. They received land or were expelled—or in the terms of the times, were offered free passage—to Sierra Leone. Self-liberated—or from their owners' point of view, fugitive—slaves came with the help of the British navy during the British-U.S. War of 1812–14 or with help of Black and White supporters via the Underground Railroad. The 1850 U.S. Fugitive Slave Act increased the number of free northern Black refugees, and the Civil War led to a further exodus in the 1860s. From Windsor through rural Ontario to Toronto and Montreal, these men and women established communities. They could form an elite of merchants, lawyers, and clerics but could not achieve political clout. Their economic position became increasingly marginal and when, after 1900, the Great Migration brought southern African Americans to the industrial cities, African Canadians departed to the United States to join these communities. In the 1920s, a new migration from "the islands," or the Caribbean, included peoples from many different backgrounds: Barbadian, Bermudian, Jamaican, Trinidadian, and Cuban, among many others.[77]

Canadians' emphasis on the contrast between Canada's free society and U.S. slavery facilitated the inclusion of Black Canadians into discourse and historiography, a "north-side view of slavery." Immigrants wrote about their support for escaping African Americans crossing Lake Ontario or the St. Clair River as a topos of their Canadianization. Publication of "fugitive slave" narratives in Ontario drew on oral traditions, a source historians did not yet accept. But such anti-slavery publications were also part of the "Ontario hegemony"; the experiences of Nova Scotian and other Blacks were marginalized or forgotten.[78]

Racism in its Canadian version was part of the experiences of men and women of African background. Around 1900, immigration bureaucrats

77 : Dionne Brand with Lois de Shield, eds., *No Burden to Carry: Narratives of Black Working Women in Ontario 1920s–1950s* (Toronto: Women's Press, 1991); Robin W. Winks, *The Blacks in Canada: A History* (New Haven: Yale, 1971; rev. ed., Montreal: MQUP, 2000); James W.St.G. Walker, *Racial Discrimination in Canada: The Black Experience* (Ottawa: Canadian Historical Association, 1985).

78 : Life-stories of the refugees were collected in 1856, when most had spent little time in Canada. Benjamin Drew, ed., *The Refugee, or the Narratives of Fugitive Slaves in Canada: Related by Themselves, with an Account of the History and Condition of the Colored Population of Upper Canada* (Boston, 1856; repr. Toronto: Coles, 1972).

excluded Black Americans from recruitment for prairie farming, though some came on their own initiative. When, in 1955, a first group of female domestics from the British "West Indies" planned to enter Canada, another generation of bureaucrats, instrumentalizing the Canadian mythology of coldness, pronounced the applicants to be unable to stand Canadian winters. They had to relent under prodding from British officials, who preferred African Jamaicans and others to go to the White Dominions rather than to Britain itself. In the early twentieth century, a supportive network of Black women spanning eastern Canada organized migration of impoverished women from the Halifax community to domestic service in Ontario households. In the mid-1960s, less-than-supportive white urban planners had the Black neighbourhood in Halifax razed in an urban renewal / cultural destruction program.[79] In contrast to the racializing institutional practices, Canadian artists painted African Canadians since the 1920s: Wyn Wood's sculpture "Head of a Negress" (1926), the Russian immigrant Aleksandre Bercovitch's "The Negro Girl" (1935), Alma Duncan's "Young Black Girl" (1940), and John Hall's "Lydia and Veronica" (1940). Collective memory did not open its gates widely to African Canadians but it left the door ajar.

Asian men and women crossing the Pacific were also racialized and excluded. The first had come as pioneers when the East India Company sent some seventy Guangdong craftsmen and sailors to Vancouver Island in 1788. The English of this expedition remained sojourners, but many of the Chinese settled and mixed with local Native peoples. Free California Chinese prospectors, merchants, and service workers joined the Fraser River gold rush in 1858 and within a year a direct shipping route from Hong Kong to Vancouver was opened. By 1860, when the trans-Pacific trip took thirty to sixty days, 1,175 Chinese lived in the Fraser Valley, but few women, who under Confucian precepts too ranked low, were among them. Chinese contract labourers, recruited in considerable numbers for railway construction, were excluded immediately after completion of the transcontinental line in 1885 by the government's first anti-Chinese law. Chinese immigrants had

---

79 : Donald H. Clairmont and Dennis W. Magill, *Africville: The Life and Death of a Canadian Black Community* (Toronto: Canadian Scholars' Press, 1974); R. Bruce Shepard, *Deemed Unsuitable: Blacks from Oklahoma* (Toronto: Umbrella, 1997); Colin A. Thomson, *Blacks in Deep Snow: Black Pioneers in Canada* (Don Mills, ON: Dent, 1979); Howard Palmer and Tamara Palmer, "The Black Experience in Alberta," in Palmer and Palmer, eds., *Peoples of Alberta: Portraits of Cultural Diversity* (Saskatoon: Western Producer, 1985), 365–93; Christiane Harzig, "'The Movement of 100 Girls': 1950s Canadian Immigration Policy and the Market for Domestic Labour," *Zeitschrift für Kanadastudien* 36 (1999): 131–46; Frances Henry, *Forgotten Canadians: The Blacks of Nova Scotia* [in the 1960s] (Don Mills, ON: Longman, 1973).

to pay a head tax of $50, which was raised to a prohibitive $500 in 1903. Exceptions were made for merchants, since commerce and the transfer of Western ideas were to continue. Subsequently, Japanese migrants came as well as, within the context of the British Empire, South Asian migrants. Sikh colonial auxiliaries, who had travelled through Canada after taking part in the pomp and circumstance of imperial ritual in London, returned in 1904 when their regiment was disbanded in Hong Kong. Some five thousand "Hindu" worked as unskilled labourers in logging, lumbering, and agriculture or moved to California, where many intermarried with women of Mexican background. In 1908, Canada's government ended immigration of "Coloureds" from the Empire, who under British law were citizens like White Canadians and thus had the right to migrate freely. To avoid a clash with the imperial government, administrative subterfuge was used: entry at the Pacific ports was made dependent on a "continuous passage," but steamers from ports in India had to stop en route for coaling. British Columbians' attempts to deport those who had already arrived to British Honduras failed.[80]

While racism was rampant, some immigrants and outside observers acknowledged the hard work and the emotional life of men and women from Asian cultures in general and from the southern Chinese provinces in particular. In British Columbia's agriculture, co-operation was frequent and joint associations of Euro- and Asian Canadian farmers emerged. Lonely immigrant men and women of European background, to their surprise comforted by Chinese servants, cooks, or restaurant owners, realized that the generic "John Chinaman" was but a stereotype and that the empathy came from these men's own loneliness. They reflected on their preconceptions: Chinese restaurants displayed "weird-looking eatables" but perhaps served "wonderful dishes" inside; Chinese merchants' wives wore "beautifully worked silk coats"; a Sikh, treated "with silent contempt by most of

---

80 : Recent re-evaluations of the Asian-Canadian experience include Hugh Johnston, *The Voyage of the 'Komagata Maru': The Sikh Challenge to Canada's Colour Bar* (Vancouver: UBC Press, 1989); Norman Buchignani, Doreen M. Indra, Ram Srivastiva, *Continuous Journey: A Social History of South Asians in Canada* (Toronto: McClelland & Stewart, 1985), 12–70; N. Gerald Barrier and Verne A. Dusenbery, eds., *The Sikh Diaspora: Migration and Experience Beyond Punjab* (Delhi: Chanakya Publ., 1989); and Karen I. Leonard, *Making Ethnic Choices: California's Punjabi Mexican Americans* (Philadelphia: Temple Univ. Press, 1992). Issues of whiteness, race, and racism are discussed in Peter Ward, *White Canada Forever: Popular Attitudes and Public Policy Towards Orientals in British Columbia* (Montreal: MQUP, 1978); Peter S. Li, *The Chinese in Canada* (Toronto: Oxford, 1988), and Li, ed., *Race and Ethnic Relations in Canada* (Toronto: Oxford, 1990); and Kay Anderson, *Vancouver's Chinatown: Racial Discourse in Canada, 1875–1980* (Montreal: MQUP, 1991).

the 'superior race,' [had] rendered valiant service to the Empire of which he is a citizen." The Punjabis, Sikhs, and Pathans were treated by Canadian authorities and Irish-Canadian labour leaders as the Irish had been treated by the English. "They must have had a severe shock as to the interpretation of British law and fair-play." High-handed authorities and underhanded White workers mistreated "Orientals." B.C. employers welcomed "this influx of Oriental labour as being cheaper than White," while England's employers opposed emigration because oversupply of labour "enables them to get rich quicker."[81] The ideas, images, and perspectives available at any one time in Canadian history were many. Some chose racializing, ethnicizing, and otherizing ones; some opted for intercultural or humanist perspectives; some mingled general prejudices with differentiated views in particular encounters.

Immigrant ethnics of European backgrounds: Subalterns creating societies

Received language plays another trick on equality of human beings and citizens when it designates early European newcomers as "firstcomers" or "founders" and nineteenth-century newcomers as "immigrant ethnics." If used in scholarly writing, the terminology undercuts analysis by hierarchization. The history of nineteenth- and twentieth-century newcomers is complex. Canada was a refuge for U.S. Americans from the 1770s to the 1970s: for the many-cultured Loyalists, for enslaved and free African Americans, for young men escaping draft into the Confederate Army during the Civil War, and for young men in the 1960s and '70s who wanted to avoid the war in Vietnam. The Dominion of Canada, in the age of nation-states, was willing to integrate newcomers according to practices of dynastic regimes by granting Mennonites, Doukhobors, and Icelanders special rights of limited self-administration. Such privileging of one group over others was anathema to theorists of democratic polities.

Late nineteenth-century immigration policy divided humanity into preferred Europeans, non-preferred (and, in the terms of the times, non-White) Europeans, and unwanted or excluded "black"-, "yellow"-, or brown-skinned

---

81 : Christian F.J. Galloway, *The Call of the West: Letters from British Columbia* (London: Adelphi 1916), 256–58, 276; Martin A. Grainger, *Woodsmen of the West* (1st ed., 1908; repr. Toronto: McClelland & Stewart, 1964), 32, 79; Basil Stewart, *The Land of the Maple Leaf, or Canada As I Saw It* (London: Routledge, and Toronto: Musson, 1908), 128–35. Hugh Tinker, "Indians in Southeast Asia: Imperial Auxiliaries," in Colin Clarke, Ceri Peach, and Steven Vertovec, eds., *South Asians Overseas: Migration and Ethnicity* (Cambridge: Cambridge, 1990), 39–56.

people. However, when after the Prairies' incorporation into Canada it became clear to policy-makers that settlers were needed in great numbers, an
advertising campaign among the four peoples of the British Isles and the
many peoples in the western and northern White part of Europe brought
less than the desired healthy masses suited for outdoor work. Anglo-Saxon
migrants came as urban labourers and their Teutonic cousins, after industrialization, found jobs at home in the Germanies. Thus, new reservoirs of
migrants had to be tapped, but Europeans on the margins, under the construction of Whiteness and of colour hierarchies, were said to be of "olive"
complexion (Italians), or dark (East Europeans), or inferior without need
for colour coding (Irish and Jews). In a masterstroke of discourse restructuring as a prerequisite for a revamping of immigration policy, the Secretary of the Interior, Clifford Sifton, in 1896 invited "stalwart peasants in
sheepskin coats, born on the soil, whose forefathers have been farmers for
ten generations." He addressed Ukrainians but avoided racialization by
reference to hardy agriculturalists—the imagery connected to British yeoman farmers. This ten-second sound bite, incorporated into the hegemonic
male national narrative, relegated women and children to oblivion. Sifton
had, in fact, invited family units, men with "stout wives and a half-dozen
children"—turning of prairie sod into farms required family labour. The
Ukrainian ethnocultural group grew when Polish, Jewish, and German-
speaking people from the multi-ethnic, multilingual, and multi-religious
societies of Eastern Europe joined it. For them, at first too few to develop
their own institutions, it was advantageous to confront mainstream society
as one sizable if composite group.[82]

The newcomers' cultural belonging—or, with a genetic undertone, their
ethnicity—was clear to themselves. Historians working from census data
find less clarity. Census-takers reckoned cultural background in the ethnic
and racial background statistics through the male line. Such gendered data
increase the size of all groups with a surplus of men who marry women from
other ethnocultural groups. A 1931 study of people of German background
in the province of Quebec found an imbalanced ratio of men to women of
145 to 100 in the child-bearing age group of twenty to thirty-nine. Since
men of German background married women of other cultures, of the 169
"German" children only 81 (47.9 percent) had German mothers, while 88
had mothers of French, British, or other background. Before the "multiple

82 : Sifton quoted in John W. Dafoe, *Clifford Sifton in Relation to His Times* (Toronto:
Macmillan, 1931), 142. Donna Gabaccia, "The 'Yellow Peril' and the 'Chinese of Europe':
Global Perspectives on Race and Labor, 1815–1930," in Jan Lucassen and Leo Lucassen,
eds., *Migrations, Migration History, History: Old Paradigms and New Perspectives* (Bern:
Lang, 1997), 177–96.

origins" category was finally introduced in 1981, many "immigrant" groups were augmented by such a "homegrown" segment.[83]

The "German" group, highly heterogeneous according to the data, will be used as an example for the construction of ethnicity. By national origin, it includes German-Germans, Austrian-Germans, Swiss-Germans, and East European descendants of eighteenth- and nineteenth-century German emigrants. A cross-tabulation of census data shows more people of German background than German-speaking immigrants, an inconsistency explained by Russian-speakers of German background. By religion, Mennonites, Hutterites, and Amish are distinct ethno-religious groups who speak particular Low German dialects and left the Germanies because of persecution. Gatekeepers of Germanness in Canada have, nevertheless, often included them into "their" group. A similar cleavage between ethnic and religious culture makes census classification of Germans of Jewish religion difficult. The Yiddish language is one of the German dialects but Germans in Europe classified Jews as of different race. Less than one quarter of those labelled "German" came directly from the German states or, after 1871, the Second Reich. The ambiguities of ethnic self-classification become evident in the 1921 and 1941 census data. In view of the Second and Third Reich's warfare and the resulting image of Germans abroad, the census takers recorded a precipitous decline in men and women of German background and a concomitant rise of other groups, in particular those of Dutch background. Ethnocultural affiliation, constructed as following the male line, depends on expediency.[84]

While French and British Canadian gatekeepers, if not all members of these groups, remained in limbo, the "ethnics" jointly with the descendents of the early newcomers created regional societies, immigrant neighbourhoods, and workers' shop floor communities. Supportive networks facilitated acculturation and insertion. Out of these many societies, Canadian society emerged; out of many local identities with origins across the globe, Canadian identities emerged in institutional frameworks established by the empires and their firstcoming personnel.[85] When, in the 1960s, the British

---

83 : For a discussion of the complex ethnocultural composition of this group see Hoerder, "German-Speaking Immigrants of Many Backgrounds and the 1990s Canadian Identity," in Franz A.J. Szabo, ed., *Austrian Immigration to Canada: Selected Essays* (Ottawa: Carleton, 1996), 11–31.

84 : Hoerder, "German-Speaking Immigrants" (1996).

85 : Hoerder, *Creating Societies* (1999). The inclusion of ethnic cultures into Canadian historiography and into the received canon of literature was pioneered by Howard Palmer and Tamara Palmer Seiler. The best introduction to the sociology of ethnocultural groups is Wsevolod W. Isajiw, *Understanding Diversity: Ethnicity and Race in the Canadian Context* (Toronto: Thompson, 1999).

and French Canadians planned to institutionalize bilingualism, the Ukrainian-Canadian group, with its highly developed institutions, demanded inclusion—was it a third founding nation? Those labelled "ethnics" no longer accepted marginalization in institutions and scholarship. In addition, since the changes in immigration regulations in the early 1960s, earlier than the change of U.S. law in 1965, immigrants from Asian societies and refugees from the Americas came in ever greater numbers. The policy changes and multicultural interaction in everyday life resulted in inclusion of the newcomers into civil society, into institutional practices, and into scholarship.

Discourses about belonging and sentiments of citizenship

Who was Canadian had been debated all along. The impact of the first newcomers, Second Peoples, or two hegemonic groups—whatever the designation—was and is acutely reflected in the institutional structure of the Dominion and of modern Canada as well as in collective memory and scholarship. Such pre-eminence is justified because of their role as institution-builders and, at the same time, it is a dead weight in memory and research. While British settler families "roughing it in the bush" established a place for themselves and French Canadian habitants in gaily coloured costumes were assigned a place by the memory-keepers, those of African, Caribbean, and Asian background and "allophones" of European background remained invisible, were made invisible. If the hegemonic, self-styled founding nations in fact remained in limbo between their old-world backgrounds and the new physical and social space, few of the marginalized used their society of origin as reference point. While they held memories of childhood socialization and usually retained some pre-migration modes of everyday life, they Canadianized and were conscious of this development. Newcomers of Asian background, in view of racism as well as of mandates of their culture of origin, had different experiences. Most Chinese migrants, for religious as well as cultural reasons, lived lives in both the society of origin and receiving community. Japanese immigrant men, under the threat of exclusion, decided to bring in wives, establish stable communities, and Canadianize. Sihk-British citizens from South Asia were made to realize that colour overrode imperial belonging and law. Only men and women of African background from the nineteenth-century United States became part of society, problems caused by Euro-Canadian racists notwithstanding. The issue of "founding" a society and of being part of creating societies was a complex one not captured in received public memory until the 1960s.

Canadian society and its historiography and Social Studies, like those of other societies, are characterized by a sequence of major signifiers. At first, religion designated people, dividing them into Catholics and Protestants or segregating them into heathens. From the eighteenth century, ethnic and imperial cultures as well as skin colour became the main demarcation lines. In the nineteenth century, ethnicity and class came to play a role with respect to both exclusion and organized activity to demand inclusion.[86] Gender, on the other hand, did not achieve serious attention until the last third of the twentieth century. By law, women's nationality and culture followed that of men. Euro-White hegemonic culture was not only British Anglican or Protestant or French Catholic—each internally heterogeneous by class—it was also male. Scholarship-sanctioned master narratives followed such societal preconceptions.[87]

Women, who make up one half of societies and family economies, politically were not part of the nation-state. In Canada, they achieved a precarious inclusion when they won the right to vote in 1918. To prevent women from joining male elites, successive Canadian governments from 1917 to 1928 and the judges of the Supreme Court in 1928 upheld a male lawyer's claim that women were not "qualified persons" within the meaning of the British North America Act of 1867. Keeping institutions a male preserve does not only imply hegemony, it also guarantees that salaries from governmental positions remain men's. A further polemic about admitting women to the Canadian population erupted in 1947–48, when Parliament debated the end of Chinese exclusion. China had been an ally in war and Asia seemed to become a promising market. Fearful of a sizable immigration, the Mackenzie King government intended to admit only sponsored "family class" immigrants from China, estimated at less than eight thousand women. Racists, mainly from among British Columbia's all-male politicians, argued that thirty thousand sponsored wives could come and give birth, perhaps to three children each: such immigration out of the womb would flood the

86 : Donald Avery, "Dangerous Foreigners": European Immigrant Workers and Labour Radicalism in Canada, 1896-1932 (1983), revised as Reluctant Host: Canada's Response to Immigrant Workers, 1896-1994 (Toronto: McClelland & Stewart, 1995).

87 : Candice Lewis Bredbenner, A Nationality of Her Own: Women, Marriage, and the Law of Citizenship (Berkeley: Univ. of California Press, 1998); Marylee Stephenson, ed., Women in Canada (Toronto: New Press, 1973); Veronica Strong-Boag, "Writing About Women," in John Schultz, ed., Writing about Canada: A Handbook for Modern Canadian History (Scarborough: Prentice-Hall, 1990), 175–200; Strong-Boag and Anita Clair Fellman, eds., Rethinking Canada: The Promise of Women's History (1st ed., 1986; Toronto: Oxford Canada, 1997; 4th ed. by Veronica Strong-Boag, Mona Gleason, Adele Perry, 2002); Royal Commission on the Status of Women in Canada [appointed by Prime Minister Lester Pearson 1967], Report on the Status of Women in Canada (Ottawa: Queen's Printer, 1970).

country. This "life-giving" clause was meant to keep "Oriental" women out of the country. Racist-sexist thought was deeply embedded in society.

Development of a comprehensive Canadian belonging and of concomitant scholarship and collective memory was retarded by the core-imposed and elite-accepted lack of a Canadian citizenship. Independent nation-states provide inhabitants with citizenship; the semi-dependent White Dominions had to assign British citizenship to its people.[88] Only after World War II was a distinct Canadian citizenship conceptualized—in a logic of death for the nation-state. After "foreign" men with non-British names had given their lives—for Canada? for a Dominion? for a British-imperial entity?—some statesmen argued that these Others had a right to be Canadians. The "life-giving" clause for exclusion of women stood thus juxtaposed with what might be called the "death-in-war" clause for admission of men to the nation-state. The citizenship law of 1949, passed eighty years after the state's establishment, was a large step toward official recognition of Canadian identity, but it still privileged immigrants from Britain. As yet, British-minded administrators, however, were not ready to give in. When the ethnicity-of-origin category "Canadian" was for the first time inserted into the census questionnaires of 1951, census-takers were instructed to mark it only "when a person insists." In a world of national chauvinisms, this might be considered an encouraging sign of national modesty, but it was meant to prevent expression of Canadianness.

The census became contested ground as to ethnocultural belonging, which continued to be reckoned through the male line. Only in 1981 was the category "multiple origin" introduced to permit expression of cultural diversity within families. In 1991, 29 percent of the respondents chose this response. While Statistics Canada finally had recognized that race-and-monoethnic measures of belonging were meaningless, politicians and gate-keepers of ethno-cultural interest groups wanted to keep their allegedly mono-cultural constituencies separate so as to be eligible for either founding nation status or multiculturalism funding. Such utilitarian considerations overrode people's identifications. A 1988 Statistics Canada trial run of a census form with one mark-in box for Canadian ethnic background and one for Canadian ethnic identity showed that the former was marked by

---

88 : British citizenship originally had been extended to and/or imposed on all colonial peoples. However, when British citizens from among non-white peoples began to migrate to the White Dominions at first and to the British core after World War II, they were stripped of their citizenship.

36 percent of the respondents, the latter by 53 percent. Canadian people, in contrast to many gatekeeping governmental and ethnic groups' bureaucrats, could easily combine Canadian belonging *and* multiple cultural backgrounds.[89]

Scholarship, and Canadian Studies in particular, thus deals with a complex concept of national belonging at best, with biased ones at worst.

> "The nation is *made* in a field of social practices, all *imbued with power of varying magnitudes and types*, that are brought into some continuing relation, practically and imaginatively. Once created, the nation partially, but not completely, shapes future social practices and identities in the space it claims and seeks to delimit. To some extent, national affiliation and identity is the result of an agreement, partly coerced, partly voluntary, to find unity in diverse personal memories and public historical narratives."[90]

If such complexity is acknowledged, scholarship and educational institutions still have to deal with persistent clichés. To take one example, in the last quarter of the twentieth century the mythology about habitants visualized in Krieghoff's 1840s paintings was still historical "knowledge" to some Canadians even though the imagery had been deconstructed since the 1960s. What might be called a toxic folklore may paralyze minds. The social sciences will constantly have to analyze the discriminatory effects of such mental petrifications produced by art and literature, to provide data for remedial action. Remedies, however, may have side effects. The term "visible minorities" was introduced to collect data for remedial anti-discrimination measures and thus was useful. However, it assumes, first, that white is not a visible colour and, second, that people of a skin colour other than "white" are "minorities" rather than equal citizens. Any representation may contain discriminatory or marginalizing connotations.

Creating social spaces in everyday lives

While legal and constitutional rules about belonging were decided at the overarching political level, native-born and foreign-born Euro-Canadians

---

89 : Monica Boyd, *Measuring Ethnicity: The Roles of People, Policies and Politics and Social Science Research* (Toronto: Univ. of Toronto, Dept. of Sociology, Feb. 1994); "Ethnicity in the Canadian Census," thematic issue, *Canadian Ethnic Studies* 35.1 (2003): 1–170.

90 : Project on Internationalizing the Study of American History, "Report on Conference II," Villa La Pietra, New York Univ., Florence, Italy, July 1998 (emphasis added, D.H.). Older definitions of nationality with emphasis on continuity are summarized in Anthony D. Smith, *National Identity* (Reno: Univ. of Nevada Press, 1991).

in the many cultural regions developed life projects and life strategies in local contexts: availability of land or jobs; the resources of family, kin, and neighbours; and adherence to particular customs and values. Since most of them neither understood nor respected as models the ways of life and social organization of First Peoples and since they had left their societies of origin because of a lack of options, they neither duplicated society-of-origin structures nor adapted to pre-existing social structures. They created local societies and connected to similar ones by networks of relationships, by feelings of a shared cultural past and a common language, and by similar interests. The geography of such networks resulted in shared or overlapping "social spaces." In the same places, men, women, and children of one culture may connect to each other, while those of another culture connect to their particular friends. In an urban neighbourhood or a farming district, neighbours may help each other regardless of culture but meet at social occasions only with co-ethnics. Thus, an Irish-Canadian space extended from the industrial towns of the St. Lawrence Valley to the shore of Lake Ontario and from Toronto to the agricultural settlements around London. The social space of French Canadian lumberjacks extended across the northern belt of forest harvesting. Asian Canadians added their social spaces from the West to the East. Such social spaces, as networks of relationships, often remain invisible to observers who are not part of the particular community—unless the members of the community are distinguished from others by physical features or dress styles.

For common Canadians, the political frame—the national polity, policies, and politicking, or in a word "Ottawa," as well as the urban elites of Montreal and Toronto—remained distant. Few immigrants, including those who explicitly Canadianized, mentioned provincial or national politics in their life writings. Still, the frame—easy immigrant admission and economic options—were implicitly present and some services were highly valued. While labourers had no support from the government and sometimes faced repression, farming families not only registered their homesteads, they also called the building material for their sod huts "government brick," cut from the government-allocated land. The federal postal service permitted contact with friends and kin who had stayed behind, whether in the plains of Ukraine, the English Midlands, or Guangdong province. In their local everyday world, subsistence, contacts to the outside world, and education of children were facilitated by low-cost government services: local roads, postmaster or postmistress, schools. Low taxes and few officials compared favourably with European and Asian societies. Before the 1920s, officials at Montreal's immigrant home and Winnipeg's immigrant sheds were helpful and well liked. Regional identification and immigrants' Canadianization came as a slowly emerging attachment to the sum of local societies, the national frame they helped to build, and the institutions developed from the top down.

Thus larger socio-economic regions—provinces and municipalities—and more intimate social spaces provided and provide a layered structure in which life courses are planned or policy decisions made. In the everyday lives of men, women, and even more so children, presumably distinct cultural groups have fuzzy borders. As early as the 1910s, one British observer gave a succinct summary of the belonging of non-British immigrants and the dual loyalty of the British ones. According to J. Burgon Bickersteth, among the majority of the people, "this cosmopolitan collection, . . . one sentiment is noticeable . . . after they have been living a few years in the country, and that is loyalty to Canada. . . . There is a very strong feeling of Canadian nationality, which is growing every year." Loyalty to the Empire, on the other hand, was strong only "among the British element." Canadianization crept upon immigrants "imperceptibly."

A century and a half earlier, this had also been the experience of French-speakers: Élisabeth Bégon, who in 1749 at the age of 53 migrated from Montreal to France, "ce pays qu'elle avait tant désiré voir," after arrival in France, "se découvre profondément canadienne et voit que son pays, les coutumes, la société de Montréal et de Québec, lui sont plus chers que la France."[91] While, internally, struggles over Canadian belonging and identity raged, from the outside "Canada" has always appeared as a distinct polity, whether hierarchically as two dependent cultures or as a society composed of many cultures. Societies of origin, whether in Europe, Asia, or the Caribbean, as well as the society south of the 49th parallel, are distinctly different. From the outside, Canadian Studies has a clearly defined subject matter; from the inside, the many parts do not always appear as a whole.

---

91 : J. Burgon Bickersteth, *The Land of Open Doors: Being Letters from Western Canada 1911-13* (London, 1914; repr. Toronto: UTP, 1976), quote p. 86; Galloway, *Call of the West*, 278; Grandpré, *Histoire de la littérature française*, quote p. 1:72.

Chapter 4

SELF-CONSTRUCTIONS: FROM REGIONAL CONSCIOUSNESSES TO NATIONAL BILLBOARDS

The question of over-arching national cultures was of paramount concern to the nineteenth-century Atlantic World's middle classes. During the Age of Democratic Revolution, from the 1760s to 1815, France, Britain, Spain, Portugal, and the Netherlands transformed their multiple regionalisms into centrally administered states as frames for commercial expansion and literary expression. Among East European peoples, chafing under the reactionary dynastic rule of the Romanov, Habsburg, and Hohenzollern dynasties, an awareness of distinct cultures, languages, and economic interests developed in the "springtime of peoples" of the 1830s. At the same time, intellectuals of the United States nationalized British English by a distinct American spelling and advocated "the American System" as economic regime. The Canadas, Italies, and Germanies, which unified only from the mid-1860s to the mid-1870s, developed their respective national consciousnesses late. Such national construction of identity and of a distinctive, recognizable way of life implies the drawing of boundaries to Others; nationalization involves loss of particularities, denigration of regional forms of cultural expression, and "specialization" as well as subalternization of groups labelled "minorities." In the case of Canada, boundaries to First Peoples and "ethnics" were fortified; those to Great Britain, however, remained under construction, and as to France, it was not clear whether a boundary to the industrial society was drawn or whether its Catholic-francophone society remained a frame of reference. After 1867, literary and artistic productions in the Canadas were many-faceted, but billboard-type nationalist, often popular sloganeering also developed.

Regional specifics, generic folklorization, few First Peoples

The production of literary and artistic works in the Old World and the New was different: "Là, il englobe un certain ensemble d'oeuvres incontestablement valables. Ici, il désigne la collection matérielle des oeuvres produites dans les limites d'un territoire national." This high-culture biased but perceptive comment by Georges-André Vachon emphasized that, from assumed need, in an unintended process of democratizing cultural production, that is, of inclusion, all cultural expressions count. During the colonial period in Quebec, after Newfoundland and Acadia the oldest of the Canadian societies, cultural production was intense and affirmative. In the Maritimes, early writers were free to satirize society. Writing in Ontario was as yet restricted to only a few authors from the British Isles. Repeatedly, opportunities for a French-English literary co-operation presented themselves, but never came to fruition.[92]

In the decades between the 1660s and 1713, the most intensive French colonizing period, the settlement project detached itself from the missionary one. Both a sedentary society and a nomadic network of coureurs des bois emerged—the first dualization of Quebec society, on which the French-British and the habitant families / *élites définitrices* dualisms were to follow. Rather than analyze the new society in terms of social groups, binary stereotypes abounded in this society's founding texts as well as in later interpretive ones. The dualist imagery overlooked the artisans and merchants and constructed the coureur des bois as "nomade qui refuse la société, ses lois et ses limites," as anti-social beings presenting a dangerous incitement to the toiling habitant to depart, too.[93] Some authors, such as John Hare, generalized positively: "Le Canadien français est voyageur dans l'âme. Pendent le régime français il ouvre presque tout ce vaste continent . . . il rêve de partir, visiter et dominer le 'pays d'en haut.' Un nouveau continent cent fois plus vaste que le territoire [de la France]." This provided options: "Si l'habitant trouve la vie dans la colonie trop difficile ou étouffante, rien ne pouvait l'empêcher de s'aventurer dans le forêt afin de partager la vie plus libre des indigènes." However, the voyageurs represented only between 7 and 10 percent of the people of Nouvelle-France.[94] From early travellers' accounts, writing developed in a utilitarian mode: "mémoires et lettres que les administrateurs et les missionnaires adressent en France.... On veut intéresser la métropole à l'oeuvre coloniale; on dit le pays, les réalisations, les besoins." Popular chansons drew on memory: "[Les faits] que nous appelons canadiennes nous viennent presque toutes de France." For common people, whether farmers or lumberjacks, long winters and secluded life in camps supported the development of an oral *culture populaire*, which adapted pre-migration cultural traditions. For women—among them Marie de l'Incarnation, Marie Morin, and Regnard Duplessis—convents provided a career opportunity and an intellectual space of their own, as well as an opportunity to become chroniclers.[95]

---

92 Pierre de Grandpré, *Histoire de la littérature française du Québec*, 4 vols. (Montreal: Beauchemin, 1967-69), 1: 28-60, quote p. 28.

93 LeBlanc in Grandpré, *Histoire de la littérature française*, 1:70, quote slightly rearranged.

94 John Hare, *Les Canadiens français aux quatre coins du monde: une bibliographie commentée des récits de voyage, 1670-1914* (Quebec: Société historique de Québec, 1964), quotes pp. 12, 14. Hare's terminology (*"mère-patrie," "le continent peuplé d'aborigènes, dans un état primitif,"* p. 12) indicates his adherence to traditional views of society.

95 : Grandpré, *Histoire de la littérature française* (1967–69), 1:28–60, quote p. 57.

The French governors had prohibited the introduction of printing presses and thus prevented independent opinions and public debate. A first (bilingual) newspaper was established only in 1764 after the arrival of the British. For several decades, the society became pluralist, but the loss of francophone elites through emigration, marginalization, and, most importantly, assimilation also led to an intermission in cultural production. French travellers from Europe bypassed the St. Lawrence Valley, preferring the more lively and exotic Louisiana, or Haiti as a free French-language African-Caribbean society after 1804. When, as a result of the ascendancy of the English-speakers, the bilingualism of the legislative assembly was challenged for the first time in 1792, Pierre Bédard caustically queried why the English had not accepted Norman as their language after 1066.[96]

In fact, the French language was on the rise among the population, which in a process of ruralization increased from 75 percent in 1763 to 88 percent in 1825: "Le Canada français évolue ainsi à contresens des grands pays occidentaux pendant plusieurs décennies." From the 1830s, both French and English Canadian writers and gatekeepers reacted, the former by underpinning the development ideologically with the concept of attachment to the soil (*terroir*) the latter by labelling the farming families a rude and primitive people. The stereotype of the habitant family was a joint creation. Up to the early twentieth century, literary authors and scholars of folklore ascribed a folk culture to them. Philippe-Joseph Aubert de Gaspé set the agenda in *Les anciens canadiens* (1863); contrary to the French-Canadian nobility's daughters after 1763, his French maidens refused to marry British men. His English translator, G.D. Roberts (*The Canadians of Old*, 1890),[97] suggested that reconciliation between French-Canadian and English-language cultures might be helpful. Instead, ethnologists provided a new twist to the English–French dichotomy. "Folk" societies, "simple" by definition of the times, were "Indian" and French-Canadian—British people's expressions appeared as too sophisticated to be labelled "folksy."[98] French-language literary productions reinforced the voyageur–habitant dualism. While the coureurs des bois were exorcized from memory by the silence of literature, Patrice Lacombe initiated the rural novel with *La terre paternelle* (1846). This genre was to dominate literary production and sales for a century. Writing in both

---

96 : Grandpré, *Histoire de la littérature française* (1967–69), quote p. 1:108.

97 : A first translation by Georgina Rennée had appeared in 1864.

98 : Marcel Rioux, "La Folklorisation d'une société," and Pierre de Grandpré, "La Tradition orale," in Grandpré, *Histoire de la littérature française* (1967–69), 1: 79–85, 86–96; Fernand Dumont, *Genèse de la société québécoise* (1st ed., 1993, 2nd ed., Montreal: Boréal, 1996), 158, 306.

English and French, Louis-Honoré Fréchette introduced British Canadians to French-Canadian folk life via *La Légende d'un peuple*, 1887, inspired by Victor Hugo, and his "the habitant as a type" sketches, *Christmas in French Canada* (1899; French translation *La Noël au Canada*, 1900). Ethnology and literary production merged in a way, when Gaspé's *Les anciens canadiens* came to be considered as a source for the study of habitant culture.[99]

Though the Loyalist migrations and the arrival of large numbers of Irish had made Quebec bi- or even tricultural, most literary histories deal with French-language authors only. After a 1830s flurry of adventure, crime, and historical romances, some authors embarked on a glorification of French male heroes such as Octave Crémazie of Montcalm. Pierre-J.-O. Chauveau (*Charles Guérin*, 1846) emphasized English oppression, but did not overlook urban industrial development, and Antoine Gérin-Lajoie's "Un canadien errant" (1842) became a popular "French-national" anthem of grievances against anglophone hegemony. By the 1860s, *Le Mouvement littéraire du Québec* had emerged. When the factory towns along the St. Lawrence River began to attract landless sons and daughters of habitant families, their customs and lore also became a theme.[100] Few writers, however, dealt with the topic of emigration to the factories of New England.[101] By interpreting society, these authors shaped its self-understanding and thus opened or closed political and life course choices.

When, in the 1830s, shipping connections to France improved and when scheduled service was established in 1855, numerous Quebecers visited France, *la patrie-mère*. Among them were historian F.-X. Garneau and nationalist writers such as O. Crémazie and J.-P. Tardivel. All realized, as Dame Bégon had in mid-eighteenth century, that they preferred life in French-Canada. Their image of France was a Quebec creation and, in consequence, some contrasted democratic life in the Canadas with the shallow and materialistic lives of French aristocrats and rich bourgeois. English Canadian

---

99 : *La terre paternelle*, first serialized, was reprinted as a book in 1877; Antoine Gérin-Lajoie, *Jean Rivard: le défricheur* (ser. 1862; repr. as book 1874) and *Jean Rivard: l'économiste* (ser. 1864; repr. as book 1876). For his poems *Fleurs boréales*, Fréchette in 1871 became the first Canadian writer to receive a prize by the Académie française. His recognition in English-Canada is demonstrated by honour's degrees as doctor of letters by McGill, Queen's, and the University of Toronto.

100 : *The Oxford Companion to Canadian Literature*, eds. Eugene Benson and William Toye (1st ed., 1983; 2nd ed., Toronto: Oxford, 1997), 269–70. Esp. Joseph-Charles Taché, *Forestiers et voyageurs* (1863; repr. as book Montreal, 1884) and works by Honoré Beaugrand, Albert Laberge, Claude-Henri Grignon, Berthelot Brunet, Damase Potvin, Ernest Choquette, Louis-Honoré Fréchette.

101 : Honoré Beaugrand, *Jeanne la fileuse: épisode de l'émigration franco-canadienne aux États-Unis* (Fall River, MA, 1878).

authors never viewed Britain in similarly critical terms.[102]

English-language writers in Quebec were few. Religious fundamentalists, such as the visiting American minister George Bourne, fuelled antagonism (1834). In contrast authors such as Mary Anne Sadlier in her romantic depiction of Irish life (1851) counteracted hate literature and added the Irish newcomers to the literary repertoire. In the Maritimes and Newfoundland, writers and journalists were less affirmative. They ridiculed stereotypes and newspapers reflected the multiple views of society. In a bilingual poem about Newfoundland, Irish-born D.R. MacConmara used English to describe the island as attractive and Irish Gaelic to describe the difficulties of everyday life, thus employing a convention of satirization common among subaltern cultures. In Nova Scotia, where a first newspaper had been published since 1715, satires on pioneer society appeared in serialized form and culminated in Thomas C. Haliburton's *The Clockmaker* (1836)—a Yankee looking at Atlantic Canada. However, myths also made their appearance and had a lasting impact. Henry W. Longfellow's *Evangeline* (1847), romanticizing the suffering of the expelled Acadians, unintentionally initiated a revival of Acadian cultural expression. The Maritime imperialists' views of Canada in the British Empire resembled French-Canadian elite dreams of France's grandeur.[103]

In 1830s Upper Canada, more than a century after the emergence of Quebec writing, the difficulties of frontier life were the major theme. John Galt and Frederick Marryat explicitly or implicitly warned prospective settlers. Susanna Moodie dramatized the life of genteel settlers, while her sister Catherine Parr Traill wrote positive accounts. All of these authors had come with financial means or, like Galt, were outside observers. Class became a topic when such gentlefolk authors complained that innkeepers and servants did not show the deference expected of such lower human beings in Britain. Ethnicity came to the fore when English and Scots, Catholic and Protestant Irish, Ulster Scots and Welsh realized that they and, more importantly, their children in school had to learn to get along with each other, had to Canadianize their distinct Old World ways of life. Acceptance of the new social landscapes was particularly difficult for half-pay officers and younger sons of the gentry, as many observers noted.[104] Gentlewomen's

---

102 : Julia Beckwith Hart, *Tonnewonte; or, The Adopted Son of America* (Watertown, NY, 1825); John Richardson, *Écaté; or, The Salons of Paris* (London, 1829).

103 : The English-language *Evangeline* was later translated into French. Napoléon Bourassa in *Jacques et Marie* (ser. 1865–66; as book 1866) also dealt with the expulsion.

104 : Dirk Hoerder, "Pluralist Founding Nations in Anglo- and Franco-Canada: Multiple Migrations, Influences, Reconceptualisations," *Journal of Multilingual & Multicultural Development* 24.6 (2003): 525–39.

writings, a distinct regional tradition, culminated in Catherine Parr Traill's writings, which included a handbook on women migrants' adaptation and amateur botanist information in the tradition of eighteenth-century learned societies.

The oral cultures of First Peoples, thinly represented in the written Euro-Canadian literatures, fared differently in each regional tradition. Early fiction in French presented romanticized stories of martyrdom among Indians; early fiction in English bloodthirsty savages. John Richardson dealt with Pontiac's uprising of 1763 (three volumes, London, 1832); U.S. author Henry W. Longfellow in *The Songs of Hiawatha* (1855) created a fictional Iroquois-Ojibway. However, from the Jesuits' *Relations*, European observers were aware of the oral traditions of the Huron and Algonkin peoples, and later of peoples further north or west. While the viceroys occasionally accepted a "Native" presence during visits of British Crown princes and other ranking persons, the federal government had established a treaty-secured distance from First Peoples by the 1870s. In literary productions, First Peoples were not part of the cultural heritage, but merely happened to live in the same territory. Confederation poets, such as Charles G.D. Roberts and Archibald Lampman incorporated Indian themes while Duncan Campbell Scott emphasized the "primitive." Juliette Gaultier, in the late 1920s, performed northern Alaskan, Copper, Inuit, Ojibway, and West Coast Native songs while attired in "traditional" Native dress. Silencing and appropriation of voice occurred at the same time. The sporadic inclusion of First Peoples' cultural-spiritual expressions into the "national" canon range from Emily Carr's paintings of Pacific Coast villages and Edwin Holgate's work to "improving whiteness by going Native" in summer camps for Ontario children from the 1920s to the 1950s, or to a New Age-type spirituality that requires drumming, dancing, feathers, hugging and "getting in touch with feelings." For twentieth-century Euro-Canadians, Aboriginal cultural self-expression remained invisible as a 1994 study by the Canadian Civil Liberties Association criticized.[105]

It might be argued that the potential for an English-French literary scene and critical social commentary was present. The social tensions expressed

---

105 : Maria Tippett, *Making Culture: English-Canadian Institution and the Arts before the Massey Commission* (Toronto: UTP, 1990), 66–78; Renée Hulan and Linda Warley, "Cultural Literacy, First Nations and the Future of Canadian Literary Studies," *Journal of Canadian Studies* 34.3 (1999): 59–86; Sharon Wall, "Improving on Whiteness: 'Going Native' in Ontario Summer Camps, 1920–1955," and Sheila McManus, "Mapping the Alberta-Montana Borderlands: Cartographies of Race and Gender in the Late Nineteenth Century," (papers presented at Univ. of Toronto, York Univ. conference "Defining Whiteness," Toronto, ON, 13–15 Oct. 2000).

in the rebellions of 1837, especially the impact of the British and British-Canadian "Family Compact" of Montreal's and Upper Canada's ruling elite became a topic for critical works.[106] In Canada's bicultural, commercial and, before 1857, political capital Montreal, the influential *Literary Garland* (1838–51) and English-language novels of manners and of social life in the two Canadas (Rosanna E. Leprohon, Frances Brooke) as well as translations from English into French and vice versa indicate coalescence. If divisive positions prevailed, literatures by the 1860s were distinctly Canadian. Positions were also gendered and literary activities part of politics. The Toronto Women's Literary Association, founded in the 1870s, a few years later became the Toronto Women's Suffrage Association.

Canada's West: New settlers, few national symbols, and the rise of a world of consumption[107]

To the regional specifics of the East, in-migrant settlers and small businesspeople added the Prairie West by creating many local societies that coalesced into a larger world. Others had established the differentiated societies from the Pacific Coast to the Rocky Mountains. The North, present in some cultural productions as region to prove masculine survival skills, remained marginal to socio-economic development. Of these regions, the prairies' settlement in particular was a trans-border phenomenon that demands analysis in comparison to U.S. developments.[108] In the North, the fur economy had declined and the mining economy was only in its initial stages. While in both Quebec and Ontario the residents created images, or "mental maps," of the landscapes they inhabited and experienced, the images of distant parts of the country like the West and the North by comparison were reported rather than experienced. Thus, "literary cartographies" or geogra-fictions emerged.[109]

Settlement of the West, in contrast to the acquisition of Quebec, began with unmitigated conquest—no Manitoba Act modelled on the Quebec Act of 1774 gave freedom of religion, law, and language. With the transfer of

---

106 : New, *A History of Canadian Literature* (1989), 54–56. Charles E. Beardsley, *The Victims of Tyranny*, 2 vols. (Buffalo, 1847); William Dunlop [Backwoodsman, pseud.], *Two and Twenty Years Ago: A Tale of the Canadian Rebellion* (Toronto, 1859).

107 : This section is based on Hoerder, *Creating Societies* (1999), Chapter 15.

108 : John W. Bennett and Seena B. Kohl, *Settling the Canadian-American West, 1890–1915: Pioneer Adaptation and Community Building; An Anthropological History* (Lincoln: Univ. Nebraska Press, 1995).

109 : Tamara Pianos, *Geografikationen in der anglo-kanadischen Literatur: Perzeptionen und Kreationen nördlicher Landschaften* (Würzburg: Königshausen und Neumann, 2000).

Rupert's Land, the distinct societies of the approximately twenty-five thousand First Peoples and of the fifteen thousand Red River Métis were destroyed. Many of the latter were employed by the Hudson's Bay Company when it traded off the lands to the new federal state without bothering to inform them—a kind of corporate takeover. A group of aggressive local expansionists and a scheming merchant, under the guise of a U.S.-inspired concept of manifest destiny, pursued their particular interests. However, with Louis Riel as spokesperson, the Métis established self-government and, had they been accorded the same respect as the people of the Maritimes or British Columbia, a negotiated entry into Confederation might have been effected. Instead, self-rule was deemed a "rebellion" against settler interests and Ontario-Ottawa imposed rule; the army was sent to quell the movement and institute White rule in 1870. A second attempt to assert Métis and Native rights in 1885 was also ended by federal troops, partly to satisfy the British-chauvinist leadership of Ontario. A trial found Riel guilty of treason and he was hanged.[110] Most scholars followed a White, Confederation-centred perspective and termed the claim for self rule a "rebellion." Nationalist Donald Creighton labelled Riel a "dictator"; only W.L. Morton called it the "Red River Resistance." First Peoples' and Métis' collective memory of Riel's execution could not become part of historiography since they had no access to the writing of national history. In contrast, Québécois memory, which constructed the hanging as one more sign of ruthless imposition of British-Canadian power, instrumentalized the death for its purposes. Only after conquest did the federal government seek compromise.[111]

Once immigrant families had set up their homesteads they formed communities, but were parsimonious in building institutions. One national institution, the North-West (later the Royal Canadian) Mounted Police, watched, often benignly, over life and enforced norms without large-scale repressive actions. From the start, the settlers' local spaces were part of

---

110 : Thomas Flanagan, *Riel and the Rebellion: 1885 Reconsidered* (Saskatoon: Western Producer, 1983), argued that several of the grievances were of the Métis' own making and that the government was on the verge of solving some of the problems. Due to the missed opportunities for reconciliation, Flanagan argued that at the centenary, Riel should not be granted a posthumous pardon. Diane P. Payment, in *"Les gens libres— Otipemisiwak": Batoche, Saskatchewan 1870–1930*, Engl. ed. *"The Free People"* (Ottawa: Environnement Canada, 1990), on the other hand, placed the emphasis on the period after the defeat of 1885 and rejected the thesis of a social and economic disintegration in favour of the struggle of the "gens libres" to remain masters of their lives.

111 : Gerald Friesen, *The West: Regional Ambitions, National Debates, Global Age* (Toronto: Penguin, 1999); Peter Charlebois, *The Life of Louis Riel* (Toronto: NC Press, 1975; rev. ed., 1978).

larger worlds: internationalized access to homestead land, families spread over continents, transatlantic labour markets for harvest workers, production for world markets. An international corporation, the Hudson's Bay Company (HBC) mediated between local, national, and worldwide markets. Transatlantic relations, in the immigrants' minds, concerned families and, sometimes, Old World politics. Another connection, the pomp and circumstance of the British Empire, remained marginal to immigrants' perceptions unless they came from the imperial core. Once farming families began to produce staples, wheat in particular, the food and implements a family could buy depended on distant markets.

National myths have constructed the HBC and the Mounties as pillars of order before the advent of regular governmental institutions. The Company's factors ruled, gave advice, and stocked provisions. They built a reputation for being well informed, judicious, and fair. Relations of trust developed in a hierarchical structure. This has been interpreted as a sign of British fair play transported to Canada. But fair play had not been part of relations between lords and tenants at the time of enclosure in England and during the Scottish Highland clearances. Rather honesty and fairness paid off in terms of transaction cost in this society in the making. No armies, police forces, or courts had to be maintained as long as mutual trust was maintained. First Peoples trading at the posts were well informed about the value of their pelts. But after the HBC sold Rupert's Land, it was reduced from an informal government to a trade and real estate company.

The North-West Mounted Police, the second pillar of order, was established in 1873. A plan to recruit half of the force from among the Métis was shelved when they claimed self-government. Instead, the force connected to the symbolism of the British troops' uniforms: red coats. It earned respect by protecting First Peoples from U.S. whisky smugglers and by protecting settlers from U.S. horse and cattle thieves. NWMP policing strategies followed customs of the land. As to social strategies, the Mounties were masculine, honest, upright—and well dressed. Ladies were said to succumb to "scarlet fever," adoring the red-coated "polite Englishmen's dashing" looks. The force obliged by hospitality—an engaging feature also practised by HBC factors. The somewhat inflated self-esteem of the force did not escape critical notice. The Mounties, as a force or as individuals, assumed tasks that later were to become the responsibility of social service agencies. For newcomers, this conduct was the opposite of the police-controlled class societies of the Old World. While masculinity entered collective memory, reality saw many of the Mounties as married, with wives as helpmates. When society diversified, the force could not mediate class differences. Among workers no image of RCMP fairness ever developed. The force accused the Rev. J.S. Woodsworth of preaching "revolutionary doctrines," and in 1918, a year after the Russian Revolution, it singled out labour unions and farmers in the "foreign settlements" as "susceptible to Bolshevik teaching." This one-sidedness did not become part of the nationalist master narrative's RCMP story.[112]

In the decades before World War I, the Dominion government continued to be of little concern in the Prairies, where people considered the Canadian Pacific Railway (CPR) "as being 'the Government.'" This specific form of nation-building was based on the political economy of the times. The Dominion-sponsored CPR connected farmers to markets across the globe, the trans-Pacific trade included. In 1891, a few grain-filled railcars left each of the many hamlets where farming families shipped their produce. The cars added up to more than twenty thousand leaving eastbound from Winnipeg and an imaginative observer such as A.M. Klein saw "all the coloured faces of mankind" when looking at the grain elevators in Montreal. Farm families were aware of their connection to world systems: each time the Empire of which Canada was a part was involved in distant wars, purchases of army supplies had immediate consequences on grain prices in the Prairies and the amount of food on a family's table as well as on machinery bought and credit risks taken. The families were also aware that the CPR exploited its monopoly and from around 1900 began to organize prairie- and nationwide to fight the monopolist.[113]

While Prairie farmers were often considered to be mainly of Ukrainian, Mennonite, and other foreign cultures, the majority of the settlers were of Ontarian or British background and English-speakers. British emigrants benefited from their country's imperial reach and developed a concomitant discourse: the English "can emigrate to any quarter of the globe without changing their flag, their allegiance, or their language. An Englishman… may choose according to his fancy, and remain an Englishman always." For those choosing Canada, this society's meaning varied by class and decade. Imperial racists aggressively slurred non-British and non-Teutonic immigrants. Status-conscious Britishers considered the Dominion suitable for British "people of small fortune, whose means, though ample to enable them to live well in Canada are insufficient to meet the demands of rising

---

112 : *RCMP Security Bulletins: The Early Years, 1919-1929*, ed. Gregory S. Kealey and Reg Whitaker (St. John's, NL: Canadian Committee on Labour History, 1994), 11-24, passim; Keith Walden, "The Great March of the Mounted Police in Popular Literature, 1873-1973," Canadian Historical Association, *Historical Papers* (1980), 33-56.

113 : Frank G. Roe, *Getting the Know-How: Homesteading and Railroading in Early Alberta*, ed. J.P. Regan (Edmonton: NeWest, 1982), 58; A.M. Klein, *Complete Poems*, ed. Zailig Pollock, 2 vols. (Toronto: UTP, 1990), 2:650; *Historical Atlas of Canada*, 3 vols. (Toronto: UTP, 1987-1993), 2:42.

expenses at home." In Britain, opponents of emigration were those who exploited their countrymen's "cheap labour." Lower-class British emigrants, reflecting on the inequities of life in Great Britain, were "sometimes rather contemptuous of the land of their birth."[114] Newcomers viewed the societies of origin and of destination in codes of class, gender, and region of socialization.

At the beginning of the twentieth century, when democratically minded farmers and workers outnumbered genteel Britishers, the "Pillars of Order" mythology succumbed to a "Democracy of Consumption," personified by Timothy Eaton and institutionalized in his mail-order company. Eaton's carried the world of consumption into Prairie homes and was vastly more important than the Ottawa government. In contrast to the CPR's freight rates, its sales policy followed the principle of honesty of the earlier pillars of society and, even more importantly, of the settler families' cash-strapped moral economy. Across the Prairies, the catalogue gave access to possibilities of consuming: it was "a book to dream over." Its illustrations overcame language and cultural barriers and were more informative than an encyclopedia. If a family had no money to spend, the catalogue and the dreams of what might be, perhaps next year, did not cost a cent. In the worlds from which immigrants came, much of Eaton's merchandise would never have even been visible to small farmers, landless labourers, or urban workers. Timothy Eaton's price and refund policies permitted marketing over long distances without personal contact with sales personnel. His symbolism appealed to many: dispatch of Eaton's delivery wagons resembled "all the showmanship… of the Royal Horse Guards… at the trooping of the colour"; Eaton's drivers stepped up to the front door of rich people's homes though delivery personnel were expected to use the service entrance; boys dreamed of becoming Eaton's drivers; immigrant women with some English guided more recent arrivals through the stores; the catalogue set women's dress styles across the country; and immigrants Canadianized their dress code by looking at the catalogue. As a text, the catalogue surpassed not only novels but also the Bible in cultural importance.[115]

The Prairies in national imagery appeared as railway tracks (stylized as "the steel"), wheat, and farm machinery. Such symbols and their reference to mass production and national wealth reflected the lives of the producer families as little as cars at the end of an assembly line mirror the lives of industrial workers. The people of the region, in 1871 less than thirty thou-

---

114 : John J. Rowan, *Emigrant and Sportsman in Canada* (London, 1876), quotes pp. 1–9.

115 : Autobiographical testimony quoted in Hoerder, *Creating Societies* (1999), 199–202; see in general Joy L. Santink, *Timothy Eaton and the Rise of His Department Store* (Toronto: UTP, 1990).

sand, numbered 1.3 million by 1911. Isolated settlements had become part of larger social spaces that coalesced into one Prairie region as part of the nation. However, in national discourse, Western regionalism received far less attention than Quebec or Ontario. In Quebec-centered discourse, the Prairie francophones are merely people "hors Québec"—they might be defined as inside of Canada or as part of "la francophonie nord-américaine." While political leaders had envisioned this process, it was the immigrant families who built these societies and contributed to Canada's economy.[116]

In the Northwest, loggers and miners took over from the missionaries. But romantic stories of explorers and fur traders "north of the 60th" parallel persisted. The North, though described as a world of tough men and few women, was the world of working-class hard rock miners, of Italian railway workers and their families strung out along the transcontinental lines, of lumbermen across the Canadian Shield and on to the Rockies. Women's life writings reflect shared but difficult living conditions. Few read such accounts. In contrast, male writers such as Robert Service made a fortune with barroom verse glorifying the North and the gold rushes.[117] Myths usually have little connection to reality—but the producers of them often strike gold by capitalizing on the spirit of the times. For example, few gold rush migrants struck it rich, yet the Klondike gold rush of 1896 became the symbol of buoyant optimism and material growth. The economically far more important large corporate producers of minerals in a global market for ores and refined metals hardly entered literary lore. Reflective scholars such as W.L. Morton have argued that Canada's distinctiveness was a response to the Northern mingling of Native and European cultures. A "learning of wilderness ways" implied "dependence on Indian inventions and skills" and an absence of Euro-Canadian institutions. Other historians wrote as if no North existed.[118]

In British Columbia, First Peoples still accounted for the majority of the population in 1891, the men and women of European background, so-called Whites, numbered but twenty-four thousand. In the construction of race in

116 : See, among others, Larry Pratt and Garth Stevenson, eds., *Western Separatism: The Myths, Realities and Dangers* (Edmonton: Hurtig, 1981).

117 : Other authors were Alexander Ross and Agnes C. Laut. See Chapter 5, this volume.

118 : W.L. Morton, "The North in Canadian Historiography," *Transactions of the Royal Society of Canada* IV, 8, Section "Proceedings" (1970), 31–40, quote p. 33. Morris Zaslow, *The Opening of the Canadian North*, 1870–1914 (Toronto: McClelland & Stewart, 1971); Louis-Edmond Hamelin, *Nordicité Canadienne* (1975; 2nd rev. ed., Montreal: Hurtubise, 1980), transl. by William Barr as *Canadian Nordicity: It's Your North, Too* (Montreal: Harvest House, 1978); and, in a popularizing and dramatizing vein, Pierre Berton, *The Mysterious North* (Toronto: McClelland & Stewart, 1956).

British Columbia, "White" included Métis, that is, the English-speaking off-spring of First Nations' women and HBC men. While in the Prairies railways meant progress, on the Pacific Coast it was trade with Asia that seemed to promise riches. Authors of Euro-Canadian background in Ontario (and Quebec), however, had no Pacific vision. Literary expression about life in British Columbia was limited to diaries and autobiographies. These presented a differentiated image of society. Many Euro-Canadians distinguished their neighbours by culture: Blackfoot, Chilcotin, Fountain, Lillooet, Similkameen, Flathead, Okanagan, Shuswap, and many more. Others, missionaries in particular, worked hard to label Native men as drunkards, Native women as slovenly. Some local observers were also capable of viewing immigrants from Asian cultures with open eyes: workers, merchants, domestics, and small traders. Cultural interaction, usually hierarchicized and mixed with racism, was the rule. Prejudiced narratives divided the Anglo community, too: English immigrants constructed themselves as superior and down-graded "Canadians" as colonials, and internal migrants from the Maritimes were labelled "fish-eaters." British migrants reflected imperial reach—they had lived in India or Ceylon (now Sri Lanka), had come with the Royal Engineers, or had been to the Australian or Caribbean colonies. The province's priests from Belgium, France, and Italy reflected the hegemonic reach and international recruitment of the Church in Rome.

In contrast to Atlanto-centric Ontario and Quebec observers, imperial and B.C. commentators placed the economy of the Pacific Coast in a hemispheric eastern perspective: Transsiberian Railway, Japan's rise to power, the economic potential of Asia. British-minded and solidly entrenched in the concept of Whiteness, they warned of Japanese and Russian immigrant "hordes" that might crowd out "the old British stock, and the old British virtue." British immigrants, who did not succeed, were particularly bitter and arrogant about the Others, who proved more adaptable. In such views, British Columbia was thinly linked to an emerging Canadian identity, potentially linked to a Pacific economy, and decidedly a hinterland of the British Empire. And yet, ironically, such men and women produced a faithful simulacrum of Britishness in Victoria.[119]

Canada's East:
Multiple literatures and hierarchies after Confederation

In the cities of the East, whether in Quebec, Ontario, or the economically stagnating Maritimes, interactions were as complex as in the Prairie West,

119 : William Newton, *Twenty Years on the Saskatchewan, N.W. Canada* (London: Stock, 1897), vi, 180–84.

the mining North, and on the Pacific Coast. In these segments of the country, few of the distinctly Canadian authors chose the culturally interactive possibilities of the Anglo-East / Quebec / Prairie West triptych as a theme. In their hegemonic and powerful yet narrow mental spaces neither the distant West nor the nearby immigrant underclasses appeared as worthy of attention. A few modest signposts indicating multiple possibilities and directions were overshadowed by nationalist billboards. Literary productions of the period were "tale-telling," to use W.H. New's phrase (1989), though a few authors broke out of the mould of "Confederation poetry" or "habitant glorification." To "unweave" the single cords of the two master narratives and literary canons, it is necessary to look at the many threads that might have become part of a canvass of cultures, had gatekeepers cared to take note of diversity even within the Anglo and French segments of society.

The so-called Confederation poets wrote in a British tradition, as did writers of Atlantic Canada. Lucy Maud Montgomery, who transmitted British-Canadian views through her bestselling children's stories to the next generations, was unconventional as regards gender roles. *Anne of Green Gables* (1908) is narrated from a women's almost proto-feminist perspective. His own boyhood socialization and resulting attachment to England was behind Stephen Leacock's *Sunshine Sketches of a Little Town* (1912). When writers such as Archibald Lampman and Duncan Campbell Scott criticized biblical mythology and organized religion, this might have been a starting point for a comparative study of belief systems: Native and European, animist and Christian. However, Scott, after becoming deputy superintendent of Indian affairs in 1923, considered his co-Canadians "primitive" peoples. Though noticeable, new trends were not generally welcomed or, perhaps, generally not welcomed.

While English-language literature was neither integrative nor forward-looking, French-Canadian cultural production was totally out of sync with societal developments. Quebec society was changing. Industry developed quickly; factories ("facteries" in Anglicized French) became ever more numerous and many men and women, who would formerly have migrated to New England, turned toward Quebec's expanding cities. The share of people living in rural communities declined precipitously from 60.3 percent in 1901 to a mere 36 percent two decades later. Nevertheless, reputable theologians such as Mgr. Louis-Adolphe Pâquet and essayists such as Edmond de Nevers constructed a missionary people with no interest in pursuit of material gain and economic progress, "détenteurs d'une culture et d'une civilisation supérieures."[120] But from the 1890s, the "romantize-the-past" mainstream faced competition from critical and realist writers. Authors born in the 1870s formed the École littéraire de Montréal (1895). Émile Nelligan, of both Irish and Québécois background, depicted Catholicism as haunting rather than comforting. But around 1910, the École returned to the traditionalist mainstream with its magazine *Le Terroir*. A more important sign of impending change was Camille Roy's essay "La nationalisation de la littérature canadienne" of 1904. He understood the colonial context of Quebec literature and called for autonomy both from Quebec's past-centred myths as well as from France. Ironically, some autonomy appeared, when sons and daughters of well-placed families began to explore metropolitan life by visiting France, and Paris in particular. Their European experience was cut short with the declaration (not "outbreak") of war in 1914, but their avant-garde review *Le Nigog* (established 1918) was intended to bring Quebec closer to modernity. Some essayists fused literary writing with political economy and action. Nationalists such as Olivar Asselin and Jules Fournier tried to direct people's discontent or *colère* against the government, which abandoned national resources to foreign companies, mainly from the United States In sympathy with Henri Bourassa, they supported francophone minorities outside of Quebec, and within the province advocated a dualist pan-Canadianism based on two peoples and the *survivance* of the smaller one.[121]

The failure of new approaches in the tightly Church-controlled society is epitomized by the "fate" or reinvention of Louis Hémon's novel *Maria Chapdelaine* (serialized 1914, published as book 1916). In London, from 1902 to 1911, French-born Hémon had written short stories on the life of lower-class men and women, including many-cultured immigrants. Like these, the depiction of the habitant family of *Maria Chapdelaine* was based on acute observation. He sympathetically described the inner life of *le menu peuple* and underclasses, who had little power over the circumstances in which they lived. While he could relate to the hardworking frontier *défricheurs*, his cliché-socialized readers placed him in the clerical tradition of glorifying peasant life and fidelity to the ways of the past. In fact, he accorded common people a place of their own in a society not ready to do so and criticized cler-

---

120 : Pâquet, *Bréviaire du patriote canadien-français* (1902), and Nevers, *L'avenir du peuple canadienne-français* (1896); Paul-André Linteau, René Durocher, Jean-Claude Robert, and François Ricard, *Histoire du Québec contemporain*, 2 vols. (2nd ed., Montreal: Boréal, 1989), quote 1:723.

121 : Ultramontane authors, Tardivel for example, demanded separation and founded the Ligue nationaliste in 1903 with the journal *Le Nationaliste* (1904). "Independence" in these terms included economic independence from U.S. capital.

ical ideology as dark clouds hanging heavily over people's life projects.[122]

In both French- and English-language literature, women writers and the topic of women's roles in society remained marginal. Joanna Wood's depictions of women in small-town Ontario reflected the community-imposed limits on independence and Quebec's first women writers did not deviate from the "Party," or Church, line. The Ursuline-educated novelist Laure Conan (pseudonym of Félicité Angers), subscribing to the trinity of family-nation-faith, had two French Canadian youths give up their "foreign" love and then marry locally and thus remain true to the nation. Blanche Lamontagne, poetess of the Gaspésie, also remained under the protective shield of pious traditionalism. In contrast, the independent-minded Ontario-born journalist Sara Jeanette Duncan travelled and lived across the Empire, in India in particular. She moved between satire of things imperial (*The Imperialist*, 1904) and descriptions of women's independence (*A Social Departure*, 1890). Her and others' travel writings about Canadians in England began to emphasize Canadianness and expected the English to accept a Canadian national-cultural identity (*Cousin Cinderella*, 1908). Women's writing brought forth male responses. The renowned constitutional historian J.G. Bourinot, in 1893, pontificated from the rostrum of the Royal Society of Canada that historical writing included "picturesqueness of narration, … [and] philosophical insight into the motives and plans of statesmen"—the male version of women's allegedly light reading. When women became active, for example, Emily Ferguson Murphy as feminist writer (*Janey Canuck*, 1910), Nellie McClung in politics, and Emily Stowe in the medical profession, reactionaries such as J.-P. Tardivel, fearing female independence, mounted opposition. As late as 1930, a Quebec law permitted a man to file for divorce in case of adultery of his wife, but a woman could file for divorce only if the husband had his "concubine" live in the same house: "quoi qu'on en dise, on sait bien qu'en fait la blessure faite au coeur de l'épouse n'est pas généralement aussi vive que celle dont souffre le mari trompé par sa femme."[123]

---

122 : Louis Hémon, *Maria Chapdelaine* (Montreal: Lux Éd., 2003). In 1913, Hémon was found dead on the side of railway tracks. The question has been raised whether trainmen threw him off while he was riding the rails. Louis Hémon, *Nouvelles Londoniennes: De Marble Arche à Whitechapel*, ed. Chantal Bouchard (Pantin: Le Castor Astral, 1991). See also his *Itinéraire de Liverpool à Québec* (Paris: Grasset, 1927; repr. Quimper: Calligramme, 1985). Nicole Deschamps, Raymonde Héroux, and Normand Villeneuve, *Le mythe de Maria Chapdelaine* (Montreal: PU Montréal, 1980); Geneviève Chovrelat, *Louis Hémon, la vie à écrire* (Louvain, Belgique: Éd. Peeters, 2003).

123 : Clara Thomas, "Canadian Social Mythologies in Sara Jeannette Duncan's 'The Imperialist'," *Journal of Canadian Studies* 12.2 (Spring 1977): 38–49; Bourinot cited in New, *History of Canadian Literature* (1989), 112; Linteau et al., *Histoire du Québec*, 1:587–99,

Women achieved voting rights in all provinces except Quebec between 1916 and 1922. There, it took two more decades of struggles of the feminist Fédération nationale Saint-Jean-Baptiste, the Montreal branch of the Conseil national des femmes, and of activists Thérèse Casgrain and Marie Gérin-Lajoie to overcome male and clerical opposition in 1940.[124] Regarding openness to new developments, whether women's rights, urbanization, or education, Quebec was *en retard* because its cultural gatekeepers were.

English-language writers, too, were *en retard*, ensconced in conventions and ambivalent about Canadianness. First, they were never quite certain whether to promote homegrown cultural activities or whether to feel inferior about them. Second, misjudging attitudes of the British government, gatekeepers believed that Canada's governing elites would be granted more of a say in matters of the Empire. Third, British law discriminated against copyright of Canadian authors while favouring not only British but also American publications.[125] Finally, the literary club movement, strongest in Ontario, reflected Central Canadian attitudes more than those of English-speakers in other regions. Signs of change came from authors who turned to the impact of scientific and technological advance on the environment and from the expanding market for books. Middle-class British Canadians formed numerous literary and arts clubs since the 1890s, usually segregated by gender and, in British Columbia in particular, often excluding the reading public of "ethnics" of European background and immigrants of Asian background. This movement to encourage and enjoy culture in Canada faced publishers who wanted clichés that sold rather than independent opinions that found unprofitable niche markets at best. Susie Frances Harrison, using a man's name—Gilbert King—as pseudonym, in her title story to *Crowded Out! and Other Sketches* (1886) attacked British publishers who accepted nothing but "wilderness" versions of life in Canada.[126]

---

quote p. 598.

124 : In Newfoundland, enfranchisement came in 1925, before the colony joined Confederation. In Quebec, propertied women had been enfranchised from 1809 to 1849—then the male legislators disenfranchised them.

125 : New, *History of Canadian Literature* (1989), 95–96.

126 : Grandpré, *Histoire de la littérature française* (1967–69), 2:89. A variant of the "wild nature approach" was the "humanized animal approach" of writers like Ernest Thompson Seton (1860-1946), the "I-am-an-Indian stance" of "Grey Owl," pseudonym of Archibald Stansfeld Belaney (1888-1938), and, as variant of the "strong male approach," the Woodcraft Indian and Boy Scout approaches: always be prepared, do a good deed daily. Belaney, born in England, migrated to northern Canada and invented a Scots-Apache parentage. He buttressed his childhood fascination with "Indians" by learning from the Ojibway and from his wife Anahareo, an Iroquois. A French-Canadian

Departures to new forms of expression and to inclusiveness as well as to new topics were, in a way, countered by a development that was meant to aid independent artistic expression in Canada. Viceroys had excluded any organizations and activities from patronage that smacked of an "ethnic component" but they might include First Peoples into the rituals of state. The latter, in distinction to immigrants, were unlikely to claim political rights but were said to be of ancient dignity. When, in 1880, the Governor General established the Royal Canadian Academy of Arts, patterned after Britain's Royal Academy of Art of 1768, it was intended to lay the "foundations for future greatness" (Earl Grey) and to exclude "alien elements." "Greatness" implied an institutionalization of taste, a government-sponsored organization of cultural gatekeepers. After 1900, the many local festivals and fairs that were a type of material-culture show from the bottom up, also took on a national guise as part of building the nation.

Central Canada's English-speaking middle class's promotion of the arts was, in part at least, meant to counter the intrusions of the city, industrial culture, and urban lower classes into the area of cultural expression. The movement came to be challenged, however, from what Ontario's self-styled "national" elites considered the margins: the West, immigrants, and the lower classes. Some immigrants formed clubs of their own. The literary society of Regina gave Icelandic-cultured Laura Salverson an opportunity to present her writing, and other clubs accepted "foreign influences" from immigrant artists. More importantly, the club movement opened the way for imports of popular culture from the United States. Thus, those who "were preservers and keepers of the established and familiar" (Tippett 1990) saw their hegemony challenged by increasingly more popular clubs promoting cultural expression.[127] Mechanics' institutes, a form of self-organization developed in Scotland, opened reading rooms for workingmen; James Woodsworth's All People's Mission in Winnipeg did so after 1904. His *Strangers Within Our Gates* (1908) and *My Neighbour* (1910) included immigrants, though as beings far inferior to Anglo-Saxons. Universities reached out to new segments of the society by their extension movement.

The emergence of a national consciousness and culture was reflected quite differently in immigrant life writings. Whether agriculturists in the West or urban dwellers in the cities of the East, newcomers immediately had to establish an economic foothold. As labourers, artisans, and farmers they worked, paid taxes, and contributed to the national economy. Once family

---

parallel was the poetry of Gonzalve Desaulniers (*Les bois qui chantent*, 1930).

127 : Maria Tippett, *Making Culture*, 6–83; Carl F. Klinck et al., eds., *Literary History of Canada: Canadian Literature in English*, 4 vols. (2nd ed., Toronto: UTP 1976, 1990), 1:197–99.

relationships had been re-established, the next goal concerned the future of the children. Immigrants petitioned for school districts, built schools, and hired teachers. In immigrant neighbourhoods, whether urban or village, some teachers reached out to the languages and cultures of the pupils of different tongues. The school system as institution, however, was geared to Britishness, or in Quebec to Catholicity. Immigrants Canadianized faster than British or French Canadians of long standing since they did not remain welded to images of imperial grandeur or Catholic rule. To them, the two hegemonic cultures remained distant. The emerging Canadian nation thus consisted of three major cultural components as well as of the marginalized Native peoples, and regionally of an Ontario core, a Quebec core or sub-centre, with many regional and local societies pursuing their own cultural projects.

Billboards of self-advertising: Canadian Firsters, English-Canada's British imperialists, French-Canada's advocates of race

Three developments strengthened the Anglo-French division, the "Canada First" and the British imperial movements as well as the re-emphasis on tradition among Quebec's French Canadians. Gatekeepers juxtaposed a putatively generic Anglo middle class and elite culture to a putatively more ancient Quebec- and Church-supported self-centredness, and the vociferous ideologues of British-Canadian imperialist or Quebec-Canadian racist hue projected messages and labels on billboards but did not talk to each other. After the turn of the twentieth century, anglophone Western women erected their own billboards.

In the 1860s, a *repli traditionaliste* (P. Savard 1984) engulfed Quebec society in a navel-gazing approach that deliberately overlooked the *choix moderniste*, industrialization and urbanization. Since modernization of production did not keep pace with the traditional pattern of reproduction, ever more children were left without land or jobs. For them the *choix moderniste* was migration to the industrial cities of New England, which deprived Quebec society of many of those ready for change. The ultra-conservative Bishop Laflèche, who could not stem the movement, much as he and others tried to, covered his defeat by rhetorically evoking fidelity to faith and *terroir* switching to a new rhetoric about missionary peoples (*peuples apôtres*) called by Providence to settle among industrial peoples (*peuples industriels*). "Mgr Laflèche va jusqu'à rêver que cette partie des États-Unis pourrait un jour s'annexer d'elle-même au Québec." Quebec's self-enclaved elites dreamt about a Catholic empire in North America. While this remained beyond their reach, they directed those they could influence, peasants without land, to colonize marginal regions in Quebec, thus sending them into poverty instead of endowing them with imperial grandeur. Many such gatekeepers, coming out of the same few *collèges classiques* and the even fewer universities, struck together in a close network—not a family compact, but a *laïques-religieux* clique.[128]

Segments of the hegemonic anglophone elites shared such self-centredness but combined it with an outward imperial mission. The Ontario-based "Canada First" movement believed in continental expansion of the province's economy and, dividing the society by race, propagandized the superiority of English-speaking Celtic, Teutonic, and Scandinavian "Northmen" over French Canadians and French-speaking Métis. Authors of the early 1900s pointed to "the danger to the Empire from the indiscriminate immigration into Canada of Russian and Galician Jews, Greeks, Germans, Dutch, Poles, Hungarians, Italians, and even Syrians and Turks," who were not the "kind of material" wanted —who, however, were badly needed to populate the cities and prairies.[129] Canada Firsters, as ideologues of race, defined large, ethnocultural segments of the state's population out of the cultural nation. With respect to class, ranking immigration officials joined the quest for exclusion. They defined self-confident and organized working-class people as "slackers" and thus excluded them from the economically productive nation. Had this ideology prevailed, Canada would have permanently relegated itself to the status of economic hinterland.

This hegemonic discourse "stemmed from a group of thinkers with roots in the Maritimes, whose careers took them into the corridors of Central Canadian political influence" (for "Central Canadian," read, "Ontario"). Most were born between 1835 and 1846: George Munro Grant, from Nova Scotia, Glasgow-educated and principal of Queen's University; George Robert Parkin from New Brunswick, Anglican and Oxford-educated, whose agrarian and anti-urban ideas influenced the Confederation poets (*Imperial Federation*, 1892, written in opposition to continentalist visions such as that of Goldwin Smith); J.G. Bourinot from Cape Breton, a constitutional historian, who sought to define the country's culture and political system; as well as the younger Andrew Macphail from Prince Edward Island, amateur historian of the imperial connection to Great Britain. From Upper Canada, George Denison of Loyalist background, military historian and propagandist of national greatness, joined the circle. So did Stephen Leacock, English

---

128 : Grandpré, *Histoire de la littérature française* (1967–69), quotes, p. 194–95.

129 : Basil Stewart, *The Land of the Maple Leaf, or Canada As I Saw It* (London: Routledge, and Toronto: Musson, 1908), viii.

immigrant, who taught at Upper Canada College, the circle's training centre for their children. Subsequently, Leacock moved to McGill as conservative political economist. The group, internally linked by marriage, "espoused the Englishness of the empire."[130]

The imperialists' visions were as large as they were contradictory, combining the fascination of technology with reverence for Victorian ideals of life and family. The CPR's engineer Sandford Fleming, sympathetic to these visions, proposed the worldwide time zones necessary for global travel and commerce. George M. Grant saw trans-Pacific commerce with China as key to Canada's future. The CPR connected London with Hong Kong and profited greatly from the government's lucrative mail contracts. Organizations such as the Imperial Federation Movement sent speakers on lecture tours throughout the Empire. As regards language, they stuck to a British English, thus consciously removing themselves from the regionally diverse Canadian English. Popular fiction in this mode of thought intensified "imperial sensibilities." Gilbert Parker, for example, after an Anglican boyhood in Ontario and stints as a journalist in Australia, in politics in England, and as propagandist in World War I North America, had his romances published in an "Imperial Edition" (1912–23). CPR-paid billboards lured immigrants into buying their passage to a New Canaan with productive mines, inland lakes, and British Columbian orchards. C.L. Cowan, missionary-to-be for the Scottish Presbyterian Church of Canada, decided to cross the ocean in 1908, when Scotland was "agog over the novel *The Sky Pilot*" and a clerk in Switzerland did so after he "saw all the beautiful posters: grow apples and get rich." In contrast, immigrants did not fare well in the writings of two clerical authors, the Rev. Charles W. Gordon (pseudonym Ralph Connor) and the Abbé Lionel Groulx. Both developed simple stories of two Canadas, Scottish British and French Catholic, and painted billboards that influenced self-images of many Canadians far more deeply than the many signposts of cultural interaction described above.

Ralph Connor, born in 1860 in Glengarry, Ontario, of immigrant parents (a Scottish Presbyterian minister and a New England mother) became an educator and missionary.[131] Steeped in a stern Scottish Protestant morality, he began to publish in 1898 and in his novels extolled the virtues of the wilderness at a time of expanding cities, and the rugged beauty of the Rocky Mountains, when few but wage-working miners and free-spending wealthy

---

130 : Maude Parkin married William Lawson Grant, the son of George M. Grant and headmaster of Upper Canada College, 1917–35. Alice Stuart married Vincent Massey and, though socially conservative, was active in Liberal politics of the interwar years.

131 : The self-chosen pseudonym "CanNor" (from *Can*ada and *Nor*thwest Territory) was adapted by Connor.

tourists saw them. Good women (resembling his mother) in domestic havens patrolled by missionaries and policemen he juxtaposed with masculine God-fearing Glengarry Scots and hardy types in the wilderness. They were morally far above foreign Slavs with minds warped by a childhood under the yoke of Old World tyrannies, living in overcrowded dirty little huts, addicted to drink and violence. His imagery struck a responsive chord in the English-language reading public: his first novel, *Black Rock: A Tale of the Selkirks* (1898), sold an unusual five thousand copies. His second, *The Sky Pilot: A Tale of the Foothills* (1899), sold even more. Connor's Scottish-Canadian folklore included an unflattering display of the English in Canada and ambivalent descriptions of Americans. His heroes and heroines, copied by many authors, became stock types in Canadian fiction and, according to critics, a cornerstone of British-Canadian national identity. Connor connected his fantasies of family, founding heroes, and famous landscapes to the earlier imagery of explorers, of Whiteness, referred to then as the White Man's Burden, of Anglo-Saxon superiority over lesser breeds, and of masculinity. This billboard, dazzling in the eyes of contemporaries, distracted many people from seeing the multiple other aspects of Canadian ways of life and of expressions in the arts and literature.[132]

Lionel Groulx was born in 1878 into a hardworking and God-fearing family, the Catholic variant and thus different from Connor's Presbyterian version. As *abbé*, he first made himself the high priest of the French-Canadian "race" and then posed as a scholar, having been appointed to the Université de Montréal's history chair by the city's archbishop. "[Il] a dû s'improviser historien," as a critical commentator noted.[133] He popularized existing thought, galvanized public opinion around his message, organized pilgrimages to historic sites, and was omnipresent in print, then radio, and finally television. Groulx painted in broad strokes, and admitted as much when, late in life, he described himself as "un écrivain engagé." Both Gordon and Groulx mythologized the present by constructing it from a mythologized past. In the wake of Bishop Laflèche, Quebec's governing classes expanded their narrow St. Lawrence valley-vision beyond the colonization projects for marginal, adjacent land to an imperial project. Brothers in mind to anglophone imperialist opponents, they began to include French-speakers

---

132 : Michael Hurley, "Ralph Connor (Charles William Gordon), 1860–1937," *Dictionary of Literary Biography* (Detroit: Gale), vol. 92 "Canadian Writers 1890–1920," ed. W.H. New (1990): 50–56; Grant Overton (1923), cited in *Twentieth-Century Literary Criticism*, vol. 31: 105–6. A many-faceted discussion of myth and memory as regards the role of Scots is Marjory Harper and Michael E. Vance, eds., *Myth, Migration and the Making of Memory: Scotia and Nova Scotia c. 1700–1990* (Halifax: Fernwood, 1999).

133 : Savard & Grandpré in Grandpré, *Histoire de la littérature française* (1967–69), 2:142.

in the Canadian West and the United States into their cultural project, their "vocation en Amérique." Groulx underpinned the ideology by a constructed history of the Americas: the role of Catholic and Romance-language Spain and Portugal had been ephemeral, but France, whose abandonment of Acadia, Louisiana, and Quebec he conveniently glossed over, kept its role by survival of its blood and culture.[134] His theme of "race," central in contemporary biological thinking and eugenics, saw French Canadians surrounded by inimical forces that threatened their very survival: Jews and all others who did not support the Church; those who succumbed to urban and industrial ways of life, secularism and materialism; those who attempted to spread Anglo-Canadian culture; and the habitants's enemies, the "coureur des bois, être si troublant, fait de parties si suspectes ... récents immigrants, encore sans profession, ... fils aussi de seigneurs et de gentilhommes ou qui s'en donnent l'air."[135] Rejuvenation of society was to come out of a nationalist youth movement, the Association catholique de la jeunesse canadienne-française (established 1904), supported by the Ligue des droits du français (1913) and the corporatist and anti-Semitic ideology of the journal L'Action Française (established 1917). Like Gordon's, this imagery struck a responsive chord but did not succeed in welding together economic modernization with a Christian social vision as enunciated in the Church's social teachings. Groulx's L'Appel de la race (1922) was a call to cling to the roots or face personal destruction. His billboard was attractive to all who disliked the socio-economic change. But there were some, such as Camille Roy, who attacked this billboard as a disfigurement of the landscape of faith and society, and others who parodied it, such as Philippe Panneton (pseudonym Ringuet) in his "Appel de la crasse" (1924).[136]

Men of other persuasions took more pragmatic approaches. In Quebec, Henri Bourassa, statesman and editor of Le Devoir from its founding in 1910 to 1932, led the struggle against British imperialism and its British Canadian propagandists. As at earlier conjunctures during which biculturalism seemed one viable option,[137] Bourassa's cautious bicultural vision

134 : Groulx, preface to the first volume of the Revue d'histoire de l'Amérique française, (1947), 3–5, as organ of his Institut d'Histoire de l'Amérique française (est. 1946).

135 : Lionel Groulx, Notre grande aventure: l'Empire français en Amérique du Nord (1535–1760) (Montréal: Fides, 1958), 185.

136 : Phyllis M. Senese, "Lionel Groulx, 1878–1967," Dictionary of Literary Biography, vol. 68 "Canadian Writers 1920–1959, first series," ed. W.H. New (1988): 152–59; Maurice Filion, ed., Homage à Lionel Groulx (Ottawa: Éd. Leméac, 1978); Julien Goyette, Lionel Groulx: Une anthologie (Montreal: Bibliothèque québécoise, 1998); New, History of Canadian Literature (1989), 154.

137 : Adam Lymburner supported a mutual respect at the time of the Constitution of 1791

of Canada could not prevail against the rabid teachings of Groulx, whose anti-Semitic attitudes Bourassa shared. Just as Garneau affirmed French culture against Lord Durham's uninformed slur of 1839, Bourassa affirmed Canadian autonomy against Laurier's lack of an independent foreign policy, epitomized in the Canadian participation in the South African war. His concept of self-determination, *maîtres chez nous*, fostered self-confidence and cultural pride. His third theme of social values in economic life and the public good, was shared by English-language pragmatists. Like French intellectuals, Quebec's commentators were oriented toward the present while Ontario's writers were concerned with the past.[138] In Ontario, opposition to Anglican orthodoxy was epitomized by Methodist Egerton Ryerson, who established Ontario's secular school system as well as an important publishing house. William Dawson (1820–99), professor at McGill and one of the founders of the resource-opening Canadian Geological Survey, represented the Scottish "Common Sense" tradition. This school of thought's empirical orientation cared little for the English-Anglican–imperial ideological cast. Dawson, opposed by imperialist Leacock, supported women's education at universities. While divisive imperial and racist propaganda dominated the discourse, the pragmatist intellectuals charted the course for future development.[139]

Into this debate, women inserted themselves. In contrast to Gordon and Groulx, who both glorified their mothers' roles as domesticated women, Nellie McClung and Emily Murphy's visions were feminist and embedded in temperance and other reform activities. Still, they also cherished billboard-type slogans. McClung's Canada was "missionary; it was rural; it was assimilative," it contained vast expanses of fields of golden wheat.[140] She combined the national with the familial, educational opportunities for women with a mothering ideal. She supported self-organized women's clubs and joined the Winnipeg Political Equality League. She defied the Conserva-

and Robert Nelson argued for official bilingualism in 1838 (Dumont, *Genèse*, 125, 184).

138 : Joseph Levitt, ed., *Henri Bourassa on Imperialism and Bi-culturalism*, 1900–1918 (Toronto: Copp Clark, 1970); Linteau et al., *Histoire du Québec*, 1:648–55.

139 : New, *History of Canadian Literature* (1989), 87–97; Susan Mann Trofimenkoff, *The Dream of a Nation: A Social and Intellectual History of Quebec* (Toronto: Gage, 1983), 218–32; Margaret Gillett, *We Walked Very Warily: A History of Women at McGill* (Montreal: Eden Press, 1981).

140 : The male counterpart was Frederick Niven who in his *Canada West*, written before but published after the onset of the Depression in 1929, remembered "the old days... when the English speech was everywhere, indomitable settlers driving the first furrows, and the wild young men, the breakers of the prairie, going on their jocund way as though to the sound of bands." He presented several such Hollywood-type pictures of the settlers.

tive Manitoba premier, Rodmond Roblin, whose support for capital aroused the ire of many small producers. By 1921, the Roblin government was out and she was in, as a member of the legislature for the Liberal Party. From her evangelical perspective, she decried poverty and deprivation but found working-class self-organization and direct actions, such as the Winnipeg General Strike, difficult to accept. She chose the side of "respectable" Canadians, who united to break the labour movement by violence and slander, and to exclude labour activists from Canada by deportation.[141] More open and welcoming was Janey Canuck, "the naive, youthful, self-confident, and brash" creation of Emily Ferguson Murphy. Murphy shared the vision of self-determined women's lives, was ready to accept massive White immigration, and was optimistic about the advantages settlers would find in Canada and Canada in them. Mass production of wheat rather than accelerating industrialization would make Canada a strong nation. However, Murphy also believed in sterilizing the mentally "unfit" and her writings contained anti-Chinese and anti-Black diatribes. Many wanted to hear her message; her *Open Trails* (1912) sold over sixty thousand copies. It was more attuned to prospects for the future than the backward-looking Scots of Ralph Connor or the near-fascist youths of Lionel Groulx.[142]

Gordon's masculinity and Groulx's corporatism could easily have led to fascist organization as it did in Europe. Neither vision helped Canadians to come to terms with industrialization, urbanization, increasing mobility, speed-up of communications, cultural heterogeneity, and new ideas about society. Nellie McClung's billboard reserved space for women and Emily Murphy democratized the characters that appeared on the posters. Had the billboard's glossy master narrative taken hold, Canada's economy would have been restricted to a grain agriculture in the very decades, 1885 to 1914, which signalled the triumph of industrialism. Workers were not part of the nation: "A Trade Union artisan who will not work more than eight hours a day ... will not work on a farm at all, and has to be fed by the public when work is slack," opined a British Canadian opinion leader, "is quantity and very bad quality ... such men are not wanted in Canada." For once, Quebec's *courant clerico-nationaliste* agreed with the anglophone hegemony

141 : Janice Fiamengo, "A Legacy of Ambivalence: Responses to Nellie McClung," *Journal of Canadian Studies* 34.4 (1999): 70–87; Veronica Strong-Boag, Introduction to Nellie L. McClung, *In Times Like These* (1915; repr. Toronto: UTP, 1972), vii–xx, and Strong-Boag, "'Ever a Crusader': Nellie McClung, First-Wave Feminist," in Strong-Boag and Anita Clair Fellman, eds., *Rethinking Canada: The Promise of Women's History* (1st ed., 1986; Toronto: Oxford Canada, 1997), 178–90.

142 : Isabel Bassett, "Introduction" to Emily Murphy, *Janey Canuck in the West* (1st ed., 1910; repr. Toronto: McClelland & Stewart, 1975), ix–xxiii.

and opposed working-class organizations. Its ideologues called on paternalist capitalists to build small factories in agricultural zones. In an extension of rural life, they would process farm products and operate only in the winter when farm families were underemployed.[143] Capitalists, who shared the opposition to labour unions, steered a different course, accepting workers regardless of ethnicity as long as wages remained low; employers did not want families but flexible young men in prime working age. Canadian imagery was complex and often exclusionist; identities sprang from many backgrounds and experiences.

The billboards' small print

While identities were developing, there were, constitutionally speaking, no Canadians at the turn of the twentieth century. The hegemonic role of British ways of conceptualizing society and empire made all inhabitants of the Empire *British* citizens; as analyzed above, no Canadian (or Australian, or Indian, or Malay) citizenship existed. Canada's national billboards might have carried a byline: "the British Attorney General determines that independent status is dangerous to the health of the Empire" or "produced in Canada under a licensing agreement from London." Canadians from backgrounds other than British were aware of the resulting problems and saw the small print loom large, since they had to bear the cost.

The imperialists' proudly proclaimed "imperial sensibilities" may look less than sensible and sensitive, but they appear as outright brutal from other perspectives. Adherence to the Empire deprived Canada and Australia of full independence, and under the concept of "Empire settlement," it deprived others of self-determination, namely British orphans and children of what reformers considered unfit parents, "surplus women" who would not find a husband in England, and disabled soldiers from imperial wars. These were sent to the "white colonies" by population planners, social cost accountants, and propagandists of British superiority. In contrast to the deportation of Acadians (and later of the South African Boers), this type of transportation was meant to be benign. White Canada's "imperial sensibilities" could accommodate the destruction of the Red River Métis' society, and could justify the exclusion of Chinese and other Asian men and women and the division of humanity into preferred and non-preferred races. In the Empire, such sensibilities permitted waging war to open China to the British opium trade and permitted establishment of indentured servitude

---

143 : Clifford Sifton, "The Immigrants Canada Wants," *Maclean's*, 1 April 1922, cited in Howard Palmer, ed., *Immigration and the Rise of Multiculturalism* (Toronto: Copp Clark, 1975), 35; Linteau et al., *Histoire du Québec*, 1:701–3.

or "second slavery" of millions of men and women from British India and China. Since Canadian history does not only start in England and Ontario, but also in the Red River Valley, in the southern provinces of China, and South Asia's many societies, the White-Anglo imperial master narrative and the distinct Quebec narrative were far too narrow to accommodate the full range of perspectives that any study of Canada would have to incorporate.

Many Canadians outside of the opinion-leaders' circles were far more open-minded. Numerous Manitoba settlers did not share the domineering attitudes toward the Métis and some British Columbians decried the harassment of Sikhs. First Peoples considered themselves allied nations rather than subjects of lesser status. French Canadians struggled for their language, culture, and legal system. Life writings show that many English, Scots, Welsh, and Irish newcomers of the 1870s and after were acutely aware of the imperial power relations and individuals' attitudes of superiority and, thus, they consciously decided to Canadianize. Immigrants of neither British imperial background nor of membership in Roman-Catholic institutions (as distinct from cultural ways of life and religious spirituality) remained critical of imperial and "national"-cultural hegemony, which is one more kind of flag-waving ethnicity.

A new image to conceptualize Canadian history and society has been the "family tree." According to this view, Canadian identity has its roots in Europe (and, perhaps, among First Peoples); out of the roots the trunk or mainstream grew, which, in turn, sprouted many different branches. Each leaf is nourished by the roots. However, did First Peoples, French, and British merge into one trunk? And, if leaves wither seasonally, does the trunk remain unchanged? If the storm of war tears off leaves, will the trunk (nation) be nourished by the mouldering leaves of soldiers' bodies? Rather, if we grope for an image, we might suggest an umbrella of institutions that covered those who held its handle but left out in the rain those without a hold. Sometimes, as in 1837, so few were in the protected position that the many left out tried to wrest the institutional umbrella from the hands of the privileged. In the family-tree image, the roots form one big tangle, but in all societies—not only in those styled immigration societies—newcomers join the mainstream-trunk with their own roots. If we stay with the biological image, society is not a giant redwood or a sugar maple but more like a tropical forest with roots, entwined lianas, and supplejacks. The cold Canadian North as a tropical forest. Images create problems. In whose minds did they develop and who accepted them?

A change from the image to what has been called hard data provides a different and disconcerting perspective. If we say the Canadian population as a whole equals 100 percent, the master narrative left out women—minus 50 percent; of the men, it left out the lower-class ones (roughly two fifths), it did not include children (roughly one third), it excluded men of skin colours other than "white" (less than 5 percent of men around 1900). The "master" narrative thus has always been a minority or a 15 percent version of Canada's society, history, and identities. It never described the trunk-mainstream of the family tree. Rather it truncated the whole story and produced dead wood.

Other, better-suited metaphors are the images of a mosaic, an ever-changing kaleidoscope, or a tossed salad. The imagery of weaving and textiles is preferable. Acting people, women and men, combine threads of many colours, some self-produced, others brought from afar or bought from someone else, perhaps into a fine tapestry, perhaps into an everyday garment. The threads keep their distinctiveness but, interwoven, they form a new whole. However, since the threads do not act themselves, this metaphor also needs to be corrected. People weave their lives into social patterns; braided lives influence each other and come out changed. When garments or tapestry are worn out, their colours fade, and a new generation will clothe itself and interweave lives.

II. FROM PRIVILEGED DISCOURSES TO RESEARCH ON SOCIAL SPACES

Before the 1920s, historiography was factual and constitutional or embellishing and idealizing. Historians often wrote with literary intentions or pretensions. Self-views changed when, from 1900, newcomers arrived in Canada in unprecedented numbers. A vigorous effort to help them become part of society came from men and women, who deep in their minds and hearts were convinced that this would involve an uplift of those of foreign customs, values, and beliefs. If this *constructive* effort was an essential part of building Canadian society, why have some historians considered the dispatch of soldiers to the *destructive* war in Europe, from 1914 to 1918, more important? Why would they consider death in war rather than building of societies as the basis of national consciousness? Common Canadians did not share the nationalist-militarist view; they accorded the 1918 "Spanish flu's" death toll "at home," far higher than that of the four years of war afar, a much more important place in memory. The privileged discourses of the two educated mainstreams—or *men*streams—monopolized knowledge production and the shaping of published national collective memory.

Research on Canada expanded, and as more and more colleges and universities were established, disciplines diversified. Bicultural Montreal's anglophone McGill University exerted a major influence on scholarship (chapter 5). A first approach to the Study of Canada was achieved by geography as a study of actual and potential social spaces (chapter 6). Distributing narratives and knowledges to Canada's peoples as a whole or to segments of them occurred in self-organized mechanics' or women's institutes, through public libraries, and in the schools and through school books. Social workers attempted to inculcate the lower classes and newcomers with what they considered Canadian values. In the upper echelons of society a new national intellectual and administrative elite formed itself (chapter 7). The studies of Canada and their multiple narratives were part of shaping Canadian society and making its elites.

Chapter 5

PRIVILEGED DISCOURSES UP TO 1920:
SCHOLARSHIP IN THE MAKING

Merchants and missionaries, officers and officials of European background, coming into contact with Native peoples, collected and classified their cultural artifacts as an approach to the study of "folk," if allegedly primitive folk. Folklore and ethnography became the anchor point for the new, as yet highly problematic discipline of ethnology, and later for an anthropology based on "Western civilization" or Euro-North American values and viewpoints as Saïd and many others have pointed out. Next, Euro-Canadian men, often self-taught, often opinionated, wrote about the history of Euro-Canada as an institutional-cultural project with emphasis on a particular region or a particular ethno-national group. Many saw culture in the several Canadas as merely derivative of Britain and France in the Old World. Outside observers attempted comprehensive descriptions for particular audiences, such as prospective British emigrants or the educated French middle class. They belonged to the periods of amateur research and of professionalization, the latter process extending roughly from the 1850s to, depending on the discipline, the 1890s or 1920s.

Religion as guide for research:
The establishment of universities up to the 1920s

Regardless of culture—Scottish, English, or French—academic research and teaching was intended to be governed by Christian principles or, more exactly, their several denominational variants. Each denomination imported a particular scholarly culture: Scottish Presbyterians' pragmatism especially from Edinburgh, Anglican orthodoxy especially from Oxford and Cambridge, Catholicity in the differing versions of several European-based Orders. The struggle for secularization began in Ontario in the 1840s. Toward the end of the nineteenth century, royal academies and professionalizing academic institutions encouraged development of the sciences and the arts and brought together top talent. They also established orthodoxies of what was acceptable and of what was marginalized or excluded.

Early colleges from Windsor, NS, to York, ON, had been orthodox and Anglican, emulating the older English universities.[144] In contrast, Method-

---

144 : The three King's Colleges at Windsor, NS, 1789 (Loyalist); York, 1827 (later Toronto); Fredericton, NB, 1828; Anglican Bishop's College in Lennoxville, QC, 1843. Robin S. Harris, *A History of Higher Education in Canada*, 1663–1960 (Toronto: UTP, 1976).

ist and Baptist colleges were to prepare men for the ministry along more participatory lines,[145] while Roman Catholic ones followed more rigorous, dogmatic lines.[146] Others pursued the liberal and democratic ideals of the older Scottish universities.[147] Scottish thought, especially Baconian science, deeply influenced the intellectual community. Francis Bacon (1561–1626) had argued that man could come to know reality by observing nature empirically, and his popularizers—educators, journalists, and clergymen—turned his theories into a philosophy: knowledge was founded upon experience and entailed nothing more than a classification of facts and phenomena. Natural theology and moral philosophy integrated the sciences and helped to accommodate new discoveries. The Scottish Common Sense school, with Thomas Reid and William Hamilton as major philosophers, was suspicious of scholasticism and theological constructions. The first principal of McGill, geologist and philosopher J. William Dawson, practised these traditions.[148]

The parallel system of higher education in Quebec had its origins in the Collège des Jésuites, founded as early as 1635, as a kind of generic *collège classique* teaching theology, classical studies, and sciences. By the mid-1660s, it recruited its professors from France, mainly sojourning men in their twenties who returned after a few years. For more practical training, the Jesuits' "hydrographic school," founded three-quarters of a century later, taught mathematics, astronomy, and physics for navigators and surveyors. This approach was a kind of applied sea-centred geography geared to commerce and communication. Mgr. François de Laval, first bishop of Quebec, founded the Grand and Petit Séminaire de Québec in 1663; the first to train priests, the latter to prepare French and Indian students for the Collège des Jésuites. After the British victory of 1759, the Jesuit institution and the Petit Séminaire became *collèges classiques*. Shortly after, in the 1770s, the pope disbanded the Jesuit Order altogether. Eighteenth-century institutions, such as the École des Arts et Métiers de Saint-Joachim and the Institut des Frères Charron, provided liberal arts, classical studies, and religious and professional training. Heterogeneity within the confines of the Catholic

---

145 : Victoria College (Coburg, ON, 1841) and Mount Allison University (Sackville, NB, 1839), both Methodist, and Baptist Acadia University (Wolfville, NS, 1838).

146 : St. Francis Xavier (Antigonish, NS, 1855) and the University of Ottawa, 1848.

147 : Dalhousie, Halifax, NS, 1818 (based on Edinburgh University, as non-denominational counterpart to King's College); McGill University, Montreal, 1821 (non-denominational, anglophone), based on the endowment of merchant McGill for public education; and Queen's University, Kingston, 1841 (Presbyterian).

148 : Robert A. Falconer, "Scottish Influence on the Higher Education in Canada," *Transactions and Proceedings of the Royal Society of Canada* 21 (May 1927): 7–20.

faith was assured through competition between men's and women's Orders: the Récollets, Jesuits, Sulpiciens, Franciscans, Ursulines, and others.[149]

Two of the three leading institutions of higher learning, the University of Toronto as a federation of colleges and Université Laval, came into being in the 1850s. Toronto's University College, as secular degree-granting institution for the denominational colleges,[150] was founded after a long struggle against religious control over higher learning.[151] In contrast, Université Laval, since 1852 the first francophone university in North America, was to be strictly Roman Catholic. Its predecessor, the Grande Séminaire, continued as its Faculty of Arts. The Université d'Ottawa, bilingual and Catholic, emerged out of the Collège de Bytown (established 1848) in 1889. A satellite campus of Laval, established in 1876 in Montreal, became the independent Université de Montréal in 1919. It received civil recognition in 1920 and the École des hautes études commerciales (established 1907, teaching since 1910) became its business school.[152] It published the first Canadian economics periodical, *L'Actualité économique*. The new anglophone organizational model, a federation of denominational colleges, including Roman Catholic ones under a secular degree-granting umbrella institution, reduced cost and permitted diversity. Of the seventeen degree-granting institutions in 1867, only four were non-denominational and one third had an enrolment of less than one hundred students. Around 1900, when the entire university enrolment amounted to 6,500 students in less than a dozen institutions, the denominational institutions were still strong, with George Munro Grant, principal of Queen's University and the "elder statesman," and with their chief administrators often drawn from the ranks of clerics.

For more than half a century, however, first among the leading universities was McGill, founded as "a private institution supported by the anglophone economic elite of Montreal" in the mid-1850s. Its "strong utilitarian ethos" led to numerous approaches to the study of Canadian society: geographers and sociologists in particular explored social spaces, the potential of the

---

149 : Marc Lebel, Pierre Savard, Raymond Vézina, *Aspects de l'Enseignement au Petit Séminaire de Québec (1765–1945)* (Quebec: Société historique du Québec, 1968).

150 : King's College (1827, Anglican; secularized 1849), Trinity College (1851, Anglican, founded to counter secularization), Victoria College (Coburg 1841, Methodist), St. Michael's (1852, Roman Catholic), Knox College (1844, Presbyterian).

151 : Organizationally as well as doctrinally, the decision of Methodists, Congregationalists, and Presbyterians in 1924 to form the United Church of Canada simplified religious diversity and indicated an ecumenical spirit.

152 : The École supérieure de commerce was founded shortly later. Robert Rumilly, *Histoire de l'École des hautes études commerciales de Montréal, 1907–1967* (Montreal: Beauchemin, 1967).

West, and the problems of the cities. Though the peculiarities of Canadian self-definitions have it that anglophone McGill is often not considered a Quebec university, interaction between McGill and Laval sociologists was close—one of the many examples of co-operation between the two language groups.

In the Prairie provinces, a third, distinct system of higher education with emphasis on agriculture, applied research, and extension services was created from the 1870s to the 1910s. The University of Manitoba, established in 1877 as the first degree-granting university, followed the federated model of denominational colleges: Saint-Boniface (Roman Catholic), St. John's (Anglican), Manitoba (Presbyterian), and, in 1888, Wesley (Methodist). The University of Alberta (founded 1906) and the University of Saskatchewan (founded 1907) were non-denominational. McGill established a branch campus in British Columbia in 1908, which in 1915 became the independent provincial University of British Columbia. Thus, Prairie developments were different, yet connected to the anglophone East. UBC was a copy of the Eastern system.[153]

Within the universities, traditional departments, especially the classics, struggled to stay centre stage in both prestige and funding when the social sciences developed. Moral philosophy became the science of an orderly social community or—with emphasis on economic well-being—"commonwealth," when it came to be recognized that even a mere subsistence base of food and housing was not available to all members of society. Such moral philosophy or ethic were expressed in the secular social reform, the Protestant "social gospel," and the Catholic Church's encyclical *Rerum novarum*. Empirical collection of data—the Baconian approach—was to provide the background for remedial action by enlightened legislators and administrators. While McGill from its beginning placed strong emphasis on natural philosophy—in the process of becoming the natural sciences—and thus could achieve a leading position in both the social and natural sciences, other institutions followed suit only much later. The two French-language universities only turned to the social sciences as late as the 1920s. Since Canada's elites accorded low priority to scholarship, until the 1970s university teachers had to be recruited from abroad, from Great Britain and France, from Rome's universities and U.S. institutions. Such scholars would not provide a perspective "from the outside," rather they were part of imperial discourses and often considered their "home" culture superior to Canada's. Young Canadian PhD candidates had to leave for universities in England, Scotland,

---

153 : Robert Choquette, *Langue et religion: Histoire des conflits anglo-français en Ontario* (Ottawa: PU Ottawa, 1977), 21-53 on the Université d'Ottawa. Doug Owram, *The Government Generation: Canadian Intellectuals and the State, 1900-1945* (Toronto: UTP, 1986), 8-9.

France, or the United States for post-graduate studies. Thus Quebec's universities remained tied to papal encyclicals, but among francophone scholars, the Association canadienne-française pour l'avancement des sciences, established in 1923, moved away from ethnocentric concerns and dogmatic interpretations. British-Canadian universities remained tied to imperial concepts and participated in the First Congress of the Universities of the Empire (1912). While in the late nineteenth century, moral philosophy and natural theology lost influence to a Darwinian ideology of self-preservation, in education Scottish common sense ideals continued their hold for several more decades.

University education received a major and brutal jolt in World War I. From youthful and imperial enthusiasm, a large number of anglophone students volunteered for service in 1914, and four years later, when the total Canadian death toll stood at sixty thousand, the ranks of students were depleted. Returning veterans, a generation welded together by wartime camaraderie and survival, enrolled in large numbers. So did an "unprecedented number of women" with a new public self-confidence and in view of the lack of *men*power. As yet, the social sciences were integrated, but specialization began, with the natural sciences and medical faculties in the forefront. In the 1920s, utilitarianism came to be seen as one aspect of a moral bankruptcy that had led Western societies into war. Some academics claimed that both specialization and vocational training strangled the quest for knowledge. Adherents of the moral-philosophy tradition called for a reintegration of knowledge to achieve intellectual coherence and moral substance in higher education. A struggle between those academics who saw themselves as guardians of tradition and those who wanted to be agents for social improvement split the scholarly community, as A.B. McKillop has argued.[154] Ethnologists and historians ranked themselves clearly on the side of tradition, they appeared as believers—in what might be called secular creeds—of White, perhaps Christian, superiority over "primitive peoples" and wrote almost biblical founding narratives of their own societies.[155]

---

154 : Marlene Shore, *The Science of Social Redemption: McGill, the Chicago School, and the Origins of Social Research in Canada* (Toronto: UTP, 1987), 6–8; A.B. McKillop, *A Disciplined Intelligence: Critical Inquiry and Canadian Thought in the Victorian Era* (Montreal: MQUP, 1979).

155 : The claim to superiority stems from the Christian Church's claim to possess the only true and truthful knowledge of this world and realms beyond this world. The Good Friday liturgy asked God to help Jews —and implicitly other infidels—to lift the veil from their eyes, to help them out of their perfidious delusion. As late as 1928, an attempt to reform the liturgy was blocked by the Pope. Ongoing research by Hubert Wolf and team, Univ. of Münster, Germany.

Folklorists to ethnologists:
Grave robbing, appropriating, researching

During the early periods of contact, whether at Tadoussac in the sixteenth century or on the Queen Charlotte Islands in 1774, or later in the Red River Valley—all of these European place names—the French, Spanish, and English visitors/explorers/intruders came for pelts. They also acquired "Indian" artifacts and described, in their own terms of reference, what they observed during their often short visits. In zones of contact/conflict with Aboriginal peoples' worlds across the globe, the missionaries and high priests of two of the three Eastern Mediterranean religions "of the Book"—Judaism, Christianity, and Islam—transposed and imposed their belief systems onto other societies. Only Jewish rabbis did not seek to convert others. Muslim leaders sought adherents for their faith among the cultures of the Indian Ocean. Particularly convinced of their religion's and thus their peoples' superiority were the Christian religious strategists. The Christian public and scholarly discourse's "white-over-pagan-red" paradigm has overshadowed conversion in the other direction, "white" into "red" or "black" into "red," as well as the development of "red-black" enclaves. Métis societies emerged from cultural fusion; "white" societies from cultural adaptation; "red" changed through contact. Among the missionaries of European background, spirituality and materialism were often closely linked. They competed with shamanic and animist belief systems; they did not necessarily need the better weaponry since they had the stronger organizations and stricter hierarchies in addition to financial backing. For the South Seas and the Pacific, Greg Dening has sensitively described the interaction and misunderstandings, the self-assured arrogance, the violence on both sides, the support and cooperation emerging out of conjunctions of interest or human solidarity. For the Pacific Coast First Peoples' societies, Douglas Cole has traced collectors' and amateurs' approaches.

Collectors of "Indian" or "Eskimo" artifacts were many: religious men, military men, trading men—and Native men hired as interpreters. Missionaries, recognizing the competing spirituality of such artifacts, destroyed them when their power permitted or sold them off when their own funds ran low. Acquisition of artifacts, whether private or commissioned by public museums, took precedence over comprehending customs and values. The latter could neither be transferred nor sold. In 1930, an anthropologist who watched a potlatch at Fort Rupert noted that while the rituals and the words spoken remained unchanged, the artifacts were gone—they were in museums from Washington to Ottawa to Berlin.[156]

Europeans' knowledge acquisition about the physical side of First Peoples' human existence involved the measuring of body parts of the living and exhibition of the bones of the dead. Local dealers, renowned European and North American collectors and eminent scholars—sometimes with the help of whole Native communities converted to Christianity—took whatever could be transported. Bodies were robbed from graves in the name of science, flesh and sinews "cleaned" from bones. Living "specimens" of Aboriginal peoples, labelled "exotic," were displayed at exhibitions or in zoos and shows—increasingly with the consent of the respective individuals, whose ways of life had already been destroyed. Examples are institutions such as the American Museum of Natural History in New York, exhibitions such as the Chicago World's Fair of 1893 and the International Colonial Exhibition in Paris of 1931, zoological gardens in Italy and Germany, and U.S. shows such as Buffalo Bill's. Carl Hagenbeck, a famous zoological entrepreneur in Hamburg, Germany, instructed his travelling collectors and expedition entrepreneurs to convince individuals, families, or groups of Native peoples to come to Europe to be exhibited in his "animal and peoples exhibitions." Many of those who came died, some returned, and few expected to be stared at by self-styled "civilized" people. A particularly well-researched incident is that of "Eskimo" ordered by the American Museum of Natural History. Canadian author Kenn Harper has described how the polar explorer Robert Peary brought six Inuit from Baffin Bay in 1897. The men, women, and children were housed in the museum's basement and remained at the mercy of the ethnologists' scientific interest and of the sensation-loving spectators. Within a few weeks, all except Minik, a boy styled "the New York Eskimo," had died. A foster family familiarized him with U.S. culture. Looking for his roots, he discovered that the bones of his father, Qisuk, were exhibited in the museum. In shock, the uprooted Minik made his way back to his people, but remained unable to recover. The story of Minik came down in different versions of memory. First Peoples' oral traditions differ as much from each other as Western people's eyewitness accounts.[157]

---

156 : Greg Dening, *The Death of William Gooch: A History's Anthropology* (1st ed., 1988; rev. Honolulu: Univ. of Hawai'i Press, 1995); Douglas Cole, *Captured Heritage: The Scramble for Northwest Coast Indian Artifacts* (Vancouver: UBC Press, 1985, repr. 1995). See also Russel L. Barsh, "Are Anthropologists Hazardous to Indians' Health?" *Journal of Ethnic Studies* 15.4 (1988): 1–38.

157 : Kenn Harper, *Give Me My Father's Body: The Life of Minik, the New York Eskimo* (Frobisher Bay: Blacklead, 1986). For a survey of exhibitions of human beings see Nicolas Bancel et al., eds., *Zoos Humains: De la Vénus hottentote aux reality shows* (Paris: Éd.

The first step in any serious study of other peoples involves learning their respective language, and some early researchers made great efforts to develop a form of writing for languages existing in spoken form only, for example Gabriel Sagard in his *Dictionnaire de la langue Huronne* (1615).[158] Most collectors, however, showed little interest in original meaning. Henry Rowe Schoolcraft, the U.S. Indian agent among the Ojibway of the Great Lakes from 1812 to 1842, recorded tales in English, and Native peoples' stories were usually retold in terms deemed appropriate for a non-Native reading public whether young or adult. They were appropriated by those taking charge of "national" cultural memory. Acting from an allegedly benevolent "salvage paradigm," folklorists and ethnologists with an antiquarian interest in customs and dresses often added a dose of sentimentalism—"the last of the Mohicans," "the last Beothuk," the noble but receding "savage" of "pure" culture.[159] They often lumped together all cultures they considered less modern than their own. Thus English Canadian folklorists studied both Aboriginal hunting and French-Canadian habitant culture, but never looked at their own culture in ethnological terms. In contrast to traditional historiography, ethnography dealt with the majority of the people rather than only with educated elites.

In the late nineteenth century, scholars of the new field of anthropology actively collected and thus preserved in written form First Peoples' cultures that their co-nationals in the missionary and artifact trades were destroying. Borderlines between scholars and grave robbers, however, were fluid. Franz Boas was involved in "salvaging" bones and artifacts from Aboriginal peoples' burial sites; museum curators bargained for bones, skulls, and skeletons. These anthropologists, intending to record oral traditions literally, were dependent on interpreters, for example of the Thompson River Indians (James Teit), of the Salish (Boas), of the Cree (Leonard Bloomfield), and of the Haida (Barbeau). Problems were numerous. German American

La Découverte, 2002); Matthias Gretzschel and Ortwin Pelc, eds., *Hagenbeck: Tiere, Menschen, Illusionen* (Hamburg: Abendblatt, 1998), 32-52; Michael Ames, *Cannibal Tours and Glass Boxes: The Anthropology of Museums* (2nd rev. ed., Vancouver: UBC Press, 1992).

158 : Elke Nowak, "'Gehet hin in alle Welt ...': Die Aneignung fremder Sprachen und die Sprachwissenschaft des 18. und 19. Jahrhunderts," *Berichte zur Wissenschaftsgeschichte* 22 (1999): 135-45.

159 : "On s'attendrit aussi sur les Indiens et sur la race des Hurons en train de disparaître. Joseph Lenoir (1822-61) écrit le *Chant de mort d'un Huron*, J.-G. Barthe (1816-93), *Fragment iroquois*, et F.-X. Garneau, le poème qui est un de ses meilleurs, Le dernier Huron." Pierre de Grandpré, *Histoire de la littérature française du Quebec*, 4 vols. (Montreal: Beauchemin, 1967-69), 1:163-64.

Franz Boas, the most original of scholars, interpreted his data to consider the Kwakwaka'wakw (Kwakiutl) the Pacific Coast's "model tribe," suitable to be exhibited at the Chicago World's Fair. His informer, George Hunt, was a Métis, whose English father, an HBC factor, and Tlingit mother had raised him at the Fort Rupert trading post. Hunt, who spoke the language fluently, married a local Kwakwaka'wakw woman and was initiated into this people's male associations. He was told by scholars to concentrate on commonplace rather than specific ceremonial objects, by exhibition curators to deliver richly ornamented ceremonial artifacts, and, depending on demand and competition between museums and private collectors, to bring as many objects as he could get, or to bring few and to concentrate on the meanings and stories associated with them. Hunt received about five dollars per cranium and often ravaged burial sites, which he said were abandoned. Some of his informants criticized him for passing on their stories, so that they lost control over the meaning and impact. In Western parlance, he committed copyright violations. When he did not deliver, the scholar-collectors hinted that his salary would be cut. He delivered what was asked of him—and was temporarily ostracized by his family for exploiting their spirituality.[160] James Teit, who also co-operated with Boas, "had a unique perspective on and entrée into local women's culture through his Salish wife, Lucy Antko," and he portrayed Native women as "strong, independent, and fully-participating members of their community."[161] Given the adoption of Christianity by some Native communities and the Canadian government's policy of civilizing "Indians," the collections and the translations preserved aspects of these cultures that might otherwise have been lost. The body of sophisticated knowledge available in the present relied on this research. Edward Sapir, as linguist in charge of the anthropology section of the National Museum of Canada from 1910 to 1925, who had the help of Charles Marius Barbeau and Félix-Antoine Savard, could arrive at a classification of First Peoples' languages that is valid to the present day (*Language*, 1921).[162]

---

160 : Edith Fowke, "Folktales and Folk Songs," in Carl F. Klinck et al., eds., *Literary History of Canada: Canadian Literature in English*, 4 vols. (2nd ed., Toronto: UTP 1976, 1990), 1:177–87; Cole, *Captured Heritage*, 61, 151–64. See in general George E. Marcus and Michael M.J. Fischer, *Anthropology as Cultural Critique* (Chicago: Univ. of Chicago Press, 1986); Scott Michaelsen, *The Limits of Multiculturalism: Interrogating the Origins of American Anthropology* (Minneapolis: Univ. of Minnesota Press, 1999).

161 : Pauline Greenhill and Diane Tye, eds., *Undisciplined Women: Tradition and Culture in Canada* (Montreal: MQUP, 1997), quote p. 18n4.

162 : David G. Mandelbaum, ed., *Selected Writings of Edward Sapir in Language, Culture and Personality* (Berkeley: Univ. of California Press, 1963); Laurence Nowry, *Man of Mana: Marius Barbeau, a Biography* (Toronto: NC Press, 1995). Barbeau was convinced

Euro-Canadian historians developed a sequence of themes according to Bruce G. Trigger: first Indians as allies; then, once First Peoples were no longer needed in Euro-imperial struggles, the antiquated Indian; the beginning of ethnohistory from Franz Boas on; the post-Innis studies of the fur trade; and finally studies of particular Native peoples. John A. Price classified historians' approaches as amateur phase, as museum phase, and, after 1940, as academic anthropology, which needed two decades to come to maturity. In the self-described superior cultures, mental change was agonizingly slow and auto-stereotyped superiority rendered the merits of others invisible.[163] In school and college teaching, biased perspectives persisted. James W.St.G. Walker's 1971 research on the most frequently assigned undergraduate texts in English and in French concluded: "The picture of the Indian as a human being ... is confusing, contradictory and incomplete... . Of the long string of epithets used to describe the Indian, 'savage' predominates [a list of two dozen negative terms] ... A corresponding, though shorter, list of complimentary terms ... [portrays the Indian] as 'brave'." Images of "noble savages" contrasted with those of "the presentation of him as a child in relation to white men." Some historians produced clichés. Harold Innis judged First Peoples to be "ignorant" of agriculture; Abbé Groulx bluntly classified Indians among the "races moins évoluées." In contrast, Harold Eccles found their agriculture to be "impressive" and their food "superior to that of Europeans." In Walker's 1982 follow-up study, historical geographers rather than historians appeared as highly aware of cultural adaptation and deliberate trading strategies. Thus college students continued to be socialized through biased official educational institutions into stereotypes about co-Canadians at a time when the Hawthorne Commission had already developed the "citizenship plus" concept.[164]

---

that the Tsimshian's songs were of Asian Buddhist origin and that their oral narratives reflected comparatively recent migrations from Asia (231, 392–93).

163 : Bruce G. Trigger, "The Historians' Indian: Native Americans in Canadian Historical Writing from Charlevoix to the Present," *Canadian Historical Review* 67 (1986): 315–42, repr. in *The Native Imprint: The Contribution of First Peoples to Canada's Character*, ed. Olive P. Dickason, 2 vols. (Athabasca: Athabasca Univ. Educational Enterprises, 1995), 1:423–50; John A. Price, "Native Studies," in Alan F.J. Artibise, ed., *Interdisciplinary Approaches to Canadian Society: A Guide to the Literature* (Montreal: MQUP, 1990), 117–147.

164 : James W.St.G. Walker, "The Indian in Canadian Historical Writing," Canadian Historical Assoc., *Historical Papers* (1971), 21–47, quotes 21–22, 23, 25, 26, and "Bibliographic Essay: The Indian in Canadian Historical Writing 1972-1982," in Ian A.L. Getty and Antoine S. Lussier, eds., *As Long as the Sun Shines and the Water Flows: A Reader in Canadian Native Studies* (Vancouver: UBC Press, 1983). See Chapter 13 for the Hawthorne Report.

Historians' promotional, compilatory, nostalgic, and constitutional narratives

While, in the nineteenth century, moral and natural philosophy provided the general frame for the world in which humans lived, historians were the keepers of collective memory; no other social sciences had yet come into existence. They thus held a powerful position in defining which events or processes, which actors, and which social groups were considered worthy of being part of collective, later national, memory. To reach out to a broader educated public, some wrote in a literary style; others, intent on a particular line of argument or political position, wrote for the academic and policy-making elites; yet others wanted to share a story, often of mainly regional significance. Even if proclaiming a faithfulness to "facts" and a belief in "objectivity," historiography has remained confined to an author's and his social group's particular convictions about society, polity, and economy. Literary historians could employ imagination as part of their craft and, using for example the Jesuits as a major source, introduced the *Relations'* imaginary elements about "Indian" ways of life into collective historical memory as facts reported by eyewitnesses—whose categories of viewing, whose gaze, was not questioned. Later documentary historians followed a more rigorous source critique, but their narratives remained incomplete. What they did not find in their written sources, which usually refer to institutions and hegemonic culture, could not enter their interpretations. Writing about the hegemonic groups, historians were far more influential than folklorists and ethnologists, but by excluding folk stories and material artifacts from the body of their sources, they were also far more narrow.[165]

Early "promotional history" (Bumsted) intended to publicize the progress of recent as well as established settlements and to attract further inhabitants and investments. Such works provided information on geography and climate, flora and fauna, before turning to prospects of the particular region. In their way, they were comprehensive. Intent to capture their audience by enthusiastic information, the authors often got lost in a welter of detail and picturesque, romantic incidents. Whether in French or Eng-

---

165 : This section is based on *The Oxford Companion to Canadian History and Literature*, ed. Norah Story (1st ed., Oxford: OUP, 1967), and *Supplement to the Oxford Companion to Canadian History and Literature*, ed. William Toye (Toronto: OUP, 1973); *The Oxford Companion to Canadian Literature*, eds. Eugene Benson and William Toye (1st ed. by William Toye, 1983; 2nd ed., Toronto: OUP, 1997), esp. J.M. Bumsted, "Historical Writing in English," 534–29, and A.I. Silver, "Historical Writing in French," 539–43; Grandpré, *Histoire de la littérature française*; M. Brook Taylor, *Promoters, Patriots, and Partisans: Historiography in Nineteenth-Century English Canada* (Toronto: UTP, 1989).

lish, most dealt with particular colonies.[166] The next, "compilatory," stage brought forth statistical accounts of Upper Canada and of all British North American colonies, as well as a comprehensive history with no literary ambitions but explicit pro-British, even "ultra-royalist" feelings.[167] Some historians of a particular colony pursued an economic history approach and included the material base of social life and of institutions into their interpretations. Newfoundland historian J.D. Prowse understood the cod fishery as part of the making of England; Duncan Campbell emphasized Nova Scotia's mercantile and industrial relations.[168] In the later nineteenth century, this approach included the West, which remained outside of "old Canada's" institution-centred or self-congratulatory local history approaches. Authors of the North, such as fur traders Alexander Ross and Agnes C. Laut, developed the theme of contact and conflict as a struggle between "savagery" and civilization or wrote vivid and picturesque stories.[169] They are almost forgotten since neither the West nor the North, in the minds of contemporary gatekeepers, could reflect progress.

Comprehensive studies of particular regions began with a perspective from the outside, with the French Jesuit P.F.X. Charlevoix's *Histoire et description générale de la Nouvelle France* (1744). Providing a wealth of information, he saw the inhabitants of the continent as the opposite of Europeans: uncorrupted, not enslaved to interest, free of the inequality on which "civilized" societies were founded. Histories written in Britain followed the "our Empire" line of argument. Subsequent authors, who dealt with the Seven Years' War and the battle on the Plains of Abraham as well as the War of 1812, usually pursued a "gallant deeds" tradition. George Heriot's *History of Canada* (1804) connected to earlier "explorer" and travel accounts by a lively interest in manners and customs of "Indians" as well as in the Euro-Indian wars; Michel Bibaud's *Histoire du Canada* (1835) was the first important

---

166 : Prince Edward Island (John Stewart, 1806), New Brunswick (Peter Fisher, 1825), Nova Scotia (Thomas C. Haliburton, 1829), northern New Brunswick and Gaspé (Robert Cooney, 1832).

167 : Upper Canada: Robert Gourlay, 1822; British North American colonies: Joseph Bouchette, 1831; comprehensive history: William Smith Jr., 2 vols., 1826.

168 : Newfoundland (Charles Pedley, 1863; J.D. Prowse, 1895), Nova Scotia (Beamish Murdoch, 1832–33 and 1865–67; Duncan Campbell, 1873), New Brunswick (James Hannay, 1879, 1897).

169 : Ross on the Oregon territory (1849), the "Far West" (1855), and the Red River Settlement (1856); Laut's "fur trade romances" included titles like *Lords of the North* (1900) and *Heralds of Empire* (1902). Other authors were James McCarroll (1871) and Joseph E. Collins (1886); Robert Service (1874–1958) published raucous writings.

work in a document-based mould.[170] Major nineteenth-century historians saw writing as a literary endeavour, for example Francis Parkman in the United States and François-Xavier Garneau in Canada. The story, seen in epic terms as struggles of strong men, had to be presented in a way to capture readers. Francis Parkman's *The Old Regime in Canada* (1874), part of his seven-volume epic *France and England in North America* (1865–92) reached the large U.S. audience and shaped memory more lastingly than Garneau's writing addressed to the small Canadian public.[171]

In Quebec, Jacques Viger's historical compilations and his manuscript manual of Canadian French with its affirmation of distinctiveness indicated a step away from metropolitan France.[172] F.-X. Garneau's magisterial *Histoire du Canada depuis sa découverte jusqu'à nos jours* (4 volumes, 1845–50), which remained unsurpassed for a century, emphasized the struggle for survival of French-Canadian culture but did not cater to the Church "qui s'était arrogé un monopole sur les âmes comme sur les biens" (Fohlen). It was a response to Lord Durham's British-centredness in his *Report* of 1839. Since Garneau saw no reason to reduce history to the building of monasteries and conversion of "savages," the Catholic Church came close to considering him as "individu dangereux" and viewed his writings "comme une perversion." Involved in political and cultural arguments, Garneau was influenced by French historians, Augustin Thierry in particular, who combined liberal politics with a romantic style.[173] In contrast to Garneau's em-

170 : Charlevoix, *Histoire et description générale de la Nouvelle France avec le journal historique d'une voyage fait par ordre du roi dans l'Amérique septentrionale* (3 vols., Paris, 1744; Engl. translation New York, 1866–72). Bibaud's *Histoire* was reedited in 3 vols., 1837, 1844, 1878.

171 : More differentiated than Parkman was, almost a century later, William J. Eccles, *La société canadien sous le régime français/Canadian Society during the French Regime* (Montreal: Harvest House, 1968).

172 : Jacques Viger, *Néologie canadienne, ou Dictionnaire des mots créés en Canada et maintenant en vogue, des mots dont la prononciation et l'orthographie sont differantes de la prononciation et orthographie françoises . . .* , manuscript 1810, 1st publ. by the Société du parler français aux Canada (Quebec, 1909–10), current ed., Suzelle Blais, ed. (Ottawa: PU Ottawa, 1998).

173 : The English translation by Andrew Bell (1860) misrepresents parts of the text. The standard edition was the nine-volume 8th rev. ed. by Hector Garneau (1944–46). Gilles Galichan, Kenneth Landry, Denis Saint-Jacques, eds., *François-Xavier Garneau: une figure nationale* (Quebec: Éd. Nota Bene, 1998). Claude Fohlen, "Problématique de l'histoire canadienne," in Fohlen, Jean Heffer, François Weil, *Canada et Etats-Unis depuis 1770* (Paris: PU France, 1965; 3rd ed., 1997), 63–96, quotes p. 66. In Grandpré's authoritative *Histoire de la littérature française* (1967–69), Arsène Lauzière reinvented Garneau as an idéologue, almost a saviour: "Quatre-vingts ans après l'impitoyable défaite des Plaines

phasis on society and culture, John M. McMullen's *History of Canada from Its First Discovery to the Present Time* (1855) stressed parliamentary institutions and imperial-colonial government as well as a distinctively British North American tradition of material progress and commercial expansion. Subsequent Quebec writers abandoned Bibaud's documentary tradition and Garneau's comprehensive liberal approach for allegiance to the clergy and advocacy of the role of Catholicism, "[histoire] prosélyte et hagiographique" in Fohlen's words. Its main proponent—after a brief critical interlude[174]— was the Abbé Jean-Baptiste-Antoine Ferland.[175] The Abbé Henri-Raymond Casgrain, "auteur de plusieurs biographies, assez fantaisistes d'ailleurs," became the centre of the École Littéraire et Patriotique du Québec which created the "unending struggles" theme: against the Indians first, against the English next, and finally against modernity as a whole. The 1860s historical novels of Antoine Gérin-Lajoie, Philippe-Joseph Aubert de Gaspé, and Charles Thibault sang paeans to the agriculturalist, though Quebec was on the verge of its first industrial revolution.[176] The one effort to bypass the "historiographie politico-militaire" was Émile Salone's history of the colonization and French historian François-Edmé Rameau's history of French-speakers outside of Europe. It was left to the Royal Commission on Relations of Labour and Capital of the 1880s to deal with social problems in Quebec (and in Canada as a whole).[177]

---

d'Abraham, son oeuvre vint assumer et parachever la restauration de la dignité personnelle du Canadien français" (1:144).

174 : The Abbé Charles-Étienne Brasseur de Bourbourg, in his *Histoire du Canada, de son Église et de ses missions*, 2 vols. (Paris, 1852), described the Catholic bishops appointed by the British administrators as incapable elderly supporters of the British. Robert Christie's six-volume *History of the Late Province of Lower Canada* (1848–55) was of lasting value.

175 : Ferland, *Cours d'histoire du Canada* (1861–65); Fohlen, "Problématique," quote p. 67; Paul-André Linteau, René Durocher, Jean-Claude Robert, and François Ricard, *Histoire du Québec contemporain*, 2 vols. (2nd ed., Montreal: Boréal, 1989), 1:379.

176 : Fohlen, "Problématique," quote p. 67. Gérin-Lajoie, *Jean Rivard: le défricheur* (serialized 1862; as book Montreal, 1876) and *Jean Rivard: l'économiste* (ser. 1864, as book, Montreal, 1876); Aubert de Gaspé, *Les anciens canadiens* (Quebec, 1863); Joseph-Charles Taché published collections of legends, *Forestiers et voyageurs* (1863); Louis Fréchette, *La légende d'un peuple* (1887).

177 : Émile Salone, *La colonisation de la Nouvelle-France: Étude sur les origines de la nation canadienne française (Paris, 1905);* François-Edmé Rameau de Saint-Père, *La France aux colonies: Études sur le développement de la race française hors de l'Europe; Les Français en Amérique; Acadiens et Canadiens* (Paris, 1859). See Jean Blain, "Économie et société en Nouvelle-France: le cheminement historiographique dans la première moitié du XXe siècle," *Revue d'histoire de l'Amérique française* 26.1 (1972): 3–32, quote p. 3; Taylor, *Promoters, Patriots, and Partisans*, 84–115.

Based on Garneau's liberalism and in reaction to Casgrain's nationalism, a new generation of francophone historians, in the last decades of the nineteenth century, considered the survival of French-Canadian ways of life and language as assured. A concerted effort to collect documents (as had been initiated by the Société historique et littéraire de Québec in 1824) was supplemented by monographs on specific aspects of French-Canadian history. The two major fields remained religious and political history. A liberal nationalism was represented by Benjamin Sulte who, inspired by Voltaire, concentrated on the common people and attacked both the Jesuits' and France's neglect of the colony in his compilatory *Histoire des Canadiens français 1608–1880* (8 volumes, 1882–84).[178] Fernand Dumont summarized the effects of Church-centred historiography: "Les historiens religieux, les amateurs de légendes et de chansons, les auteurs de romans historiques et les poètes exaltent les origines au point d'élaborer un véritable mythe de l'âge d'or … qui rejoint les utopies de la vocation agricole et de la mission providentielle. Loin d'être reprise de soi en vue d'un avenir, la mémoire est inversion du projet et évasion dans le passé." Like Krieghoff's paintings these writings added to the dead weight burdening the choices of the living.[179]

Authors of British background wrote from a Whig perspective of progress toward responsible government. Regional, United Colony, as well as transcontinental perspectives were part of the political-societal debates. The "participant historians" (Bumsted) from Garneau to John G. Bourinot developed lively writing styles and covered all of Canada. Bourinot's sober and well-researched *Canada under British Rule, 1760–1900* (1900) radiated "a real satisfaction with Canadian parliamentary institutions and with Canadian achievements in the arts and in science." Among authors of British background, a "Whig interpretation" of history held sway: "the contemplation of freedom broadening down from precedent to precedent toward an agreeable present" combined with a belief "in democracy and in social and economic progress" (Windsor 1965). Five decades after Garneau's professionalism, Bourinot's and William Kingsford's works mark the breakthrough to professional historiography among English-language writers. But a major and lasting problem emerged: the sheer quantity of "national" history written by Ontario-socialized and -based scholars established "an equation of Ontario's past with the nation's past" (McKillop 1988).[180]

---

178 : Other authors included Louis-Philippe Turcotte, Laurent-Olivier David, and Joseph-Edmond Roy.

179 : Fernand Dumont, *Genèse de la société québécoise* (Montreal: Boréal, 1996), 316.

180 : Bourinot's interests ranged far beyond the constitutional. See his "Our Intellectual Strength and Weakness: A Short Review of Literature, Education and Art in Canada," in *Transactions and Proceedings of the Royal Society of Canada* (1983), 3–36; Kingsford, *His-

From the mid-1870s to the 1910s, during Macdonald's national policy and Quebec elites' *repli traditionaliste*, skilled amateur historians and journalists, whether adherents of the Canada First or of the Ultramontane ideologies, engaged in nationalist "drum-and-trumpet" historiography, which was frequently imbued with the piety of a particular denomination. In British Canadians' versions, the Church played no role but God's providence seemed to make English-style responsible government the Dominion's destiny. Perspectives included regional ones, contentious English-French juxtapositions, and some integrative ones. Romantically, Charles R. Tuttle aimed at "the inculcation of a higher and nobler sentiment of patriotism" and wanted to create "admiration" among U.S. readers. J. Castell Hopkins simply opined that Canada was "great."[181] In this climate of opinion, local historians, memory-keepers, and boosters combined to develop sites of historic importance, sites that would chain the present to the past through reverence. In a utilitarian view, such sites would encourage tourism and attract provincial or federal funding. Ideologically, selection of sites followed a "battlefield-and-ruins" approach.[182] Designation of particular sites or events as worthy of commemoration involves the power of establishing selection criteria and control over historic memory. Subsequent generations, who may want to commemorate different aspects of the past, face positions occupied by history hewn in granite and cast in bronze. War memorials glorifying death might be supplemented with or be replaced by memorials for those who advocated peace and created societies.[183]

---

tory of Canada (10 vols., 1887–98). Kenneth N. Windsor, "Historical Writing in Canada to 1920," in Klinck et al., *Literary History* (1965), 1:223–64, esp. 233, quote p. 229; A.B. McKillop, "Historiography in English," *Canadian Encyclopedia*, quote p. 2:993.

181 : Tuttle, *An Illustrated History of the Dominion 1535–1876* (1877); Hopkins, *The Story of... Half a Continent* (1899), *Progress of Canada* (1890), and *Canada: An Encyclopedia*, (6 vols., 1897–1900); Windsor, "Historical Writing" (1965), quote p. 231.

182 : In 1907, the federal government established the Quebec (later National) Battlefield Commission in preparation for the 1908 Quebec Tercentennial and the preservation of the Plains of Abraham and, in 1910, the Federal Historic Sites and Monuments Board of Canada.

183 : The battle over memory is also waged in schoolbooks. The Grade 8 text by J. Bradley Cruxton and W. Douglas Wilson, *Flashback Canada* (Don Mills, ON: Oxford, 2000), covering the 52 years from 1867 to 1919, devoted 58 of 344 pages of text to the five years 1914–19. The authors use the term "war breaks out"—volcano-like—instead of "war was declared." They include a long section on the heroism of Canadian soldiers at the battle of Vimy Ridge, 9 April 1917, long celebrated by military historians as a feat central to Canadian nation-building ("Brigadier-General Alex Ross said, 'I thought then... that in those few minutes I witnessed the birth of a nation.'" p. 308). However, they also include a thoughtful personal memory (p. 327): One of the perhaps

The increasingly professional historians could rely on the Federal Archives Branch organized in 1872, which later became the National Archives of Canada, and on materials collected by amateur historical societies such as the Literary and Historical Society of Quebec (established 1824), the historical societies of New Brunswick (1874), Nova Scotia (1878), and Ontario (1888; till 1899 under the name Pioneer and Historical Association), and the Manitoba Historical and Scientific Society (1875) founded by George Bryce, who in his history of Manitoba (1882) relied on solid documentation though he also intended to promote the "infant" colony. Writing from outside the Ontario consensus, he wanted to capture social dynamics rather than reduce history to politics and constitutions (*A Short History of the Canadian People*, 1887). Quebec historians of the period emphasized "la petite histoire et … la couleur régionale." The Champlain Society, founded in 1905 with the support of the Canadian Bank of Commerce in Toronto, engaged in publication of splendid Canadiana.[184]

Regional and national historiographies travelled separate yet partly parallel paths. Regional and local historical societies often included women and were concerned with whole lives. National historiography reduced social life to politics, but from politics alone people cannot chart life courses. Yet local history, as regards aspects of identity construction, buttressed nationalist themes. Ontario writers emphasized nation-building in terms of Britishness: the United Empire Loyalists, the feats of the War of 1812, the pioneer settlers. Since in these struggles the Iroquois played a role, they were accorded the place of manly warriors. Native women, even outstanding diplomats such as Mary Brant, were not mentioned. White pioneer women were accorded a role in establishing a Protestant Canada, Christian values, and British nationality. This approach was repeated by authors in the Prairies as well as in British Columbia and, even more explicitly, it was played out in parts of the Empire with large non-White populations.[185]

---

600 war veterans still living in 1999, proud of his medals, remarked, "All those men who were killed. How unnecessary. . . . A very terrible thing that a man has to give his life." He added thoughtfully, "I would feel compassionate toward any teenager who considers November 11th [Armistice Day] just another holiday," and added as his personal view that to the soldiers and their families the deaths, wounds to body and soul, and heroism continued to have meaning. "Some in hospitals throughout the country are still suffering. We have to remember those fellows." In contrast to such differentiated views, one-sided official narratives, which privilege the nation-through-death-in-war ideology over individuals' and families' sufferings and over life projects cut short, should not have a place in collective memory.

184 : Pierre Savard in Grandpré, *Histoire de la littérature française* (1967–69), 2:135.

185 : Donald Wright, "Gender and the Professionalization of History in English Canada

Academic historiography owed its existence to the rapid expansion of English-Canadian university curricula after 1880 with McGill and the University of Toronto as forerunners, but Queen's, Dalhousie, and Manitoba of almost equal importance. At the University of Toronto, William Ashley was appointed in 1888 to teach history and political economy, and George M. Wrong in 1892 a lecturer of history. At McGill, principal J.W. Dawson took great interest in history, and in 1895 Charles W. Colby became lecturer. English-socialized academics in Canada observed the country's development with skepticism. Emigrant Oxford scholar Goldwin Smith considered Canada to be a mere string of regions that, in their own best interests, should aim for continental integration with the United States. Nationalist historians, such as George M. Grant of Queen's University, rejected such views. Some of Quebec's French-language historians concerned themselves with "l'idéal de développement telle que proposée par l'état métropolitain," that is, France, rather than with Quebec's "période close, refermée sur elle-même." When, in Anglophonia, revisionist critical approaches such as William D. LeSueur's interpretation of the revolt of 1837 (1908) undermined societal myths, powerful families—the Mackenzie one in this case—prevented publication.[186]

Social history made its first inroads. Wrong's study on the interaction of the British and French, a social history of a seigneury taken over by a Scottish family (*A Canadian Manor and Its Seigneurs*, 1908) stood equal to Joseph-Edmond Roy's *Histoire de la seigneurie de Lauzon* (5 volumes, 1897–1904). Even these renowned scholars, however, were not immune to casting the habitant family as symbol of a conservative romanticism. Wrong criticized the exploration-and-politics approaches, and like O.D. Skelton from Queen's University, demanded inclusion of trade, commerce, and industrial life into the writing of history. Such a socio-economic approach was pursued by George Bryce (University of Manitoba) in his *Remarkable History of the Hudson's Bay Company* (1900) and by Adam Shortt (Queen's University) in a study of Canada's economic and financial investment (1889).[187] Shortt

before 1960," *Canadian Historical Review* 81 (2000): 29–66; Cecilia Morgan, "History, Nation, and Empire: Gender and Southern Ontario Historical Societies, 1890-1920s," *Canadian Historical Review* 82 (2001): 491-528; Adele Perry, *On the Edge of Empire: Gender, Race, and the Making of British Columbia, 1849-1871* (Toronto: UTP, 2000); Margaret Strobel, *European Women and the Second British Empire* (Bloomington: Indiana Univ. Press, 1991).

186 : Windsor, "Historical Writing" (1965), 247; Blain, "Économie et société" (1972), quote p. 5.

187 : Adam Shortt, *The Evolution of the Relation between Capital and Labor* (Kingston, OT: 1889).

had taught himself at the Walkerton, Ontario, Mechanics' Institute and studied at Edinburgh and Glasgow. He remained imbued with the Scottish tradition of connecting philosophy and economy, of combining ethics with empiricism. Like Wrong, he had trained for the ministry first, but became an economist with an historical perspective. As co-editor of *Canada and Its Provinces* (1914–17) he combined nation-state with provincial-regional approaches to history.

Wrong, who had intended to keep Canada's relations with Great Britain before the public mind, came to realize that Canadians were "a people quite different from the English."[188] With other historians he used the Historic Landmarks Association of Canada (established 1907) to found the Canadian Historical Association in 1922 and the *Canadian Historical Review* emerged from Wrong's annual *Review of Historical Publications Relating to Canada* (1897) in 1920.[189] By that time, the French-Canadian counterpart, the *Bulletin des recherches historiques* (founded 1895) had appeared for a quarter of a century. After 1900, the major private publishing houses for works of history were established[190] and three English-language multi-volume series on Canadian national history appeared.[191] English Canadian historians could pre-empt the institutions since in Quebec Abbé Lionel Groulx reduced historiography to "advocacy history," that is, passionate pleas for *survivance* and Quebec-Canadian nationalism. The titles of his books evolved from *Nos luttes constitutionnelles* (1916) to *La Naissance d'une race* (1919). Only Thomas Chapais at Laval based his lectures on respect between the two major ethnic groups. His work was attacked immediately and under the impact of the anglophones' abrogation of French-language instruction in schools

188 : Windsor, "Historical Writing" (1965), quote p. 257.

189 : The *Review* was and is owned by the University of Toronto Press, not the Canadian Historical Association (CHA), and long had a self-perpetuating editorial board. For a short survey of the CHA see Donald Wright, *The Canadian Historical Association: A History* (Ottawa: CHA, 2003).

190 : UTP, 1901; McClelland & Stewart, 1906. Ryerson Press, 1919, emerged out of Toronto's Methodist Book Room, established 1829.

191 : The twenty-volume "Makers of Canada" series (Toronto: George N. Morang, 1903–8; new ed., 1926), inspired by Carlylean hero worship, presented a literary view of history. Of the 27 "founding" personalities, all of them men, six were French-Canadian and so were several of the authors: "The history of an individual is often the history of a nation," thought one of the contributors. G.M. Wrong and H.H. Langton edited *The Chronicles of Canada* (32 vols., Toronto: Glasgow, Brook, 1914–16) for the general public. For professionals A. Shortt and A.G. Doughty edited *Canada and Its Provinces: A History of the Canadian People and Their Institutions* (23 vols., Toronto: Glasgow, Brook, 1914–17).

from Ontario to Manitoba, Quebec's historians, other social scientists, and cultural activists became even more nationalist.[192]

Refraining from nationalist pronouncements, a closer look would discern a multiplicity of French dialects—in France the Parisian "high" dialect became the society's standard language only in the twentieth century. It would also see that English came in lower-class and elite accents, and that Gaelic-speakers from Brittany via Wales and Ireland to Scotland had also arrived. About 1900, linguists began to chronicle the differences between British and Canadian English, and English immigrants were realizing that they had to adapt their vocabulary and pronunciation to Canadian usage. A century after Viger had emphasized Quebec's distinct French, the Abbé Camille Roy began an effort to purify the French-Canadian language through the Société du parler français (established 1902), which in 1912 organized a continent-wide congress.[193] Such differentiation remained alien to academic historians in the two versions of the nationalist mood.

Until the 1910s, the study of the past was characterized by three different approaches to Canada as a state and a nation, all premised on assumptions of its future course of development. Regionalists, sometimes with a sense of boosterism, concentrated on one part of the country. Continentalists for economic or geographic reasons dealt with North America as a whole and assumed implicitly or explicitly that integration with the United States would be inevitable. Nationalists operated from a concept of regions coalescing into a nation, a cultural nation that would remain distinct from the United States. This Canadian "nationalist" approach differed from "nationalist" historiography in Europe, which often claimed a place of superiority for one particular nation and thus justified expansionist strategies. Imperial issues assumed a new dimension around 1900, with the British Empire's Egyptian campaign and Canada's involvement in the war in South Africa and in World War I. Imperialists approached the history of Canada as part of the Empire rather than on its own merits. Anti-imperialists rejected the British connection but often assumed Canada to be too small for independent nation status and thus looked toward the upcoming empire, the United States. This historiography limited itself to British Canada and pursued a parliamentarist approach based on British institutions. French Canadian historians, who for good reasons rejected such British-centredness, limited themselves to French-Canada and emphasized British oppression with occasional references to France or an outreach to Rome. Even chronological

---

192 : Groulx, *Histoire du Canada français depuis la découverte* (4 vols., 1950–52); Chapais, *Cours d'histoire du Canada* (8 vols, 1919–34).

193 : M.H. Scargill, "The Growth of Canadian English," in Klinck et al., *Literary History*, 1:265–73.

emphasis differed: French-language historians dealt with Nouvelle-France and the British colonial period, English-language historians with constitutional events of 1840 and 1867. Neither side turned to a bicultural Canada as a whole.

With so much speculation, historiography has justly been described as the last of the "amateur disciplines in the universities," a field that was "underdeveloped."[194] While critics acerbically commented that men, methods, and ideas were imported, George Wrong, O.D. Skelton, and Adam Shortt, as well as George Bryce, Edmond Roy, and Thomas Chapais left important studies and approaches and established scholarly associations and journals.[195] The British tradition of a quest for responsible government and active citizenship included a democratizing element, but before the 1920s stopped short of considering enfranchisement of the people in general. Reference to French political thought since the Revolution of 1789 might have opened up theory to an appreciation of popular vote. But no French-Canadian political theory emerged; in fact, Quebec's Catholic Church had supported the papal court's opposition to democratizing and nationalizing movements in Italy.

Hegemonic scholarship and subalterns' lesser discourses

The privileged discourses within Canada's historico-political scholarship were one aspect of establishing a segment of the people as the political nation. While they explain one of several variants of Canadian identity, for modern Canadian Studies they are but founding myths. Five decades after Confederation, the English-Canadian historiographic orthodoxy was characterized by four aspects: institutional—responsible government; biographic—great makers of Canada; imperialist—British superiority; and gendered and racialized—male and White. French Canadian historians, under the clerical paradigm, established a different orthodoxy. This political history approach was tempered by an awareness of the importance of economic factors and of the peopling of the state. Those who were privileged to shape such discourses were few. Professors from Dalhousie, New Brunswick, Laval, Bishop's, McGill, Queen's, Toronto, Western Ontario, and, as the only university west of southern Ontario, Manitoba, established the opinion-

---

194 : William Kilbourn and Henry B. Mayo, "Canadian History and Social Sciences (1920–1960)," in Klinck et al., *Literary History* (1965), 2:22–52, quotes pp. 23, 43. See also A.B. McKillop, *A Disciplined Intelligence, and McKillop, Matters of Mind: The University in Ontario 1791–1951* (Toronto: UTP, 1994).

195 : On Wrong and Shortt see Carl Berger, *The Writing of Canadian History: Aspects of English Canadian Historical Writing Since 1900* (Toronto: Oxford, 1976), 1–31.

forming periodicals: *Queen's Quarterly* (1893), McGill's *University Magazine* (1901–20), the *Canadian Forum* (1920), *Dalhousie Review* (1921), and, finally, the *University of Toronto Quarterly* (1931).

Subaltern groups began to develop their own discourses—separately since they had no access to the institutions. Usually they were neither read nor heard by the gatekeepers of privilege. First Peoples' narratives and symbolic expressions, though sporadically noticed, were not incorporated. The White lower classes of European background had little or no time to write, but oral testimony is accessible through the published hearings of the Royal Commission on Relations of Labour and Capital. Non-English but English-language newcomers, the Scots and Irish as well as the United Empire Loyalists (UEL) laid claim to a part of nation-building in ethnocentred historical studies and, for the Scots, publicans even succeeded in erecting a national billboard. N.F. Davin for the Irish (1877), and W.J. Rattray for the Scots (1880–83), as well as UEL associations struggled to establish these three groups' pre-eminence in public discourse.[196] Beyond these, only the somewhat exotic Doukhobors and Mennonites attracted attention among English-language writers.[197] No French Canadian authors dealt with immigrants. On the national level, royal commissions on Chinese immigration (1885), on Chinese and Japanese immigration (1902), and on Italian labourers in Montreal (1904), while meant to engage in fact-finding, became cliché-imposing institutions.[198]

Middle-class and elite Euro-Canadian women inserted or attempted to insert themselves in male discourses.[199] They carved a niche for themselves in amateur and professionalizing historiography by forming their own network, the Women's Canadian Historical Society, for example in Toronto

---

196 : Nicholas Flood Davin, *The Irishman in Canada* (London: Sampson Low, Marston & Co.; Toronto: Maclear, 1877); William Jordan Rattray, *The Scot in British North America*, 4 vols. (Toronto: Maclear, 1880–83); and *The Scotsman in Canada*, 2 vols., by the poet W. Wilfred Campbell and the scholar George Bryce (1911); Alexander C. Casselman, "The German United Empire Loyalists of the County of Dundas, Ontario," *U.E. Loyalist Assoc.* (Toronto) 3 (1900): 53–76.

197 : Aylmer Maude, *A Peculiar People: The Doukhobors* (London: Constable, 1905); (Rev.) A.B. Sherk, "The Pennsylvania Germans of Waterloo County, Ontario," *Ontario Historical Society Papers and Records* 7 (1906): 98–109.

198 : Royal Commission on Chinese Immigration, *Report and Evidence* (Ottawa 1885; repr. New York: Arno, 1978); Royal Commission on Chinese and Japanese Immigration, *Report* (Ottawa: Dawson, 1902; repr. New York: Arno, 1978); Royal Commission Appointed to Inquire into the Immigration of Italian Labourers to Montreal and the Alleged Fraudulent Practices of Employment Agencies, *Report* (Ottawa: Dept. of Labour, 1904).

199 : Beverly Boutilier and Alison Prentice, eds., *Creating Historical Memory: English-Canadian Women and the Work of History* (Vancouver: UBC Press, 1997).

in 1895 (*Transactions* 1896–1914) and in Ottawa (*Transactions* 1901–54). In Manitoba, the provincial librarian William J. Healy compiled *Women of the Red River: Being a Book Written from the Recollections of Women Surviving from the Red River Era* for the Women's Canadian Club. Intended to insert only the superior women into the narrative, it began with "The First White Woman in the West"—a major theme of the Whiteness discourse of the times. Though subaltern to men, the women did make a statement: published in September 1923, demand for the volume was so high that a first reprint was necessary in November 1923, a second in November 1924.[200] The superior yet subaltern women's perspective was nationalist and British, heroic and male as Mary L. Campbell's "Origin of the Canadian People" (1901) indicated. Nevertheless, she carefully distinguished the several groups from the British Isles, differentiated Irish by region, mentioned German and Dutch immigration, and, as regards the French, commented, "it was not French character but rather French rule and institutions which were 'found wanting.'" For her, amalgamation of all into one nation was the issue of the day.[201] Women, who had been part of working life outside of the home all along, whether in agriculture, textile production, or creating societies, achieved federal enfranchisement in 1918. In 1921, they elected Agnes Macphail as first woman to Parliament, and in 1930 Cairine Wilson was named the first woman Senator. A Canadian Women's Press Club formed in 1904, and in 1928 *Chatelaine* was established. But a report in 1984 still had to call discrimination against women in academia a "national disgrace."[202]

Native peoples, whose exclusion, too, has been a disgrace, developed their own narratives about the visiting Europeans or ruling Euro-Canadians. Christian ways of worship were understood as a different ritual system, rather than as a different belief system with a different God, expressed in a different theology, and administered by a distant Church hierarchy. "Transubstantiation seemed not unlike ritual cannibalism, the priests' celibacy seemed equivalent to the shamans' practice of seeking extrahuman power through sexual abstinence."[203] With the seemingly inexplicable rise of ill-

---

200 : Winnipeg: Russel, 1923; repr. for the Centennial 1967.

201 : *Women's Canadian Historical Society of Ottawa Transactions* 1 (1901): 137–146.

202 : Thomas H.B. Symons and James E. Page, *Some Questions of Balance: Human Resources, Higher Education, and Canadian Studies* (Ottawa: Assoc. of Universities and Colleges of Canada, 1984), 187–214, quote p. 187. See also Marianne G. Ainley, ed., *Despite the Odds: Essays on Canadian Women and Science* (Montreal: Véhicule, 1990).

203 : New, A History of Canadian Literature (1989), quote p. 21. A pioneering study is Cornelius J. Jaenen, "Amerindian Views of French Culture in the Seventeenth Century," *Canadian Historical Review* 55 (1974): 261–91. A new approach is represented by Paul, *We Were Not the Savages* (2000). Its many expressions are collected in Dickason, *Na-*

nesses and the ravages of epidemics at the time of contact, baptism as a cur-
ative ritual was worth a try. The surviving Native peoples developed their
own interactions with the newcomers. They integrated the Native and European worlds into a fur economy. Some changed their spiritual preferences
and the respective material expressions to Christian ones. When families
decided to honour their dead by tombstones, they gave the traditional burial chests to museums. Euro-Canadian society incorporated Native peoples'
customs and words, and later generations would not know the origins of
such cultural practices, incorporated beyond recognition.

If Euro-Canadian culture held the power, Native peoples held on to their
views of themselves as independent polities or, individually, as human beings. When asked during the Prince of Wales' visit of 1860, for example,
to be present in the background or as an exotic but choreographed fore-
ground, they pursued their own agenda: Native peoples in Halifax made a
point by greeting the Prince before the official Euro-Canadian committee.
The Iroquois cast themselves as allied nations, subjects of Queen Victoria
in their own right, with no British-Canadian mediation wanted. At Quebec's tercentenary in 1908, First Nations' pageantry nearly stole the show:
eye-catching costumes, dramatic role playing as fierce warriors—or as pious
Christian converts. Vigorously inserting themselves into the program, they
performed better than the White participants. On the less spectacular level
of everyday individual lives, a Mohawk woman, Eliza Sero, in 1921 contested
government seizure of her seine net in court, arguing that the licensing law
did not apply to Mohawks, who historically had been allies and had never
accepted the status of subjects. That Eliza Sero lost her case underlines the
pervasiveness of racial understandings in law and political theory.[204] Several decades were to pass before such a position was debated seriously in
government and in public opinion.

Better known than Eliza Sero is E. Pauline Johnson, or Tekahionwake
(1862–1913), poetess, journalist, and performer. To earn her living, she had
to face both racism and sexism, and underwrite the cost of systemic inequality imposed on non-White women. Her "dual identity" in the White
and Aboriginal world made her part of White women's aspirations and yet
excluded her from them. She remained single and independent, though she

---

tive Imprint (1995). See also James P. Ronda, "'We Are Well As We Are': An Indian
Critique of Seventeenth-Century Christian Mission," *William and Mary Quarterly* 3.34
(1977): 66–82.

204 : Ian Radforth, *Royal Spectacle: The 1860 Visit of the Prince of Wales to Canada and the
United States* (Toronto: UTP, 2004); H.V. Nelles, *The Art of Nation-Building: Pageantry and
Spectacle at Quebec's Tercentenary* (Toronto: UTP, 1999); Constance Backhouse, *Colour
Coded: A Legal History of Racism in Canada, 1900–1950* (Toronto: UTP, 1999), 103–31.

sometimes had to rely on friends. In her writings, however, she often presented motherhood as normative. Was this out of respect for Aboriginal women's roles as significant matrons with power and influence? In contrast to White women presented by Euro-Canadian female authors before Nellie McClung and Emily Murphy, her Aboriginal female characters were physically strong, engaged in outdoor activities, and passionate in their views. They were also more eroticized than the White women modelled on the stereotype of passivity of the Victorian age. As English and French cultural expressions were often more interactive than collective memory has it, so were Euro-Canadian and First Peoples' cultural expressions.[205] Subalterns' perspectives, often as partial as those of the master narrators, provide a contribution toward a more complex and complete societal self-understanding.

Outside perspectives: Observers' interpretations of Canada

From the outside, Canada appears as a whole. Its society is bounded by the east and west coasts, by the 49th parallel and the frozen North. Visiting observers watch people rather than digest the exclusionary master narrative. Internally, scholars or amateurs who stood outside of a particular hegemonic discourse could employ broader perspectives. Thus, a professor of medicine at McGill, Andrew Macphail, though of nationalist persuasion, wrote several well-researched historical studies and reached beyond the confines of the discipline by combining personal memoir, biography, historical detail, and novelistic techniques (*The Master's Wife*, 1939). From outside, the Jesuits' observations ("relations" rather than analyses) integrated views of everything that seemed different or worthwhile of note in a country that was foreign to them—"foreign country studies."[206]

Around 1900, visitors from Great Britain in particular left accounts of Canada which may be divided—according to their authors' interest in a particular knowledge segment—into accounts of missionaries, of sportsmen, of

---

205 : Veronica Strong-Boag and Carole Gerson, *Paddling Her Own Canoe: The Times and Texts of E. Pauline Johnson (Tekahionwake)* (Toronto: UTP, 2000). See also Mary Ellen Turpel, "Patriarchy and Paternalism: The Legacy of the Canadian State for First Nations Women," *Canadian Journal of Women and Law* 6.1 (1993): 174–92, who from her Aboriginal perspective distances herself from white feminists.

206 : Early examples of such country descriptions include Pierre Boucher, *L'Histoire véritable et naturelle des moeurs et productions du pays de la Nouvelle-France vulgairement dit le Canada* (1662), and le Père Charlevoix, a professional writer, who wrote a synthesis in French of the colonial project (1744), a biography of Marie de l'Incarnation and, later, histories of Saint-Domingue and of Japan.

settlers, of the politically-imperially minded, of engineers.[207] Railway engineers, who travelled across the country, wrote summaries of their knowledge/experience. Basil Stewart of the Grand Trunk Pacific Railway may serve as one example. He published books about Cyprus, Japanese colour prints, religion, and the Great Pyramids, and authored a *Handbook on Railway Surveying* (1909). In 1908, his *The Land of the Maple Leaf, or, Canada as I Saw It* appeared simultaneously in London (Routledge), Toronto (Musson), and New York (Dutton). In the introduction he candidly set forth his personal reasons for writing the book as well as his views on "race." Too many colourful accounts serving the interests of "the various transportation Companies" and the "Immigration Department of the Dominion Government" circulated "to entice a population into Canada." Though travel was indeed low-priced, immigrants met with disillusion when intending to settle: "a person should know beforehand what kind of life and what conditions he [or she] may expect to find." While immigration of Russians, Germans, Italians, or Jews presented dangers to the Empire, the thirteen million Britishers "on the verge of starvation" would make "good material" (pp. vii-viii). In a chapter on "Modern Empire Building," Stewart compared the United States and Canada to the benefit of the latter, then described a westward journey from Montreal to British Columbia to provide his readers with facts on history and "the North American Indians." He addressed labour and the economy in the chapters on railway construction camps, "the labour problem," and "protection or free trade." In conclusion, he discussed Canada's role in the imperial defence, explained "why the Englishman is despised in Canada," and asked what the future would bring. His and many other outsiders' accounts provide fascinating glimpses into a society in the making. This approach might be called an "images in the making" literature containing insights beyond established discourses and scholarship.

In contrast, André Siegfried's *Canada, les deux races. Problèmes politiques contemporains* (Paris, 1906; English as *The Race Question in Canada*, London: Nash, 1907) was an analytical discussion and later influenced Marshall McLuhan. Siegfried, born into an Alsatian textile producer family, was displaced to Le Havre after the annexation of Alsace by Prussia in 1870. He was French and Protestant, anti-clerical and republican, widely travelled and thoughtful. With some exaggeration, Frank Underhill called him the Tocqueville of Canada. Since in Siegfried's opinion both French culture and Protestant culture were superior to Anglo and Catholic ways of life, he was

---

207 : Dirk Hoerder, unpubl. bibliography of accounts on early travel to Canada East up to the 1840s, missionaries in the Northwest, early observers and settlers in the pre-1890s Prairies.

neutral indeed. He visited Canada in 1898 and 1904, after the Riel and school conflicts and before the conscription crisis of 1914. He discussed the "psychological formation," church, schools, and national sentiments, then moved on to constitution and political parties. Of the latter's appeal to the material interests of voters, he remained highly critical. Next he commented on the "balance of the races" and the "civilization" of Canada and finally turned to its external relations. Siegfried, like Stewart, published a variety of "country studies," ranging from Africa to the United States; in contrast to Stewart he achieved scholarly distinction.[208] Such perspectives by authors socialized outside of a particular social and ethnic group within the country provide contrasting understandings and interpretations. On a scholarly level, such diversity of perspectives developed from the 1960s when Canadian Studies outside of Canada came into being (chapter 12).

---

208 : Siegfried later published *Canada*, Engl. transl. by H.E. Hemming and Doris Hemming (London, 1937), and a revised second edition under the title *Canada: an International Power* (London, 1947). On Siegfried and McLuhan see Richard Cavell, *McLuhan in Space: A Cultural Geography* (Toronto: UTP, 2002), Chapter 8.

Chapter 6

SUBSTANTIAL RESEARCH: THE SOCIAL SPACES OF THE GEOLOGICAL SURVEY OF CANADA

The details of Canada's physical geography or flora and fauna interested neither historians nor billboard-erecting talking heads nor writers of *belles letters*, who preferred the discourses and myths about the North, *le terroir*, or roughing it in the bush. However, from the eighteenth century, inquisitive observers, women with (self-)education from the leisured classes and men of the Hudson's Bay Company with their native wives, began to study the natural history of Canada and sent lively descriptions or dried specimens to French, British, or U.S. scholars. Women of Lady Dalhousie's circle were among the founders of what might be called Canada's first learned society, the Quebec Literary and Historical Society; others were among the founding members of the Botanical Society of Canada (established 1860).[209] These eclectic amateurs, curious about everything, came to be labelled unscientific when professionalization of knowledge acquisition demanded rigorous methodologies and full-time work. In the process, allegedly emotional women were also excluded from the pursuit of rational, that is, allegedly male methods of study.

The making of maps: Physical, social, and mental

Into the early nineteenth century, the natural sciences and physical geography were called "natural philosophy" rather than exact sciences. Exploration of new geographies and spaces involves a great number of contrasting and conflicting perspectives. Canada's physical geography, surveyed and divided into sections, became agricultural land and attracted settlers; divided into woodlots, it attracted investors and loggers; or, if classified as mineral-bearing, it attracted capital and miners. Physical landscapes became social spaces. The geological study of the Canadian Shield, the Prairies, and the Rockies set parameters for human habitation and local-global economies. In this respect government administrators and immigrant miners were intellectually ahead of those developing the national lore, and Native peoples held to their own spatial narratives.

---

209 : Marianne G. Ainley, "Last in the Field? Canadian Women Natural Scientists, 1815–1965," in Ainley, ed., *Despite the Odds: Essays on Canadian Women and Science* (Montreal: Véhicule, 1990), 25–62, esp. 27–29. A medical doctor, Abraham Gesner, in 1836, had published his *Geology and Mineralogy of Nova Scotia*, and in Upper Canada, a scholarly migrant, John Rae, had studied the geology from the 1820s. In 1827, the Natural History Society of Montreal had been established which came to publish *The Canadian Naturalist and Geologist*.

Maps contain ambiguities; cartography has been Eurocentric for centuries. "Recognition of the ideological, religious, and symbolic aspects of maps, particularly when linked with a more traditional appreciation of maps for political and practical purposes, greatly enhances the claim that cartography can be regarded as a graphic language in its own right."[210] Early maps have been called "imagined evocations of space"—but would not a late twentieth-century map of seventeenth-century Canada that merely charts routes of European colonizers and obliterates First Peoples' cultural spaces be anything but a self-serving imagination, an instrument of power? Over time, the continent of North America assumed many shapes in the mental maps of newcomers, depending on historic conjuncture and specific interests. For "explorers" it was a barrier on the way to India, for sixteenth-century fishermen a useful littoral zone, and for fur companies a profit-generating resource area. Some came to terms with this continental space and utilized it. Others searched desperately for a gap in the land mass to continue to the fabulous riches of the East—or riches *belonging to peoples in the East*. Finding the way "East" required a "Northwest Passage"—where is East, where is West?

"Continents appear to be natural and organic. They seem discrete physical units that exist prior to and independent of the sense humans make of them and the sovereignties into which humans divide them. Countries shift boundaries. Nations rise and fall, but continents persevere through much longer time spans."[211] Sixteenth- and seventeenth-century Europeans would hardly discuss their own continent in terms of a bounded physical space. Rather, they would speak of Europe's dynastic realms or, for example, the cultures of the Eastern Mediterranean or, in the west, of the Bourbon dynasty. Their maps were open ended because their knowledge was open ended. Physical features in cartography depended on oral reports or hearsay, and the imaginary creatures that cartographers inserted into land and water made these spaces dangerous or safe, inviting or forbidding. The physical spaces unknown to continental Europeans, especially the newly found Americas, were incorporated into minds and empires at a time when dynastic states were changing from itinerant rule and ephemeral marriage alliances to settled courts with a new social group of administrators who were responsible in particular for finances. These, facing the inefficiency of rule according to the nobility's standards of manly warfare and of honour, developed rational and standardized methods of counting, measuring, and

---

210 : J.B. Harley and David Woodward, *Cartography in Prehistoric, Ancient, and Medieval Europe and the Mediterranean* (Chicago: Univ. Chicago Press, 1987), quote p. 4.

211 : Richard White, "Is there a North American History?" *Revue française d'études Américaines* 79 (Jan. 1999): 8–28, quote p. 11.

surveying as well as data-interpretation by accounting, organizing, and spa-
cializing—the sciences of revenue economics (*Kameralwissenschaften*). Rulers supported the sciences and profited from them; Samuel de Champlain,
for example, was the Bourbon king's official geographer. The new type of
economically responsible rule, mercantilism, involved a shift from honour
to commerce, from the haphazard to the long-term, from ostentatious consumption to attention to a positive bottom line. This conceptual change was
to have lasting influences in the construction of the Americas.

European ship captains, travellers, and early geographers set out to explore what they did not know. They set out to learn about the facts of nature
in order to master nature. They had methods of mapping but no knowledge
of the languages of resident peoples. Thus they could not enquire. Nor did
they want to enquire, given that they felt superior. On the other hand, those
who could not afford to dream of possibilities in unknown spaces but on a
day-to-day basis had to organize their own and the explorer's survival, did
enquire: early sailors asked for food and cures against scurvy, early settlers
for seeds adapted to soils and climate, early fur traders for routes and animal habitats. These men might use violence, might rob and rape. But some
did learn languages and developed pidgin or patois forms of communication. They sought out women of the resident peoples for sex, but more importantly as partners for a temporary commercial strategy or a life course,
or the fur trade segment of their life course. Resident women had connections to supplies and sociability; the migrant men the connections to markets. Both combined different geographical knowledges. However, once the
European newcomers had established not only their societies and polities
but also their power of rule and definition, the learning processes ended
and the European measuring methods were transferred to North America:
grid pattern and concession lines imposed on landscapes and cultures. The
straight lines lasted, as did the inconsistencies: today's straight streets in
Toronto, for example, at some intersections shift by a few dozen yards: once
upon a time, surveyors had used a natural curving rather than a constructed
straight baseline. Inscribing such lines permanently on a changing social
space, in this case, has resulted in a modern traffic hazard. More decisive
was the incongruity of measuring imposed on previously inhabited social
space: when surveyors crossed into settled Métis land in the Red River Valley to carve out a Manitoba territory, they were warned off by the residents.
Since behind the measuring men were local men with acquisitive interests
and a state with its honour, they had to prove their power. Thus the socio-
political map of the Red River Valley was changed at the cost of lives. In
a later phase, street corners and other spaces became the sites for monuments to some feat in history. This created mental hazards. At the cost of

detriment to historical memory, spaces were ascribed with meaning, an occupying force of monuments narrowed later generations' options to define spaces according to their perspectives.

In the nineteenth century, missionaries and travellers described the spaces they traversed as rugged and inhospitable. The same spaces provided First Peoples with sustenance. The travelling men created the printed lore that was to become part of literary and everyday stereotypes. From mid-century, geographers investigated and described the new territories. Only after their information had been compiled and digested centrally would administrators come to establish institutions and to raise imposts. Since as yet no separate economic and social sciences existed—except for their applied version as accounting sciences—geography was comprehensive. It dealt with physical geography and its actual usages by residents as well as with potential usages by expected newcomers. As "a synthesizing field" it was descriptive, analyzing, applied, and future-oriented—the latter to the potential detriment of resident men and women. "Geographers seek to understand the actual settled land …, the differing character of the earth's surface (regional variety), and the complex, interlacing relationships between man and land." They "recognize that most of even these physical influences are filtered by man's heavy cultural conditioning. Algonkians and Europeans lived in the same St. Lawrence lowlands, experienced the same landforms and much the same climate, but responded to common influences in radically different ways. And man also creates his environments: to a considerable extent man is a captive of his own creations."[212] Settlers, miners, and small-town businessmen from many cultures of the world arrived captivated by their preconceived notions of the spaces.

Exploring the territorial and economic basis for nation building

From the 1840s, steamboats, railway, steam engine, and the telegraph brought Canada closer to "the ambit of European … exploitation." The United Colony government established the Geological Survey of Canada (GSC) in 1841/42, which only a decade later represented Canada at international exhibitions in London (1851) and Paris (1855). Minerals played a vital part in the transportation revolution: coal released industries from dependence on rivers and water power, coke from dependence on woods and charcoal, and steel from wooden machinery. Recognizing the importance

---

212 : R. Cole Harris and John Warkentin, *Canada before Confederation: A Study in Historical Geography* (1974; rev. ed., Ottawa: Carleton, 1991), quote p. v. For an attempt to view a landscape from a First Peoples' point of view see Conrad Heidenreich, *Huronia: A History and Geography of the Huron Indians 1600–1650* (Toronto: McClelland & Stewart, 1971).

of transportation to Canada's economy, entrepreneurs quickly adopted new means of communication. Only eight years after the steamboat's invention in Britain, a first steamer connected Quebec with Montreal and as of 1816 steamships had plied the Great Lakes. The first railway was opened in 1836, but as yet the markets of the Atlantic colonies and Lower and Upper Canada remained separate. The forges of Saint Maurice in Quebec, the iron works at Furnace Falls (Lyndhurst) in Upper Canada, and the coalfields at Pictou and at Sydney, Nova Scotia, assumed new importance and required "a practical science of ore-finding and mine development." This practical science could rely on the more theoretical science of geology, a term first used in the mid-seventeenth century and given institutional support by the Geological Society of London (established 1807). It could rely on mapping in France (first geological map, 1780, by Guettard and Monnet) and in Britain (English county maps since 1794; Scottish Board of Agriculture ones with soil and rock exposures). A first public museum on geology and mapping was opened in London in 1841. In other, thinly settled societies, geographers pursued similar objectives. The Swedish scientist Johan Wilhelm Zetterstedt, for example, travelled through the northern Västerbotten district in the 1830s to describe which areas were suitable for farming and which would support farming families only marginally.[213]

The GSC's staff was part of the Atlantic World. William Edmond Logan, a Montrealer educated at Edinburgh, was appointed its first director in 1842. While neither British nor French cultural and political elites were ready to take the colony seriously, the economic elite certainly did once solid information about mineral resources permitted solid projections of investments and profits. Government-employed geologists were to advance the mining economy and as early as 1855, Commissioner J.C. Taché in his *Esquisse sur le Canada* described the United Colony's historic development and economic potentialities. Logan followed with a magisterial *Report of the Progress from Its Commencement to 1863; Illustrated by 498 Wood Cuts in the Text and Accompanied by an Atlas of Maps and Sketches* (1863), generically cited as *Geology of Canada*. Just as the Canadian Pacific Railway was to create the poster-view of Canada to profit from immigrants' fares, the GSC created the resource-image to attract investments.[214] By the early 1900s, political

213 : Morris Zaslow, *Reading the Rocks: the Story of the Geological Survey of Canada, 1842–1972* (Ottawa: Macmillan, 1975), 6–10, quotes pp. 6, 9. Zetterstedt, *Resa genom Umeå Lappmarker i Vesterbottens Län, förrättad aer 1832–1833* (Oerebro: N.M. Lindh, 1833).

214 : The GSC's impact on patterns of investments was strong. When, after the U.S. Upper Michigan peninsula's mining boom, the Canadian government received applications for mining concessions north of Lake Superior and Lake Huron, the GSC staff suggested licences to be granted to bona fide operators for 21 years and lots of 5 x 2 miles, one licence per claimant. Zaslow, *Reading the Rocks* (1975), 58–59.

economists would criticize the dependence on foreign capital and the siphoning off of profits to the metropoles, but cultural producers remained dependent on the young-immature-nation cliché. Culture, technical developments, and geographic-economic exploration became linked by early photography, developed both in England and in France, when entrepreneurs in culture introduced this means of communication to Canada. William Notman's studio in Montreal chronicled private and public events beginning in the 1850s and by 1858 the government detailed a photographer, Humphrey Hime, to its Manitoba expedition.

Geology and geography as studies of the natural environment, of social spaces, and of economic potential formed the base from which Canada's nineteenth-century scientific community developed its international reputation. Geologist John William Dawson (1820–99), Nova Scotia-born and Edinburgh-trained, became both a leading scholar in the most advanced applied science of the times as well as superintendent of education in Nova Scotia. As principal of McGill University since 1855, he for almost four decades shaped the scientific development from "natural philosophy" to an array of disciplines, though as a devout Christian, he never accepted Darwin's evolutionism. Academic disciplines systematized the knowledge acquisition begun by the amateurs of the natural, geographic, and literary societies.

After 1867 and the acquisition of Rupert's Land, the GSC expanded to operate from coast to coast. In the Maritime provinces, it could rely on the data collected by the Nova Scotia Institute of Natural Science (established 1862) as an offshoot of the Literary and Scientific Society of Halifax. Westward, numerous expeditions pressed forward to facilitate the government-encouraged railway construction. In 1872, the GSC reached the headwaters of Peace River, in the '80s the delta of the Mackenzie River, and in the '90s the Hudson Bay and the Labrador region. Finally, with the northern and Arctic waters exploration from 1897 to 1904, the GSC contributed to Canada's claims for authority over the Arctic. The Survey also turned again to the settled regions of Ontario and Quebec because advances in data-collection and theoretical concepts pointed to the likelihood of usable mineral deposits along the southern margin of the Precambrian strata.[215]

The GSC's headquarters remained in Montreal and its younger staff consisted mainly of McGill graduates. McGill Principal J.W. Dawson's son George Mercer Dawson, after studying geology at McGill and in London, joined the GSC in 1875.[216] Though suffering from a physical handicap, he ex-

---

215 : Zaslow, *Reading the Rocks* (1975), 60–175.

216 : George's son, William Bell Dawson, in turn, became a geographer but combined this training with that of engineer. As employee of the CPR he was involved in mediating

plored the West as far as the Queen Charlotte Islands (1878), became British commissioner on the natural resources of the Bering Sea, a charter member of the Royal Society of Canada, as well as a member of the Ethnological Survey of Canada. French Canadians on the staff mapped Quebec's regions from the 1880s.[217] When Prime Minister Laurier pressed for more French Canadians to be appointed to the GSC, Dawson commented that the request was reasonable but that few could be hired because few were "educated in science."[218] As in all of the sciences, women had been absent except as librarians and as temporary researchers since the 1880s. Even women with a university degree in the natural sciences were expected to retire into homemaking after marriage. If career-oriented, they had to remain single and to accept positions as assistants of the men—"anonymous assistants" since their names often did not appear in publications. Only two women outside of the GSC succeeded in organizing private expeditions: Elizabeth Taylor, daughter of the U.S. consul in Winnipeg, to the Mackenzie River in 1892; and Mina Benson Hubbard, after the death of her husband during a Labrador expedition, to Labrador and northern Quebec in 1905.[219]

"The Survey played an important role in making an interested world aware of Canada's potentialities" through reports, articles, lectures, and "especially through its exhibits at great international fairs." It hosted the International Committee on Geological Nomenclature (Ottawa, 1905) and the International Geological Congress (Toronto, 1913).[220] French geographers such as Elisée Reclus (*Nouvelle Géographie Universelle*, 19 volumes, 1875–99), his brother Onésine, as well as Pierre Deffontaines contributed to a knowledge of Canada in France through "sociétés de géographie" organized in French cities, and

---

between the government and the company about the shoddy quality of construction of the railway's western sections.

217 : Especially Abbé J.C.K. Laflamme, N.J. Giroux, and E.R. Faribault.

218 : Zaslow, *Reading the Rocks* (1975), 179–80, 202; Douglas Cole and Bradley Lockner, eds., *To the Charlottes: George Dawson's 1878 Survey of the Queen Charlotte Islands* (Vancouver: UBC Press, 1993); Dawson with A.R.C. Selwyn, *Descriptive Sketch of the Physical Geography and Geology of the Dominion of Canada* (1884).

219 : Ainley, "Last in the Field?" (1990), 31–36, and Ainley, "D'assistantes anonymes à chercheurs scientifiques: une rétrospective sur la place des femmes en sciences," *Cahiers de recherche sociologique* 4 (1986): 55–71; Alan Cooke and Clive Holland, T*he Exploration of Northern Canada, 500 to 1920: A Chronology* (Toronto: Arctic History Press, 1978), 265, 303–4.

220 : The GSC did, on occasion, produce flawed results, as when a piece of crystalline limestone from the Ottawa River was misinterpreted as a fossil and named "Eozoon Canadense" (1858) or when glittering deposits of undefined nature were said to contain diamonds in 1912.

the group Les amis du Canada began to meet from 1885. German geographers explored the Arctic from the 1880s.[221] The GSC's transatlantically trained staff included a Paris-educated Polish migrant as early as 1844, recruited men from Scotland and Germany, and used the latest Swedish technology. The surveyors' Three-Mile (-to-an-Inch) Sectional Maps of the West completed the intellectual-scientific appropriation of the landscape and a museum became "a comprehensive collection of all aspects of the Canadian scene, of natural and human history." The field staff showed interest in every aspect of life, collected samples of rocks and minerals, plants, animals, fishes, birds, Indian and Inuit artifacts, studied languages and legends. This National Museum of Canada (first the Victoria Memorial Museum) became independent of the GSC in 1947.[222] At the turn to the twentieth century, the GSC turned from systematic mapping and description to theory, explaining how, where, and why mineral deposits occur. From 1887, its "Section of Mines" applied the results and published the "Statistical Report on the Production, Value, Exports and Imports of Minerals in Canada." In 1907, the GSC was merged into the newly created Department of Mines. The mining industry also organized and devoted its annual meetings both to technological or scientific developments and to pressure the government for "favourable concessions."[223] The staff of the Survey thus continued to tread a thin line between a narrow approach as handmaid to economic interests and as a broad scholarly institution.[224]

While in the master narrative of historical memory the GSC has received little attention, the utilization of the spaces it mapped through railway construction and farming has become part of the national lore and is inscribed on the country's landscape. Societal Studies would conceptualize all aspects of this process. The natural sciences and applied research contributed to the emergence of agriculture in the Prairies. Research into patterns of

---

221 : Zaslow, *Reading the Rocks* (1975), 3, 192, 285–308; Jean-Pierre Augustin and Vincent Berdoulay, *Modernité et tradition au Canada: Le regard des géographes français jusqu'aux années 1960* (Paris: Harmattan, 1997).

222 : Of its four divisions—mineralogy, geology, biology, anthropology—the latter was divided in 1911 into an archeology and an ethnology section, headed by Harlan I. Smith and Edward Sapir respectively.

223 : General Mining Association of Quebec, 1891; Mining Society of Nova Scotia, 1892; Ontario Mining Institute, 1894; Federated Canadian Mining Institute, 1898. Zaslow, *Reading the Rocks* (1975), 74–81.

224 : The GSC seems not to have been involved in early conservation attempts. The Commission of Conservation (est. 1909) dealt with resource management, depletion of natural resources, water management, reforestation, and public lands. This approach was expanded to cities by the Civic Improvement League of Canada (est. 1915): public health, sanitation, poor housing, and unsafe water.

climate and the breeding of new strains of wheat, by Charles Saunders for example, was the basis for the fourth phase of the staple economy after fish, fur, and timber. Without the scientific input of the agricultural extension services of Prairie universities, society would have developed differently. Production of wheat grew almost thirty-fold in the fifteen years from 1896 to 1911, from 8 to 231 million bushels. It provided a living for more than a million men, women, and children.

In the twentieth century, the GSC's methods and its role changed profoundly. In 1919, the first aerial survey of Canada was undertaken and expeditions discarded horses in favour of planes.[225] In the 1930s, the minister of mines announced, "We have across the northern part of Canada from coast to coast geological conditions that would challenge the courage, the enthusiasm and the capacity for effort of the Canadian people for thousands of years."[226] Without any boosterism, the "geographic interpretation" of Canadian history and identity has remained a major historical contribution to the present as evidenced, for example, in the work of John Warkentin and R. Cole Harris.[227]

The human implications of surveying a territory

First Peoples and Métis knew the territory the men of the Survey were describing. While a history of the GSC's European-background staff mentioned "Indians" only as guides and packers carrying essential supplies, Native peoples, in fact, advised the exploring scholars on routes, helped them to organize their trips, and could chart roads and railway lines. Their input

---

225 : Systematic scientific aerial photography began in the mid-1920s and was expanded during World War II as well as in anticipation of the Cold War to undertake the Arctic charting. K.R. Greenaway (RCAF) and S.E. Colthorpe (USAF), An Aerial Reconnaissance of Arctic North America, for Joint Intelligence Board (1948); Moira Dunbar (Geophysics Section, Defense Research Board) and Keith R. Greenaway (RCAF), Arctic Canada from the Air (Ottawa: Canada Defense Research Board, 1956).

226 : Zaslow, Reading the Rocks (1975), 359–82. During the Depression, the Survey was at first downgraded, then received a large grant to hire unemployed university students. It was further expanded during World War II because of the demand for minerals and to achieve independence from foreign suppliers.

227 : John Warkentin, ed., Canada: A Geographical Interpretation, prepared under the auspices of the Canadian Association of Geographers (Toronto: Methuen, 1970), French ed. Le Canada: Une interprétation géographique (updated ed., 1968, 1970); and Warkentin, Canada: A Regional Geography (1st ed., 1997), rev. ed. as A Regional Geography of Canada: Life, Land, and Space (Scarborough, ON: Prentice-Hall, 2000). Historical Atlas of Canada 3 vols., (Toronto: UTP, 1987–1993), changing editors from volume to volume, vol. 1: "Origins to 1800," ed. R. Cole Harris.

to imagining the landscapes was large. Many immigrants showed great respect for their knowledge and the men of the Survey considered "Indian" and Inuit peoples human beings with rights, opinions, and a dignity of their own. During a visit to the Qu'Appelle River region and its peoples, one exploring crew, "much alarmed at the unrest," suggested to end all activities until a federal-Native treaty could be concluded. Others demanded that smugglers, often from the United States, should be prevented from selling whiskey and that, in view of the extermination of the buffalo by U.S. hunters and tourists, food should be supplied to famine-threatened peoples. In the Arctic, A.P. Low, as sympathetic observer of Inuit life, commented on missionaries' criticism of "Eskimo" morals: "who is to say what is right in this respect among a people situated as they are." He understood White-Native hierarchies. "As a people, they are very hospitable and kind; but like other savages would probably soon tire of continuous efforts to support helpless Whites cast upon them, especially when the guests assume a superiority over their hosts."[228]

The ways of life of First Peoples were an integral part of the world the geologists and geographers investigated. G.M. Dawson compiled a comprehensive report on the customs, vocabulary, and everyday life of the Haida; expanded the vocabulary to related terms of other Northwest Coast peoples, and later prepared a rudimentary Cree vocabulary. Diamond Jenness, who had come to Canada via New Zealand, as successor to Sapir published the first survey, *Indians of Canada* (1932). On the other hand, the Indian Act of 1876 and the Department of Indian Affairs centralized its administration of Native men, women, and children even further after the bitter protests of 1885 and after the near-starvation caused by the extinction of the buffalo. The bureaucrats interfered into very private matters, Indian agents often were arbitrary, and the system became overpowering. Laws discouraged the hunting and gathering way of life in the Prairies and, in 1884, forbade the "potlatch," the ritual distribution of wealth in the Pacific Coast's sedentary societies. "As band Councils continued to oppose imposed regulations, the administration responded in 1898 by granting the Superintendent General overriding powers." In order to change landscapes and social spaces according to Euro-Canadians' interests, the Indian Act was amended in 1911 to allow parts of reserves without surrender by Native peoples to be reassigned both by municipalities and by companies for purposes of building roads, railways, or other infrastructures in the "public" (in other words, Euro-Canadian) interest. To prevent independent articulation of First People's

---

228 : Zaslow, *Reading the Rocks* (1975), 16, 174-75, quote p. 174; Dirk Hoerder, *Creating Societies* (1999).

interests, the government prohibited usage of band funds for litigation to reclaim alienated land. "In 1927, political organization beyond local levels of government were in effect banned when Amerindians were denied the right to raise funds without permission," a state of affairs (in other words, of oppression) that lasted until 1951.[229]

The GSC's surveys permitted a measuring of the land grants to the railways and thus profits for the private corporations. Immigrant farming families shared the advantages of the science of map-making, reflected in the six-mile (ten-kilometre) townships in much of Canada. All they had to do was select their land and find the surveyor's stakes. Finding these stakes was a sign that the first inhabitants had lost their stake. Their knowledge of the land was no longer needed and their ways of living off and in it came to an end. Human lives, applied research, and bureaucratic management of resources had become entwined and were permeated by power relationships—and centralized knowledge meant power. The Study of Canada implies the shaping of Canadian society. The interlacing of concepts and consequences, of activities and acquisitions, of research and human management was reflected in the organizational structure of Canada's government. Its Department of Mines and Resources, as of 1937, consisted of a resource unit, the Mines and Geology Branch; of a resource and landscape unit, the Lands, Parks, and Forests Branch; of a measuring unit, the Surveys and Engineering Branch; and of two human management units, the Indian Affairs Branch and the Immigration Branch. The power to exclude and to include had become vested in bureaucratic organization embedded in a national discourse on a hierarchy of races.

---

229 : Dickason, *Canada's First Nations* (1992), 273–89, 319–38, quotes pp. 323, 328.

Chapter 7

LEARNING AND SOCIETY: SOCIAL RESPONSIBILITY, EDUCATIONAL INSTITUTIONS, ELITE FORMATION

Interactions between hegemonic views of scholarship and society's self-perceptions were many. Self-organized citizens had begun to collect useful or interesting information in the early nineteenth century; they developed local and larger movements for self-instruction throughout the century. Their Enlightenment-influenced concept of an evolution of humankind to better social organization and material security based on knowledge resulted in "institutes" for self-education and in a movement for public libraries. Provincial governments institutionalized compulsory education systems. While these disseminated knowledge, they also opened a way to impose particular versions of history, visions of a moral society, or belief systems, whether religious or nationalist, onto the minds of children. On the level of colleges and universities such society-wide conglomerates of "facts" and norms would socialize future elites and form their minds. Curricula could be bound to the past or be future-oriented.

An informed society:
Nineteenth-century movements for self-instruction

The urban and small-town middle-class club movement collected and spread knowledge, as did agricultural improvement since the early 1800s.[230] By mid-century the movements diversified into class and gender: mechanics' institutes appeared in the 1840s, farmers' associations somewhat later, and gender-based women's institutes in the 1890s. Many of these associations opened, usually modest, libraries to permit members to improve their education. From the 1880s, public libraries opened their doors to men and women who would not easily be able to buy books. Centralization of taste, literary and art forms, and cultural hegemony was attempted through late nineteenth-century elite institutions such as the Royal Canadian Academy of Arts.

The movement to establish mechanics' institutes emerged in London, England, in 1823, from an initiative by George Birkbeck, as voluntary as-

---

230 : The first agricultural college was opened at Ste. Anne de la Pocatière, Quebec, 1859. Ontario followed suit with the Ontario Agricultural College in 1874. In the Prairies, Manitoba Agricultural College was founded in 1906, the College of Agriculture at the University of Saskatchewan in 1910, the College of Agriculture in Alberta in 1912, and in BC at the British Columbia College in 1915.

sociations of artisans and mechanics and, eventually, all working men, for instruction in the elementary and scientific principles underlying their work. Spreading through the English-speaking world, such institutes were centres for adult education in economics, history of science, and social history, and they became meeting places of early labour unions. In bicultural Montreal, the Institut canadien, established as a centre of patriotism and culture in 1844, came under the influence of Louis-Joseph Papineau and was associated with the newspaper *L'Avenir* (established 1847). The initiative, meant to improve the situation of the common people, did not emanate from them but met a demand as is indicated by the success of the so-called Parti rouge which advocated reforms, supported a more open U.S.-style political system, and could send eleven members to Parliament in 1854. The establishment, the old parties, and the Church combined in condemnation: the Church placed books written by its members on its Index of forbidden books. Similar organizations were founded in other cities and towns, the Toronto Canadian Institute, for example, about 1850.[231]

From the small-town and rural farmers' institutes, a first Women's Institute emerged in Stoney Creek, Ontario, in 1897.[232] This initiative came out of the agricultural world where women's labour had a more central place than in urban middle-class contexts or among artisans, mechanics, and urban skilled workers. It intended to spread ideas for good home management and, in the arena of politics, to struggle for better sanitation. The initiative spread first in Ontario, then in other provinces, and coalesced into the Federated Women's Institutes of Canada in 1919, based in Winnipeg and led by Emily Murphy. While mechanics' institutes had their origins in England, a woman from British Columbia founded a first rural women's institute in England in 1915. By 1933, the Associated Countrywomen of the World formed, with headquarters in Stockholm. These associations expanded their activities to include agriculture, industry, citizenship, and culture. Women's Labour

---

231 : Jim Blanchard, "A Bibliography on Mechanics' Institutes with Particular Reference to Ontario," in Peter McNally, ed., *Readings in Canadian Library History*, 2 vols. (Ottawa: Canadian Library Assoc., 1986, 1996), 1:3–18; C. Bruce Fergusson, *Mechanics' Institutes in Nova Scotia* (Halifax: Public Archives, 1960); Sybil Grimson, "Mechanics' Institutes," *Encyclopedia Canadiana*, 10 vols. (Toronto: Grolier, 1970), 6:416. Specialized studies include L.P. Jolicoeur, "Les Mechanics' Institutes: Ancêtres de nos bibliothèques publiques," *Assoc. Canadienne des Bibliothécaires de Langue Française, Bulletin* 10 (1964): 5–9; Nora Robins, "The Montreal Mechanics' Institute, 1828–1870," *Canadian Library Journal* 38 (1981): 373–80; G.R. Selman, "Mechanics' Institutes in British Columbia," *Continuous Learning* 10 (1971): 126–30; Fernand Dumont, *Genèse de la société québécoise* (1st ed., 1993; Montreal: Boréal, 1996), 243–52, 317–19.

232 : The temperance movement, with the Women's Christian Temperance Union established in Owen Sound, ON, in 1874, was also influential.

Leagues, modelled on the British Labour Leagues as auxiliaries to the Independent Labour Party, emerged in Canada prior to World War I. Membership remained small, but in 1923–24, under an initiative of the Communist Party of Canada, the locals federated and began to publish *The Woman Worker*. In general, women increasingly rejected restriction to the sphere of the home and by 1912 one out of every eight women was a member of some organization.[233]

The movement to establish public libraries developed out of English and Scottish social reform and was taken up in Toronto and Montreal. Similarly some Catholic Orders addressed a broader public through libraries. In 1840s Montreal, the Sulpiciens and the Natural History Society of Montreal did so. A Canadian observer summarized British developments and drew lessons for Canada: from 1849, municipalities by act of parliament had the right to levy a small rate for a library and by 1880 libraries were flourishing, providing "agreeable and wholesome literary food …, which has helped to preserve them [the readers] from grosser temptations, and to enlarge, if not elevate, their mental vision." On this principle, Canadian libraries were to include "Literature of Public Questions" as well as fiction that, though perhaps of no interest to "the lawyer," would definitely attract "the ladies"; they were to exclude "all works which have a tendency either to subvert the public morals or to encourage the spread of infidelity." Reading matter was to inculcate students with the principle of knightly chivalry "to defend the weak, resist the oppressor, to add to courage humility, to give to man the service and to God the glory," and to further industrial as well as wider education.[234]

While the aim—education and moral guidance—was clear, the practical side was contested: who would pay and who would select the reading matter? When, in 1850s Ontario, Methodist Egerton Ryerson attempted to induce all towns to establish libraries, the main response was a demand for provincial funds. After the 1882 Free Libraries Act, the citizens of Toronto in a refer-

---

233 : "Women's Institutes," *Encyclopedia Canadiana* (1957 ed.), 10:353–54; "Mechanics' Institutes," ibid., 6:416 (Sybil Grimson); and "Mechanics' Institutes," *Canadian Encyclopedia*, ed. James H. Marsh, rev. 2nd ed., 4 vols. (Edmonton: Hurtig, 1988), 2:1319 (Chad Gaffield); rate of organization: "Women's Organizations," ibid., 4:2329 (Wendy Mitchinson); Linda M. Ambrose, "Ontario's Women's Institutes and the Work of Local History," in Beverly Boutilier and Alison Prentice, eds., *Creating Historical Memory: English-Canadian Women and the Work of History* (Vancouver: UBC Press, 1997), 75–98.

234 : Alpheus Todd, "On the Establishment of Free Public Libraries in Canada," *Royal Society of Canada Proceedings and Transactions* 1, Sec. 2 (25 May 1882): 13–16, quotes ibid.; James Bain, "The Public Libraries of Canada," in *Canada: An Encyclopedia of the Country*, ed. J. Castell Hopkins, 6 vols. (Toronto: Linscott, 1898–1900), 5:207–11.

endum overwhelmingly endorsed establishment of a public library.[235] The new public library acquired the Mechanics' Institute's building and its substantial library of more than 7,400 volumes. A "limited number" of French and English books were added in the early years, but, under continuous financial difficulties, few or no acquisitions were made until after World War II. In the 1910s, the library's "national story hours" familiarized children with Canada's heroes and history. Public libraries thus negotiated between class and nation, between lore and information.[236]

In Montreal, the Church opposed such free access to information. This largest city in Canada, ninth in size in North America, had grown from 268,000 inhabitants in 1901 to 470,500 in 1911, with 63 percent francophone. In 1880, authorities had refused the offer of the Institut canadien to donate its library of 10,000 volumes to the city. Two decades later, the mayor solicited a Carnegie library grant on condition that the city would assume the cost of maintenance. Catholic journalists railed, "nous sommes menacés d'une bibliothèque Carnegie ... un foyer d'infection," and so did the clergy, which had just had to accept a public hospital: "Un hôpital sans Dieu; une bibliothèque où le prêtre ne soit pas admis à traiter des questions de morale." Debates raged for a decade and a half about public access to reading, censorship, and the Church's "Index." Then the proposal was defeated. The Chambre de commerce advocated a more narrow approach for a library with books about "sciences pratiques, industrielles et commerciales," and in 1903 the Société Saint-Jean-Baptist opened a "biliothèque technique au Monument National." Its holdings were modest, some 4,000 volumes in 1907. Thus Quebec remained "outside the continental trend known as the 'Public Library Movement.'"[237]

To expand the public library system to rural Canada, the Carnegie Foundation offered grants for demonstration services at the (Lower) Fraser Valley Regional and the Prince Edward Island libraries. Once established, the services were to be funded by local taxes. The pilot project indicated "an enormous book hunger in rural areas" and a need for regional or province-wide libraries "that could deliver adequate services." While some observers voiced fears of U.S. or Carnegie imperialism due to possible American

235 : Behind the initiative was John Hallam, who had come as a poor immigrant from Lancashire, England, and through self-education became a merchant and alderman.

236 : Barbara Myrvold, "The First Hundred Years: Toronto Public Library 1883–1983," in McNally, *Canadian Library History*, 1:65–79.

237 : Marcel Lajeunesse, "Les Bibliothèques publiques á Montréal au début du XXe siècle: essai d'histoire socio-culturelle," in McNally, *Canadian Library History*, 2:173–98, quote p. 176.

content of book selection procedures, this project became a model for other rural regions. The widespread demand for public access to educational materials in self-funded township and city libraries resulted in contests between adherents of practical information and those advocating instruction in line with particular moral principles. The institute and public library movements were both means of self-organization and means of inculcation of national and religious belief systems.[238]

Schools: Dissemination of whose identity-providing narratives?

Public education, too, was contested ground: whose values were to be taught, who was to be in control of schools as an institution, and what kind of identities would pupils have at the end of their education? In the mid-nineteenth century, the Roman Catholic, the Anglican, or one of the numerous Protestant churches set the educational agendas. When in Quebec a report of 1842 showed that only 5 percent of the school-age children attended primary school, the legislature passed laws to improve attendance but hesitated to establish a Ministère de l'instruction publique until 1868. But the Church, in what might be termed the Conquest of 1875 and the battle at the capital of Quebec City, defeated all reforms. In consequence of this educational *enclavement*, funds spent on Catholic pupils amounted to only half the sum spent on Protestant pupils (under their own commission) and by 1900 Quebec's francophone population of 1.3 million sent 722 students to university; the anglophone one of 0.2 million sent 1,358 students. Demands by trade unions and some liberals (designated as "radicals") to make school attendance compulsory could not prevail. A law of 1907 mandated that illiterate working children, age twelve to sixteen, had to attend evening classes—after ten hours of work six days a week. In 1910, the minimum working age was raised to fourteen, if only in industrial employment, and employment of illiterate children under the age of sixteen was prohibited. School attendance was low; teachers' salaries were even lower. The Church hired women whom it paid half or a third as much as men, and as a result children often waited for teachers, who never came because they would not be able to live off the wage. About 1930, women teachers in the Catholic system received on average $387 annually, compared to $1,068 in Protestant schools; nuns worked for less. Children with an education had to face the problem that Quebec's French had not followed the evolution of metropolitan French.

---

238 : Maxine K. Rochester, "Bringing Librarianship to Rural Canada in the 1930s: Demonstrations by Carnegie Corporation of New York," in McNally, *Canadian Library History*, 2:241–63.

Their dialect was difficult to comprehend for people from France and other parts of the Francophonie—enlistees from Martinique, shipped to France in the 1940s via Quebec, remembered "les Québécois dont l'accent le fasait rire aux larmes." Low educational attainment resulted in low income levels: French Canadians on average earned less than recent immigrants. Educational disadvantage turned firstcomers into latecomers in the nation.[239]

In multi-denominational but Anglican-ruled Ontario, Egerton Ryerson confronted the British state church represented by Bishop John Strachan as early as the 1820s with the demand for non-denominational education. He incorporated educational ideas from Prussia and Ireland, from Massachusetts and New York, into Ontario's School Act of 1841. The school system became uniform, tax-supported, non-denominational, and compulsory. Private schools could continue to operate if parents paid for them. In rural Canada, schooling was not a high priority for parents who valued the labour of their children and had little cash to pay school rates. Thus, beginning with New Brunswick in 1784, provinces set aside land, the income from which would contribute to teachers' salaries. From 1871, the Prairie provinces provided a quarter section for a school building in each township and, upon petition of local parents, provided grants-in-aid for teachers' salaries. The community was responsible for the building and its maintenance. Such local self-organization led to pro-and-con debates within communities, since all adults, parents of school-age children or not, had to contribute. This stood in contrast to European rural societies, where common people had no say regarding educational facilities. *Hors Québec*, free tax-supported schools had become the rule by the 1880s.

In Quebec's schools, language usage depended on the respective community's language and religion, with the majority of the schools in the French language. The educational rights of French-speakers in bilingual regions outside Quebec as well as of immigrant children were contested. The Manitoba Act of 1870 provided constitutional guarantees for separate schools for the Roman Catholic francophone Métis population and the Northwest Territories Act of 1875 (as amended in 1877) provided for French and English, Roman Catholic and Protestant schools. From 1867, Section 93 of the British

---

239 : Paul-André Linteau, René Durocher, Jean-Claude Robert, and François Ricard, *Histoire du Québec contemporain*, 2 vols. (2nd ed., Montreal: Boréal, 1989), 1:267–79, 537–59, 601–29. Number of students: Marcel Rioux, *La Question du Québec* (Paris: Éd. Seghers, 1969), transl. by Hames Boake as *Quebec in Question* (Toronto: Lewis and Samuel, 1971), 61. Susan Mann Trofimenkoff, *The Dream of a Nation: A Social and Intellectual History of Quebec* (Toronto: Gage, 1983). For the enlistees see Raphael Confiant's novel *Le Nègre et l'Amiral* (Paris: Grasset, 1988), 393.

North America Act empowered the federal government to intervene in provincial school systems to protect educational needs of minorities. In a first controversy in New Brunswick, where Acadian and Irish Catholics could no longer send their children to "separate" Roman Catholic schools when the provincial government mandated uniform "non-sectarian" education, the federal government did not intervene. In Manitoba, where the English-speaking population had increased tenfold within a decade, a law of 1890 abolished both the dual school system and French as official language. Denominational schools could continue to operate if parents paid both the rate for the public schools and the cost of their separate school. To redress this violation of the Manitoba Act, the federal government intervened only when ordered by the courts in 1896: to the non-denominational public schooling, religious instruction could be added after classes; where 10 or more pupils spoke French or another non-English language, instruction was to be "upon the bilingual system." This downgraded the French language to one of many languages but upgraded immigrants' languages. As regards the Northwest Territories, where the right to French-language instruction had also been drastically curtailed, the 1905 federal autonomy bill for Saskatchewan and Alberta contained a clause, drafted by Henri Bourassa and Charles Fitzpatrick, both from Quebec and both Catholic, to reinsert the compromise of 1877. But the Anglophile Secretary of the Interior, Clifford Sifton, vigorously opposed such equality of languages. In Ontario, where the French-speakers had increased to 10 percent of the total population, the provincial government in "Regulation 17" of 1913 restricted French to the first two years of elementary instruction. Quebecers, such as Bourassa, who saw Canada as a pact between two cultural groups, lost out once again and the Catholic Ultramontanes once again had their suspicions officially confirmed by Ontario's British-minded elite.[240] In the midst of conflicts, Quebec's government voted for a $400,000 compensation to the Jesuit Order for lands that had reverted to the colony more than a century earlier, when the Pope had temporarily disbanded the Order (1888 Jesuit Estates controversy). Ontario and other Protestant provinces were enraged. Whenever a choice between conflict or compromise had to be made, the hardliners among Ontario's and Quebec's elites chose conflict.

The second major issue of the "school question" was the presence of immigrants. Some educators viewed them as "the ignorant peasantry of central and eastern Europe and Asia" (Manitoba Department of Education, 1906); others considered "the immigrants as a 'challenge and invitation' to

---

240 : R. Douglas Francis, Richard Jones, Donald B. Smith, *Destinies: Canadian History Since Confederation* (Toronto: Holt, Rinehart, 1988), 29, 80–86, 135–37, 189–99.

Canadian institutions," which could be met successfully (Superintendent of Education, Northwest Territories, 1898).[241] In the debates about employing mother-tongue teachers to reach out to non-English speaking pupils, French spokesmen rejected association with the "other ethnics" rather than forging alliances. Ukrainian, German, and Mennonite immigrants, who were close to reaching "institutional completeness," successfully requested mother-tongue instruction. A report on the languages used in 1913 concluded, in keeping with the contemporary Anglo-conformity, that English was learned best if taught without reference to any other language.[242] During the World War I hysteria, the remaining separate schools in the Prairie provinces came under provincial supervision.[243] The Ukrainian Canadians, in Europe pressured by the Habsburg and Romanov Empires to shed their cultural independence, vigorously asserted their identity. Their newspaper *Novyny* angrily editorialized: "The minister of education lies when he says that Alberta is an English province. Alberta is a Canadian province, where everyone has equal rights, including the Ukrainians." This posed the issue squarely: was Canada to be Canadian or British?[244]

In the 1920s, the issue of whose culture was to be taught received a new dimension when class was added to ethnicity. Alfred Fitzpatrick, principal

241 : Marilyn Barber, "Canadianization through the Schools of the Prairie Provinces before World War I: The Attitudes and Aims of the English-Speaking Majority," in *Ethnic Canadians: Culture and Education*, ed. Martin L. Kovacs (Regina: Canadian Plains Research Centre, 1978), 282–283, quotes pp. 282, 286; Lovell Clark, ed., *The Manitoba School Question: Majority Rule or Minority Rights* (Toronto: Copp Clark, 1968).

242 : Barber, "Canadianization," 292. The debates are analyzed by Raymond J.A. Huel (Saskatchewan), Cornelius J. Jaenen (Manitoba), Martin L. Kovacs (Hungarians), and Savelia Curnisky (Ukrainians), as well as by Nanciellen C. Sealy's study of New Brunswick, in Kovacs, *Ethnic Canadians*, 295–369. Chad Gaffield contextualized the conflict in social stratification, *Language, Schooling, and Cultural Conflict: The Origins of the French-Language Controversy in Ontario* (Montreal: MQUP, 1987), transl. as *Aux origines de l'identité franco-ontarienne: Éducation, culture et l'économie* (Ottawa: PU Ottawa, 1993).

243 : See C.B. Sissons, *Bi-Lingual Schools* (1916), O.D. Skelton, *Language Issue* (1917), and J.T.M. Anderson, *The Education of the New Canadian* (1918). Robert England's *The Central European Immigrant in Canada* (Toronto: Macmillan, 1929) closed the debate. Vera Lysenko's *Westerly Wild* (1956) provided a sympathetic fictional assessment of a bilingual woman teacher's impact on her pupils in a Saskatchewan town. In the 1970s, two sensitive literary accounts were published: Gabrielle Roy, *Ces enfants de ma vie* (Montreal: Stanké, 1977) and John C. Charyk, *Those Bittersweet Schooldays* (Saskatoon: Western Producer, 1977). See also "Education and Ethnicity," ed. Cornelius J. Jaenen, special issue of *Canadian Ethnic Studies* 8.1 (1976).

244 : William A. Czumer, *Recollections about the Life of the First Ukrainian Settlers in Canada*, transl. by Louis T. Laychuck (Ukrainian orig., 1942; Edmonton: Canadian Inst. of Ukrainian Studies, 1981), 104–12, 118–119.

of Frontier College, in keeping with the ideas of the nineteenth-century Mechanics' Institutes and of modern socialist thought, argued that working people were entitled to education. Education was to be part of an improvement plan that would start with living conditions and would include all "foreigners," even those in camps and bunkhouses. Fitzpatrick, aware of gender, demanded access for women to education and to a broad range of jobs. For decades to come, however, working people's and women's life-worlds were not even reflected in school texts.[245]

School texts are highly important in fashioning discourses, myths, and knowledges. They reach young people at the crucial age of formatting the basic categories into which later information is sorted and of acquiring the methods and theories—programs in modern parlance—to digest information and narratives. Bureaucracy-sanctioned schoolbooks had a monopoly over children's minds. Nineteenth-century English-language ones were imports from the United States; then, in 1846, some thirty titles were adopted from the highly developed Irish educational system. British models informed the Canadian-produced texts of the 1850s: John Lovell's *Series of School Books*, James Campbell's Canadian National Series, and the influential Ontario Readers (since 1884).[246] French-language schoolbooks, published in larger numbers since the 1860s, were first produced with a private publisher, Beauchemin, then religious organizations controlled the market.[247] Regardless of language, the textbooks were written by middle-class men from the two hegemonic cultures for whom Others, whether women, workers, newcomers, or Native peoples, were not part of the world to be learned.

Since Canada's knowledge production, including the construction of the two master narratives, was centred in Ontario and Quebec, the viewpoints from the two Central Canadas were advertised as generically Canadian. In Ryerson's Ontario, Christianity in its Anglican or Protestant version was to inculcate a "new nationality," a sense of Canadian identity in contrast to what was provided by the imported U.S. texts and the loyalism-to-Britain

---

245 : Alfred Fitzpatrick, *The University in Overalls: A Plea for Part-Time Study* (Toronto: Hunter-Rose, 1920); Kenneth W. Osborne, *"Hard-working, Temperate and Peaceable": The Portrayal of Workers in Canadian History Textbooks* (Winnipeg: University of Manitoba Press, 1980).

246 : Many surveys were dull and fact-ridden (e.g., W.H.P. Clement's of 1897 and W.H. Withrow's of 1878); only Charles G.D. Roberts' *A History of Canada* (1902) achieved literary standards.

247 : Frères des écoles chrétiennes (1877), Congrégation de Notre-Dame (1881), Librairie Saint-Viateur (1887), Frères de l'instruction chrétienne (1900), Frères du Sacré-Coeur (1902). Fernand Dumont (*Genèse*, 10) remembered such Quebec-national history from his 1920s school years.

homilies. His successor, G.W. Ross, subscribed to a pan-Canadianism and to an industrial society that included an English-French co-operation, but which remained firmly bound to an empire-centred as well as Canada First ideology. In the peculiar Canadian setting, conservative British Canadian parents accused him of weakening the ties to Great Britain while Franco-Ontarians felt that their culture did not receive adequate respect. Ontario's educators felt that "Canadian patriotism should be comprehensive, respectful, intelligent, and at the same time intense," a goal to which militarist aspects, in the French-Canadian version *virilité* and *réveil nationaliste*, were added after 1900. In Quebec's schools, Christianity in its Catholic version included loyalty to the local priest and other notables as well as to the empire of the Church. The separate educational projects remained compatible, as Geneviève Laloux-Jain argued. In neither of the two cultural regions could reformers prevail. For nationalist reasons, Émile Dubois demanded a practical education, "de préparer la jeunesse à 'lutter pour conquérir notre place au soleil', puisque 'nos rivaux, par la force des circonstances, plus que par la supériorité intellectuelle, ont de l'avance sur nous'." In anglophone Canada, H.H. Miles's textbooks provided a balanced view of a bicultural Canada. As professor of mathematics at Bishop's College, Quebec, he lived outside of the historians' established discourses and inside a bicultural province. Anglophone pragmatists unceremoniously juxtaposed material aspects to *valeurs spirituelles:* "poems are good; so are potatoes, and if we must choose between them it must be potatoes."[248] Canadian civic culture and practical information on country and society had to develop in spite of the school system.

Children, whether of immigrant or Canadian-born parents, found few Canadian things or values in their texts or in the institutional set-up. Immigrant pupils feared the ridicule of their English Canadian classmates and the arrogance of teachers, whether a Finnish girl in Timmins, Jewish Leah Rosenberg in Toronto, a Russian-Jewish and an Icelandic girl in Winnipeg, or German-born boys in northern British Columbia. Such discrimination countered the billboard versions of English-British-Canadian culture and

---

248 : Geneviève Laloux-Jain, *Les manuels d'histoire du Canada au Québec et en Ontario (de 1867 à 1914)* (Quebec: PU Laval, 1974), esp. 21–58, quotes pp. 28, 49. See also Marcel Trudel and Geneviève Jain, *Canadian History Textbooks: A Comparative Study, Studies of the Royal Commission on Bilingualism and Biculturalism,* no. 5 (Ottawa: Queen's Printer, 1970). Bernd Baldus and Meenaz Kassam, "'Make Me Truthful, Good, and Mild': Values in Nineteenth-Century Ontario Schoolbooks," *Canadian Journal of Sociology* 21 (1996): 327–58. Miles, *A School History of Canada* (1870), *The Child's History of Canada* (1870), and an English-language history of French-Canada to counter biases of previous English writing on the French regime (1872).

fairness that educators propounded as the model for acculturation. In 1914, a Ukrainian Canadian complained, "We help Canada rise / In Commerce and all things," but do not get recognition, "We will tell the whole world: / 'English culture is peculiar.'" A woman teacher of Italian background could not understand why the Ontario Department of Education's manual of 1934, six and a half decades after Dominion status, demanded: "The teacher should not fail to emphasize the extent, power, and responsibilities of the British Empire, its contributions to the highest form of civilization, the achievements of its statesmen and its generals, and the increasingly important place that Canada holds amongst the Overseas Dominions." Immigrants, socialized by gatekeepers into a male imperial British world, were nevertheless excluded as "ethnics" from the Canadian institutions and elites.[249] Children had to learn everything they never needed to know about the British Isles, Great Britain's institutions, and the manly reach of the British Empire. Such narratives and billboards without relation to their everyday lives, disconcerted schoolchildren across the Empire—in Australia, Jamaica, and elsewhere.[250]

As usual, other options were available in the marketplace of ideas and textbooks. After the carnage of World War I, the Canadian branch of the International League for Peace and Freedom commissioned an analysis of textbook contents. The League advocated feminism, pacifism, and social justice, saw war "as essentially a masculine affair," and espoused an amalgamation of Prairie co-operativism and socialism. Inculcation of pupils with nation-

---

249 : Hoerder, *Creating Societies*, 99–100, 105–17, 128–30, 231–32; Czumer, *Recollections*, 104–12, 118–119; Penny Petrone, *Breaking the Mold: A Memoir* (Toronto: Guernica, 1995), 165–91; Baldus and Kassam, "Ontario Schoolbooks." Margaret Atwood, *Survival: A Thematic Guide to Canadian Literature* (Toronto: Anansi, 1972), 29. See also Mary Two Axe Earley, Zonia Keywan, Helen Potrebenko, "Ethnicity and Femininity as Determinants of Life Experience," *Canadian Ethnic Studies* 13.1 (1981): 37–42: Potrebenko remembered, "At school I learned that everything English was good and the exact opposite of Ukrainian. So if Ukrainian men were chauvinists, English men were not. . . . English society was free and democratic unlike the autocratic paternalism of Ukrainians, . . . By the time I learned the truth, I was a long way from home." She learned about weak women and strong boys, but in her experience boys were stupid rather than strong. Quote p. 40.

250 : Australia: Jill Ker Conway, *The Road from Coorain* (New York: Vintage, 1989), 96–104; Jamaica: Edward Pilkington, *Beyond the Mother Country* (London: Tauris, 1988), 11, and Cindy Hahamovitch, "Jamaicans Jump Jim Crow: Caribbean Encounters in the World War II South [of the U.S.]," unpubl. paper, Soc. Science Hist. Assoc., annual meeting, Pittsburgh, Oct. 2000. The children of native elites, for example in India, also learned little about South Asian but much of British history. Clark Blaise and Bharati Mukherjee, *Days and Nights in Calcutta* (New York: Doubleday, 1977; Markham: Penguin, 1986), 170–71.

alist history was criticized by H.G. Wells in Great Britain, John Dewey in the United States, and Agnes Macphail of the Progressive Party in Ottawa. The League of Nations set up a Committee in Intellectual Co-operation to encourage textbook revision in member states. In Canada, the committee, which in 1933 surveyed history and social studies texts, was quickly labelled "dangerously unpatriotic, anti-British, and subversive of respectable values." Not daring to hire an outspoken reformer, the League recruited Peter Sandiford, professor of education at the University of Toronto, to direct the survey. His team concluded that regarding the teaching of internationalism and peace a few texts were excellent, a few were fair, others just satisfactory, and others inadequate.[251] Thus, at least some textbooks placed Canada in an internationalist and peace-supporting perspective.

Applied scholarship I: The training of social workers

Around 1900, socio-economic changes coincided with new roles for experts and academics. The economic and immigration boom from the late 1890s to 1912 brought tremendous growth in "machine technology, the scale of industrial plants and primary resource production." The new industrial jobs and the growth of the cities induced a large-scale internal rural-urban as well as a mass proletarian transatlantic migration. From 1891 to 1911, the share of city dwellers in the total population grew from 31.8 to 45.2 percent. Given that wages were low, labourers not yet organized into unions, and living conditions unsanitary, the economic boom resulted in social "problems" or, phrased more neutrally, "issues." Academics addressed these, particularly in Montreal, while for labourers from Asian societies in Vancouver, only the church missions and their social services indicated interest. Impoverished miners in the Rockies set up mutual aid associations, hungry harvest workers from the Prairies drifted to the cities each winter, the abominable living conditions in Winnipeg resulted in the 1919 General Strike—but academic institutions with a problem-analyzing, though not necessarily -solving capability were concentrated in Central Canada's cities.[252]

Which group of experts was to take the lead in addressing the socio-economic changes and the resulting inequalities? At the end of the nineteenth century, the "businessman reformer, the church philanthropist, and the amateur enthusiast" had been considered the true experts. Under such reasoning, only bankers possessed the knowledge to organize governmental

251 : Ken Osborne, "An Early Example of the Analysis of History Textbooks in Canada," *Canadian Social Studies* 29.1 (1994): 21–25, quotes pp. 21, 22.

252 : Doug Owram, *The Government Generation: Canadian Intellectuals and the State, 1900-1945* (Toronto: UTP, 1986), quote p. 17.

bank regulations. It is a characteristic of privileged discourses that outside actors with greater perspectives are usually not called in. Under such beliefs, academics realized "that they and their ideas were becoming, if not irrelevant, at least marginal to the society around them" and they "began to search for a new role for themselves in society and for new solutions to the problems confronting Canada." A professionalization, a move from privileged discourses to substantial research in the social sciences, was to effect a shift from haphazard approaches to the "visible miseries and immoralities of city life" to fundamental urban reform and efficiency in the public interest. To challenge the role of the businessmen and philanthropists, constructed as "natural" experts, the concept of university-trained experts demanded "a new role for the intellectual community in order to assist society and to reassert the importance of intellectual leadership in Canada." Old-style gatekeepers and society as a whole would have to accept "that the scientific technique was valid as a means of assessing social problems."[253]

Government-sponsored as well as individual fact-finding missions had been undertaken since the 1880s: the 1889 Royal Commission on Relations of Labour and Capital, and Herbert B. Ames's *The City Below the Hill* were two. *A Sociological Study of a Portion of the City of Montreal, Canada* (1887), and J.C. Chapais's jeremiad against "le luxe, l'ivrognerie, l'amour de plaisir" in *La Revue canadienne* were others. Distinct from U.S. discourses, misery was not reduced to individual failings, but seen as a threat to and responsibility of the whole nation. Some conservative talking heads, such as George Munro Grant, principal of Queen's University, cast society as a whole in the guise of a slum: society would become "a city of pigs." Around 1900, social studies, not yet the social sciences, emerged. While the churches were skeptical of positivist sociology as developed by Comte and Durkheim, some clerics understood the need to analyze society's problems. Concerned Protestant scholars, empirically if accidentally observing poverty in Montreal's working-class quarter, had established a service centre, a "Settlement House," in 1891. The Montreal Charity Organization Society, founded in 1901, was also modelled upon the first such U.S. organization in Buffalo (established 1879). In Catholic thought and practice, the Société de Saint-Vincent de Paul attempted to regulate and professionalize distribution of alms. Charity expenditures, ineffective in the elite's view, "prompted the city's anglophone social-welfare leaders to push for the creation of a department of social service." Such organized charity was meant to introduce a "scientific mode" of thought and action into social work and to restore each client "to a state of independence and self-reliance by some means

---

253 : Owram, *Government Generation*, quotes pp. 13, 41.

other than monetary" (emphasis added). Montreal's charity organization, an Anglo-Protestant initiative, crossed the Anglo-French divide and invited French-language Montrealers to participate. The renowned Université de Montréal economist Édouard Montpetit joined the board of directors. The social responsibility movement involved a comparatively small circle of men and thus the scholar-reformers knew each other and did not draw rigorous boundaries between disciplines. In an elite manner, they filled positions at new (and at old) universities with their students or from universities abroad where they themselves had studied. As a rule, connections between scholars, non-academic social reformers, social workers, municipal administrators, and federal politicians were close.[254]

Reacting to demands by theologians and ministers close to the Protestant "social gospel" and the Catholic *Rerum Novarum* thought, universities moved in the 1910s to institute training programs for social workers and coordinating centres for social-welfare efforts. Commissions of the Methodist and Presbyterian Churches compiled data from detailed empirical studies and in 1914 a first Social Services Congress convened in Ottawa. In the context of its affiliated theological colleges and their interest in the "social question," McGill University established a Department of Social Study and Training. Its first director, John Howard Toynbee Falk, exemplifies the internationalism of such endeavours, the social selectivity of the new social service elite men, and World War I influences on mentalities. He had experience with poverty in Liverpool, England, had worked with the Red Cross and the Patriotic Fund during the war, and had been active in relief work for Russian refugees. "Relief," whether from urban poverty or wartime displacement, was the catchword of the day in the advanced Atlantic World, from the Urals to the Rocky Mountains. War had breached class barriers, had brought women and men from different classes in contact with each other, the argument went, and since the better-placed had learned how "the other half" lived, middle-class social workers were to become interpreters between classes. When Governor General Lord Byng, distant from the quarters of the poor, lauded a Canada without slums, Falk invited him to tour Montreal's poverty-stricken quarters. Byng reversed himself and came to support social reform. The scholarship-policy connection was functional.

Co-operation among reformers, however, was fraught with incompatible visions and attitudes. Deeply humane visions vied with cold planning

---

254 : Owram, *Government Generation*, 3–49, quoting G.P. Grant p. 3, Chapais p. 21; Marlene Shore, *The Science of Social Redemption: McGill, the Chicago School, and the Origins of Social Research in Canada* (Toronto: UTP, 1987), quotes pp. xiii, xiv.

approaches, Christian or socialist mutuality with concerns for an ordered society. In addition, the "young" country's "vast geography, small population, and even smaller pool of investment capital" suggested a need for large-scale state intervention into the economy. With its institutions still evolving and a total population—compared to the United States—just the size of a "sample" for scholarly research, some considered Canada a laboratory for ameliorative social programs.[255] The sample's problem groups, in this reasoning, were the urban underclasses and allegedly genetically or racially inferior immigrants from so-called non-preferred countries. Before World War I, the Scottish-educated McGill moral philosopher, William Caldwell, charted a trajectory to a more equitable society in his *Pragmatism and Idealism* (1913). After 1918 and in reaction to the 1919 Winnipeg General Strike as well as widespread work stoppages in Montreal and urban discontent elsewhere, well-established and conservative advocates of an "order" that was never properly defined reacted with invoking a threat of "Bolshevism" and calls for a policing of society. The step from policy to police often is but a small one. As yet, the farmers' discontent and the beginnings of their co-operative movements seem to have been too distant to be visible to these urban elites.

Rather than espousing a U.S.-style individualism, the social reformers proposed stateside social intervention in terms of the British Independent Labour Party's programs. They abandoned the idea of local communal "settlement house" projects in favour of the state as the only institution with the resources and power to shape the evolution of society. In this respect, Scottish-influenced scholars and France-educated economists such as Édouard Montpetit concurred. If, in Europe, the state had abandoned the economy, "il a aussi abandonée les hommes à leur propres forces, c'est-a-dire condamné les faibles à la defaite, en rejetant l'intervention de l'État." State intervention—along lines suggested by social scientists—could ensure "la paix sociale" and if the state had the power, it also had the responsibility. Advocates of "order" concurred that, in view of the growing strength of working-class organizations in Canada and socialist parties in Europe, state intervention was needed. Queen's University's political economist O.D. Skelton argued that top-down state intervention was needed to defeat bottom-up socialist ideas. "Only action by the state to ensure the efficiency and humanity of capitalism would offer the possibility of long-run social

---

255 : The concept is still in use almost a century later. After the re-election of George W. Bush in November 2004, Raymond Chrétien, former ambassador to the U.S., commented: "Le phénomène d'américanisation du Canada, visible dans les années 1990s, est aujourd'hui terminé. Il y a un nouveau sentiment nationaliste chez les Canadiens, fiers de vivre dans un laboratoire social." *L'Express* no. 2785, 15 Nov. 2004, p. 14.

stability and continued immunity from the class hatreds and social convulsions of European society."[256]

From such nationwide perspectives, everyday social work seemed inefficient. It would also not help social scientists in academia to pursue their careers. Thus, after a short experimental period, McGill's administrators divided the Department of Social Study and Training into an academic Department of Sociology and an affiliated underfunded School of Social Services. U.S. sociologists, too, were dissociating themselves from reform- and practice-oriented activities in the 1920s and, in the Depression decade after 1929, it seemed more prestigious to develop research projects than to deal with the indigent on a day-to-day basis. McGill's Board of Governors closed down the School of Social Services in 1931. The field had "evolved from a Christian doctrine of social concern into a subject that venerated science and implicitly criticised social reform." Protestant churches withdrew when secular organizations assumed leadership. A more ominous side emerged when experts in Great Britain, the United States, and Canada turned to a social Darwinist approach centered on social and human "efficiency" and economic productivity. Falk and similar experts saw the impoverished, handicapped, sick, and imprisoned as parasites feeding on society. Convinced that international stability and peace depended on economic productivity, reformers initiated programs to combat wastefulness and inefficiency.[257]

Expressed positively, the men of this social group shared a commitment to prevent a repetition of the horrors of war. Equity, international arbitration, and early attention to potential social problems were seen as prerequisites for a social management that would benefit all. The initiative for a research agenda that covered much or all of society, a study of Canada, thus occurred in overlapping contexts and climates of opinion: internationally as effort to develop a material and social basis for human life that would prevent another world war, economically and socially in terms of efficiency and profitability, politically and in social philosophy as a shift from a Christian social gospel movement to a Fabian collectivism and social responsibility.

---

256 : Owram, *Government Generation*, 50–79, quotes pp. 30–36. Barry G. Ferguson, *Remaking Liberalism: The Intellectual Legacy of Adam Shortt, O.D. Skelton, W.C. Clark and W.A. Macintosh, 1890–1925* (Montreal: MQUP, 1993).

257 : Shore, *Science of Social Redemption*, 26–67, quote p. xiv.

Applied scholarship II:
Transforming researchers into the federal elite

In various ways, reformers and academics organized themselves to achieve political clout. In 1913 the Canadian Political Science Association (CPSA) was founded, in 1915 the Civic Improvement League of Canada. While both quickly became defunct under the impact of the war, the role of the state in wartime, both as revenue-collecting institution to finance the military and as responsible for sending young men to their death in battle, had a major impact on the relationship between the state and the citizens, academics and policy-makers, women and men. In contrast to liberal concepts, the state intervened in all realms of society. Two elites—students and businessmen—were particularly affected. Students, the intellectual elite of the next generation, enlisted in high numbers and died in high numbers. The business elite reaped unusually high profits from war-related production. In response to the latter, the government first imposed a business profits tax, and second introduced a federal income tax, thus reversing the nineteenth-century liberalist credo that the state should not interfere with private property. Issues of class and of community were debated. At first, the tax applied to a high-income segment of the population only, a mere 0.5 percent of the population. Critics of society, such as Toronto journalist Samuel T. Wood, commented that while the people of Canada had "not undertaken the creation of dukes, . . . they have created several millionaires who are quite as costly and burdensome." A political scientist emphasized the long-term policy implications: "Necessity has brought now what justice might have called for in vain some years longer." Citizens as taxpayers asked what they would get in return: the nation-state, rather than drawing upon men in wartime, would come to be expected in peacetime to protect citizens' individual life projects during economic or individual crises by delivering social security.[258]

Progressives, whose calls for an active role of the state had been rejected by the reigning liberalist discourse and practice, found the wartime involvement of the state in the economy impressive. A heterogeneous new philosophy of state and society emerged. Charles Gordon, the creator of the Scottish billboard version of Canadian identity (chapter 4) and a famous World War I military chaplain, was shocked by the Winnipeg General Strike and tried to bring labour and capital together. His novel *To Him That Hath* (1921) was based on his experience in the Manitoba Council of Industry. Progressives believed that the mobilization of social and economic forces by the state was congruent with domestic aims of effective use of resources

---

258 : Owram, *Government Generation*, 80–106, quotes p. 81.

(including human beings), orderliness in society, and civil service reform. After 1918, however, reformers split into an idealist conservative segment (Leacock, *The Unsolved Riddle of Social Justice*, 1920), a liberal, moderate faction (Mackenzie King, *Industry and Humanity*, 1918), and a radical faction (Bland, *The New Christianity*, 1918). Commitment to reform, as so often happens, stopped short of changing gender roles. For example, academic and policymaker Adam Shortt, married to Elizabeth Smith, one of Canada's first female graduates in medicine and a leading feminist, rejected enfranchisement of women. While service to society and political community had become a dignified role, the traditional gender division placed men in well-paying and policy-setting government positions and women in low-paying or unpaid social service.

Academics, with first an interest in policy-making and then in many cases a position in government, had formulated their goals at the founding of the CPSA in 1913. Adam Shortt, civil service commissioner in Ottawa, in full agreement with Édouard Montpetit, explained: "It is through a select, active minority that the most effective and progressive ideas as to political and social welfare must be introduced." The CPSA was to bring together academic experts, men of the educated elite, and political leaders to approach social problems and developments from a scientific point of view. As academics of high renown, Shortt and O.D. Skelton set out to create a Canadian service elite in politics and policy-development.[259] While in Europe, nationalism reigned paramount, the Canadian elite was, in a way, cosmopolitan. Shortt, an Ontario-born Scots Presbyterian, graduated from Queen's, studied in Edinburgh, and then returned to Queen's in 1888. Conservative Stephen Leacock, of a well-to-do English family that had emigrated to Canada to try farming, was educated at Upper Canada College and the University of Chicago. William Ashley, historian and political economist at the University of Toronto, accepted the first chair in economic history in the United States at Harvard in 1892. James Mavor, Scottish-born and educated at Glasgow University, filled Ashley's University of Toronto position. William Lyon Mackenzie King studied political economy at the University of Toronto, Chicago, and Harvard. To provide service to the poor, he worked as a volunteer in an immigrant neighbourhood in Chicago. He was Canadian deputy minister of labour relations in 1900, but also took employment with the Rockefeller Corporation at the height of its attempt to smash labour unions. R.M. MacIver of the University of Toronto's Department of Political Economy, Scottish-born

---

259 : Owram, *Government Generation*, 50–64. In a parallel development in the U.S., the "Wisconsin idea" rallied professors of the University of Wisconsin to progressive reformers. In 1912, a liberal professor, Woodrow Wilson, was elected president.

and educated, served a stint at Oxford and migrated to Toronto in 1915. Was he "impeccably Canadian" as Doug Owram, steeped in the peculiar British-Canadian discourse, commented? Or was he an immigrant Scot? The most important francophone member of the new elite was economist Édouard Montpetit, educated in Montreal and Paris and professor of political science at the Université de Montréal since 1910. Before the background of abject urban poverty in Canadian cities as well as the Russian revolutions of 1905 and 1917, the group was united by a consensus that socialism was not the product of conspiratorial agitators but a result of a flawed economic regime. The group, after all, might be called "Canadian" with respect to the solutions it advocated, although Ukrainian and Chinese immigrants as well as Native peoples would have reason to disagree.[260]

The new theory of a reforming, intervening *Modern State* (1926) was developed by R.M. MacIver, who consciously revised the traditional social-justice philosophy to emphasize the role of the new social sciences. He rejected state-centred idealism and cultural nationalism, and anticipated the idea of the modern welfare state: "[t]he state has purpose and value only in the service it provides" to individual citizens. But he also posited the "individual's supremacy over the collectivity." The university-trained operators of the service structures and arbiters of regulation and self-determination would be the experts dividing their time between institutions of learning and of policy-making. However, into this elite's social discourse, the national collectivity crept back in through biological concepts of nationhood and society. Sociologist C.A. Dawson mused that this service elite would be "part of something infinitely stronger and larger" than the individual. Men thus were constructed as quasi-immortal, because after death, their achievements and service remained alive in the nation. Nation-building, maleness, and death-in-war were still entwined.

Ten years after the crisis of war, the crisis of the capitalist system, the Depression of 1929, hit people in Canada and people worldwide. Material lives—food, clothing, and housing—moved to the forefront of concern in the circles of the government men and those to the Left of them. The failure of the so-called practical men—businessmen, entrepreneurs, investors, and bankers—became even more evident than at the time of the "social problem" debate in the 1880s. No social engineering could redress the problem; a managerial state was needed. While the Liberal Party under Mackenzie King rejected far-reaching reforms, committed reformers such as socialist

---

260 : Owram, *Government Generation*, 11–14, 30–36. For the development of economic history in the U.S. see Naomi R. Lamoreaux, "Economic History and the Cliometric Revolution," in Anthony Molho and Gordon S. Wood, eds., *Imagined Histories: American Historians Interpret the Past* (Princeton: Princeton, 1998), 61–84, esp. 60–63.

Frank Underhill and conservative Harold Innis argued that social well-being "was increasingly defined not in the spiritual or moral terms of an earlier generation but in terms of material standards of living" for the living generation. Frank Underhill (University of Toronto) and Frank Scott (McGill) joined with University of Toronto economist Irene M. Biss (married to Spry), Eugene Forsey, Harry Cassidy, and Graham Spry to form the League of Social Reconstruction. From the Prairies, the intellectuals and politicians of the Co-operative Commonwealth Federation—outsiders to the Central Canada orthodoxy—made their way to the capital and inserted their views. A liberal consensus was forged by Vincent and Alice Massey (née Parkin) in the Liberal Party's study groups. Such intricate government-academia relationship raises the question of societal commitment versus scholarly detachment, of democratically elected versus self-selected experts. In any case, scholars were highly influential in charting a course for Canadian society and policies.[261]

The social service elite, "government men" in Owram's term or "new mandarins" in Granatstein's, also "created a foreign policy for Canada that was at once nationalist and internationalist, aggressive and responsible, practical and idealist"—no mean achievement. International relations involved the reform of the Empire into a Commonwealth, establishment of the League of Nations, the advent of fascism in Europe, a strong Right wing in Canada, and the declaration of World War II. At the 1926 Imperial Conference, the equality-of-status doctrine for relations among what were called the White Dominions was accepted and in 1931 the Statute of Westminster created the British Commonwealth. The Canadian government in 1927 for the first time appointed an ambassador to Washington, D.C., rather than being represented by Great Britain's ambassadorial staff. After World War I, the government's almost isolationist attitude notwithstanding, social reformers felt close to the League of Nations and advocated peace through international co-operation. Charlotte Whitton, who had co-edited *Social Welfare* and had served as secretary to a cabinet minister, was appointed to the League's Child Protection Committee. Once, however, dogmatic racism asserted itself in this elite. When, in the 1930s, the refugee-generating fascist states were surrounded by refugee-refusing democracies, Canada among them, the immigration bureaucrats rejected admission of Jewish refugees from the Holocaust, commenting that "none is too many." In addition, men

---

261 : Owram, *Government Generation*, 107–91, quote p. 171; Linda Kealey, ed., *A Not Unreasonable Claim: Women and Reform in Canada 1880s–1920s* (Toronto: Canadian Women's Educational Press, 1979); Kealey and Joan Sangster, eds., *Beyond the Vote: Canadian Women and Politics* (Toronto: UTP, 1989); and Kealey, *Enlisting Women for the Cause: Women, Labour and the Left in Canada, 1890–1920* (Toronto: UTP, 1998).

of the Christian orders kidnapped Native children from their families and cultures to re-program them in boarding schools according to White religious images and methods reflecting the uncharitable violence of the Old Testament.[262]

The academics-administrators-policymakers formed "a coherent group." Many had studied at Oxford, its weak social sciences and political economy notwithstanding, and perhaps succumbed to some "imperial mystique," Scott, Underhill, Massey, Spry, and Pearson among them. The university was open to young Canadians without sufficient means but with excellent credits through imperial scholarships, the Rhodes ones in particular. As a student group, they became a "clearing house of intelligence," formed common attitudes, ambitions, and ideals, established a network of international contacts, and after return to Canada could capitalize on the Oxford "prestige factor." The men, "policymakers rather than bureaucrats," were united by work and friendship and "operated almost anonymously within a tight and private little world—offices moments away from each other, homes nearby, clubs close at hand." Their wives, many also university graduates, formed their interrelated network and organized the group's social life. In sociological terms, the group was anything but representative of Canadians: Roman Catholics were underrepresented, as were French-speakers. Canadians from Ukraine or Italy, from China or British India were not represented. It may be argued that the Ottawa men, or better the Ottawa families, took Canadian society as a whole into account; they shared the notion "that public service was a civil virtue."[263]

The Study of Canada in the social sciences, the scholars' self-interest to cast themselves as a group of experts and to take jobs in the government, as well as the discourse about the course of the nation, shaped Canadian society and polity. Harsh exclusions did take place: some institutions rigorously persecuted socialists, deported immigrants on welfare, racialized men and women from East and South Europe and, much more so, immigrants from societies and cultures in Asia. The view of society based in British backgrounds, in its everyday applied version, became an anglophone Canadian mentality that shaped the federal state's and society's institutions and the

---

262 : Irving Abella and Harold Troper, *None Is Too Many: Canada and the Jews of Europe 1933–1948* (Toronto: Dennys, 1983); Linda Jaine, ed., *Residential Schools: The Stolen Years* (Saskatoon: Univ. Extension Press, 1995); Agnes Grant, *No End of Grief: Indian Residential Schools in Canada* (Winnipeg: Pemmican, 1996).

263 : J.L. Granatstein, *The Ottawa Men: Civil Service Mandarins 1935–1957* (Toronto: Oxford, 1982), quotes pp. xii, 2, 10; Owram, *Government Generation*, 130, 144–46; Barry Ferguson and Doug Owram, "Social Scientists and Public Policy from the 1920s through World War II," *Journal of Canadian Studies* 15.4 (1980–81): 3–17.

underlying values. Such social commitment was shared by the few French Canadians in this elite, if not by Quebec's provincial elite. This Canadianness was shaped in the frame of worldwide economic forces and Canada-wide struggles for material justice.

Four aspects of the world of the scholar-policymakers merit more attention than they have received, since they were to have far-reaching consequences for Canadian society and Canadian Studies. The Ottawa families' men were influential, but their wives were highly educated and, in distinction to London, the men did not withdraw into exclusively male clubs. The women, too, shaped the climate of opinion. Irene Biss stood up to Harold Innis; Alice Massey influenced the "brain trust" of the Liberals, the Port Hope circle; and Charlotte Whitton was a leading social reformer and, later, mayor of Ottawa. Secondly, the Ottawa families—not merely Granatstein's male mandarins—shared a common lifestyle. Raising their families, many employed a full-time maid and some a nanny in addition. When by the late 1940s and early 1950s, domestic servants and caregivers were in short supply, Ottawa men breached the racial barriers to bring in caregivers of other than imperial "white" skin colour, the "first 100 girls" from the West Indies.[264] Thirdly, Canadian diplomats including Lester Pearson were instrumental in inserting the human-rights clause into the charter of the United Nations. Raising the banner of equality for people of all cultures abroad raised the question of equality of ethnocultural groups in the many-cultured Canadian society internally. The service women from the West Indies and all other earlier immigrants had to be accepted as equal in status. Fourth, to rephrase a famous Western book of religion, the public servants, like God, who looked on the results of his labours and found them to be good, found the results of their labour to be good, too. In later decades, to spread the word, they appropriated funds, if for the development of Canadian Studies abroad rather than for apostles. Internally, inclusion of all was achieved in steps by the citizenship legislation of 1947, in the multicultural policies of the 1970s, in the "citizen plus" concept for First Peoples, and finally in the cultural diversity of schools.

---

264 : Christiane Harzig, "'The Movement of 100 Girls:' 1950s Canadian Immigration Policy and the Market for Domestic Labour," *Zeitschrift für Kanada-Studien* 19.2 (1999): 131–46.

III. THE STUDY OF CANADA: THE SOCIAL SCIENCES, THE ARTS, NEW MEDIA, 1920s–1950s

Until the 1950s, statewide or "national" Canadian culture developed in a dialectic of supra-national power relations that included imperial strategies and cultural hegemonies, as well as economic penetration / "investment," and of sub-national self-assertion of ethnocultural groups and women's expressiveness. Canadian nationhood included an awareness of the state's limited significance among the big economic-cultural actors in the Atlantic World. The Pacific and African ones hardly counted at this time.

While interests, social groups, and regional specifics varied widely from Halifax to Victoria, national political, scholarly, and literary-cultural elites had consolidated by the 1920s in Ottawa, Montreal, and Toronto. New literary styles emerged and artist groups expanded from Ontario to "the rest of Canada." Scholars and writers responded to perceived problems, such as the alien immigrant (male, singular), urban poverty (families, plural), or the promise of the West turning into a revolt of Prairie citizens. The social sciences and the humanities were divided. Self-reflections of writers and artists in novels, poetry, and fine art were segregated into "fiction" or *belles*—jamais *laide*—*lettres*. A third field, mass communication—the press, telephone and telegraph, film and radio, television—emerged only from the 1930s. A concept of interlinked discourses might have shaped research.

After about 1920, professional scholars' analyses replaced amateurs' often thoughtful writings. The historical, social, political, and economic sciences were an integrated field with different questions and approaches, and studied Euro-Canadian society as a whole. The division or even fragmentation into separate disciplines was yet to come. Sociologists looked at issues from settlement in the West to the urban worlds of recent immigrants and, after the beginning of the Great Depression in 1929, to causes of and remedies for unemployment. Political economists placed Canada in the context of world markets and dependency relationships to foreign capital. Historiography, far less analytical, remained close to literature. While based on data, it produced narratives called national but still centered on the St. Lawrence Valley and Ontario. Through the economics of communication, the production of culture and power in communication, political economy connected to communications theory. The humanities, enamoured with mother country or *patrie* "high" literature, disregarded Canadian writing. English- and

French-language literary works were not translated into the respective other language—another missed opportunity for interaction. A "misguided belief" in a "one-way bilingualism in Quebec" assumed that Quebecers were able to read English-Canadian literature in the original, with no "reciprocal expectation" about English Canadians' linguistic capabilities and interest in French-Canadian writing.[265]

French-language scholars' contributions remained largely separate from those of English language, and only in the 1940s did Quebec's Catholic universities establish social science faculties. In bicultural Montreal, some exchange took place between the influential McGill University and the emerging Université de Montréal, while the University of Toronto and Université Laval remained ensconced in their respective culture's approaches. McGill assumed leadership in sociology, the University of Toronto in political economy. Canadian scholarship in English language, distant from the British court and from British life, remained free from court scholarship. Rather, given the country's dependency on an export economy of raw materials in which much of the profits accrued to the respective metropolitan core, it developed an innovative political economy approach to society. At the Université de Montréal, the study of *relations industrielles* as a field of enquiry between economics and sociology became a research topic.

Social scientists asked: How may we improve what we are? Historians, in contrast, wanted to know: How did we become what we are? Thus, implicitly, the writing of history involved a diagnosis of the present and assumptions about the direction of society's evolution. Historians' discourses were shaped by perceived traditions, social scientists' discourses by perceived contemporary problems, and literary writers could deal with everything of interest to them, but, in view of recognition to be achieved and in order to earn a living, they had to insert their texts into ongoing discourses and cater to the tastes of prospective readers. Seemingly, the natural sciences, also still a more or less integrated field, were more rigorously empirical. In 1908, McGill's New Zealand-born scientist Ernest Rutherford received the Nobel Prize for his physics of atoms (*Radio-Activity*, 1904, revised 1905). However, research into the nature of matter undercut Newtonian determinism, the "laws" of natural science. Both in the social and natural sciences, processes of observation influenced analytical results, as formulated by Werner Heisenberg in the "principle of uncertainty" (*Unschärferelation*, 1927). Modern discourse theory could have emerged at this juncture of scholarship and

---

265 : Philip Stratford, comp., *Bibliography of Canadian Books in Translation: French to English and English to French* (1st ed., 1975; rev. ed., Ottawa: Humanities Research Council of Canada, 1977), esp. "Foreword," i-viii, quote p. iv. As regards translations of literary works, bicultural Canada in international comparison ranked between Iceland and Albania.

science. But rationalism and traditionalism imposed limits of acceptable discourses, formed "climates of opinion" (Carl Becker), "grids of meaning" (Foucault 1966), "frames of remembrance" / "cadres sociaux" (Halbwachs 1997).[266]

On the whole, scholarship and literary production remained male-stream. Immigrants from cultures other than British or French were often considered "problems," contributions by them in their languages were not noticed by those restricted to one of the two hegemonic languages. Marginalization and exclusion of "Others" remained an unquestioned practice. A few women succeeded in entering academia but were barred from faculty clubs and thus could neither socialize nor join get-togethers with invited speakers.[267] One-sidedness was deeply inscribed and engendered in nineteenth- and twentieth-century bourgeois society. If university libraries are filled with erudite studies that present "part-ial" views only, remedial work is necessary. Veneration of the past, of the *patrimoine*, often merely cloaks one-sidedness.

The male and female worlds were said to be structured along binary oppositions of reason/emotion, objective/subjective, intellectual knowledge / sensitive experience. They were complementary but mutually exclusive, and women could not become "knowers." Only later did theorists of knowledge production take note of the intimate relation between knowledge and interests. The division into gendered spheres happened to protect men's job markets. Gender separation increased whenever a particular field passed from practical wisdom to theory and construction, from "amateur" to "professional." While as amateurs, men and women had shared the recording of natural and social phenomena and the shaping of collective memory, only men became professionals in academia. Outside of the established Central Canadian cores of knowledge production, women's research capabilities were at least somewhat appreciated, whether in the Maritimes or the Prairies. Other models of gender relations were available even in the centres of the power of definition, as McKillop has persuasively argued in "The Ar-

---

266 : See *American Historical Review*, 37(2): 221 36, for Carl Becker's 1931 Presidential address to the American Historical Association; Maurice Halbwachs, *La mémoire collective* (new rev. and augmented ed., Paris: Michel, 1997).

267 : As students, women had first been admitted to Mount Allison University, NB, in 1858 to classes; in 1875, Mount Allison was the first university in the British Empire to grant a B.Sc. degree to a woman. Dalhousie University, Halifax, followed in 1882; McGill in 1884; U of T—after much opposition—in 1885. By 1920, one-sixth of the students enrolled were women. Royal Commission on the Status of Women in Canada, *Report on the Status of Women in Canada* (Ottawa: Queen's Printer, 1970), 164.

rival of Women."[268] In their reminiscences, women who did gain access to the professions indicated a self-understood feeling of equal capability rather than a railing against male oppression, an awareness of being assigned a secondary place sometimes expressed with anger but more often with bemused observation of men's self-delusions. Women had to insert themselves judiciously. Subsequent writing by men often rendered women's achievements invisible by not citing them. Men symbolically annihilated women's role in scholarship.

Exclusion from visibility of women's and immigrants' contributions to Canadian scholarship and literary production occurred even though the compilers of the first surveys of Canadian writing disparagingly posited that cultural production had been limited and that a "dragnet approach" had to scrape together all kinds of genres and publications rather than to concentrate on "high" culture as surveys of national culture in Europe would have done. This lament, on the positive side, meant comprehensive approaches to literatures. From a Canadian Studies perspective, such inclusiveness resulted in a complex societal rather than a narrow (middle-) classist and culturally elitist perspective. Compilations such as Norah Story's *Oxford Companion* included the writings of foreigners, travellers and visitors, sojourners and immigrants. To intra-societal views these add the perspective from the outside based on different socializations and discourses. In his *History of Canadian Literature*, W.H. New (1989) included inventions and discoveries—insulin, snowmobile, penicillin—and achievements such as Norman Bethune's medical help during the Chinese Revolution. Not only are these developments part of Canadian society and thus part of Societal and Cultural Studies, their previous exclusion also indicates power and hierarchization in national memory production.[269]

---

268 : Lorraine Code, *What Can She Know? Feminist Theory and the Construction of Knowledge* (Ithaca: Cornell, 1991); A.B. McKillop, *Matters of Mind: The University in Ontario 1791-1951* (Toronto: UTP, 1994), Chapter 6, pp. 124–46. See also Database on Canada's Women Writers before 1940 on Simon Fraser University website (as of 2002) compiled by Carole Gerson (www.lib.sfu.ca/canadaswomenwriters).

269 : Pierre de Grandpré, ed., *Histoire de la littérature française du Quebec*, 4 vols. (Montreal: Beauchemin, 1967–69); Carl F. Klinck et al., eds., *Literary History of Canada: Canadian Literature in English* (1st ed., Toronto: UTP, 1965, rev. 1967); Norah Story, ed., *The Oxford Companion to Canadian History and Literature* (1st ed., Oxford: Oxford, 1967); New, *A History of Canadian Literature* (1989).

Chapter 8

DATA-BASED STUDIES OF SOCIETY:
POLITICAL ECONOMY, HISTORY, SOCIOLOGY

At the turn to the twentieth century, the study of societies, whether those of France, Germany, England and Scotland, the United States or Canada, was one integrated field though scholars varied in combinations and approaches. English-language political economy and the social sciences emerged out of social reform and out of the Scottish tradition of a moral philosophy of society. Studies of society emerged from Schools of Divinity, denominational colleges, and departments of "Metaphysics, Ethics, and Civil Polity." In Canada, where research approaches were "colonial" (V. W. Bladen) to the 1920s, during the phase of Canadianization, the social sciences—political science, political economy, sociology, and anthropology—remained a closely related field of research, a "family affair." In the small community of scholars, the men knew each other; with the felicitous organizational setup of the joint annual meetings of most scholarly associations at The Learneds, communication was easy. During their three-martini conference lunches, as one woman sociologist put it, "the boys" decided where to place their graduates.

The men did accept some women, preferably as research assistants or editors of journals. However, the women did not necessarily content themselves with the assigned roles. Some remained single and, in the entwined legal and discourse systems of the times, thus kept their own stature.[270] Helen MacGill Hughes, whose mother, Helen Gregory MacGill, was the first woman judge in British Columbia and whose sister, Elsie G. MacGill, was the first woman to graduate in engineering, turned to sociology through an interest in Chinese migrants and anti-Oriental legislation, and pursued her doctorate at Chicago (1935). With her fellow student-husband, Everett C. Hughes, she moved to McGill. They studied economic change in a market town turned industrial, Cantonville, and she enjoyed "the challenge and delight of doing it all in French." She was not, however, named as co-author of *French Canada in Transition* (1943). Later, back at the University of Chicago, she worked as liaison between the Sociology Department and the *Encyclopedia Britannica* and as managing editor of the *American Sociological Review*.[271] Aileen Dansken Ross, from an established Montreal family, de-

---

270 : Susan Hoecker-Drysdale, "Women Sociologists in Canada: The Careers of Helen MacGill Hughes, Aileen Dansken Ross, and Jean R. Burnet," in Marianne G. Ainley, ed., *Despite the Odds: Essays on Canadian Women and Science* (Montreal: Véhicule, 1990), 152–76. I am grateful to Jean Robertson Burnet, whom I interviewed on 9 November 2000.

271 : Helen M. Hughes, "Maid of All Work or Departmental Sister-in-Law? The Faculty Wife Employed on Campus," *American Journal of Sociology* 78 (1975): 767–72, and

veloped an interest in socio-economic planning while touring the Soviet Union in the early 1930s, when the far-reaching changes still fascinated reformers, planners, and pioneers to a degree that some called this society "the other America." She studied at the London School of Economics and the University of Chicago, and received her doctorate for research on French-English relationships in Quebec's Eastern Townships (1948). She taught at McGill and studied, among other topics, intercultural relations in Montreal and the role of the middle classes in social transformations.[272]

Jean Burnet, born of Scottish immigrant parents, could tie into the Scottish intellectual tradition and, since her father was a printer, into the printers' tradition of reading. She studied at Chicago with Everett Hughes and enjoyed the hospitality of the Hughes family. Fluently bilingual, she taught at University of Toronto after 1945 and, while for Hughes and Ross Canada was one topic among many, for Burnet it remained *the* topic. Her doctoral research into social transformation in a Prairie community, Hanna, Alberta, may be considered the antecedent of 1970s social history. She experienced minoritization in its many guises: as a woman she had to enter the faculty club by the back door (like "negroes" in the United States), was told that too many "Asians and women" were on the staff, and as single woman, had to do the "daily chores" on the department shop-floor: activate members, send out mailings, do editorial work. Single women experienced such pressure even more than wives of male faculty, who were expected to devote themselves to home, husband, and children. Like any subaltern, she was paid less than the masters of the discourse.[273] Eva R. Younge (of Danish background) co-authored with C.A. Dawson *Pioneering the Prairie Provinces, the Social Side of the Settlement Process* (1940). As research assistant, she found little time to publish under her name, and later taught at the McGill's School of Social Work. Economist Rosemary Clark, wife of sociologist Delbert Clark, taught extension classes. In political economy, Irene M. Biss assumed a professorship at University of Toronto and was a member of the League for

Hughes "On Becoming a Sociologist," *International Journal of the History of Sociology* 3 (Fall / Winter 1980–81): 27–39.

272 : Aileen D. Ross, "Sociology at McGill in the 1940s," *Society: Newsletter of the Canadian Sociology and Anthropology Assoc.* 8 (1984): 4–5.

273 : Jean Burnet, "Minorities I Have Belonged To," in Danielle Juteau-Lee and Barbara Roberts, eds., "Ethnicity and Femininity," topical issue of *Canadian Ethnic Studies* 13.1 (1981): 24–36, esp. 30–31; Burnet's *Next-Year Country: A Study of Rural Social Organization in Alberta* (Toronto: UTP, 1951) was the third volume of a series directed by S.D. Clark and "sponsored by the Canadian Social Science Research Council through a special grant from the Rockefeller Foundation relating to the background and development of the Social Credit Movement in Alberta" ("Preface," p. v).

Social Reconstruction. After her marriage to Graham Spry, she taught at Cambridge, University of Saskatchewan, and University of Ottawa. In the 1960s and '70s, she lectured worldwide for the Associated Country Women of the World.[274] Mary Quayle Innis, as wife of Harold Innis, was constrained by duties in the family of which he was not an "active member," as one female colleague remembered. Nevertheless, she published *An Economic History of Canada* (1934) and was also a writer of short stories, poet, and arts patron. For the Canadian Federation of University Women she edited *The Clear Spirit: Twenty Canadian Women and Their Times* (1966).[275] Women were less influential in historiography, a field that had assigned itself the goal of preparing a master narrative, not a mistress narrative.[276]

In international comparison, Canadian social scientists' emphasis on communities and social relations was remarkable. In Germany, the field was state-centred (*Staatswissenschaften*) and combined demography (*Bevölkerungswissenschaft*), public law, constitutional theory (*allgemeine Staatslehre*), economics (*Volkswirtschaftslehre* or *Nationalökonomie*), Max Weber's sociology of the polity (*Staatssoziologie*), and the political sciences. Critical scholars who placed societal interests before those of the dynastic state were labelled socialists of the lectern (*Kathedersozialisten*). In the United States, the Chicago "School of Sociology" developed from a nucleus of scholars in divinity and philosophy who were interested in the effects of urbanization and industrialization on the moral character of society. The originally broad research came to focus on immigrant assimilation. Britain's influence on Canada was complex. Positively, the pragmatist approaches of Scottish scholars exerted a lasting influence; negatively, the aversion of many English professors to U.S.-style empirical sociology retarded development. French-Canadian sociology was based on Pope Leo XIII's call for social justice in his encyclical *Rerum Novarum* of 1891. In the 1910s, political economy emerged from a critique of U.S. capital's penetration into Quebec's economy; from the 1940s, sociology became acceptable and was influenced by the French school of the *Annales: Économies - Sociétés - Civilisations* (later *Annales Histoire - Sciences Sociales*) and its broad multidisciplinary

---

274 : Duncan Cameron, ed., *Explorations in Canadian Economic History: Essays in Honour of Irene M. Spry* (Ottawa: PU Ottawa, 1985).

275 : Innis, *An Economic History of Canada* (Toronto: Ryerson, 1934, rev. ed., 1943). Two of her short stories were reprinted in Donna Phillips's representative selection *Voices of Discord* (Toronto: New Hogtown Press, 1979).

276 : Margaret Andrews, "Attitudes in Canadian Women's History, 1945–1975," *Journal of Canadian Studies* 12.4 (1976): 69–78; Donald Wright, "Gender and the Professionalization of History in English Canada before 1960," *Canadian Historical Review* 81.1 (2000): 29–66.

long-range perspective to complex societies. In the 1940s and '50s, scholars from the two language groups co-operated, in particular McGill's Carl A. Dawson; Georges-Henri Lévesque, a Dominican priest from Lille, France, who introduced Laval to sociology; Jean-Charles Falardeau of Laval; and political economist Édouard Montpetit of the Université de Montréal. Lévesque invited Everett Hughes to teach at Laval in 1942–43 and to develop a program of social science research for Quebec. These men, with S.D. Clark from University of Toronto, probably influenced most sociology appointments into the 1960s.

When Harold Innis and Donald Creighton are named as founding fathers of a distinctively (English-language) Canadian approach to the study of societies, this Torontonian perspective hides the contributions of McGill and Laval sociologists. It misses the input of the League for Social Reconstruction and the Co-operative Commonwealth Federation (CCF) and of Westerners such as William L. Morton. Long before Creighton, a woman, Scottish geographer Marion Newbigin, proposed a Laurentian approach in her *Canada: The Great River, the Land and the Men* (1926). In francophone scholarship, the seminal Édouard Montpetit is almost forgotten. In the training of Canadian elites, Groulx's nationalization of Quebec history resembled Ontario's Upper Canada College-driven Anglo-imperialization. An impetus to modernize, came, as so often happens, from the outside, from Paris where Émile Salone's study of France's regime and British "conquest" interpreted colonization as a social and economic process. But historians "d'une certain grandiloquence" diffused their version of a dichotomous history through the *collèges classiques*. Groulx's Rome-inspired search for the "golden age of the French Canadian nation" overshadowed sophisticated work in the social sciences.[277] The manifold colonial limitations as well as innovative input from European and U.S. intellectual centres resulted in a Canadian academic tradition, dependent and yet distinct.

Canadian universities and U.S. foundations, 1920s–50s

From the 1920s to the 1950s, the U.S. Carnegie and Rockefeller foundations provided 7.3 and 11.8 million dollars respectively to Canadian institutions for education, the social sciences, and research on U.S.-Canadian relations. In the field of education, Canada was part of the Carnegie Foundation's continental approach to civic virtue and self-improvement. It funded

---

277 : Salone, *La colonisation de la nouvelle-France: Étude sur les origines de la nation canadienne française* (Paris, 1905; repr. Montreal: Boréal Express, 1970). Michael D. Behiels, "Recent Quebec Historiography," *History and Social Science Teacher* 17.2 (1982): 73-82, p. 73.

assessments of the state of Canadian public libraries, of educational developments in Quebec, and of the need for public libraries in the Maritimes, where a strong American influence on the region's cultures was recognized. Research libraries "as repositories of knowledge and culture that could provide the basis for intelligent and well-informed human action" were the recipients of Rockefeller Foundation grants. Scholars would be the mediators of "intelligent" action, a concept fitting Canadian intellectuals' notions of their role as a national elite. Finally, in the 1950s, "les études Carnegie" of Laval scholars explored socio-economic factors that influenced school attendance, the choice of professions of graduates from the *collèges classiques*, attitudes of teachers, and educational ideologies. Laval's Catholic educators, increasingly critical of the Church, began to suggest the replacement of traditional curricula with new ones befitting a society entering the age of technology.[278]

In research, the U.S. foundations supported social science projects since, from a U.S. perspective, 1920s Canada was a kind of laboratory in which social developments could be studied *in statu nascendi*. In the United States—not to mention Europe—patterns were more fixed.[279] The interest stemmed from an assumption that understanding of social problems would prevent warfare. The men and the few but often highly influential women in the foundations did represent "a vested interest in the present organization of society and in protecting their gains by alleviating disruptive elements"; the concepts of free and of capitalist societies were congruent. Philanthropy was a form of investment according to business lines to "help solve some of humanity's most pressing problems" and to "enhance social stability." The "'well-being of mankind' . . . was conceived in terms of the values of the

---

278 : Charles R. Acland and William J. Buxton, "A Neglected Milestone: Charles F. McCombs' Report on Canadian Libraries, 1941," in Peter McNally, ed., *Readings in Canadian Library History*, 2 vols. (Ottawa: Canadian Library Assoc., 1986, 1996), 2:265–74; Buxton and Acland, *American Philanthropy and Canadian Libraries: The Politics of Knowledge and Information; Accompanied by Charles F. McCombs' "Report on Canadian Libraries" Submitted to the Rockefeller Foundation in 1941* (Montreal: McGill Univ. Graduate School, 1998); Arthur Tremblay, "La recherche pédagogique," in Louis Baudouin, ed., *La recherche au Canada français* (Montreal: PU Montréal, 1968), 99–125, pp. 118–19.

279 : The recipients of the grants are listed in the Massey Commission's *Report on National Development in the Arts, Letters and Sciences 1949–51* (Ottawa: King's Printer, 1951), 436–42. The Rockefeller Foundation and Carnegie Foundation for the Advancement of Teaching as well as the Russell Sage Foundation and the Laura Spellman Rockefeller Memorial Fund and other major philanthropic foundations were being re-organized along bureaucratic lines. Coordination was undertaken by the U.S. Social Science Research Council (est. in 1923) and, considerably later, the Canadian Social Science Research Council (est. in 1940).

middle classes, or what Terry Eagleton . . . refers to as the 'hegemonic project of bourgeois society'." Thus the philanthropists have been called "sophisticated conservatives" among whom critical stances were fully acceptable.[280] In the United States, the Carnegie Foundation supported Gunnar Myrdal's research on social inequality, which resulted in his famous *An American Dilemma: The Negro Problem and Modern Democracy* (1944). While the trusts behind the foundations did certainly not advocate social peace and equity, the foundations' personnel came from the enlightened elites in search of stable internal and external peace. It might be argued that everyman and everywoman, whether citizen or newcomer, did expect a certain predictability of social and economic developments in order to chart a life course. The exploited and impoverished, however, had little reason to accept a stability that placed them at the bottom of the society.

The foundations' continentalist, but never annexationist or domineering, approach resulted in funding for social science studies on the development of many-cultured stratified urban populations and on the settlement of the West by immigrants from many cultures. The Rockefeller Foundation's grants of the 1930s supported the interdisciplinary "Social Science Research Project" (SSRP) based at McGill University, which could literally capitalize on its long history of high standards and in the process perpetuate its hegemonic position. The Carnegie Foundation's Canadian-American relations research, established by J.B. Brebner and published in 25 volumes from 1936 to 1945 with James T. Shotwell as editor, brought together scholars from the United States and Canada. For sociological research, Carl Dawson, who had studied in Chicago, hired mainly Chicago-trained staff. While the influence of the southern neighbour was already being feared in the realm of popular culture, a community of scholars was still functioning. In scholarship, no "American imperialism" was noticeable at the time when U.S. expansion into the Caribbean and Asia had been under way for four decades. U.S. scholars and the foundations' officers were more innovative than the Canadian scholars. They suggested the study of the Social Credit movement to Harold Innis and S.D. Clark, and funded Leonard Marsh's pathbreaking unemployment study. In a way, the enlightened conservatives supported social reform in order to achieve stable social processes that would benefit

---

280 : Theresa Richardson and Donald Fisher, eds., *The Development of the Social Sciences in the United States and Canada: The Role of Philanthropy* (Stamford, CT: Ablex, 1999), esp. Richardson and Fisher, "The Social Sciences and Their Philanthropic Mentors," 3–21, quotes pp. 7–8, and Fisher, "A Matter of Trust: Rockefeller Philanthropy and the Creation of the Social Science Research Councils in the United States and Canada," ibid., 75–93.

their corporate interests as well as sizable segments of the people of Canada or the United States.[281]

From social reform to sociology: The city and the West

The problems of urban poverty in many industrializing cities of the Atlantic World of the 1880s and the issue of farming families deprived of a livelihood by mechanization of agriculture across much of the northern hemisphere in the 1920s provided the two major impulses for the emergence of sociology as a discipline. Montreal's impoverished lower-class families had been visible to urban reformers and sociologists since the 1880s, Charles Booth and Henry Mayhew documented poverty in London, and Jacob Riis photographed slums in New York City. Arnold Toynbee's "settlement house" in London—a centre for reformers, often from universities, to live and work in the slums—formed the model for the settlement houses in New York and Chicago. At the latter, Jane Addams, Sophonisba Breckenridge, and many other women collected "the facts" on social problems, the empirical data to convince legislators to pass reform measures. From such data, the men at Chicago University wrote their books. The University, originally a Baptist institution, was established in 1892 with Rockefeller money. Its Divinity School and Department of Sociology, in close co-operation, taught under the influence of modernist ideas and the social and psychological thought of John Dewey. This soon-to-be famous "Chicago School of Sociology" attracted a number of Canadian Baptists and initiated research projects on immigrants, in the climate of opinion of the times often seen as a "problem."[282]

Montreal scholars aware of these issues founded L'Association canadienne pour l'étude et la diffusion des sciences sociales in 1892 and the Quebec Société d'économie sociale et politique in 1905. Out of such *Rerum Novarum*-inspired study circles and the French "université ambulante" (1905), L'Action

281 : Donald Fisher, *Fundamental Development of the Social Sciences: Rockefeller Philanthropy and the United States Social Science Research Council* (Ann Arbor: Univ. of Michigan Press, 1993); Charles R. Acland and William J. Buxton, "Continentalism and Philanthropy: A Rockefeller Officer's Impressions of the Humanities in the Maritimes, 1942," *Acadiensis* 23.2 (1994): 72–93. Watson Kirkconnell and A.S.P. Woodhouse, *The Humanities in Canada* (Ottawa: Humanities Research Council of Canada, 1947), mimeographed draft, was begun in the autumn of 1944 by the Humanities Research Council of Canada with the support of the Rockefeller Foundation. It is an organizational, often very general survey.

282 : Stow Persons, *Ethnic Studies at Chicago, 1905–45* (Urbana, IL: Univ. of Illinois Press, 1987).

sociale catholique emerged in Quebec in 1907, which, under the tutelage of Abbé Paul-Eugène Roy, restricted itself to an "apostolat social." In 1911, a Jesuit École sociale populaire (Abbé Hudon) followed in Montreal, with a library reminiscent of the independent mechanics' institutes. In 1920, the Jesuit R.P. Papin-Archambault used such *action-catholique* social thought to organize the first *Semaines sociales du Canada*, subsequently held annually.

Until 1920, sociology as a field had been taught, with few courses, only at the innovative University of Manitoba. In 1922, McGill hired sociologist Carl A. Dawson both for its social work program and to teach sociology. Dawson, a Prince Edward Island Methodist, like many university teachers and reformers had been a minister. Influenced by social-gospel thought, he had studied at University of Chicago's Divinity School with Albion Small, one of many sociologists who originated from a pious rural background. Supervised by Robert Park, he wrote his dissertation on "The Social Nature of Knowledge," arguing that "all culture and knowledge, morals and ideals had social origins." Also influenced by Herbert Spencer's *The Social Organism* (1860), he adopted a biologist "human ecology" approach, according to which higher forms of life push out lower ones. Like Roderick McKenzie at the University of Manitoba and Harold Innis at University of Toronto, Dawson assumed that societies develop toward progressively higher stages. This ideological bias notwithstanding, he thoughtfully explained the growth of cities and regions and analyzed metropolitan dominance over hinterlands.[283]

McGill's new 1920s generation of scholars had "a strong sense of service to the community," in a sense centered on the nation, as the university wanted "to make Canada a front-ranking industrial nation." All resources and disciplines were to be marshalled to this end. Sociology, which replaced geography as the leading field of research, jointly with social work would be the instrument to achieve "human efficiency." While the political economy of staples production looked into the past to understand present international dependencies, sociology and social work were present-oriented tools for repair, "since the war had created severe economic problems in the city, resulting in widespread work stoppages in 1919, murmurings about Bolshevism, and fears of social upheaval." The city's anglophone elite pushed for cost-effective and coordinated social services, and in 1919 established the Montreal Council of Social Agencies. Ahead of other provinces, the government, with Louis-Alexandre Taschereau as premier, passed a public

---

283 : Marlene Shore, *The Science of Social Redemption: McGill, the Chicago School, and the Origins of Social Research in Canada* (Toronto: UTP, 1987), xv-xvi.

assistance law in 1921. When the Catholic bishops rejected government surveillance of Catholic charity institutions, Taschereau stood firm.[284]

At McGill, where teaching had been interdisciplinary, Dawson modelled the new Department of Sociology on that of the University of Chicago. Queen's and the University of Toronto's social work and sociology departments, on the other hand, remained more British-oriented. French-language sociology connected to French academics, especially Frédéric LePlay, engineer, economist, and Catholic social thinker, whose teachings found institutional incorporation in the *Société de l'économie sociale*.[285] In an attempt to influence political and social developments, McGill sociologists undertook two large and complementary research projects, the Social Science Research Project (SSRP) on urban unemployment and immigration, and the rural Frontiers of Settlement study. Similar to the Geological Survey of Canada, both dealt with (human) community and its (regional) territorial basis as foundations of society. Such society-oriented research had to struggle against the past-oriented classical philology departments. In the course of a review of the university's programs to assess whether they were capable of "training leaders befitting Canada's new international status" and whether McGill was keeping its place in the competition with the Université de Montréal, the Dean of Arts, Ira Mackay, commented that issues such as immigration, population, and land settlement were not worth the expense for a whole department. To strengthen their position in the University and to counter the trend toward specialization, social scientists through personal networks secured large grants from the U.S. Social Science Research Council (SSRC)[286] and the Rockefeller Foundation. On this basis, the new sociology department, modelled on the University of Chicago's and Yale's interdisciplinary social science programs as well as on the Institute of In-

---

284 : For earlier developments see chapter 7 "Applied Scholarship I: The Training of Social Workers." Shore, *Science of Social Redemption*, quotes p. xiii. Henri Bourassa opposed this measure as statism and lay interference with religious activities.

285 : S.D. Clark, "Sociology in Canada: An Historical Overview," *Canadian Journal of Sociology* 1 (1975): 225–234; his "The Changing Image of Sociology in English-Speaking Canada," 4 (1979), 393–403, is a rambling memoir. "Socio-National Factors and the Development of Sociology / Les facteurs socio-nationaux et l'évolution de la sociologie," topical sections in *Canadian Journal of Sociology / Cahiers canadiens de sociologie* 1 (1975–76): 89–124, 223–34, 343–85, 499–528.

286 : After the American Council of Learned Societies had been established in 1919, the American Political Science Association, the American Economics Association, and the American Sociological Association established the U.S. Social Science Research Council in 1923.

tellectual Co-operation in Paris, examined "the problems that Canada was experiencing as it became more urbanized and attempted to absorb a large and diverse immigrant population into the economic mainstream and forge a national identity." The U.S. SSRC also reasoned that social improvement was "impeded by lack of knowledge about human behaviour" and that the philanthropic foundations should foster "national research and reform."[287]

The social sciences received a problem-laden methodological input from World War I research on men's capability for industrial production and warfare. Jointly, social and natural scientists had measured work processes and developed the concept of scientific management. They had also undertaken medical and emotional testing of recruits and, during the post-war efforts to restrict immigration to the United States, natural scientists received funding to study migrants. But Mary Van Kleeck, the SSRC's director of industrial research and a former social worker, shifted funding to social scientists. Foundation officers assumed that "the social sciences could utilize all of Canada as their laboratory, a laboratory that was 'unrivalled' because the country was young, in the process of active development, and less bound by traditions than other civilizations." In response, McGill scholars suggested projects ranging from the folklore of Native peoples to classification and measurement of emotions. In this context, the Frontiers of Settlement project, initiated by Isaiah Bowman, the Canadian-born founder of the American Geographical Society, selected Canada as the site of a detailed study in the frame of comparative research on a global settlement belt from Patagonia, via the Peace River District in British Columbia and Alberta, to Siberia and Manchuria.[288] C.A. Dawson and economist W.A. Mackintosh, professor of political and economic science at Queen's, developed as guiding hypothesis a concept of a life cycle of a region from sparsely settled to

---

287 : Shore, *Science of Social Redemption*, xvii-xviii, 8-13, quotes pp. 196, 197. The conceptualization of societies as laboratories acquired a much more ominous meaning in the period of World War II and the Cold War when both U.S. Army and U.S. foundations looked for basic models of social organization with a specific *leitmotif* in each society. The interest behind the research was to facilitate (1) analysis of "enemy societies" like Nazi Germany and imperial Japan as well as after 1945 communist societies and (2) military administration of occupied societies. In the period of decolonization under the global hegemony of the two superpowers, the U.S. and the S.U., the "national interest" behind the U.S. research changed to prediction—"early warning"—of revolutionary movements in developing societies within the U.S. sphere of interest. Thomas Zitelmann, "'Area Studies' in den USA: Strategie und Wissenschaft," *Gulliver* 11 (1982): 140-49.

288 : Shore, *Science of Social Redemption*, 203-4; Isaiah Bowman, *The Pioneer Fringe* (New York, 1931); W.L.G. Joerg, ed., *Pioneer Settlement: Cooperative Studies by 26 Authors* (New York, 1932).

world-market integrated, and of the importance of communication links for the expansion of isolated settlements.

Like the perceived urban problems, the West with its potential to permit economically secure lives for farming families, whether immigrants or internal migrants, ranked high in scholarly and public attention. The West's problems soon became evident, too, first through the struggles of the farming families against the railway and elevator corporations from the early 1900s on. Influences from the U.S. farmers' Granger movement reached Canada's West. Among Quebec's small farmers, co-operative movements emerged, especially in fire-insurance and dairying, but in view of the provincial government's opposition it could achieve a certain institutionalization only in 1919. At the beginning of French-language sociology stood the work of French-trained Léon Gérin on rural life,[289] which could connect to the studies of historians Joseph-Edmond Roy and George Wrong on *seigneuries,* published in 1897–1904 and 1908 respectively. Later, after the Great Depression, Everett Hughes from McGill, at the suggestion of Georges-Henri Lévesque of Laval, developed a "Programme de recherches sociales pour le Québec,"[290] which suggested the study of social dynamics in rural and urban parishes with emphasis on communities as well as on families. Sociological and anthropological approaches still were two aspects of the same field.

Regarding the shaping of agriculture in the West, Canadian academics, hoping that as efficiency-oriented scholars they would have an influential role in developing "the machinery directing and controlling immigration," used an administrative shift of responsibility for natural resources from the federal government to the provincial ones to insert themselves into the new-settlement and resource-exploitation policies. Dawson, who wanted governments both to observe empirically and to control benignly, emphasized the influence of the natural and the cultural environment on human behaviour in his ecological theory. He expected the evolutionary process "to establish an equilibrium and a harmonious social order." The massive research, completed between 1929 and 1931 (9 volumes, W.A. Mackintosh

---

289 : Gérin, a civil servant, never held a university post. Etienne Parent, editor of *Le Canadien*, has also been called an early sociologist. The Union catholique des cultivateurs had a mere 5,000 members in 1924. Paul-André Linteau, René Durocher, Jean-Claude Robert, and François Ricard, *Histoire du Québec contemporain*, 2 vols. (2nd ed., Montreal: Boréal, 1989), 1:555–63.

290 : *Cahiers de l'école des sciences sociales, politiques et économiques de Laval* 2.4 (1943). See also Claude Couture and Claude Denis, "La captation du couple tradition-modernité par la sociographie québécoise," in Terry Goldie, Carmen Lambert, Rowland Lorimer, eds., *Canada: Theoretical Discourse / Discours thérétiques* (Montreal: Assoc. for Canadian Studies, 1994), 105–32.

and W.L.G. Joerg, editors), was outdated by the time of publication, in view of the Depression-induced restructuring of agricultural production in the late 1930s and '40s. Influenced by R.D. McKenzie's theory on the expansion of Western civilization as a product of metropolitan dominance supported by "tributes" from subordinate regions ("The Concept of Dominance and World Organization," 1927), Dawson combined rural with urban sociology and attempted to explain general patterns of settlement. This research connected to the Canadian-American relations study of the Carnegie Endowment for International Peace. Marginal regions were left to anthropologists to collect folklore.[291]

Throughout the 1920s, the McGill sociologists also examined the ecological history of Montreal and the social conditions of its segmented districts, and in the early 1930s research was expanded and consolidated into the Social Science Research Project under a Rockefeller grant. Dawson, in "The City as an Organism" (1926), suggested that Montreal was a fertile ground to test the Chicago School's theories on metropolitan regions. Everett and Helen MacGill Hughes studied urban "race" relations and the effects of industrial change in a French-Canadian community. Their approach was contextualized in theology students' investigations of poverty, social workers' interest in all facets of social welfare, and sociology students' "natural areas" (Robert Park) concept. It was also contextualized by Montreal's role as the main centre for wheat shipment from the Prairies to Europe (until Vancouver via the Panama Canal captured a part of the business), as a banking and industrial centre, and as a service centre with educational institutions, hospitals, and a high level of cultural production. Massive rural–urban migrations and low industrial wages involved emergence of slums, social problems, and the mixing of many-cultured rural internal and transatlantic migrants. The researchers hypothesized that stable neighbourhoods would have all the institutions needed by a community, while deteriorating or slum ones would be characterized by "imposed" or "elevating" institutions. Institutional completeness is a characteristic of self-determined societies; institutional deficiencies open communities or regions to outside imposition.

Fabian-society influenced Leonard Marsh, from the London School of Economics, was hired for the SSRP, but McGill's board of governors withdrew support. Marsh then used his experience with social security in Britain to undertake a study of employment from the double perspective of the demand for labour by major industries and of supply from school graduates and immigrants. This approach involved a shift from emphasis on local

---

291 : Shore, *Science of Social Redemption*, 147–183, quotes pp. xvii, 119. The future U of T sociologist S.D. Clark wrote his MA thesis under Dawson on "The Role of Metropolitan Institutions in the Formation of a Canadian National Consciousness" (1935).

poverty to questions of immigrant adjustment and international industrial development. In 1931, 13.5 percent of Montreal's population was in-migrants of neither French nor British cultural background, for most of whom no jobs had been available in their societies of origin. When in Montreal's bicultural scholarly community no qualified French Canadian researchers could be found, William Roy, a scholar from New England of French-Canadian background, was hired. Out of the SSRP came Marsh's *Canadians In and Out of Work* (1940) and the Hughes' *French Canada in Transition* (1943). Marsh did not shy away from questions of class and, refusing to blame individuals, he incorporated the role of larger socio-economic forces and advocated remedial political strategies, "collectivist" ones as his critics among colleagues, in the university's governing institutions, and in the general public charged.[292]

Self-organized collective action from the working classes remained anathema to most academics as well as the clerical and commercial elites. Based on the encyclical of Pope Pius XI, *Quadragesimo Anno* (1931), and similar in spirit to U.S. foundations, anglophone Canadian social scientists, and Ottawa men, *L'Action Catholique* in the 1930s attempted to insert a new dynamism into religious activities. Its activists strove for world peace by pacifying the working classes, the poor, and the discontented through politics and programs of inclusion. This spawned a new attention to the labour movement. As in other ideologically past-oriented societies, new developments came from the outside: the early Quebec labour organizations from the United States and French syndicalism, which by the time it reached Quebec, "parlait lui aussi anglais." Among Catholic reformers, some argued that unions under the lead of a priest (*aumônier*) should counsel workers. Priests trained in social action helped to establish unions in Chicoutimi and Thetford Mines, of which the former expanded into the Fédération ouvrière mutuelle du Nord. Others joined into the Ligues du Sacré-Coeur and, in 1921, the Confédération générale des travailleurs catholiques du Canada emerged. But two decades later its mere forty-eight thousand members were divided into some two hundred fifty associations. French-Canadian nationalism, as the ideological basis for *"enquêtes"* on economic problems, motivated L'Action française (established 1917), which by the mid-1920s, however, turned against internal dissidents, considered working men and women "our human capital," and blamed all social evils on British rule and Confederation. *L'Action française* had to dissolve in 1928 after the Vatican condemned its equivalent in France as semi-fascist. Thereafter, two further movements attempted to alleviate social problems. Conservatives constructed urban

---

292 : Shore, *Science of Social Redemption*, 195–272. Later studies on Montreal were published by Terry Copp and Bettina Bradbury.

labourers as originating from common people in rural communities, and Abbé Ivanhoë Caron began a colonization enterprise, "un retour à la terre," in northern Quebec in the 1930s. The province's government, aware of the resulting penury and, sometimes, starvation, did not intervene against the scheme. In contrast, Jeune Canada (established 1932), connecting to the Association catholique de la jeunesse canadienne-française of twenty years earlier and initiated by a manifest of André Laurendeau, might be considered a precursor of the "*dégel*" of the 1960s: "les lendemains sont lents et mettent souvent plus d'une génération à venir."[293]

On the level of university education, Édouard Montpetit from the École des Hautes Études Commerciales established the École des Sciences Sociales at the Université de Montréal in 1920.[294] Under prevailing power relations, the École, for a quarter century, could offer only a two-year program of night classes taught in the spirit of *Action sociales* concepts of popular education and reform. This may explain why McGill could not hire a qualified French-language scholar in the 1930s. By 1940, the program included politics and diplomacy, administration and accounting in business, journalism, sociology, and public administration. From 1943 to 1948, the Université de Montréal faculty added an Institut de Sociologie, an École de Relations Industrielles, and an École de Service Social and in 1952 renamed the school École des Sciences Sociales, Économiques et Politiques. At Université Laval, Georges-Henri Lévesque institutionalized the École des Sciences Sociales, Politiques et Économiques in 1938 (in 1943, Faculté des Sciences Sociales) and Jean-Charles Falardeau, whose 1941 MA thesis had dealt with the organization of society as outlined in Marxist materialism, became its first full-time sociologist. At both universities the staff remained small—three full-time positions each in the mid-50s. Looking back from the 1950s, Falardeau commented that Quebec's climate of opinion had accustomed students and academic teachers to "theoretical, apologetic, and sentimental" thinking rather than to empirical observation. He succeeded in making Laval's sociology department the leading francophone one and, in Quebec's tradition of public debate, he was briefly co-editor of *Cité Libre*. The development

---

293 : Jean Hamelin and Nicole Gagnon, *Histoire du catholicisme québécois: le XXe siècle*, vol 1: "1898–1940" (Montreal: Boréal, 1984); Jean-Charles Falardeau, "Vie intellectuelle et société entre les deux guerres," in Pierre de Grandpré, *Histoire de la littérature française du Quebec*, 4 vols. (Montreal: Beauchemin, 1967–69), 2:187–98, quote p. 195.

294 : The Oblate Order established an École des Sciences Politiques et Sociales at the bilingual University of Ottawa. Maurice Tremblay and Albert Faucher, "L'Enseignement des sciences sociales au Canada de langue française," in Massey Commission, *Studies: A Selection of Essays Prepared for the Royal Commission on National Development in the Arts, Letters, and Sciences* (Ottawa: King's Printer, 1951), 191–204.

of French-language academic sociology may be divided into three periods. From Gérin's work to the 1930s, rural themes dominated. In the faculties of sociology at Montréal and Laval, interest in rural issues continued, but industrial and urban issues came to the fore and Falardeau directed parish, community, and family studies. Gradually, as research shifted to social organization and institutions, a critical sociology of religion also emerged. From the late 1940s, research focused on what came to be called the "national" question. The Hughes' research on ethnicity as a factor in the division of labour was re-interpreted by Université de Montréal sociologists as confirmation of the disadvantaged position of French Canadians, and the concept of "ethnic class" emerged. While scholars underrated stratification within the French-Canadian group, they did demonstrate higher levels of property ownership, power, and wealth among Quebec's English Canadians.[295]

After the "social surveys" about problems of the poor in Vancouver, Regina, Hamilton, London, Toronto, and elsewhere—which resembled publications of Chicago's Hull House reformers and Paul V. Kellogg's work with the *Survey*—and after the one single scholarly effort to study the working classes, R.H. Coats' study of the cost of living (1915),[296] the most important work of Montreal's sociology and relations between classes was Leonard Marsh's famous *Report on Social Security for Canada*, published in 1943.[297] Just as French-Canadian thought continued to refer to *Rerum Novarum*, this document on government involvement in the welfare of Canadian citizens was deeply influenced by British ideas. William Henry Beveridge's report *Social Insurance and Allied Services* (London, November 1942) advo-

---

295 : Jacques Dofny and Marcel Rioux, "Les classes sociales en Canada français," *Revue française de sociologie* 3 (1962): 290–300, repr. in English in Rioux and Yves Martin, eds., *French Canadian Society* (Toronto: McClelland & Stewart, 1964) and in Rioux and Martin, eds., *La société canadienne-française: études choisis* (Montreal: Hurtubise, 1971), 315–25.

296 : *Report of the Royal Commission on Relations of Labour and Capital*, 2 vols. of reports, 5 vols. of evidence (1889), abridged edition *Canada Investigates Industrialism*, Gregory Kealey, ed. (Toronto: UTP, 1973); Methodist Church of Canada and Presbyterian Church of Canada, *Reports of Investigations of Social Conditions and Social Surveys* (Toronto, 1913–14); Methodist Church of Canada, Dept. of Evangelism and Social Service, *Christian Churches and Industrial Conditions* (Toronto, [1921]); see also Mary Jennyson, Study of the Canadian Settlement Movement, mimeographed manuscript, n.d., MHSO. Allen F. Davis, *Spearheads for Reform: The Social Settlements and the Progressive Movement 1890–1914* (New York: Oxford, 1967), esp. 12–14, 64–65; Richard Allen, *The Social Passion: Religion and Social Reform in Canada* (Toronto: UTP, 1971), 10–15.

297 : The federal government had adopted a law instituting old-age pensions in 1927, which were limited, however, to persons over 70 years of age disposing of less than $365 annually and payments were limited to $20 per month.

cated a comprehensive national welfare project, incorporating health and unemployment insurance, protection against the consequences of industrial injuries, and old-age pensions. Beveridge, an Oxford-educated economist born in India, had developed his lifelong interest in the causes and cure of unemployment as a resident at the Toynbee Hall settlement house. The *Report* was highly controversial in the British government and immensely popular among the people at large. Marsh's *Report* proceeded from the concept of a responsibility of the whole of society for the welfare of each of its members. Christian ethics via British Fabianism had made the transition to Canadian policy advocacy.[298] But, in contrast to the lively British debates, Marsh's pivotal study became a "neglected classic" (Helmes-Hayes and Wilcox-Magill), the most forgotten study (Burnet) of Canadian society. The author of the next major study, John Porter (*The Vertical Mosaic*, 1965), seemingly was not even aware of Marsh's work.[299] If the impositions of the Roman Catholic Church retarded francophone scholarship, the lack of memory of genuine Canadian traditions among English-language researchers retarded anglophone scholarship.

While sociology was in full swing at McGill, at the University of Toronto it remained part of the Department of Political Economy until 1963, and its four academic teachers came from different backgrounds and approaches. Jean R. Burnet remembered that as students, "we had to give each of them a hearing and reconcile their views as best we might." The Methodist Victoria and the Catholic St. Michael's colleges discouraged students from taking sociology courses. No national scholarly organization of sociologists existed until, in 1955, a number of young rebels, both franco- and anglophone, some of them bilingual (such as Jacques Brazeau), founded the Anthropology and Sociology Chapter within the Canadian Political Science Association. In 1963, J.R. Burnet became editor of the new *Canadian Review of Sociology and Anthropology*. By the 1950s, the Prairie universities' sociology departments liberated themselves from the hold of University of Toronto and McGill dons. But when the 1960s expansion of the field necessitated hiring more young faculty than the old far-too-small Canadian institutions could provide, with the University of Alberta in the lead they hired U.S. graduates in numbers that turned the new independence into just another dependence.[300]

---

298 : While the Chicago School never discussed government intervention, the international context came to the U.S. through President Franklin D. Roosevelt's and Eleanor Roosevelt's call for social welfare programs when Prime Minister Mackenzie King visited Washington. Fearing to be outflanked by the Conservatives, King in the throne speech of January 1943, echoed the U.S. goal of freedom from fear and want.

299 : Shore, *Science of Social Redemption*, 271.

300 : Burnet, "Minorities I Have Belonged To," esp. 25–27.

Political economy: Staples, markets, consumption, and cultural change

Next to sociology, political economy was a pillar of Societal Studies in Canada. Since historiography remained limited to politics and constitutional rule, W.A. Mackintosh demanded consideration of the "Economic Factors in Canadian History" (1923).[301] Two decades earlier, Quebec economists had analyzed industrialization and the influx of American capital. But neither in Quebec's institutionalized religion-based discourse nor in Ontario's monolingualist scholarly community could this urban industrial and present-centered approach gain influence. Rather, Harold Innis's past-oriented as well as pathbreaking staples approach, first enunciated in 1930, became the discipline's reigning paradigm, though at the time of the 1921 census less than a quarter of Canada's net domestic income was produced in agriculture, forestry, fishing, and hunting or trapping. The limited interest of researchers in industrialization combined with the Prairie-centered "golden wheat" rhetoric and Quebec's "*terroir*" mythology perpetuated a discourse, if a highly innovative one, about a raw-material driven Canadian economy and a Quebec economy "*en retard.*" Just as the data did not support the emphasis on staples in the present, they did not support Quebec's economic stagnation in the past. Its economic growth, noticeable after 1871, accelerated after 1896 and surpassed the Canadian average, even though it remained below that of Ontario.

Influx of American and British capital had been at the centre of economist Errol Bouchette's *L'Indépendence économique du Canada français* (1905). Diagnosing increasing dependence, he called for an economic renewal and for abandoning the *anciens canadiens* mythology. His anti-foreign call for economic self-determination, *Restons maîtres chez nous!*, came to be cited again and again, and in the process was appropriated by the keepers of memory to nationalist propaganda with a culturalist undertone, "notre maître le passé," and parish-centered discourse of "*antiétatisme*," which then was meant to preclude state action to regulate capital. Labour, in contrast, was still being regulated by precepts of the Church. The biblical struggle against evil, once waged by missionaries against Native peoples, had long become a struggle against modernization. However, economist-journalist Henri Bourassa suggested strategies to come to terms with economic penetration, with the heavily British and U.S. capitalization of industry: since the public good deserved consideration in matters economic, Quebecers would have to reduce the power of outside investors and achieve economic prosperity

---

301 : *Canadian Historical Review* 4 (1923): 12–25.

within their own socio-economic frame. In a similar vein, the Chambre de Commerce de Montréal as early as the 1880s had called for better technical and commercial education,[302] and Édouard Montpetit advocated experimental and empirical approaches: "l'économie politique est avant tout une science d'observation, très proche de la vie qu'elle s'efforce de pénétrer"; it was a sociological science.[303] With these exceptions, industrialization was not a topic for francophone and anglophone scholars of the first half of the twentieth century.

Harold Innis addressed the relationship between society, economy, and state in global dependency relationships, as well as privileged knowledge production. From pulp as raw material for newsprint he moved easily to communication and culture. Historiography of production processes may not easily overlook the producers, and each production regime resulted in distinct settlement patterns, social relations, and working families' lives. But no working-class historiography emerged. Rather, economic history (with W.J. Ashley and James Mavor at Toronto, Adam Shortt at Queen's, and Stephen Leacock at McGill) and the study of labour economics (with John Davidson at the University of New Brunswick) coalesced into an integrated political economy that only dissolved under the impact of the Cold War in the 1950s into economics (capitalist versus communist systems) and political science (Free West versus totalitarian systems).

The political economy of raw material production or of "staples"—fish, fur, lumber and timber, pulp and paper, and wheat—as a decidedly historical approach was of high contemporary political relevance in view of Canada's continuing dependent position in the world economy. Harold Innis turned the University of Toronto's Department of Political Economy, which he joined in 1920, into the leading one in the field.[304] He had studied political science at McMaster and in his PhD thesis at the University of Chicago (published 1923, the year Mackintosh took historians to task for their neglect of

---

302 : Charles Bilodeau, "L'histoire nationale," in Massey Commission, *Studies*, 217–30, quote p. 217; Linteau et al., *Histoire du Québec*, 1:433–35.

303 : François-Albert Angers, "Naissance de la pensée économique au Canada français," *Revue d'histoire de l'Amérique française* 15.2 (1961): 204–29, esp. 207–211. Montpetit's heavy teaching load and numerous appointments to government commissions prevented him from leaving a broad range of publications—for a long time he was as forgotten as Leonard Marsh.

304 : Ian M. Drummond, in his dry *Political Economy at the University of Toronto: A History of the Department*, 1888–1982 (Toronto: UTP, 1983), listed the major U of T appointments. Innis was head of the department 1937–52; it became a producer of PhDs in the 1940s. The department survived the Cold War but was divided into economics and political science in 1982.

economic factors), he dealt with the history of the Canadian Pacific Railway (CPR), a core element of Canada's political economy. Given the physical size of the country, transportation was a key element in its history. Canoes, via waterways and portages, had carried furs to markets and information in many directions. Horses had relieved prairie farmers from walking the endless miles to the next store. Administrative and spiritual personnel, judges and ministers, went "circuit" riding to their dispersed clienteles. Railways provided access to markets for farming families; for federal politicians they were the steel to forge the many regions into one national economy. In the West, where political institutions were not highly visible, the CPR was considered "the government." Railways were also a means of communication, by travel to kin and friends, by excursions into different parts of the country, or through the transport of the mails and in a "virtual," speedier way through the parallel telegraph wires. Finally, railways were the country's capitalist corporations par excellence.

Innis's next publication, *The Fur Trade in Canada* (1930), dealt with the western half of an Atlantic staples trade centered on European metropoles.[305] The trade's eastern half, also London-centered, comprised Scandinavia and the whole of Siberia. The fur trade globalized the northern hemisphere just as, at the same time, plantation economies globalized the southern hemisphere. The concept of "fur empires" placed Canada in a perspective of Atlantic economies, understood its dependency toward Europe, and emphasized the internal east-to-west advance of exchange, cultural contact, and communication. Arthur R.M. Lower added the lumber economy in a continental and Atlantic perspective with his *The North American Assault on the Canadian Forest* (1938) and *Great Britain's Woodyard: British America and the Timber Trade* (1973). The close connection between politics and economics as well as between both and cultural production is indicated even by the titles of Innis's books, *Political Economy of the Modern State* (1946), *Empire and Communication* (1950), *The Bias of Communication* (1951), *Changing Concepts of Time* (1952). From this emphasis on communication and power a new field was to emerge: Marshall McLuhan's research on technology and communication.[306]

---

305 : William Eccles, "A Belated Review of Harold Adams Innis, *The Fur Trade in Canada,*" *Canadian Historical Review* 60 (1979): 419–41, provides a critical assessment.

306 : Historians who accused Innis of being a "nationalist" mix two discourses: the study of society as a whole and an attitude of nationalism toward the society. Innis was fully aware of the consequences of both nationalism and dogmatic religion. He noted: "War, fetid smell of nationalism the breeding ground of the pestilences of the west, the worship of which kills its millions where the worship of the church in the inquisi-

By understanding the role of raw materials in the global economy, Innis also understood the role of capital—low capital-formation in the raw-material-providing periphery-implied investments from Europe (or later the United States) and thus profits that accrued to the financial and processing core. Innis analyzed the dependent position of Canada in the British Empire and in the world economy—he could have connected to the earlier research by Quebec economists. Later, dependency theorists would elaborate on Latin American countries' relations to the North Atlantic powers, the United States in particular. While Innis understood the relationships between production, politics, and cultural expression, like other economists of the time he hardly looked at loggers in bunkhouses, fishing families on the Atlantic coast, or farming families in the prairies, or at the role of women and of gender relationships. Thus John Hartley's comment is well taken, that in tracing the history of Canadian Studies, scholars should not engage in "ancestralization" and turn Innis into a scholarly superman.[307]

Other political economists decentered the field from its concern with staples. They expanded the empirical and theoretical perspectives to analysis of power concentrated in big cities, by developing the metropolitan-hinterland thesis. They could thus come to terms both with the Atlantic World's metropoles and peripheries and Canada's commercial and manufacturing cores' relationship to the agricultural and logging hinterlands. Yet others concentrated on land policy and agriculture, banking and capital formation, the state and economic life. A major shift occurred in response to the economy's collapse after 1929. A group of social scientists and economists, who might be called "state theorists," elaborated on the role of state intervention into the economy and on the relationship between Canada's colonial economy and the imperial centre. In 1946, W.L. Morton, from the University of Manitoba, wrote a brief but incisive indictment of the staples and Laurentian approaches. Their perspective of heroic entrepreneurial activity overlooked the exploitation of the supplying regions as well as the commercial centres' cultural hegemony over the hinterlands. Ideologically, the staples approach had buttressed the economically dominant position of English-speaking Central Canada. Later, as professor at Trent University,

tion killed its thousands." William Christian, "The Inquisition of Nationalism," 62-72, quote p. 62, in "Harold Innis 1894-1952," topical issue of *Journal of Canadian Studies* 12.5 (1977).

307 : Jane Jenson, "From Silence to Communication? What Innisians Might Learn by Analysing Gender Relations," in Charles R. Acland and William J. Buxton, eds., *Harold Innis in the New Century: Reflections and Refractions* (Montreal: MQUP, 2000), 177-95; John Hartley, *Tele-ology: Studies in Television* (London: Routledge, 1992), 17.

Morton participated in establishing the most comprehensive Native Studies and history-based Canadian Studies program in the country.[308]

From this sophisticated analytical level, several authors pointed to the uneven development across Canada and to the connections between region and class. G.F.S. Stanley in *The Birth of Western Canada* (1936) provided an early re-statement of regional economic and political history. W.L. Morton followed suit with his *Manitoba: A History* (1957). The St. Lawrence perspective was challenged by a reassessment of regionalism: resource exploitation concentrated wealth and power in some regions. Metropolitan centres and their immediate supply belts, with differentiated class structures, relegated other regions to permanent underdevelopment with islands of highly concentrated resource exploitation. A vast differential separated the commercial-financial core and the labour- and product-supplying regions, with respect to class and culture as well as resources available for education, recreation, and social benefits.[309] Morton integrated his commitment to regional distinctiveness into a comprehensive study of *Canadian Identity* (1961). To the staples thesis he added the uniqueness of Canada as a northern land. Politically conservative, he argued that the Canadian monarchy was founded on allegiance rather than on contract, thereby hiding the experience of French Canadians and the immigrants. In a country of "economic hazard, external dependence and plural culture, government has needed to possess an objective life of its own." This may explain in part why he, the Westerner, joined with Ontarian Creighton to edit the eighteen-volume Canadian Centenary Series (since 1963). Morton defined history as "what the community thinks about itself, how it sorts out ideas." He was certainly active in providing historical memory with new directions.[310]

Even Morton did not address the question of the economy of Prairie farming families and other western producers before they became cogs in staples production. Most settler families and working men came without any capital, registered for a quarter section, and began to build local societies. With

308 : W.L. Morton, "Clio in Canada: the Interpretation of Canadian History," *University of Toronto Quarterly* 15 (April 1946): 227–34, repr. in Carl Berger, ed., *Approaches to Canadian History: Essays by W.A. Mackintosh and Others* (Toronto: UTP, 1967, repr. 1979), 42–49.

309 : Wallace Clement, "Regionalism as Uneven Development: Class and Region in Canada," and Patricia Marchak, "A Contribution to the Class and Region Debate," in "Perspectives on Regions and Regionalism in Canada," ed. William Westfall, *Canadian Issues / Thèmes Canadiens* 5 (1983): 68–80, 81–88; W.L. Morton, *The Canadian Identity* (Madison: Univ. of Wisconsin Press, 1961; rev. ed., Toronto: UTP, 1972), quote p. 111.

310 : Morton cited by A.B. McKillop in *Canadian Encyclopedia*, 3:1393; Lyle Dick, "'A Growing Necessity for Canada': W.L. Morton's Centenary Series and the Forms of National History, 1955–80," *Canadian Historical Review* 82 (2001): 223–52.

the neighbours often miles away, even the emergence of a barter economy was difficult. Thus a society of "open doors" and an economy of mutualist help developed. Agrarian produce was exchanged, and fish from Lake Winnipeg and Lake Manitoba was sold over great distances with, at the beginning and into the twentieth century, few cash exchanges involved. Labour was a means of exchange, bartered in times of low demand on the homestead. Since such surplus labour was in demand elsewhere, it involved migration of farmers in between sowing and harvest to rail construction or, in winter, between harvest and sowing to lumbering. Staples production was seasonal and required high mobility and flexibility. It involved reallocation of labour between women and young children on the one hand, and adolescent children (especially boys) and men on the other. This gendered local economy, which involved child labour, has been neglected by economists who selected national-perspectives or global-dependency approaches. A second aspect overlooked in the political economy of production, capital formation, and the export trade is the consumption or reproductive side of family economies, the sphere ascribed to women. Once families had some cash available, native-born and immigrant families alike were interested in spending options and in improved standards of living. In 1884, Eaton's distributed its first mail-order catalogue, which for decades was to exert a strong impact on the Canadian consumer economy and culture from Ontario to the Rocky Mountains. It Canadianized patterns of consumption.[311]

Quebec was part of the staples production and of the St. Lawrence entryway approach. But the study of its nineteenth-century economy remained separated from the study of Canada's other regions. Industrialization implied both social changes and the influx of capital, the latter to the benefit of U.S., British, and Anglo-Canadian financiers. Scholars such as Robert Rumilly have argued that an indigenous French-Canadian entrepreneurial class emerged from the mid-1870s on. Quebec's government, however, preferring large capital to the more limited resources of local investors, deprived the latter of the possibility to accumulate and to expand out of enclosed Quebec into the national economy. Next to the economically informed essayists and editors Bouchette and Bourassa, Quebec's socio-educational system in the six decades from 1900 to 1960 produced only three economists: Montpetit, mentioned above, François Vézina and François-Albert Angers. A few other "précurseurs sans audience" devoted part of their research to economics.[312]

---

311 : Dirk Hoerder, *Creating Societies*, chapters 13–15. See chapter 4 here.

312 : Angers, "Naissance," 207–211; Jean Blain, "Économie et société en Nouvelle-France: le cheminement historiographique dans la première moitié du XXe siècle," *Revue d'histoire de l'Amérique française* 26.1 (1972): 3–32, quote p. 23; Robert Rumilly,

However, Pierre-Georges Roy and Antoine Roy's inventories of notary and probate records provided a basis for local studies of a region's political economy,[313] and several major works on the ironworks of Saint-Maurice and on population development indicated a shift in scholarly interests.[314] Two major English-language studies by women from McGill, on New France and the Quebec City, were unfortunately never published.[315] French-language scholars never arrived at an overarching interpretation that might have challenged the Laurentian or staples approaches: "Cette Nouvelle-France, glorieuse par ses hommes entourés d'obstacles vaincus, n'allait pas non plus se laisser entamer par le modèle du *staple* . . . une optique matérialisante qui ne pouvait que répugner . . . une explication axée sur le voluntarisme incarné dans la 'race'," Blain commented acerbically. Paul-Emile Renaud's early structuralist approach did not resonate with his peers.[316] The dominant French-Canadian voluntarist ideology featuring strong if losing men in agriculture paralleled U.S. (male) popular beliefs in individualism and literary works on the "orphan hero."[317]

While scholars could navigate in the realm of comprehensive theories or enclose themselves in lamentations, the common people's everyday world consisted of the global and the local, for native-born and immigrants alike and regardless of languages or cultures: worldwide economic trends, a war afar (but in the British Empire) increased grain prices, numbers of urban jobs, family incomes. A recession in the Western world deprived families of income and food to eat. Local life-worlds made survival or economic security possible, and consisted of a vicinity accessible through roads and markets, and of schools for the next generation. The national level provided a

---

Histoire de l'École des hautes études commerciales de Montréal, 1907-1967 (Montreal: Beauchemin, 1967).

313 : Pierre-Georges Roy was named archivist of Quebec in 1920.

314 : Benjamin Sulte, *Les forges Saint-Maurice* (1920), Joseph-Noël Fauteux, *Essai sur l'industrie au Canada sous le régime français*, 2 vols. (1927); Georges Langlois, *Histoire de la population canadienne-française* (1934); Albert Tessier, *Les forges du Saint-Maurice, 1729-1883* (1952).

315 : Elizabeth Jean Lunn, "Economic Development in New France, 1713-1760" (PhD diss., 1942); Allana Reid, "The Development and Importance of the Town of Quebec, 1608-1760" (PhD diss., 1950). The same was true for English-language research in McGill's sociology department undertaken by women.

316 : Blain, "Économie et société," quote p. 27; Renaud, *Les origines économiques du Canada: l'oeuvre de la France* (Paris, 1928), distinguished between *longue-durée* economic and social forces and incidental ones like wars, conquests, and epidemics.

317 : David W. Noble, *The Eternal Adam and the New World Garden* (New York: Braziller, 1968).

framework, but in farming families' collective memory only two branches of the federal government had any impact. First, allocation of homesteads gave them an economic foothold; second, the postal service provided communication links to kin and friends in the next town or a continent off (the Universal Postal Union was established in 1878). The social and the economic were intricately entwined. Monolingualism, a mark of elite gatekeepers, was a disqualifier at the local level. Multilingualism, a rudimentary one at least, was required to communicate with neighbours or to do business at a store. Common people's social lives were centered not only on economic survival but also on communication. This was captured, at least in part, by the sociologists of rural life in the Prairies and Horace Miner's study of the seemingly traditional rural parish of Saint-Denis in the mid-1930s, which found major changes in patterns of consumption and a decline of self-sufficiency.[318] The political and social economy research as part of the Study of Canada was vastly more comprehensive than the emphasis on the staples approach suggests.

Political history and political science: Institutions, revolt of the West, Cold War

The closely entwined development of national governmental institutions, the export economy, and population growth explain the connections between political-institutional historiography, world-market–oriented political economy, and a sociology concerned with peopling the country and its cities. In the 1920s, increasingly differentiated research methodologies as well as the new global power constellations changed co-operation between the fields, once combined as "Metaphysics, Ethics, and Civil Polity" at University of Toronto in one department. Canada's involvement in World War I induced political and constitutional historians to assess the Canadian nation-state's position in international relations rather than as a subaltern part of the British Empire.[319] First, the "annex to Great Britain" view had to cope with the advance of the United States from powerful neighbour to world power and largest creditor state. Still, the imperial approach continued to be reinforced by in-migration of scholars from English and Scottish universities. Second, the questions of and funding by U.S. foundations

318 : Hoerder, *Creating Societies*, chapter 5, 14; Horace Miner, *St. Denis: A French-Canadian Parish* [in Kamouraska] (Chicago: Univ. of Chicago Press, 1939).

319 : William P.M. Kennedy, *The Constitution of Canada 1534-1937: An Introduction to Its Development, Law, and Custom* (1922; 2nd ed., London: Oxford, 1938); Chester Martin, *Empire and Commonwealth: Studies in Governance and Self-Government in Canada* (Oxford: Clarendon, 1929).

strengthened a continental approach to U.S.-Canadian relationships. Third, a nationalist school concentrated on the biography of founding fathers in a literary style. Furthermore, specialized historiographic subfields evolved and French-Canadian historical writing remained Quebec-centered. Finally, the discontent of the West with the CPR's corporate-capitalist government expanded from legal challenges to co-operative and farmer-labour movements, and crested in a broad protest movement that gave impetus to a new social history.

The "Canada as part of the British realm" approach concerned itself with the meaning of Canada's new constitutional position. Rejecting interpretations of colonially minded academics, these historians still argued that Canada remained British rather than becoming American. Among supporters of this view were W.P.M. Kennedy and O.D. Skelton, the latter also Secretary of State for External Affairs and biographer of Wilfrid Laurier (1921). This school's most original historian was Chester Martin from Manitoba who became head of the University of Toronto's History Department. In *The Foundations of Canadian Nationhood* (1954), "he pursued and marked out the origins of the process by which the world's greatest empire transformed itself into a community of self-governing nations."[320] Martin avoided a Whig success story, but did bemoan, in a dream of what might have been, the "loss" of the thirteen colonies in 1776. Political historian to the bone, he dismissed all economic factors as "specious" to the story of a nation.[321]

The continentalist school of historians discussed North American similarities and Canadian-American relations. It reflected the increasing interdependence of the U.S. and Canadian economies, or perhaps the dependence of the latter on the former. While J.W. Dafoe's *Canada: An American Nation* (1935) popularized this perspective, John B. Brebner's *The North Atlantic Triangle* (1945) was the major scholarly statement. Political scientists of the Canadian Institute of International Affairs considered Canadian-American relations the central theme of Canada's foreign policy ("Canada and World Affairs" series). 1930s research emphasized south-north connections between the regions of Canada and their U.S. counterparts south of the border, tended to minimize differences, and produced seminal studies on cross-border migration. To this school Canada appeared as closer to the

---

320 : William Kilbourn and Henry B. Mayo, "Canadian History and Social Sciences (1920-1960)," in Carl F. Klinck et al., eds., *Literary History of Canada: Canadian Literature in English*, 4 vols. (2nd ed., Toronto: UTP, 1976, 1990), 2:22-52, quote p. 24.

321 : Other historians included Reginald Trotter; Chester New, author of a biography of Lord Durham (1929); and William Smith, who published *The Political Leaders of Upper Canada* (1931).

United States than to Great Britain as regards class divisions, political institutions, religion, and education.[322]

Among French Canadian historians, the amateur Jean Bruchési, who attempted to remain true to the sources, in his often-reprinted *Histoire du Canada pour tous*[323] took a position closer to Chapais' open-minded *Cours d'histoire du Canada* (1919–33) than to Groulx's ideological pronouncements. Gustave Lanctot published a study of women's migration to Nouvelle-France, a biography of François-Xavier Garneau, and destroyed legends in *Faussaires et faussetés en histoire canadienne* (1948). The Abbé Arthur Maheux, critical of Quebec historians' self-centeredness, in his *Pourquoi sommes-nous divisés* (1943) called for school curricula based on everyday life and the economics of production and consumption—another call that went unheeded.[324] In contrast, Martinique-born Robert Rumilly, who reached Quebec via France in 1927 and gravitated politically to the far Right, despite his lack of scholarly training published a *Histoire de la province de Québec* in forty-two volumes. Some French Canadian historians founded the Société canadienne d'histoire de l'Église catholique in 1933. Michel Brunet, who in 1959 critically commented on the views of English Canadian historians' and French Canadian elites' views of Quebec's peoples, did subscribe to the conquered-people view of French Canadians.[325]

Anglo-Canadian historiography, *en retard* if compared to political economy and sociology, brought forth an overarching interpretation only in the late 1930s. The soon-to-be-dominant Laurentian or Canadian nationalist school was embodied in Donald Creighton's *The Commercial Empire of the St. Lawrence, 1760–1850* (1937), an empire French and British in sequence. Though seemingly related to Innis's political economy of the fur

---

322 : Marcus Lee Hansen with John B. Brebner, *The Mingling of the Canadian and American Peoples* (New Haven: Yale, 1940); Leon E. Truesdell, *The Canadian-Born in the United States: An Analysis of the Canadian Element in the Population of the United States, 1850 to 1930* (New Haven: Yale, 1940). French-Canadian migrations were studied later. See Yolande Lavoie, "Les mouvements migratoires des Canadiens entre leur pays et les États-Unis aux XIXe et au XXe siècle: Etude quantitative," in Hubert Charbonneau, ed., *La population du Québec: Etudes rétrospectives* (Montreal: Boréal, 1973), 73–88.

323 : 1st ed., 1934, 2nd 2-vol. ed., 1936, numerous subsequent editions.

324 : Gustave Lanctot, *L'Administration de la Nouvelle-France* (1929), *François-Xavier Garneau* (in English 1926, in French 1946), *Filles de joie ou filles du Roi* (1952), *Une Nouvelle-France inconnue* (1952), *Histoire du Canada*, 3 vols. (Montreal: Beauchemin, 1959–63), English as *History of Canada*.

325 : Michel Brunet, "The British Conquest: Canadian Social Scientists and the Fate of the Canadiens," *Canadian Historical Review* 40 (1959), 93–107, repr. in Berger, *Approaches*, 84–98.

trade, Creighton erected a new billboard that replaced Ralph Connor and Lionel Groulx's decaying ones and overshadowed Nellie McClung's vision of women's participation. "Parce qu'un pays n'est rien sans un mythe fondateur, on peut presque dire que Creighton . . . a créé le Canada," noted a French historian, and a Canadian journalist stated: "The mythology, the truisms, the folk wisdom we all take for granted, he invented. . . . His image of Canada has penetrated deep into popular culture: some of us were educated by Creighton long before we could read. We are all Creighton's children. He has enchanted us."[326]

Creighton's lasting fame is testimony that many of his readers preferred enchantment to historical information. His synthesis was a step backwards to male heroes and to adventures of discovery:

> "Whether the hero's name was Cartier or Mackenzie, Champlain or Simon McTavish, some half-remembered merchant or nameless coureur de bois, whether his journey and his mastery were mainly one of stout limb and heart or one of the willing imagination, it mattered little; in the hero's act of penetration and possession of the land of the St. Lawrence there lay the central secret of Canadian history."[327]

A less dramatic perspective might have taken the British Atlantic seaboard colonies as a starting point: their ports were open to the transatlantic trade all year, and the St. Lawrence was frozen for half a year. In Creighton's panorama, the railways extended the penetration of the riverain commerce across the Laurentian shield. To the U.S.'s "wild west" this juxtaposed Canada's "last best west" as realm of large private corporations, whether Hudson's Bay Company, the North West Company, or the Canadian Pacific Railway. Since men and penetration were the subject, consumption and women's raising of children were not deemed worthy of attention. The children would be Canada's peoples and history-makers of the next generation. Large commercial networks and, subsequently, benign government control was thus said to have achieved what in the United States had involved haphazard advance based on individuals' guns and the army's collective firepower. The Red River Métis' repression was conveniently bypassed in this story. This literary and artistic Laurentian docudrama Creighton subsequently expanded in *Dominion of the North* (1944), then narrowed his vision.

---

326 : Laurence Cros, *La Représentation du Canada dans les écrits des historiens anglophones canadiens* (Paris: Univ. de Paris 3, [2000]), quote p. 273; Heather Robertson, "The Man Who Invented Canada," *Saturday Night* (Oct. 1977), quotes pp. 20 and 25, as quoted in Cros, ibid.

327 : Kilbourn and Mayo, "Canadian History and Social Sciences," quote p. 36.

While for Innis Canada's development necessitated a new North American (that is, non-European) economy, ecology, technology, and institutions, in Creighton's British-European mind-frame it necessitated a great White man. Prime Minister *John A. Macdonald* (two volumes) in this larger-than-life account evolved from *The Young Politician* (1952) to *The Old Chieftain* (1955). Far-sighted but French-speaking men, such as *intendant* Jean Talon, were not part of this perspective. Creighton's hero "embarked upon the immense journey to possess and subdue the inland kingdom to which the river was the key." On the positive side, Creighton connected the economic actors—merchants and traders—with the political ones, and Macdonald's close linkages to corporations could serve as an example for a political economy of nation-building from the top down.[328]

At the same time, historical writing diversified with reasoned syntheses and the exploration of specific themes in the 1940s and, with numerous publications, in the 1950s.[329] Arthur Lower reflected on economic and social developments in his *Canadians in the Making* (1958), the first comprehensive social history. Others included culture, the visual arts for example. Sociologist S.D. Clark dealt with religious pluralism in *Church and Sect in Canada* (1948) and C.D. Sisson's *Life and Letters of Egerton Ryerson* (two volumes, 1937, 1947) provided an epitaph for this Methodist minister, journalist, politician, and educator, who considered himself the chief guardian of both the Ontario conscience and its non-sectarian education. Studies in intellectual history, often of high quality, appeared parallel to studies in regional and local history, especially on British Columbia (Margaret Ormsby, 1958), Manitoba (W.L. Morton, 1957), and Saskatchewan (studies by Jean Murray, 1950s); on the Old Province of Quebec (Hilda Neatby, 1966) and the Atlantic Provinces (W.S. MacNutt, 1965); and, finally, on the North (Morris Zaslow, 1971). Women entered the field, emphasizing region or, if bilingual, included Quebec into English-language writing.[330] Hilda M. Neatby, for example,

---

328 : "Harold Innis 1894–1952," topical issue of *Journal of Canadian Studies* 12.5 (1977): introduction. Cros, *Représentation,* quote p. 273. Carl Berger, "Donald Creighton and the Artistry of History," in Berger, *The Writing of Canadian History: Aspects of English Canadian Historical Writing Since 1900* (Toronto: Oxford, 1976, 2nd ed., 1986), 208–37.

329 : Kilbourn and Mayo, "Canadian History and Social Sciences," 32–34; Berger, *Writing of Canadian History,* on Lower, 113–36. Old approaches remained powerful in imperial and military history: C.P. Stacey, *Canada and the British Army* (1936); A.F. Duguid, *Official History of the Canadian Forces in the Great War* (1938). In 1945, the Army General Staff re-established its Historical Section.

330 : Beverly Boutilier and Alison Prentice, eds., *Creating Historical Memory: English-Canadian Women and the Work of History* (Vancouver: UBC Press, 1997); Veronica Strong-Boag and Anita Clair Fellman, eds., *Rethinking Canada: The Promise of Women's*

who had studied at the University of Saskatchewan, the Paris Sorbonne, and the University of Minnesota, taught at a sequence of Prairie universities starting in 1926.[331]

Political science, concerned with institutions, at its inception was an offshoot of late nineteenth-century constitutional history. For half a century, its strongholds were at the University of Toronto and McGill, with smaller departments at Dalhousie University and in the West, the universities of Saskatchewan and British Columbia. The Canadian Political Science Association (CPSA), re-established in 1929/30 after its brief pre-World War I existence, was to integrate economics, sociology, and anthropology with political science. Its *Canadian Journal of Economic and Political Science* (*CJEPS*, 1937–66) combined the political and economic sciences.[332] Publications increased in the 1940s, although as late as 1950 only thirty political scientists taught at all Canadian universities. The field remained English-speaking; the *CJEPS* was bilingualized a year before it suspended publication. In 1967, political science and economics split into distinct disciplines and subdisciplines, such as business history (Norman S.B. Gras), emerged. A 1976 call by Daniel Drache to reunite the fields was significantly published in the interdisciplinary *Journal of Canadian Studies*. In result, a political economy section re-emerged within the CPSA.[333]

Political historians and scientists published the "Canadian Government Series" (established 1946; first editor R. MacGregor Dawson). One-volume syntheses of Canadian nation-building included Arthur Lower's *Colony to Nation* (1946), an economic and social study that juxtaposed "the predominantly static, Catholic, and rural French-speaking community and the predominantly dynamic, Calvinist, and commercial English-speaking community," and Edgar McInnis's *Canada: A Political and Social History* (1947), with emphasis on international relations. Other scholars turned to political

History (1st ed., 1986; Toronto: Oxford, 1997; 4th ed. by Veronica Strong-Boag, Mona Gleason, Adele Perry, 2002); Wright, "Gender and the Professionalization;" Michael Hayden, ed., *So Much to Do, So Little Time: The Writings of Hilda Neatby* (Vancouver: UBC Press, 1983); Dianne M. Hallman, "Cultivating a Love of Canada through History: Agnes Maule Machar, 1837-1927," in Boutilier and Prentice, *Creating Historical Memory*, 25–50; Cecilia Morgan, "History, Nation, and Empire: Gender and Southern Ontario Historical Societies, 1890-1920s," *Canadian Historical Review* 82 (2001): 491-528.

331 : Hilda Neatby, "National History," Massey Commission, *Studies*, 205-16.

332 : The annual *Contributions to Canadian Economics* began to appear in 1928.

333 : Peter J. Smith, "Some Observations on the Revival of Canadian Political Thought," introduction to "Canadian Political Thought," topical issue of *Journal of Canadian Studies* 26.2 (1991): 3-4, 179-80; Daniel Drache, "Rediscovering Canadian Political Economy," *Journal of Canadian Studies* 11.3 (1976): 3-18.

biography and, if vastly more sophisticated than the authors of the Makers of Canada series (1903–08; revised edition, 1926), continued to exclude the vast majority of the citizens from a role as political actors.[334]

Just as nation-building had deeply influenced pre-1920s historians, the discontent in the West induced historians from the 1930s to the 1950s to new theory-building. Farming families' grievances, articulated since 1900, gained momentum in the 1920s and burst forth as "the revolt of the West" in the Depression decade. Provincial United Farmers parties had achieved voter recognition since 1919 and an election victory in Ontario. The Progressive Party (founded 1919) and the Co-operative Commonwealth Federation (founded 1932) responded to voter discontent, and Left-leaning intellectuals formed the League for Social Reconstruction (1932). Resulting from the workers' strikes, the farmers' protests, and the new parties, elites ready to cope rather than antagonize passed social legislation: minimum wages and old-age pensions in 1929, and marketing controls such as the Bank of Canada and the Canadian Wheat Board in the 1930s. In two provinces, voters impatient for change carried right-wing parties to power, in Alberta Social Credit with William "Bible Bill" Aberhart in 1935 and in Quebec Duplessis's Union Nationale in 1936. Groulxian Rex Desmarchais expanded his demand for social change (essays *Tentatives*, 1937) to a call for violent upheaval. He wanted a dictatorial elite to turn Quebec into an independent Catholic nation (*La Chesnaie,* 1942). Thus, Quebec thought remained marginal once again.

New ideas came from the West; a new regionalism of both farmers and social scientists provided a counterweight to the Laurentian synthesis. W.L. Morton, in particular, but also George Bryce had argued that the West was as distinctive as Quebec. The historiography of the two Central Canadas, Ontario and Quebec, in contrast was a "nationalized regionalism" since the respective historians mistook their part of Canada for the nation, thus "otherizing" the Rest of Canada. Neither Maritimers nor Westerners accepted this claim, but the Ontario and Quebec historians had the printing presses, publishing houses, and best-funded and most prestigious universities. They could impose discourses. The Ontario-socialized writer Mazo de la Roche, on re-reading her second novel, *Possession*, realized that by setting it in Nova Scotia, "I had gone terribly wrong." Its "strangeness" had led her to include "guidebookish" descriptions into a book that would have been

---

334 : Kilbourn and Mayo, "Canadian History and Social Sciences," quote 2:30; J.M.S. Careless, *Brown of the Globe* (2 vols., 1959–63); Roger Graham, *Arthur Meighen* (3 vols., 1960–65); Donald Kerr, *Sir Edmund Head* (1954); W.S. MacNutt, *Days of Lorne* (1955); Elizabeth Wallace on Goldwin Smith (1957); William Kilbourn, *The Firebrand: William Lyon Mackenzie and the Rebellion of Upper Canada* (1956); William Eccles, *Frontenac: The Courtier Governor* (1959).

"quite able to stand on its own." Thus her third novel is again set in Ontario, "the province I knew so well." Had the Ontario establishment realized as openly as de la Roche its "special" view as well as the capability of Canada to stand on its own—or the Quebec elites the ability of French Canadians in the many other regions to speak for themselves—the development of Canadian identities would have provided more options, might have been more inclusive.[335]

Regional historians drew on U.S. traditions and the Canadian sociologists' Frontiers of Settlement research. For once, no British influence was noticeable; rather Frederick Jackson Turner's interpretation of the role of the West ("the frontier") in American history and Charles A. Beard's attention to the economic factors in the American constitution-writing process were the landmarks. Chicago sociologist R.D. McKenzie's theory of the growth of cities, industries, and of economic concentration influenced Canadian ideas about metropolitan dominance over "the natural region" and about internal divisions of labour. Since emphasis on regions implies variations in landscapes, this approach, like the ecology-related staples approach, has been called "environmentalist," sometimes with an undertone of determinist "biotic" factors, to use the term of the times. However, cultural aspects and power hierarchies were part of this approach. Viewed from the "outlying regions," Central Canada's domination made Confederation an instrument of injustice, as even a conservative Westerner such as William Morton noted. Like Carl Dawson in sociology, historians Frank Underhill, Arthur Lower, and A.L. Burt explored the power and influence of metropolitan centres in the development of Canada. Morton's *The Progressive Party in Canada* (1950) provided a sympathetic account of the demands for inclusion beyond the hinterland role of wheat-staple production that made the West part of the Canadian political process. The definitive statement of the hegemony of metropolitan planning and control was J.M.S. Careless's "Frontierism, Metropolitanism, and Canadian History" (1954).[336] This economic approach was supplemented by sensitive community studies such as Jean Burnet's *Next-Year Country* (1951). Anglophone historians constructed the study of prairie farmers as emerging from a tradition of research on early Upper Canada settlers (Gerald Craig) and forgot to mention the important social histories on *seigneuries* in French Canada.

---

335 : de la Roche, *Ringing the Changes: An Autobiography* (Toronto: Macmillan, 1957), 166–67, 175.

336 : *Canadian Historical Review* 35 (March 1954): 1–21. For a short survey of scientific development see Suzanne Zeller, *Land of Promise, Promised Land: The Culture of Victorian Science in Canada* (Ottawa: CHA, 1996).

While regionalist scholarship included farmers, or better, farming families, as actors in the building of Canada, the class basis of scholars' socialization led them to bypass labour union and working-class history altogether. The federal immigration paradigm that excluded as much as possible single mobile working men as an unstable "element" may have functioned as an additional blindfold, and lower-class men and women had little means to make their voices heard. Canadian labour relations, after 1902, had come under the sway of the powerful and expansionist American Federation of Labour, whose "international unions" incorporated Canadian workers in subaltern locals under the guise of international solidarity. In scholarship, labouring people were merely one party in "industrial relations," and meanings of language changed: "industry" no longer referred to work as in "industrious labourer" but to capital and production, as in "industrial combine."[337] While reformers and social scientists had studied "the poor," if not class relations, historians and political scientists remained silent about Canada's labouring people until after 1900. Influenced by labour relations in the Rockefeller Trust, W.L. Mackenzie King introduced the Industrial Disputes Investigation Act of 1907 both to mediate between what he considered the four parties to industry, and to curb Western Canadian miners' militancy. In his four-cornered scheme of industrial relations, King had power represented twice, as capital and as management, labour being the third party, society as a whole with its interest in continuous functioning of the economy being the fourth. This concept of mediation lacked insight into power relations.[338] In scholarship, "industrial relations" research had been introduced by the Wisconsin School of Labour Economics in the 1880s, at Princeton University in the 1920s, and finally at Cornell University's New York State School of Industrial and Labor Relations. In Canada, Queen's University took the lead by establishing its Industrial Relations Section in

---

337 : Social Service Council of Canada, *A Résumé of Labour Legislation in Canada, 1922* (Toronto, n.d.); Craig Heron, *The Canadian Labour Movement* (Toronto: Lorimer, 1991); Jean Hamelin and Noël Bélanger, eds., *Les travailleurs québécois 1851–1896* (Montreal: PU Québec, 1973); Fernand Harvey, ed., *Le mouvement ouvrier au Québec: aspects historiques* (Montreal: Boréal Express, 1980); Eugene A. Forsey, *The Canadian Labour Movement, 1812–1902*, and Irving Abella, *The Canadian Labour Movement, 1902–1960* (Ottawa: CHA, 1974, 1975); Kenneth W. Osborne, *"Hard-working, Temperate and Peaceable": The Portrayal of Workers in Canadian History Textbooks* (Winnipeg: Univ. of Manitoba Press, 1980).

338 : W.L. Mackenzie King, *Industry and Humanity: A Study in the Principles Underlying Industrial Reconstruction* (1918; repr. Toronto: UTP, 1973); Reginald Whitaker, "The Liberal Corporatist Ideas of Mackenzie King," *Labour / Le Travailleur* 2 (1977): 137–69; Bruno Cartosio, "Strikes and Economics: Working-Class Insurgency and the Birth of Labor Historiography in the 1880s," in Dirk Hoerder, ed., *American Labor and Immigration History, 1877–1920s: Recent European Research* (Urbana: Univ. of Illinois Press, 1983), 19–42.

1937. Université Laval and the Université de Montréal followed in 1944. The University of Toronto's Department of Political Economy set up the separate Institute of Industrial Relations in 1946, while McGill, the leading university in sociology, followed only in 1948. Among historians, attention to reform and labour emerged belatedly. Social democratic historian Kenneth McNaught, in his *A Prophet in Politics* (1959), provided a retrospective on the reform impetus, elevating J.S. Woodsworth to near-sainthood. Only in 1960 did economist and historian Harry Clare Pentland come up with an innovative synthesis, *Labour and Capital in Canada, 1650–1860*. He perceptively commented: "Historians have paid considerable attention to the English capital that made possible Canada's canal and railway building in the eighteen-forties and -fifties, and some attention, too, to the Scottish contractors who supervised the work. But there has been almost complete neglect of the real builders of Canadian public works, mainly Irish, who toiled with pick and shovel." Creighton, the gatekeeper king, had expressed fears of the concept of class in historical writing in his 1957 Presidential Address to the Canadian Historical Association.[339]

The combination of Western upbringing, broad scholarship, and the role of scholars in the Canadian political elite is epitomized by Frank Underhill. Born in Ontario and educated a Victorian liberal, he assumed his first teaching appointment at the University of Saskatchewan (until 1927). Observing working-class militancy, he turned to the British tradition of Fabianism and served as president of the League for Social Reconstruction. With J.S. Woodsworth and John W. Dafoe he was active in the Progressive movement, and in 1933 authored the founding manifesto of Canada's first social democratic party, the Co-operative Commonwealth Federation. Subsequently, as an academic gadfly at the University of Toronto, he predicted the dissolution of Canada's ties with Great Britain and its ever closer relationship with the United States—a prediction that almost got him dismissed from the scholarly British fan club, the University of Toronto faculty. From his 1920s socialist sympathies he moved to liberalism and later became a sympathetic but pointed critic of the Left. In the 1950s, when Washington had become the major external metropolis, he supported U.S. Cold War positions.[340] His interaction with scholars from political science, political

339 : H. Clare Pentland, *Labour and Industrial Capitalism in Canada, 1650–1860* (1960), re-edited as *Labour and Capital in Canada 1650–1860* (Toronto: Lorimer, 1981), and Pentland, "The Lachine Strike of 1843," *Canadian Historical Review* 29 (1948): 255–77, quote p. 255; Stuart Mealing, "The Concept of Social Class and the Interpretation of Canadian History," *Canadian Historical Review* 46 (1965): 201–18, citing Creighton, "Presidential Address" 1957.

340 : R.D. Francis, *Frank H. Underhill: Intellectual Provocateur* (Toronto: UTP, 1986).

economy, sociology, and anthropology reflect pre-1940s interdisciplinary connections, his shift to the Right reflects the mood of the intermediary decades before 1960s scholarship.

As yet marginal: Immigrants in scholarship

The Study of Canada, fixed on the two hegemonic groups and on perceived social problems of Others, never included the voices of peoples speaking other languages. While the new migrant family-created societies of the Prairies became part of the research, scholars did not mention society's underside of persecution of socialists, deportation of impoverished immigrants, racialization of men and women from East and South Europe and, much more so, immigrants from cultures in Asia.[341] "Before 1970 ethnic history and ethnic studies in Canada [including Quebec] remained a highly neglected field of academic inquiry," according to Howard Palmer[342] and Sylvie Taschereau.[343]

During the seven decades from Sifton's call for Ukrainian peasant families in the 1890s to the appointment of the Royal Commission on Bilingualism

---

Underhill, *In Search of Canadian Liberalism* (1960). He summarized his views on *Canada and the U.S. in Canadian Political Parties* (pamphlet, 1957) as North American (but not a U.S.-American) in terms of the "great refusal of 1776" to reciprocity of 1911.

341 : For a more extended discussion of immigration and ethnic history see Hoerder, "Ethnic Studies in Canada from the 1880s to 1962: A Historiographical Perspective and Critique," *Canadian Ethnic Studies* 26.1 (1994): 1–18. A broad assessment is John Berry et al., eds., *State of the Art Review of Research on Canada's Multicultural Society* (Toronto: UTP, 1994).

342 : Howard Palmer, "Canadian Immigration and Ethnic History in the 1970s and 1980s," *Journal of Canadian Studies* 17 (1982), 35–50, and "History and Present State of Ethnic Studies in Canada," pp. 167–183, in Wsevolod Isajiw, ed., *Identities: The Impact of Ethnicity on Canadian Society* (Toronto: Martin, 1977), and "Recent Studies in Canadian Immigration and Ethnic History," in Valeria G. Lerda, ed., *From Melting Pot to Multiculturalism: The Evolution of Ethnic Relations in the United States and Canada* (Rome: Bulzoni, 1990); Jean Burnet, "The Late Emergence of Ethnic Studies in English-Canadian Sociology," unpubl. paper, MHSO, n.d. [c.1980]; Roberto Perin, "Clio as an Ethnic: The Third Force in Canadian Historiography," *Canadian Historical Review* 64 (1983): 441–67; essays by Alan Anderson and Norman Buchignani in special issue on "Multiculturalism," *Journal of Canadian Studies*, vol. 17, no. 1 (Spring 1982).

343 : Sylvie Taschereau, "L'histoire de l'immigration au Québec: Une invitation à fuir les ghettos," *Revue d'Histoire de l'Amérique Française*, 41 (1988): 575–589; Danielle Juteau, The Sociology of Ethnic Relations in Quebec: History and Discourse, mimeographed, Dept. of Sociology, Univ. of Toronto, 1991; Michael Behiels, *Quebec and the Question of Immigration: From Ethnocentrism to Ethnic Pluralism, 1900–1985* (Ottawa: Canadian Historical Assoc., 1991).

and Biculturalism in 1963, four distinct periods of investigation and scholarship may be discerned.[344] The beginning of a debate about immigrants has sometimes been traced to J.S. Woodsworth's positive if biased *Strangers Within Our Gates* and Ralph Connor's anti-immigrant novel *The Foreigner*, both published in 1909. At the same time, Emily Greene Balch in the United States wrote her thoughtful and oft-cited *Our Slavic Fellow Citizens* (1910). But a first phase of "investigations" covered the years before and just after the turn of the century. A second phase, from 1907 to 1929, brought forth more substantive works of educators and writers with specific interests, for example missionary work, procurement of settlers able to buy land, and recruitment of families to fill the empty spaces that seemed to threaten the unity of Canada. Scholars from the social sciences and literary authors paid considerable attention to Prairie settlement through the 1930s and into the 1940s. Wartime unity from the top down—or segregation into camps—marked the end of the period, and Vera Lysenko's *Men in Sheepskin Coats* (1947) and Everett C. Hughes' "The Study of Ethnic Relations" (1948)[345] indicate the turn toward the fourth period. The 1950s and early 1960s were characterized by publications that, though mainly undistinguished, by their sheer quantity indicated an impending qualitative change. This periodization is based on studies in English language, whether published in Canada or abroad; French-language studies appeared only from the mid-1960s.[346] Studies by immigrant scholars in their own respective language could not become part of received scholarship since the gatekeepers of the craft could not read them, excepting publications on Scots, Welsh, English, Irish, and French in their native languages.[347] Thus, a tradition of historiography

---

344 : Donald Avery and Bruno Ramirez distinguish three phases: early "British and French ethnocentric and patriotic works," scholarly controversies in reaction to the mass arrival of immigrants, and a post-1945 reassessment of the immigration experience. "Immigration and Ethnic Studies," in Alan F.J. Artibise, ed., *Interdisciplinary Approaches to Canadian Society. A Guide to the Literature* (Montreal: MQUP, 1990), 77–116, esp. 93–96. See also Howard Palmer, "Reluctant Hosts: Anglo-Canadian Views of Multiculturalism in the Twentieth Century," 81–118, in Second Conference on Multiculturalism: *Report* (Ottawa, 1976).

345 : *Dalhousie Review* 24 (1948): 477–482.

346 : Rosaire Morin, *L'immigration au Canada* (Montreal: Éd. de l'Action Nationale, 1966), and Jeremy Boissevain, an anthropologist from the University of Amsterdam, *Les Italiens de Montréal: L'adaptation dans une société pluraliste* (Ottawa: Queen's Printer, 1965, also publ. in French, 1971). A few novels of immigrants' experiences in French language, dating from the 1920s, indicate a public interest in questions of ethnicity and acculturation in French Canada to which no scholarship was ready to respond (see chapter 9).

347 : On Jews: Abraham Rhinewine, *Der Yid in Kanada*, 2 vols. (Toronto: Farlag Kan-

added its weight to the existing linguistic hegemony. To trace relationships between perceptions of scholars and the wider public, novels about the ethnic experience need to be part of the evaluation of societal incorporation or exclusion of newcomers.[348] During these decades the basic interpretations and terminologies emerged: Howard Kennedy's "New Canadians," James Woodsworth's "Coming Canadians," and Kate A. Foster's "Canadian Mosaic."[349]

The first period, from the 1880s to about 1905, was characterized by a view of foreigners as a problem. At best, this view was coupled with the intention of helping to solve some of the difficulties, particularly through education. At worst, "les travailleurs sociaux, économistes ou sociologues qui ont écrit sur le sujet ne se sont intéressés qu'aux aspects pathologiques."[350] The two major themes were alleged moral and social misconduct, and the pros and cons of bilingual teaching in education. As in the United States, where the compendious governmental reports on questions of "race" and immigration found their high point in the forty-one-volume Dillingham Commission *Report* (1911/12), Canadian activities began with governmental investigations of those outsiders considered most offensive, "Orientals" and Italians: Chinese immigration 1885, Chinese and Japanese immigration 1902, Chinese

---

ada, 1925, 1927); Benjamin Gutelius Sack, *Geshikhte fun Yidn in Kanade: fun di friste unheybn bis der letster tsayt* (Montreal, 1948), as *History of the Jews in Canada* transl. from the Yiddish by R. Novek, Montreal: Harvest House, 1965). On Magyars: Ödön Paizs, *Magyarok Kanadában: Egy most készülö országról* (Budapest: Athenaeum, 1928); Jenö Ruzsa, *A Kanadai Magyarság Története* (Toronto, 1940). On Doukhobors: V.A. Sukhorev, *Istoriya Dukhobotsev* (Grand Forks, BC, 1944). On Poles: B.J. Zubrzycki, *Polacy w Kanadzie* (1759–1946) (Toronto: Kongres Polonji Kanadyskiej, 1947). On Russians: G. Okulevich, *Russkie v Kanade* (Toronto: Federatsii Russkikh Kanadtsev, 1952). On Italians: Guglielmo Vangelisti, *Gli Italiani in Canada* (1st ed., n.p., Italy, 1955; 2nd rev. ed., Montreal: Chiesa italiana di N. S. della Difesa, 1958).

348 : For studies of ethnic groups in English-Canadian or French-Canadian literature and for ethnic literatures see John P. Miska, *Ethnic and Native Canadian Literature: A Bibliography* (Toronto: UTP, 1990); Tamara J. Palmer, "Ethnic Response to the Canadian Prairies, 1900–1950," *Prairie Forum* 12 (Spring 1987): 49–74; Joseph Pivato, ed., *Contrasts: Comparative Essays in Italian-Canadian Writing* (Montreal: Guernica, 1985); Jars Balan, ed., *Identifications: Ethnicity and the Writer in Canada* (Edmonton: Canadian Inst. of Ukrainian Studies, Univ. of Alberta, 1982).

349 : Howard Angus Kennedy, *New Canada and the New Canadians* (Toronto: Mousson, 1907); James Shaver Woodsworth, *Strangers Within Our Gates, or Coming Canadians* (Winnipeg: Methodist Church, 1909, repr. Toronto: UTP, 1972); Kate A. Foster, *Our Canadian Mosaic* (Toronto: YWCA Dominion Council, 1926).

350 : Taschereau, "L'histoire de l'immigration," 577, subsumes under this judgment the scholarship of the whole first half of the twentieth century.

immigrants' property losses during the 1907 riots, the Italian *padrone* system in 1904. The North-West Mounted Police in its annual reports often labelled immigrants as deviant.[351] The debate on the "school question" involved a controversy between educators who felt they were dealing with Europe's "ignorant peasantry" and those who viewed the immigrants as a challenge. A survey published in 1913 by Norman F. Black concluded this period. In Canadian literature, immigrants hardly made a debut. Only Mary Esther MacGregor (pseudonym Marian Keith) described the "insularity" of settlers from the British Isles, whose Scottish, English, and Irish distinctiveness and ethnic chauvinism as yet precluded a monocultural charter-group stance.[352]

In the second period, "a charitable, if prejudiced social survey approach" emerged. Reformers were interested in the spiritual salvation and social well-being of the foreign-born. Some wanted to develop social policies and Canadianization programs. The pamphlets of nativists and exclusionists were shrill and uninformed.[353] Howard A. Kennedy's sweeping survey of the Western Canadian scene was intended to provide more information for immigrants than did government publications. He interpreted the mass arrivals as comparable to the "Aryan flood that laid the foundations of Europe," to "the taking of England by the Angles and Saxons," and to the westward movement in the United States, which "gave new homes and new life, prosperity and independence, to millions of the struggling poor of Europe." Once settled, the newcomers provided business with "a vast new source of food supply for Europe and Asia," which would result in Canada's "rapid rise" to a "commanding position in the politics of the globe."[354] In 1909, authors with opposing approaches published a romantic account of the Brit-

---

351 : Royal Commission on Chinese Immigration, *Report and Evidence* (Ottawa, 1885; repr. New York: Arno, 1978); Royal Commission on Chinese and Japanese Immigration: *Report* (Ottawa: Dawson, 1902; repr. New York: Arno, 1978); Royal Commission Appointed to Inquire into the Immigration of Italian Labourers to Montreal and the Alleged Fraudulent Practices of Employment Agencies (Ottawa: Department of Labour, 1904); *Royal Commission to Investigate the Losses Sustained by the Chinese Population in the City of Vancouver on the Occasion of the Riots in that City, Sept. 1907*, 4 vols. (Vancouver, 1908). Canadians' resort to violence against immigrants was investigated by the government of India: *Report of the "Komagata Maru" Committee of Inquiry* (Calcutta, 1914).

352 : Mary Esther MacGregor, *The Silver Maple: A Tale of Upper Canada* (New York[?]: 1906 or 1908 [?]).

353 : For example Stephen Leacock, "Canada and the Immigration Problem," *National and English Review* (April 1911), 316–327, and George Exton Lloyd, "Immigration and Nation Building," *Empire Review* (Feb. 1929), 105–106.

354 : Kennedy, *New Canada*, quotes pp. 13–17.

ish "pioneers" in Lord Selkirk's colony (founded 1812, George Bryce), with no attention to the neighbouring French-Métis and Roman Catholic Saint-Boniface (founded 1818), and a factual though biased report on "strangers" in Winnipeg after 1900 (J.S. Woodsworth). The Methodist minister Woodsworth, under the influence of the university settlement house movement in East London and New York's reformers, was superintendent of Winnipeg's All People's Mission[355] in North End since 1904, when the city was the gateway and the tollgate to the prairies. Woodsworth's ethos and his textbooks for practical work proceeded from Leviticus 19:34: "The stranger that sojourns with you shall be unto you as the homeborn among you, and thou shalt love him as thyself."[356] While the propagandist of the Empire, Rudyard Kipling, had rephrased the text to imply more distance: "The stranger within my gate / He may be true or kind, / But he does not talk my talk - / I cannot feel his mind." Woodsworth tried to understand immigrant men and women, and *Strangers Within Our Gates* was hailed by contemporary reviewers as a "pioneer sociological study."[357]

Utilitarian works on land granting policies, the economic value of settlers, and their "national character" also appeared.[358] Labour migration to Canada roused the interest of scholars abroad with a sociological study of Canadian immigrant navvies published in New York, a study on Native workers on the Pacific Coast published in Berlin, and another on Chinese "coolie" migration published in London.[359] While settlers came within the framework of the Atlantic economies, workers were part of a worldwide migration pattern supported by capital flows and military moves within the British Empire.[360] The controversy about immigrants from Asia was reflected in increased

---

355 : Isaiah 5-7: "My house shall be called a house of prayer for all people."

356 : Cf. also Deut. 13:12-13. Richard Allen, "Introduction" to the reprint edition of Woodsworth, *My Neighbor* (Toronto: UTP, 1972), vi-xix.

357 : Cited in Marilyn Barber's "Introduction" to the 1972 edition of *Strangers*. Biographies of Woodsworth have been published by Olive Ziegler (1934), Frank H. Underhill (1944), Grace MacInnis (1953), and Kenneth McNaught (1959).

358 : Peter H. Bryce, *The Value to Canada of the Continental Immigrant* (Ottawa: privately published, 1928); Robert England, *The Central European Immigrant in Canada* (Toronto: Macmillan, 1929).

359 : Edmund W. Bradwin, *Bunkhouse Man: A Study of Work and Pay in the Camps of Canada, 1903-1914* (New York, 1928; repr. Toronto UTP, 1972); Rajani Kanta Das, *Hindustani Workers on the Pacific Coast* (Berlin, 1923); Persia Crawford Campbell, *Chinese Coolie Emigration to Countries Within the British Empire* (London: King, 1923).

360 : Dirk Hoerder, "Migration in the Atlantic Economies: Regional European Origins and Worldwide Expansion," in Hoerder and Leslie P. Moch, eds., *European Migrants: Global and Local Perspectives* (Boston: Northeastern Univ. Press, 1996), 21-51.

scholarly and polemical output in the 1920s.[361] Robert England, teacher and later Continental Superintendent of the Canadian National Railway's Colonization Department, concisely summarized the issues in terms echoed by the American foundations when supporting research on the process of settlement: "In these vast plains of Western Canada there is being wrought an experiment in racial [i.e. ethnic] co-operation deserving to be more widely known." He added: "There is no experiment in the British Empire like it; nor is there one that will test so severely, and perhaps endanger, our British ideals and those things we love."[362]

At the time of the Diamond Jubilee of Confederation in 1927, the stage was being set for a new level of scholarship, ironically by another bitter debate over the qualities of immigrants and over immigration policy as part of nation-building. Essays appeared under topics such as "Moulding a Nation" or "The Case for a Quota." Serious contributions were published mainly in the *Queen's Quarterly* and *Dalhousie Review*, the more one-sided pieces in the appropriately titled *National and English Review* or the *Empire Review*.[363] This third period encompassed the prolific 1930s and the war years of the 1940s. The policy to populate the West had achieved its results: "New Canadians" were settled in large numbers, but social, economic and political discontent was high. During the post-World War I depression, coupled with a tight money policy, wheat prices tumbled by 45 percent, the Social Gospel approach lost its impact, and the Winnipeg General Strike was ended by troops. Rather than a new "problems" approach, a political economy and class-based approach emerged; the League for Social Reconstruction mediated between politics and the social commitment of academics.

The inclusiveness of research expanded. Studies of the "visible" groups, "Black people" and "Orientals," now differentiated into Chinese, Japanese and Sikhs, included reformist authors who "wanted to improve race relations through objective description and analysis of the Japanese Canadian community and its history" (Young et al. 1938).[364] Of the groups of Euro-

---

361 : Hilda Glynn-Ward (= Hilda G. Howard), *The Writing on the Wall* (Vancouver: Sun, 1921; repr. Toronto: UTP, 1974); S.S. Osterhout, *Orientals in Canada: The Story of the Work of the United Church of Canada with Asiatics in Canada* (Toronto: Ryerson, 1929).

362 : England, *The Central European Immigrant*, 8–10.

363 : Select Committee on Immigration, *Report* (Ottawa, 1928). E.K. Chicanot, 1929; W.A. Carrothers, 1929; W. Burton Hurd, 1929; Arthur Lower, 1930. See above for the exclusionists' writings.

364 : African-Canadians: Ida Greaves, 1930; MA theses by Wilfried E. Israel, 1928, and Harold H. Potter, 1949. Asian-Canadians and Japanese "relocation:" H.F. Angus, 1931 and 1933; Forrest E. LaViolette, 1948; historiographical survey by W. Peter Ward, *The Japanese in Canada* (Canada's Ethnic Groups, no. 3; Ottawa, 1982). One study on Chinese

pean background, the Scots, Jews, and Ukrainians received the most attention with a "contribution history" approach, or one of predominating filiopietism. Research was also devoted to the ethno-religious groups.[365] On a provincial rather than national level, research into the impact of ethnocultural groups was initiated in the mid-forties by the Historical and Scientific Society of Manitoba under the lead of Margaret Stovel McWilliams. Almost forgotten today, she was also one of the few authors to pay attention to women's history and "had aided in the writing" of *Women of the Red River* (1923). The emphasis on integration motivated detailed research on specific economic opportunities. Usually of "applied" and local significance, such studies were a facet of pre-1960s multidisciplinary Ethnic Studies.[366]

Fiction about newcomers, that is, the emotional, playful, tentative and tantalizing incorporation of the immigrant experience, was less than developed.[367] Thus, Watson Kirkconnell, translator, scholar, and humanist, set out to spread knowledge about immigrants' cultures, but rather than their own writings he focused on literature in their European cultures of origin.[368] Educated in the Anglo-Canadian tradition, Kirkconnell almost accidentally came into contact with immigrant cultures and, while teaching at Winnipeg's Wesley College, he translated verse from some fifty European

---

immigration done at the University of Toronto was published in Shanghai (Tien-Fang Cheng, 1931). Charles H. Young, Helen Richmond Young Reid, William A. Carrothers, ed. by H.A. Innis, *The Japanese Canadians* (Toronto: UTP, 1938). Even those concerned with problems—the Canadian National Committee for Mental Hygiene—rather than publishing denigrating pamphlets hired sociologists to study the two groups, Japanese and Ukrainians, considered the most difficult ones to Canadianize.

365 : A statistical basis for studies of specific groups was provided by Census Monographs (1921 to 1941 census). The author (Hurd, 1929) was heavily anti-alien; see similar publications 1937 and 1941. No analysis of the 1951 census exists. Donald Avery *"Dangerous Foreigners": European Immigrant Workers and Labour Radicalism in Canada, 1896-1932* (Toronto: McClelland & Stewart, 1983), 115.

366 : McWilliams, *Manitoba Milestones* (1928); Beverly Rasporich, "Retelling Vera Lysenko: A Feminist and Ethnic Writer," *Canadian Ethnic Studies* 21 (1989): 38–52; R.S. Elliot, for example, studied immigrant truck farming, *The Marketing of Fresh Fruits and Vegetables in Greater Winnipeg* (1946).

367 : For an interpretation see Tamara Palmer, "Ethnic Character and Social Themes in Novels about Prairie Canada in the Period from 1900 to 1940" (MA thesis, York Univ., 1972), and Dick Harrison, *Unnamed Country: The Struggle for a Canadian Prairie Fiction* (Edmonton: Univ. of Alberta Press, 1977).

368 : J.R.C. Perkin, ed., *The Undoing of Babel: Watson Kirkconnell, The Man and His Work* (Toronto: McClelland & Stewart, 1975), and Kirkconnell's autobiography, *A Slice of Canada: Memoirs* (Toronto: UTP, 1967), containing a complete listing of his works.

peoples into English.[369] While some clerics, professors, and politicians denounced the "mass of foreign ignorance and vice," Kirkconnell "set out to combat ignorance" and bring about "sincere co-operation whether in the New World or in the Old." He pointedly informed his readers from the two dominant groups that the volume of the New Canadians' writings had surpassed that published in Quebec-French for three decades and, in the West, was actually surpassing that of the Anglo-Canadians. He advocated a cultural "confederation" with "recognition" of the immigrants' history, languages, and literatures in schools and universities, a "co-operative existence" that presaged a policy of multiculturalism. At the same time, John Murray Gibbon, publicity agent for the CPR first in Europe then in Montreal, prepared his *Canadian Mosaic*, a historical, ethnographical, and literary portrait of some thirty ethnic groups. This informative but highly eclectic study of 1938 intended to make Canadians understand themselves as people of many backgrounds.[370]

Kirkconnell's commitment to international understanding, however, had rigorous limits. After an early uncompromising critique of fascism, he moved to a rigorous Canadian-Unity stance during World War II. He still helped to convince native-born Canadians of the loyalty of the immigrants, as these groups themselves struggled to do. At the same time, U.S. magazines such as *Common Ground* and the "Nation of Nations" series of Slovene-American writer Louis Adamic attempted to bring the literature of new Americans to the attention of the old, to prevent the American Dream from turning "into the Nightmare of Intolerance."[371] But from 1939 to 1945 these humanitarian approaches served the purpose of wartime uniformity of public opinion.[372] Kirkconnell changed to a rabid Cold War position and with other eminent native-born Canadian authors supported persecution of the political Left

---

369 : Kirkconnell, *European Elegies* (Ottawa: Graphic, 1928), the book had been rejected by several major European publishers. W.H. New, "Watson Kirkconnell," in *Dictionary of Literary Biography*, 68:188–193; N.F. Dreisziger, "Watson Kirkconnell and the Cultural Credibility Gap between Immigrants and the Native-Born in Canada," in Kovacs, ed., *Ethnic Canadians*, 87–96, esp. 89–91.

370 : Janet McNaughton, "John Murray Gibbon and the Inter-War Folk Festivals," *Canadian Folklore* 3 (1981): 67–73.

371 : See the essays by Gudrun Birnbaum, William C. Beyer (quote p. 233), and John L. Modic in *Louis Adamic: Symposium* (Ljubljana: Univerza Edvarda Kardelja, 1981).

372 : In the United States, Foreign Language Information Service, reorganized as Common Council for American Unity in 1940; in Canada, Committee on Co-operation in Canadian Citizenship, Communities of Recent European Origin, established in January 1942 by the Department of National War Services.

among the New Canadians, including their cultural expressions.[373] Only a few authors remained critical toward the internal consequences of war, the exclusionist-initiated debate of the late 1920s having been transformed to a "Canadian-All" stance in the 1940s. It excluded those perceived as radical as un-Canadian.[374] On the positive side, Laura Goodman Salverson's and Vera Lysenko's immigrant novels presented early ethnic women's points of view.

The fourth period, the two decades between the sociological approach and the emergence of multiculturalism, began with a lull of research in the immediate post-war years and the considerable output of the 1950s remained undistinguished. Noteworthy was the attention paid to ethno-religious groups; to politically "clean" groups, such as Dutch and Icelandic immigrants; and to Hungarian Canadians after the stream of refugees from the 1956 anti-communist uprising. A modest interest in the history of labour and the Left also became noticeable. But an account of the communist movement by an activist and D.C. Masters' study of the Winnipeg General Strike devoted little space to immigrants.[375] In contrast to the intellectually fascinating thirties, the Cold War and the right-wing backlash to the Depression reforms resulted in intellectual drabness. Immigrant groups hid their radical pasts; academics practised thought-control.

The works of lasting significance were a mere half dozen publications: Jean Burnet's investigation of rural social organization in Alberta (1951), which linked the sociology of the 1930s to the community studies of the 1960s; W.L. Morton's *The Progressive Party of Canada* (1950); two sociological studies of specific groups, LaViolette on the Japanese (1948) and Peterson on the Dutch (1955); and a few essays on methodological questions, Vallée et al. on ethnic assimilation and differentiation (1957) and the study of group formation by Breton and Pinard (1960). Given the increased awareness about the impact of gender in the writing of history, it is noteworthy

---

373 : Cf. for earlier developments Avery, *"Dangerous Foreigners."* Myrna Kostash, in *All of Baba's Children* (1977), wrote about the suppression of the Ukrainian-Canadian Left and, more than 30 years after the events, was bitterly criticized for deviating from the group's self-description.

374 : Kirkconnell, *Canadian Overtones* (Winnipeg, 1935), 3–6; *The Ukrainian Canadians and the War* (1940), *Canadians All* (Ottawa: Minister of National War Services, 1941). See also such publications as R.A. Davies, *This Is Our Land: Ukrainian Canadians Against Hitler* (Toronto, 1943), or John M. Gibbon, *The New Canadian Loyalists* (Toronto, 1941). For new approaches see Louis Dudek and Michael Gnarowski, eds., *The Making of Canadian Poetry* (Toronto: Ryerson, 1967), Chap. "Other Canadians," and Balan, ed., *Identifications* (1981).

375 : Tim Buck, *Thirty Years, 1922–1952: The Story of the Communist Movement in Canada* (Toronto, 1952); D.C. Masters, *The Winnipeg General Strike* (Toronto: UTP, 1950). Further publications appeared only in the late 1960s.

that Vera Lysenko, in an approach much broader than that of Paul Yuzyk (1953), combined scholarship with literary reflections of the immigrant experience. Thirty years later Myrna Kostash and Helen Potrebenko took up this comprehensive perspective that had not been forthcoming from established (mainly male) scholarship.

To summarize, the semi-colonial attitude of historians as well as politicians prevented recognition of non-British and non-French achievements. The efforts to Canadianize immigrants were undercut by the mentally dependent officials who did not even think of adding a category "Canadian" to ethnic affiliations in the census forms until 1951. On the French-Canadian side, introspection prevented any active input into immigration scholarship. Finally, in the early 1960s, a new generation of scholars developed innovative social, historical, and humanities-based Ethnic Studies approaches. Their extensive reference to U.S. research indicated that the support of an outside perspective, of a non-colonial discourse, was helpful to propose new ideas in Canada.

Twice marginalized: "Indians" and folk and the emergence of anthropology and ethnohistory

The "Canadians All" stance never included "Indians," and the research field "ethnology" never achieved the status of the nationhood narratives of historiography. Ethnologists and anthropologists, with few exceptions, were slow in freeing themselves from preconceptions about lesser peoples and, thus self-encapsulated, developed no refined methodologies similar to those of sociologists for the study of the urban poor or marginal western farming families. The collectors' and scholars' pursuit of people's "original" cultures was an approach first criticized by the Swedish *folklivs-forskning* of Sigurd Erixson and by Polish ethnologists, who approached regional peasant cultures in their societies with analytical rigour.

When in the 1930s it became evident that First Peoples would not assimilate and that decimated though they were, there was no reason to assume they would die out, scholarly interest grew. The museum or collecting phase of dealing with "folk" and first cultures gave way to a university-centered phase. Building on the work of Edward Sapir on languages, and on Franz Boas for anthropological theory, scholars came to reject the concept of a unilinear development of humankind according to which some peoples had evolved less far along one single upward-bound timeline. External influences could activate different potentialities of an existing culture; economic, social, and religious practices might have different behavioural outcomes among different peoples; and cultures evolved in response to collective needs. Like Johann Gottfried Herder did for the peoples of East Central Europe, Boas argued that First Peoples' cultures may be understood only in their own terms of reference.

To ethnology, which collected the "lore"—the knowledges and wisdoms— of local and regional societies, many women scholars contributed: from the 1900s, Violetta Halpert and Ethel Mackenzie, whose husbands Herbert Halpert and W. Roy Mackenzie are better remembered; Helen Creighton in Nova Scotia from the late 1920s;[376] and from the 1950s, Catherine Jolicoeur among New Brunswick's Acadians and Jean Heffernan among miners and the Irish in Nova Scotia. The multi-talented Edith Fowke—active in the Co-operative Commonwealth Federation, the Fellowship of Reconciliation, and the Women's International League for Peace and Freedom, the Co-operative Committee for Japanese Canadians, the *Canadian Forum*, and the Woodsworth Memorial Foundation—introduced common Canadians to many-cultured voices through her CBC program *Folk Song Time* in the 1950s. She translated French-Canadian songs into English to familiarize monolingual British Canadians with this cultural output of their country. All of these women were close to the communities whose traditions they collected. But they saw them in terms of traditions rather than in terms of evolution toward urban, industrial, and consumer lives.[377]

From the 1930s, scholars refined approaches. Starting either from Harold Innis's study of the fur economy or from Thomas F. McIllwraith's archaeological-anthropological work, they relied on archaeological artifacts and the archives of the Hudson's Bay Company but rejected First People's oral testimony as a valid source to study pre-contact cultures, the fur economy, or early Native–European cultural exchange. While U.S. scholar George T. Hunt still concentrated on conflict (*The Wars of the Iroquois*, 1940), and Léo-Paul Desrosiers noted the Iroquois' contribution to the evolution of

---

376 : Beginning her work in the late 1920s, Creighton received support from the Rockefeller Foundation and the National Museum. Creighton, *A Life in Folklore* (Toronto: McGraw-Hill Ryerson, 1975). Ian McKay, *The Quest of Folk: Antimodernism and Cultural Selection in Twentieth-Century Nova Scotia* (Montreal: MQUP, 1994), has criticized Creighton for creating a "false identity" of a united, anti-modern folk.

377 : Pauline Greenhill and Diane Tye, eds., *Undisciplined Women: Tradition and Culture in Canada* (Montreal: MQUP, 1997), essays by Ronald Labelle on Jolicoeur, 28–38, Fowke, 39–48, Diane Tye on Jean D. Heffernan, 49–64. Edith F. Fowke and Carole Henderson Carpenter, *A Bibliography of Canadian Folklore in English* (Toronto: UTP, 1981); Fowke, *Folklore of Canada* (Toronto: McClelland & Stewart, 1976); Kenneth S. Goldstein, *Canadian Folklore Perspectives* (St. John's, NL: Dept. of Folklore, Memorial University, 1978); Magnus Einarsson, *Everyman's Heritage: An Album of Canadian Folk Life* (Ottawa: National Museum, 1978); Carole H. Carpenter, *Many Voices: A Study of Folklore Activities in Canada and Their Role in Canadian Culture* (Ottawa: National Museum, 1979); and several serial publications and journals.

Nouvelle-France but remained welded to stereotypes (*Iroquoisie*, 1947), Jacques Rousseau, in *L'Hérédité et l'homme* (1945), rejected all racist pronouncements whether in traditional ethnographical research or in Groulx-style "historiography." However, the new approaches, best exemplified by Alfred G. Bailey's *The Conflict of European and Eastern Algonkian Cultures, 1504–1700* (1937), received little recognition until the general climate of opinion changed in the 1960s.[378]

Research centres included the National Museum / Museum of Civilization and the Canadian Centre for Folk Culture Studies in Ottawa (Marius Barbeau); the Archives de folklore at Laval since 1944 (Luc Lacourcière), with a journal of the same title since 1946; and such regionally specialized centres as the Department of Folklore at Newfoundland's Memorial University since 1962 (founded by Herbert Halpert); the Centre d'études acadiennes / Centre for Acadian Studies at the University of Moncton; the Centre for the Documentation of Traditional Culture at Trois-Rivières (founded 1970, Robert-Lionel Séguin and Maurice Carrier); the Centre franco-ontarien de folklore at Sudbury's Laurentian University (founded by Germain Lemieux); the folk life sections of the Manitoba Museum of Man and Nature; and the Provincial Museum of Alberta (now the Royal Alberta Museum). Other centres, sometimes amateurish, concentrated on a particular ethnic ("our") group. Umbrella organizations emerged from the 1950s: the Canadian Folk Music Society (founded 1957), the Canadian Folk Arts Council (founded 1964), and the Folklore Studies Association of Canada (founded 1975). While the development of the field was done by both women and men, institution-building was a male affair.[379]

The archaeological approach to Aboriginal cultures, pioneered in the National Museum by Harlan I. Smith, brought forth publications on peoples across Canada, and Ontario in particular. The "fur trade" school argued that traditional inter-tribal relations became quickly obsolete when the trade, far more important than French-British imperial competition and warfare, changed the parameters of relations between different Native peoples. In the 1950s and '60s, First Peoples came to be recognized as well-versed traders in the works of Edwin E. Rich, Abraham Rotstein, Arthur Ray, and Donald Freeman. Rather than juxtaposing cultures, these scholars developed the concept of a "transitional economy" in which First Peoples acted on principles different from their European trading partners but demanded

---

378 : Alfred G. Bailey, "Retrospective Thoughts of an Ethnohistorian," Canadian Historical Association, *Historical Papers* (1937), 15–29, repr. Toronto: UTP, 1969.

379 : A recent critical evaluation and assessment of the discipline's development (not available to the author at the time of writing) is provided by Julia Harrison and Regna Darnell, eds., *Historicizing Canadian Anthropology* (Vancouver, BC: UBC Press, 2006).

"good measure."[380] As regards religiosity, Jacques Rousseau questioned the "Christianity triumphant" approach in 1951: First Peoples experimented with different spiritualities and were able to incorporate aspects from other belief systems, the Christian one in this case, without renouncing those of their own. In contrast to such competence for plurality, mono-religious missionaries with their One God and Holy Trinity were convinced of both their own superior spiritual power and the inevitable waning of animist spirituality. Native religious practices were rendered invisible. Anthropologists, in contrast, were aware of power relations: only in the period of subordination of First to Second Peoples did the former become susceptible to Christian indoctrination or conversion. "Ethnohistory" overcame the preconception of First People's societies as static. In the United States of the 1960s, the American Indian Movement's struggle for respect within the context of the Civil Rights Movement resulted in similar yet distinct scholarly developments.[381]

The separate study of Euro-Canadian folk and its lore and art continued to concentrate on objects, tales, and songs, and thus also continued to be descriptive. Analysis of relations and meanings was sorely missing. Even though in nineteenth-century Europe, folk culture had been considered the basis of bourgeois culture, its study remained marginal. Once middle-class intellectuals had established their master narrative as a means to oppose dynasties' and nobilities' hegemonic narratives and public displays, they turned folk traditions into usable pasts to buttress the story of "a people," "a nation"—no research and analysis needed. The field could have been an interdisciplinary undertaking *par excellence*, involving history, language, literature, anthropology, psychology, and sociology, as a basis for understanding one's own and neighbouring cultures. Rather, common people's expressions were designated as "naive" or simple, and contrasted to "artificial" cultures of courts and nobilities. In a scholarly perspective, folk expression is communal, regional ("vernacular"), and traditional, if adaptable; it is passed on

---

380 : The fur-trade studies were published from 1960 to 1983. See Bruce G. Trigger, "The Historians' Indian: Native Americans in Canadian Historical Writing from Charlevoix to the Present," *Canadian Historical Review* 67 (1986): 315–42; John A. Price, "Native Studies," in Artibise, *Interdisciplinary Approaches*, 117–147, esp. 130–32, for the archaeological approach.

381 : The results of the new approach were published only since the mid-1970s. Important works are Bruce G. Trigger, *The Children of Aataentsic: A History of the Huron People to 1660* (Montreal: MQUP, 1976), and David Blanchard, "Patterns of Tradition and Change: The Re-Creation of Iroquois Culture at Kahnawake" (PhD diss., Univ. of Chicago, 1982). Other studies were, in the U.S., Calvin Martin (Berkeley, 1978); Stephen Krech III (Athens, Ga., 1984); W.H. McNeill (Garden City, 1976); and in Canada, Adrian Tanner (St. John's, 1979); Denys Delâge (Montreal, 1985); Lucien Campeau (Quebec, 1979).

intergenerationally in everyday life by communities rather than individuals. "Artful" expression may be meant to adorn or beautify everyday life: carved spoons, polished tools with complex inlays, complex quilts, hunting decoys, a weather vane. Ritual expression may give meaning to events, seasons, festivities. It may transform material or spiritual meaning into symbolic form: embroidered dresses that signify a stage in the life cycle, painted eggs that reflect the spirituality of Easter celebrations, thanksgivings to celebrate the end of a period of hard work such as harvest fests, or songs that simplify repetitive work or provide a work rhythm. Supra-regional but culture-specific folk art includes, for example, artisanal or working-class trade union banners, shop signs symbolically representing craft and solidarity, and lumbermen's songs as well as sailors' rituals. Such expressions may have a Christian mythological or a hierarchical-dynastic background, such as reverence for the pomp and circumstance of Catholic bishops or affective expressions toward a distant ruler—the British monarch for example. Such types of affirmative expressiveness by common people are usually encouraged or orchestrated from the top down through local transmitters such as clerics, teachers, or other representatives of power and institutions.

In Societal Studies, research on "traditional" popular expressiveness still remains a sideline, and connections to twentieth-century popular culture are rarely drawn. Nor is the connection between cultural expression of First Peoples, First Immigrants, and Present Newcomers often made. Hegemonic peoples, even the respective underclasses, usually are not part of "folk" studies since by definition they rank above "folk." Thus, in Canada, the least studied group is the English.[382]

---

382 : Dirk Hoerder, "Pluralist Founding Nations in Anglo- and Franco-Canada: Multiple Migrations, Influences, Reconceptualisations," *Journal of Multilingual and Multicultural Development* 24.6 (2003): 525–139.

Chapter 9

DISCOURSE-BASED REFLECTIONS ABOUT SOCIETY: WHERE WERE THE HUMANITIES?

"Nations are to a very large extent invented by their poets and novelists" (Huxley 1959)—unless colonizing imperial bards and administrators impose their invention. Group cohesion, as any First People's person knows, emerge from "shared stories," which "lie at the heart of a culture's identity." Theorists and ideologues of the White Atlantic "discovered" such insights only in the 1980s.[383] This discourse theory, the analysis of meanings of spoken and written words, is a complex theorization of what historians, unless they made themselves into ideologues, have used as theoretical-methodological basis of their craft: a critique and contextualization of any source used, a search for implied and hidden meanings. Narratives are acted out in everyday practices and they vary between social spaces. Stories in Montreal, Ottawa, Moose Jaw, and Victoria are different, yet they coalesce into national or, more cautiously, countrywide ones. While recent theorists have discussed the "invention" of tradition, invention is but a special case. Rather, shared stories may be elaborated, developed, or be reduced to a simplifying billboard message.[384]

While scholars in the social sciences took Canada to be one whole with many regions and social strata with subaltern and hegemonic ethnocultural groups, while they understood it as a society developing almost like an experiment but in need of regulation when larger disparities between the parts came to be observed, scholars in the humanities hardly noticed Canada; though, as Marlene Shore cautiously noted, they did not stagnate *entirely*. Humanities scholars succumbed to the fallacy that "high" literature

---

383 : Aldous Huxley, *Texts and Pretexts* (London: Chatto and Windus, 1959), quote p. 50; Jerry Diakiw, "Children's Literature and Canadian National Identity: A Revisionist Perspective," *Canadian Children's Literature* 87 (1997): 44–52, quote p. 37; Cruikshank, *The Social Life of Stories* (1998); Jennifer S.H. Brown and Elizabeth Vibert, eds., *Reading Beyond Words: Contexts for Native History* (Peterborough, ON: Broadview, 1996); Benedict Anderson, *Imagined Communities: Reflections on the Origin and Spread of Nationalism* (London: Verso, 1983).

384 : Eric J. Hobsbawm and Terence Ranger, eds., *The Invention of Tradition* (Cambridge: Cambridge, 1983); Werner Sollors, ed., *The Invention of Ethnicity* (New York: Oxford, 1989); Kathleen N. Conzen, David Gerber, Ewa Morawska, George E. Pozetta, Rudolph J. Vecoli, "The Invention of Ethnicity: A Perspective from the U.S.A.," *Journal of American Ethnic History* 12 (1992): 3–41.

afar was more important than shared stories at home.[385] They fixed their gaze on Britain and the Empire or on France and Rome. The recently much-theorized concept of "gaze," as appropriation of the spheres of distant Others in terminologies and hierarchies imposed by the gazer, has a counterside. The blinders, focusing the gaze on "ancient" cultures and beliefs of British Celts and Roman Popes, may result in the symbolic annihilation of Self. The appropriating gaze of Canada's cultural elites implied a *dis*regard of Canada as a viable culture and crowded Canadian experiences out of the storage space of collective memory.

Recognition, acceptance, and analysis of one's own material and discursive cultures, not necessarily agreement with all of its expressions and positions, provides an understanding of the present from which perspectives, projects, and courses for the future may be charted by individuals, social groups, and political institutions. "*Je me souviens*" may be a resource. While the social sciences were retarded by the Cold War mentalities of the 1950s, the self-blindfolded humanities had never cared to look at "local" Canadian literature, arts, and media. They could not recognize the tantalizing options provided by alternative expressions and visions as in the Little Magazines, Little Theatres, or the *presse d'opinion*.

Until the mid-twentieth century, most of the literary and artistic cultural production and consumption was Central Canadian, anglo- as well as francophone.[386] Since Ontario's products increasingly supplied national demand, some adjustments to an Anglo-national discourse occurred. Since both hegemonic elites were linguistically challenged when it came to cultural productions in immigrant languages, and since they were nearly blind as regards First Peoples' cultures, all of these many-faceted productions remained outside recognized "national" culture. In contrast to high-culture-fixated European states, in Canada funding went to more popular expressions, such as the festival movement—pageants and ceremonies of Anglo or

---

385 : Marlene G. Shore, *The Science of Social Redemption: McGill, the Chicago School, and the Origins of Social Research in Canada* (Toronto: UTP, 1987), 7.

386 : Scholars do not agree on whether the two major Canadian literatures follow "a single basic line of ideological development, creating a whole spectrum of common images, attitudes and ideas" (Ronald Sutherland) or follow diverging or even conflicting lines: relations between human beings and social-physical environment in English-language writing, relations of human beings to destiny or the absolute in French-language writing (Jean-Charles Falardeau). Canadian literatures are more complex than the binary linguistic division implies and Philip Stratford pleaded for a differentiated analysis of "how exchanges take place" or "why exchanges do not take place" and suggested that differences may elucidate Canadianness. "Canada's Two [Major] Literatures: A Search for Emblems," *Canadian Review of Comparative Literature* 6 (1979): 131–38, esp. p. 138.

French historical meaning. Meant to entrench two particular versions of cultural expression, it was as elitist as the European setting, from the perspective of newcomers and First Peoples.

The colonial mindset of cultural producers, scholars, and archivists is reflected in the lack of a national bibliography or register of art works. Only in 1939 did the *University of Toronto Quarterly* (established in 1931) add an annual but non-cumulative survey, "Letters in Canada."[387] First surveys of "Canadian" literature, confined however to one of its languages, appeared in the 1920s and '30s. Only toward the end of Canada's first century did critical evaluations of discourses appear. Guy Frégault's *La guerre de la conquête* (1955), for example, questioned the heroic version of French-Canadian historical narrative. Alain Grandbois, in *Né à Québec* (1933), used a biography of the seventeenth-century priest and explorer Louis Joliet to illustrate "how history turns into story and legend."[388] Studies of British-Canadian mythologies were conspicuously absent.

Myth-based views of society stimulated social movements. The policy of settling the West, perhaps mixed with Quebec's ruralism, led to a Country Life Movement to counter the drift to cities. It upheld rural values, fit well with the golden-wheat rhetoric, and its *Farm and Ranch Review* (Calgary) quoted Greek philosopher Socrates in support of farm life. A healthy-outdoor-life advocacy of medical doctors in Britain had a far more utilitarian goal: under the concept of "empire settlement," they shipped men slightly disabled from imperial wars and unmarried women to Canada and other "white colonies." They wanted to rid British society of invalid men and "useless" women, both considered costly burdens to society. The colony-nation and the centre of the Empire were entwined, to the detriment of the former. Dumping people considered superfluous at "home" was enveloped in stories of empire and health.

From the 1920s on, concepts of the Canadian space changed. Excursions to the British and French metropoles became fashionable for young men and women of means, and English and Scottish harvest workers "visited" Canada. The latter were forced to reflect on their status as colonials or Britishers, to negotiate the usage and construction of spaces. Furthermore, the two wars brought Canadians into closer contact with Europe than intended by

---

387 : A few early bibliographic surveys, beginning in 1837 with the *Catalogue raisonné d'ouvrages sur l'histoire de l'Amérique et en particulier sur celle du Canada* by Georges Barthélemi Faribault, were concerned with French-language publications only with the exception of Henry J. Morgan, *Bibliotheca Canadensis* (Ottawa: Desbarats, 1867). See Guy Sylvestre, "La recherche en littérature canadienne-française," in Louis Baudouin, ed., *La recherche au Canada français* (Montreal: PU Montréal, 1968), 149–61, esp. p. 155.

388 : New, *A History of Canadian Literature* (1989), quote p. 141.

many. Internally, the spread of the automobile permitted local and regional mobility and increased urban–rural leisure and rural–urban shopping excursions. In literature and history, the North assumed a new significance, as it did for the economy. Distances between regions shrank.

One, two, many literatures—or none?

Far into the twentieth century, gatekeepers welded to the two European reference cultures would call their own groups "founding peoples" to keep other groups in subaltern position. Rather than laying foundations, they had not cut loose from dependency. Their faithfulness to Mother Britain or Father (*patrie*) France, however, went unrewarded. The educated public in the metropoles was not interested in what it considered bush and backwoods, as even Susanna Moodie noted—Moodie, whom Northrop Frye called "a [gentry-class] British army of occupation in herself, a one-woman garrison." Calls by perceptive members of the elite, such as Thomas D'Arcy McGee, for genuinely Canadian writing went unheeded.[389]

In such "frames of remembrance," universities did not teach Canadian literature for five decades after Confederation and little of it for another five decades.[390] In 1919, Nova Scotian J.D. Logan at Acadia University offered a "History of Canadian Literature" in its relations to English and American literature. In his Anglo-Maritime tradition, Logan understood Canada's poetic spirit to be Celtic and engaged in a quest for genuine democracy. In this perspective, Acadian and other French-language poetry would be mere folklore.[391] By the 1920s, Douglas Bush called attention to a distinctive and mature Canadian literature. Later, Northrop Frye angrily noted that "the advantages of having a national culture based on two languages" had been offset by the elites' total neglect of this potential. The two groups had been described in Hugh MacLennan's *Two Solitudes* (1945) as interactive yet autistic cultures. Northrop Frye commented that separate languages, codes, and styles could imply "the death of communication and dialogue."

---

389 : David Staines, "Canada Observed," in Staines, ed., *The Canadian Imagination: Dimensions of a Literary Culture* (Cambridge, MA: Harvard, 1977), 1–21, esp. p. 7; Northrop Frye, "Conclusion," in Carl F. Klinck, ed., *Literary History of [English-] Canada* (1st ed., Toronto: UTP, 1967), 821–49, quote p. 839. Philip Stratford, in contrast, argued that both Canadian literatures "remained quite derivative" to World War II ("Canada's Two [Major] Literatures," quote p. 131).

390 : Isolated courses were taught in 1906–07 at the MacDonald Institute of the Ontario Agricultural College and in 1907–08 at McGill.

391 : Gwendolyn Davies, "J.D. Logan and the Great Feud for Canadian Literature: 1915–1923," *Canadian Issues / Thèmes Canadiens* 17 (1995): 113–28.

Difficulty of communication protected Quebec culture from Americanizing influences, though not its economy from U.S. investments.[392]

While in academia Canadian literature was symbolically annihilated, authors and their reading public knew that their particular version of literature was alive and well, and saw the need to act and to organize, as did publishers,. To counter the neglect, their rhetorical invocation of a "Canadian spirit" in prose, verse, and painting was sometimes overly nationalist or "plain boosterism" (New 1989). As forums, they established *The Canadian Bookman* in 1919, the *Authors' Bulletin* in 1922 (renamed *The Canadian Author and Bookman* since 1943), and the Canadian Authors' Association in 1921. Critic William Arthur Deacon became the pro-Canadian influential literary editor of *Saturday Night* (1922–28) and of the *Globe and Mail* (1936–60). Lorne Pierce, the editor of Ryerson Press (1922–60), launched the nationalist "Makers of Canada" series in 1923. The "prix David" gave respectability to literature in Quebec, and Albert Lévesque in 1930 founded an influential publishing house to re-edit important but forgotten works. While the Académie canadienne-française was established in 1944, the Governor General's Awards for literature, initiated in 1937, for more than two decades honoured English-language works only. Parallel to the slow appreciation of Canadian writing and art, a rapid turn to U.S. imports was noticeable. Canadian readers bought eight U.S. magazines for each Canadian one in 1929 and spent one hundred dollars on U.S. magazines for each dollar spent on British magazines.[393]

While public spending on and academic recognition of Canadian cultural products was low, new expressive trends abounded, in particular with respect to writing by and about independent women (often designated "ladies" in contemporary parlance). The Persons Case about the status of women was a real-life satire starring an all-male cast, whose plot would have been considered too cliché-laden if invented by a writer. Around 1910, the "second industrialization" brought forest, mining, and hydroelectric industry; U.S. investments, critically debated by Errol Bouchette, became more important than British ones. In response, some authors proposed critical and iconoclastic views of the period's discourses but, in general, imperial values and other certainties collapsed only during World War I. French Canadians refused to fight what they considered to be a British affair even though the

---

392 : Desmond Pacey, "The Study of Canadian Literature," *Journal of Canadian Fiction* 2.2 (1973): 67–72; Bush, "Is There a Canadian Literature?" *Commonweal* 6 Nov. 1929; Staines, "Canada Observed," 4; Marine Leland, "Quebec Literature in Its American Context," in Staines, *Canadian Imagination*, 188–225; Frye, "Conclusion," quotes pp. 824, 831.

393 : J.M. Bumsted, *The Peoples of Canada: A Post-Confederation History* (Toronto: Oxford, 1992), 224.

struggle involved liberation of France from the German Reich's occupation.[394] After the war, Canada joined the League of Nations independently from Britain. Internally, the Winnipeg General Strike pitted classes against each other, and hysterical fears of Bolshevism and Soviet-style revolution gripped parts of the middle classes. Discerning political activists organized an Independent Labour Party, and in 1921 the new Progressive Party garnered sufficient votes and seats to become the Official Opposition.

New topics included Native peoples and the Euro-Canadian world outside of Ontario and Quebec, the West in particular. A Euro-Canadianized version of First Peoples' cultures was incorporated into Canada's historical ancestry, but some of their customs, the potlatch for example, remained prohibited. After 1900, Edmund Morris was commissioned to paint "Indian chiefs"; Iroquois were invited to give speeches in their own languages at the 1908 Quebec tercentenary; and in an anthropological vein, Edward S. Curtis produced a "documentary" film on the Kwakiutl (1913), but the traditions were re-enacted before the camera. What had been cultural practice with an element of impressive showmanship changed to theatre in front of the lens, and to the aesthetics of visual reproduction. However, the film *Nanouk of the North* (*Nanouk l'Eskimo*) did show the everyday life of a family on the Hudson Bay's east coast (United States, 1921, Robert Flaherty), and in 1924 Georges Bugnet published a sympathetic Métis story, *Nipsya*. Only in the 1950s did realist works appear about problems in Native societies, as at the Skeena River, portrayed in Hubert Evans's *Mist on the River* (1954), or on Inuit society and on the Montagnais Cree, portrayed respectively by Yves Thériault's *Agaguk*, (1958) and *Ashini* (1960, English, 1972). With Thériault, of French-Acadian and Montagnais ancestry, Native Canadians made their entry into the received canon of literature.

The West, as a topic and as a billboard, became part of the literary struggle about Britishness. Frederick Niven, an immigrant Scot, in *Canada West* (1930) dreamed of "the old days . . . when the English speech was everywhere, indomitable settlers driving the first furrows, and the wild young men, the breakers of the prairie, going on their jocund way." Progress, he feared, might "spell problem," since recent settlers were not of the right type. Young newcomers from the "preferred races," rather than "tackle the job," wanted to acquire telephones, electric light, and other amenities. Only the non-preferred East Europeans, with their "trivial" demands upon life, accepted the "dreary toil and spiritual stagnation." To prevent that "the non-preferred [should] overbalance the preferred," the government would

---

394 : During the war "great events" and "our heroes" type of writings appeared, like John McCrae's *In Flanders Fields* (1919) and Billy Bishop's *Winged Warfare* (1918).

have to orchestrate their absorption carefully. The book, sometimes classified as non-fiction, appeared in print only after the beginning of the Depression in 1929, when collapse of the capitalist world brought Niven's hardy yeoman farmers to penury.[395]

Other writers, including French-language ones, provided a sensitive understanding of the emotional and physical hardships of frontier settlement and included the many cultures of the settlers. In addition, from commercial motives, the CPR promoted intercultural understanding in the 1920s. Immigrants began to publish extensively. Those from France and writing in French, for example immigrant Manitoban Maurice Constantin-Weyer and Georges Bugnet (*La Forêt*, 1935), transcended the Quebec-Ontario dichotomy.[396] French migration to Manitoba was also the subject of Alfred Glauser's *Le vent se lève* (1942); Alberta became the social space of Magali Michelet's *Comme jadis* (1925) and of André Borel's Swiss newcomers.[397] Gabrielle Roy, from Saint-Boniface, belonged to those francophones defined in reductionist perspective as "hors de Québec." In a literary masterpiece, she described a multi-ethnic community in northern Manitoba where she had been a teacher (*La petite poule d'eau*, 1951; in English as *Where Nests the Water Hen*, 1951).[398] French-speaking immigrants found a place in literature, too.[399] Much of this writing had to be published in France, even Gabrielle Roy's first novel, since, even into the 1930s, Quebec publishers were not yet ready for perspectives from the outside.

While some young intellectuals left Quebec and chose France as a second home to escape the mind-numbing ecclesiastical atmosphere, *le roman paysan* and *les romans idylliques et doctrinaires*, including the "romantisme féminin des années 30," still extended the past into the future and called upon the living to pursue the ancestral ways.[400] This genre, of no value

---

395 : Frederick Niven, *Canada West* (London and Toronto: Dent, 1930), 34–46.

396 : Constantin-Weyer, *Manitoba* (Paris, 1924), an autobiographical novel on a French immigrant in Manitoba; *Un homme se penche sur son passé* (1928) and *L'Epopée canadienne* (Paris, 1931) about French immigrants in Manitoba.

397 : Borel, *Croquis du Far-West Canadien* (Paris: Attinger, 1928) and *Le Robinson de la Red Deer* (Paris: Attinger, 1930).

398 : See also Roy, *Rue Deschambault* (Montreal: Beauchemin, 1955; published as *Street of Riches*, Toronto: McClelland & Stewart, 1957), which includes sketches of immigrant families in St. Boniface, Manitoba.

399 : Damase Potvin in *Le Français* (Montreal: Garand, 1925) described French immigrants in Quebec; Maurice de Goumois, *François Duvalet* (Quebec: L'Institut Littéraire du Québec, 1954), dealt with French immigrants in northern Ontario.

400 : Authors included Robert de Roquebrune [Robert Laroque, pseud.], Félix-Antoine Savard, who glorified the struggle of a French-Canadian peasant and his sons against

according to Quebec's major literary history, collapsed when "le malaise de la littérature de terroir" could no longer be overlooked.

> En un siècle où les campagnes se sont mises à se dépeupler au profit des villes, le roman ne pouvait pas s'en tenir à exalter le courage du paysan, les hautes vertus de la vie rurale ou de la colonisation, la fidélité à la terre. Les déceptions, l'ennui, l'impatience, les vices, l'accablement désolé sous le poids de la misère et de l'adversité, sont aussi des réalités auxquelles la littérature doit faire droit.[401]

Albert Laberge depicted the ugly, unrewarding, wearying toil of farm life; Claude-Henri Grignon's *Un homme et son péché* (1933) provided a psychological portrait "de l'avarice terrienne"; and Phillipe Panneton (pseudonym Ringuet) in his empirically-based *Trente Arpents* described a farmer who, cheated of his land by a village notable, has to migrate to New England. To Quebec's elites the process of rural impoverishment was known. Horace Miner's sociological study of the Saint-Denis parish in Kamouraska (1939) had analyzed the decline of self-sufficiency, and in a novel Adélard Dugré had discussed the influence of the city on rural lifestyles. Germaine Guèvremont in *Le Survenant* (1945, in English *The Outlander*) delivered the final blow to true-to-the-land tradition. Later, Jean-Paul Désbiens continued the analytical approach in his autobiographical *Sous le soleil de la pitié* (1965), which described the difficult life of a Quebec family in the 1930s.[402] Rodolphe Girard's satiric *Marie Calumet* (1904), about a priest's housekeeper who considered all bodily functions of the priest "holy enterprises," resulted in vitriolic attacks from the Church, and Girard had to resign his job as a journalist.[403] Finely crafted regionalist novels included those of Adjutor Rivard (*Chez Nous*, 1914) and a first turn to urban life in Arsène Bessette's *Le débutant* (1914). Writers such as Grignon and Jean-Charles Harvey commented critically on the narrow school system and its basically negative

---

an English intruder (*Menaud, maître-draveur*, 1937), as well as poets Nérée Beauchemin and Gonzalve Desaulniers.

401 : Pierre de Grandpré, ed., *Histoire de la littérature française du Québec*, 4 vols. (Montreal: Beauchemin, 1967–69), 2:282.

402 : Laberge, *La Scouine* [Bitter bread] (1918); Ringuet, *Trente Arpents* [Thirty acres] (1938, Engl. 1940); Dugré, *La campagne canadienne* (1925). New, *History of Canadian Literature* (1989), 103.

403 : Paul-André Linteau, René Durocher, Jean-Claude Robert, and François Ricard, *Histoire du Québec contemporain*, 2 vols. (2nd ed., Montreal: Boréal, 1989), quote p. 1:563. Girard, as late as 1946, could republish *Marie Calumet* only in a cleansed version.

education.[404] A new genre, novels with psychological depth, was established by Girard, Hector Bernier, and Gaétane de Montreuil. Had scholars in the humanities emphasized this broad array of new Quebec-Canadian voices, the cliché of a "Québec en retard" might have been revised earlier.

Journalists and public speakers, called "premiers inquiéteurs," and the *presse d'opinion* moved to new questions. Debating magazines, often short-lived, such as *Idées* (1935–39), *La Relève* and *La Nouvelle Relève* (1934–41, 1941–48), and *Gants du ciel* (1943–46), stood in opposition to those in power and provided forums for new ideas. At *Le Devoir* (founded 1910), perhaps the "founding" journal of this type, Georges Pelletier succeeded Bourassa as editor in 1932. Olivar Asselin, editor of *Le Canada* (1930–35), founded the weekly *l'Ordre* in 1934 and attempted to insert freedom of thought and freedom of expression into the ossified society. The few women journalists left the corners assigned them to deal with family problems rather than idealizations, with social questions, and with politics. Writers used irony, critical comment, and discerning judgment to counter other young publicists' sympathy for corporatism and Groulxian billboards. Through sheer quantity, but also by use of new communication technology, these predominated at a time when U.S. firms, accounting for one third of all capital invested in Quebec, had the support of the government. They exported profits just as the agrarianized society exported people without jobs to the factories of New England: "Omniprésence et omnipotence croissante des cartels américains, prolétarisation des populations urbaines, insatisfaction et déracinement des rureaux," in the words of sociologist Falardeau.[405] While Quebec's debating gave voice to dissent, most of the English-language university magazines were conservative. Opinion-pronouncing rather than debating, they included the *University of Toronto Quarterly* (1895–96, re-established 1931) and McGill's more influential *University Magazine* (1901–20), edited from 1907 by imperialist Andrew Macphail. The *Dalhousie Review* (established 1921), more Canada-centered, discussed international affairs and Canadian literature.

---

404 : Grignon, *Un homme et son péché* (1933); Jean-Charles Harvey, *Les Demi-civilisés* (1934, transl. as *Sackcloth for a Banner*, 1938, and as *Fear's Folly*, 1982). Gérard Bessette pursued this theme as well as that of censorship in *Les pédagogues* (1961) and *Le librairie* (1960, Engl.: *Not for Every Eye*, 1962).

405 : Falardeau in Grandpré, *Histoire de la littérature française*, 2:189. See for the whole development in Grandpré: Pierre Savard, "Le Journalisme (1860-1900)," 1:312-324, and Savard, "L'Essai (1860-1900)," 1:325-30; Pierre de Grandpré, "Journalisme et Éloquence, de 1900 à 1930," 2:149-175, Jean Marcel, "La Critique et l'essai, de 1900 à 1930," "Essayistes et Critiques, de 1930 à 1945," and "L'Essai, de 1945 à nos jours," 2:176-85, 323-44, 3:265-339; Jean-Louis Gagnon, "Le Journalisme, de 1930 à 1945" and "Le Journalisme, de 1945 à nos jours," 2:317-22, 3:253-64.

Until the early 1930s, Quebec's governments' programs of social assistance, from welfare via protection against workplace accidents to rural credit, were ahead of those of other provinces. But politics regressed when Maurice Duplessis's Union National held power from 1936 to his death in 1959, with one single interruption. After the new developments of the 1910s and '20s, and the upsurge of the early 1930s, the educational system, published opinion, as well as intellectual life in general were stifled again for a quarter century. Duplessis looked upon cities, especially bi- or multicultural Montreal, at scholars and universities, and at labour unions as "his natural enemies," and treated them as such. He countered the lively debates with a "Padlock Law" (1937–57), which allowed the government to imprison for a year, without appeal, anyone who published or distributed new ideas labelled as "communism or bolshevism."[406]

English-language writing, freed to some degree from its Ontario fetters, exhibited a broad range of topics and genres, but also suffered from problems similar to those of Quebec prose. Romanticism and melodrama sold well. But narrow Protestantism and sententious moralism scared many readers away. Many stories, of which *Sunshine Sketches of a Little Town* (1912) by British immigrant and conservative McGill economics teacher Stephen Leacock is the best example, bypassed city life in favour of small-town romance, though occasionally coupled with satire. Regional melodrama involved Celtic lore about Cape Breton society, Prairie romances such as those of Robert J.C. Stead, wild Northwest stories, or chivalry tales from the Pacific Coast (Robert A. Hood). By this time, the Nouvelle-France imagery had achieved such a hold on English-Canadians' minds that Philip Child, Franklin D. McDowell, and Alan Sullivan could use it as a setting for novels.[407] Christian authors' positive portrayal of animals in "dog biography," as Norah Story aptly called it, and nature and wildlife narratives in general, contrasted with a sinister account of West Coast pagan culture.[408] Racial stereotypes abounded in English-Canadian writing. Leacock wanted masses of immigrants, but Britishers only, and Macphail held forth in 1920: "There are breeds of men as there are strains of animals and classes of plants.... when mental attainments and physical courage count for naught,

406 : Leland, "Quebec Literature," 188–225.

407 : Jessie Archibald, *The Token: A Tale of Cape Breton Island in the Days Before Confederation* (1930); Child, *Village of Souls* (1933); McDowell, *The Champlain Road* (1939); Sullivan, *Three Came to Ville Marie* (1941).

408 : Russell R. Cockburn, *Malley: The Story of a Dog* (1939); K. and F. Conibear, *Husky* (1940); Bruce McKelvie, *Huldowget: a Story of the North Pacific Coast* (1926).

the lower breeds will prevail."[409]

Realist urban writing took into account social problems, such as long hours and miserable working conditions of clerks in stores and banks, life in Montreal slums, or the decline of small towns upon departure of the younger generation for the more promising cities.[410] Some authors satirized urban or small-town notables, elites, and the last true believers in the British Empire, such as W.H. Moore in *Polly Masson* (1919). Morley Callaghan wrote on criminal behaviour and redemption in the cities. The ambivalent attitude to newcomers from the United States is reflected in the writings of Mazo de la Roche (e.g. *Jalna*, 1927). Such writing, like that of Quebec authors, does not deserve the label "colonial." The incisive socio-political criticism after World War I, as in Douglas Durkin's novel on the Winnipeg General Strike (*The Magpie*, 1923) and Charles Y. Harrison's attack on the bureaucracy of war and the plight of demobilized soldiers (*Generals Die in Bed*, 1930), was part of larger Western trends, the proletarian and the anti-war novels. By the 1930s, the consequences of exploitation and of the Great Depression assumed an ever increasing presence in literature. Alan Sullivan published an early novel about the expansion of industries in 1922 (*The Rapids*) and others followed suit. But radical criticism was labelled as "dangerous" or "socialist" rather than being taken seriously by elites or read by the public. Under the impression of the inequities of global, national, and regional expressions of the capitalist economy in the 1930s, some cultural producers turned further to the Left and attempted to reach broad segments of the population, "the masses."

A third kind of literature in Canada, similar to the novels by francophone newcomers, was produced by first- and second-generation new Canadians writing in English. Frederick P. Grove, of German background but self-described as Swedish, created men in the West braving snowstorms on their way home to a frightened wife, but also described the increasing use of machinery and the generational change in long-settled families.[411] B. Mabel

409 : Terrence L. Craig, *Racial Attitudes in English-Canadian Fiction, 1905–1980* (Waterloo, ON: WLU Press, 1987), quote p. 6. Howard Palmer, *Patterns of Prejudice: A History of Nativism in Alberta* (Toronto: McClelland & Stewart, 1982); Peter Ward, *White Canada Forever: Popular Attitudes and Public Policy Towards Orientals in British Columbia* (Montreal: MQUP, 1978); Patricia Roy, "White Canada Forever: Two Generations of Studies," *Canadian Ethnic Studies* 11.2 (1979): 89–97.

410 : Isabel Ecclestone Mackay, *The House of Windows* (1912); John P. Buschlen, *Canadian Bankclerk* (1913); Robert J.C. Stead, *Grain* (1926). On bank clerks see also Adam J. Tolmie's autobiography, *Roughing It on the Rails* (Bloomfield, ON: Silverthorn, 1983).

411 : Grove, *Over Prairie Trails* (1922); *Settlers of the Marsh* (1925; repr. 1966) among others. His autobiography, *In Search of Myself* (1946), fabricated a life: The German

Dunham and Martha Ostenso, of Norwegian background, wrote on Ontario Mennonites and Norwegian immigrants respectively. The highly literate Mennonites also published extensively in their particular Dutch-German dialect.[412] Laura Goodman Salverson of Icelandic background and Vera Lysenko of Ukranian background wrote sensitive novels and an autobiographical account. Other Western settlers—lumberjacks in the north and immigrant miners in the Rockies—also found a place in literature, for example in a now forgotten "Novel of Canadianization."[413] Some writers came to include urban immigrants and their social spaces, in particular the poor neighbourhoods in Montreal, Toronto, and Winnipeg, but also the upwardly mobile and their (lack of) ethics.[414] Gender relations between Old-World authoritarian fathers and their wives and children raised concern, as did discrimination against immigrants.[415] In their own languages, the ever lar-

---

Felix Paul Greve faked suicide in 1909, migrated to Canada, and re-emerged as "Swedish-born" Frederick P. Grove. Klaus Martens, *Felix Paul Greves Karriere: Frederick Philip Grove in Deutschland* (St. Ingbert: Röhrig, 1997).

412 : Dunham, *The Trail of the Conestoga* (1924); Ostenso, *Wild Geese* (1925). Harry Loewen, "Canadian-Mennonite Literature: Longing for a Lost Homeland," in Walter E. Riedel, ed., *The Old World and the New: Literary Perspectives of German-Speaking Canadians* (Toronto: UTP, 1984), 73–93.

413 : Salverson, *The Viking Heart* (1923; rev. 1947) and the autobiographical *Confessions of an Immigrant's Daughter* (1939; repr. 1981); Lysenko, *Yellow Boots* (1954) and *Westerly Wild* (1956), on Ukrainians in Manitoba; Augustus Bridle, *Hansen: A Novel of Canadianization* (1924), on Norwegians among Anglo-Saxons; Nellie L. McClung, *Painted Fires* (1925), on a Finnish girl in Western Canada, and *Clearing in the West: My Own Story* (1935) on Ontarians in Manitoba; Angus Graham, *Napoleon Tremblay* (1939), a picaresque novel about French-Canadian lumberjacks; Ethel Chapman, *The Homesteaders* (1931, repr. Toronto, 1936), on human relations among newcomers to whom mutual help is more important than acquisition of wealth; Wilfried Eggleston, *The High Plains* (1938), an autobiographical novel about an English immigrant in Alberta; Edward McCourt, *Home Is the Stranger* (1950), on Irish in Saskatchewan; Magdalena Eggleston, *Mountain Shadows* (1955), on Eastern Europeans in the Crow's Nest Pass.

414 : Georgina Sime, *Our Little Life* (1921), on urban immigrants' expectations; John Mitchell (pseud. Patrick Slater), *The Yellow Briar: A Story of the Irish in the Canadian Countryside* (1933), on an orphan of 1847; Frederick John Niven, *The Transplanted* (1944), on a post-1870 Scot's experiences; Morley Callaghan, *The Loved and the Lost* (1951), on Afro-Canadians in Montreal; Henry Kreisel, *The Rich Man* (1948), on a Canadian-Jewish immigrant who revisits Europe; Mordecai Richler, *Son of a Smaller Hero* (1955) and *The Apprenticeship of Duddy Kravitz* (London, 1959; French transl.: *L'apprentissage de Duddy Kravitz*), on Jews in Montreal; Adele Wiseman, *The Sacrifice* (1956), on a Jewish immigrant's experience in Winnipeg; John Marlyn, *Under the Ribs of Death* (1957), on Hungarians in Winnipeg.

415 : For example in Ostenso, *Wild Geese* (1925), and in French-Canadian writing Grignon, *Un homme et son péché* (1933). Some women's autobiographical prairie writ-

ger "rest" of Canadian society reflected on its experiences, as did Stephan G. Stephansson in his poetry *Andvökur*, Y.Y. Segal in *Vun Mein Velt*, and Illia Kyriak in a three-volume realist novel of Ukrainian pioneer life in Vegreville, Alberta.[416] As yet, no literature dealt with immigrants from Asia.

Margaret Atwood has argued that "both earlier and later immigrants come unprepared and are confused by what they find." However, autobiographies and letters, in which immigrants make sense of their recent or lifelong experiences, show a high degree of coping and coherence. Of course disasters, whether individual such as the death of a loved one, socio-economic such as the Great (or a small) Depression, or natural such as the drought of the 1930s, do result in disjuncture. Studies of communication between immigrants and their kin and friends at home by letter, by personal visit, or in the present by telecommunication, show that many newcomers arrive with relatively detailed information about what awaits them. For most immigrants, the issue was not mere "survival" but, in their own views, at least, the active creating of a family economy and communal or even Canadian belonging.[417]

Comparable perhaps to Quebec's *presse d'opinion*, new developments in English writing and even in immigrant writing received a boost from the Little Magazines of cultural producers ready for innovation, but without access to major publishers or unwilling to use the established channels. *Preview, First Statement, Direction,* and *Contemporary Verse* published poetry, short fiction, and programmatic essays that were part of the 1930s social protest movements. Like the social scientists who developed innovative research designs and wanted to influence society, writers, artists, and broadcasters moved away from middle-class and elite aesthetics. The Little Magazines, Little Theatres, the avant-garde urban artscape attempted to address a broader public, sometimes defined as proletarian, more often

---

ings dealt with men so attached to buying ever more machinery that the family economy collapsed.

416 : Stephansson, *Andvökur* (*Wakeful Nights*, Icelandic, 6 vols., 1909–38); Segal, *Vun Mein Velt* (*Of My World*, Yiddish, 1918); Illia Kyriak (transliteration varies), *Syny zemli*, 3 vols. (1939–45), translated and abridged as *Sons of the Soil* (Toronto, 1959, repr. 1983).

417 : Margaret Atwood, *Survival: A Thematic Guide to Canadian Literature* (Toronto: House of Anansi Press, 1972), Chap. 7 "Failed Sacrifices: The Reluctant Immigrant"; Unpublished bibliography of immigrant life-writings accumulated for Dirk Hoerder, *Creating Societies: Immigrant Lives in Canada* (Montreal: MQUP, 1999). The best contextual analysis of immigrant communication is the introduction to Walter D. Kamphoefner, Wolfgang Helbich, and Ulrike Sommer, eds., *News from the Land of Freedom: German Immigrants Write Home*, transl. from the German by Susan Carter Vogel (German orig., 1988; Ithaca: Cornell, 1991).

generically defined as "the common people." Or, they simply wanted to experiment with new forms. Radical poets and writers published *Masses* (1932–34) and *New Frontier* (1936–37) with Dorothy Livesay, Leo Kennedy, and A.M. Klein as authors. Klein wrote trenchant social allegories, Sinclair Ross narratives of domestic pressure, Mary Quayle Innis and Dyson Carter short stories sympathetic to the proletarian cause. Novelists turned to the working classes. Irene Baird wrote on chronic unemployment and labour unrest in Depression Vancouver (*Waste Heritage*, 1939) and Morley Callaghan questioned conventional moral judgments in problem-fraught interactions and explored society's dispositions to women and class, priests and prostitutes, and Blacks, often in bar or street corner settings (*Such Is My Beloved*, 1934; *They Shall Inherit the Earth*, 1935). Hugh Garner, from the 1940s turning to Toronto's Irish-cultured Cabbagetown, soon displayed a conventional gruff toughness, and Prairie writers turned to struggles for survival with a whiff of sentimentalism.[418]

The dissenting Little Theatres developed under the influence of German *agit-prop* troupes and expressionism. The New Theatre in Winnipeg, with Laura Goodman Salverson among its activists, staged working conditions of immigrants, especially Ukrainian Canadians, and the Progressive Arts Club in Vancouver staged Clifford Odets's *Waiting for Lefty*. Montreal's New Theatre Group, as was to be expected, ranked among Duplessis's natural enemies. Toronto's Theatre of Action, many of whose actors would become well-known TV stars or public personalities later, produced Oscar Ryan's *Eight Men Speak* on the simultaneous 1931 arrest of eight communists. Toronto police, mentally not far from Duplessis, closed the show after the first performance. Painters such as Charles Comfort and Paraskeva Clark turned to industrial subjects and the working classes. The new poetry was anthologized by Arthur J.M. Smith (*The Book of Canadian Poetry*, 1943) and John Sutherland (*Other Canadians*, 1947), while the new prose was anthologized only much later by Donna Phillips. A long-range perspective was provided by Margaret Fairley (*Spirit of Canadian Democracy: A Collection of Canadian Writings from the Beginnings to the Present Day*, 1945).[419] While Smith simply distinguished between a "native" nineteenth-century romantic tradition and a "modern, cosmopolitan" development since the 1920s, Sutherland in

---

418 : James Doyle, *Progressive Heritage: The Evolution of a Politically Radical Literary Tradition in Canada* (Waterloo, ON: WLU Press, 2002); David Frank, "The Progressive Tradition in Canadian Literature" (review essay), *Labour / Le Travail* 52 (Fall 2003): 245–51; New, *History of Canadian Literature* (1989), 154–57.

419 : Phillips, *Voices of Discord* (Toronto: New Hogtown Press, 1979). Raymond Knister, of German background, had edited *Canadian Short Stories* (1928) with a major introductory essay that provided an overview of the genre.

a more critical stance challenged Canadian authors "to transcend colonialism" for a "universal civilizing culture of ideas." Sutherland, who was aware of the growing U.S. influence, demanded a fusion between English- and French-Canadian literatures and a replacement of old-style poetry, whose "viewpoint becomes more frozen and immovable every day," by poetry addressed to proletarians, to the common people, to average Canadians. These voices, labelled "dissenting" or sometimes "communist," were more Canadian than British in style. While these authors, some close to the Communist or the Socialist Party, foregrounded class, new developments after a hiatus of two decades would be post-colonial.

Many dissident writers drew inspiration from or were part of the increasing mobility from rural or small-town to city life and the non-continuous communication between the two spheres. Internal migrants, socialized into the world views of neighbours, teachers, and/or clergy and lacking contact with urban modernity, experienced shock when entering the vibrant intellectual life of the cities. Better communication and resulting choice of options would have eased the transition. The "underlying assumptions" of traditionalist authors, such as the Confederation poets, "were coming to have less and less meaning" to readers to whom "the decorative beauty of their verse" and their prestige still appealed. In reaction to the national stances of the Group of Seven, *The Canadian Bookman*, and the Canadian Authors' Association, Arthur J.M. Smith and Frank R. Scott founded *The Fortnightly Review* (1925–27) as a literary supplement to the *McGill Daily*. Other, often mimeographed sheets appeared from Toronto to Vancouver. Small presses emerged—at the beginning, First Statement Press and Contact Press—and experimented with new forms of writing and thinking, forms that established publishers would not touch for fear of the ideas, the aesthetics, or commercial viability. While Smith became a scholar in the humanities, significantly with a position at Michigan State University in the United States rather than in Canada, Scott became a lawyer, professor of law, and Canadian civil rights activist. With the authors of the *Review* they formed the "Montreal Group" of anglophone poets who wanted to address modern society and free themselves from Victorian conventions. Through the small presses, Little Magazines, and Little Theatres, Canadian writing and performing took up cosmopolitan influences and looked to the future rather than to the past.[420]

---

420 : Louis Dudek and Michael Gnarowski, eds., *The Making of Modern Poetry in Canada* (Toronto: Ryerson, 1967), 45–61; Fred Cogswell, "Little Magazines and Small Presses in Canada," in *Figures in a Ground: Canadian Essays on Modern Literature Collected in Honour of Sheila Watson*, eds. Diane Bessai and David Jackel (Saskatoon: Western Producer, 1978), 162–173, quote p. 164.

Western farmers, ethnic groups, women, and British Columbia authors also had to organize publication outlets for themselves. The farmers' co-operative and the farmer-labour movements of the 1930s established small presses, especially Western Producer in Saskatoon, and in the 1950s Peguis Publishers and Queenston House. In British Columbia, Campbell River's Ptarmigan Press and Vancouver's Orca Sound Publications, New Star Books, and Evergreen were active. Ethnic groups' presses and subsequent research centres included the Manitoba Mennonite Historical Society, Derksen Publisher in Steinbach, the Central and East European Studies Society and the Canadian Institute of Ukrainian Studies in Edmonton, and the Polish Alliance Press in Toronto. Regional and local public research institutions provided support for commercially non-viable texts, for example, the Provincial Archives of Alberta, the Glenbow Institute, the Regina School Aids Publishing Company, and the University of Regina's Canadian Plains Research Centre. Later, in Toronto, the Women's Press was founded and other small but influential presses such as House of Anansi, Sono Nis Books, and Talon Press (later Talonbooks). These literary movements democratized Canadian culture and were non-colonial.

To evaluate the different forms of cultural production, a "great mouths–Little Magazines" juxtaposition may be helpful. While propaganda-spewing, billboard-creating English-language imperialists and race-conscious propagandists of Nouvelle-France's achievements overshadowed diversity and innovation, the Little Magazines, Little Theatres, and immigrant authors addressed both open-minded and marginalized segments of Canada's peoples. This cultural scene was increasingly concerned with Canadian themes in juxtaposition to cross-border extension of American culture and to commercialized culture.[421] Cultural producers had to make a living from their products, had to market them in a changing climate of opinion of ever fewer readers interested in ye-olde-British or *foi-et-terroir* Nouvelle-France themes. U.S. publishers were ahead of Canadian literary scholars when they published Canadian novelists and when the U.S. *Atlantic Monthly* accorded a Canadian author an important major prize. The interwar years were a Canadian period with British influence on the decline and U.S. influence as yet far from its apogee. Living under Depression conditions, the broad mass of Canada's peoples, however, may have had little time for cultural consumption.

The one innovative and integrative approach in the humanities was proposed by Northrop Frye. "Literature is conscious mythology," he argued, "as society develops, its mythical stories become structural principles of

---

421: Maria Tippett, *Making Culture*, 16.

story-telling, its mythical concepts, sun-gods [or snow and Indians] and the like, become habits of metaphorical thought. In a fully mature literary tradition the writer enters into a structure of traditional stories and images." It might be debated whether fully developed myths are indeed a sign of "maturity." Common Canadians, who left life writings, evidenced no overarching myths and thus could mediate between social settings and individual experience in a more differentiated way than national conventions of literary writing permitted. To such "integrative" myths Frye juxtaposed destructive "ideologies"—probably in reaction to the disasters of the fascist and Stalinist versions. But was dependency on Britain and France a past-centered myth or was it an ideology? Michael D. Behiels interpreted that "mythologies coordinate us with nature and our shared primal and primary concerns. Ideologies apply and adapt mythologies but in doing so they falsify the primary concerns since ideologies promote differences and segregation while myths promote human solidarity." Frye's perceptive insights, his "imaginative creations," tried to focus "on the human condition itself" (O'Grady 1999). As a result of his emphasis on myths and essentialist archetypes, Frye's Cultural Studies project, "to contribute to the discussion, within a very broad constituency of educated citizens, of fundamental socio-political issues such as societal cohesion amid cultural diversity, the validation of structures of power and the idea of progress," has received scant attention in the social sciences. Thus, this one valiant start in humanities theorizing ended in abstraction.[422]

Images large and small:
The nationalization of the arts

Canadian art and its narratives had begun in a missionary and colonizer vein. One of the very first paintings, "La France apportant la foi aux Indiens de la Nouvelle-France" (post-1666), was symptomatic. Produced by seventeenth-century visiting French clerics and from the early eighteenth century by laymen or imported from France, les beaux-arts de la décoration religieuse set the tone for more than two centuries. The British-Canadian counterpart from the Maritimes to forts on the Great Lakes was the later-emerging landscape genre of educated English, often military officers who

---

422 : Northrop Frye, "Conclusion," quotes pp. 824, 836; Michael D. Behiels, "Introduction. Canadian Thinkers in the 20th Century," *Journal of Canadian Studies* 34.4 (1999): 9–13, quote p. 10; Jean O'Grady, "The Poetic Frye," ibid., 15–26; Douglas Long, "Northrop Frye: Liberal Humanism and the Critique of Ideology," ibid., 27–51, quote p. 27. Mazo de la Roche, *Ringing the Changes: An Autobiography* (Toronto: Macmillan, 1957), 186–89.

learnt to sketch topographies as part of their training. Native peoples' spiritual artwork was hardly perceived by the newcomers, some of their utilitarian ornamental styles were adapted and Europeanized. As another element, regional forms of folk art emerged. Since the small communities could not yet support resident artists, travelling ones produced portraits and other paintings on command.

In the first half of the nineteenth century, a democratization and Canadianization, if in a colonial context, occurred when amateur gentlemen of means and leisure founded art clubs: the Halifax Chess, Pencil and Brush Club (1787) whose members concentrated on water-colours; and the British- and French-Canadian-supported Toronto Society of Arts, and the Montreal Society of Artists (both 1847). Exhibitions included artists from northeastern U.S. cities and itinerant painters. Joseph Légaré, who had restored and collected paintings brought by clerics fleeing revolutionary France, turned to provincial Canadian themes in baroque style. Cornelius Krieghoff's ahistorical pastoralism hierarchized culture by creating the quaint habitant families for a paying English-Canadian public. Paul Kane, from Toronto, painted Plains peoples as statue-like heroes. By mid-century the world of art stabilized and Upper Canada's society copied exhibition societies flourishing in English counties. The Provincial Exhibition added an art section in 1846, offering prizes to amateurs and, from 1852, to professionals.[423]

In the next decades, the dual colonial legacies gave way to increasingly Canadian settings. U.S. styles of art became admissible as another foreign influence. The anglophone Art Association of Montreal, today the Musée des Beaux-Arts de Montréal, held a first exhibition in 1860 in the Mechanics' Institute. The Society of Canadian Artists (founded 1867) reflected the new national consciousness, but restricted to Canadian members and under the impact of the recession of the 1870s, it soon entered a phase of stagnation. In 1877, Lord Dufferin initiated the National Gallery and the Royal Canadian Academy of Arts, which held its first exhibition in 1880. The opening of the West resulted in a thematic shift to large-size landscape painting and in a spatial shift from Montreal, the port for European-based vessels, to Toronto, the inland harbour connected via Duluth to Winnipeg. A London-born Scot, John A. Fraser left Montreal to participate in the founding of the Ontario Society of Artists (1872), out of which the Ontario College of Art

---

423 : Provincial exhibitions were part of a nationalizing moment bringing together producers from agriculture and industry. Local exhibitions were meant to further pride in achievements of the community, to advance knowledge through exchange of information and sharing of experiences. Elsbeth A. Heaman, *The Inglorious Arts of Peace: Exhibitions in Canadian Society during the Nineteenth Century* (Toronto: UTP, 1999).

developed.[424] Under the influence of both the U.S. Hudson River school and sophisticated English water-colour techniques a landscape school emerged in the 1860s among mostly British immigrants, a few German ones, including Otto Jacobi and Albert Bierstadt, and U.S. immigrants, including Robert Duncanson, the first African-American painter of national renown. When the transcontinental railways provided access to the Rocky Mountains, enthusiastic and heroic paintings of their impressive grandeur were produced by the hundreds. An urban counter-movement turned to the "dignity of labour" (J.R. Harper) and to common people in small towns and rural settings. Urbanity also induced many painters to visit Paris. Social themes included everyday life and large machines, a young woman teacher facing the old men of the school board in "A meeting of the School Trustees" by Robert Harris (1885), and "Mortgaging the Homestead" by George Reid (1890). When the Pacific Coast's First Peoples and their ceremonial poles attracted the attention of Emily Carr after 1900 as "relics" of a different spirituality, the Nootka adopted her as Klee Wyck, the Laughing One, but Euro-Canadian critics and collectors showed no interest. By the 1930s she proclaimed Pacific Coast Native art as the oldest art of the West and a better model than old European styles.[425]

In the early twentieth century, international and national developments merged. Toronto's Canadian Art Club (established 1907), for example, introduced impressionism and Scandinavian landscape painting. The Group of Seven coalesced in the Toronto of the 1910s, initiated by a summer tourist guide, Tom Thompson, who painted in spring and fall and thus reflected the brilliant colours of the changing seasons of Algonquin Park, Georgian Bay, and the North.[426] Originally mainly commercial illustrators, the Group's members held a first exhibition in 1920. Reflecting a simple nature-loving life in the bush, one of the myths of Canadian identity, they became known as "northern enthusiasts" and proclaimed an independent, colourful "Canadianism of the eye" (New 1989) at a time when French surrealism and German expressionism captured the art world. The ever-changing members

---

424 : In 1900, the Art Museum of Toronto (later Art Gallery of Ontario) was established.

425 : Dennis Reid, *A Concise History of Canadian Painting* (1973; 2nd ed., Toronto: Oxford, 1988), and Reid, "Nationale Bestrebungen: Die Entwicklung einheimischer Strukturen zur Förderung der Malerei in Kanada," in *Kanadische Malerei: 19 und 20 Jahrhundert* (Stuttgart, 1983); J. Russell Harper, *Painting in Canada: A History* (1st ed., 1966; 2nd ed., Toronto: UTP, 1977). For music see Helmut Kallmann, *A History of Music in Canada, 1534–1914* (Toronto: UTP, 1960). While Reid and Harper employed a European-influence perspective, Kallmann structured his study according to regional Canadian developments.

426 : The Group originally included Tom Thompson, Franklin Carmichael, A.Y. Jackson, Franz Johnston, Arthur Lismer, Lawren Harris, J.E.H. MacDonald, and Frederick Varley.

of the Group fanned out to paint the Pacific Coast, the Rocky Mountains, the Arctic, the Maritimes, the Canadian Shield, and the St. Lawrence. At first rejected by critics, they blended commercial art nouveau with Scandinavian symbolism and made cottage country seem like untamed nature. By claiming a national mission they made a profitable business out of their art. In Montreal, artists, including some professionals, formed the Beaver Hall Group, which became the most significant women's group of painters of the 1920s and '30s. Sarah Robertson and Lilias Torrance Newton were members. In the early 1930s, the Group of Seven held a retrospective at the National Gallery (1936) and the national Canadian Group of Painters was founded (1933). Urban themes or small-town scenes with at least some human beings in the picture never gained the same following the landscape schools had. Quebec's agrarian ruralism had its counterpart in an Ontario and national grandeur-of-landscape ruralism. But international war as well as transnational art produced new styles and themes: battlefield scenes and munitions factories of the two World Wars, French-European and North African influences from Tangier, and portraits of African Canadians.[427]

Painting has dominated the discourse about Canadian art, but a far more democratic development, photography, and a master-narrative imposing monument art also emerged. In 1880, a French inventor developed the folding "tourist" camera, and in 1888 George Eastman of Rochester, NY, began to market a small camera that empowered common people to create images. Given that amateur photos, not considered art, have never been collected, it is impossible to say how self-created photographs influenced discourses and self-views. Their impact was ephemeral. In contrast, permanency was the goal of those with the power of definition, who erected historical monuments from the mid-1890s. Monuments impress particular aspects of the past on passers-by. War memorials, for example, commemorate dead soldiers as heroes of the nation, but annihilate memory of their widows and children and of crippled surviving veterans. Federal and provincial legislative buildings might reflect a sovereign people but were ornamented to impress respect for institutions. The symbolisms of Parliament in Ottawa (completed 1866) and of the Palais législatif de Québec (constructed since 1883) were carefully conceptualized "je me souviens" themes in architecture, paintings, and ornaments, including Robert Harris's "The Fathers of Confederation" (1883) in Ottawa. Manitoba's legislative building with two large male bison in front is a good example of cliché-ridden public artwork ·

---

427 : Among the new painters were Carl Schaefer, Charles Comfort, David Milne, Louis Muhlstock, Adrien Hébert, James Wilson Morrice, and as only woman Pegi Nicol MacLeod.

built at a time when it was expected that the population would reach several million a decade or two later. Gothic-type new churches, château-style hotels, and classicist railway stations supplemented the eclectic borrowing from across the ages and societies. It merits emphasis, however, that borrowing, like translation, implies adaptation to Canadian usages.[428]

Art schools became forums for debates about styles in a secularized Canadian society in an international context. Quebec's École du Meuble (Montreal) and the Écoles des Beaux-Arts (Quebec, 1922; Montreal, 1923) were staffed with cosmopolitan teachers who, like creative artists across the country, discarded the orthodoxy of the Group of Seven and of Quebec religious art. They experimented and moved in many directions. Examples are Lawren Harris's turn to geometric abstractions, Emily Carr's stylized landscapes, a Montreal group's French-inspired surrealist painting (retrospectively styled the "automatists"), and anglophone Paris-trained artists' turn from the figurative to the abstract. Some walked borderlines: Ozias Leduc painted religious motives for public exhibition, though privately he produced symbolist art. Toronto's John Lyman formed an "École de Paris" and the Contemporary Art Society (1939). By 1938, when the Eastern Group could mount its first exhibition of abstract painting, it was obvious to many that the nationalist Canadian Group of Painters had lost its hold on the public's appreciation of themes. In reaction to the paralyzing Duplessis government in Quebec, fifteen artists, seven of them women, in a mimeographed manifesto called *Refus global* (1948) attacked the less than holy trinity of Church, State, and Business and the shallowness of cultural production imposed by them. Painters Jean-Paul Riopelle and Paul-Émile Borduas as well as the playwright Claude Gauvreau were at the forefront.[429] In a kind of unlimited artistic individualism—which got Borduas sacked from his teaching post at the École du Meuble—the group demanded a liberating, spontaneous, anarchic personal style that could never be realist. This avant-gardist self-expressive style limited the audience of *Refus*, and few non-Quebec artists participated.

An unexpected development had its origins in the Cold War and fears of "Hot War" of the late 1940s. Canada's Arctic shores assumed military importance for the distant early warning (DEW) line, a protection against the perceived threat of Soviet Union missile attacks. Huge U.S. military installations and their environmentally destructive debris disrupted Inuit life. To foster economic activity in the communities, distant from markets and communication, the federal government, the Hudson's Bay Company, and

---

428 : Linteau et al., *Historie de Québec*, 1:732–34.

429 : Patricia Smart, *Les femmes du Refus Global* (Montreal: Boréal, 1998).

the Canadian Handicrafts Guild jointly encouraged a revival of traditional Inuit and Native art. Certification of artworks prevented cheap imitations under the rampant free market ideology. West Coast and Arctic as well as Iroquoian art came to replace the Group of Seven's dazzling nature paintings as quintessentially Canadian in the view of many collectors. The new "Indian and, especially, Inuit art was literally brought into existence by a collaboration between European-trained and traditional native artists, assisted by government."[430]

Communication as a resource and as a tool of power:
From common people's telecommunication
to global communication theory

Production, whether of art or wheat, distant from consumers, required networks of communication. So had everyday life in the thinly settled First Nations' North America through the ages. Along thin lines, knowledges spread across Native peoples' social spaces and, subsequently, through Native–European contact or conflict zones. All necessitated long-distance oral communication including multiple translations or re-lations. Communication, particularly over long distances, has often been taken to be technologically defined. However, the step from oral and written modes to wire and electronic ones accelerates only speed. Through the ages, traders—whether Chinese or Arab seafarers, African or European caravan owners, or Native Americans—had exchanged information between cultures and across great distances. Eurasian merchants' hand-written, often-copied travel manuals supplemented oral information and provide historians with sources. In contrast, the knowledges of peoples without writing, such as the fishermen of the northern Atlantic, the peoples of North America or Africa, for lack of written documents hardly entered historical memory.

Societies relying solely on oral transmission could flexibly adapt knowledges to particular societal needs, but they were deprived of the possibility of accumulating data. With writing and print, the nineteenth-century network of historical and scientific societies, including those in the Canadas, collected whatever "useful information" they could find. Aware of the existence of parallel, overlapping, and conflicting knowledges, French Enlightenment philosophers began to compile an encyclopedia meant to be "universal." The escalating speed of collection of knowledge across the world made *savants* realize that multiple systems of knowledge storage and the

---

430 : Bumsted, *Peoples of Canada*, quote p. 383.

fragmentation of the world's intellectual inheritance into particular national systems of categorizing resulted in "disorderly" procedures and systems. The resulting "universal encyclopedia," with its centralization, privileged accumulating Western peoples over non-accumulating ones.[431]

In North America, exchanges between Native peoples involved long-distance (or "tele-") communication as well as mediation between language groups. The fur trade created a transcontinental, transoceanic, and intersocietal macro-region of communication. Native hunters responded to demands in London or Paris, with information relayed through the trading companies' factors. Resident women and sojourning European traders formed partnerships and families to communicate about regions and practices of supply, to negotiate differences of culture, and to connect to distant markets' networks of communication. Knowledges were shared among participants, yet were not under the control of central places and central actors. Another type of long-distance communication connected immigrants with kin "at home," that is, the former home, by written letter or oral information during visits. Immigrant letters transmitted relatively realistic information in terms of options for life projects. News about a particular locality, whether Ontario's Hastings County or Alberta's Lethbridge, indicated options to the recipients, often prospective migrants. To recipients with little knowledge of Canadian geography, such options appeared as located in "Canada" rather than a specific locality. They were thus generalized to a part of the continent or an imagined larger society and were contrasted, more often favourably than not, with conditions among subaltern peoples in the European empires or the southern provinces of China. In the process, a "Canada" emerged in the minds of kin and friends in Europe and, after 1858, among Chinese and other peoples in Asia. Both information and images were local in scope and life-project-oriented. The importance of such telecommunication, necessary to keep family relationships functioning intercontinentally, is evidenced by the high value farming families "in the middle of nowhere" accorded to the federal post service. "Ottawa's" one local service, the mail delivery and collection, was of utmost importance for making sequential migration possible. In Canadian society, the combination of stores, printed Eaton's catalogues, and the mail permitted tele-trading, the rise of mail-order buying. For "locals" it provided connections to the larger world of

---

431 : Dirk Hoerder, *Cultures in Contact: World Migrations in the Second Millennium* (Durham: Duke Univ. Press, 2002), 28–38; Hans Dieter Hellige, *Weltbibliothek, Universalenzyklopädie, Worldbrain: Zur Säkulardebatte über die Organisation des Weltwissens* (Univ. Bremen: artec-Paper 77, June 2000).

consumption and, since mail-order catalogues were like illustrated encyclopedias, to the larger world of knowledge.[432]

After "tele-orality" and "tele-writing," the telegraph and the telephone emerged as the next stage of communication. Telegraphy, used since the mid-nineteenth century, was at first expensive and thus implicitly undemocratic, but it had an immediate impact on common people when newspapers began to receive and exchange information by wire, when trains began to function on standardized time, and when international market developments, such as a rise or fall of wheat prices, could be communicated by telegraph. A Scottish Canadian engineer, thinking in continental and global terms, proposed standardized global time zones and implemented transcontinental and trans-Pacific telegraphy in the interests of profits for his CPR and the interests of British imperial connections.[433] Telecommunication by reported word or written letter was in the hands of those who sent and received messages. With technology, contents of messages and selection of what was considered relevant for transmission passed into the hand of engineers and corporation staff. During the Métis' struggle for self-government in 1870, Whites sent calls for federal troops through railway-owned telegraph lines, and White-written stories about the struggle were spread through the wires. It has been said that the Métis lost the media battle—but they never even had access to the connecting telegraph.[434]

The telephone reached small communities in the West in the 1930s. It was easily accessible, if at first through a party line that permitted an unwanted democracy of shared information. Party lines, it has to be explained to a generation of cellphone users, connected many people's telephones through a single wire, with the connections being established by an operator in person, usually a woman, and not by an anonymous mechanical switchboard. Thus the operator knew who was calling whom and, given the technology of the times, anybody picking up the phone when someone else was on the line could listen in. Such breaching of privacy permitted quick spread of information across communities and gossip to reign over community mores. For the average Canadian, the oral, letter, and telephone communication was far more important than printed literature. Imagery and themes differed: priv-

---

432 : On farmers and the mail see Hoerder, *Creating Societies*, 196–204; Helbich et al., *News from the Land of Freedom*.

433 : The literary reflection of this is Jules Verne's *Le Tour du monde en 80 jours* (1873), also indicating French-British competition in worldwide influence.

434 : Jean-Guy Rens, *L'Empire invisible: histoire des télécommunications au Canada*, vol. 1: "De 1846 à 1956," vol. 2: "1956 à nos jours" (Sainte-Foy: PU Laval, 1993), 1:5–276 (vol. 1 Engl. as *The Invisible Empire: A History of the Telecommunications Industry in Canada, 1846–1956*, Montreal: MQUP, 2001).

ileged discourses and myths of golden wheat or others in the print media, children's illnesses, the next weekend's social, a sharing of farm implements, a joint outing in personal telecommunication. The telephone could mean survival: a call to a midwife or doctor in time of impending birthing could make the difference between life and death for a pregnant woman and/or her infant.

The new technologies for communication required investments that, as far as they were raised within Canada, could only come from the two central Canadas. Social scientists and political economists were aware that access to and power over means of communication could be a resource for many or a profit centre for a few. The sociologists of the Frontiers of Settlement project had understood how development of isolated farming communities was dependent on information connections through local, regional, or statewide focal points of transportation and communication to larger markets. In terms of power, Canada's rural hinterlands depended on the metropoles. On a further level of analysis, political economists, with Harold Innis in the lead, came to understand that the central Canadas in turn were a hinterland to more powerful central places like New York and Washington, D.C. Thus the study of mass communication has always been linked to questions of power. What had been the control of the British navy and merchant marine over transport routes came to be the U.S. head start over routes of news transmission.[435]

A communications theory, based on distribution of and access to knowledge, emerged as a corollary to Harold Innis's research on the staples economy. The fur economy had required hemispheric communication systems to coordinate producing and marketing practices effectively and profitably. A century and a half earlier, Adam Smith, theorizing the role of free markets, had discerned free and complete access to information as a decisive prerequisite. Asymmetrical access to information in the frame of concentrations of power would skew information levels and informed decision-making. Innis recognized the global aspect of communication, the importance of particular segments of knowledge for particular economic sectors, and the power of centralized political institutions, whether empires or ideological institutions such as the Roman Catholic Church. In control over the

---

435 : Half a century after Innis, the U.S. economists Joseph Stiglitz, George Akerlof, and Michael Spence, received the Nobel prize in economics of 2001 for their 1970s research on market failure through "asymmetrical information." Among the participants in market economies, those on one end of a market transaction usually know more than those at the other end. Consumers, usually knowing less about a product than the seller or producer, are placed in dependent position. Small countries with low levels of information inflow are dependent on nodes of information exchange in particular cities, whether London, Paris, Moscow, or Hong Kong.

staples economy as in the hold over souls, knowledge about opportunities, competition, and cost advantages determined success or failure. Globalized knowledges were segmented according to economic pursuit or ideological interest.

The fur trade and the cod fishery may serve as examples for hemispheric communication transmission through networks. Information from trapping or hunting groups from eastern Siberia via Scandinavia and the Hudson Bay to the Yukon accumulated in many regional trading nodes. It was compacted and made digestible to distant recipients and forwarded through sea-going ships. Finally it was centralized in the head offices of the fur trade corporations. Many different interests shaped content and strategy of communication. Quality and quantity of fur was only one element. In the core, company directors had to inform and satisfy shareholders; in the periphery, hunting families had to communicate with neighbours to make a living and, in an ideal model, to avoid either reducing fur-bearing animals beyond stock recovery or overstocking the market. This involved multiple translations between value systems—the human aspect that Innis overlooked. Cree women and Scottish traders or Ojibwa women and French Canadian men had to work out strategies of cultural, emotional, and material interaction. They influenced as well as depended on decisions in some central office in Europe, whose actors had never seen Canada (or Siberia). The demands of European fashions needed to be telecommunicated to and translated into hunting strategies a continent away. Speed of information transmission was important for quick reaction to distant occurrences. An inter-tribal war that prevented Native peoples from supplying furs could cause havoc with profits in London; an inter-imperial war in the Atlantic World that prevented fur-laden ships from sailing could wreak havoc in fur-supplying family economies.

Nodes of information exchange, whether an HBC trading post, a port city, or a capital of financial transactions, held an advantage through economies of scale and overlapping information-producing systems. The smaller or more peripheral a unit, the greater its marginality to the axes of communication. It was Innis's achievement to introduce this concept into scholarship, though given Canada's peripheral position in the British Empire, in Euro-Atlantic knowledge production, and for U.S.-American interests, few scholars at the time took note of his findings and built on it. The bias in favour of size and central location (a monopoly) was also structured, Innis argued, by the medium of communication. Any one medium was either biased in terms of control, time, or space. Those spatially concentrated "favor growth of religion, of hierarchical organization, and of contractionist institutions," or, simply, the state. Those "easily transportable," such as paper, "favor administration over vast distance" and thus growth of empires with widely stretched-out administrations. Innis also compared oral and written transmission and found the former more easily adaptable to the present, the latter more likely to require exegesis and, as in the bureaucracies of states and Churches, specialized personnel wielding power over interpretation and selection of information. Communication thus fosters particular types of cultural organization; particular means and systems of communication pattern or "bias" the messages they convey.[436]

In view of the cultural-societal, technological, and personal life changes wrought by the new twentieth-century media of communication, interpreters of the new technologies emerged. In the 1960s, Marshall McLuhan, building on Innis, proposed an integrative approach.[437] Abandoning Innis's eclectic global approach, he concentrated on the relations between means of communication and contents. He reconceptualized Innis's opposition of space and time, his implications of marginalization, and his neglect of human actors into a time-space continuum, and argued that the modes of human perception, sight, touch, sound, and smell, are interdependent. Each medium developed a particular grammar that shaped the content of information, "the medium is the message" in his all-too-often cited adage. The shaping of messages occurs only through the signifier/signified dichotomy, but also by the respective technology, orality, and hand-copied texts in a first stage, moveable type and print as second stage, and wire as well as wireless transmission as the third. In the age of television as the major everyday conveyance of information, his emphasis on the visual was well taken. Moving pictures convey mobility and speed in ways totally different from a printed explication of speed. "Hot" media provide highly defined information, a photograph for example, and thus reduce audience participation, while "cold" media are more open and permit and/or require intensive audience participation.

Media "are vast social metaphors that not only transmit information but determine what is knowledge; that not only orient us to the world but tell us

---

436 : Innis, *Empire and Communication* (1946), *The Bias of Communication* (1951), and two collections of essays. James W. Carey, "Harold Adams Innis and Marshall McLuhan," *Antioch Review* 27 (Spring 1967): 5–39, quote p. 9.

437 : Opinion on Innis and McLuhan ranges from "abstruse and controversial" (J.W. Carey) to a positing of a "Canadian School" of media research comparable to the "Frankfurt School" (Stamps). Judith Stamps, *Unthinking Modernity: Innis, McLuhan, and the Frankfurt School* (Montreal: MQUP, 1995). Most useful are Graeme Patterson, *History and Communications: Harold Innis, Marshall McLuhan, and the Interpretation of History* (Toronto: UTP, 1990); Donald F. Theall, *The Virtual Marshall McLuhan* (Montreal: MQUP, 2001). A new interpretation is presented by Richard Cavell, *McLuhan in Space: A Cultural Geography* (Toronto: UTP, 2002).

what kind of world exists; they not only excite and delight our senses but, by altering the ratio of sensory equipment that we use, actually change our character." Communications media and technology were thus conceptualized as an extension of the mind, and since they shape the messages, they alter the mind.[438] When McLuhan shaped his argument and television was shaping lifestyles, his stimulating and aphoristic writing hit a responsive chord. After his *Understanding Media* (1964), San Francisco public relations experts promoted him, and Tom Wolfe featured him in the New York *World Journal Tribune's* Sunday edition. These media (as messages) shaped the public perception of his often-aphoristic statements. Recently, Richard Cavell, while acknowledging that McLuhan was "skimming along the surfaces," provided a new post-modern reading of his spatiality: "As a side of dynamic social interaction, acoustic space provides a critical context for understanding the materiality of spatial relations in a cultural geography where all time is now and all space here."[439] McLuhan's stimulating thought was an important step toward communication theory and influenced Foucault, Derrida, and Lefèbvre, who theorized the discursive aspects of communication processes. Whether selection of a type of medium implies a "communication determination," as McLuhan argued, is still an open question. His major achievements were his imaginative phrasing, his opening of new vistas by crossing of disciplinary boundaries, and his sweeping synthesis of patterns and technologies of communication across centuries.

New nationwide media:
Whose investments, power, and contents?

The new visual media, which changed everyday lives of common people as much as the telephone had done, were the 1950s stage of a sequence of telecommunication technologies: first the press, vastly cheaper and easier to print through the invention of the rotating printing machine; next the acceleration of photos to pictures in motion; then the radio broadcasting of news; and, finally, TV broadcasting of images.

---

438 : McLuhan, *The Mechanical Bride* (1951), *The Gutenberg Galaxy* (1962), *Understanding Media* (1964). Carey, "Innis and McLuhan," quote p. 18.

439 : Theall, *The Virtual McLuhan*, 81-94, 254-56; Cavell, *McLuhan in Space*, xiii, 227; David Crowley and David Mitchell, "Communications in Canada: Enduring Themes, Emerging Issues," in Terry Goldie, Carmen Lambert, Rowland Lorimer, eds., *Canada: Theoretical Discourse / Discours théorétiques*. Selected proceedings of the conference entitled "Theoretical Discourse in the Canadian Intellectual Community," Assoc. for Canadian Studies, Gray Rocks Inn, Saint-Jovite, Quebec, 25-27 Sept. 1992 (Montreal: Assoc. for Canadian Studies, 1994), 133-52.

Based on the new print technology, a mass press had developed since the 1880s: magazines such as *Revue canadienne* (1864–1922), the *Canadian Magazine* (1893–1939), *Maclean's* (since 1896), and *Canadian Forum* (since 1920). *Chatelaine*, addressing women, followed in 1928. These and the ever more numerous dailies required increasing investments. Starting in 1903, the Canadian Associated Press provided the first wire service to which, two decades later, William Stephenson added a wire-photo process. The press relied on every technological innovation possible, but did not necessarily present new ideas. When innovation did occur, it was gendered. Women were news when struggling for their rights, were potential readers, and, as spenders of most families' consumption budgets, were the target for advertisers. But they were refused jobs in editorial offices. Ella Cora Hind, who did not accept rejection, began to work as agricultural editor at the *Free Press* (Winnipeg) and founded the Canadian Women's Press Club in 1904. Motivated by current ideas about the worldwide interconnectedness of agricultural settlement, she travelled widely to observe agricultural methods and progress both from a nationalist and an economic perspective.[440]

In the 1920s, concern over U.S. influences in press publishing increased by leaps and bounds in English-language Canada while Quebec publishers were protected by the language barrier. Influential Canadians argued that the depiction of U.S. opportunities and products resulted in (1) a pull and a loss through emigration of population in general and of highly qualified personnel ("brain drain") in particular; (2) a loss of purchasing power through advertisements which lured Canadian consumers to U.S. products; (3) Canadian authors published in U.S. magazines because they paid better honoraria; and (4) in terms of culture and morality, U.S. magazines were said to contain contents not in keeping with British imperial and/or British-Canadian sentiments, to undermine Canadian feelings of belonging through a process of Americanization, and to distribute "salacious" materials that would "dissipate" the morals of the youth in general and young women in particular. Economically, U.S. publishers, first, had the advantage of economies of scale, that is lower overhead costs because of their far larger market. Second, they benefited from considerably higher advertising revenues. Third, to avoid Canadian tariffs, U.S. publishers printed special editions in Canada and repatriated the profits. When the Mackenzie King government abolished the limited customs protection for Canadian magazines, sales of U.S. magazines within two years, more than doubled to $5.9 million in 1937.

---

440 : Hind, *A Story of Wheat* (1932) and, on her travels, *Seeing for Myself* (1937). Kay Rex, *No Daughter of Mine: The Women and History of the Canadian Women's Press Club, 1904-1971* (Toronto: Cedar Cave Books, 1995).

In the wartime 1940s, *Reader's Digest* established a Canadian subsidiary and *Time* began to distribute a Chicago-printed Canadian edition. By the mid-1950s, U.S. magazines, imported or in Canadian editions, controlled over 80 percent of the market, and *Time* and *Reader's Digest* gobbled up 37 percent of Canadian advertising revenues. Canadian readers preferred U.S. magazines just as newspaper publishers often preferred U.S. wire services.

Canadian publishers and financiers never considered a Canadian press conglomerate but turned to a U.K.-Canada axis. They were dependent on British capital and on British notions of social standing—they sought titles of nobility. From the 1930s on, the accelerating process of concentration was controlled by Canadians with British connections: Ontario-born Max Aitken, later Lord Beaverbrook, became a London press czar; Roy Thomson, later Baron Thomson of Fleet, began to build a Toronto and Canadian chain and after World War II expanded to Great Britain; and Conrad Black, later Baron Black of Crossharbour and author of an appreciative biography of *Duplessis* (1977). In the English-language press, the Canadian contents issue has never been resolved, but Quebec held its linguistic advantage.[441]

As to radio broadcasting, a one-way oral telecommunication, the share of Canadian contents is difficult to determine for lack of sources. In 1920, the Marconi Company opened the first Canadian Radio Station in Montreal; the first French-language station (CKAC) began emissions in 1922. By 1931, 28 percent of all Quebec households owned a receiver with a metropolis–hinterland dichotomy evident: 40 percent in Montreal, 8 percent in rural regions.[442] In broadcasting it was not U.S. but potential religious control that prompted an intensive debate about power and contents. The group later known as Jehovah's Witnesses prepared to open radio stations in the 1920s. The established churches evoked the spectre of sectarian control and a government commission on broadcasting (the Canadian Radio Broadcasting Commission), with Sir John Aird as chair, began to investigate. Noting that the privately owned film industry of Canada had recently been swallowed by a U.S. distribution chain, Aird's Commission, his background in corporate capitalism notwithstanding, recommended a government-controlled national broadcasting system to prevent another economic and cultural activity being siphoned off. To prod the government into action because "it's the state or the States," Graham Spry and Alan Plaunt co-founded the Canadian Radio League in 1929. Spry, a journalist of the Winnipeg *Free Press*, was a member of the League for Social Reconstruction and co-authored *So-*

<hr/>

441 : Isaiah A. Litvak and Christopher J. Maule, *Cultural Sovereignty: The "Time" and "Reader's Digest" Case in Canada* (New York: Praeger, 1974), 14–39; New, *History of Canadian Literature* (1989), 166–67; de la Roche, *Ringing the Changes*, 120.

442 : Linteau et al., *Historie de Québec*, 1:459.

cial Planning for Canada (1934). Rejecting U.S. models of private ownership for the British one of public ownership, the 1932 broadcasting act provided for the English-language Canadian Broadcasting Corporation (CBC) and French-language Radio-Canada, both founded in 1936, a few months before the BBC. Like the railways, the CBC reached across regions and time zones and it spread Canadian perspectives across the international borders.

Public ownership, premised on airwaves as "a scarce natural resource to be exploited in the public interest," was to extend access to all Canadians as fast as technically feasible. The government assigned to broadcasting the goal of "fostering a national spirit and interpreting national citizenship" (which still happened to be British), of protecting Canadian "identity and sovereignty from incursions of the U.S. broadcasting empires," of providing employment for Canadian cultural producers, whether artists, writers, and musicians, technicians, and other broadcasting personnel. Public CBC television followed in 1952 but an act of 1958 permitted private stations under regulation of the Canadian Radio Broadcasting Commission.[443]

As to film, Canadian Studies has to analyze the southward cross-border sale of this thriving medium in 1923. After the Eastman Kodak camera democratized the taking of photographs, a new technology permitted the debut of "pictures in motion," or film. As in the case of many technological and medical breakthroughs, the Canadian input is almost forgotten. While the French Louis Lumière is usually credited with opening the first cinematography in Paris in 1895, the Ottawan Holland brothers, Andrew and George, had opened a Kinetoscope Parlor on New York's Broadway a year earlier. By 1896, when French, American, and British technologies were available, travelling "shows" rather than cinemas emerged. Within two years, they crossed the continent, often as part of vaudeville theatres, and reached Vancouver. In only six years, from 1897 to 1903, entrepreneurs and cameramen developed the major Canada-centered applications of the new medium: nature documentary with scenes from Niagara Falls by French and American firms and of the Rockies by the CPR; event documentary of the Klondike gold rush; information and propaganda, for example about Canadian troops in the Boer War (Edison, New York); a Massey-Harris commissioned advertising film on agricultural machinery (Edison); and amusement films thriving on imagery known to audiences, for example *Sleighing-Ottawa* (Edison).

The most important international impact of Canadian film production was a positioning of Canada as an immigration country. *Ten Years in Manitoba,*

---

443 : David Ellis, *Evolution of the Canadian Broadcasting System: Objectives and Realities 1928–1968* (Ottawa: Dept. of Communications, 1979), quotes p. 75; New, *History of Canadian Literature* (1989), 152–53, 181–82.

made by farmer James S. Freer in 1897, was used by the CPR for a lecture and film show tour in Great Britain in 1898–99. Both the tour's success and the increasing immigration of "Americans," seen as a threat to the "British" character of the West, induced the government to sponsor another tour in 1902, and the CPR to commission a series of thirty-five films, *Living Canada*, to stimulate British immigration. When several of the short films, made by the Bioscope Company of Canada as a subsidiary of a British company, harped on winter and snow (*Run of a Snowshoe Club, Quebec Fire Department on Sleds*), the CPR prohibited any further winter scenes, since the deeply ingrained ice-and-coldness cliché was bad for business. The films, often taken from flatcars, showed Canada from Quebec City to Victoria with sites frequently selected by local tourist bureaus.[444]

By 1903, storefront motion-picture theatres were a common feature in cities and touring companies reached out to smaller towns. A lively Canadian film production emerged, often visualizing and dramatizing existing oral-memory imagery to further a particular interpretation of Canadian history: *Hiawatha, the Messiah of the Ojibway* (1903), by Joe Rosenthal and E.A. Armstrong, based on Longfellow's fictionalized Iroquois-Ojibway poem; *Evangeline* (1907, U.S. company), also based on Longfellow; *Mes espérances* and *Quebec: The Tercentenary Celebration*, both by Ernest Ouimet; *The Canadian National Exhibition at Toronto* and *Calgary Stampede* (both 1912); films of the Rockies expanded on Ralph Connor's fiction of hardy men in the mountains; *The Battle of the Long Sault* about the mythologized Dollard des Ormeaux (1913); *Madeleine de Verchères* (1913), and many others. Canadian-made local-interest films emerged, first in Newfoundland (Harry Winter). American and British companies took up "typically" Canadian topics: moose hunt, salmon fishing, *Honeymoon at Niagara Falls* (Edison, 1907), winter carnival. They also produced dramatic films that added to or Americanized clichés about Canada: *Cattle Thieves* (1909), *Canadian Moonshiners* (1910), and *Fighting the Iroquois in Canada* (1910) among them. The Canadian Northern Railway commissioned films of its routes in 1909 and, under the auspices of the CPR's Colonization Department, another promotional immigration series of thirteen films was produced from 1910. The provincial and federal governments sponsored promotional films, for ex-

444 : The gala opening of the films in London took place in the presence of the Canadian High Commissioner, Lord Strathcona, who under his own name, Donald A. Smith, had been a CPR executive. When the film company re-released the films on its own account later, it used the sales appeal of the classic imagery: *Montreal on Skates* and *Winter Sports in Canada*. Subsequently, the series was expanded with funding from the Anglo-British Columbia Packing company to include a film *Catching Fifty Thousand Salmon in Two Hours*. Peter Morris, *Embattled Shadows: A History of Canadian Cinema 1895–1939* (Montreal: MQUP, 1978), 34.

ample on British Columbia (1908), and to propagandize World War I. Cultural producers, especially in Montreal, set up several Canadian film companies and, for distribution, film "exchanges," cinema chains, and luxury cinema theatres emerged under the lead of Ernest Ouimet (Montreal) and Jules and Jay Allen (Brantford). However, gatekeepers of what they considered culture and morals did not take well to some of the Canadian content shown and, following Quebec's lead of 1911, all provinces had passed censorship laws by 1914. Cultural autonomy in film production ended, when the U.S. Famous Players company acquired control of film distribution in Canada in 1923.[445]

Cross-border moves accelerated southward, the Canadian automobile industry was swallowed by U.S. General Motors, and the Canadian labour unions had come under the sway of the American Federation of Labor. Film actors and entrepreneurs addressing popular audiences migrated to Hollywood, Mary Pickford for example, as well as Jack Warner and Louis B. Mayer, the later film tycoons; those geared to upper middle class audiences chose to go to Great Britain. The federal government set up the Canadian Government Motion Picture Bureau (1923), after "the film image of the nation . . . [had] passed into others' control." Themes included "the familiar motifs of trapper, Mountie, wicked French-Canadian half-breed and snow," and "the reality of daily life again ran up against the image of reality, and sometimes the celluloid won" with the help of so-called "authentic costumes" of the actors.[446]

In the context of the arrival of the sound motion picture (1927) and the Aird Commission report on broadcasting (1928), a cross-section of film producers founded the National Film Society (1935, renamed Canadian Film Institute in 1950) with a mandate "to encourage and promote the study, appreciation and use of motion and sound pictures and television," then an experimental communications technology, "as educational and cultural factors in the Dominion of Canada and elsewhere." From 1938, Odeon Theatres competed with U.S. distribution companies and the British government exempted Commonwealth-produced films from the "British quota" clause directed against Hollywood. Vincent Massey, Canada's High Commissioner in London, wanting to expand Canadian film audiences in Britain and impressed by the 1930s British documentary films, arranged for its

---

445 : Morris, *Embattled Shadows*, 1–56, 243–73; Yves Lever, *Histoire générale du cinéma au Québec* (Montreal: Boréal, 1988); Marcel Jean, *Le cinéma québécois* (Montreal: Boréal, 1991).

446 : New, *History of Canadian Literature* (1989), quote p. 144; Morris, *Embattled Shadows*, 259–73. Pierre Berton, *Hollywood's Canada: The Americanization of Our National Image* (Toronto: McClelland & Stewart, 1975).

most famous director, John Grierson, to survey Canada's film industry. In response to his report, the government established the National Film Board (NFB, 1939) with the goal to encourage film production and to interpret "Canada to Canadians and to other nations." Such support carried "nation building beyond steel rails and tariffs into the realm of culture, the arts, education and creative expression of all kinds."[447]

With declaration of war in 1939 and the Cold War after 1945, the experimental and innovative phase of the 1930s came to a sudden end. Grierson, who had made working-class films in Britain and had been named first commissioner of the NFB, was named director of the Wartime Information Board (1943–45) and was requested to produce patriotic film propaganda. He did pursue his own internationalist perspective and to that purpose cooperated with the Rockefeller Foundation, whose internationalist social management approach fit the (democratic) nations-at-war attitude. When in February 1946 Igor Gouzenko, a minor official of the Soviet embassy in Ottawa, defected and revealed the operation of a spy ring, a "Red Scare" was orchestrated and U.S. and Canadian police investigated Grierson's activities and accused him of "communist sympathies." By association, they implicated the NFB and "the purges . . . in effect shut down a distinctively indigenous cultural entity in the name of the Cold War produced within the context of American mass culture."[448] In the early 1950s, the government allocated $250,000 to the NFB "to produce films in support of democracy in the Freedom Speaks program," one of the Cold War propaganda battles.[449]

While the documentary generation of the 1930s had considered film-making to be a public service, in the 1950s it became artistic self-expres-

---

447 : This government support was to have unexpected consequences in U.S.-Canada relations in the 1980s. Under the Foreign Agents Registration Act of 1938, the United States Justice Department labelled If You Love this Planet (1982) and the NFB-supported films Acid Rain: Requiem or Recovery (1982) and Acid from Heaven (1981) as "propaganda films by agents of a foreign government" and placed restrictions on their distribution. If You Love this Planet, which won an Oscar for best documentary short film, showed nuclear critic Helen Caldicott, president of U.S.-based Physicians for Social Responsibility. Charles R. Acland, "National Dreams, International Encounters: The Formation of Canadian Film Culture in the 1930s," Canadian Journal of Film Studies 3.1 (1994): 3–26, quote p. 5.

448 : Richard Cavell, ed., Love, Hate, and Fear in Canada's Cold War (Toronto: UTP, 2004), quote pp. 17–18; Reg Whitaker and Gary Marcuse, Cold War Canada: The Making of a National Insecurity State, 1945–1957 (Toronto: UTP, 1994).

449 : In 1949, another round of accusations of communist leanings began. The Canadian Department of National Defence refused permission to NFB personnel to work on defence films. To head off accusations based on rumour, Ross McLean, the NFB commissioner, invited the RCMP to conduct security screenings of NFB personnel.

sion. Government involvement continued[450] and with approval of the Department of External Affairs, the NFB began an ambitious series of thirteen films on "The Commonwealth of Nations" (1958). The project was embroiled in political controversy when the White South African government objected to *Black and White in South Africa*, a film on apartheid. External Affairs agreed to prevent the NFB from distributing the film abroad. Internally, the Duplessis government's Service du cinéphotographie à Québec (1941, renamed Office du film du Québec in 1961) countered the Anglo bias of films but also Canada-wide themes and in 1954 it prohibited the showing of some NFB films in the province. Though renowned Quebecers such as Pierre Juneau and Guz Roberge were named to the NFB to assure Quebec content in films, agitation for a separate francophone NFB branch continued.[451] In the post-war era, the mass media underwent a further revolutionary change by the rapid spread of television. Large-scale emissions in the United States began in 1946; CBC in 1952. Within five years, three million TV sets were sold and the Canadian market, at the time of one set per family, was saturated. Intra-family battles about which program to turn to was also an issue of Canadian versus American programs, with the young as well as the lower classes turning to the latter. Such seeming disavowal of Canadian culture led to the appointment of the Royal Commission on National Development in the Arts, Letters, and Sciences in 1949.

Gendered cultural elites: Nationalists, reformers, radicals

Throughout the first half of the twentieth century, nationalizing tendencies were strong but regional distinctiveness remained. Internally migrating scholars from the Prairie periphery undercut the Ontario-centeredness by emphasis on the West, the North, and hinterland contributions. The "Ontario-centeredness" gave way to "from Ontario outward." Canadian culture and scholarship stood poised between U.S. and British influences, with influence from France on French-language scholars. The National Archives, established in 1872, provided a source collection for collective memory; since 1916, the National Research Council supported Canadian research,

---

450 : To counter the invisibility of Canada in Hollywood productions, a so-called Canadian Co-operation Project encouraged references to Canada—critics commented that in U.S. films gangsters would announce that they were headed for Canada instead of Detroit.

451 : *The NFB Film Guide: The Productions of the National Film Board of Canada from 1939 to 1989* (Ottawa: NFB, 1991), xxv- lxxx, esp. xxvii-xxxix, quote p. xxiv; Acland, "National Dreams"; David Cameron, *Taking Stock: Canadian Studies in the Nineties* (Montreal: Assoc. for Canadian Studies, 1996), quote p. 16-17.

especially research on Canada; but a repository for cultural production, a National Library, was established only in 1953. Montreal's McGill University, in the social sciences, was the node of exchange with the Université de Montréal and Laval. The universities of the Maritimes, another cultural cluster, appeared as a regionalized sub-centre. Their emphasis on Celtic roots, comparable to Quebec's *survivance*, provided a contrast to Ontario's Englishness. To escape from their increasingly marginal location, Maritimers out-migrated to Ontario's colleges, where many became propagandists of Empire. From the regional and economic margin they catapulted themselves to the crest of imperial ideology production.[452]

The emergence of the scholarly elite and political "government men" (chapter 7) in the 1920s had its parallel in the development of a cultural elite. Discussing the processes involved, Maria Tippett and Mary Vipond emphasized the continued predominance of English language and British background. In stereotypical gender division, men established the institutions but networks involved women and such families educated daughters like sons into elite status. In terms of achievement, family networks seem to have been able to negotiate and integrate, and to avoid male posturing. This required well-educated and active women, as Linda Kealey and Joan Sangster pointed out. However, French-background culture still devalued women's human capital, and provided separate and unequal career opportunities only in the female religious orders.[453] In the West, farming women's input into the material family economy precluded education, and "ethnics" remained excluded from cultural production. The autobiographies of Louise Lucas and Michael Luchkovich indicate the struggles for inclusion.[454] In the two cultural centres, Alice Massey and Thérèse Casgrain, to give two examples, achieved advisory political influence, Agnes Macphail and Cairine Wilson became the first women in the House of Commons and the

---

452 : Danielle Lacasse and Antonio Lechasseur, *The National Archives of Canada 1872–1997* (Ottawa: Canadian Historical Assoc., 1997).

453 : Tippett, *Making Culture*; Mary Vipond, "The Nationalist Network: English-Canada's Intellectuals and Artists in the 1920s," *Canadian Review of Studies in Nationalism* 8.1 (1980): 32–52; Linda Kealey, ed., *A Not Unreasonable Claim: Women and Reform in Canada 1880s–1920s* (Toronto: Canadian Women's Educational Press, 1979); Kealey and Joan Sangster, eds., *Beyond the Vote: Canadian Women and Politics* (Toronto: UTP, 1989); and Kealey, *Enlisting Women for the Cause: Women, Labour and the Left in Canada, 1890–1920* (Toronto: UTP, 1998). Danielle Juteau and Nicole Laurin, *Un métier et une vocation: Le travail des religieuses au Québec de 1901 à 1971* (Montreal: PU Montréal, 1997).

454 : J.F.C. Wright, *The Louise Lucas Story: This Time Tomorrow* (Montreal: Harvest House, 1965); Michael Luchkovich, *A Ukrainian Canadian in Parliament: Memoirs of Michael Luchkovich* (Toronto: Ukrainian Canadian Research Foundation, 1965).

Senate, and women also added their voice as journalists. It seems that while the English-speaking elite coalesced into networks based on family socializing, French-Québécois men were divided into competing networks. Quebec's uncompromising power elites relegated the innovative academic analysts and writers of the debating press to distinct circles within this distinct society. English-speaking elite men were aware of "the 'intimate, trusting, confident, strong but really unorganized' web of personal relationships and friendships which linked together a 'network' of professionals, academics, businessmen, and other members of the English Canadian élite in 'informal patterns of communication'."[455]

Institution-building formalized such interconnectedness in historiography and the social sciences, among writers and publishers, among social reformers, among artists. Only the humanities lacked not only coordination but also basic research. In politics and the media, the League of Nations Society in Canada was established in 1921; the Canadian Institute for International Affairs (CIIA), first a section of the British IIA, became independent in 1928; and the Canadian Radio League lobbied for new media. The Association of Canadian Clubs (reorganized 1925/26) and the fellows of the Royal Society of Canada ensured coordination. The founders and members of these associations, Vipond noted, "were of the same class and background as the business, political, and professional leaders across the country. Family, marriage, war service, university, clubs, outlooks—all tied them together." Like all of the elite, the intelligentsia formed itself "by both birth and merit," was urban in residence, and organizationally remained almost exclusively male up to the 1960s, though the CIIA encouraged membership of "well-informed men and women" and women edited some associations' journals.[456] Within the organizations, the men formed "interlocking directorates" as one of them, Brooke Claxton, noted. In view of the "more rapid change than they had ever known before," they believed it their duty both to articulate sensible responses and to develop new institutions. "They saw themselves performing the critical function of crystallizing community identity by dispensing meaningful symbols and articulating common goals."[457] In Quebec's distinct development a dualism between the old-style

---

455 : Graham Spry cited in Vipond, "The Nationalist Network," quote p. 32.

456 : An Institute of Pacific Relations remained a U.S. organization with some Canadian members mainly from the Pacific Coast urban elites. Asian immigration had been curbed—in this respect the elites remained racist. E.D. Greathed, "Antecedents and Origins of the Canadian Institute of International Affairs," in Harvey L. Dyck and H. Peter Krosby, eds., *Empires and Nations: Essays in Honour of Fredric H. Soward* (Toronto: UTP, 1969), 91-115.

457 : Vipond, "The Nationalist Network," quotes pp. 33 (Claxton), 34, 38 (Mackenzie).

lawyer-notary-doctor triad, and a new media elite emerged. With increasing popular literacy, the latter based its influence on the mass circulation as well as the opinion press. Numerically, but certainly not as regards achievements, the francophone academic elite was small.[458] In both national and Quebec-centered perspectives, traditionalist and nationalist intellectual, clerical, and political leaders faced modernist outward-reaching businessmen, reform politicians, and journalists and editors. The modernizing forces, however, were far stronger in Anglophonia. Such distinct development of the two elites may be explained with Bourdieu's concept of "social habitus." Individuals with high social capital could and did live and act in more than one culture, could negotiate interculturally between English and French, between tradition and modernity; those who neglected development of flexibility-providing social capital were unable to deal with more than one habitus.

After the collapse of the capitalist system in 1929, many reformers turned to radical politics, while some farmer and labour activists had long been radical. The otherwise accommodative elite segments could not digest such challenges and the Liberal federal and right-wing Quebec Duplessis governments persecuted activists of the Left, hindered working-class organization, and repressed protest movements, using the RCMP to spy on Labour and the police to disperse the unemployed men's "on to Ottawa trek" in 1935. Ukrainian Canadians, the Icelandic Canadian poet S.G. Stephansson, and a large segment of Finnish Canadians supported the Communist Party. Of the latter, some re-migrated to Soviet-ruled but Finnish-settled Karelia to help build a workers republic.[459] While the Communist parties in Western societies had often responded sensitively to local conditions and were able to advance labour organization through their high organizational skills, the Soviet International's directives proved disastrous when, after labelling the

Women working as editors got little public recognition as, for example, Bess Housser, painter and editor of the art page of *Canadian Bookman*, was known as wife of Fred Housser, author of *A Canadian Art Movement*, 1926, a first study of the Group of Seven (ibid., 41). Both Mary Quale Innis and Jean Burnet worked as editors, thus, in addition to their research contributions, rending service to the men in the professions.

458 : Linteau et al., *Histoire du Québec*, 1:517-35.

459 : Donald Avery, *"Dangerous Foreigners": European Immigrant Workers and Labour Radicalism in Canada, 1896-1932* (1983), revised and expanded as *Reluctant Host: Canada's Response to Immigrant Workers, 1896-1994* (Toronto: McClelland & Stewart, 1995). See also his "British-Born 'Radicals' in North America, 1900-1941: The Case of Sam Scarlett," *Canadian Ethnic Studies* 10.2 (1978): 65-85; Michael G. Karni, ed., *The Finnish Diaspora*, 2 vols. (Toronto: MHSO, 1981); Varpu Lindstrom-Best, *Defiant Sisters: A Social History of Finnish Immigrant Women in Canada* (Toronto: MHSO, 1988).

non-communist Left "social fascists" during the so-called "Third Period," they demanded unconditional support of the Soviet Union's Pact with fascist Germany in the "Popular Front period." More typical of the Left, activists' complex intellectual ties were connections to the experimental culture of France and Paris in particular, and to British Fabianism, European writers, and African-American spirituals. They espoused a philosophy of social work and the literary expression of the Little Magazines. Some of the women radicals anticipated the feminist movement of the 1970s. Internationally, many radicals espoused the Republican cause in the Spanish Civil War. But during the Red Scare of the Cold War years, Canada's governments attempted to extinguish such activities.

Many of the reformers had deliberately reached out to Canadians in general through adult education and the schools. So did public librarians, such as Lawrence J. Burpee from Ottawa. The journal of the Association of Canadian Clubs, *Canadian Nation*, edited by Graham Spry, reached a circulation of 37,000 in 1929 and the *Canadian Magazine* (1893/1895–1937) was even more popular. Both might be called popular Canadian Studies magazines dealing with all aspects of society. Unrecognized by the humanities, such magazines were instrumental in developing a Canadian symbolism that also fit those immigrants' perspectives who had no British- or French-colonized mindsets.[460]

The study of Canada: Problems and perspectives at the turn of the Sixties

Canada's economic, social, political, and cultural trajectory was subject to the decisions of states or groups within the dominant industrial countries and to global economic cycles as well as to ideologies and discourses of internal elites and to everyday practices and adaptations of every Canadian. External influences and gatekeeper governance brought forth economic problems, cultural dependency, and identity-politics, but the gatekeepers were successfully challenged by Canada-centered cultural activities producing symbols and narratives. In the 1950s, when reformers and radicals had pointed to the need for change for several decades, when society needed to be shaped, and when visions were in demand, the social sciences abdicated

---

460 : Ronald L. Faris, "Adult Education for Social Action or Enlightenment? An Assessment of the Development of the Canadian Association for Adult Education and Its Radio Forums from 1935 to 1952" (unpubl. PhD diss., Univ. of Toronto, 1971); Owram, *Government Generation*, 152–59; Vipond, "The Nationalist Network," 38–41, 45–48; Hoerder, *Creating Societies*. The magazine's original title to 1895 (vol. 5) was *Canadian Magazine of Politics, Science, Art and Literature*.

their role by dividing themselves into disciplinary fiefs and the weak human-ities remained colonially minded. The concept of holistic, Canada-centered social sciences had given way to fragmented disciplines. All specialization involves distortion and R.A. MacKay, as president of the Canadian Political Science Association, had warned in 1944 of its intellectual dangers.[461]

The federal political elites had responded with accommodations to the system and the culture to internal and external exigencies. But the long Liberal rule under Mackenzie King (1921–1948, with two interruptions) had certainly not created structures for a genuinely open society. After World War II, another external development coalesced with internal de-mands for change. Visionary policy-makers under the lead of Lester Pear-son actively involved Canada in drafting the United Nations' Charter. John P. Humphreys, law professor at McGill, in 1946 was appointed first direc-tor of the Human Rights Division for the UN Secretariat. In consultation with the Commission's chair, Eleanor Roosevelt, and in co-operation with French lawyer René Cassin, he drafted the Universal Declaration of Human Rights, which, adopted by the General Assembly on 10 December 1948, was heralded as the "Magna Carta of mankind" and initiated a revolutionary change in international law. Among the second generation of "government men," formed by the Depression years and the human suffering involved, an awareness had formed that inequities external to as well as inside Canadian society demanded remedial action by the federal government. The prin-cipled stand taken in the debates about the UN Charter would also apply to marginalizations and discriminations at home. This perspective would inform the new generation of scholars of the 1960s and 1970s, who chal-lenged the master narratives of Canada and its francophone Quebec. They expanded the narrow gatekeeper versions of national memory and social participation to inclusiveness and to analysis by class, ethnicity and/or race, and gender. Scholars in education would add "generation" as a category.

Frank Scott, anglophone Quebecer and the most satirical as well as most constitutionally versed critic and reformer, had fought the repres-sive Duplessis government and worked with Thérèse Casgrain, advocate of women's suffrage, who had broadcast the "Fémina" program in the 1930s. His student, Pierre Elliott Trudeau, as prime minister from 1968, ended pol-itical dependency by repatriating the Constitution and calling for a Charter of Rights that would include all Canadians. Scott commented:

---

461 : Daniel Drache, ed., *Staples, Markets and Cultural Change: Selected Essays by Harold Innis* (Montreal: MQUP, 1995), "Introduction - Celebrating Innis: The Man, the Legacy, and Our Future," xiii-lix, esp xxii; Mel Watkins, "Innis at 100: Reflections on His Legacy for Canadian Studies," *Canadian Issues / Thèmes Canadiens* 17 (1995), 173–82. Owram, *Government Generation*, 271–2.

Changing a Constitution confronts a society with the most important choices, for in the Constitution will be found the philosophical principles and rules which largely determine the relations of the individuals and of cultural groups to one another and to the state. If human rights and harmonious relations between cultures are forms of the beautiful, then the state is a work of art that is never finished. Law thus takes its place, in its theory and practice, among man's highest and most creative activities.

Such an integrated approach to the social sciences, the humanities, and legal as well as constitutional discourses characterizes a Transcultural Societal Studies. However, in an intermediate period, the broadly conceived Study of Canada would become an underfunded Canadian Studies project based increasingly on the discourse-based literary scholarship, many innovative societal approaches notwithstanding.[462]

---

462 : Frank R. Scott, *Essays on the Constitution: Aspects of Canadian Law and Politics* (Toronto: UTP, 1977), quote p. ix, and Scott, *Canada Today: A Study of Her National Interest and National Policy* (1938; rev. ed., 1939; French as *Canada d'aujourd'hui*, Montreal: Éd. du Devoir, 1939), with an introduction by Édouard Montpetit; Scott, *The Canadian Constitution and Human Rights* (Toronto: CBC, 1959). Sandra Djwa, "'Nothing by Halves': F.R. Scott," *Journal of Canadian Studies* 34.4 (1999), 52–69: and Djwa, *The Politics of Imagination: A Life of F.R. Scott* (Vancouver: Douglas & McIntyre, 1987).

IV. THE THIRD PHASE: MULTIPLE DISCOURSES ABOUT INTERLINKED SOCIETIES

In the 1960s, decolonization of Canadian society, its opening to new ideas and practices, its changed lifestyles (chapter 10) were reflected in a "Canadian Studies" approach which, as inter- or transdisciplinary research, was faced with institutional obstacles. While society changed, its teachers in schools and researchers in universities were part of the pre-1960s socialized generation, were mainly men, and had to work in institutional frames and with teaching aids perpetuating long outdated British and French-Catholic frames of thought. The educational apparatus remained stationary until, at the end of the '60s, critics' efforts and struggles began to initiate changes. "Le Québec en retard" became a stock in trade of any debate but, in the Anglo-Franco hierarchy, the colonial backwardness of "Ontario *en retard*" or "Anglophonia *en retard*" was hardly mentioned. One reform effort, the expansion of the universities, seemed to address the issue. But, because of the Anglo-Canadian *retard*, teaching staff, unfamiliar with Canadian life and institutions, had to be imported. At first at least, these men—there were still only a few women in academia—could not contribute to the debate about directions for social and political developments, could not develop projects for a new Canada.

Given the fragmentation of the social sciences from the 1940s and the mind-numbing Cold War frame of thought in the 1950s, the Study of Canada, called Canadian Studies since the 1960s, had to be redeveloped, had to be newly institutionalized. But with intra-academic competition for funding, funding restrictions from the mid-1970s, as well as in an intellectually extremely complex and sometimes recriminatory climate of opinion, the practitioners of Canadian Studies could not easily chart a course for the field (chapter 11).[463] At the same time, the Study of Canada became an academic endeavour outside of Canada and developed distinct, sometimes country-specific perspectives (chapter 12). While the 1960s seemed propitious for a trajectory toward an integrated study of society, the two

---

463 : The McGill Institute for the Study of Canada / L'Institut d'études canadiennes, in the English version of its name connects to the broad social science approach of the field. An introduction to the field is provided by David Taras and Beverly Rasporich, eds., *A Passion for Identity: An Introduction to Canadian Studies* (3rd ed., Toronto: Nelson, 1993).

hegemonic Canadas had to pursue different decolonization projects, and in addition the worldwide decolonization debate brought about an awareness that ethnicizing some Canadians of European background, racializing Asian Canadians, and colonizing "the Indians" was colonialism, too. While the elites of the "Third World" or "non-White" colonies could attack the oppressive European colonizer powers, the Canadian elites had to deal with their own self-colonized mindsets. Since external and internal colonialism had to be addressed at the same time, debates, sometimes acrimonious, emerged whether "Canada" could be a reference point or Canadianness a goal, or whether any reference to this nation-state with its colonized "minorities" would merely be a perpetuation of oppressive structures. Negatively as well as positively, "Canadian Studies" as an attempt to achieve a self-understanding was unique. "Country Studies" elsewhere looked from the outside at a political unit rather than at a differentiated society. As outlined in chapter 1, British Studies had begun as a projection of Britain to the outside and continued as a New Left-initiated recognition of internal diversity. American Studies had for some time been attempting to fuse historiography with the humanities; in Canada the former was powerful, the latter non-existent. The earlier Study of Canada, geography included, had implied a more inclusive and multi-perspective approach than any other Country Study. In the disciplines, however, the new approaches initiated methodological and theoretical debates that resulted in a rewriting of history and a reconceptualization of the study of society since the 1980s (chapter 13). These achievements might be theoretically integrated into Transcultural Societal Studies (chapter 14).

Chapter 10

DECOLONIZATION: THE CHANGES OF THE 1960S

The 1950s have been described as "quiet and uninspiring" or as a "period of gestation"; the 1960s as the decade of a liberating burst of intellectual and cultural activity. "There was more ferment under the surface in 1950s Canada than is usually recognized; few 'revolutions' are truly sudden" (Bumsted 1992).[464] In a global perspective, peoples' struggles for decolonization rearranged relations between the formerly colonized peoples and the Euro-North American power core. Internally, Canadian society decolonized itself and, simultaneously, recognized that it comprised more than two cultures. In international affairs, Lester B. Pearson, Liberal Prime Minister 1963–68, trained under the old "mandarin" O.D. Skelton and one of the most active reformers, affirmed Canada's independent position and, internally, distinctly Canadian symbols. As president of the UN Assembly in 1952, he refused to budge to U.S. pressure concerning the Korean War. In 1956, he negotiated the dispatching of a UN peacekeeping force to get the invading Israeli, British, and French troops out of Egypt. He was awarded the Nobel Peace Prize in 1957. Such opposition to British policies came late. Canada's dualism might have evolved differently, had prime ministers from the 1880s on heeded French-Canadian demands to refuse support for British colonialism.

On the level of cultural symbols, the 1963 initiative to rid Canada of British signifiers and to introduce the maple leaf flag caused die-hard supporters of British symbolism to mount an interminable "flag debate." They held high military-style designs and "founding race" concepts. As so often, when High Priests Of The Past reify symbols, their concepts were patently false or, more charitably, uninformed, while the allegedly new and dangerous reforming ideas had a long history. St. George's cross, as English national symbol, lacked historical content: George never was in England and never did slay a dragon. One version of George's life and death maintains that as a Christian Turkish-born prince in Palestine, he plundered the other religions' temples until he was finally slain by an angry crowd of those he oppressed. The new symbol, the maple leaf, dated at least from the 1860 visit of the Prince of Wales. While most Torontonians flew banners of St. George, St. Andrew, and St. Patrick, a group of "Native Canadians" signified their belonging by a maple leaf banner. To the charge of being nativist, they responded that any foreign-born person was welcome as long as they felt

---

464 : J.M. Bumsted, *The Peoples of Canada: A Post-Confederation History* (Toronto: Oxford, 1992), quote p. 369. As regards feminism see Valerie Korinek, *Roughing It in the Suburbs: Reading "Chatelaine" Magazine in the Fifties and Sixties* (Toronto: UTP, 2000).

Canadian. In the 1960s, "God Save the Queen" seemed somewhat outdated but a new national anthem, too, caused debate. "The Maple Leaf Forever" fit the new flag but was a paean to British heroism. Thus in 1967 Parliament selected "O Canada," written by Calixa Lavallée and Adolphe-Basile Routhier in 1880 and translated into English by R. Stanley Weir.[465]

The mood for change was bipartisan. Progressive-Conservative Prime Minister John Diefenbaker (1957–62) changed the socio-political terms of reference for all of society. The *Bill for the Recognition and Protection of Human Rights and Fundamental Freedoms* of 1960 turned principles into actual law. To establish the frame for an "equal partnership," the Liberal Pearson government established the Royal Commission on Bilingualism and Biculturalism, chaired by André Laurendeau and Davison Duncan, and premised on cultural duality. Shortly after its *Report*, the Official Languages Act of 1969 made Canada a bilingual country, if on the federal level only. Since the internally subalternized "ethnics" had vigorously protested the two hegemonic cultures' self-centeredness, the bicultural Trudeau government proclaimed the policy of multiculturalism in 1971, followed by the Multiculturalism Act of 1988.

An exuberant, liberating spirit burst forth during the Centennial of 1967. Actors were many: women, cultural groups, perhaps workers, but probably more so the new middle classes, all of them unwilling to swallow the daily porridge served up by English-minded gatekeepers or the quaint images projected onto the screen by their French-Canadian brothers-in-spirit. Discourse has named the '60s the years of the "quiet revolution" in *Quebec*, but was there not also a breakthrough in staid and sober, perhaps somewhat dull, Ontario? Did not the liberating spirit sweep the whole of the country? Loudly focusing on Quebec society's changes detracted from the English-Canadian, Ontario-centered discourse's need for renewal. The gatekeepers' larger-than-life picture of Canada the Good, Canada as in olden times, resembled an amateur 8-mm film projected onto an Imax screen. Accordingly, no audience showed up.

Research reveals a curiously dichotomous climate of opinion. In interviews, scholars who participated in the innovations of the 1960s remembered a "spirit of exuberance" and expressed a proud memory of achievements, of re-making colonial society as well as scholarship into a world of its

---

465 : Ian Radforth, *Royal Spectacle: The 1860 Visit of the Prince of Wales to Canada and the United States* (Toronto: UTP, 2004), 275-57. In 1908, the symbol was used for a book title, Basil Stewart, *The Land of the Maple Leaf, or Canada As I Saw It* (London: Routledge and Toronto: Musson, 1908). The *National Anthem Act* was passed in 1980.

own.[466] In contrast, texts on Canadian Studies reflect numerous grievances: foreign domination, departmental and disciplinary fiefs, and deans hostile to innovation. In retrospect, the achievements, including those of many of the U.S. immigrant scholars, are incontestable, but a reluctance to institutionalize interdisciplinary programs is evident. The specific conjuncture of national self-assertion and decolonizing movements at the time of Canada's late self-liberation explains the ambiguities.

Post-colonial scholarship had to move in two directions, at times seemingly mutually exclusive. First, a brief discussion of the contested term *post-colonial* is necessary.[467] It is used here to signify a society and its cultural discourses from the point of time at which colonial political dependency ended and from which mental dependency on the former colonizing power was dissolved. The term posits that even after independence, formerly colonized societies grapple with the institutional, legal, everyday, and mental structure developed under colonialism. It secondly posits that no simple colonizer–colonized dichotomy exists but that relationships depend on social status, gender, and region. It thirdly posits that colonized societies may, at the same time, be colonizers of ethnocultural groups living within the state's boundaries. This complexity is reflected in the intra-Canadian debates. While scholarly and literary writing freed itself from bondage to Britain and France, from its inception the "new Canadian" approach faced the accusation of again establishing "hegemony" from those labelled "other ethnics," from women, and from Native peoples. The drawn-out debate whether Canadian Studies per se are nationalist, misses the point. Research incorporating all cultures in Canada and recognizing that "Canadian culture" has its origins in many societies across the globe is anything but "national(ist)." It explores, how, within this society and the bordered state, the many-cultured inputs through communication transformed themselves by fusion or coalesced into a mosaic of discernable pieces. Once again, the view from the outside is helpful: Canada's society is different from that of the neighbouring United States and from any other society. Societies are unique, but not exceptional. Internal Canadian Studies, as a quest "to understand ourselves," may betray a lingering cultural essentialism; as a quest to understand the many selves that, in constant evolution, add up to Canadian

---

466 : The author is grateful to Jean Burnet, Daniel Drache, Jim Frideres, Wsevolod and Christina Isajiw, John Lennox, Kenneth McRoberts, Richard Seaborn, and John Wadland for agreeing to be interviewed.

467 : The debate was initiated by Frank Birbalsingh, "National Identity and the Canadian Novel," *Journal of Canadian Fiction* 1.1 (1972): 56–60. A recent comprehensive anthology is Laura Moss, ed., *Is Canada Postcolonial? Unsettling Canadian Literature* (Waterloo, ON: WLU Press, 2003).

society at any given moment, it is analytically sound.[468] Interminable debates about Canadian identity, about "who we are," merely detract from the issue "how do we explain the differences." In post-national times, when the cloning of a territory's many-cultured inhabitants into "nationals" has come to an end, there are as many answers as there are people in the country. Canadianness is relational rather than essentialist.[469]

Nationalizing the material and the cultural: The Marsh and Massey recommendations

Policy, concerned with the economic basis of society in the first half of the twentieth century, turned to the questions of culture, a national one rather than a sum of regional and U.S. imported components. The Royal Commission on National Development in the Arts, Letters and Sciences (1949), chaired by Vincent Massey and Georges-Henri Lévesque, but popularly called the "Massey Commission," debated the issues.[470] In a perspective that combined the material and the cultural, the *Massey Report* of 1951 appears as the cultural equivalent to the *Marsh Report* on social security of 1943. Material security is the basis for other aspects of a society's culture.

The British North America Act of 1867 had assigned responsibility for social security, then meaning charity and medical care, to the provinces. According to the local-responsibility approach of British Poor Law and Catholic-French parish-centeredness, care for the needy was assigned to those who knew them and, incidentally, could control them. In view of the

---

468 : See for some aspects of the debate Ian Angus, "Missing Links: Canadian Theoretical Discourse," *Journal of Canadian Studies* 31.1 (1996): 141–58; Jocelyn Létourneau, "L'Avenir du Canada: par rapport à quelle histoire?" *Canadian Historical Review* 81 (2000): 230–59.

469 : Discussions of Canadian nationhood are legion and often still refer to one language group only. Philip A. Massolin, *Canadian Intellectuals, the Tory Tradition, and the Challenge of Modernity, 1939-1970* (Toronto: UTP, 2001), and Ian Angus, *A Border Within: National Identity, Cultural Plurality, and Wilderness* (Montreal: MQUP, 1997), deal with intellectual debates and frames of reference of British Canada. David Chennells, *The Politics of Nationalism in Canada: Cultural Conflict Since 1760* (Toronto: UTP, 2001), explores the competing nationalisms, British and Aboriginal, French- and British-Canadian, pan-Canadian and Québécois, and the tensions between stable federal governance and popular as well as populist and xenophobic expression or vociferousness. He juxtaposed citizens' "exclusive nationalism" and Quebec's "ethnic delegate representation" to the federal elites "imposed statecraft" and "affiliative trusteeship."

470 : Vincent Massey, in 1952, became the first native-born Governor General; five decades later Adrienne Clarkson who as a child had come with her refugee parents from Hong Kong, became the first (non-British) foreign-born Governor General.

impact of industrialization and high mobility, this approach was outdated from the start. Working-class and farmers' self-help and mutual aid organizations challenged the concept of charity as a prerogative of the better-off. A conceptual change did not emerge from future-oriented policy-making, but under the impact of war. During World War I, the provinces under the lead of Manitoba passed pension acts for civilian widows, deserted wives, and war-widows; the Liberal federal government offered support. Means tests that could easily be humiliating reflected the hold of the traditional Poor Law's mentality of control. When the Great Depression of the 1930s created havoc in people's lives, Leonard Marsh's report advocated comprehensive social security legislation. Hailed in public, lawmakers were slow in reacting.[471] A century and a half after the Enlightenment's declaration of individuals' political human rights, a "second generation of human rights" began to be operationalized: the right of individuals to material security.[472] Debate about third-generation human rights, the right of individuals and groups to cultural self-expression free from national or nationalist restraints and the right to personal development, began only another half century later.

Cultural self-determination in Canada was premised on factors different from other societies of the Euro-North American world. Canada was (1) a state with two national cultures as well as other, at the time, not recognized ones; (2) a society with elites mentally dependent on three outside structures, namely Britain, France, and Roman Catholicism; (3) a society of strong regional and accepted diversity with settlement patterns extending over comparatively large and thinly connected spaces; and (4) a state with a neighbouring polity in which economies of scale permitted cheap production and transborder export of culture. Communication about society or particular aspects of it, whether in the press, the literature, the arts, or other expressions, thus followed a trajectory different from debates in countries with high centralization, consumer density, and mono-national or corporation-controlled cultural markets. The glacially slow movement

---

471: More than a decade after the beginning of the Depression, the federal government passed an Unemployment Insurance Act in 1940. From 1951, a women- and children-centered "Family" Allowances Act, a federal-provincial social security plan including medical care, and a universal old age pension system became effective.

472 : In the 1930s, when basic premises were questioned, the constitutional-political and economic relations between the federal government and the provinces were investigated by the Rowell-Sirois Commission, appointed in 1937. Its *Report* (1940) suggested that the federal government assume sole power of collecting income taxes and in return provide "adjustment grants" to poorer provinces. It advised against cost-sharing programs.

toward political independence from 1867 to the Statute of Westminster in 1931 had been preceded among immigrants of non-British Isles background by an awareness of "Self" different from Britain. On the gatekeeper level, such difference was recognized only in 1948 in Massey's *On Being Canadian*. As (Anglo-) Canadian High Commissioner in London from 1935 to 1946, he recognized the hollowness of British Prime Minister William Pitt's dictum from the time of the Constitution Act (1791) that Canadian institutions were to be the "image and transcript of the British Constitution." In his single-gender perspective, Massey noted that military service had made Canadian men live in parts of Canada "they had never seen before and knew little about" and when abroad they had recognized similarities among themselves and differences from others. His view from the outside, from London, provided him with a fresh perspective. Cautiously distancing himself from nation-state monoculturalism, Massey recognized and accepted diversity of cultures: "Canada is the richer for them."[473]

The mandate of the Massey-Lévesque Commission recognized that (1) "it is desirable that the Canadian people should know as much as possible about their country, its history and traditions; and about their national life and common achievements"; (2) "it is in the national interest to give encouragement to institutions which express national feeling, promote common understanding and add to the variety and richness of Canadian life, rural as well as urban"; and (3) federal agencies in the cultural sector should be effective "in the national interest." Additionally, the mandate included (4) a study of Canada-UNESCO relations, (5) suggestions for "making available to the people of foreign countries adequate information about Canada," and (6) internally, to recommend "measures for the preservation of historical monuments."[474] The "Culture Commission" comprised an eminent sociologist from Laval, a civil engineer from Montreal, a university president from British Columbia, and historian Hilda Neatby from a Prairie institution.[475]

---

473 : Vincent Massey, *On Being Canadian* (London: Dent, and Toronto: Dent, 1948), quotes pp. 6, 19, 188 (Pitt citation).

474 : Order in Council (PC 1786), 8 April 1949, repr. in Royal Commission on National Development in the Arts, Letters, and Sciences, *Report on National Development in the Arts, Letters and Sciences 1949–51* (Ottawa: King's Printer, 1951), xi-xiii, expansion of the mandate, xxi. A popular summary of the report is Albert A. Shea, ed., *Culture in Canada: A Study of the Findings of the Royal Commission. . .* (Toronto: Core, 1952). It has been suggested that Hilda Neatby drafted much of the report.

475 : The Quebec government under Prime Minister Duplessis considered both the Massey-Lévesque inquiry into culture and the Rowell-Sirois Commission's report on taxation to be out of the sphere of federal jurisdiction and, in reaction, established its Royal Commission of Enquiry on Constitutional Problems (Tremblay Commission) in 1953, which reported in 1956.

When the Commission received its mandate, one version of Canadian culture operated through "corporate recognition": the Masseys financed performance halls in Toronto, Massey Hall and University of Toronto's Hart House.[476] The Massey-Harris firm's "corporate investment . . . helped to confirm the [Group of Seven] painters' value in the public mind"; one of its members, Lawren S. Harris was of the family. On suggestion of ethnologist Marius Barbeau, the CPR enabled the Hart House String Quartet to perform Canadian folksong-based compositions of Ernest Macmillan and Claude Champagne in the 1920s. The CPR's publicity director, John Murray Gibbon, had been president of the Canadian Authors' Association; the chairman of the Committee on Canadian Studies, T.H.B. Symons, came from Ontario's influential Bull family; Margaret Atwood is related to the Killam family of financiers and patrons of culture (Izaak W. and Dorothy B., née Johnston). Compared to this elite, "much of Canadian life was being lived out on another level," as W.H. New (1989) noted. Popular culture had no supporters in the Commission: "The culture lobby identified its vested interests with the contemporary aspirations of the Canadian nation" (Litt 1992). The Commission recommended funding for universities, cultural organizations, and research. In fact, the corporation–culture connection was complex. Artists, demanded Lawren Harris, were to contribute "consciously and designedly to the growth of a more highly socialized democracy by forming a nationwide and inclusive organization . . . to serve the cultural needs of the Canadian public." From the multi-ethnic West and speaking for "those Canadians who have a distinct national [rather than Central Canada-based] consciousness," the Co-operative Commonwealth Federation demanded efforts "to encourage national culture and strengthen national feeling" in the 1949 election campaign. Everywhere in the Western world, the post-war decades were characterized by increasing presence of the state in the everyday lives of people as regards social security and material well-being. Should culture be left to private business or free markets?[477]

476 : Named after Vincent Massey's grandfather Hart A. Massey (1823–96).

477 : New, *A History of Canadian Literature* (1989), quotes pp. 149, 150; Paul Litt, *The Muses, the Masses and the Massey Commission* (Toronto: UTP, 1992), quote p. 248; Bumsted, *Post-Confederation History*, quoting Harris p. 384; Maria Tippett, *Making Culture*, quote on CCF, p. 182. The elite had insisted on a second volume to the Massey Commission's *Report*. As *Studies: A Selection of Essays Prepared for the Royal Commission on National Development in the Arts, Letters, and Sciences* (Ottawa: King's Printer, 1951), this did contain some thoughtful and informed essays but also a number of talking heads' ruminations. The author of the "study" on English "Canadian Letters," for example, opined: "The Canadian reading public is ignorant" (p. 70). See also Sarah M. Corse, *Nationalism and Literature: The Politics of Culture in Canada and the United States* (Cambridge: Cambridge, 1997).

The Commission's mandate and report fit the spirit of the times. Decolonization movements challenged the legacies of imperialism. The colonized peoples of the British, French, and Dutch empires, still struggling for independence, held the Afro-Asiatic Conference in Bandung, Indonesia in April 1955; Aimé Césaire published "Culture and Colonisation" in *Présence Africaine* in Paris (1956); and francophone African and African-Caribbean intellectuals developed the concept of Negritude. Euro-White intellectuals saw this as a threat; even Jean-Paul Sartre thought that he could and should devise the philosophical guidelines for Negritude.[478]

The Massey *Report* was crafted with a mixture of nostalgia and critique. At mid-twentieth century, the commissioners pursued ideas of the nineteenth-century English cultural philosopher Matthew Arnold. Nostalgia for amateurs' community-based cultural expressions was outdated in an age of nationwide radio and literatures. At the same time, the *Report* critically noted that in the Empire's "white" Dominions, the colonial-minded elites were responsible for a lack of countrywide cultural institutions. This facilitated new imperial penetration by U.S. culture-producing corporations. With 150.7 million Americans as consumers (in contrast to 14 million Canadians), U.S. cultural producers faced considerably lower overheads and as additional bargain, could sell to English-speaking Canadians.[479] Such cultural imports could not simply be labelled "alien": Canadian consumers bought them, provincial governments supplied schools with U.S. textbooks, and children were thus socialized into U.S. worlds from an early age. By its critique of professionalized and big-city mass culture the *Report* positioned commercialization south of the 49th parallel. But, Canadian cultural producers, too, were part of bottom-line accounting. They could not earn a living unless working for wages, for example as teachers or commercial illustrators. By juxtaposing high (British-Canadian) culture to mass (U.S.) culture, the Commission opened its work to charges of elitism. To prevent Canada from becoming an external cultural province of the United States, the Commission recommended "forming the national tradition for the future," including the Canada Council (established 1957) and the National Library (established 1953) with funding that prevented political and administrative

478 : Jules-Rosette Bennetta, *Black Paris: The African Writers' Landscape* (Urbana: Univ. of Illinois Press, 1998), 53–56; Aimé Césaire, "Culture and Colonisation," *Présence Africaine* (Paris: Présence Africaine, 1956), 190–205, see also Césaire, *Discours sur le colonialisme* (1955; 6. éd., Paris: Présence africaine, 1973), 58 pp., Engl.: *Discourse on Colonialism*, transl. from the French by Joan Pinkham (New York: Monthly Review Press, 2000).

479 : The Committee was careful to list U.S. contributions, in particular foundation support, and explicitly took note of the shortcomings of Canadian institutions in this respect. Massey Commission, *Report*, 13–16, 436–42.

interference. Before multicultural plurality became acceptable in society, it emphasized "all the complexities and diversities of race, religion, language, and geography." However, following Matthew Arnold's three-class model of high elite, "populace," and an emerging non-conformist, energetic, moralist, and commercial middle class, the Commission held the middle class responsible for culture.[480]

While the Culture Commission avoided both a discussion of culture in the marketplace and of the mass media, Quebec's Tremblay Commission took a comprehensive but nationalist position: "the nation is a sociological entity, a community of culture which forms and renews itself down through the years by the common practice of the same general concept of life." Defining culture as "a way of being, thinking and feeling," as "a driving force animating a significant group of individuals united by a common tongue, and sharing the same customs, habits, and experiences," the Bilingualism and Biculturalism Commission, discussing non-hegemonic cultures in Canada in 1969, went another step further: each group contributes to the "cultural enrichment of Canada."[481] Scholars of decolonization theorized:

> Two factors are crucial in the relationship of identity discourses to cultural narratives: (1) that the discourse promotes a collective representation of the group in question, and (2) that the discourse furthers the interests of the group. The first factor, collective representation, involves the positive redefinition of a marginal or oppressed group. The second brings us into the realm of performance by questioning whether identity claims have social and political relevance and force.[482]

The Culture Commission's debates were part of an identity discourse as the federal Cultural Policy Review Committee acknowledged in 1982 and as Veronica Strong-Boag, like other feminists, emphasized. Citing Franz Fanon's *The Wretched of the Earth* (1966), she argued that in failing to confirm its distinctiveness, "English Canada has faced the dilemma of cultural dependence less successfully than Quebec."[483]

---

480 : Litt, *Muses*, 249–250; Massey Commission, *Report*, quotes pp. 4, 5. The Commission was critical of U.S. culture but probably not "anti-American," a problematic ideological term, as Richard Cavell posited in his edited volume *Love, Hate, and Fear in Canada's Cold War* (Toronto: UTP, 2004).

481 : Bumsted, *Peoples of Canada*, quote p. 382 (Tremblay Commission); Royal Commission on Bilingualism and Biculturalism, *Report*, Book 4: "The Cultural Contribution of the Other Ethnic Groups" (Ottawa: Queen's Printer, 1970), quote p. xxi.

482 : Bennetta, *Black Paris*, quote p. 241.

483 : Veronica Strong-Boag, "Cousin Cinderella: A Guide to Historical Literature Per-

The Canada Council, as an independent and endowed agency, accelerated the pace of the development of the arts, humanities, and social sciences nationwide without nationalist undertones. Even though, in view of the burgeoning artistic and scholarly life, its endowment soon proved inadequate, its grant policy became a success story and Quebec's Ministry of Culture, established in 1961 by the Liberal Lesage government, was similarly successful. From 1968, the new Social Sciences and Humanities Research Council funded research and the Canada Council limited itself to culture in the sense of the humanities. Cultural production and distribution remained contested: the Fowler Commission (established 1955) dealt with radio and television broadcasting, the O'Leary Commission (established 1961) with magazine publishing, and the Laurendeau-Dunton Commission (established 1963) with bilingualism and biculturalism. The concern about radio, television, and magazine publishing emanated from the impact of U.S. culture and economics of culture. It came either without ulterior motives as cross-border broadcasting or as a corporate profit strategy. Of all Canadian TV programs in the early 1950s, on average 48.5 percent were produced in Canada, 47.9 percent in the United States, and 3.6 percent elsewhere. But while French-language stations drew only 8.4 percent of their programs from the United States, English-Canadian ones imported 53.1 percent. The issue of belonging and identity remained squarely on the agenda, as does the question whether Canadian Studies involves the study of Canada or the study of reception of U.S. cultural products in Canada.[484]

The shift from "high" cultural production (literature, music, painting, performing) and distribution (magazines, book publishing) to the new "media culture" for "the masses," including spectator sports and "folk" expression, disempowered established critics who "relied on highly restrictive . . . canons and categories." The flowering cultural production became increasingly inclusive. From Margaret Atwood's national *Survival* it expanded to Michael Ondaatje's global worlds of Canadians from many cultures.

---

taining to Canadian Women," in Marylee Stephenson, ed., *Women in Canada* (Toronto: New Press, 1973), 262–90, quote p. 263; Federal Cultural Policy Review Committee (Applebaum-Hébert Committee), *Report of the Federal Cultural Policy Review Committee* (Ottawa: Supply and Services, 1982).

484 : The 1958 and 1968 broadcasting acts permitted operation of a network of private stations and required both private and public broadcasting to include distinctively Canadian content. David Ellis, *Evolution of the Canadian Broadcasting System: Objectives and Realities 1928-1968* (Ottawa: Dept. of Communications, 1979), 75; New, *History of Canadian Literature* (1989), 152-53, 181-82; Bumsted, *Peoples of Canada*, 389-93. In 1983, the Applebaum-Hébert Committee recommended that CBC be reduced in size and be partly privatized.

Autobiographers from among common people had noted worldwide origins of local Canadian lifeways for a century.[485]

The centennial's new climate of opinion

By the late 1960s, Canada was vastly different from what the Massey Commission had assumed in 1951 and from what W.L. Morton had described in his thoughtful *The Canadian Identity* in 1961. A new kind of Canadian Studies was needed to integrate everyday material lifestyles with literary and popular cultural expression. Adults born in the 1920s or earlier had had their life courses interrupted by the 1930s Depression and 1940s war years. Many had delayed formation of family or if married, conception of children. In a mere decade and a half after 1951, new patterns of procreation and of immigration changed population composition. Numbers grew by 25 percent to 20 million. After the "baby boom," one third of society was under fourteen years of age and 3.5 million voluntary and refugee migrants, allowing for emigration and U.S.-bound transit migration, brought a net gain of 2 million "New Canadians" by 1971. To allay traditionalists' fears of "racial" change, Liberal Prime Minister Mackenzie King had announced an immigration policy in 1947 that would reflect the present population's cultural composition. However, pressures from the imperial core as well as from Commonwealth countries combined with demand in particular labour market segments undercut the intended cultural-racial restrictions. First came "displaced persons" from the war in Europe and the Nazi labour camps. Working-age men were preferred, but other family members followed because humanitarian precepts precluded the intentional separation of families. Such "victims of war," often seen as psychologically troubled, were inoculated with massive doses of Canadianization. Next, given the suburban and centre-city construction boom, Italian and Portuguese men from the building trades migrated. Then came "coloured" people, admitted at first in small numbers only, from the West Indies and India, Pakistan, and Ceylon (now Sri Lanka), often as household help for those (White) families whose double income permitted them to hire modestly waged caretakers for their children.[486] Within a dozen years, the Commonwealth countries Hong

---

485 : Bumsted, *Peoples of Canada*, quote p. 383.

486 : Franca Iacovetta, "The Sexual Politics of Moral Citizenship and Containing 'Dangerous' Foreign Men in Cold War Canada, 1950s–1960s," in "Negotiating Nations: Exclusions, Networks, Inclusions," eds. Christiane Harzig, Dirk Hoerder, Adrian Shubert, *Histoire sociale / Social History* 34 (2000): 361–89; Christiane Harzig, "MacNamara's DP Domestics: Immigration Policy Makers Negotiate Class, Race, and Gender in the Aftermath of World War II," *Social Politics* 10.1 (Spring 2003): 23–48, and "'The Movement of 100 Girls:' 1950s Canadian Immigration Policy and the Market for Domestic

Kong, Jamaica, Trinidad, and India, as well as the U.S.-dependent Philippines had replaced Europe and the United States as the leading sources for immigrants.

The baby boom children, raised according to Dr. Spock's maxims, changed relations between generations. They strained educational institutions and as adolescents increased consumption. High productivity, rising employment with ever more women entering the labour market, and rising incomes, achieved through labour's organizing and strikes, brought "affluent" lifestyles. Old-style neighbourhoods were replaced by nodes of activity connected by streets. The downtowns' daytime populations lived in office towers and underground shopping malls, and left in the evenings. A vast suburbanization movement meant privately developed "green ghettos" with standardized bungalows, satirized by U.S. singer-songwriter Malvina Reynolds as "little boxes," and without public facilities and shops. Designed by men, the boxes' kitchens became ever smaller, segregating women into cubicles, while the basement hobby rooms for men, sometimes designated "the family room," expanded in size. The twice-daily population exchange between suburban homes and downtown jobs demanded construction of freeways, which divided older neighbourhoods into unconnected segments. Physical communication between the two poles of life was by *auto*mobile: a self-mobile without draft horse but still requiring a driver. The medium, in the context of a discourse on individual freedom, influenced the way of life. The male one person per car lifestyle emerged. Collectively the caged-in individualist drivers crowded onto the "free"-ways to settle down in rush-hour traffic jams. The wives and mothers, at the time with no second car, were imprisoned in suburbs with no public transportation. In Canada's previous staple economies no product would have been treated with as little concern.

New immigrants and baby boomers-turned-parents reduced the number of children per couple when practices, possibilities, and prohibitions of procreation changed. Since the early 1960s, the "pill" for women—with no equivalent for men, since research follows patterns of gender interests—changed intimate relationships. Decriminalization of abortion and of sex outside of marriage began in the 1960s. Law was brought into sync with life. Child raising involved increasing costs when proud parents and aspiring teenagers became marketing targets and tuition rose. Parents and educators initiated a movement to democratize the educational system. In rural communities this involved introduction of bussing since centrally located larger schools provided more options. For all it involved "the right to learn, to play, to laugh, to dream, to dissent, to reach upward, and to be himself

Labour," *Zeitschrift für Kanada-Studien* 36.2 (1999): 131–46.

[sic]" in the frame of an interdisciplinary education attuned to the needs of individual students with the twin goals of "social responsibility" and personal development.[487]

What did these changes of lifestyles, of youth–adult relationships, of the size of the young generation, and of ever more heterogeneous cultural composition of society mean for the teaching about Canada? Were teachers to socialize the young into a pre-1960s world? Mass communication brought new visions, new options, and consumer culture into homes. When in 1952 the CBC opened its first two television stations in Montreal and Toronto, a mere 146,000 Canadians, 1 percent of the population, owned receivers. Five years later, forty-four stations reached three million TV sets, and living habits changed. As the automobile had permitted an outward reach, TV implied an inward turn combined with a decline in interpersonal oral communication: TV dinners and snacks, TV soap operas and news, TV advertising. During the one-TV-set-per-home stage, families congregated to watch in silence while eating precooked dinners. From the detached bungalow, that is, separation from neighbours, followed the detached single-person, TV-equipped room within the bungalow: after the one-person-per-car, the one-person-per-room lifestyle. Such sociological perspective of culture as a way of life needs to be expanded by a humanities perspective on the TV programs' contents. In terms of information, TV presented (world) news in a more lively way than newspapers, but, to adapt McLuhan's dictum, it also changed the message. In terms of cultural-national content, U.S. programs entered ever more Canadian homes.[488]

Under the new openness, politics also changed: the Conservatives had renamed themselves "Progressive Conservatives" in 1942; the Prairie-based Co-operative Commonwealth Federation changed itself to nation-wide New Democratic Party in 1961; Quebec's Duplessis regime collapsed and the Church no longer had the resources either to hold on to power or to fund its social activities, thus making room for Jean Lesage's Liberal government from 1960 to 1966. Few had foreseen, "just how ready Quebec was for change, or how easily the traditional institutions and ways would crumble once they were confronted by an activist government composed of people from Quebec's new middle and professional classes." Had Can-

---

487 : Emmett M. Hall and Lloyd Dennis, *Living and Learning: The Report of the Provincial Committee on Aims and Objectives of Education in the Schools of Ontario* (Toronto: Newton, 1968).

488 : "The medium is the message," Marshall McLuhan, *Understanding Media: The Extensions of Man* (New York: McGraw Hill, 1964); for lifestyle changes see, for example, the study of Toronto's wealthy residential area, Forest Hill Village: John R. Seeley, R. Alexander Sim, Elizabeth W. Loosley, *Crestwood Heights: A North American Suburb* (Toronto: UTP, 1956).

ada-centered humanities taken note of the many dissenting voices in 1930s and 1940s Quebec, this development might have come as less of a surprise. The only other movement deemed worthy of the name of revolution or, disparagingly, "rebellion," was the student movement. Hegemonic terminology thus suggested that English-speaking Canada, British-dependent and riddled with remnants of Victorian concepts, was not in need of revolutionary change.[489]

Young people, in this age of optimism and humanism, lived in a world extolling free capitalist democratic societies but tolerating massive social inequalities; they observed U.S. imperialism as epitomized by the war in Vietnam; they learnt about the first (Western) world's hegemony over the third (non-White) world. In 1962, Jacques Berque, professor at the Collège de France and specialist on Algeria's war of independence, lecturing at the Université de Montréal on colonialism and decolonization, suggested to the students they decolonize themselves. The "radicals of the sixties," the Student Union for Peace Action (founded 1965) and non-organized militants, including African-Caribbean students, often espousing an "avant-garde of the proletariat" rhetoric, were particularly active at Simon Fraser, York, Montréal, and Sir George Williams (now Concordia) universities. But a decolonization debate evolved only in Quebec. Québécois radicals saw themselves as the "white niggers" of North America, a self-designation that Blacks in the United States could only view as self-pity.[490]

The 1960s witnessed a nationwide and "ethnic" "explosion of artistic activity." While a call by Frank Scott for a national gathering of writers had still failed in 1946, the first Canadian Writers' Conference came together at Queen's University in 1955[491] and George Woodcock founded *Canadian Literature* as a national review in 1959. An outside view from France had synthesized French-Canadian literary production in a context of the Americas by 1954, but the first major Canadian histories of English- and French-language literature appeared only in the mid-60s.[492] Academics in the

---

489 : Bumsted, *Peoples of Canada*, 323.

490 : Al Purdy, *The New Romans: Candid Canadian Opinions of the U.S.* (Edmonton: Hurtig, 1976); Dennis Forsythe, ed., *Let the Niggers Burn: The Sir George Williams University Affair and Its Caribbean Aftermath* (Montreal: Black Rose, 1971); Pierre Vallières' autobiographical *Nègres blancs d'Amérique* (Montreal: Parti pris, 1968), Engl.: *White Niggers of America* (Toronto: McClelland & Stewart, 1971).

491 : George Whalley, ed., *Writing in Canada* (Toronto: Macmillan, 1956).

492 : Edward D. Blodgett, in *Five-Part Invention: A History of Literary History in Canada* (Toronto: UTP, 2003), pp. 20–22, lists all literary histories of Canada, parts of Canada, particular genres or ethnicities or Canadian literature as parts of larger entities which have appeared since the mid-nineteenth century. Auguste Viatte, *Histoire littéraire de*

humanities could no longer shut out life around them and by 1970, "virtually every Canadian university offered an undergraduate course in Canadian literature." Margaret Atwood, in *Survival: A Thematic Guide to Canadian Literature* (1972), constructed a "collective persona in positing the central image of Canada (and Canadian literature) as survival within the context of victimization." While gatekeepers, living in the twilight of colonial dependence, may have considered Canada a "space in which we find ourselves lost," and may have needed literature "not only [as] a mirror" but "also [as] a map, a geography of the mind," immigrants, in life writings, novels, and poems, had long created their own spaces without reference to either hegemonies or feelings of victimization. The publication date of *Survival* indicates the paradoxes involved in achieving a genuinely Canadian cultural identification. By the time it was finally conceived, and meant to be liberating from Anglo- or Franco-dependence, it implicitly posited supremacy of two national Euro-Canadian perspectives. Thus it was challenged by men and women from the so-called "non-preferred" cultures of Europe and the newcomers from Asia, the Caribbean, and Latin America. They may have been invisible to Anglos but, recognized as being present, they did not accept the label "visible minorities." But they, too, were enmeshed in discourses, which could be censorious or even did end in self-censorship.[493]

Lively debate and innovation, beginning in Quebec with *Refus Global* (1948), involved all other cultural activities and was acceptable to corporate sponsorship. William Ronald, of the Simpson Company's display department in Toronto, persuaded the company to hold an "Abstracts at Home" exhibition in 1953. Though this did not strike a sympathetic chord with the public, Montreal's famous *art abstrait* show followed in 1959, and on the West Coast, Scottish-born Jack (J.W.G.) Macdonald, influenced by Kandinsky, experimented with new styles. In the performing arts, a club organized by English dance teachers in 1938 became the Royal Winnipeg

l'Amérique française (Paris: PU France, 1954); Pierre de Grandpré, ed., *Histoire de la littérature française du Quebec*, 4 vols. (Montreal: Beauchemin, 1967–69); Alfred G. Bailey, "Overture to Nationhood," in Carl F. Klinck, ed., *Literary History of Canada: Canadian Literature in English* (1st ed., Toronto: UTP, 1967), 1:69–81; Klinck, *Giving Canada a Literary History. A Memoir*, ed. Sandra Djwa (Ottawa: Carleton, 1991). For the arts see J. Russell Harper, *Painting in Canada: A History* (1966; 2nd ed., Toronto: UTP, 1977); Dennis Reid, *A Concise History of Canadian Painting* (1973; 2nd ed., Toronto: Oxford, 1988). A survey of Canadian music appeared earlier but did not go beyond 1914: Helmut Kallmann, *A History of Music in Canada*, 1534–1914 (Toronto: UTP, 1960).

493 : Bumsted, *Peoples of Canada*, quotes pp. 403–4; Atwood, *Survival* (Toronto: House of Anansi Press, 1972), 18–19, 32–42, quote p. 18; Dirk Hoerder, *Creating Societies: Immigrant Lives in Canada* (Montreal: MQUP, 1999); Mark Cohen, *Censorship in Canadian Literature* (Montreal: MQUP, 2001).

Ballet by 1953; the Russian-born English choreographer Rudolf Nureyev developed Toronto's National Ballet of Canada beginning in 1951; and Latvian-born Ludmilla Chiriaeff founded Montreal's Les Grand Ballets Canadiens in 1958. The Little Magazines and Little Theatres of the 1930s found their 1960s equivalent in the alternative theatres and publishers. Popular sports, beyond the cultural imagination of the new cultural producers, were addressed by the Task Force on Sports for Canadians (established 1969). The film industry, however, could not regain the ground lost to the U.S. companies in the 1920s.

The exuberance of the new Canada, its chorus of decolonizing voices, crested in the 1967 Centennial's "bipartisan extravaganza." Its centrepiece, the International Exposition at Montreal ("Expo 67"), introduced Canada to the world and, with fifty million paying visitors, Canadians to themselves. The theme, "Man and His World," fit the period's optimism—and gender stereotype. Buckminster Fuller's geodesic dome for the American Pavilion, Moshe Safdie's innovative Habitat '67 city housing complex, and the Canadian Pavilion, an inverted pyramid named Katimavik—Inuit for "meeting place"—were architectural masterpieces cited for a generation or longer. Pierre Elliott Trudeau was elected prime minister in 1968 and remained in office, with one short interruption, until 1984. He, his wife, and their children, idolized in what has been called Trudeaumania, symbolized the new Canada. His death in 2000 "fut pour tout Canadien. . . quelle que fût son allégeance politique, un deuil personnel," as the death of the Liberal Laurier, also an agent for change, had been for an earlier generation of Canadians.[494]

However, international violence overcame national exuberance. In the United States, Martin Luther King and Robert Kennedy were assassinated in 1968; students and demonstrators were clubbed and shot down at the Democratic Party's Chicago convention in 1968 and Kent State University in 1970. On the first notable "9/11,"—September 11, 1973,—Chilean president Allende was murdered in a coup promoted by the U.S. State Department and with support from the CIA. The worldwide economic crisis, brought about by a corporation-induced rise in oil prices, became a lasting recession. In Canada, funding for social and cultural programs dwindled. Literally, its affluence and happy consumption, which had never reached all segments of society, was overshadowed by dark clouds: growing pollution, a concept that entered households at a considerably slower pace than material amenities. While a century earlier the Geological Survey had turned physical

494 : Bumsted, *Peoples of Canada*, 406–13; Jean-Charles Falardeau, "Vie Intellectuelle et société entre les deux guerres," in de Grandpré, *Histoire de la littérature française*, 2:187–98, quote p. 188. Trudeau had studied labour struggles: Pierre Elliott Trudeau, ed., *La Grève de l'amiante [1949]: Une étape de la révolution industrielle au Québec* (Montreal: Éd. Cité Libre, 1956), Engl.: *The Asbestos Strike* (Toronto: Lewis & Samuel, 1974).

geography into spaces to be inhabited, habitation turned some spaces into physical wastelands. The new identities were fragmented.

A different centennial: The weight of the past in the socialization of new generations

The spirit of the Centennial and the movement for democratization of schools were neither reflected in children's literature nor in teaching methods and texts. The new, future generation was still "steeped in the liquid of imperialism" (Arthur Lower), parameters for identification with Canada were not delineated (Ramsay Cook), Canada remained a "state invisible to its own citizens" (Frank Davey). Neither infants' picture books nor juvenile novels with Canadian content existed. Pioneering authors of the 1970s assumed that "all readers were white, Christian, and native speakers of English or French"; subsequently, "lack of leadership from professional Canadian historians . . . caused writers of Canadian historical fiction for children to distort Canadian history." Similarly, schoolbooks passed outdated concepts to pupils, including ever more immigrants from ever more cultures in the world. Once graduated, they would shape the future of the society. Only from the mid-1970s did self-representational texts for the young reflect Canadian experiences in increasingly diversified variations.[495] Educators were aware that a "Canadian belonging" required knowledge about the society, its many regional variants, and its ethnic diversity. Only a few of the early twentieth-century school texts had treated Canada as a whole, and in the 1940s studies for the federal Department of Education and the Canada and Newfoundland Education Association found both French- and English-language history textbooks wanting.[496]

---

495 : Joyce M. Bainbridge, "The Role of Canadian Children's Literature in Identity Formation," *English Quarterly* 34.3–4 (2002): 66–74, citations and quote pp. 67–68; Bainbridge and Brenda Wolodko, "Canadian Picture Books: Shaping and Reflecting National Identity," *Bookbird* 40.2 (2002): 21–27; Heather Kirk, "No Home or Native Land: How Canadian History Got Left Out of Recent Historical Fiction for Children by Canadians," *Canadian Children's Literature* 83 (1996): 8–25, quote p. 8; Marisa Bortolussi, "Culture and Identity in Canadian Children's Literature," *Canadian Literature*, Supplement 1 (May 1987): 138–45; Jerry Diakiw, "Children's Literature and Canadian National Identity: A Revisionist Perspective," *Canadian Children's Literature* 87 (1997): 36–49; Sheila Egoff and Judith Saltman, *The New Republic of Childhood: A Critical Guide to Canadian Children's Literature in English* (Toronto: Oxford, 1990).

496 : Charles Bilodeau, *Rapport du Comité des manuels d'histoire du Canada* (Toronto: Société canadienne d'éducation, 1946) = "Report of the Committee for the Study of Canadian History Textbooks," *Canadian Education* 1 (Oct. 1945): 1–34; Alf Chaiton and Neil McDonald, *Canadian Schools and Canadian Identity* (Toronto: Gage, 1977), pp. 6–56. Hilda Neatby, *So Little for the Mind* (Toronto: Clarke, Irwin, 1953).

Traditional concepts circumscribed child rearing in the 1950s. The federal Department of Health and Welfare's *The Canadian Mother and Child* (1940) / *La mère canadienne et son enfant* (1941), authored by Ernest Couture, was a "forbidding, austere, and grey" text with out-of-date photography. It counselled men to be forbearing with their pregnant wives' whims. Whose mental health did the "Department of Health" address? That of male cultural dinosaurs in gatekeeping positions? Under such prescriptions, children might try to save their sanity by mental emigration out of the home to the lively broadcasts from south of the 49th. Change came fast when Doctor Benjamin Spock published his folksy and non-prescriptive *Common Sense Book of Baby and Child Care* in New York in 1946. A French translation came only a quarter century later and was published in Paris rather than in Quebec. Spock—non-coercive since he wrote in reaction to the authoritarian personality traits that were assumed to have made fascism's spread possible—still had an eye on contemporary images of masculinity. "You can be a warm father and a real man," he counselled. Spock's *Child Care* came to outsell the Bible in Canada. While grade one students came from this new socialization, the schools remained traditional.[497]

Aware of the traditionalism current when the nation was gearing up for the Centennial, A.B. Hodgetts initiated the "National History Project" to take stock of what was being taught. English-language schoolbooks remained British- or U.S.-oriented; the Catholic teaching manuals were in dire need of reform. Lloyd Reynolds's research findings of—*nota bene*—1935, that newcomers from the British Isles had more difficulty than other immigrants coming to terms with Canadian society, had had no impact on educational thought. The gatekeepers symbolically annihilated his results and valued their inflexible world views over children's options and life projects. Thus an "education for life in Canada" paradigm could not take hold and, after examining course materials and teaching methods across all provinces, Hodgetts in 1968 issued his "strong indictment" under the title *What Culture? What Heritage?* Future-oriented research in education was as lacking as research in the humanities. Educators, whether in schools or academia, like Canadian Studies scholars need to ask: What aspects of culture are being transferred to the next generation and how are they modified both in the process of teaching and of being decoded and received? How do

---

497 : Later editions as *Pocket Book of Baby and Child Care*; French transl.: Paris, 1972. Bumsted, *Peoples of Canada*, 360–62. Spock's advice has often been labelled as "permissive," as "irresponsible, undisciplined, and unpatriotic." However, the "accusation came for the first time in 1968—22 years after the book came out—from several prominent individuals who objected strongly" to Spock's opposition to the war in Vietnam. Childcare is political, indeed (quote from 1985 edition, p. xv).

adolescents' desires to become independent affect societal-cultural development? In Hodgetts's words, the task "of transmitting the cultural heritage"
has to foster "the development of responsible democratic citizens." But, "we
are teaching a bland, unrealistic consensus version of our past; a dry-as-
dust chronological story of uninterrupted political and economic progress
told without the controversy that is an inherent part of history."[498] In history textbooks, workers and the concept of class were not mentioned at
all; women were "seriously underrepresented." Another decade later, texts
edited by men, according to Ruth Pierson and Beth Light, still devoted few
pages to women or had one woman scholar add an essay on the topic. For the
Bilingualism and Biculturalism Commission, Marcel Trudel and Geneviève
Jain once again confirmed the problem: "Canada" was not taught in Canadian schools.[499] The education establishment responded to the multiple
indictments with a turn to "social issues" with neither depth nor theory: the
master narrative gave way to a broadly inclusive hodgepodge.[500]

The "no Canadian literature" paradigm also remained prevalent in colleges in the 1960s: the number of undergraduate-level courses on Can-

---

498 : A.B. Hodgetts, *What Culture? What Heritage? A Study of Civic Education in Canada*
(Toronto: OISE, 1968), quotes pp. iii, v, 5–6 (Report) 115; John C. Johnstone, *Young
People's Images of Canadian Society: An Opinion Survey of Canadian Youth, 13 to 20 Years
of Age*, Studies of the Royal Commission on Bilingualism and Biculturalism 2 (Ottawa:
Queen's Printer, 1969). See also Rowland Lorimer, *The Nation in the Schools* (Toronto:
OISE, 1984), and Ken Osborne, *In Defence of History: Teaching the Past and the Meaning
of Democratic Citizenship* (Toronto: Our Schools / Our Selves Education Foundation,
1995).

499 : Kenneth W. Osborne, *"Hard-working, Temperate and Peaceable": The Portrayal of
Workers in Canadian History Textbooks* (Winnipeg: Univ. of Manitoba Press, 1980); Linda
Fischer and J.A. Cheyne, *Sex Roles: Biological and Cultural Interactions as Found in Social
Science Research and Ontario Education Media* (Toronto: Ontario Minister of Education,
1977), cited in Ruth Pierson and Beth Light, "Women in the Teaching and Writing of
Canadian History," *History and Social Science Teacher* 17 (1982): 83–93, quote p. 83;
Marcel Trudel and Geneviève Jain, *Canadian History Textbooks: A Comparative Study*,
Studies of the Royal Commission on Bilingualism and Biculturalism 5 (Ottawa: Queen's
Printer, 1970); Geneviève Laloux-Jain, *Les Manuels d'histoire du Canada au Québec et en
Ontario (de 1867 à 1914)* (Quebec: PU Laval, 1974).

500 : "Social Studies Curricula in Canada," eds. Alan Sears, Gerry Clarke, Andrew S.
Hughes, topical issue of *Canadian Social Studies* 31.1 (Fall 1996): 14–45; Alan Sears,
"What Research Tells Us about Citizenship Education in English Canada," *Canadian So-
cial Studies* 30.3 (1996): 121–27; Bob Davis, *Whatever Happened to High School History?
Burying the Political Memory of Youth: Ontario, 1945–1995* (Toronto: Lorimer, 1995). See
also Ken Dryden, *In School: Our Kids, Our Teachers, Our Classrooms* (Toronto: McClelland
& Stewart, 1997). A comparable perspective on the U.S. is provided by Eric D. Hirsch,
Jr., *Cultural Literacy* (Boston: Houghton Mifflin, 1987).

adian literature was minuscule; a large part of the Canadian reading public "would turn instinctively to England, France, and the United States"; even in Quebec "la littérature canadienne-française n'a été l'objet d'un véritable enseignement universitaire." When in 1961 Clara Thomas planned a Canadian literature course at Toronto's new York University, the department's chairman, freshly imported from Britain, vetoed the topic and categorically stated that there was not sufficient material to fill a course.[501] In contrast to historians and literary scholars, geographers, perhaps remembering the achievements of the Geological Survey and its approaches, had moved from a preoccupation with the physical features of landscapes to human usages and social spaces. Their concept of space involves agency of all members of society. An inclusive "citizenship education," as the goal of schooling came to be called,[502] seems easy to describe: How did we become what we are—which achievements and which problems are part of our past? Which of the values we are embedded in do we want to continue into the future and how do we negotiate conflict between values? Individuals as well as society as a whole need options and social capital in order to develop. For migrants the issue of "how did we become what we are" involves two tracks as well as integration: how did our parents become what they were in the society of origin; how did our new environment, Canada or a particular region of it, become what it is? For the young, curricula need to be future-oriented: where do we, as individuals and society, go from here?

Academia: From decolonization to recolonization?

If schools had evolved slowly, the core of knowledge production, the university system, underwent massive change in all Western societies from the 1940s to the 1970s. In Canada, scientific and technological research had been boosted by World War II spending. Student enrolment grew by fifty-three thousand from 1945 to 1951 under a veterans' rehabilitation program; doubled in the '50s; and, with the baby boom generation, tripled in full-time undergraduate study and increased six-fold in graduate study in the '60s. From among the growing middle class ever more women entered colleges

---

501 : Alec Lucas, "Missing: Canadian Literature," *Canadian Forum* 51.605 (June 1971): 6–8; interview D. Hoerder with Clara Thomas, 24 Nov. 2000; Guy Sylvestre, "La recherche en littérature canadienne-française," in Louis Baudouin, ed., *La recherche au Canada français* (Montreal: PU Montréal, 1968), 149–61, quote p. 149.

502 : Yvonne Hébert, "Identity, Diversity, and Education: A Critical Review of the Literature," *Canadian Ethnic Studies* 33.2 (2001): 155–85; Michel Pagé, Fernand Ouellet, Luiza Cortesão, eds., *L'éducation à la citoyenneté* (Sherbrooke: Éditions du CRP, 2001); Yvonne M. Hébert, ed., *Citizenship in Transformation in Canada* (Toronto: UTP, 2003).

and universities. New concepts of social justice mandated easy and equal access to improved education as a means to satisfy rising social aspirations.

Internationally, higher education came to be considered the key to economic productivity in industrial societies. Rather than emanating from a concern for young people, this strategy was part of the Cold War as well as a reaction to decolonization. First, the Atlantic World's ideologues feared that "the communist system" was moving ahead of "the free world," that is, the capitalist economic system, after the USSR launched the world's first space satellite, Sputnik, in 1957. Second, the decolonizing third world changed the parameters of international competition. To keep their technological advantage, the first and second worlds invested in education and training. Both blocs, under diametrically opposed ideological and rhetorical strategies, practised "global apartheid" (Richmond) to segregate people (of colours other than "white") into low-value-added production work. Intentionally, this accelerated the "brain drain" toward the United States; unintentionally, it stimulated the massive south–north migrations that were to change the composition of societies of the Western White world. Expanded educational facilities were to improve competitiveness of the capitalist countries—with limited admission for "foreign students" from the "developing world," then still labelled "underdeveloped."

Within Canada, these parameters mandated a massive expansion of educational systems in general and universities in particular. By region, both Quebec and the West from Manitoba to British Columbia had comparatively few academic institutions. In Quebec, Bill 60 of 1964 finally placed education under provincial responsibility and a Ministry of Education and Culture—the first after the ephemeral one of 1868 to 1875—was established. Paul Gérin-Lajoie, as minister, secularized education on recommendation of the Parent Commission, and in 1967 replaced the traditional *collèges classiques* with the science-oriented *collèges d'enseignement général et professionel* (CEGEP). The Université de Montréal was secularized and the multi-campus Université de Québec (founded 1968) became the first public university. Education and scholarship caught up with the rest of Canada within a few years.[503] Numerous new universities were founded in the West, but

---

503 : From within the Church, Jean-Paul Désbiens' *Les Insolences de Frère Untel* (1960, Engl. *The Impertinences of Brother Anonymous*, 1962), first serialized in *Le Devoir*, had attacked the control of the clergy. Though writing from an elitist and nationalist perspective and rejecting the popular *joual*-French, the author was banished to Rome. Commission royale d'enquête sur l'enseignement dans la province du Québec (1961–66), chaired by the vice-rector of Université Laval Alphonse-Marie Parent, *Rapport Parent*, 5 vols. (Quebec, 1963–66); Paul-André Linteau, René Durocher, Jean-Claude Robert, and François Ricard, *Histoire du Québec contemporain*, 2 vols. (Montreal: Boréal, 1979, 1991), 2:659–72.

also in cities such as Toronto, Winnipeg, and Montreal with high numbers of lower-middle class and recent immigrant high school graduates. In Ontario, newly founded universities ended the monopoly of the University of Toronto.[504] Nationwide, the Canadian Association of University Teachers, founded in 1951 in reaction to a history of infringements on academic freedom by denominational bodies, university administrators, and wealthy benefactors, defended academic freedom as well as freedom of expression in general.[505] As recommended by the Massey Commission, universities received federal funding (after 1966 under federal-provincial cost-sharing programs), which in the "affluent years" achieved for teaching what in the interwar decades U.S. foundations' grants had achieved for research.

Colleges and universities were unprepared for innovation and the massive increase in enrolment. While public discourse and scholars had discussed and, to some degree, invented a *Québec en retard*, this gaze at "the Other" had served to hide the educational and ideological shortcomings of an *anglophonie en retard*. From the late nineteenth century, the underdeveloped system of tertiary education had forced students to go abroad for graduate and post-graduate studies. It also had necessitated the hiring of academic personnel from England and Scotland, as well as in Quebec from France. Canada's two elites had turned their societies into educational hinterlands; the reliance on colonizer cores aggravated dependency relationships. Of English immigrant teachers many had little knowledge of Canadian society but inflated concepts of Britishness, they "give the impression that they are superior to their surroundings and live 'apart' from common life," commented William Caldwell of McGill. The marketplace of ideas had offered other options: "Our university must be a national one, not a colonial one," noted an observer in the University of Toronto's *Varsity* in 1888. Almost a century later, the Committee on Canadian Studies stated that as a

---

504 : Victoria University (founded 1903, closed after the est. of UBC in 1915, reest. in 1920 as two-year college affiliated with UBC) 1963; Calgary, 1966. In the cities: York, Toronto, 1959; Winnipeg, 1967; Univ. du Québec, Montreal, 1968. In Ontario: Carleton, Ottawa, 1957; Waterloo, 1959; Trent, Peterborough, 1963; Guelph, 1964. In Manitoba, the Collège universitaire de Saint-Boniface of 1910, as the oldest educational institution in Western Canada, received neither attention from anglophone reformers nor from historians of education.

505 : Michiel Horn, *Academic Freedom in Canada: A History* (Toronto: UTP, 2000); Steve Hewitt, "'Information Believed True': RCMP Security Intelligence Activities on Canadian University Campuses and the Controversy Surrounding Them, 1961-71," *Canadian Historical Review* 81 (2000): 191-229; Mathew Evenden, "Harold Innis, the Arctic Survey, and the Politics of Social Science During the Second World War," *Canadian Historical Review* 79.1 (1998): 36-67.

consequence "of these colonial attitudes . . . universities were slow to develop roots in their own country."[506]

When during the expansion in the 1960s some 23,250 new full-time university teachers were hired, the Anglo-Canadian *retard* came into view. Far too few Canadian-trained graduates and Canadian-born graduates of British or, increasingly, U.S. universities were available. Again, teaching staff had to be hired from Britain, in the process of abdicating its imperial role, and from the United States, just then assuming the imperial lead of the Western world. At the crucial stage of its own decolonization, Canada had to rely on scholars from the old and new imperial powers to teach its young generation. University administrators, with a deference typical of the colonized, offered generous salaries and teaching conditions to U.S. personnel, while paying Canadians lower salaries, restricting them to lower-ranking positions, and assigning them the largest classes and least-esteemed topics: hinterland–metropolis relations in academia. Many newcomers from the United States did not care about the differences between the two societies; argued, in keeping with the modernization paradigm, that Canada could close the gap, the *retard*, in half a generation; did not join Canadian professional organizations. Some Americans in Quebec were more sensitive to French distinctiveness than anglophone Canadians, but most saw no need to keep lines of communication open with French Canadian colleagues.[507]

In the 1950s, neither the few Americans nor U.S. textbooks had "swamped the Canadian faculty or the Canadian content of courses." Less than two decades later, a venomous debate about the Americanization of academia erupted after Robin Mathews and James Steele from Carleton University edited a factual as well as polemical dossier on the influx from the United States. The issue quickly broadened: penetration of U.S. capital into the Canadian economy; the control of the Canadian labour movement by the so-called international U.S. unions; the mass import of U.S. popular culture and cultural products. Ian Lumsden's critical *Close to the 49th Parallel*, edited for the University League of Social Reform in 1970, found a ready

---

506 : Thomas H.B. Symons, *To Know Ourselves: Report of the Commission on Canadian Studies*, French: *Se connaître: le rapport de la commission sur les études canadiennes*, 2 vols. (Ottawa: Assoc. of Universities and Colleges of Canada, 1975), vol. 3 by Symons and James E. Page, *Some Questions of Balance: Human Resources, Higher Education, and Canadian Studies* (Ottawa: AUCC, 1984), quotes 3: 33 (Varsity), 34. Marlene Shore, *The Science of Social Redemption: McGill, the Chicago School, and the Origins of Social Research in Canada* (Toronto: UTP, 1987), Caldwell quoted p. 35.

507 : Jean R. Burnet, "Minorities I Have Belonged To," in Danielle Juteau-Lee and Barbara Roberts, eds., "Ethnicity and Femininity," topical issue of *Canadian Ethnic Studies* 13.1 (1981): 24–36, quote p. 28.

audience.[508] Some of the criticism was undifferentiated, bandying about examples of American arrogance but making no mention of refugee scholars who, as opponents of the Vietnam War, repudiated U.S. policies.[509] Some U.S. radicals, however, remained imperial-minded. The heroes of the U.S. New Left, Jerry Rubin and Abe Hoffman, were booed off stage by York University students for their disparaging comments about Canada.[510] Critics of Americanization had the data on their side, the composition of university faculty "was strikingly different from that of other . . . industrialized nations": in 1976, 98 percent of the professoriate at U.S. universities was American, 92 percent at British universities was British, in Canada only 72 percent of full-time university teachers were Canadians.[511] Of some 32,500 full-time staff members, whose citizenship was known, 12 percent held U.S. citizenship, 4.7 percent were British, 1.9 percent other Commonwealth, and 1.4 percent Belgian and French. The Prairie provinces, with their southward-oriented economies and experience of Ontario hegemony, had an above-average representation of U.S. academics. Canadian scholars demanded a "repatriation" of the universities, and accused U.S. expatriates of turning "us" into "exiles in our land" and Canadian administrators of risking "annihilation" of academic life. Institutions, dropping the second-language requirement for the bachelor degree, estranged students "from Canada's other language."[512] Many newcomers showed limited interest in adjusting to the world of their students.

508 : Mathews and Steele, eds., *The Struggle for Canadian Universities: A Dossier* (Toronto: New Press, 1969); Ian Lumsden, ed., *Close to the 49th Parallel, Etc.: The Americanization of Canada* (Toronto: UTP, 1970); Gary Teeple, ed., *Capitalism and the National Question in Canada* (Toronto: UTP, 1972); Leo Panitch, ed., *The Canadian State: Political Economy and Political Power* (Toronto: UTP, 1977). A thoughtful subsequent report is Anthony H. Richmond, *The Employment of Foreign Academics in Canada: A Report to the Royal Society of Canada* (mimeographed; n.p.: RSC, May 1983). See also the journalistic text by David J. Bercuson, Robert Bothwell, J.L. Granatstein, *The Great Brain Robbery: Canada's Universities on the Road to Ruin* (Toronto: McClelland & Stewart, 1984).

509 : As during the U.S. Civil War, Canada provided refuge to anti-war young American men and, in some cases, their families, perhaps a total of half a million.

510 : James Dickerson, *North to Canada: Men and Women against the Vietnam War* (Westport, CT: Praeger, 1999); interview with John Wadland, 7 Dec. 2000.

511 : In 1969-70, only 57% of full-time faculty members had held Canadian citizenship. The increase to 72% reflected naturalizations more than different hiring patterns.

512 : "Reflections on the Symons Report," Stephen Clarkson, Antoine Sirois, John Woods, David Cameron, *Journal of Canadian Studies* 11.4 (1976): 1-2, 50-72, esp. 56-68, quotes pp. 59, 60, 61. Admission of academic migrants became more restrictive as of April 1977, amended in 1981 (Richmond, *Employment*, 1). In the 1980s and '90s, higher salaries and better research facilities drew Canadian talent to the United States.

A retrospective from the 1990s provides a more differentiated view. Opposition to the hiring of U.S.-born scholars grew when the first generation of graduates trained in Canada entered the job market in the early '70s. By then, acculturation of many U.S. scholars was underway; those who arrived with young families intended to stay; single men married Canadian women. The Anglo-Canadian *retard* had meant that U.S. scholarship was more advanced and that no Canada-centered textbooks existed. Furthermore, immigrant U.S. nationalists had the support of Canadian empiricists, who recognized the U.S. head start in methodology and, paradoxically, of Canadian Marxists, who considered Canada merely one more example of capitalist societies. For U.S. scholars, naturalization was problematic since their country did not accept dual citizenship. The anti-American stance may also have hidden lingering anti-British sentiments among young postcolonial Canadian scholars who, facing powerful colonially minded senior colleagues, could not express such a position.

While Anglo-Canadian universities underwent a de-Canadianization or recolonization process, Quebec's intellectuals developed a sophisticated Quebec-centered research domain. The French-language humanities were protected from threat of hegemonic U.S. English-language scholarship; in the social sciences, the Lévesque-Hughes-Falardeau tradition of the 1940s and '50s served as a basis. While Ontario's social scientists did not study "le Canada comme société distincte," their francophone compatriots "ont largement contribué . . . à articuler des interprétations de la société québécoise comme totalité," and the sovereignty debates further encouraged research on Quebec society. By the 1980s, the Institut québécois de recherché sur la culture (1979) and Quebec Studies had come into being.[513]

De-Canadianization in anglophone Canada varied between disciplines. In the humanities, immigrant or transitory British academic staff reinforced the mentality of people of British background, which prevented Canadian scholars from valuing their country's literature. In the social sciences—economics, political science, and sociology—the loss of Canadian perspectives involved many factors, as the Committee on Canadian Studies, established in 1972, was to point out.

---

513 : Fernand Harvey, "Pour une histoire culturelle du mouvement des études canadiennes," *ACS Newsletter* 10.1 (Spring 1988): 13–17, quote p. 15. Jean-Paul L'Allier, Pour l'évolution de la politique culturelle (= *"Livre vert"*) (Quebec: Ministère des Affaires culturelles, mai 1976); *La politique québécoise du développement culturel* (= *"Livre blanc"*), 2 vols. (Quebec: Éditeur officiel, 1978). Jacques Portes and Sylvain Simard, eds., *La Coopération universitaire entre la France et le Québec: bilan et perspectives* (Paris: Centre de coopération universitaire franco-québécois, 1987), 13–22, noted that from 1965 to 1973, when the exchange program was well-funded, Quebec became better known in France through scholarly writing.

Chapter 11

VISIONS AND BORDERLINES:
CANADIAN STUDIES SINCE THE 1960S

The Study of Canada, in its first two phases, had been a transdisciplinary undertaking with a view into the many regional, cultural, social "parts" of Canada as well as an implicit concept of one integrating or integrated country. It had struggled with privileged and narrow discourses, which mistook a part—whether elites, men, one of the two central Canadas, or politics—for the whole. In the 1960s, the flexible research organization had given way to staked territories in public discourse and in scholarly disciplines. The spokespersons of "founding peoples," "First Peoples," and "ethnic groups" engaged in rhetorical battles about their relative positions in the society and in struggles about access to society's resources. Reflected in academia, the emerging Canadian Studies did not achieve a comprehensive view of all of society: Native Studies, Quebec Studies, Ethnic Studies developed in parallel. Some reduced the positioning to the two hegemonies, to a conflictual Quebec versus Rest-of-Canada culture or, vice versa, anglophone Rest-of-Canada versus Quebec stance.

Women, First Peoples, "ethnics," students, and many others through self-organization made their voices heard and reduced the talking heads to their little forts. Still, innovative courses for a study of the society, often by young researchers, faced numerous obstacles. If Canada as a nation-state had finally liberated itself from its triple colonial London-Paris-Rome dependency, the ambivalence of decolonization challenged pride in Canadian achievements. Liberation from colonial mindsets and master narratives had to negotiate the simultaneous recognition of the multiple internal decolonization processes of ethnocultural groups with fuzzy boundaries: of women, of the young generation, of the many-cultured First Peoples. The Canadian state was divided into provinces and, along different lines, into regions—heterotopia, as Richard Cavell suggested—the nation into gender spheres, many cultural origins or backgrounds, and highly differentiated identifications and interests.[514]

To develop Canadian Studies implied overcoming numerous practical problems. First, to know Canada necessitated knowledge of, at least, the two major languages and admission to academia of scholars with knowledge of the non-hegemonic languages and women's discourses or other idioms. In

---

514 : Richard Cavell, "Theoretizing Canadian Space: Postcolonial Articulations," in Terry Goldie, Carmen Lambert, Rowland Lorimer, eds., *Canada: Theoretical Discourse / Discours théorétiques* (Montreal: Assoc. for Canadian Studies, 1994), 75–104, quote p. 88.

the 1961 census, only 31 percent of Canada's people considered themselves able to speak French, if as a second or third language. Among scholars, exchange in the official languages was limited and access to sources in "non-official" languages more so. It also needs re-emphasizing that many of the numerous languages are gendered, and that language usage varies between generations. Second, in some disciplines about half of the teaching staff—hired from abroad—knew too little about Canada to teach about its societies or to understand its discourses and, of the Canada-socialized half, many were still rooted in pre-1960s scholarship. Third, the transdisciplinary 1920s research structure had given way to rigorous separation between disciplines, to specialized methodologies and theorizations. Disciplines demanded discipline. Scholars hardly attempted to cross borderlines; neighbouring scholarly expanses came to be considered unfriendly territory. Those who subscribed to the decolonizing and later post-colonial approaches saw their concepts shut out from orthodoxy-occupied and heavily guarded research fields and institutions. Fourth, the innovators, combining social history with cultural studies and discourse theory, faced a weakening from within. New talking heads turned from empirical research and grounded theory to instant jargon-laden post-modern rhetoric. In this tangle of interests, Canadian Studies could not achieve full recognition as an integrative national and yet post-colonial field of study and Transcultural Societal Studies remained a distant goal.

Frames of meaning: The simultaneous centering and decentering of Canada

Several characteristics distinguish Canadian Studies from Country Self-studies elsewhere. First, because of its triple dependency, the two hegemonic White gatekeeper elites and peoples never developed a unitary nationalist authoritarian discourse and identity that precluded negotiation altogether. If identity-constructions are contested, essentializing versions are constantly being questioned. Those who recognized the many-cultured composition of society did not face a phalanx of powerful nationalists who constructed every single pattern of thought and deed as stemming from time immemorial, from ancestral ways, God-given commandments, genetic or bloodlines. *Vieille souche* and British-blood defenders could do no more than lament the decline of the nation or formulate twisted referenda questions. Second, the combination of long-recognized regionalisms and of increasingly perceived cultural difference between groups of many backgrounds, as well as between genders and generations, further undercut single-track readings of the story of Canada. Third, it is worth repeating that Canada had introduced its own citizenship only in 1947, and that for the first time in their history

Canadians could call themselves "Canadian" in the 1951 census. Memory—
je me souviens—may be a suffocating corset (accepted because it provides
"beauty" in the eyes of the beholders); memory may be a construction to
impose power or to give sense to a complex and contradictory past; memory
may be an instrument to come to terms with what is, with what individuals
or segments of society want to come into being.

The hypothesis of an openness particular to Canadian society and discourse is supported by the absence of controversial debate at the introduction in 1971 of the policy of multiculturalism within the frame of bilingualism. From a Euro-national perspective the policy implied a revolutionary
reconceptualization of society, but in Canada's press and public discourse
it elicited little comment. The policy, new to self-understanding at society's top level, merely recognized what had long been everyday practice
of many Canadians. Analyzing comparatively how the Canadian, Swedish, and Dutch societies reconceptualized themselves from (bi)national to
multicultural—before the backdrop of other societies incapable of change—
Christiane Harzig found that in these (comparatively small) societies the
state-wide administration's personnel, too small to undertake a major policy
review, perceived the need for new approaches. Thus they commissioned
scholars, outsiders to bureaucratic discourse and practice, to provide analyses and recommendations. These were publicly debated and transformed
into long-range policies. The process required a readiness of administrators, policy-makers, and politicians for change; it required massive travails
to change school texts and patterns of narratives among adults. In all three
societies, historical memory played an important role. While in Canada (as
in the United States) an immigration discourse was present, in Sweden and
in the Netherlands (as in all European societies) memory of the massive intra-European migrations and cultural exchanges had been expunged. The
nineteenth-century nationalization of historiography had involved a hom-
ogenizing of complex pasts by deleting difference. In the 1970s, Swedish
and Dutch historians reintroduced the memory of migration—immigration
had been high in both societies in the seventeenth century and beyond—and
thus initiated new self-conceptualizations. From being a confining burden,
political culture turned memory into a creative, strategic resource to en-
vision, shape, craft, and construct the present and to make the future a project as a negotiated trajectory from the past via the present.[515]

---

515 : Christiane Harzig, *Einwanderung und Politik, Transkulturelle Perspektiven, Band 1:
Historische Erinnerung und Politische Kultur als Gestaltungsressourcen in den Niederlanden,
Schweden und Kanada* (English: Immigration and Policy-Making Transcultural Perspectives, Volume 1: Historical Memory and Political Culture as Creative Strategic Resource
in the Netherlands, Sweden, and Canada) (Göttingen: V&R Unipress, 2004), 241–59.

The extended, occasionally tedious, debates about Canadian identity reflect a shift from the nationalist authoritarian "he/she is and thus shall" to a flexible "he/she may select between options." Societies and states that emphasize monocultural or essentialized nationality deprive themselves of a choice between the potentialities of "diversity is our strength." By 2001, the United Nations Educational, Scientific and Cultural Organization (UNESCO) passed a Universal Declaration of Cultural Diversity. In Canada, as in many other societies, this had been lived experience. In an essay contest for a Canadian equivalent of monocultural "as American as apple pie," a Canadian student provided a far more modest statement: "as Canadian as possible under the circumstances." Among scholars, Maurice Careless and Ramsay Cook introduced the concept of "limited identities." A young student of Cook, Gerald Friesen from the West, added regionalism, and David Cameron suggested that the conceptual change from "identity" to "roles" may be "a celebration of one's identity, not its denial," and involves recognition that "our political identity is multiple." Eighteenth-century beginnings had made it so; nineteenth-century immigration and regionalism added to it; the twentieth-century constitution and bill of rights ensures that so it will remain. "An identification with the country can exist in happy harmony with a range of other affiliations of this sort, or one can experience disjunctions or tensions among them." Accommodating "multiple sets of identities . . . [is] no mean accomplishment." That such accommodations were always "peaceful and humane," as the masters of the narrative had suggested, would elicit scorn from people of skin colours other than "white," from women, from the underclasses. Still, in relation to other societies, these developments were less fraught with violent repression.[516]

During the period of thoughtful and theory-informed debates, institutionalization of Canadian Studies was slow. Thus, the Association of Universities and Colleges of Canada in 1972 appointed its oft-cited Commission on Canadian Studies (CCS) with T.H.B. Symons as Chair (and often only actor). The *Report* of 1975 presented a vast collection of data on teaching

---

516 : J.M.S. Careless, "'Limited Identities' in Canada," (1971) repr. in Carl Berger, ed., *Contemporary Approaches to Canadian History* (Toronto: Copp Clark, 1987), 5–12, and Careless, "Limited Identities—Ten Years Later," *Manitoba History* 1 (1981): 3–9; Ramsay Cook, "Canadian Centennial Celebrations," *International Journal* 22 (1967): 659–63; David R. Cameron, *Taking Stock: Canadian Studies in the Nineties* (Montreal: ACS, 1996), quotes pp. 10–13; Linda Hutcheon, "As Canadian as . . . Possible . . . Under the Circumstances!" in Gerald Lynch and David Rampton, eds., *The Canadian Essay* (Toronto: Copp Clark, 1991), 332–51. For a literary author's statement see Robert Kroetsch, "Disunity as Unity: A Canadian strategy," in Kroetsch, ed., *The Lovely Treachery of Words: Essays Selected and New* (Toronto: Oxford, 1989), 21–33.

and research with a wordy introductory reflection on "the rationale for Canadian Studies."[517] The CCS positioned Canadian Studies as a present-oriented quest "to know ourselves" and asked how the educational system transmitted information or feeling about Canada to the next generation. Self-knowledge was not to imply self-centeredness, it was to place state and society in the wider world. But the CCS derived its concept of "identity" from Greek philosophy and thus posited itself in Western philosophy. Scholars' opinions on the field varied widely: Canadian Studies should discover and inculcate Canadian identity; Canadian identity is known and word about it should be spread; Canadian Studies should combat threats "of imperialism, continentalism, regionalism, centralization, federalism, or whatever" to Canadian identity. In the climate of opinion of the times, women, the working classes, Native people, and urban Canada also did not figure prominently in the scholars' quest for self-knowledge. The *Report* devoted a mere seven lines to Native Studies but two full pages to Northern Studies. Scholars—like the Ottawa men—"have an opportunity to identify the long-term decisions that a society must make and to work toward an understanding of the issues involved in advance of the time for public decision." Rather than the "patriotic appeals" characteristic of old-style Country Studies, the CCS argued compellingly for "the importance of self-knowledge, the need to know and to understand ourselves: who we are; where we are in time and space; where we have been; where we are going; what we possess; what our responsibilities are to ourselves and to others."[518]

Among the reasons for the neglect of Canadian Studies, the CCS listed the "high representation of non-Canadians in the administrative positions of universities and of individual departments" and "Canadian faculty members . . . indifferent to Canadian studies." It defied logic that some Canadian

---

517 : Thomas H.B. Symons, *To Know Ourselves: Report of the Commission on Canadian Studies*, French: *Se connaître: le rapport de la commission sur les études canadiennes*, 2 vols. (Ottawa: AUCC, 1975), quote 1:1. Hereafter cites as *CCS Report*. Of five projected volumes, a third appeared in 1984: Symons and James E. Page, *Some Questions of Balance: Human Resources, Higher Education, and Canadian Studies*. Then publication ended. See also Page, *Reflections on the Symons Report: The State of Canadian Studies in 1980. A Report Prepared for the Department of Secretary of State of Canada* (Toronto: Canadian Studies Program, Seneca College, 1980); Stephen Clarkson, Antoine Sirois, John Woods, David Cameron, "Reflections in the Symons Report," *Journal of Canadian Studies* 11.4 (1976): 1-2, 50-72; "Point-Counterpoint: Looking Ahead into the Past," topical issue of *Journal of Canadian Studies* 30.1 (1995).

518 : *CCS Report*, 1:11-15, 90-92. A study by the AUCC on *The University and the Canadian North*, funded by Ford Foundation and the Department of Indian and Northern Affairs, concluded in 1973 that applied research was necessary, among other topics on the health of the Inuit.

scholars disdained Canadian Studies but valued European Studies at British universities or American Studies around the world. Such men sported an "attitude that Canada is not a sufficiently interesting subject for study and research"—they had their minds set in colonial-dependency mode.[519]

The happy realization of the 1970s that Canadian literature could be dated from Marie de l'Incarnation or Susanna Moodie soon had to come to terms with contributions in languages other than French or English, whether Native or other. Some scholars from the "founding nations," proud of having discovered their Canadian roots as distinct from an imperial or clerical mould, resented such questioning of their group's claim to fame at the very moment of self-assertion. The *retard* of this intellectual achievement meant that it came at the "wrong" time, too late for exclusive appreciation, overshadowed by post-colonial conceptualizations. Canadian Studies as "a form of self-studies [was] created as part of a decolonization process." If this endeavour has sometimes been labelled "nationalist," it was meant to achieve independence and recognition of complexity. In an international perspective, liberation from Britain and France as well as the U.S. warfare in Vietnam "helped to create the mental space within which our country was able to strengthen a consciousness of itself and its own achievements." Self-knowledge, from the start, referred to "our many selves."[520]

An institutionalized quest "to know our many selves" or disdain for Canadian Studies?

If Canadian identity is complex, then its study will be complex. Innovation began at two new universities, Carleton and Trent (of which Symons was founding president). Both created Native *and* Canadian Studies departments; Trent in this sequence, Carleton vice versa.[521] In a collection significantly taking an outsider's perspective, *Outside the Lines: Issues in Interdisciplinary Research*, Jill Vickers discussed the "collective scholarly activity" at Carleton under president Claude Bissell and director R.L. (Rob) McDougall. She discerned the "gentlemanly nationalism" of the "Founding Era" (1958–68), multidisciplinary with English and French, history and journalism, and the social, political, and economic sciences, as well as geography. The program

---

519 : *CCS Report*, 1:15–20, 26–28.

520 : Jill Vickers, "Another Look at Interdisciplinarity," *ACS Newsletter* (Spring 1994), 14–15, quote p. 14; Cameron, *Taking Stock*, 7:

521 : Stanley E. McMullin in "The Waterloo Experience," *ICCS Contact* 8.2 (Autumn 1989): 4–6, noted that the University of Waterloo initiative for the teaching of Canadian Studies began in 1970 in reaction to Mathews' and Steele's critique of the Americanization of Canadian universities.

was to "reflect the cosmopolitan origins and interests of the country" and to investigate the hidden aspects of the past.[522] The second, "Political Era" (1969–75), under the influence of Quebec separatism, involved a nationalism aimed at defining Canada and a preoccupation with political violence. Traditional unspoken politics of research were challenged by outspoken approaches from the Left by Pauline Jewitt, Enoch Padolsky, and Patricia Smart. "The Seedbed Era" (1975–82) focused on art history, music, law, film, linguistics, and mass communication. The tenacious opposition of scholars trained in a Euro-nationalist tradition was finally overcome in "The Era of New Scholarship" (since 1983), when Native and Women's Studies were "hearing silenced voices," when affirmative action admissions helped Native and north-of-sixty students, when activists suggested new ways of multiple heritage conservation.[523]

At Trent University, the faculty established the *Journal of Canadian Studies* in 1966 (at first in English only), and Native Studies in 1969, as well as Canadian Studies in 1972. W.L. Morton and T.H.B. Symons taught Canadiana, John Wadland inter- (not multi-) disciplinary courses. While Carleton's Jill Vickers emphasized achievements, Trent's Alan Wilson noted first, the many obstacles: charges of providing only "some lowest common denominator of pious generalities about the Canadian experience" (Jacques Barzun) and of being a vehicle of anti-Americanism. Second, he emphasized utilitarian aspects: in the post-war period, labour markets extended across the country and those who moved needed knowledge about the whole of the country, not just about one segment. While the Massey Commission had still referred to military service as nationalizing experience, the National Film Board had pursued the same goal by cross-country films that permitted those who lived in one region to visualize others. Third, language qualifications would have to include French and English for all, perhaps Celtic in the Maritimes, other European languages—Yiddish included—in the Prairies, and Asian languages at the Pacific Coast. Innovation required retooling for hegemony-challenged scholars.[524]

Many innovators of the late 1960s merit attention. Geographers such as John Warkentin (York University) and Leonard Evenden (Simon Fraser

522 : Thus the *Carleton Library Series* (since 1963) reintroduced "classics" of Canadian writing.

523 : Jill Vickers, "Thirty-Five Years on the Beaver Patrol: Canadian Studies as a Collective Scholarly Activity," in Liora Salter and Alison Hearn, eds., *Outside the Lines: Issues in Interdisciplinary Research* (Montreal: MQUP, 1996), 78–85, quote p. 80.

524 : Alan Wilson, "Canadian Studies at Trent," *Journal of Canadian Studies* 15.3 (1980): 39–46, quotes pp. 40, 42; interview with John Wadland, 7 Dec. 2000.

University) left a deep impact on the study of Canada.[525] International scholars had expanded the perspectives, for example Scottish James W. Watson, who after working with the Geological Survey in Ottawa returned to Edinburgh, and German geographers Carl Schott, Karl Lenz, and Alfred Pletsch. They were instrumental in establishing Canadian Studies in Edinburgh, Marburg, and Berlin. Geographers' turn from the physical to the historical-cultural resulted in an empirically grounded early recognition of how landscapes were constructed, how social spaces changed over time, how natural environment and human activity interacted. Warkentin became first director of Canadian Studies at the newly founded York University. But even at this institution, the history faculty, many of whom had just fled the stale Creightonian University of Toronto's history department, was reluctant to accept an interdisciplinary approach. Only Ramsay Cook acted as interlocutor of both French- and English-Canada and never accepted the study of a part as an equivalent for the whole. At some Prairie universities, innovators challenged hegemonies: at the University of Alberta, Henry Kreisel established a program of Canadian literature, and the University of Calgary became the major centre of western as well as trans-Canadian ethnic history. The interdisciplinary approach of James Frideres in sociology, Howard Palmer in history, Anthony Rasporich as student of labour and the working classes, and Tamara Palmer in literature re-centered Anglo predominance to many-cultured input. Such scholars kept their distance from earlier—halfway—innovators, such as W.L. Morton from Manitoba (later Trent), who had introduced the West to Canadian history but had remained conservative in interpretation, or Watson Kirkconnell (Winnipeg), who had introduced minority literatures to the canon but had excluded ethnic writers on the Left. In the "far west" sat British Columbia with its trans-Pacific connections: Simon Fraser University joined the Canadian Studies movement; UBC followed in the late 1980s with emphasis on multidisciplinary approaches, and in the 1990s with an internationalist approach to Canadian Studies. In the early 1970s, designated Canadian Studies programs were available at four universities in the Atlantic Provinces, at nine Quebec, twenty Ontario, and ten western ones. As regards disciplines, the shift from the social science-based study of Canada of the interwar years to literature-

---

525 : John Warkentin, ed., *Canada: A Geographical Interpretation*, prepared under the auspices of the Canadian Association of Geographers (Toronto: Methuen, 1970), French ed. *Le Canada: Une interprétation géographique* (1970), rev. ed. as *Canada: A Regional Geography* (1997), and further rev. as *A Regional Geography of Canada: Life, Land, and Space* (Scarborough: Prentice-Hall, 2000); Allen Seager et al., eds., *Alternative Frontiers: Voices from the Mountain West* (Montreal: ACS, 1997).

based, identity-discussing Canadian Studies is striking.[526]

While interdisciplinary-minded scholars were in the lead of developing Canadian Studies as a comprehensive field, bounded disciplines were still in poor shape. In the departments of English in the early 1970s, only 8 percent of the courses dealt with Canadian literature in a substantial way, though enrolment and PhD topics indicate that student interest was higher. French-Canadian universities did better. They dealt with literatures in both languages and the University of Sherbrooke offered a bilingual program in Canadian literature. But Quebec's institutions suffered from the "haphazard conservation methods and cataloguing practices of most libraries." As to art, not only were there few courses offered, but also little research in Canadian art history was undertaken. As a result, no curators for galleries or museums were being trained and no Canadian art archives of national scope had been established.[527] In geography, less than one quarter of undergraduate courses dealt with Canada. Since research in urban geography was virtually absent, policy-makers were left without information for decision-making. Historiography "sailed along as majestically, as securely, and as inflexibly as the Royal Navy" (Alan Wilson) and the discrepancy between enrolment in Canadian history courses (34 percent of the students) and courses offered (20 percent of the total) once again emphasized the generation gap between teachers and students. While in their briefs to the Commission historians had named only military history as deserving more attention, the CCS recommended courses on the different "historiographical traditions" of both linguistic communities, on regional, urban, economic, labour, and social history, as well as on the history of "the Native peoples, the French-speaking minorities outside of Quebec and the English-speaking minority within Quebec" and the "many other diverse cultural groups that have

---

526 : This section is based on interviews with John Lennox (21 Nov. 2000), Clara Thomas (24 Nov. 2000), John Warkentin (30 Nov. 2000) of York Univ.; John H. Wadland (7 Dec. 2000) of Trent Univ.; Tamara Seiler (23 March 2001) of the Univ. of Calgary; Allan C.L. Smith (19 March 2001) and Richard Cavell (2 April 2001) of UBC. I am deeply indebted to all of them for sharing their memories and analyses with me. All of them were more informative and lively than any published account of the emergence of Canadian Studies, whether the Symons or the Cameron reports.

527 : CCS Report, 1:30–52, quote p. 52; Alec Lucas, "Missing: Canadian Literature," Canadian Forum 51, no. 605 (June 1971), 6–8. The departments of "performing, fine, and applied arts" hardly bothered to reply to the CCS queries (1:92–98). The CCS Report (1:88–90) noted that the study of "interpretation and translation" should be self-evident in a bilingual country but that programs were being developed only recently. Linguistics was missing, but see M.H. Scargill, Modern Canadian English Usage: Linguistic Change and Reconstruction (Toronto: McClelland & Stewart, 1974).

made their home in Canada." Women might have added to the list.[528]

As regards political economy, the social sciences, and anthropology, the CCS's results were even bleaker. Academics had abandoned the Canada-specific political economy of the interwar years. Even to conceive of economics and politics as interrelated was dangerous to careers in the Cold War-imposed frame of reference, which juxtaposed non-political free and affluence-producing Western economies to politicized deprivation-generating Socialist countries' economies. With the exception of research on petroleum and agricultural economics at two Prairie universities, researchers paid "inadequate attention . . . to resource economics, despite the enormous importance of this field to Canada." They preferred abstract models to empirical research.[529] The "intellectual habits and practices of Canadians" rather than immigrant U.S. academics in the social sciences made the field "a passive appendage of its American counterpart." In addition, non-Canadians among the faculty amounted to nearly 45 percent in sociology and 60 percent in anthropology by 1973/74. Many of the migrant U.S. sociologists belonged exclusively to U.S. professional associations; few published in the *Canadian Review of Sociology*. Anticipating discourse-theory, the CCS emphasized, "these disciplines are highly sensitive to the particular society in which they are located, particularly when that society [i.e. the United States] is large, self-contained and preoccupied with its own affairs." Scholars had a responsibility "to speak about society to society."[530]

In political science, the reigning paradigm that nation-states developed specific political cultures was undercut by a Cold War corollary that styled the United States as the model of democracy, and "the exclusive American possession of superpower status in the international system of national political science communities" had "a profound impact upon the development of the discipline around the world" (Alan Cairns). Proximity of language and academic institutions as well as widespread use of U.S. texts in Can-

---

528 : *CCS Report*, 1:56–65.

529 : *CCS Report*, 1:65–71, quote p. 67; Alan C. Cairns, "Political Science in Canada and the Americanization Issue," *Canadian Journal of Political Science* 8.2 (June 1975): 191–234.

530 : CCS Report, 1:71–78; Jean R. Burnet, "Minorities I Have Belonged To," in Danielle Juteau-Lee and Barbara Roberts, eds., "Ethnicity and Femininity," topical issue of *Canadian Ethnic Studies* 13.1 (1981): 24–36, esp. 29–30; R. Alan Hedley and T. Rennie Warburton, "The Role of National Courses in the Teaching and Development of Sociology: The Canadian Case," *Sociological Review* 21.2 (May 1973): 299–319; Jan J. Loubser, *Canadianization of the Social Sciences* (Ottawa: SSFC-FCSS, 1978); G.B. Rush, E. Christensen, J. Malcomson, "Lament for a Notion: the Development of Social Science in Canada," *Canadian Review of Sociology and Anthropology* 18 (1981): 519–44.

adian classrooms resulted in "a unidirectional integration of political science and other social sciences on both sides of the 49th parallel." The "rich and voluminous" U.S. literature, an advantage of the size of the scholarly community, made Canadian political science "fundamentally imitative." By 1973/74, more than one third of full-time faculty members were not Canadian: U.S. citizens held 22 percent of the positions. The CCS demanded that students be taught "the federal system of government, the operation of Parliament, the role of the country's political parties . . . the distinguishing features of Canada's political culture," as well as about "bilingualism, multiculturalism, and regional economic disparities." An "understanding of the distinctive political culture of this country" was important since the media presented "a mass of information" that "conditioned" many "to think almost completely in terms of American political ideals, terminology, institutions and practices."[531]

In research, few scholars remembered "the earlier traditions of political and social inquiry that were established in the formative years" of the 1920s and '30s. Such symbolic annihilation explains why a leading sociologist such as Carl Dawson was neither read nor cited; why John Porter had not heard of Leonard Marsh; why Jean Burnet, linking the two generations of sociologists, received a lifetime achievements award only a decade and a half after retirement; and why few Canadian scholars in 2000 could name H. Clare Pentland as a political economist. In submissions to the CCS, the internationally famous political scientist C.B. McPherson "pointed to the unrealized possibilities in the distinctive Canadian tradition of political economy" and sociologist Raymond Breton acerbically summarized:

> For an ethnically differentiated society, . . . there is little to contribute to the analysis of multi-ethnic societies. For a regionalized society there is little study of regional inequalities and of social integration. For a society with regions different in their ecology, culture, and history, there is little attention paid to comparative social structure. For a rapidly changing society, there is little on the study of the evolution and change of social institutions, patterns of power relationships, and demographic trends. For a society that has in many

531 : Denis Smith, "What Are We Teaching? The Nationalization of Political Science," *Canadian Forum* 51.605 (June 1971): 4–5, quote ibid.; Donald Smiley, "Must Canadian Political Science Be a Miniature Replica?" *Journal of Canadian Studies* 9.1 (Feb. 1974): 31–41; similar conclusions had been reached by W.H.N. Hull, "The 1971 Survey of the Profession," *Canadian Journal of Political Science* 6.3 (March 1973): 89–95, and Paul Fox et al., *Report of the Committee on Canadian Content*, submitted to the Canadian Political Science Assoc., Aug. 1974; CCS Report, 65–71, quote p. 69.

ways a distinctive history and a distinctive combination of economic, cultural, ecological, and demographic conditions, there is little . . . that is distinctively Canadian.

Had discipline-ensconced scholars seized the opportunities of interdisciplinary Canadian Studies, the evaluation might have been more positive.[532] Arthur Tremblay noted that any *en retard* position could quickly be remedied by a major co-operative research effort, and A.B. Hodgetts called for an interprovincial Canadian Studies Consortium to overcome the *retard* of anglophone teaching.[533]

Creating national and pluralist Canadian and Canadian Studies institutions

To overcome the deficiencies, the federal government, Canada Council, and private foundations established a "Canadian Studies enterprise" (Cameron). Coordination, however, was often lacking. The Canada Studies Foundation (CSF, established 1970) was to achieve what well-conceived decolonized curricula could have provided all along: comprehension of Canada and its people. It provided teachers with classroom materials, furthered communication through its periodical *Contact*, and under the impact of Hodgetts and Gallagher's *Teaching Canada for the '80s*, funded cross-regional and cross-cultural projects. "Pan-Canadian Studies," according to the CCS and the Massey Commission, would have to involve interregional student exchange.[534] Then in 1986 the federal government abolished the CSF.

Organizational activities were intense but diverse. The Association of Community Colleges of Canada (established 1970) coordinated Canadian Studies activities and launched *Communiqué: Canadian Studies*, a bibliographical quarterly (1974); then began a Canadian Studies Project, soon renamed Canadian Studies Bureau, temporarily with a Quebec office. Funded

---

532 : *CCS Report,* 1:27-28, 52–56, 65–78; Raymond Breton, "The *Review* and the Growth of Sociology and Anthropology in Canada," *Canadian Review of Sociology and Anthropology* 12.1 (Feb. 1975): 1–5, quote pp. 1–2.

533 : Arthur Tremblay, "La recherche pédagogique," in Louis Baudouin, ed., *La recherche au Canada français* (Montreal: PU Montréal, 1968), 99–125; A.B. Hodgetts, *What Culture? What Heritage? A Study of Civic Education in Canada* (Toronto: OISE, 1968), 118; *CCS Report,* 1:112-22, "Study of Official Languages."

534 : Around 1970, foreign student Vijay Agnew noted that few of her co-students at Wilfrid Laurier University had travelled outside of Ontario (*Where I Come From.* Waterloo, ON: WLU Press, 2003, 10). Around 2000, according to oral information from Winnipeg scholars, a large part of first-year students at Manitoba's universities had never travelled outside of the province.

by the U.S. Kellogg Foundation and since 1978 by the Secretary of State, this initiative also fizzled in 1986.[535] The Association for Canadian Studies (ACS), founded in 1973 as a learned society, launched *Canadian Issues* and the *ASC Newsletter* and—coordination or bureaucratization?—set up a Council of Canadian Studies Programs Administrators. But the renowned Trent-based independent *Journal of Canadian Studies* remained the major periodical in the field. The ACS restricted itself to "internal studies," that is, Canadian Studies by Canadian scholars, at a time when U.S. Canadian Studies specialists had been active for several years and when similar associations developed in a number of countries. When the International Council for Canadian Studies was created, renowned Canadians took leading roles, John Lennox and Paul-André Linteau to name just two, but ACS for much of its history remained aloof from outside perspectives.[536]

Beyond the Canada Council, the federal government—mindful of the provincial responsibility for education—provided no Canadian Studies funding structure. Thus projects succeeded each other without continuity.[537] Among private foundations, the Bronfman family's CRB Foundation, in addition to strengthening the unity of the Jewish people, set itself the objective to enhance Canadian identity by the TV *Heritage Minutes*, the quarterly *Heritage Post*, and the Heritage Learning Resources Project. Such a "heritage approach" also inspired the government-funded Heritage Canada Foundation (established 1973), which rather than encouraging historical monument adoration concerned itself with preserving small-town

---

535 : Cameron, *Taking Stock*, 36–38, 112, 122. Cameron, a political scientist trained outside of Canada (London School of Economics), began his career at Trent University and in 1977 became Director of Research of the Pepin-Robarts Task Force on Canadian Unity. Research for his report on Canadian Studies was completed as of 1994. Colin Howell and Martha MacDonald, "Diversity, National Unity and Self-Awareness: The Cameron Report on Canadian Studies," *Journal of Canadian Studies* 30.4 (1995–6): 3–4. *CCS Report*, 1:126–27; A.B. Hodgetts and Paul Gallagher, *Teaching Canada for the '80s* (Toronto: OISE, 1978).

536 : Cameron, *Taking Stock*, 123–29; *The Association for Canadian Studies: A Brief History 1973-1988* (1988); James Page, in his *Reflections*, reviewed the ACS. Discussions of the author with ICCS delegates, 2002-4.

537 : In 1978, a pilot project of the Secretary of State to improve and expand Canadian Studies; 1981, under an initiative by David Cameron, a National Program of Support for Canadian Studies; 1984, a revamped version, the Canadian Studies and Special Projects Directorate; then again a Canadian Studies Program. In 1991, the Department of Multiculturalism and Citizenship was temporarily established; the Secretary of State's Multiculturalism Directorate was replaced by Canadian Heritage in 1996.

main streets and memories of everyday life.[538] In this medley of activities, a few cultural institutions and collaborative editorial projects stand out. The Historic Sites and Monuments Board of Canada (established 1919) began to modernize but, far more importantly, the Canadian Institute for Historical Microreproductions (established 1978) undertook to reproduce all early Canadiana and the multimedia Jean Talon Project set out to gather and digitize information on twentieth-century Canada. The *Dictionary of Canadian Biography* (since 1966), of necessity, is restricted to "important" men and—far fewer—women. *The Canadian Encyclopedia* (Edmonton: Hurtig, 1985), a private undertaking, and the three-volume *Historical Atlas of Canada* (1987–93) have become major reference works. "Reference tools" and "reference institutions" to aid collective memory have long been the "heritage" of other societies; in Canada they date, with few exceptions, from the Centennial or after. Only the National Archives of Canada (established 1872, secured by law in 1912) and Statistics Canada (established 1918) came early. Belatedly, the National Library of Canada was added in 1953. The 1990 Museums Act created the Canadian Museum of Civilization as well as the National Museum of Science and Technology and the National Gallery. The National Film Board was expanded into the Film Board and Telefilm Canada. In Europe, dynasties had begun to develop research aids and repositories even before the nation-state came into existence, and in the United States, scholars had begun to do so from the time of the Constitution in 1789 on. In Canada, the century-long lack of easy access to data complicated research, increased cost, and reduced quality. Such research tools impact on society; as Cameron emphasized, "the thing being studied is in part being created by the process of enquiry itself." This holds true vice versa: if no archives of collective memory are created, the thing to be studied remains vague.[539]

Scholars' best efforts notwithstanding, the field remained marginal to the disciplines and to deans' funding priorities. Thus, from the *CCS Report* of 1975 to Cameron's *Taking Stock* in 1996, the "Canadian Studies enterprise"

---

538 : Cameron, *Taking Stock*, 135–37, chapter 11 on book and digital publishing. In 1978, the Social Sciences and Humanities Research Council was established as central funding agency for scholarship. But in 1992, the federal government closed down the Science Council and the Economic Council of Canada—the province of Ontario had terminated its Economic Council in the mid-1980s—at an incalculable loss to the country according to Cameron (*Taking Stock*, 37). The province of Quebec established its own academic granting council in 1984, Fonds pour la formation de chercheurs et de l'aide à la recherche, with three special programs Québec-Acadie, Québec-Ontario, Québec-Ouest canadien.

539 : Cameron, *Taking Stock*, quote p. 4, 121, 137–40, 163, Chap. 9–10.

could not decide whether the goal was a "shared concern to strengthen citizenship and public values" or, as one of Cameron's colleagues at the University of Toronto felt, "remedial courses about neglected areas." Was the field to affirm identities—"there have been periods in our history when substantial portions of the Canadian community have known who they were and what they stood for"—or to question them since such periods "have rarely been defining moments for the community as a whole"?[540] A comparison of Canadian Studies with Women Studies indicates that the latter, backed by a political movement, prospered. The former, under the broad post-national frames of thinking and the narrow self-enclosure of the disciplines, was not high on the agenda.

The CCS's goal of "knowing our place in the world" involved problems specific to countries with powerful neighbours. Rather than a binary internal–external "us and them" dichotomy, a hierarchicized triangle of Canada, United States, and other foreign countries had to be studied both in politics and in culture. Furthermore, the all-important internationalization of research was turned on its head by Americanization and U.S.-centeredness. A nation-state assertiveness could not counterbalance the infringing U.S. perspective. In political economy, for example, research confined to Canada misses the destinations for the staple goods, of communication technology, of inventions and international trade. Social science research remains incomplete unless it includes all cultural backgrounds of Canadians, their society of residence, their ongoing ties to friends and kin in the societies from whence they came, and perhaps societies of transition in which they spent a part of their lives. Like Aboriginal Canadians' stories, a comprehensive narrative of Canada weaves together the threads of the life stories of all Canadians into a society-wide cloth. Teaching such complex stories may be difficult but offers pupils and students of all backgrounds possibilities for identification.[541] The whole of Canada emerges from regional and cultural nodes of research activity: Quebec, British Columbian, or Acadian Studies, women, labour, and Ethnic Studies, Aboriginal and global worlds. The Atlantic provinces were part of the Atlantic World and British Columbia is not

---

540 : Cameron, *Taking Stock*, quote p. 3; Howell and MacDonald, "Diversity, National Unity and Self-Awareness," 3–4. U of T review of the Canadian Studies program of University College, 1996–97. I am grateful to the Chair, Ian Radforth, for sharing his information and papers submitted to the review board.

541 : Citizens' Forum on Canada's Future (Keith Spicer, chair), *Report to the People and Government of Canada* (Ottawa: Minister of Supplies and Services, 1991); Cameron, *Taking Stock*, 31–49, 68, 87; Leon Fink, "Losing the Hearts and Minds, or How Clio Disappeared from Canadian Public Schools," review essay, *Labour / Le Travail* 43 (Spring 1999): 211–15.

only a Canadian but also a Pacific Rim community. Canadians use technology produced across the world, eat food from many parts of the globe, and as children they express themselves in classrooms among peers from dozens of societies and cultures.[542]

The traditional picture of a binational Canada was easy to grasp, if not necessarily valid; the "study of Canada in the world and the World in Canada" is far more difficult to comprehend, but it certainly is not superficial. Students recognized its validity to their lives and indicated high interest in courses on multicultural, Aboriginal, women's, and regional history and life. However, since universities did not offer interdisciplinary PhD programs, no younger scholars pushed the field ahead. In Jill Vickers's words, the Anglo-Canadian nationalist founding impulse "to know ourselves" continued as a lasting influence and, since the founders were Euro-Canadian, so was the field. In contrast to the founders, "Canadian" history and culture is both global and Canadian.[543]

---

542 : Cameron, *Taking Stock*, 25–34; *CCS Report*, 78–112. The regional studies programs in the early 1990s included Saint Mary's Atlantic Canada Studies Program, Simon Fraser's BC Studies Certificate, Regina's Canadian Plains Studies Program, Université du Québec à Trois Rivières' Programme d'études québécoises. Francophone universities outside of Quebec included French-Canadians from across Canada: Université Sainte-Anne, NS; Glendon, York Univ., Toronto; Faculté Saint-Jean, Univ. of Alberta; Collège universitaire de Saint-Boniface, Univ. of Manitoba, with its Centre d'études franco-canadiennes de l'ouest modelled on the Centre de civilisation canadienne-française at the Univ. of Ottawa. A different, supranational approach was pursued by McGill's North American Studies Program.

543 : Jill Vickers, "Where Is the Discipline in Interdisciplinarity," in *Interdisciplinarity: Working Documents* (Montreal: ACS, 1992), 5–41.

Chapter 12

VIEWS FROM THE OUTSIDE: THE SURGE OF INTERNATIONAL CANADIAN STUDIES

The Massey and the Canadian Studies commissions had demanded "the promotion abroad of a knowledge of Canada" and, internally, an understanding of Canada in larger cultural and institutional contexts. The origins of Canada's federal and Quebec's provincial institutions as well as of its religious denominations lay in Europe. U.S. political thought and economic policy were "of immediate relevance to an understanding of Canada." From the mid-nineteenth century on, cultural heritages "have been and continue to be intimately related to developments in [all] other parts of the world," and from the time of the staple economies, multinational companies connected Canada to many parts of the world. Twentieth-century refugees came from international conflicts. Last, but first, the social spaces in which "Canada" emerged had been home to First Peoples when the earliest newcomers arrived.[544]

"Canadian Studies outside of Canada" (rather than the nation-outward perspective of "Canadian Studies abroad" or even "Canadian Studies in foreign countries") emerged as a combination of initiatives in particular countries, of response or pro-activeness by Canadian institutions, of external cultural policies in a global setting, and of United Nations' activities.[545] In 1966, UNESCO passed its Declaration of the Principles of International Cultural Co-operation. While the Canada Council was established in this frame, other countries' external cultural policies stemmed from different contexts and intentions. The United Kingdom had established the British Council to counter German fascist propaganda in 1935/36; the United States began its

---

544 : Thomas H.B. Symons, *To Know Ourselves: Report of the Commission on Canadian Studies*, French: *Se connaître: le rapport de la commission sur les études canadiennes*, 2 vols. (Ottawa: Assoc. of Universities and Colleges of Canada, 1975), 1:85–88, 2:1–56, quote 2:2. Hereafter cited as *CCS Report*. See also Applebaum-Hébert Committee, *Report*, 313–39: "International Cultural Relations." *ICCS Contact CIEC*, vol. 1 (1982-), first as *International News Canadian Studies / Nouvelles internationales des études canadiennes*, since vol. 3 (1984) *ICCS Newsletter / Bulletin du CIEC*, since vol. 8 (1989) current title.

545 : This section relies on Paul D. Schafer (for the Department of External Affairs, DEA), *Canada's International Cultural Relations*, mimeographed (Ottawa: Supply and Services, March 1979); "Canadian Studies at Home and Abroad," ed. James de Finney, Gregory Kealey, John Lennox, Tamara Palmer Seiler, *Canadian Issues / Thèmes Canadiens* 17 (1995); Luca Codignola, *La constitution d'une identité canadiste. Les Premières années, 1981-1991* (Ottawa: ICCS, 1991); interviews with former DEA officials Brian Long, Commonwealth of Learning, Vancouver, 3 April 2001, and Richard Seaborn, 23 Sept. 2003. See also David R. Cameron, *Taking Stock: Canadian Studies in the Nineties* (Montreal: ACS, 1996), 130-135.

Fulbright program of scholars' and students' exchanges in 1946 to spread the message of democracy—and perhaps its hegemony—in post-World War II societies; and France had supported French culture and language in particular regions of the world since its second phase of imperial outreach in the 1870s. Regarding Canadian Studies, initiatives began from the outside. In China and India, migration of students and researchers provided incentives: in 1941 Chian Wei Chang, later an eminent scholar in China, had been the first Chinese to obtain a doctorate in Canada. In the 1960s, when highly educated young Indian men—few women at the time—began to search career opportunities in Canada, their decision sparked an interest among their academic peers remaining in India. In the Netherlands, the memory of asylum in Canada for the Dutch royal family during the country's occupation by Nazi troops and the liberation by, among others, Canadian soldiers had resulted in respect and interest. Elsewhere, scholars concentrating on the United States turned their attention to the whole of North America and included Canada as well as, although less often because of the different language and culture, Mexico. The Canadian government began its first initiatives in cultural external policy in 1963.[546]

There were also far earlier beginnings. European educated middle classes' interest developed in the context of "exploration" of the geography of other continents and of a juxtaposition of "the civilized" looking at the "uncivilized." From mid-eighteenth century, travel accounts in French and English were translated into German and other languages, and became a basis for a geography and sociography of North America.[547] After 1900, the academic field of "Romance Philologies" in Germany began to include French-Canadian literature and language in its agenda as useful knowledge. In the period of economic competition between European states and empires, interest in culture (*Kulturstudien*) remained a sideline. It was the economic sciences that concentrated on Canada as immigration country, agricultural exporter, and potential market for German industrial products. In this respect, it re-

546 : Wang Tai Lai and Claude-Yves Charron, "Ten Years of Canadian Studies in the People's Republic of China," *ICCS Contact CIEC* 9.1 (Spring 1990): 14–18; Om P. Juneja, "Canadian Studies in India: Dynamic and Diversified," *ICCS Contact CIEC* 10.2 (Fall 1991): 7–10.

547 : As has been mentioned above, from the 1880s, German geographers developed an interest in the Arctic and the publications from two major expeditions established, (1), a lasting tradition of geographical research which became part of the discipline in Canada and, (2), an interest in Native peoples since geographer Franz Boas, during one of the expeditions, changed his research interest to ethnology. While the geographic tradition remained part of German scholarship, Franz Boas, of Jewish faith, emigrated to the United States and was one of the founders of ethnographic and ethnological research.

sembled British imperial scholarship. When, during World War I, Canada remained part of the British Empire, that is, of the enemy nations, the academic approach changed. Since its political direction had been misunderstood, "English Philology" needed to help the German nation and the political elite understand the culture and mentality, the "literatures" of the British colonial empire. This might be called "preparedness scholarship" for the next struggle. The racist thinking of the period and antagonism to the "soft" English led to the "finding" that anglophone writing was mainly Scottish and Irish, strong and harsh. Using British-Canada's colonial dependence on "England," some German academics declared Anglo-Canadians to be incapable of pursuing "their duty" of developing a culture of their own. However, parallel to the nationalist and racializing interpretations, several solid studies on English-Canadian and French-Canadian writing and on German Canadians appeared.[548] While the United States from the early 1950s established "American Studies" in the new Federal Republic and elsewhere in Europe, and while the tradition-bound Country Studies of Britain continued to plough ahead, Canadian Studies no longer existed. Once again, the exception was geography, especially at the University of Marburg, where a new generation of scholars built on previous achievements. A donation by a Canadian businessman, Alan Coatsworth, in 1949 permitted the establishment of an interdisciplinary Canadian Studies library.[549]

Motivation to engage in the study of Canada outside of Canada varied from country to country and within countries between institutions. At first, Canada was studied as part of North America, of the Commonwealth, or of *la Francophonie* in the world. Outside of Canada, the "ice and snow" image and "vast expanses" rhetoric lingered. U.S. texts about "our 'neighbor to the north', made up of friendly people who are 'just like us'," remained vague; French texts cliché-ridden—"Vue d'Europe, l'histoire canadienne semble essentiellement une affaire d'hommes. Comme si les grands espaces et la rudesse du climat n'avaient guère engendré que l'endurance, du courage physique et une certain rudesse, tous caractères que l'on accorde plus volontiers aux masculin." Rhetorically, the author then added: "Double cliché sans

---

548 : Introducing the recently settled and allegedly immature cultures of North America into the "English Philologies," concerned with the ancient and high culture of Britain, was innovative and thus resented by the traditional British-centered philologists. In a curious twist of power relations in academia the innovators had to ally themselves with the "new Germany," that of the Nazi Party, to gain a foothold in the university system. As a result, a mere ten years later, the field collapsed, tainted by the association.

549 : Konrad Groß, "Die Entwicklung der Kanadastudien," *Gulliver* 19 (1986): 30–36; Dirk Hoerder and Konrad Groß, eds., *25 Years Gesellschaft für Kanada-Studien: Achievements and Perspectives* (Augsburg: Wißner, 2004).

profondeur, évidemment"—but do modern societies still have to repeat such stereotypes? Canadian Studies outside of Canada challenge such stereotyping. In contrast to Canadian Studies from the inside, in their view "Canada is there," as a polity, a society, and an economy. The identity-searching debates—"where is Canada?" and "who are we?"—are at best of secondary concern, if any. If a generic Canada is part of scholars' and students' mental maps, regional or other differentiation may follow. Vice versa, internal emphasis on the many regions, cultures, and generations may obstruct the view onto the whole. "Deux observateurs du Canada, l'un étranger, l'autre indigène, disposant des mêmes données, ne trouvent pas de réponses identiques. Chacun filtrera au travers de sa culture" (P. Savard 1984).[550]

Canadian foreign policy and
Canadian Studies outside of Canada

While the Americanization of Canada's universities was being criticized, Canadian Studies received an impetus from the United States. When Carleton and Trent scholars began their Canadian Studies activities just two years before the Canadian Association for Canadian Studies (ACS) was founded, the William H. Donner Foundation (New York), upon initiatives of U.S. Canadianists, funded the Center of Canadian Studies within the School of Advanced International Studies at Johns Hopkins University, Baltimore, in 1969. In the following years, the Donner, Rockefeller, and Carnegie foundations, as well as the U.S. Office of Education, established Canadian Studies centres, especially at the University of Rochester, NY, and at Duke University, NC. Scholars founded the Association for Canadian Studies in the United States (ACSUS) in 1971.[551] From 1975 to 1980, similar associations

---

550 : Marian C. Salinger and Donald C. Wilson, *The Portrayal of Canada in American Textbooks* (Durham: Duke Univ., Center for Intl. Studies, 1990), 25; Pierre Savard, "Le Canada sous la loupe des savants étrangers / Some Views on Canadian Studies, Yesterday and Now," *ICCS Newsletter* 3.2 (Oct. 1984): 30–32, quote p. 31; Raphaelle Rérolle in *Le Monde* "Livres," 5 April 2002. See also Edelgard Mahant and Graeme S. Mount, *Invisible and Inaudible in Washington: American Policies toward Canada* (Vancouver: UBC Press, 1999).

551 : *CCS Report*, 2:6–7; William Metcalfe, "'Modified Rapture!' Recent Research on Canada in the United States," *Intl. Journal of Canadian Studies* 1–2 (1990): 203–216; Karen Gould, Joseph T. Jockel, William Metcalfe, eds., *Northern Exposures: Scholarship on Canada in the United States* (Washington, D.C.: ACSUS, 1993); John G.H. Halstead, *Labor of Love: A Review of Canadian Studies Programs in the United States*, Report of.a Canadian Studies Visiting Committee, 1991 (Washington, D.C.: ACSUS, 1991). See also "Canada in the Americas," *Intl. Journal of Canadian Studies* 13 (1996). Textbooks expressly written for U.S. students include William Metcalfe, ed., *Understanding Canada: A Multidisciplin-*

were founded in Great Britain, France, Italy, Japan, the German-speaking countries, Australia, and New Zealand. Jointly with ACS they formed the International Council for Canadian Studies / Conseil international d'études canadiennes (ICCS-CIEC) at a 1981 conference in Halifax.[552]

This surge of international Canadian studies meant that the ICCS began to function a mere eight years after self-organization of Canadian scholars in the ACS.[553] While ACS long expressed misgivings about the "outsiders," individual Canadian scholars were prominent in the ICCS. James E. Page, collaborator of Symons, and Pierre Savard, one of Quebec's best-known historians, were elected as the first two presidents, and Paul-André Linteau as first editor-in-chief of the *International Journal of Canadian Studies / Revue internationale d'études canadiennes (IJCS/RIEC)*. The journal's first issue presented European scholars' views of the study of Canada (volumes 1 to 2, 1990). The ICCS Council placed great emphasis on bi- and multiculturality but, in its first ten years, seated only three women and no "minority" person, visible or non-visible. While separatist Quebec scholars often eschewed international activities, Canadianists in other countries made a conscious effort to deal with Canada as a whole in both official languages. Viewed from the outside, Canada was one country, internally diverse and often characterized by differences from the United States.

At the time of the Commission on Canadian Studies' critique of Canadian Studies in Canada, officials in the Department of External Affairs (DEA) had already begun to address both the issue of developing Canadian Studies

ary Introduction to Canadian Studies (New York: New York University Press, 1982), and Joseph K. Roberts, *In the Shadow of Empire: Canada for Americans* (New York: Monthly Review, 1998).

552 : British Association for Canadian Studies, BACS, 1975; L'Association française d'études canadiennes, AFEC, 1976; Associazione Italiana di Studi Canadesi, AISC, 1978; Japanese Association for Canadian Studies, JACS, 1979; Association for Canadian Studies in German-Speaking Countries / Gesellschaft für Kanada-Studien in deutschsprachigen Ländern, GKS, 1980; Association for Canadian Studies in Australian and New Zealand, ACSANZ, 1980; Association for Canadian Studies in Ireland, ACSI, 1982. Associations in the Nordic countries (1984), the People's Republic of China (1984), the Netherlands (1985), India (1985), Israel (1985), Spain (1988), Brazil (1991), Venezuela (1991), Russia (1992) as successor organization to the ACS of the Soviet Union, Korea (1992), Mexico (1992). The ICCS-CIEC also admits associated members. Associations in Western Europe, East Central Europe, and Latin America have formed regional co-operative associations.

553 : Though the ICCS-CIEC, in addition to member organizations' contributions, depended on funding from Canada's DEA, no government influence was ever exerted. Interview with Kenneth McRoberts, editor *Intl. Journal of Canadian Studies*, 9 Nov. 2000. Some funding strategies, however, are influenced by long-term policy goals.

abroad and the needs of Canadianists in other countries.[554] Aware of U.S. ignorance about Canada, embassy officials provided support to U.S. scholars from the late 1960s on. The Chair in Canadian Studies, established at the University of Edinburgh in 1975, has been considered the official beginning of DEA's support for Canadian Studies outside of Canada. Geographer James Wreford Watson, of Scottish background and born in China, had studied both in Edinburgh and Canada. He had served in the federal Department of Mines and Natural Resources, and from 1954 on, taught at Edinburgh University where he launched the Centre of Canadian Studies in 1973.[555] DEA's Bureau of Public Affairs (later the Bureau of International Cultural Relations) included a Cultural Affairs Division (established 1965) and an Academic Relations Division.[556] The budget of just over CA\$2 million in 1973/74 (less than 1.5 percent of DEA's total) compared to US\$220 million (1974) for the United States Information Service.[557] At first, DEA concerned itself with book donations to libraries and with support for academic exchange. Interaction between politics and academic interests were played out when, after Quebec's second referendum, ACSUS planned a Quebec-U.S. conference to discuss possible bilateral relations in case of Quebec's independence. Canada's Washington embassy opposed the conference while the Department of Foreign Affairs and International Trade (DFAIT), to its credit, though unhappy about the timing, considered it a matter of academic freedom and thus eligible for support.[558]

---

554 : DEA was renamed Department of Foreign Affairs and International Trade, DFAIT, in 1995; Foreign Affairs Canada / Affaires Étrangères Canada, FAEC, in 2004. Cameron held an influential position in the ministry for a number of years. James E. Page, after the end of his term as ICCS president, became Director of Canadian Studies at the Department of the Secretary of State. In an earlier initiative, Prime Minister Mackenzie King had established a Chair of Canadian Studies at Harvard University in 1945, to be filled annually by an eminent Canadian scholar. Such rotatory appointments preclude continuity.

555 : Biographical note on J.W. Watson, *Intl. News Canadian Studies* 3.1 (April 1984): 7-9. Some political manoeuvring seems to have taken place. Secretary of State, Allan MacEachen from Cape Breton, lobbied for a Celtic Studies Chair in the Maritimes and—it has been said—felt that if Scotland were involved in Canadian Studies, Canada, that is, federal funding agencies, might become more easily involved with Celtic Studies.

556 : The Academic Relations Division through its Historical Section contributes to scholarship by compilation of documents on external relations.

557 : In 1991-92, Canada's spending on international cultural affairs was still lower than in 14 other countries (Harry H. Chartrand), though lower spending does not automatically imply fewer results.

558 : Analysis of the complex forces supporting or contesting the support structure for Canadian Studies within DEA would require a social history of the administration

Scholars who deal with the culture of another country or promote and import ideas and other cultural products need to negotiate between cultures. They may also face demands for loyalty imposed by governments. Thus, some states' laws consider a scholar or cultural producer with a DEA grant an "agent of a foreign power." Under this clause, in 1983 the United States banned Canadian films about acid rain made with public funding. In societies with intellectual traditions that were decidedly on the Left but which, in their respective educational systems, pursued strategies far more elitist than those in Canada, visiting Canadian artists or scholars found it difficult to insert themselves without openly criticizing such class-based selectiveness. DEA's diplomats had to balance the French-English dichotomy. Programs, first directed toward France, Belgium, and Switzerland (1963), then toward Italy, Germany, and The Netherlands (1965), pursued the following objectives:[559]

> (1) to foster the realization of Canada's short- and long-term interests, particularly peace, security, order, sovereignty, identity, unity, and good government;
>
> (2) to strengthen Canada's image abroad as a country with a dynamic cultural life as well as strong bilingual, multicultural, and democratic traditions;
>
> (3) to expose people in all parts of the world to the diversity, originality, and excellence of Canadian achievements in all sectors of cultural life;
>
> (4) to contribute to Canada's domestic development through the opening up of international markets for cultural products as well as through the provision of economic opportunities for the training and professional development of Canada's creative talents;
>
> (5) to share as many experiences and engage in as much co-operation as possible with other countries;

and of negotiating conflicting goals: Embassies, forced to react to whatever was on the agenda, advocated a "current issues" approach; Cultural Affairs and Academic Relations officials insisted on a long-range strategy with emphasis on teaching, that is, outreach to students; scholars preferred funding for research; ranking utilitarian-minded DEA administrators wanted to address only those countries relevant to their political and economic strategies. After the expensive Centennial, rigorous cost cutting hurt external cultural policy. To avoid sudden interference with long-range objectives, Academic Relations officials developed a prioritized long-range agenda and had to circumvent exclusion of regions considered marginal, like Eastern Europe before 1989 or Latin America, from cultural programs.

559 : "Objectives," 1979 version from Schafer, *International Cultural Relations*, 41.

(6) to promote the rights of freedom of expression, freedom of movement, and freedom of program selection for Canada's creative talents abroad as well as for foreign talents in Canada;

(7) to expose Canada's creative efforts to the highest possible standards of international assessment and informed criticism;

(8) to make the experience of Canada's cultural community as well as the experience of cultural communities of other countries as rich and productive as possible from an intellectual, social, aesthetic, and humanistic point of view.

Such multicultural exchange projects — as compared to cross-border cultural propaganda — gave Canadian external cultural policies a distinct advantage.

Cultural external policy mandated exchange as a two-way process. It was intended to strengthen the "third option" policy, which *cautiously* positioned Canada as "distinct from but in harmony with the United States."[560] Policymakers referred to "communication between people," interdependence, and problems facing mankind (such as nuclear testing). They came to include Third World countries since development aid, if technical and economic only, would underestimate the intellectual-cultural aspects of the respective people's aspirations. The policies also had an explicit internal dimension: "We cannot convey a higher standard of concern for the greater good if we neglect it within our own borders—much less, if we allow multinational corporations to make a mockery of it abroad." In contrast to the humanities-based approach of American Studies, DEA subscribed to the inclusive Canadian tradition of "history, politics, literature, sociology, economics" as the prime disciplines of Canadian Studies. The image of Canada presented was to be non-partisan and credible, not "a vehicle for selective Government messages, propaganda or an expurgated image." By 1976, DEA officials were far more positive about Canadian Studies than the CCS in 1975. They noted "a self-confidence in Canadian creativity and scholarship" that "has to a large extent replaced the obsessive quest for national identity."[561]

A systematic development of Canadian Studies in other countries was the next goal. Under the lead of Richard G. Seaborn and Brian Long, with support

---

560 : An early U.S.-centered "head-start" program, intended to reduce the lack of understanding of difference, promoted Canadian culture in the sense of arts and literature. Soon issues high on the public agenda received attention: acid rain, free trade, fishery, among others. Thus the humanities-centered program expanded to include political science, environmental studies, and economics.

561 : George A. Cowley, Freeman M. Tovell, and John W. Graham, "Recent Growth of Interest in Canadian Studies Abroad," *International Perspectives* [a journal of External Affairs] (Sept./Oct. 1976), 27–43, quotes pp. 33, 34, 40, 42.

of René de Chantal, Joseph Jurkovic, and Janet Bax, a cost-effective program emerged. Since the establishment of Chairs was expensive and, as one-person enterprises, not necessarily effective for building multidisciplinary centres; since sending professorial faculty abroad for a year at the time, analogous to the U.S. Fulbright program, involved cost and rotation, in 1976 DEA decided to provide faculty abroad with the opportunity to add a Canadian specialization to their expertise through short-term grants (Faculty Enrichment / Research Programs, FEP/FRP). At first, this program addressed Canada's major partners, the United States, Great Britain, France, Germany, and Italy, as well as Japan. For Israel, a private Jewish-Canadian initiative had already established cultural relations. With the growing importance of the European Union, the program was expanded. While Canada's International Development Agency (CIDA) restricted its funding to Commonwealth countries, in particular "white" Australia and New Zealand, in 1982 open-minded DEA officials seized the opportunity of an increase in funding to include China and India as well as Mexico, Brazil, Argentine, Venezuela, and Peru into the FEP/FRP. Policy-makers argued for grants based on academic merit rather than on short-term Canadian political or economic interests. When in 1995 DFAIT's Trade section began to follow the U.S. line on free trade and reduced funding for cultural and academic affairs, several of the international Canadian Studies associations strongly supported DEA's Cultural Affairs Division and the program remained intact.[562]

DEA's policies had to counter first, CIDA's emphasis on White Commonwealth countries; second, Canadian academics' continentalist perspective stemming from their graduate studies at U.S. institutions mandated by Canada's institutional academic *retard*; and third, the imperial mind-frame which induced (and induces) many British Canadian scholars to conceptualize academic relations along a Britain–Canada–Australia / New Zealand axis. DEA's multidirectional approach was thus "foreign" to many scholars in 1970s and '80s Canada. A new U.S.-centeredness became apparent when DFAIT's Academic Relations Division planned to involve Alberta more actively. The province not only showed little interest in contacts with Europe because of its oil industry's southward U.S. connection, it also emphasized that most of its recent immigrants came from Asian cultures. The federal government, in view of the increasing trans-Pacific trade, upgraded cultural relations to Asian societies. But size mattered and only the large embassies in India, Japan, and China have Cultural Affairs personnel. The smaller Southeast Asian countries remain cut off from direct access to cultural exchange. In Europe, the German-language Canadian Studies

---

562 : Interviews with Brian Long, 3 April 2001, and Richard Seaborn, 23 Sept. 2003.

Association could serve three societies and, after 1989, support the development of Canadian Studies in East Central Europe. Differences between Asian cultures precludes any such role for one embassy or scholarly association. In Latin America, too, academic and cultural relations centre on larger countries, and a hemispheric Network of Canadian Studies emerged in 2004. The position of Cuba under the U.S. embargo, the cautious Canadian criticism of this policy, and efforts of individuals resulted in some research relations, and one Cuban Canadian Studies institute joined ICCS-CIEC as associate member. In 2000, the international Canadian Studies associations published sixteen journals in thirteen countries in addition to the ICCS's journal and those published in Canada.

Since Canadian Studies scholars outside of Canada, like policy-makers and ambassadorial staffs, are responsive to issues with *temporary* high public visibility, research and conferences often reflect public debates. Thus the francophone-anglophone controversy and Quebec culture have received considerable attention, the Maritimes less so.[563] The West, as a social-cultural region, and the North, first a challenge for geographers then as imagery in literary expression, have been and are prominent in teaching and research. The field's breadth is evidenced by the international Canadianists' disciplinary affiliations: political science, law, and public administration, 17 percent; history, 11 percent; sociology and anthropology, 11 percent; economics and commerce, 10 percent; geography, 5 percent; social services and education, 10 percent; literature, 24 percent; language, 4 percent; library science, 1 percent; arts and recreation, 5 percent; philosophy and religion, 2 percent; and science and technology, 1 percent (1996/97 figures, rounded). The editor of the *International Journal of Canadian Studies* summarized the goals of Canadian Studies abroad:

> [It] offers fresh perspectives on a cultural scenario that is distinctly Canadian but at the same time shaped by multicultural diversity and openness. Rather than merely duplicating 'domestic' approaches, Canadianists abroad should aim, from their detached vantage point, at placing Canadian arts and literature [and any other topic] in an international context and challenging canonized views.

With almost seven thousand Canadianists in twenty-six countries in the year 2000, approaches are bound to be comprehensive.[564]

---

563 : One—German-language—example is Udo Kempf, ed., *Quebec: Wirtschaft - Gesellschaft - Politik* (Hagen: ISL-Verlag, 1999).

564 : Walter Pache, introduction to vol. 6 of the *Intl. Journal of Canadian Studies* (Fall 1992): 5-7. In 1988 the National Library and the ICCS signed an agreement to provide

Perspectives from the outside: Topics and questions[565]

A wide range of topics of mutual interest characterizes the research on Canada by scholars outside of it who often closely co-operate with Canadian academics. Since each side has to translate its questions and approaches into frames of reference intelligible to the other, new perspectives often emerge from a search for common ground.[566] Thus scholars in India perceived Canadian literature in English—like its U.S. counterpart—not only as part of "British seed planted in American soil," but also as a part of a Commonwealth literature: "like India's own complex literary heritage, Canadian literature—or literatures, more precisely—are written in more than one major language and reflect a regionally diverse and multicultural society." At the end of the 1980s, some fifty universities in India offered courses on Canada's literatures and several universities offered programs including politics, history, economics, and sociology as well as, in one case, Women's Studies. Regionalism also ranked high in India–Canada comparisons. An intra-Canadian perspective traditionally focused on Britain and Australia, and would not easily subsume Canadian writing under "new literatures in English." Quebec's literature appeared as part of a *francophonie*, formerly colonial, or, even broader, in the context of a Romania.[567]

A similarly comparative yet totally different approach emerged between Ireland, Scotland, the Maritimes, and Quebec. Gaelic and French as minority languages and literatures were compared in complex contexts of bilingualism framed by specific economic, political, historical, legal, and cultural structures. In contrast to the Commonwealth-literatures approaches in India, the Gaelic-Acadia-Quebec circum-Atlantic theme emphasized ethnohistory and folklore, rural industries and fishery. Analytical concepts of subaltern societies and marginalization or of family economies in a rural–urban continuum, were missing. "Folk" was used as self-referential axis to establish historical traditions distinct from English or British.[568]

---

comprehensive bibliographic access to Canadian Studies materials published outside of Canada. Günter Grünsteudel's *Canadiana-Bibliographie 1900–2000* (Augsburg: ISL-Verlag, 2001) listed almost 5,000 titles published in German-language countries alone.

565 : In the following two sections I rely on my knowledge of developments in the German-language association, other European associations, some information about Latin America, and little about Canadianists in Asia.

566 : Information from reports to the *ICCS Contact CIEC*, published since 1982.

567 : C.D. Narasimhaiah, C.N. Srinath, Wendy Keitner, eds., *Glimpses of Canadian Literature*, cited in *ICCS Newsletter* 6.2 (Fall 1987): 12–13. The title could not be verified by a bibliographical search.

568 : One example was the Quebec-Ireland-Canada series of colloquia in the late 1980s.

Centering on power rather than on folk, Italian Canadianists such as Luca Codignola and many others noted that, until the 1960s, Rome—if ranking behind Paris and London—had been Canada's "third capital abroad." Since then, numerous Italian and Canadian researchers have studied Canadian history with sources from the Vatican archives that had previously "been used in a very narrow, ecclesiastical and hagiographical fashion." These studies investigated a quasi-linear dependency relationship rather than a Catholic space similar to a Gaelic space.[569]

From Japan a trans-Pacific perspective emerged that did involve an interest in multicultural policies despite the Japanese government's attempts to keep the country as homogenous as possible. As in other Asian societies, research often dealt with two distinct but interrelated North American cultures. In the same hemisphere, but with a different outlook, Australian scholars overcame their disinterest and British-centeredness when the country had to rethink its position in the changing economic macro-regions and "White Australia" concepts. Suddenly Canada appeared as a "Pacific neighbour," and marginal regions in Canada were compared to marginal regions in Australia, Newfoundland to Tasmania for example. Federal–provincial or –state relations were problem-laden in both countries. Later, scholars compared Aboriginal issues and land rights in both countries as well as labour movements in the two British-background societies.[570]

From a U.S. perspective, proximity induced scholars to study interdependence and, in applied research, to engage in comparative policy studies. Research on borderlands includes the Vancouver-Seattle region with its lumber and fishing industries as well as ecological concerns, the ranching borderlands from Alberta to Montana, the Detroit-Windsor industrial region, and the Maritime–New England connections. The political border

569 : Luca Codignola, "The View from the Other Side of the Atlantic," *Intl. Journal of Canadian Studies* 1-2 (1990): 217-58, CD-ROM edition. Researchers include Gabriele Scardellato and Roberto Perin.

570 : Katsumi Ito, *Issues of Canadian Studies* (title translated from Japanese, most articles in Japanese) (Tokyo: Japanese Association for Canadian Studies, 1987), cited in *ICCS Bulletin* 7.1 (Spring 1988); Peter Crabb, ed., *Theory and Practice in Comparative Studies: Canada, Australia and New Zealand.* Papers from the First Conference of the Australian and New Zealand Association for Canadian Studies, Sydney, Aug. 1982 (Sydney: ACSANZ, 1983), esp. Crabb, "Canadian Studies in Australia and New Zealand: Aiding Understanding among Pacific Neighbours," 12-18; Rita M. Bienvenue, "Comparative Colonial Systems: The Case of Canadian Indians and Australian Aborigines," ibid., 242-56; Bruce H. Bennett, "Australian Studies and Canadian Studies: Reports, Responses, Problems, Prospects," *Journal of Canadian Studies* 26.4 (1991/92), 33-52; Gregory S. Kealey and Greg Patmore, eds., "Australia and Canada: Labour Compared," special issue of *Labour / Le Travail* 38 (1996).

divides legal systems and administrative regulations, but similar economic and social formations bring about shared practices and interests. A concept of eastern North America as a culturally and economically triply divided macro-region has been proposed by Marc Egnal. As regards comparative policy studies, health care has been prominent, including "Canada-bashing" comments on socialized medical services.[571]

Political scientists in Latin America analyze the trilateral Canada–United States–Central and South American power hierarchies and diplomatic relationships. International relations of post-dependency Canada involved new policies toward Latin American states since 1968. Canada's policy of trade diversification, which targeted states from Mexico to Brazil, also meant increasing Canadian government and NGO involvement. After the end of the Cold War, Canada finally joined the Organization of American States, a decision many Latin countries had urged on Canada since OAS's founding in 1948. Relations that appear as "intermittent, distant, and ambivalent" from a Canadian perspective are considered as hesitant or as intentional neglect in Latin American perception. Diplomacy and trade are increasingly supplemented by intersocietal strategies of exchange and knowledge production. The "information age" based on communication technologies and on advanced communication theory and technology in Canada involves rapidly increasing exchanges with commercial value and cultural content. This is facilitated by networks of Latin American (mostly refugee) migrants in Canada. Communication, foreign policies, and cultural perceptions mirror stereotypes politicians, cultural producers, and people in general have of "the Other" rather than merely each other. Thus mutual (mis-) perceptions— "the Arctic meets the Caribbean"—rank high in research ever since the "great White men" cliché of diplomacy collapsed.[572]

---

571 : From among many studies: Karen Gould, Joseph Jockel, William Metcalfe, eds., *Northern Exposures: Scholarship on Canada in the United States* (Washington, D.C.: AC-SUS, 1993); Donald K. Alper and Robert L. Monahan, "The Attraction of a New Academic Frontier: The Case of Canadian Studies in the U.S.," in Allen Seager et al., eds., *Alternative Frontiers: Voices from the Mountain West* (Montreal: ACS, 1997), 173-83. Marc Egnal, *Divergent Paths: How Culture and Institutions Have Shaped North America* (Oxford: Oxford, 1996). A U.S.-Canadian co-operative collection of essays is Chad Gaffield and Karen L. Gould, eds., *The Canadian Distinctiveness into the XXIst Century / La Distinction Canadienne au Tournant du XXIe Siècle* (Ottawa: Univ. of Ottawa Press, 2003).The McGill Institute for the Study of Canada also deals with practical aspects of the future of Canada–U.S. relations, for example pharmacare in both countries.

572 : This has been collated from research proposals to the ICCS 2005 conference "Canada from the Outside In: Images, Perceptions, Comparisons" by Raul Rodriguez Rodriguez (Havana), Canada's Latin America Policy: Perceptions from the South; Gilberto Lacerda Santos (Brasilia) and Delia Monteiro (Mexico City), Voir et être vus dans

Obvious topics for external perspectives on Canada are international relations and Canada's position as a "middle power" with a "third option" policy. The "middle power" concept has often been approached in a comparative perspective as a contrast to U.S. super-power politics. Wilfried von Bredow and his co-authors, for example, argue that Canada's foreign policy, in the frame of asymmetric U.S.–Canadian relations, is multilateral and thus comparable to Germany's and the Swiss Federation's multilateralism. To counterbalance U.S. unilateralism, the three countries attempt to assume a larger role in international politics. Switzerland and Canada, but not Germany, are in a process of enlarging the traditional state-centered security agenda toward "human security." University students in the German-language countries, however, indicate a growing interest in Canada since DFAIT's anti-personnel-mine treaty negotiations under Lloyd Axworthy. The human security issue fits with Pearson's stand as regards the UN Charter, and reflects the moves to a further expansion of human rights.[573]

Human rights and the equality of all human beings also explain a renewed interest in First Peoples. Attention to "Indians," of long tradition, had established clichés and narratives that recent scholarship has to counter. Since the mid-nineteenth century, "Indians" in many European cultures and, because of the author Karl May, in Germany in particular, appeared in literature as exoticized Others, were reduced to images in children's books, and—with women left out—became "brothers" for boys in puberty who wanted to conquer the great wide world mounted on horseback, with an eagle's feather indicating their prowess. As one critic noted, the nineteenth- and twentieth-century literature "teaches us about ourselves": German or European history as expressed in "Redskin" heroes whose aggressiveness or humanity depended on the respective political regime and the climate of opinion. "Indianthusiasm" imagines people "as figures of the past, implying that anybody truly 'Indian' will follow cultural practices and resemble even physically the lifestyles and physiognomy of First Nations peoples before contact." Modern ethnology and anthropology devote much print to counter such images. In the 1960s, an ethnographic "endangered peoples" approach introduced the public to peoples across the globe whose cultural or sometimes physical survival was threatened. From the 1980s, First Peoples' modern writings became available in translations. Numerous liter-

---

la Société d'information: la construction d'un espace virtuel d'échange entre le Canadá et l'Amérique-latine comme stratégie pour l'avancement des études canadiennes; and Maria Teresa Aya Smitmans (Bogotá), "Canada and Colombia: Where the Arctic Meets the Caribbean: a Look at the Northern Country through the Prism of Human Security."

573 : Wilfried von Bredow, ed., *Die Außenpolitik Kanadas* [The Foreign Policy of Canada] (Opladen: Westdeutscher Verlag, 2003).

ary, linguistic, and anthropological studies appeared and authors, scholars, and elders were invited for readings and conferences. The appropriation of voice, the misrepresentation of culture, the "imaginary ethnology" came to a belated end. Comparisons to Aboriginals elsewhere began, especially in Australia and New Zealand.[574]

In France, Canadian Studies emphasized Quebec and Acadia but soon became inclusive of all aspects of the many regional societies. Particularly noteworthy is the critical assessment of the Canadian self-historiography and its perspectives. French and French Canadian scholars as well as those *hors du Canada* frequently employ comparative or integrative perspectives of a global *francophonie*, sometimes with a core-periphery undertone or intentional hierarchization, "les littératures et cultures francophones *hors d'Europe*."[575]

Outside of Canada, interest in Canadian literatures received a boost from Canada's presence in the international media during the Centennial, especially Expo '67 in Montreal. Scholars in Europe, often in close co-operation with Canadian colleagues, seized upon Margaret Atwood's *Survival* of 1972. In the post-national climate of opinion, regional literatures—first of the Prairie West, then of Acadia[576]—proved attractive to both researchers and students. In view of the specifics of national scholarly discourses, a comparison of literary histories of Canada compiled outside of Canada with those from the inside would reveal multiple perspectives—in this respect, too, diversity may be a strength. By the 1990s, multicultural literatures or, better, the many Canadian literatures, as well as intercultural communication, were high on the agenda. In societies in which monocultural ideologies held sway, such interest was sometimes motivated by hopes that societies would follow the Canadian path of development. In Latin America, where societies and societal discourses had developed the concept of *métissage* in the 1940s, interest focused on differences or similarities between the societies and their cultural productions.

---

574 : Hartmut Lutz, "Receptions of Indigenous Canadian Literature in Germany," in Hoerder and Groß, *25 Years Gesellschaft für Kanada-Studien*, 129–46.

575 : Claude Fohlen, "Problématique de l'histoire canadienne," in Fohlen, Jean Heffer, François Weil, *Canada et Etats-Unis depuis 1770* (Paris: PUF, 1965; 3rd rev. ed., 1997), 63–96; Laurence Cros, *La Représentation du Canada dans les écrits des historiens anglophones canadiens*. Collection des Thèses du Centre d'Études Canadiennes de l'Université de Paris III, no. 4 (Paris, [2000]); Robert Dion, Hans-Jürgen Lüsebrink, János Riesz, dir., *Écrire en langue étrangère: Interférences de langues et de cultures dans le monde francophone* (Montreal: Nota Bene, 2002).

576 : A complete edition of Acadian writings is being prepared at the Univ. of Dresden, Germany, under the editorship of Ingo Kolboom—to give only one example.

The development of Canadian Studies in particular countries and macro-regions, to some degree, reflects not only Canada's position in the world and Canada's foreign policies, but also an interest in Canada's mineral resources and policies. A conference theme such as "India and Canada: Partners for the Future" (Delhi, 1988) was typical. The Undersecretary of State for External Affairs, J.H. Taylor, in an address to the ICCS delegates in 1987 diplomatically kept all options open. He began with a concise statement of interest: "The more Canada's history, literature, economy, and geography are understood and appreciated in your countries, the more likely it is that we can effectually manage our relations with your countries." He then cited a legislative committee:

> Notre pays reste un fervent défenseur de l'atlantisme. Nous tenons à nos racines européennes. Les institutions, les lois, la culture et les traditions européennes ont toujours été les piliers de la société canadienne. C'est cet héritage qui, lors des deux guerres mondiales, a fait traverser l'Atlantique à peu près d'un million de Canadiens, dont plus de 100,000 ne sont jamais revenue.

To this extremely conservative perspective of death and nation he then immediately added:

> The development of Canada itself can be seen as a reaching out to the Orient, a bridge between the Atlantic and Pacific. Canada has always been a nation of immigrants and refugees and, for more than a decade now, more of our new citizens have come from Asia than from anywhere else. Since 1982 our two-way trade across the Pacific exceeded our trade across the Atlantic.

Once upon a time the flag followed the trade, or advanced before it. Now Country Studies seems to do so.[577]

Multicultural diversity in the Atlantic World
. . . and beyond

The nation-state approach to history and culture was challenged when new concepts emerged in Canada about nationhood and newcomers in the 1970s and, subsequently, elsewhere. In the study of transatlantic migration, the corollary of the nation-framed perspective led to one emigration and one

---

577 : J.H. Taylor, "Canada's Foreign Policy: An Internationalist Approach," *ICCS Bulletin* 6.2 (1987): 33–38, quotes pp. 34–35.

immigration approach, with North American immigration historians often not versed in the language of the newcomers and thus unable to understand their culture. This frame led to a nation-to-ethnic-enclave paradigm of migrant experiences. The emphasis on relations between ethnic groups in Canada, and the growing awareness among some European scholars of interrelated movements of people of different cultures between Europe's regions as well as across the Atlantic, undercut the constructed dichotomy of European emigration and North American immigration countries. A co-operative research project of scholars from most European cultures (rather than nations) and the two North American societies developed a complex model of the North Atlantic migration system,[578] of intra-European migrations and cultural exchange parallel to a new post-national historiography,[579] and of communication across language boundaries in Europe's many-cultured regions, in particular the people in the southeast. The research did connect to the empirical work of the Chicago School of Sociology but revised its U.S.-centered "assimilation" paradigm to a complex understanding of acculturation and insertion.[580]

---

578 : Ralph Davis, *The Rise of the Atlantic Economies* (London: Weidenfeld & Nicolson, 1973); Dirk Hoerder, ed., *Labor Migration in the Atlantic Economies: The European and North American Working Classes During the Period of Industrialization* (Westport, CT: Greenwood, 1985); *ICCS Newsletter* 4.1 (April 1985).

579 : In several European states, post-nationalist historians rewrote the respective master narrative as to reinsert the many-cultured past. Yves Lequin, ed., *La mosaïque France: histoire des étrangers et de l'immigration* (1988), rev. as *Histoire des étrangers et de l'immigration en France* (Paris: Larousse, 1992); Colin Holmes, *John Bull's Island: Immigration and British Society, 1871-1971* (London: Macmillan, 1988), and Linda Colley, *Britons: Forging the Nation, 1707-1837* (New Haven: Yale, 1992); Jan Lucassen and Rinus Penninx, *Newcomers: Immigrants and Their Descendants in the Netherlands 1550-1995* (Dutch orig. 1985; rev. ed., Amsterdam: Het Spinhuis, 1997); Anne Morelli, ed., *Histoire des étrangers et de l'immigration en Belgique de la préhistoire à nos jours* (Brussels: Centre Bruxellois d'Action Interculturelle, 1992). Several recent studies cover Europe as a whole: Klaus J. Bade, *Migration in European History*, transl. Allison Brown (Oxford: Blackwell, 2003); Heinz Fassmann and Rainer Münz, eds. *European Migration in the Late Twentieth Century: Historical Patterns, Actual Trends, and Social Implications* (Aldershot: Elgar, 1994); and many others.

580 : Dirk Hoerder and Armin Hetzer, "Linguistic Fragmentation or Multilingualism among Labor Migrants in North America," in Hoerder and Christiane Harzig, eds., *The Immigrant Labor Press in North America, 1840s-1970s: An Annotated Bibliography*, 3 vols. (Westport, CT: Greenwood, 1987), 2:29-52; William I. Thomas and Florian Znaniecki, *The Polish Peasant in Europe and America*, 5 vols. (1918-20; 2-vol. ed., New York: Knopf, 1927); Hoerder, "From Migrants to Ethnics: Acculturation in a Societal Framework," in Hoerder and Leslie P. Moch, eds., *European Migrants: Global and Local Perspectives* (Boston: Northeastern Univ. Press, 1996), 211-262; Hoerder, "Labour Markets - Com-

On this basis, the European Network for Canadian Studies' (ENCS) international symposium "Recasting European and Canadian History: National Consciousness, Migration, Multicultural Lives" in 2000[581] applied Canadian and European many-cultured approaches to the history of societies.[582] European societies had never been as homogeneous as the nation-state approach suggested. Intra-European migrations were large and multi-directional, cultural interactions the rule. National cultures, constructed in the nineteenth century, rested on regional diversity and continued to do so in the twentieth century. The new national cultural consciousness, developing from the 1780s to the 1830s, was made into a political nationalism and, in some cases, an expansionist chauvinism from the 1870s to 1918. Developments in Italy and Germany, like those in Canada, followed a different chronology; they unified as states only in the 1860s and '70s: in Italy a north-south dichotomy remained, in Canada the distinct Quebec society, in Germany multiple regional and religious differences. Upon analysis, the earlier unified states (not "nations") appeared as diverse, too: Great Britain consisted of several distinct ethnicities, France incorporated minority populations, the Austro-Hungarian Empire was a self-avowed "state of many peoples" (*Vielvölkerstaat*). In small numbers, migrants from China, Africa, and other macro-regions were part of Europe's socio-cultural and economic developments. Thus the theoretical debate on ethnicity in nation-building will have to include everyday ethnocultural interaction and conflict, exclusionist gatekeeper discourses, and scholarship, as well as the top-down (para-) military ethnic "cleansing"—annihilation and murder is the correct term. In contrast to the impetus from the identity debate in Canada, multicultural "guestworker" immigration and reform parties, whether Left

---

munity - Family: A Gendered Analysis of the Process of Insertion and Acculturation," in Wsevolod Isajiw, ed., *Multiculturalism in North America and Europe: Comparative Perspectives on Interethnic Relations and Social Incorporation* (Toronto: Canadian Scholar's Press, 1997), 155–83, and Hoerder, "Segmented Macrosystems and Networking Individuals: The Balancing Functions of Migration Processes," in Jan Lucassen and Leo Lucassen, eds., *Migrations, Migration History, History: Old Paradigms and New Perspectives* (Bern: Lang, 1997), 73–84.

581 : The ENCS quinquennial conferences, held since 1990, were originally proposed by Cornelius Remie from the Association for Canadian Studies in the Netherlands. Remie was the Network's coordinator to early 2005.

582 : "Negotiating Nations: Exclusions, Networks, Inclusions," eds. Christiane Harzig, Dirk Hoerder, Adrian Shubert, *Histoire sociale - Social History* 34 (2000), and Hoerder with Harzig, and Shubert, eds., *The Historical Practice of Diversity: Transcultural Interactions from the Early Modern Mediterranean to the Postcolonial World* (New York: Berghahn, 2003), and Harzig, Danielle Juteau, Irina Schmitt, eds., *The Social Construction of Diversity: Recasting the Master Narrative of Industrial Nations* (New York: Berghahn, 2003).

or Green, provided the impulse for a grounded reconceptualization of European societies' self-representations.[583]

Many present-day Canadian historians incorporate First Peoples' input; some European academics expanded the emergence of their civilizations to many origins. Italian and Iberian culture emerged in the vibrant Arab and Islamic-Judeo-Christian exchange of the Mediterranean World. The corporatist-religious ethnic coexistence in the Ottoman Empire provided a model for multi-faith polities in the modern societies of the Eastern Mediterranean. East Central Europe was and is an area of mixed settlement. Regional and national identifications emerged under Central and West European Romanticism, in which the cognitive level of Enlightenment rationalism merged with an affective level and in which elite constructions coincided with popular practices. The period, characterized by the emergence or construction of national consciousness (Hroch 1985), from the 1870s also involved state- or empire-wide imposed homogenization strategies: Russification, Magyarization, and Germanization in the European variants, Americanization and Anglo-conformity in the United States and Canada. The construction of Britain, France, or the United States as model nation-states or first democracies (Seymour M. Lipset) involved a hierarchization rather than analysis. Starting from the theoretical debate about "imagined communities" and the *Report* of the Bilingualism and Biculturalism Commission, the ENCS scholars suggested new policies of incorporation and of representation of collective memory for media and classroom teaching.[584]

In Canadian society, it was argued, the concept of citizenship was place-sensitive, and the universe of political discourse was dominated for the first three decades of this century by disputes over the factors contributing to regional inequalities. In Europe, non-place sensitive subject status and internally unequal economic development increased emigration potential and thus contributed to the peopling of many societies, Canada included. Other cultural affirmations, reflecting the mobilization of linguistic, religious, or class identities, were expressed in regional discourses and claims on the state in the name of fair treatment of regions and their inhabitants. In Canada, this led to accommodation, if still exclusive, of cultural groups of Asian background; in Europe to warfare and refugee-generation, which in turn increased propensity to emigrate to North America. From the 1950s,

---

583 : Essays by Norbert Rehrmann, Fikret Adanir, Michael John, Paul E. Lovejoy, Peter S. Li, Adam Walaszek in Hoerder, Harzig, Shubert, *Historical Practice of Diversity*.

584 : Essays by Jane Jensen in Hoerder, Harzig, Shubert, *Historical Practice of Diversity*; by Veit Bader, Minoo Moallem, Tariq Modood, Marie McAndrew, Sarah van Walsum, Danielle Juteau, Christiane Harzig, Tim Rees in Harzig, Juteau, Schmitt, *The Social Construction of Diversity*.

a structural reconfiguration of nation-states brought new representations of the national collectivity. In post-colonial countries such as France, Britain, and—differently—Canada, politicians and scholars debated new, and potentially conflicting, connections between different forms of pluralism such as dualism, multiculturalism, and multinationalism. In Sweden and the Netherlands, which experienced sizable immigration from the 1960s to the 1980s, and in Canada, policies were implemented to account for the changing social and cultural composition of the population. Political culture allowed for profound changes in self-representations, which incorporated diverse cultural practices or at least acknowledged differences. While Canada in such developments did not serve as a model, it did serve as a yardstick of self-reconceptualization. Thus, none of these countries' self-studies—and the same holds true for other countries—were limited to a nationally bounded social space. Canadian history and society involves Europe, Latin America, and Asia; Canadian developments influence other societies; Swedish society was part of the Baltic region; Dutch society connected first to the neighbouring German-language and the Scandinavian region, then to the colonies in Southeast Asia and the Caribbean. Canadian Studies and the study of ethnic relations in Canada were an influential precursor of research into multicultural everyday practices and literary expressions, first in terms of a mosaic, of pieces of many colours, then in terms of globally extended integrated lifeworlds of common people as well as cultural producers.

Canadian literatures, viewed from the outside, have appeared societally rooted, not as a high-culture *Überbau* distant from some material "basis." E.D. Blodgett has discussed "Canada as Alterity: The View from Europe, 1895–1961." Evaluations depended on the starting point of the perspective taken. Thus, a Swiss author began his text with: "Petits pays, petits resources, petites gloires, n'est-ce pas?" (Rossel 1895).[585] To European observers the two distinct literatures were complementary rather than separate; more attention was paid to writings in French, often in the context of a larger *francophonie*. The liberating spirit of the 1960s in the Atlantic World and in Canada at the Centennial, in particular, resulted in scholarly developments that paralleled those in Canada. While Margaret Atwood, Margaret Laurence, Alice Munro, and Gabrielle Roy received the bulk of the critical attention at first, literary historians and other scholars soon turned from the two internally diverse mainstreams first to Métis and Native Canadians,[586] then

---

585 : Edward D. Blodgett, *Five-Part Invention: A History of Literary History in Canada* (Toronto: UTP, 2003), 239–62, citation p. 240.

586 : To cite only a few works, Robert Kroetsch and Reingard M. Nischik, eds., *Gaining Ground* (Edmonton: NeWest, 1985), looked at European contributions to Canlit Studies;

to the many literatures in Canada, and from there to everyday communication in more than one language, thus integrating language, literature, and social sciences, and their translation into daily usages.[587] The *International Directory of Canadian Studies 1997–1999* listed scholars engaged in the study of multiculturalism from thirty of sixty-eight countries with scholarship in Canadian Studies.[588] The "petit pays—petit ressources" position has been replaced by "interactivity/métissage" perspectives.

This high level of interest induced the ICCS in 2000 to embark on a co-operative research project, "Transculturalisms." Five teams, each composed of scholars from many countries, analyzed

> the patterns of cultural transfer in Canada and in other countries; the impact of transculturalisms on so-called 'national' cultures, with an emphasis on Canadian culture from historical and contemporary perspectives; the intermingling of cultures (cultural *métissage*) and its impact on Canadian or foreign national identity; the effectiveness or ineffectiveness of cultural 'protectionist' policies within and outside Canada; and the influence of Canadian culture on the world cultural market in the 20th and 21st centuries. [589]

A British-German-Canadian team analyzed patterns of intergenerational transfer among youth from many cultures in schools and found local–global relationships that extended from London, Hamburg, or Calgary to many localities across the globe. Communication in peer groups, often through long-distance cell phone calls, occurred in frames of reference of adaptations of imagery from youth magazines, fashions, and other pictorial expressions, but usually not in terms of the "popular" or "high" literatures that Canadian or other Societal Studies analyze. Such youth cultures, not

---

Narasimhaiah, Srinath, Keitner, eds., *Glimpses of Canadian Literature*, analyzed reception in South Asia; Wolfgang Klooß, *Geschichte und Mythos in der Literatur Kanadas: die englischsprachige Métis- und Riel-Rezeption* (Heidelberg: Winter, 1989), was one of the first to turn to Métis literature in the Prairies.

587 : Universität Saarbrücken, Université de Montréal, École Supérieur de Commerce de Lyon: A "Séminaire tri-nationale: Communication économique interculturelle: L'État et l'économie en France, en Allemagne et au Canada" proposed "l'analyse des interactions communicatives dans le contexte de l'économie internationale, surtout dans les domaines du marketing, de la communication (à travers les médias), des ressources humaines et de l'organisation d'entreprise" (May 2003 and May 2004).

588 : Compiled by Linda M. Jones (Ottawa: ICCS, 1999).

589 : ICCS Executive Committee, "Transculturalisms: Proposal for a Research Project Undertaken by International Research Teams," May 2000.

easily comprehensible to adults—the parents included—form an internally plausible whole for those who live it.[590]

A Canadian-Latin American team, which approached *"métissage culturel* and its impact on Canadian or other national identities," noted that debates on the effects of globalization often began from very local or regional perspectives. Methodologically, studies of *métissage* imply "interdisciplinary and transcultural translation." If cultures can no longer be reduced to one "type," national or other, the complex frames of reference and codes need to be comprehensible to multiple audiences. Thus, Quebec French-Canadian cultural productivity has received an important stimulus from Haitian writers or, more complex, "les romanciers québéco-haïtiens," who by fragmenting a White, *vieille souche*, or other French-language discourse increase options and socio-discursive frames of reference. If French Quebecers of long tradition or English Canadians in Ontario fear for the loss of a way of life they liked—and which was likeable—it is important to remember that the newcomers arrive from cultures whose traditions, values, and ways of life were lost when European colonizers arrived. Multicultural diversity may add to a whole as in a finely crafted mosaic. *Métissage* may be the result of power and violent penetration. It may be interactive and translatable.[591]

590 : Phil Cohen, Michael Keith, Les Back, *Issues of Theory and Method* - Working Paper 1, and *Between Home and Belonging: Critical Ethnographies of Race, Place, and Identity* - Working Paper 2 (mimeographed - London: Centre for New Ethnicities Research, Univ. of East London, 1996 and 1999); "Transculturalisms / Les transfers culturels," *Intl. Journal of Canadian Studies* 27 (2003); Dirk Hoerder, Yvonne Hébert, Irina Schmitt, eds., *Negotiating Transcultural Lives: Belongings and Social Capital Among Youth in Comparative Perspective* (Göttingen: V&R Unipress, 2004. Canadian edition, UTP 2006).

591 : Transculturalisms Project, theme session "Canadian Métissage/Hybridity: Between, Among, Within Cultures," by Sneja Gunew, quote p. 1; theme session "Les Amériques: traversées et transmutations," by Zila Bernd; theme session "Migrations et métamorphoses de la littérature québécoise," by Simon Harel.

Chapter 13

AGENCY IN A MULTICULTURAL SOCIETY:
INTERDISCIPLINARY RESEARCH ACHIEVEMENTS

In the 1960s and '70s, with discourses and policies of inclusiveness developing, the majority of scholars still were men from the native-born middle classes of British or French background. They considered their experience generically "Canadian" and that of all Others as "special." This attitude is "natural" and general during early childhood. York University's feminist scholar Vijay Agnew, socialized in India in an upper middle-class family, remembered: "I believed that the values by which I was raised were universal." Her rethinking began when, as a foreign student in Canada, none of her cultural ways of life fitted and when her Canadian peers—from their perspectives—asked her about India's society as a whole. Perspectives resulting from experience may be differentiated in the development to mature adulthood. Often, childhood self-centeredness remains, and for those invested with power in society, it turns into an interest-driven frame of mind. In everyday life, self-universalization results in making all other experiences invisible or, in social research, in the "specializing" of women, ethnics, working classes, and First Peoples. Such "specializing" occurs within hierarchies and usually involves a subordinating of the "Others." However, unquestioned self-centering had been placed on the agenda of debate as early as 1908, when the only early (British-) Canadian author of children's literature, Lucy M. Montgomery, has her *Anne of Green Gables* say: "There's such a lot of different Annes in me. I sometimes think that is why I'm such a troublesome person. If I was just the one Anne it would be ever so much more comfortable, but then it wouldn't be half so interesting." Thus multilayered personalities and perspectives had a place in literature for young people. Anne refused to be a straight jacketed master narrative.[592]

Traditional scholars searched for the simple, the one comfortable but uninteresting Anne or, in their mental worlds, the John A. or Mgr. B. Writing about complex personalities and providing an inclusive view of the many agents in history and society demanded complex research and multiple approaches. Thus, after the master-narrative had been unmasked, it took decades of detailed research to fill the narrative's many gaps until "people's"

---

592 : Vijay Agnew, *Where I Come From* (Waterloo, ON: WLU Press, 2003), 2; Montgomery, *Anne of Green Gables* (1908; Toronto: Ryerson, 1942, repr. 1960), 205–7.

histories of Canada could be written.[593] Those who felt decentered melo-dramatically decried the new inclusiveness as "privatizing the mind," as "sundering" or even "killing" Canadian history.[594] Sundering what, the broken relationship between two founding nations? Interest in history had been smothered by the 1950s' bland Anglo- and Franco-male version of history, "profoundly out of step with what was happening in the rest of the world . . . Mainstream Canadian historians had no idea how to make up for the shortfall" (Bumsted 1992).[595] The new multi-faceted practices and perspectives brought forth an outcry against "mosaic madness" (Bibby 1990), a "lament for a nation" (G. Grant 1965), a comment on "the unbearable lightness of being Canadian" (Gwyn 1995), and a labelling of multiculturalism as an "illusion" (Bissoondath 1994).[596] As in the fable about the emperor without clothes, the masters of the narrative, dethroned, defrocked, and undressed, did not take lightly to the changes in society.

Amateur historians, Barry Broadfoot and Rolf Knight among them,[597] began to weave common people's stories into the tapestry of history. A new image, meant to be inclusive, welcomed immigrant cultural groups as new branches of "the family tree." But such men and women came with histor-

---

593 : J.M. Bumsted, *The Peoples of Canada*, 2 vols. (Toronto: Oxford, 1992); Margaret Conrad, Alvin Finkel, Cornelius Jaenen, *History of the Canadian Peoples*, 2 vols. (Toronto: Copp Clark, 1993); Dirk Hoerder, *Creating Societies: Immigrant Lives in Canada* (Montreal: , 1999); Gerald Friesen, *Citizens and Nation: An Essay on History, Communication, and Canada* (Toronto: UTP, 2000). In contrast to Creightonian hero-worship, contextualized biography is capable of providing complex narratives and analyses as, for example, in Brian Young, *George-Etienne Cartier: Montreal Bourgeois* (Montreal: , 1981).

594 : Michael Bliss, "Privatizing the Mind: The Sundering of Canadian History, the Sundering of Canada," *Journal of Canadian Studies* 26.4 (1991/2): 5–17; J.L. Granatstein, *Who Killed Canadian History?* (Toronto: HarperCollins, 1998). Granatstein, a fan of big rhetoric, in *The Great Brain Robbery* (Toronto: McClelland & Stewart, 1984), written with David J. Bercuson and Robert Bothwell, discussed "Canadian and Other Useless Studies" (130–46) and predicted the "ruin" of Canada's universities. See "Point-Counterpoint: Sundering Canadian History," *Journal of Canadian Studies* 27.2 (1992): 123–30.

595 : Interview with John Wadland, 7 Dec. 2000; Bumsted, *Peoples of Canada*, quote p. 415–416.

596 : Reginald W. Bibby, *Mosaic Madness: The Poverty and Potential of Life in Canada* (Toronto: Stoddard, 1990); George P. Grant, *Lament for a Nation: The Defeat of Canadian Nationalism* (Toronto: McClelland & Stewart, 1965; repr. Ottawa: Carleton, 1995); Richard J. Gwyn, *Nationalism without Walls: The Unbearable Lightness of Being Canadian* (1995; new ed., Toronto: McClelland & Stewart, 1996); Neil Bissoondath, *Selling Illusions: The Cult of Multiculturalism in Canada* (Markham, ON: Penguin, 1994).

597 : The "Knight" family, Depression-time immigrants from Germany, chose the English name over their German birth name "Krommknecht," which would have translated into "hunch-backed handyman."

ies of their own. In this image, not only the trunk would be rooted, each branch would have its own roots. Canadian society and Canadian Studies incorporate many histories. South Asian and Chinese experiences, African-Caribbean origins, and Latin American refugee-generating regimes are all aspects of Canadianness. Each arrival and incorporation involves changes of memory and actual self-views. To present, for example, a scholarly portrait of Caribbean culture in Toronto or Chinese culture in Vancouver requires a selection from what is available in the society of origin and what is transported and desirable or useful in the new surroundings, as well as a translation for readers with different symbols and codes. Translation implies Canadianization and at the same time diversification of Canadianness. Everyday lives as well as all forms of artistic and literary production involve little lineage in a particular tradition and much cross-fertilization, *métissage*. In historiography, each newcoming group, whether Jewish or Jamaican, requires a new look at Canadian colour coding, the Atlantic World's discourses, and narrative self-representations.

In past-oriented societies, categories are linear in terms of imperial, national, religious, or other organizing principles. Socialization into one dominant tradition reduces the resources of the mind for coming to terms with the complexity of a society. "Specializing" of Others becomes a survival strategy for one-track mindsets. In contrast, emphasis on the multiple allows negotiation, provides options to explore or accommodate the many facets of societal life, and to use "categories" that overlap rather than provide neat little boxes. In people's lives the specific, the societal, and the global interact; projecting lifeways and making decisions is multi-layered. Analytical approaches reflect complex lives and are cogently grounded. Scholars working within hierarchizations and disciplinary boundaries live in bounded spaces and thus their findings are of bounded validity.[598] Northrop Frye's and Marshall McLuhan's vivid, transdisciplinary re-interpretations of self-representations and communication were part of an innovative global world of scholarship: British cultural studies, German critical theory, French structuralism and post-structuralism, American mass communications research, semiotics in linguistic, and communications theory as well as discourse theory. Subaltern studies, feminist approaches, and youth research claimed equality and thus specialized the male narrative—one special case among many. None of the new approaches claimed universal truth or posited generic validity. By the 1980s, Canadian research had absorbed British

---

598 : As the 1930s writers and scholars who created Little Magazines and Little Presses to publish unconventional thought, authors in the 1970s created their own presses, the Canadian Women's Educational Press and New Hogtown Press in Toronto or New Star in Vancouver, for example.

and U.S. material-culture and social-history approaches, but less so French discourse theory. Given the Canada-specific identity discourses, perhaps no discourse theory was needed; the referential character of each statement may have been lived—though not cherished—reality.

Past-oriented societal sciences:
A gendered history of the people[599]

Writing about the past is a humanities and a social sciences endeavour. Narrative history might resemble a realist historical novel, might appear as historical romance—a handsome hero rescuing a beautiful maiden or a threatened society from evil forces. It might be a tale of exploration or a dissemination of ideology. It might also be a mix of genres and thoughtfully reflect and explore past options. Just at the time when the nationalist version of the story of Canada seemed to be reaching its apogee—Arthur R.M. Lower's *Colony to Nation* (1946), W.L. Morton's *The Canadian Identity* (1961) and *Kingdom of Canada* (1963), Creighton's *Canada's First Century* (1970)—lingering doubts about its validity came to the fore. Ramsay Cook and Maurice Careless, who provided the bridge between the old guard and the new social historians, called for an understanding of "regional, ethnic, and class identities" and suggested that "in these limited identities" rather than in any heroic imagery Canadianism might be found. Even this cautious term raises questions: why are such identities "limited"? Is national identity unlimited? Is it the standard? The perspective is in the eye of the beholder, the logic in the mind of the logician or more exactly in the categories with which he or she grew up. "Layered identities" (Robert Irwin) may be a more adequate term.[600]

Young researchers, such as Michael Bliss, "thought that the older historians' apparent obsession with their role as national sages, as definers and interpreters of the Canadian experience, was probably wrong-headed,

---

599 : The following sections outline developments. It is impossible to cite the full range of publications in the several fields of research.

600 : Cook, "Canadian Centennial Celebrations," *International Journal* 22 (1967): 659-63, quote p. 663; J.M.S. Careless, "'Limited Identities' in Canada" (1969, publ. 1971), repr. in Carl Berger, ed., *Contemporary Approaches to Canadian History* (Toronto: Copp Clark, 1987), 5-12. After only a single decade of social history, Careless, in "Limited Identities - Ten Years Later," *Manitoba History* 1 (1981): 3-9, decried that "such things as national concerns are by and large passed over and discounted" (p. 3). Cook, with more analytical balance, remembered "The Golden Age of Canadian Historical Writing" (*Historical Reflections* 4, Summer 1977: 137-49). Robert Irwin, "Breaking the Shackles of the Metropolitan Thesis: Prairie History, the Environment, and Layered Identities," *Journal of Canadian Studies* 32.3 (1997): 98-118.

perhaps even unprofessional." According to Jean-Paul Bernard, the entrenched position of the "nation-building" and *"survivance nationale"* approaches resulted in pent-up questions and arrested development. Innovation came with the expansion of the profession. In 1960, the old-style narrators of Great White and Black-robed men had all the particular sources at their disposal. The profession consisted of some 160 historians who knew each other and formed a closed circle. In 1976, more than a thousand historians—men and some women—spread across Canada and, at new institutions, could work unencumbered by intra-departmental orthodoxies. Their sources were not easily accessible and thus their enterprise was time-consuming. Neither archivists nor statisticians had bothered to collect documents on everyday life or provide bibliographies on common people.[601] New textbooks, thus, were slow to come. In the United States, a new synthesis was achieved earlier since publishers, addressing the far larger textbook market, realized the sales potential of surveys that included women and "ethnics."[602]

To some degree, the new historiography and the social sciences merged. The writing of history required social science categories and theorization; present-oriented societal research required explication of historical contexts. Historians in many parts of the Western World, regardless of specific national-cultural discourse, left the state-centered institutional-history confines to write broadly conceived social histories. While the class-gender-race/ethnicity trilogy replaced the unitary-nation tenet, theorizations varied from country to country. In Western Europe, inspired by the English New Left and, ironically, recognizing the "totalitarian" Eastern European socialist scholarship's "democratic" inclusion of the working classes, the historiography of labouring people became the most innovative subfield. French historians intensified research about the slowly evolving, *longue durée*, material base of societies and of everyday life: *"histoire totale"* in the

---

601 : Bliss, "Privatizing the Mind," quote p. 7; Jean-Paul Bernard, "L'historiographie canadienne recente et l'histoire des peuples du Canada (1964–94)," *Canadian Historical Review* 76 (1995): 321–53; Douglas Owram, "Narrow Circles: The Historiography of Recent Canadian Historiography," *National History* 1 (Fall 1997): 5–21, p. 8. For a thoughtful and vivid critique see Laurence Cros, *La Représentation du Canada dans les écrits des historiens anglophones canadiens*. Collection des Thèses du Centre d'Études Canadiennes de l'Université de Paris III, no. 4 (Paris, [2000]).

602 : In an early remedial effort McClelland & Stewart had begun to publish the series "Generations: A History of Canada's Peoples" with federal support. Each volume was concerned with a particular ethnocultural group; some provided critical insight, others were detail-filled histories of the "we were there, too" type. The overarching interpretation is Jean R. Burnet with Howard Palmer, *"Coming Canadians:" An Introduction to a History of Canada's Peoples* (Toronto: McClelland & Stewart, 1988).

Annales tradition. French theorists of discursive patterns of expression and modes of thought—Barthes, Derrida, Foucault, Bourdieu—revealed the un-analyzed "grids of meaning" of words and language. Their theories imposed self-reflection on scholars. A new generation of historians set out to change the "archive of memory" and "the habitus" of knowledge producers. Nationalist historians, suddenly without the pedestal of "objectivity," had reason to be fearful—though it was not history that was being killed, but their version of it.

In Canada, the new generation rather than waging battles about access to established structures and institutions moved to establish their own. The stimulating *Histoire Sociale / Social History* (established 1968) bypassed the staid *Canadian Historical Review*. On the geographic margins of Canada's knowledge production *B.C. Studies* (established 1968) and *Acadiensis* (established 1971) positioned themselves. The Prairie journals *Saskatchewan History* (1948), *Alberta History* (1952), and *Manitoba History* (1980) asserted claim to a historical memory unencumbered by centralist viewpoints. [603]Within the Canadian Historical Association, the Urban History Committee, the Committee on Canadian Labour History, and the Canadian Committee on Women's History created spaces for themselves.[604] Students of immigration and ethnicity bypassed ethnocentric approaches and formed the Canadian Ethnic Studies Association with its (at first mimeographed) journal, *Canadian Ethnic Studies / Études ethniques du Canada* (established 1969). Research on the role of literary expression in the creation of hybrid cultures, on the impact of women in processes of acculturation, on generational differences between immigrant parents and Canadian-schooled children, and on integration through working-class experiences, made the field transdisciplinary and multilingual.[605]

---

603 : On regions see Berger, *Contemporary Approaches*, 13–87, with essays by E.R. Forbes on the Maritimes, Serge Gagnon on New France, Gerald Friesen on the Prairie West, Allan Smith on British Columbia. J.M.S Careless, "Frontierism, Metropolitanism, and Canadian History," *Canadian Historical Review* 35 (March 1954): 1–21.

604 : Cf. *Urban History Review / Revue d'histoire urbaine* (est. 1972) and *Labour / Le Travail: Journal of Canadian Labour Studies* (est. 1976). To 1984, the French segment of the journal's title—*Labour / Le Travailleur*—reflected the then current male perspective. Women established the Canadian Women's Educational Press in 1974.

605 : Summaries of the innovations include Bernard, "L'historiographie;" Gregory S. Kealey, "The Writing of Social History in English Canada, 1970–1984," *Social History* 10 (1985): 347–65; Ronald Rudin, *Making History in Twentieth-Century Quebec* (Toronto: UTP, 1997), and Rudin, "Revisionism and the Search for a Normal Society: A Critique of Recent Quebec Historical Writing," *Canadian Historical Review* 73 (1992): 30–61. A bibliographic survey is M. Brook Taylor and Douglas Owram, eds., *Canadian History: A Reader's Guide*, 2 vols. (Toronto: UTP, 1994), and a new edition: J.L. Granatstein and

In Quebec, "la prise de conscience d'une histoire québécoise, fondée sur la recherche et non plus exclusivement sur l'idéologie, est recente," as French historian Claude Fohlen noted. The departments of history of the Université de Montréal and de Laval date only from 1946 and 1947 respectively. Inter-disciplinarity followed: L'Institut québécois de recherche sur la culture, established by sociologist Fernand Dumont in 1979; Le Centre interuniver-sitaire de recherches sur les populations, established 1972 by historical demographer Gérard Bouchard; and Le Centre interuniversitaire d'études québécoises (Université de Québec à Trois-Rivières and Université Laval) established by Normand Séguin and historical geographer Serge Courville. Again the generic and the specific were contested. Scholars did not agree whether "Quebecers" referred to all people in the province, to French- and English-speakers separately, or to men and women of French background only. Such self-centered debates reduced outward-directed perspectives. The *Revue d'histoire de l'Amérique française*, which during its first twenty-five years had devoted one third of its space to Quebec increased coverage of the province to more than four-fifths of its space by the late 1970s. Quebec historians polarized around the issue of belated or retarded development and who was to blame. Guy Frégault, Maurice Séguin, and Michel Brunet—the so-called Montreal school—held British "conquest" responsible for all problems, and traced *survivance* to "l'agriculturalisme, l'anti-étatisme et le messianisme." Espousing a traditional interpretation, "[ils] partagent… l'idée que la recherche était utile dans la mesure où elle pouvait aider les intérêts de la collectivité nationale."[606]

The revisionist Laval school, trained by Marcel Trudel and including Fer-nand Ouellet and Jean Hamelin, saw Quebec's history as self-created, or perhaps self-inflicted. "Préférant les approches pluridisciplinaires," they turned to economic questions and agency of particular segments (rather than simply classes) of society. A differentiated assessment of the change from French to British regime from 1759 to 1763 cleared the way for an understanding of the rebellion of 1837/38 as pivotal reference date with the role of the emerging francophone *petit bourgeoisie* and the Parti patriote at the centre. In a model-type gendered approach, Allan Greer interpreted the

Paul Stevens, eds., *A Reader's Guide to Canadian History*, 2 vols. (Toronto: UTP, 1982). See also André Beaulieu, Jean Hamelin, Benoît Bernier, *Guide d'histoire du Canada* (Quebec: PU Laval, 1969), rev. as Jacqueline Roy, ed., *Guide du chercheur en histoire cana-dienne* (Quebec: PU Laval, 1986); Alan F.J. Artibise, ed., *Interdisciplinary Approaches to Canadian Society: A Guide to the Literature* (Montreal: MQUP, 1990).

606 : Claude Fohlen, "Problématique de l'histoire canadienne," in Fohlen, Jean Heffer, François Weil, *Canada et Etats-Unis depuis 1770* (Paris: PU France, 1965; 3rd rev. ed., 1997), 63–96, quotes p. 68.

conflict as *une mutation politico-sociale* at the time of Queen Victoria's accession to the throne in 1837. Men, aghast at having a seventeen-year-young
woman head the kingdom, released a tempest of anti-women statements:
"Le résultat fut que le sexe devient de plus en plus la principale ligne de par-
tage entre gouvernants et gouvernés à l'âge des grandes révolutions bour-
geoises." Maleness was evoked in a rhetoric of independence, honour, and
masculine values. For women, only the sphere of religious orders was left
for careers outside of male control.[607]

Hamelin and Ouellet, influenced by the *Annales* school, studied the province's internal economic history and social relations. Jean-Pierre Wallot and
Gilles Paquet countered with a study of Quebec in the Atlantic economy and
emphasis on competition between the anglo- and francophone bourgeoisies. Gilles Bourque, from a Marxist perspective, emphasized class struggle
both between French and British Canadians and within each group. Louise Dechêne argued that the Montreal entrepreneurs, whatever their linguistic background, above all were rational businessmen. Later, Kathryn A.
Young (1996) expanded this approach to economic anthropology. Similarly,
habitants and farmers rationally pursued the welfare and security of their
families. A new religious history differentiated between people's spirituality, parish organization, and *curé* influence, as well as structures and power
politics of the Church. In the debating tradition, lively exchange ensued,
but in retrospect the interpretations appear as complementary rather than
conflicting. Robert Mandrou's concept of *mentalités* and Fernand Braudel's
longue durée of material conditions of life informed research. The propon-
ents of rational choice theory, if eschewing ideological pronouncements, did
not always take into account that agents of historical processes negotiate
many interests, values, and loyalties. Multiple rationales compete with each
other and outcomes evolve from non-rational preferences. The high-quality
research shifted emphasis from colonial Nouvelle-France to nineteenth- and
twentieth-century Quebec and, according to Paul-André Linteau, involved
a change of parameters from Quebecers as "an ethnic group to the population of a territory." The revisionists, many of them students at the new Université de Québec à Montréal, introduced new courses, captured the edi-

---

607 : Rudin, *Making History*; Michael D. Behiels, "Recent Quebec Historiography," *His-
tory and Social Science Teacher* 17.2 (1982): 73–82; Fohlen, "Problématique," quote p. 69.
See also Serge Gagnon, *Quebec and Its Historians 1840 to 1920*, transl. by Yves Brun-
ette (Montreal: Harvest House, 1982); Fernand Ouellet, "La recherche historique au
Canada français," in Louis Baudouin, ed., *La recherche au Canada français* (Montreal: PU
Montréal, 1968), 87–98. Greer, *The Patriots and the People: the Rebellion of 1837 in Rural
Lower Canada* (Toronto: UTP, 1993); Danielle Juteau & Nicole Laurin, *Un métier et une vo-
cation: Le travail des religieuses au Québec de 1901 à 1971* (Montreal: PU Montréal, 1997).

torial positions of the *Revue d'histoire de l'Amérique française* (*RHAF*), and arrived at a new synthesis, the two-volume *Histoire du Québec contemporain* by Linteau, René Durocher, Jean-Claude Robert, and François Ricard (1979, 1989), which perhaps overemphasized the normalcy of Quebec's development in an Atlantic context. New sociological journals and the *Cahiers de géographie du Québec* permitted interdisciplinary approaches.[608]

In anglophone Canada, too, narratives had to be expanded and reconceptualized. A pre-1960s' Marxist tradition of Labour Studies—Fred Landon, J.I. Cooper, Stanley Ryerson, and H. Clare Pentland—supported by U.S. foundation grants, had espoused an industrial relations approach. The category of class was re-introduced into historiography by Stuart R. Mealing, Jean-Pierre Wallot, and, with emphasis on ethnicity, John Porter. In the 1970s, young scholars influenced by the English New Left, especially E.P. Thompson and E.J. Hobsbawm, and trained at U.S. universities by Leftist scholars such as Herbert Gutman, expanded research from labour's organizing and shop-floor resistance to working-class culture. Traditional in their emphasis on production, scholars such as Gregory S. Kealey, Bryan Palmer, and Russell G. Hann, at first, did not look at reproduction and thus excluded gender from the analysis. Even in their work an Ontario-centeredness is noticeable, if in an international perspective of labour militancy. Others turned to Western radicalism and labour in the Maritimes. Jacques Rouillard studied labour in Quebec and the emigration to New England factories.[609] Women's work was studied by women historians. Source and essay

---

608 : Paquet and Wallot, "International Circumstances of Lower Canada, 1786–1810: Prolegomenon," *Canadian Historical Review* 53 (1972): 371–401, and *Patronage et pouvoir dans le Bas-Canada* (*1794–1812*): *Un essai d'économie historique* (Montreal: PU Québec, 1973); Wallot, *Un Québec qui bougeait: Trame socio-politique au tournant de XIXe siècle* (Montreal: Boréal Express, 1973); Dechêne, *Habitants et marchands de Montréal au XVIIe siècle* (Paris, Montreal: Plon,1974; Engl., Montreal, 1992); Kathryn A. Young, "'. . . Sauf les perils et fortunes de la mer': Merchant Women in New France and the French Transatlantic Trade, 1713-1746," *Canadian Historical Review* 77.3 (Sept. 1996): 388–407; Bourque, *Classes sociales et question nationale au Québec (1760-1840)* (Montreal: *Parti pris*, 1970); Rudin, *Making History*, quoting Linteau p. 191, and 201–16 for an acrimonious debate about revisionist historiography as prop for sovereigntism. Another critical discussion is Claude Couture and Claude Denis, "La captation du couple tradition-modernité par la sociographie québécoise," in Terry Goldie, Carmen Lambert, Rowland Lorimer, eds., *Canada: Theoretical Discourse / Discours théorétiques* (Montreal: ACS, 1994), 105–31. For further literature see Fernand Ouellet, *The Socialization of Quebec Historiography Since 1960* (North York: York Univ., 1988), rev. from "La modernisation de l'historiographie et l'émergence de l'histoire sociale," *Recherches sociographiques* 26.1-2 (1985): 11–83.

609 : Gregory S. Kealey, "Stanley Ryerson," *Studies in Political Economy* 9 (1982): 103-72; S.R. Mealing, The Concept of Social Class and the Interpretation of Canadian History,"

collections appeared, and so did syntheses beginning with those by Fernand Harvey and Donald Avery.[610] In a high-strung debate about whether
the concept of "class" was applicable to Canadian history, the "anti-class"
forces overlooked context: the European concept referred to rigid barriers
and pronounced consciousness, the North American concept to sociological
categories and militancy.[611]

CHR 48 (1965): 201–18; John Porter, *The Vertical Mosaic: An Analysis of Social Class and
Power in Canada* (Toronto: UTP, 1965); Jean-Pierre Wallot, "Le Canada français: classes
sociales, idéologies et infériorité économique," *RHAF* 20 (1966): 477–98. Jacques Rouillard, *Les travailleurs du coton au Québec, 1900–1915* (Montreal: PUQ, 1974), and Rouillard, *Ah! Les États: Les travailleurs canadiens-français dans l'industrie textile de la Nouvelle
Angleterre d'après le témoignage des derniers migrants* (Montreal: Boréal, 1985). The Re-
groupement des chercheurs en histoire des travailleurs québécois (est. 1972) brought
together historians of labour and industrial relations. Gérard Dion, "La recherche en
relations industrielles dans les universités du Québec," in Baudouin, *La recherche au
Canada français*, 71–86.

610 : A first collection of essays was Gregory Kealey and Peter Warrian, eds., *Essays
in Canadian Working-Class History* (Toronto: McClelland & Stewart, 1976). Fernand
Harvey, ed., *Le mouvement ouvrier au Québec* (Montreal: Boréal Express, 1980); Donald Avery, *"Dangerous Foreigners": European Immigrant Workers and Labour Radicalism in
Canada, 1896–1932* (Toronto: McClelland & Stewart, 1983), rev. and expanded as *Reluctant Host: Canada's Response to Immigrant Workers, 1896–1994* (Toronto: McClelland
& Stewart, 1995); Bryan D. Palmer, *Working-Class Experience: The Rise and Reconstitution
of Canadian Labour, 1800–1980* (Toronto: Butterworth, 1983); Craig Heron, *The Canadian Labour Movement: A Short History* (Toronto: Lorimer, 1989); Linda Kealey, *Enlisting
Women for the Cause: Women, Labour and the Left in Canada, 1890–1920* (Toronto: UTP,
1998); Russell G. Hann et al., comp., *Primary Sources in Canadian Working-Class History,
1860–1930* (Kitchener: Dumont, 1973); Laurel Sefton MacDowell and Ian Radforth, eds.,
Canadian Working Class History. Selected Readings (Toronto: Canadian Scholars' Press,
1992). For a popular survey see Desmond Morton with Terry Copp, *Working People: An
Illustrated History of Canadian Labour* (Ottawa: Deneau & Greenberg, 1980).

611 : Review essays by year of publication: Gérard Dion, "La recherche en relations industrielles;" David J. Bercuson, "Recent Publications in Canadian Labour History," *The
History and Social Science Teacher* 14:3 (Spring 1979): 179–183; Irving Abella, "Labour
and Working-Class History," in *Reader's Guide to Canadian History*, 2:114–36; Gregory
S. Kealey, "The Structures of Canadian Working-Class History," in W.J.C. Cherwinski
and Kealey, eds., *Lectures in Canadian Labour and Working-Class History* (St. John's: Memorial Univ., 1985), 23–26, and Kealey, "Writing About Labour," in John Schultz, ed.,
Writing about Canada: A Handbook for Modern Canadian History (Scarborough: Prentice-
Hall, 1990), 145–174; Bettina Bradbury, "Women's History and Working-Class History," *Labour / Le Travail* 19 (1987): 23–43; Bryan D. Palmer, "Working-Class Canada,"
in Berger, *Contemporary Approaches*, 124–42, and Kenneth McNaught, "E.P. Thompson
vs. Harold Logan: Writing about Labour and the Left," ibid., 143–64; Jacques Ferland,
G.S. Kealey, and B.D. Palmer, "Labour Studies," in Artibise, *Interdisciplinary Approaches*
(1990), 9–38.

If the West and the North had only recently been added to the history of the Central Canadas, a "new regionalism," or urban history, re-focused historiography on population centres and pivots of power. The vast physical spaces—eastern rural and western wheat-growing as well as the northern expanses—that had dominated images of Canada receded in favour of cities as markers of Canadian society and discourse about it. Once again, J.M.S. Careless set the tone early, and studies of working-class urban living conditions placed Canada in a global perspective: early twentieth-century Montreal shared with Calcutta the distinction of the highest infant mortality rate in the world (Terry Copp, Michael J. Piva). Urban historians and geographers who analyzed cities as social spaces rather than merely as power centres often worked from outside the traditional discourse-producing institutions in Toronto and Montreal (G. Stelter at Guelph, A. Artibise at Winnipeg). Innovation became mainstream in the 1990s when the federal government needed policy-related research. Canada's population doubled in the last third of the twentieth century with most of the immigrants going to the cities. Research addressed metropoles' multicultural gendered living in an internationally comparative perspective of global urbanization processes.[612]

Historians reconceptualized their questions in terms of a transcultural history of society. The shift from great statesmen (or great villains) and the resulting determinist actor–victim dichotomy to differentiated views of many-cultured actors in an uneven field of power relations does not only give back agency to all members of society, it also gives back responsibility and thus results in new evaluations of achievement or failure. However, historians have yet to incorporate the reorganization of memory resulting from population recomposition by migration. If the grandparents of half of Canada's pupils and students and a large segment of the parental generation grew up outside of Canada, would not historians have to provide bi- or multifocal narratives of the past? To students of immigrant background, "Elgin" or "Simcoe" signify no more than the name of streets. For students from South Asia, to take only one example, the hybridity and power

---

612 : Careless, *The Rise of Cities: Canada before 1914* (Ottawa: Canadian Historical Association, 1978); Gilbert A. Stelter, "Urban History in Canada," *The History and Social Science Teacher* 14:3 (Spring 1979): 185–194, and Stelter, "A Sense of Time and Place: The Historian's Approach to Canada's Urban Past," in Berger, *Contemporary Approaches*, 165–80; Alan F.J. Artibise, "Canada as Urban Nation," in Stephen R. Graubard, ed., *In Search of Canada* (New Brunswick, NJ: Transaction, 1889), 237–64. An authoritative collection of essays is Stelter and Artibise, eds., *The Canadian City: Essays in Urban History* (Toronto: McClelland & Stewart, 1977), rev. and enlarged as *The Canadian City: Essays in Urban and Social History* (Ottawa: Carleton, 1984).

relations in British India and its dissolution/deconstruction into multiple successor states may be of far more importance. Even a multiculturally educated Canadian writer, North Dakota-born Clark Blaise, had to realize after many years of marriage with India-socialized Bharati Mukherjee: "So much of Bharati was unknown to me because I had not been able to appreciate the texture of her first twenty-one years." Transcultural learning through a year-long stay in India made Blaise aware of the limitations of his own socialization. This society, which "I thought I knew profoundly," in comparative perspective appeared as a segment of "that whole bloated, dropsical giant called the West."[613] Historians, too, will have to incorporate the many pasts of their students, interwoven in personal identities and acted out in Canada.[614] They will also have to develop popularizing narratives to achieve impact on collective memory.[615]

Present-oriented societal sciences:
From Cold War camp to social spaces

In the 1960s and '70s, the social sciences stood at the verge of a rapid process of innovation, induced both through new theorizations and through the several societal liberation and civil rights movements. They were also fettered by the ever more pronounced distinctiveness of disciplines that cemented traditional non-theorized assumptions and prevented an integrated study of societies as in the 1920s and '30s. At this point, the "Americanization" of personnel and textbooks militated against a study of Canada and those who did emphasize Canada were accused of a "nationalist" turn in an age of decolonizing internationalization. While the reinsertion of the category of class had been a major achievement in social science historiography, gender was at the fore in the social sciences. Women's history as well as ethno-class concepts in sociology indicate the transdisciplinary aspects of the research.

Still, borderlines between disciplines were strong, ethnology and anthropology remained concerned with societies of low structural hierarchiza-

---

613 : Clark Blaise and Bharati Mukherjee, *Days and Nights in Calcutta* (New York: Doubleday, 1977; Markham: Penguin, 1986), quote p. 138.

614 : Historians' organizational and physical meeting places are contested ground. As late as the mid-1990s, a visiting Canada Council scholar in the U of T's Department of History observed how some of the department's retirees, traditional imperial historians, transformed the "Commons" room into a British-style male club at lunchtime. While the new generation of historians avoided the room as a meeting place, students did use the Commons without bothering about the old men's corner.

615 Pierre Berton's highly popular works provide but an adventure-story type of history.

tion and institutionalization; political science, economy, and sociology with specific aspects of highly differentiated geographically spread-out societies. In the former, historical depths remained "natural" since the societies studied were considered traditional; in the latter, "short-term" approaches to actual phenomena could not recognize change over time: snapshot science rather than moving pictures. While in the context of de- and re-colonization of academia the quest "to know ourselves" had been considered legitimate, in the 1980s it appeared not only as "nationalist" but also as "White studies." Acrimonious debates pitted traditional (Right) nationalists against Left nationalists who supported cultural independence, even protectionist measures, in the context of a globalizing U.S. culture and the U.S. military-industrial complex. Such self-assertion came when the student generation developed an international music culture with a cosmopolitan array of choices between Liverpool's Beatles and Caribbean or Latin American bands. However, profits accrued to U.S. corporations that owned the record distribution business. Evolving from "vernacular" to young people's mass-consumption music, it lost its countercultural aspect of talking back, of giving cohesion as well as voice to particular local-social and generational segments of society.

Ethnologists and anthropologists at the Canadian Centre for Folk Culture Studies at the Canadian Museum of Civilization continued the focus on Native, French-Canadian, Anglo (Celtic), and other societies. The first English-language research centre was established at Memorial University of Newfoundland as late as 1968. In terms of gender, Elli-Kaija Kongas-Maranda became the first woman with a full-time professorial position (Laval, 1976). Theoretical advance was slow. First, modernization "theory" juxtaposed the traditional and the modern with teleological implications. It assumed a timeless golden age of (coloured) Native cultures before contact or of (White) Celtic- or French-Canadian society before multiculturalism. Second, the benevolent gaze onto other societies easily turned into intellectual colonialism, which assumed "folk" cultures to be less socio-culturally advanced than the researchers' cultures, and which cast power impositions as victimization paradigms or history-of-the-unfortunate approaches. The gaze onto "heritage"—*patrimoine* but not *matrimoine*—still searched for "pure" traditions; "folk" remained an undifferentiated whole without stratification and diversity. Third, structural functionalism proceeded from the hypothesis that customs that persist over time must benefit society in a stabilizing way. This school never asked to whom in society such benefits accrued. Finally, some researchers were instrumental in popularization of cultures, even in creating provincial (Euro-) "folk" types labelled authentic (e.g. "Celtic" or "Acadian") by concentrating on the picturesque and thus deflecting attention from regional marginalization. In contrast, critical scholars realized their own interpretations as culture-based, contextualized "traditional" cultures in larger economic–societal–legal exchange frames, and understood that particular phenomena or processes may have more than one valid meaning. Each perspective onto the Other involved constant translation of the culture studied into the language and mental frames of the researcher's culture. Anne Cameron's *Copper Woman*, for example, was criticized for changing Aboriginal people's stories into forms acceptable to Euro-Canadian readers. Only slowly were Canadian market, kinship, and institutional relations and cultures of European-Canadian and, subsequently, Asian and other backgrounds studied from anthropological perspectives.[616]

Market relationships, including the aspects of transport and communication, had been the strength of the field of political economy before the 1950s mentally restrictive Cold War axiom of free Western capitalist versus economically determinist Eastern socialist societies destroyed the research agenda. In contrast, the field of economics, in a narrow sense, passed through quantification and abstraction to advocacy scholarship for free competition and free markets, in the process turning Adam Smith's invisible hand to the highly visible fist of the most powerful state economies, and subsequently the multinational companies. Only in the 1970s did a young generation of internationalist as well as of nationalist-minded New Left scholars return to Innis's Canadian political economy. These anglophone scholars ignored earlier Quebec scholarship, whether of Édouard Montpetit or theorists of penetration of U.S. capital into the weaker Canadian economy. Such capital-centered research had emerged in Quebec three decades

---

616 : Michael C. Howard and Patrick C. McKim, *Contemporary Cultural Anthropology* (Toronto: Little, Brown, 1982); Pauline Greenhill and Diane Tye, eds., *Undisciplined Women: Tradition and Culture in Canada* (Montreal: MQUP, 1997), esp. essays by Laurel Ducette, "Reclaiming the Study of Our Cultural Lives," 20–27, Diane Tye, "Lessons from 'Undisciplined' Ethnography: The Case of Jean D. Heffernan," 49–64, Christine St. Peter, "Feminist Afterwords: Revisiting *Copper Woman*," 65–72, Pauline Greenhill and Diane Tye, "Critiques from the Margin: Women and Folklore in English Canada," 167–86; Michael Behiels, ed., "Futures and Identities: Aboriginal Peoples in Canada," *Canadian Issues* 21 (1999); Janice Acoose / Misko-Kìsikàwikhwè (Red Sky Woman), *Iskwewak: kah' ki yaw ni wahkomakanak: Neither Indian Princesses Nor Easy Squaws* (Toronto: Women's Press, 1995); François-Marc Gagnon, *Ces Hommes dit Sauvages: L'histoire fascinante d'un préjuge qui remonte aux premiers découvreurs du Canada* (Montreal: Libre Expression, 1984); Emma LaRocque, "The Colonization of a Native Woman Scholar," in Christine Miller and Patricia Chuchryk et al., eds., *Women of the First Nations: Power Wisdom, and Strength* (Winnipeg: Univ. of Manitoba Press, 1996), 11–18.

before Innis's work on the pre-industrial staples economy. Daniel Drache and Mel Watkins, Charles R. Acland and William J. Buxton among others, expanded "staple approaches" to include political, cultural, and constitutional questions; differentiated between Quebec, Ontario, and "hinterland" developments and traditions; and reformulated the metropolitan–hinterland dichotomies. Drache summarized Canadian research about centre–margin relations, about dependency theory and domination strategies.

These political economists, in a Marxist variant of the Scottish moral philosophy tradition, developed their research strategies from a human-value positioning that prioritizes satisfaction of basic needs for all members of a society. They addressed particular societal formations, especially the bourgeois-capitalist one, as an integrated socio-economic regime involving uneven development, concentration of economic-political power, and social inequalities. Its inequities notwithstanding, capitalism appeared as capable of containing the diversity of class and group interests by satisfying a sufficient number of social groups. This "societal science" could easily incorporate McLuhan's examination of mass culture and commodification of cultural products, as well as material and cultural domination by the U.S. state and multinational companies. Thus, not only did political economy remain a bourgeoning field in Canada when it was shunned as "Marxist" elsewhere, it also achieved integration of cultural-societal-economic-political factors into an empirically grounded science of society.[617] Yet in societal practice, a women's consumer movement of the late 1940s, under the paralyzing and mind-numbing Cold War frame of thought, was labelled dangerous, foreign, and radical and wiped off the political agenda by the political institutions.[618]

---

617 : Daniel Drache, "Rediscovering Canadian Political Economy," *Journal of Canadian Studies* 11.3 (1976): 3–18; Drache, ed., *Staples, Markets and Cultural Change: Selected Essays by Harold Innis* (Montreal: MQUP, 1995), esp "Introduction," xiii–lix; Wallace Clement and Daniel Drache, *The New Practical Guide to Canadian Political Economy* (Toronto: Lorimer, 1985); Mel Watkins, "Innis at 100: Reflections on His Legacy for Canadian Studies," *Canadian Issues / Thèmes Canadiens* 17 (1995): 173–82; Charles R. Acland and William J. Buxton, eds., *Harold Innis in the New Century: Reflections and Refractions* (Montreal: MQUP, 2000), esp 2–28. For Quebec, Édouard Montpetit's "L'économie politique," *Revue canadienne* 52 (1907): 154–68, 259–68, was the seminal text. Jacques Parizeau, "La recherche en science économique," in Baudouin, *La recherche au Canada français,* 57–70; François-Albert Angers, "Naissance de la pensée économique au Canada français," *Revue d'histoire de l'Amérique française* 15.2 (1961): 204–20.

618 : Julie Guard, "Canadian Citizens or Dangerous Foreign Women? Canada's Radical Consumer Movement, 1947–1950," in Marlene Epp, Franca Iacovetta, Frances Swyripa, eds., *Sisters or Strangers? Immigrant, Ethnic, and Racialized Women in Canadian History* (Toronto: UTP, 2004), 161–89.

The Canadian Political Science Association, which reorganized in 1967, reinserted a political economy section only a decade later, in 1976. The discipline "Americanized" with respect to personnel, "behaviouralist" quantification, and allegedly value-free research. As for methods, an "individualistic" school collected empirical data by administering questionnaires to individuals, an "institutional" school relied on document analysis to discern collective behaviour as expressed in political institutions. In French-Canada, where the first political science faculty was established only in 1954 at Laval, scholars remained comparatively independent of U.S. influence. Both of Canada's intellectual-linguistic communities published in the *Canadian Journal of Political Science / Revue canadienne de science politique* (1968). The search for distinctiveness came as a response to U.S. hegemony and its Vietnam War rather than as a reaction to the presence of U.S. scholars at Canadian universities. Canada's self-positioning as a middle power in global politics, in scholarship brought forth an independent reformulation of political theory and a comparative study of polities—with Quebec scholars concentrating on their society. In the field of the study of administration, research on "Ottawa men" or "federal mandarins" neither anticipated a sociology of institutions nor theorized administrators as "inhabitants of structures" with distinct signifying systems and legal codifications. No integrative Canadian Studies approach to the political apparatus emerged. Instead, the self-confined "conflict of the two founding nations" approach resulted in circular debates about identity and perceptive but drawn-out strategies of constitutional reform.[619] Separate yet related, a unique internationalist approach to citizenship and social incorporation emerged. With a population originating from across the globe, some political and social scientists expanded the assimilative Canadianization-paradigm of the 1950s to equity in political representation, global division of power, and good

619 : C.B. Macpherson, "After Strange Gods: Canadian Political Science, 1973," in Thomas N. Guinsburg and Grant L. Reuber, eds., *Perspectives on the Social Sciences in Canada* (Toronto: UTP, 1974), 52–76; "Citizenship and Rights," topical issue of *International Journal of Canadian Studies* 14 (1996); Harold D. Clarke and Marianne C. Stewart, "Public Beliefs about State and Economy: Canada and the United States in Comparative Perspective," *Intl. Journal of Canadian Studies* 13 (1996): 11–40; Jean Laponce, "Using Footnotes to Trace the Evolution of Political Science from 1935 to 1989," *CPSA Bulletin* 19.1 (March 1990): 4–7; Kent R. Weaver, "Solitudes, Hierarchies and Continentalism: Recruitment of Political Science Faculties in Canada and the United States," *CPSA Bulletin* 23.2 (Nov. 1994): 88–91; Marc Renaud, Pamela Wiggin, and Jocelyn Charron, "Social Sciences in Canada: Changing Landscapes, Changing Challenges," *Canadian Journal of Policy Research* 3.2 (Fall 2002): 96–104.

governance.[620] Will Kymlicka, Charles Taylor, John Ralston Saul, and the expatriate Canadian John Kenneth Galbraith, who addressed political philosophy in a multicultural and concerned society, achieved international recognition.[621]

The local-and-global-governance perspective transcended the disciplinary boundaries of political science in favour of integrative studies of society including economics and sociology. Only by the late 1950s had sociologists, concentrated at McGill and University of Toronto, in the narrow disciplinary sense emerged as a community of their own. While McGill established an independent Department of Sociology, other universities kept some links to related disciplines intact, often with economics, and at UBC with anthropology. However, unexpected societal reactions slowed teaching. Student interest in sociological data—one way "to know oneself"—induced lively discussions about their new thought on social issues, from sex to religion, in public and at home. Parents and large parts of society, not yet ready to analyze their own everyday and intimate lifestyles, organized a backlash against sociology. Government institutions, which began to draw on political and economic scientists, hardly listened to sociologists, though politicians began to adopt sociological catchwords. Still intent on dissociating themselves from social welfare and social reform, English-language scholars distanced themselves from the earlier positioning as society's preceptors and eschewed any influence. In contrast, French Canadian scholars valued involvement in restructuring Quebec's society. From a commitment to Christian social reform, it critiqued the inflexible institutionalized Catholicism, and many sociologists entered the civil service or shared their expertise in the Parent Report on education (Guy Rocher) and the Rioux Report on teaching the arts. Jean-Charles Falardeau from Laval suggested that sociologists took over the counselling and discourse-influencing roles of the pre-1960s priest-lawyer-journalist combine. Sociologists joined the

---

620 : John Goldlust and Anthony Richmond, "Factors Associated with Commitment To and Identification With Canada," in Wsevolod Isajiw, ed., *Identities: The Impact of Ethnicity on Canadian Society* (Toronto: Martin, 1977), 132–153, and Goldlust and Richmond, "A Multivariate Model of Immigrant Adaptation," *International Migration Review* 8 (1974): 193–225; Richmond, *Global Apartheid. Refugees, Racism, and the New World Order* (Toronto: Oxford, 1994); Jay Drydyk and Peter Penz, eds., *Global Justice, Global Democracy* (Halifax: Fernwood, 1997); Wilfried von Bredow, ed., *Die Außenpolitik Kanadas* (Opladen: Westdeutscher Verlag, 2003).

621 : Will Kymlicka, *Liberalism, Community, and Culture* (Oxford: Oxford, 1989), and Kymlicka, *Multicultural Citizenship: A Liberal Theory of Minority Rights* (Oxford: OUP, 1995); Charles Taylor, *Multiculturalism and the "Politics of Recognition"* (Princeton: Princeton, 1992); John Ralston Saul, *The Unconscious Civilization* (Concord, ON: Anansi, 1995); John Kenneth Galbraith, *The Culture of Contentment* (Boston: Houghton Mifflin, 1992).

debates in *Cité Libre, Parti Pris,* and *Socialisme.* In academia, *Recherches sociographiques,* established in 1960 by Laval's Department of Sociology and Anthropology, began publication four years earlier than the *Canadian Review of Sociology and Anthropology,* and, since 1969, *Sociologie et sociétés* provided a second forum. Differences between the two linguistic—or, better, discourse-defined—"camps" were large. The U.S.-influenced *Review* published quantitative micro-empirical research; French-language sociologists preferred macro-level, conflict-oriented, and organizational analyses. Among anglophone sociologists only those engaging in ethnic-relations research and studies of good governance pursued multidisciplinary strategies. When the federal government needed information as well as non-partisan policy recommendations on bilingualism, sociologist Jean Burnet directed the research. Like Ramsay Cook in historiography, she bridged the generational gap in sociology.[622]

The study of society, in Canada's human geography approach, pioneered by the Geological Survey, involved the concept of social spaces long before Henri Lefèbvre theorized the field. Scholars from Germany and France contributed. Raoul Blanchard, for example, brought an original, outside perspective and methodology to "social and economic change in terms of geographic context, [and to] the social meaning of co-existent lumber and agricultural activity." Geographers such as R. Cole Harris (UBC), Len Evenden (SFU), and John Warkentin (York University) became central to an interdisciplinary Canadian Studies effort and published textbooks for students long before the other social sciences including history did so. In the field of human geography, scholars continued the integrative social science traditions of the 1920s. Geography, not considered an enemy by Cold Warriors, could develop without ideological blindfolds.[623]

622 : Jean-Charles Falardeau and Frank E. Jones, "La sociologie au Canada," *Transactions of the Third World Congress of Sociology* (Intl. Sociology Assoc., 1956), 7:14–22; Mabel F. Timlin and Albert Faucher, *The Social Sciences in Canada: Two Studies* (Ottawa: SSRCC, 1968); Guinsburg and Reuber, *Perspectives on the Social Sciences;* "Socio-national Factors and the Development of Sociology / Les facteurs socio-nationaux et l'évolution de la sociologie," topical sections in *Canadian Journal of Sociology* 1 (1975–76): 89–124, 223–34, 343–85, 499–528; Georges-Henri Lévesque et al., eds., *Continuité et rupture: Les sciences sociales au Québec [Colloque du Mont-Gabriel, 1981],* 2 vols. (Montreal: PU Montréal, 1984); Danielle Juteau, *The Sociology of Ethnic Relations in Quebec: History and Discourse* (Toronto: U of T, Dept. of Sociology, 1991); Fernand Duval and Yves Martin, eds., *Imaginaire social et représentations collectives: Mélanges offerts à Jean-Charles Falardeau* (Quebec: PUL, 1992).

623 : Henri Lefèbvre, *The Production of Space* (London: Blackwell, 1991); R. Cole Harris and John Warkentin, *Canada before Confederation: A Study in Historical Geography* (1974; rev. ed., Ottawa: Carleton, 1991), and Warkentin, *A Regional Geography of Canada: Life,*

The quasi-separation of much of scholarship from society and the distinctive as well as separating intra-disciplinary refinement of methodologies and theories occurred at the very time when transdisciplinary discourse theory and societal reform movements pointed in the opposite direction. The demands for inclusion by the young, the women, and the culturally or racially marginalized challenged scholarship. When academia refused to act or moved only slowly, activists inserted themselves and created Women's Studies, Native Studies, and Ethnic Studies. "Diversity can be closed, in which case it is merely a collection of varying solitudes, or it can be open, in which case its value as a source of creative inspiration is most fully realized. . . . Canadian cultural policy should come down on the side of open diversity," the Federal Cultural Policy Review Committee commented in 1982 and added: "The present inequitable access of women to all levels of responsibility and activity in the cultural sector [the economy, and politics,] deprives Canadian society as a whole of a vital dimension of human and artistic experience."[624]

Self-articulation of women and mainstreaming gender

Women struggled for power to control *their* own lives, as opposed to traditional national definitions of power as control over *others'* lives. One major prerequisite for changed gender roles was the reduction of the number of children per couple and thus of time for child care, and improved contraception gave women control over their reproductive capabilities. A second prerequisite, the recasting of gender roles, had not been achieved. Household-labour-proof husbands or partners were, with few exceptions, the only model on the market; magazine editors contextualized ads for women's shampoo by how-to articles, but refrained from explaining how to shave when advertising razor blades for men. Florence Rae Kennedy, a U.S. African-American lawyer, activist, civil rights advocate, and feminist, is known for her comment: "Honey, if men could get pregnant, abortion would be a

Land, and Space (Scarborough, ON: Prentice-Hall, 2000); Jean-Pierre Augustin and Vincent Berdoulay, *Modernité et tradition au Canada: Le regard des géographes français jusqu'aux années 1960* (Paris: Harmattan, 1997); Chad Gaffield, "The New Regional History: Rethinking the History of the Outaouais," *Journal of Canadian Studies* 26.1 (1991): 64–81, quote p. 65; J. Lewis Robinson, *Concepts and Themes in the Regional Geography of Canada* (Vancouver: Talonbooks, 1983); Thomas Greider and Lorraine Garkovich, "Landscapes: The Social Construction of Nature and the Environment," *Rural Sociology* 59.1 (1994): 1–24.

624 : Canada. Federal Cultural Policy Review Committee (Applebaum-Hébert Committee), *Report of the Federal Cultural Policy Review Committee* and companion volume *Summary of Briefs and Hearings* (Ottawa: Supply and Services, 1982), quote p. 9.

sacrament." In the Atlantic World, Simone de Beauvoir's *The Second Sex* (1949) and Betty Friedan's *The Feminine Mystique* (1963) shaped debates. A quarter century after its Universal Declaration of Human Rights, the UN declared 1975 to be International Women's Year.[625]

Terms of reference of the Royal Commission on the Status of Women in Canada, established in 1967 with five women and three men as commissioners, postulated equality of opportunity rather than mere equality at birth, but not yet equality of outcome. Nation and gender remained entwined: "the full use of human resources is in the national interest" and for women to enter the paid labour force it was necessary that "the father and society" share childcare. "To overcome the adverse effects of discriminatory practices," the state would have to enter the sphere of gender roles, which were "based on traditions and myths." Ethnologists of traditional societies would have had a heyday had they turned to the societies of Western males. In "a world organized and ruled by men[, these] will be naturally inclined to keep women in subjugation. As John Stuart Mill put it [in 1869]: 'Men do not want solely the obedience of women, they want their sentiments . . . not a forced slave but a willing one.'" Political institutions, "our government bodies," are "not unlike stag parties but the stakes here are human dignity and social progress."[626] Women's oral archives of memory, as subversive as those of any other subaltern group, had long held such views. Male historians had always been careful to exclude oral narratives from acceptable evidence.

Women established the National Action Committee on the Status of Women in 1971 and the Canadian Advisory Council on the Status of Women in 1973 as forums of their own, and to monitor implementation of the Commission's recommendations.[627] They had work on their hands. One of the "stag parties," the Supreme Court, in a 1973 case of a woman who had worked the family farm jointly with her husband for twenty years and claimed an "undivided half-interest in the property" after separation, decided that "her various services in connection with her husband's ranching activities did not give her any beneficial interest in the property claimed." Courts hand

---

625 : Gloria Steinem, *Outrageous Acts and Everyday Rebellions* (New York: Holt, Rinehart & Winston, 1983, repr. New York: Signet, 1984), 4–8, quote p. 8; de Beauvoir, *The Second Sex* (Paris: Gallimard, 1949); Friedan, *The Feminine Mystique* (New York: Norton, 1963).

626 : Royal Commission on the Status of Women in Canada, *Report on the Status of Women in Canada* (Ottawa: Queen's Printer, 1970), quotes pp. xii, 1, 3.

627 : Canadian Advisory Council on the Status of Women, *As Things Stand: Ten Years of Recommendations* ([Ottawa: CACSW, 1983]); Jill Vickers, Pauline Rankin, and Christine Appelle, *Politics as if Women Mattered: A Political Analysis of the National Action Committee on the Status of Women* (Toronto: UTP, 1993).

down rulings (note the hierarchy), they do not provide justice, as a saying among law experts has it. In reaction to such decisions, family law reform began with an Ontario act of 1978. The Supreme Court was equally one-sided in a 1973 appeal of a Native Canadian woman, Jeannette Corbière-Lavell, to have her Indian status restored, which she had lost upon marriage to a non-Indian. She charged sex discrimination since Native men did not lose status when marrying a non-Native woman. Her claim was rejected, with the justices commenting that the Bill of Rights did not override discriminatory legislation. Such "blatant use of double standards" accelerated women's protests, but they also had to deal with their own colour-coded standards. White British and French Canadian women, with easier access to institutions than Native, immigrant, and in particular "coloured" Canadian women, often assumed to speak for "generic woman" when pursuing their particular interest.[628]

In view of such sociological, historical, and legal issues, as well as concepts of good governance, social science scholarship on gender roles and equality could have taken off—but with few exceptions the take-off was limited to the few women admitted as scholars to academia.[629] Some intellectuals did defect from *l'ancien régime*, to use Tocqueville's concept. Historian Ramsay Cook, for example, included women among agents in society.[630] Much of the research in early Women Studies was remedial. "We-were-there-too" perspectives, so-called contribution history, filled the many gaps left by the master narrative. Upon the English- and French-language "Great Women" approach (Andrews), which included the "first White woman in Native women's spaces" subgenre, followed a burgeoning of research, which Veronica Strong-Boag noted as early as 1973, primarily concerned with exploited working women. Within a mere decade and a half after the mid-1960s, such studies provided the data for complex analyses and theory. Male historians,

---

628 : CACSW, *As Things Stand*, 12–13, quote p. 13; Kenneth Coates, "Being Aboriginal: The Cultural Politics of Identity, Membership, and Belonging among First Nations in Canada," *Canadian Issues* 21 (1999): 23–41. Federal Bill C-31 (1985) returned Indian status to thousands of such Native women and their children.

629 : Lionel Gendron ventured forth with *Qu'est-ce qu'une femme* (Montreal: Éd. de l'homme, 1961), an old-style male physiology approach to women's behaviour and being. Women did not have to ask what a man is; on pain of punishment, the less powerful observe and know the powerful far better than vice versa.

630 : Alexis de Tocqueville, *L'Ancien Régime et la Révolution* (1856). Cook re-edited Catherine Cleverdon's *The Woman Suffrage Movement in Canada* (1950; Toronto: UTP, 1974) and provided a study of a western reformer, "Frances Marion Beynon and the Crisis of Christian Reformism," in Carl Berger and Ramsay Cook, eds., *The West and the Nation* (Toronto: McClelland & Stewart, 1976).

theoretically no further advanced, had had a century and a half to collect their version of the facts.[631]

Theorizations and methodological innovations emerged from a thoughtful debate on the consequences of the staples thesis for women's history. The Innis school had had nothing to say about women or families. However, the fur trade was mediated by Native women as partners of Scottish or French Canadian traders. In the cod fishery, men left families for extended periods of time or, if fishing locally, divided the processing of the catch with the families. Western grain-producing agriculture was family work. The lumber economy, like the building of railways, impacted family life through long absences of husbands, fathers, or sons. Women became (temporary) heads of households; children grew up with only one parent present. Innis, sensitive to power in communication, might have asked who in a family has what information, processes it how, and connects to whom?[632] A second, contested, theorization related gendered strategies in politics to the ability to bear children. Mary O'Brien argued "that men create institutions to carry their projects forward in time," while women create genetic-personal continuity and, by implication, may not need political structures. However, self-organization had been essential to achieve suffrage. Political strategies emerged from cultural habitus. Anglophone women struggled for individual women's equality, francophone women for liberation based on collective rights. Third, life culture-based research reintegrated the spheres of production and reproduction. While economists had never looked at family economies, scholars using life-course approaches, sensitive to continuing role differences between women and men, reconceptualized the implicitly male three-stage model of youth–working age–retirement into a complex model interweaving childcare, work in and out of the home, and care for aging parents. The recognition that retirement pensions were based on the male life-course model indicated how individual life courses and institu-

---

631 : The Corrective Collective, *Never Done: Three Centuries of Women's Work in Canada* (Toronto: Women's Educational Press, 1974); Margaret Andrews, "Attitudes in Canadian Women's History, 1945–1975," *Journal of Canadian Studies* 12.4 (1976): 69–78; Mary Quayle Innis, ed., *The Clear Spirit: Twenty Canadian Women and Their Times* (Toronto: UTP, 1966). Veronica Strong-Boag, "Cousin Cinderella. A Guide to Historical Literature Pertaining to Canadian Women," in Marylee Stephenson, ed., *Women in Canada* (Toronto: New Press, 1973), 262–90, pp. 277–81, provided a list of a broad range of works. Alison Prentice, "Writing Women into History: The History of Women's Work in Canada," *Atlantis* 3.2 (1978): 72–84.

632 : Strong-Boag, "Cousin Cinderella," 264; Jane Jenson, "From Silence to Communication? What Innisians Might Learn by Analysing Gender Relations," in Acland and Buxton, *Harold Innis in the New Century*, 177–95.

tional arrangement are inextricably interwoven.[633]

A gendered study of family discourses indicates the differences between authoritarian and negotiating strategies, between closing and opening spaces in intergenerational transfer of values. Fathers usually would order children to do certain things; mothers, who shared the commitment to parental power unequivocally, would, however, phrase a question: "should he —or she—do so?" Thus men asserted authority; women left room to negotiate. Similarly, gatekeeper pronouncements preclude debate; societal negotiating spaces permit intergenerational and intergroup evolution. The study of society and its history was as heavily sexualized as reproduction: in the traditional narrative, male explorers penetrate the continent along the great river. After settlement, lonely males with an axe over their shoulder would walk off and be swallowed by the almost impenetrable, dark forest. They might be lost forever or they might, at one point, chop down the enveloping trees, clear a living space and, with light coming in, create a living space for a new family or, possessively, their family.[634]

By the 1980s, women had incorporated themselves into historiography.[635] Collections of essays provided a survey of the state of the art. From women's history, gender history emerged, and from the history of femininity emerged the history of masculinity. Masculinity, part of biographies of "great White men" and of "frontier" and "the Great North" accounts, lost its dominance over the discourse. The biological category of sex was deconstructed and

633 : Janice Acton, Penny Goldsmith, and Bonnie Shepard, *Women at Work: Ontario 1850-1930* (Toronto: Women's Educational Press, 1974); Alison Prentice and Susan Mann Trofimenkoff, eds., *The Neglected Majority: Essays in Canadian Women's History*, 2 vols. (Toronto: McClelland & Stewart, 1977); Marie Lavigne and Yolande Pinard, eds., *Les femmes dans la société québécoise* (Montreal: Boréal Express, 1977; rev. ed., 1982); Francine Barry, *Le travail de la femme au Québec: L'évolution de 1940 à 1979* (Montreal: PUQ, 1977); Linda Kealey, ed., *A Not Unreasonable Claim: Women and Reform in Canada 1880s-1920s* (Toronto: Women's Educational Press, 1979); Collectif Clio (= Micheline Dumont, Michèle Jean, Marie Lavigne, Jennifer Stoddard), *L'histoire des femmes au Québec depuis quatre siècles* (Montreal: Quinze, 1982, Engl. 1987; rev. ed., 1992); Louise Tilly and Joan Scott, *Women, Work and Family* (New York: Holt, Rinehart & Winston, 1978); Dirk Hoerder, "Reconstructing Life Courses: A Historical Perspective on Migrant Experiences," in Victor W. Marshall, Walter R. Heinz, Helga Krueger, Anil Verma, eds., *Restructuring Work and the Life Course* (Toronto: UTP, 2001), 525-39.

634 : Mary O'Brien, *The Politics of Reproduction* (Boston: Routledge, 1981); Vickers et al., *Politics as if Women Mattered*, 3-4; Strong-Boag, "Cousin Cinderella," 281-85.

635 : Strong-Boag, "Cousin Cinderella," and Beth Light and Strong-Boag, *True Daughters of the North: Canadian Women's History; An Annotated Bibliography* (Toronto: OISE Press, 1980); Ghislaine Houle, *La femme au Québec* (Quebec: Bibliothèque nationale du Québec, 1975).

revealed as another social convention. In conjunction with legal changes—the decriminalization of homosexuality—gay and lesbian inclinations came into the open and Queer Studies emerged. However, generational difference was, as yet, not fully represented. Research focused on the worlds of adults: children were subsumed under family history, youth lifestyles downgraded to the status of subculture.[636] Women's caucuses emerged in many professional associations; approaches varied from Marxist feminism to traditional middle-class positions. By the 1990s, the category of gender had become mainstream, even if not yet accepted by all of the former "first," now oppositional, sex.

From First Peoples in a fourth world to participants in an open society

In the global division of First or capitalist, Second or socialist, and Third or colonized/decolonizing Worlds, as well as intra-Canadian "founding peoples" claims, Native Canadians inserted themselves as First Peoples in a Fourth or internally colonized World. Inter-tribal self-organization began during the hardships of the 1930s in connection with labour militancy on the Pacific Coast and in the late 1950s among Prairie groups. The activists of the 1960s could build on three decades of struggles, and could relate to the U.S. civil rights and American Indian movements as well as on demographic growth since the late 1940s. Economic development in the North involved extractive industries and the war-related construction of first, the Alaska Highway and, second, the Distant Early Warning (DEW) anti-missile system. The resulting temporary concentrations of English-speakers as well as the new technologies and consumer goods in Native people's communities infringed on ways of life and rights or presumed rights. Intergenerational change followed: Native children grew up with English as their first language. This implies both loss of culture-specific ways of expression and a new facility to press Native demands in the hegemon's language.[637]

Efforts to create Native country-wide organizations had to negotiate diversity of cultures and regional interests, competing traditionalist and modernizing philosophies, reserve or urban ways of living, and indigenous, Catholicized, and other belief systems. A first National Indian Council of 1961 strove for unity among peoples, betterment of their position in

---

636 : Strong-Boag, "Cousin Cinderella," 273–75; Ruth Pierson and Beth Light, "Women in the Teaching and Writing of Canadian History," *History and Social Science Teacher* 17 (1982): 83–93, esp. 91; Peter Dickinson, *Queer is Here: Nationalisms, Sexualities and Literatures of Canada* (Toronto: UTP, 1999).

637 : Cruikshank, *The Social Life of Stories* (1998), xiv.

society-at-large, improved relationships to non-Indians, and a revision of White people's images of Native peoples. This initiative from urban groups, premised on overcoming the threefold division into status and non-status Indians and Métis, foundered in 1968. But it showed the way. The Assembly of First Nations (at first National Indian Brotherhood) representing status Indians, the Native Council of Canada (at first Canadian Métis Society) representing Métis and non-status Indians, and the Inuit Tapirisat (former-ly Inuit Brotherhood) emerged as national political and cultural organiza-tions by 1971 and often spoke with a common voice.

Incorporation of this part of Canada's population into academia was as slow as that of women and "ethnics." Since no interdisciplinary transcultur-al study of society existed, Native peoples together with White "folk" con-tinued to be segregated into anthropology and ethnohistory, fields that had moved from "gaze" to analytical, partly archaeology-based research. Sev-eral scholars had raised their voices against restrictions on First Peoples' cultures by Second Peoples' laws, but to no avail. Alfred Bailey's important study on European–Native conflict, hardly noticed in 1937, was reprinted in 1969.[638] The first Native Studies departments at North American universi-ties were established at the University of Minnesota in 1964 and at Trent University in 1969.[639] The Canadian Bill of Rights of 1960 made discrimina-tion liable to prosecution, and the militant U.S. American Indian Movement achieved strong media presence.

The government's Indian Affairs Branch—rather than academics claim-ing to study the state and its nations—initiated a major scholarly survey of First Peoples across the country, undertaken from 1964 to 1969 by Harry B. Hawthorn (UBC) and Marc-Adélard Tremblay (Laval). The multidisci-plinary research involved some fifty ethnologists as well as Stuart Jamie-son (economics), Alan Cairns (political science), and Kenneth Lysyk (law). While the *Report's* "citizenship plus treaty rights" Aboriginal rights con-cept was meant to reflect changed governmental attitudes, Indian Affairs Minister Jean Chrétien's "White Paper" of 1969 ignored the implications. In terms of human rights and political theory, the White Paper's reasoning was sound. It proposed individual equality before the law, full access to all

---

638 : Alfred G. Bailey's *The Conflict of European and Eastern Algonkian Cultures, 1504-1700* (1937). Bailey had studied both with Innis and McIllwraith.

639 : Three major surveys appeared: Dickason, *Canada's First Nations* (1992; 3rd ed., 2001); J.R. Miller, *Skyscrapers Hide the Heavens: A History of Indian-White Relations in Can-ada* (3rd ed., Toronto: UTP, 2000); Arthur Ray, *I Have Lived Here Since the World Began: The Illustrated History of Canada's Native Peoples* (Toronto: Key Porter, 1996). Howard Adams, in *Prison of Grass: Canada from a Native Point of View* (1st ed., 1975; Saskatoon: Fifth House, 1989), rewrote Canadian history from First Peoples' perspectives.

social services, and non-discriminatory governmental and administrative practices. In terms of cultural and political plurality, it ignored treaty rights and cultural contexts. It was a "thinly disguised programme of extermination through assimilation" according to Harold Cardinal's *The Unjust Society.* As president of the Indian Association of Alberta, he demanded treaty-based inclusion and rejected both separatism and the "Uncle Tomahawks'" integration on White People's terms.[640] A general debate about policies ensued and three co-operative research and impact-assessment projects were undertaken in the next decades: McGill University's Program in Anthropology and Development presented a study on the impact of rapid technological change (Norman Chance et al.), the impact of the James Bay hydroelectric development was assessed (Richard Salisbury et al.), and Justice Thomas Berger held hearings on the Mackenzie Valley Pipeline project.[641] When the *Report* of the Royal Commission on Aboriginal Peoples (RCAP) had also been published in 1996, Alan Cairns suggested a Canadian Studies project to reactivate the "citizen plus" concept to counter the "termination of federal services" ideas circulating in the bureaucracy as well as the public and administrative disregard for Native peoples.[642]

Social scientists in anthropology, law, cultural studies, and other fields have been slow in bridging the distance between the Euro-Canadian Self and the Native-Canadian Other. As Olive Dickason noted:

> The rise of states has inexorably led to the subordination of non-state societies, usually resulting in their disappearance or their incorporation to a greater or lesser degree into the

---

640 : Harry B. Hawthorn, *A Survey of the Contemporary Indians of Canada*, 2 vols. (Ottawa: Indian Affairs Branch, 1966–67), cited as *Hawthorne Report*; "White Paper" = *A Statement of the Government of Canada on Indian Policy* (Ottawa: Queen's Printer, 1969); Harold Cardinal, *The Unjust Society: The Tragedy of Canada's Indians* (Edmonton: Hurtig, 1969).

641 : Norman Chance, *Developmental Change among the Cree Indians of Quebec* (Ottawa: Queen's Printer, 1970); Richard Salisbury, *A Homeland for the Cree: Regional Development in James Bay, 1971–1981* (Kingston: MQUP, 1986); Thomas Berger, *Northern Frontier, Northern Homeland: The Report of the Mackenzie Valley Inquiry* (Ottawa: Supply and Services, 1977), cited as *Berger-Report.*

642 : Royal Commission on Aboriginal Peoples (RCAP), co-chairs René Dussault and George Erasmus, *Final Report*, 5 vols. (Ottawa, 1996), cited as *RCAP, Report*; Alan C. Cairns, *Citizens Plus: Aboriginal Peoples and the Canadian State* (Vancouver: UBC Press, 2000); Ken Coates, "Writing First Nations into Canadian History: A Review of Recent Scholarly Works," *Canadian Historical Review* 81 (2000), 99–114. Since then, applied research assumed new dimensions, whether pursuing advocacy approaches sympathetic to First Peoples or keep-things-as-they-are ideas of the bureaucracy.

dominant group. Non-state societies had once been in a position to live and let live because of their ability to fragment; but that asset proved to be a fatal liability in the face of the agglomerative tendencies of institutional and territorial states.

The discourses to construct *The White Man's Indian* in the United States have been explicated by Robert F. Berkhofer, and in Canada by Cornelius Jaenen, Olive P. Dickason, and François-Marc Gagnon. They attempted to narrate First Peoples' spirituality, perceptions, customs, and everyday lives in terms of indigenous frames of reference. This ethnosemantic approach, which requires fluency in the languages of the people studied, accepts oral traditions as a source. In a parallel, unrelated development, sociologists and anthropologists in France looked at Western cultures' discourses, symbolic expressions, and patterns of meaning behind the surface of words (Foucault 1966, Bourdieu, and others). While the French work is widely accepted as critical discourse theory, White scholars and judges still debate the accuracy of the oral narratives of First Peoples (or Western lower classes and White women).[643]

As early as 1974, Cornelius J. Jaenen questioned the direction of scholars' gaze by looking at Nouvelle-France through the eyes of Native peoples. First Peoples appropriated "technologies" such as iron knives, needles, and pots; they were impressed by the highly developed French ceremonial and ritual practices; and they admired the French for taking care of Native old and sick people left behind by their kin. They would not understand French concepts of personal property and noticed the low morals of French men when approaching Native women. If the French were as rich as they claimed, why were some of them poor and why could poor people not simply take what they needed? If France was the paradise the newcomers described, why did they leave? If they wanted Native people to send their children to missionary schools, why did they not offer reciprocity by sending French children to learn in Native societies? Why did parents hand children to nursemaids? Why were offenders punished but their victims not comforted? Why were French standards of personal hygiene so low? The empirical data First

---

643 : Berkhofer, Jr., *The White Man's Indian: Images of the American Indian from Columbus to the Present* (New York: Vintage, 1979). Jaenen, *Friend and Foe: Aspects of French-Amerindian Cultural Contact in the Sixteenth and Seventeenth Centuries* (New York: Columbia Univ. Press, 1974); Gagnon, *Ces Hommes dit Sauvages: L'histoire fascinante d'un préjugé qui remonte aux premiers découvreurs du Canada* (Montreal: Libre Expression, 1984); Dickason, *The Myth of the Savage* (1984), quote p. 278. See also Michael Behiels, ed., "Futures and Identities: Aboriginal Peoples in Canada," *Canadian Issues* 21 (1999): 14-22, and Kenneth Coates, "Being Aboriginal," ibid., 23–41.

Peoples had about Second Peoples indicated that some exchange was useful but that in other respects keeping a distance was healthy.[644]

Scholars re-evaluated the arrival of Europeans and their invasion of Native peoples' lands at the Atlantic coast as well as the subjugation of the Plains Cree from the early seventeenth- to the mid-nineteenth century.[645] "Encapsulation" of resident societies by more numerous and powerful newcomers was analyzed worldwide, and world systems approaches were applied to First Peoples.[646] Women scholars studied Native women's roles in an intercultural exchange. By forming partnerships with traders of European background they negotiated between cultures, and accommodated different belief and trading systems as well as patterns of everyday life. They provided the newcomers with access to trading networks, and resident peoples with access to larger markets. "Tender ties" emerged, until White Christian missionaries gained control of naming, and otherized Native women as slovenly and sexually accessible "squaws." In the late twentieth century, Native women criticized paternalist Native chiefs as well as the lack of legal protection for Native women in Euro-Canada's laws.[647]

While it is well known that European and Aboriginal approaches to historical time and memory differ, few Native historians have been hired into academia. Daniel N. Paul has presented *A Mi'kmaq Perspective on the Collision between European and Native American Civilizations* and the RCAP *Report* contrasted Western historians' "sense of distance" to processes they

---

644 : Jaenen, "Amerindian Views of French Culture in the Seventeenth Century," *Canadian Historical Review* 55 (1974): 261–91; Denys Delâge, *Le pays renversé: Amérindians et Européens en Amérique du nord-est 1600-1664* (Montreal: Boréal, 1985); Leslie F.S. Upton, *Micmacs and Colonists: White-Indian Relations in the Maritimes, 1713-1867* (Vancouver: UBC Press, 1979); John W. Grant, *Moon of Wintertime: Missionaries and the Indians of Canada in Encounter since 1534* (Toronto: UTP, 1984).

645 : Francis Jennings, *The Invasion of America: Indians, Colonialism, and the Cant of Conquest* (Chapel Hill: Univ. of N.C. Press, 1975); Bruce G. Trigger, *Natives and Newcomers: Canada's 'Heroic Age' Reconsidered* (Montreal: MQUP, 1985); John L. Tobias, "Canada's Subjugation of the Plains Cree, 1879-1885," *Canadian Historical Review* 64 (1983): 519–48.

646 : Eric Wolf, *Europe and the People without History* (Berkeley: Univ. of California Press, 1982); Richard White, *The Roots of Dependency: Subsistence, Environment, and Social Change among the Choctaw, Pawnees, and Navajos* (Lincoln: Nebraska Univ. Press, 1983).

647 : Sylvia Van Kirk, *"Many Tender Ties": Women in Fur Trade Society in Western Canada, 1670-1870* (Winnipeg: Watson, 1980), and Van Kirk, *Towards a Feminist Perspective in Native History* (Toronto: OISE, 1987); Jennifer S.H. Brown, *Strangers in Blood: Fur Trade Company Families in Indian Country* (Vancouver: UBC Press, 1980); Adele Perry, *On the Edge of Empire: Gender, Race, and the Making of British Columbia, 1849-1871* (Toronto: UTP, 2000); Mary Two Axe Earley in Danielle Juteau-Lee and Barbara Roberts, eds., "Ethnicity and Femininity," topical issue of *Canadian Ethnic Studies* 13.1 (1981): 37-38.

study with an Aboriginal "sense of immediacy." A historian at his desk may have more distance to his prospective audience than a storyteller in front of attentive listeners.[648] But climates of opinion—as during the Cold War, for example, with its threats of dismissal for dissenting university teachers— impressed immediacy on "Western" academics. An appreciative audience, reflected in high sales of their books, may also influence their narratives. Academics have been and are much closer to their topics and to the economic, social, and political world around them than they like to admit.

N. Ross Crumaine and Marjorie M. Halpin's *The Power of Symbols* and many other studies applied the Native and European concepts of symbolic representation to First Peoples' arts, orality, religions, and everyday practices. Julie Cruikshank, who lived with three female Yukon elders for several years, in her sensitive study described how she would ask questions as an anthropologist with her research interests in mind. Rather than provide an answer, the elders would respond with a story, "consciously providing me with a kind of cultural scaffolding, the broad framework I needed to learn before I could begin to ask intelligent questions." Researchers need "to become familiar with the pivotal narratives 'everybody knows'." Cruikshank came to reject the scholar-respondent hierarchy and observed how the elders "kept redirecting our work away from secular history and toward stories about how the world began and was transformed to be suitable for human beings." Scholars need to be aware that through childhood socialization they are deeply embedded in Christian or other mythologies about the origins of the world, and phrase their hypotheses accordingly.[649]

Issues of memory and voice are common to all cultures. If people tell stories and engage in rituals, what cosmology, customs, and traditions shape memory? The pompous rituals of monarchy, the purifying dances of shamans, the ceremonial parades during state visits, the rules to be observed in passage from childhood to puberty, all have meanings not accessible to cultural outsiders, and, due to transmission of encoded memory over generations, sometimes not even to insiders. Memory as reflected in oral history, the Royal Commission on Aboriginal peoples noted, is "facts enmeshed in the stories of a lifetime." So are Euro-Canadian life writings, in which people reflect on their lives and attempt to make sense out of disjuncture or conjuncture and to devise a communication strategy that will reach their

648 : Paul, *We Were Not the Savages* (1993, 2000); *RCAP, Report* (1996), 1:33.

649 : N. Ross Crumaine and Marjorie M. Halpin, *The Power of Symbols: Masks and Masquerade in the Americas* (Vancouver: UBC Press, 1983); Cruikshank, *The Social Life of Stories* (1998), quote p. 27, 46. See also Jennifer S.H. Brown and Elizabeth Vibert, eds., *Reading Beyond Words: Contexts for Native History* (Peterborough, ON: Broadview, 1996). Michel de Certeau, *The Practice of Everyday Life*, transl. from the French original, *Arts de faire*, by Stephen Rendall (Berkeley: Univ. of California Press, 1984).

addressees. And so is national collective memory as reflected in historians' narratives.[650]

Just as Euro-Canadian gatekeepers felt threatened by new narratives that undercut their control over society's self-views, First Nations elders fear losing the power to influence lives or their private meanings if they share their stories with outsiders. While control over family-wide stories may be legitimate, unless some members are shortchanged, control of society-wide stories, given the multiple social groups involved, appropriates voice without legitimization. If rewriting a story of First Peoples to fit a particular—for example a Euro-Canadian—cosmology is considered acceptable, then rewriting the Bible in terms of Aboriginal people's cosmology must also be acceptable. The issue of voice is many-layered. Who may speak for whom? Who has the power to speak for "someone" else regardless of the feelings of the "someone"? Narrators of the master narrative often have the power to take away other peoples' languages.[651] Mi'kmaq poet Rita Joe noted:

> I lost my talk
> The talk you took away.
> When I was a little girl
> At Shubenacadie school.
>
> You snatched it away:
> I speak like you
> I think like you
> I create like you
> The scrambled ballad, about my world.
>
> Two ways I talk
> Both ways I say,
> Your way is more powerful.
> So gently I offer my hand and ask,
> Let me find my talk
> So I can teach you about me.[652]

---

650 : *RCAP, Report* (1996), 1:32–42, quote p.33; Dirk Hoerder, *Creating Societies* (1999), 15–23.

651 : Robert Bringhurst's *A Story as Sharp as a Knife: The Classical Haida Mythtellers and Their Worlds* (Vancouver: Douglas & McIntyre, 1999) sparked a bitter reaction from some of the Haida, though a century ago a storyteller had told the stories to one of the collectors for Boas and they had been transcribed with unusual accuracy. See comment by Mark Abley, *Times Literary Supplement*, 5 May 2000.

652 : Rita Joe, cited in *RCAP Report*, 3:603. For Mexican Americans Maya Angelou in her poem "Equality" expressed the same experience: "You declare to see me dimly.../ Though I stand before you boldly," in *I Shall Not be Moved* (New York: Random House,

Redefining ethnocultural belonging
and transcultural identities

While the Massey Commission intended to decentre Britain, it did not plan to decentre British- and French-Canadian cultures. It saw no role for a cultural "third force," for those segregated as "other ethnics." A decade and a half later, the Bilingualism and Biculturalism Commission's terms of reference also referred only to the two hegemonic groups. During its hearings, those Canadians who had not been totally excluded but had been specialized into the category "allophones," with the Ukrainian-Canadian organizations as a spearhead, articulated their belonging and demanded space for their cultural expressions. In the 1960s climate of opinion, the Commission hired sociologist Jean Burnet to provide information on Canada's peoples as a whole and on their full range of diversity. Aware of the narrowing of perspectives from the 1920s Study of Canada to a British-/French-Canadian master narrative, Burnet initiated a massive research effort, and as a social scientist effected the inclusion of literature, poetry, and the arts into the agenda of cultural studies / studies of ethnic cultures. The originally unplanned but subsequently most famous fourth volume of the *Report* synthesized scholarship on the "other ethnics," a term adopted from the census categories English-French-Other, which was neither theoretically supported nor meant as oppositional. In reaction to this culturally inclusive report and to self-organization of both "ethnics" and "First Nations," the dominant groups' gatekeepers began to redefine these as "founding nations," a term that had first appeared in the late 1940s.[653]

A second important change involved the reconceptualization of immigration policies. More than twenty years after Canadian diplomats had been instrumental in having discrimination by race and ethnicity proscribed in the Charter of the United Nations, the government opted for a culturally neutral points system with family sponsorship clauses. Exclusion of immigrants

---

1990). A few historians have attempted to let people speak for themselves through their lifewritings, among others Rolf Knight and Barry Broadfoot by collecting them, Dirk Hoerder by fashioning a Canadian narrative from them, and Gerald Friesen by suggesting that texts of peoples' lives and the ways in which they are told as well as the media used establish a framework for citizenship and for Canada.

653 : Royal Commission on Bilingualism and Biculturalism, *Report*, 4 vols. (Ottawa: Queen's Printer, 1967-70), Book 4: "The Cultural Contribution of the Other Ethnic Groups" (1970). Interview with Jean Burnet, 9 Nov. 2000. In the Commission's research department, director Michael Oliver attempted to limit data collection to the hegemonic groups. Evelyn Kallen, *Ethnicity and Human Rights in Canada* (2nd ed., Toronto: Oxford, 1995); Dirk Hoerder, "Ethnic Studies in Canada from the 1880s to 1962: A Historiographical Perspective and Critique," *Canadian Ethnic Studies* 26.1 (1994): 1–18.

from cultures other than European had been reduced step by step: of Chinese in the late 1940s, of Japanese subsequently, and of "coloured" West Indians when labour demand in domestic service and in caretaking was reflected in a quota for women in the context of the British Empire-turned-Commonwealth. It was expanded later to women from the Philippines, other Southeast Asian societies, and from Latin America, in the context of global disparities in standards of living. The Progressive Conservative government's 1960 Bill of Rights revised Liberal Prime Minister Mackenzie King's 1947 discriminatory preference for immigration from Europe. The points system's elitist aspects—high points for high educational levels—which according to some gatekeepers' secret hopes would still favour immigrants from Europe, were balanced by the possibility of bringing in family members without regard to education and skills and, to a lesser degree, by Canada's commitment to re-settle refugees. High educational attainment, unbeknownst to advocates of a "White Canada," was also a characteristic of many Asian and Latin American middle classes.

The new attention to the many cultures required public display in order to achieve general acceptance in society's discourses. In a first step, "ethnic culture" was appended to the Massey Commission's high culture as folk culture. Following a prototype of public display—the "Folklorama" held in Winnipeg since Manitoba's centennial in 1970—other provinces have supported ethnic and Native folk expressions. This maintained the hierarchization of high and folksy versions of culture, and was perhaps also a reaction to the mass-produced culture of the U.S. and Canadian capitalist economies. In a second stage, the Trudeau government's 1971 policy of multiculturalism on a bilingual basis privileged the two official languages, but considered cultures as equal. The policy that institutionalized modern Canadian cultural self-representations has been criticized as denigrating Quebec culture to one of several ethnic cultures, as placing "ethnics" in unchangeable slots, and as fragmenting Canadian society. From its intentions, it merely removed the pedestal from under British- and French-Canadian self-aggrandizement. There was no reason why Italians in Montreal, Ukrainians in Toronto, Chinese in Vancouver, African Caribbeans, or any other group should consider their culture inferior. In *Citizens and Nation*, Gerald Friesen suggests that the "everyday history" of "everyday Canadians," their agency and creativity, is "a crucial strength of Canada" and results in "the nation."[654]

The goals of the policy on "multiculturalism in a bilingual framework" emphasized integration and cultural communication. The government of-

---

654 : Gerald Friesen, *Citizens and Nation: An Essay on History, Communication, and Canada* (Toronto: UTP, 2000), quote p. 228.

fered: (1) support for those cultural groups "that have demonstrated a desire and effort to continue to develop, a capacity to grow and contribute to Canada"; (2) measures to "assist members of all cultural groups to overcome cultural barriers to full participation in Canadian society"; (3) programs to "promote creative encounters and interchange among all Canadian cultural groups in the interests of national unity"; and (4) programs to "assist immigrants to acquire at least one of Canada's official languages."[655] The policy's dynamism emerged from the emphasis on interactive cultural processes, respect for plural identities, and help to achieve full participation. Its reference point was Canadian society as a whole. The policy was deeply humanistic in taking human cultural identities as valid constructs and in considering diversity as an increment of socio-cultural options. For groups with a long presence in Canada and the concomitant Canadianization over generations, cultural expressions such as artifacts, folk dances, and ceremonially revived foodways had become "symbolic" or visible. Such "symbolic" expressions insert subordinated cultures into hegemonies, but do not change actual lifeways or express "foreign" patterns of belonging. On this level, Folklorama-type celebrations served as focuses. For recently arrived individuals and ethnocultural groups, who still lived pre-migration or even ancestral ways, the policy of multiculturalism meant liberation from subaltern status and from the pressure to assimilate unconditionally.

Criticism of the policy centered on the alleged shallowness of folk art and on the divisiveness of cultural plurality. However, the colourful beauty of embroidered dresses or painted Easter eggs appears as superficial only to those who have not learned to decipher the complex Christian spiritual coding of the eggs and the social status and celebratory connotations of the dresses. Furthermore, if colourful fall foliage as painted by the Group of Seven turns national symbol, there is no reason to denigrate other colourful human artifacts. Furthermore, the message of symbols is more easily accessible than complex literary expression of, for example, a Michael Ondaatje or Margaret Atwood. As to divisiveness, British and French Canadian gatekeepers' fears of a fragmentation of national cultures were reinforced by fears of the gatekeepers of ethnic cultures that the policy of cultural interaction would make boundaries between ethnocultural groups permeable. Their advocacy of cultural retention involved economic interest. Ethnocultural producers and mediators—journalists, teachers, functionaries, and priests or pastors— as well as owners of small businesses catering exclusively to the tastes of

---

655 : Announcement of Implementation of Policy of Multiculturalism within Bilingual Framework. Canada, *House of Commons Debates* (8 Oct. 1971), p. 8545–48, 8580–85. The federal *Multiculturalism Act* was passed in 1988.

their group can earn a living only if "defections" from the group are discouraged, if hybridity is prevented. For every traditionalist who lamented the decline of a nation there was a traditionalist who lamented the decline of an ethnicity. Paradoxically, a common chorus line emerged. Interest-driven ethnocultural *enclavement* undercut the policy's integrative goals.[656]

Many scholars experienced the new perception of culture as a challenge. Parallel to the Bilingualism and Biculturalism Commission's researchers, John Porter studied economic stratification and found a "vertical mosaic." Though ethnic occupational differentiation had declined from 1931 to 1961, the longest-settled groups still commanded positions above all others. Canada's democratic structures were class-based and provided unequal access to power. Subsequent research modified Porter's findings, and recent economic growth through immigration and newcomers' innovations resulted in a comparatively dynamic society in which skilled and professional immigrants may reach the average national income within a decade.[657] In addition, U.S. and Canadian scholars began a transborder co-operation. In Canada, policy-making was more innovative, in the 1960s U.S. scholarship was more advanced, and young academics crossed the border in both directions. Since, in contrast to U.S. immigration history, British and French Canadian scholars had not deemed the "other ethnics" worthy of attention, no entrenched positions existed at Canadian universities. In contrast to the Americanization of the social sciences, in Ethnic Studies questions and hypotheses emerged from Canadian discourses and were studied in Canadian contexts with Canadian data. Canadian-born researchers, such as Raymond Breton, Danielle Juteau, Cornelius Jaenen, and Howard and Tamara Palmer, and U.S.-born scholars, such as Robert Harney, Warren and Madelaine Kalbach, Nathan Keyfitz, Wsevolod Isajiw, and Jeffrey Reitz forged ahead of U.S. methodologies and theories.

---

656 : Alan B. Anderson and James S. Frideres, *Ethnicity in Canada: Theoretical Perspectives* (Toronto: Butterworth, 1981); Raymond Breton, Wsevolod W. Isajiw, Warren E. Kalbach, Jeffrey G. Reitz, *Ethnic Identity and Equality: Varieties of Experience in a Canadian City* (Toronto: UTP, 1990); Wsevolod W. Isajiw, ed., *Multiculturalism in North America and Europe: Comparative Perspectives on Interethnic Relations and Social Incorporation* (Toronto: Canadian Scholar's Press, 1997); Friesen, *Citizens and Nation*; Wsevolod W. Isajiw, *Understanding Diversity: Ethnicity and Race in the Canadian Context* (Toronto: Thompson, 1999).

657 : John Porter, *The Vertical Mosaic: An Analysis of Social Class and Power in Canada* (Toronto: UTP, 1965); A. Gordon Darroch, "Another Look at Ethnicity, Stratification and Social Mobility in Canada," *Canadian Journal of Sociology* 4 (1979): 1–25; David Ley and Heather Smith, "Immigration and Poverty in Canadian Cities, 1971–1991," *Canadian Journal of Regional Science* 30 (1997): 29–48. See also Vic Satzewich, *Racism and the Incorporation of Foreign Labour: Farm Labour Migration to Canada since 1945* (London: Routledge, 1991).

This vibrant young group of researchers faced scholarly associations dominated by older colleagues. The Inter-University Committee on Canadian Slavs (IUCCS), a respectable as well as insurgent group with a tradition of opposing the British-colonial tradition, had achieved academic recognition and even political status in the late 1960s. In 1973, the young insurgents transformed the IUCCS into the Canadian Ethnic Studies Association (CESA). Their mimeographed Calgary-based publication, still busy with making bibliographic information on ethnic groups accessible to students, became the well-renowned journal *Canadian Ethnic Studies*. In the gendered social conventions of the time, the wife of one of the insurgent-innovators—holding a natural sciences degree but no job, since she cared for the children—in her "spare time" created CESA's logo. The Association's U.S. equivalent, the Immigration and Ethnic History Society, remained Atlanto-centric.[658] Canadian ethnic and multicultural studies achieved worldwide leadership, due in part to the transnational composition of the scholars. Robert Harney established the Multicultural History Society of Ontario with its journal *Polyphony* (1978); Howard Palmer discussed the de-centering of mono- or biculturalism by immigration; Danielle Juteau analyzed the relations and interactions between groups and their self-creation; Tamara Palmer expanded Canadian literatures to include the many-cultured publications of Prairie-centered authors. Jointly they developed the then-innovative "impact of ethnicity on Canadian society" approach (W. Isajiw).[659] Canadian ethnic research became Transcultural Societal Studies before the term was ever discussed.

Recognition of ethnocultural diversity induced the federal government to sponsor "ethnic chairs" at universities, whose appointees were to devote their research to particular cultural groups in order to expand the Canadian narrative. The program, centered on groups of European background, was terminated before cultural groups from Asia, the Caribbean, Africa, or

---

658 : Interview with Wsevolod and Christina Isajiw, 19 Aug. 2002. See *Journal of American Ethnic History* for U.S. developments.

659 : Howard Palmer, *Immigration and the Rise of Multiculturalism* (Toronto: Copp Clark, 1975); Danielle Juteau-Lee, ed., *Frontières ethniques en devenir / Emerging Ethnic Boundaries* (Ottawa: Éd. de l'Université d'Ottawa, 1979), esp. 1–19; Tamara Palmer, "Ethnic Character and Social Themes in Novels about Prairie Canada in the Period from 1900 to 1940" (MA thesis, York Univ., 1972), and Tamara Palmer Seiler, "Multi-Vocality and National Literature: Toward a Post-Colonial and Multicultural Aesthetic," *Journal of Canadian Studies* 31.3 (Fall 1996): 148–65; Cornelius Jaenen, "Ethnic Studies: An Integral Part of Canadian Studies," in Isajiw, *Identities*, esp. xi; Dirk Hoerder, "German-Speaking Immigrants [in Canada]: Co-Founders or Mosaic? A Research Note on Politics and Statistics in Scholarship," *Zeitschrift für Kanadastudien* 14.2 (1994): 51–65.

Latin America received equal support.[660] In a way, this belated recognition came too late. By this time, scholars considered boundaries between groups as constructed. Upon analysis, such lines dissolved into borderlands. Pointedly, funding for boundary-reinforcing "ethnic chairs" came when multicultural and interactive metropoles needed attention. Two decades later, Citizenship and Immigration Canada conceived (1994) and funded (1996) the Metropolis Project on migration, diversity, and changing cities. Academic researchers responded and the project received international acclaim. The research philosophy of the project's initiator, Meyer Burstein, called for interagency and governmental co-operation to develop successful migration and integration policies, for academic research, and for input from NGOs, the private sector, and the public at large.

The ethno-immigrant identities, like the two ethno-national ones, that allegedly divided Canadian society into many segments have been considered essentialist and were said to have been transported to Canada in the process of migration. However, nineteenth-century and later migrants departed their lands of origin with regional belongings: Chinese came from one of the Empire's southern regions; German speakers left as Swabians, Hessians, or Mecklenburgers; Irish with different religious-regional-cultural affiliations. Settling in an urban or a rural community, they lived among neighbours who had limited geographical and societal categories available to position them, who could not deal with sub-national diversity. Thus, a process of construction of ethnic identities began as part of communication between groups in Canada. Neighbours as well as bureaucrats labelled the newcomers according to polity of background: Chinese, German, British, Japanese, Syrian, or other. The regionally grounded immigrants realized the value of such labels when entering politics. In voting there was advantage in numbers. Thus the multitude of groups of regional origin reconstructed themselves as sizable groups of national origin.[661] The emergence of ethnic

---

660 : In 2003, three Chairs dealt with Gaelic, Celtic, and Irish, and nine Chairs with other European cultures, two with Jewish Studies. For Africa only one Chair existed; for Asia three Chairs devoted to South Asian cultures. Another ten Chairs dealt with ethnic relations and specific aspects of ethnic culture in Canada; one Chair was devoted to Native Studies.

661 : Dirk Hoerder and Inge Blank, "Ethnic and National Consciousness from the Enlightenment to the 1880s," in Hoerder et al., eds., *Roots of the Transplanted,* 2 vols. (Boulder: East European Monographs, 1994), 1:37–110; Hoerder, "From Migrants to Ethnics: Acculturation in a Societal Framework," in Hoerder and Leslie P. Moch, eds., *European Migrants: Global and Local Perspectives* (Boston: Northeastern Univ. Press, 1996), 211–262; Hoerder, "Labour Markets - Community - Family: A Gendered Analysis of the Process of Insertion and Acculturation," in Isajiw, *Multiculturalism in North America and Europe,* 155–83.

identity is influenced and circumscribed by the receiving society. Religion also played a role: German and Irish newcomers, for example, formed two distinct groups each, one Catholic, one Protestant. Racial thought segregated some: in the case of the Jewish faith, religion was often constructed as "racial" difference. Combined with geographic distance, racialization resulted in macro-groups. While newcomers from Europe were categorized by nation of origin, newcomers from Asia were often summarily labelled as "Oriental" or "Asiatic" races. The combination of national origin and ethnic enclave simplifies cultural markers. Such simplifications were important to quantifying scholars: the replication of the "ethnics'" (self-) ascriptions in the census questionnaires simplified complex life stories.[662] Simplification may skew data; simplification is also needed to cope with complex embedded lives and to transmit complex collective memories.

Embedded lives is a term different from *part of a group*, which assumes that the group is bordered. In his study of "a border within," Ian Angus assumes an "us" as an ethnocultural group and a "we" as a civic nationalism of the whole society. But cultural groups may also be defined by gender, a specific period's socialization experience, or a stage in the lifecycle (such as adolescence) or other conditions. Individuals have different group affiliations at the same time; borders are "fuzzy" as the British sociologist Robin Cohen put it. It is neither an Anglo nor a Franco nor an "ethnic" way of life that is "threatened" as some people feel, because these ways of life are always transitory. Canada, tied together by rails, was the work of many-cultured "ethnic" work gangs; Toronto's present shape is the work of Italian and Portuguese construction workers; Montreal's francophone community is not only *vieille souche* but also Haitian. "Embeddedness" permits support and flexibility; group constructions may permit sheltered space but as structure, like the steel girders of a high-rise, cannot bend to new exigencies—change may come through expert restructuring or through a wrecking crew. People as agents in or of their own lives usually prefer flexibility; as citizens they look for options for civic participation.[663]

---

662 : Gordon E. Priest, *Ethnicity in the Canadian Census* (Toronto: U of T, Dept. of Sociology, 1990); Monica Boyd, *Measuring Ethnicity: The Roles of People, Policies and Politics and Social Science Research* (Toronto: U of T, Dept. of Sociology, Feb. 1994); "Ethnicity in the Canadian Census," thematic issue of *Canadian Ethnic Studies* 35.1 (2003): 1–170, esp. essays by Richard Y. Bourhis, "Measuring Ethnocultural Diversity Using the Census," 9–32, and Madeleine Kalbach, "The Intergenerational Transfer of Ethnic Identity in Canada at the Turn of the Twenty-First Century," 135–48.

663 : Ian Angus, *A Border Within: National Identity, Cultural Plurality, and Wilderness* (Montreal: MQUP, 1997), 135–69; Robin Cohen, "Fuzzy Frontiers of Identity: The British Case," *Social Identities* 1 (1995): 35–62; Metropolis Project and Multicultural-

Decentering hegemonies: The humanities as discourse-centered societal sciences

Social and historical categories as the basis of societies' scholarly, literary, political, and popular narratives are shifting complexes of social meanings that vary from one social space to another, and are constantly being transformed by political contact and conflict, published and everyday discourse, and everyday practices. "National identity" is one such category and when, from the 1960s on, it began to expand from privileging British- and French-Canadian to more inclusiveness, the traditional beneficiaries of the narrow meaning attempted to buttress their claims by the designation "founding nations." To use modern imagery, while the gatekeepers tried to format the minds of all members of society without ever giving them access to the source code, those excluded had been aware that for their distinct historical memory no plug-ins were provided and they were left to work with shareware. For decades, subaltern groups had posited their claims for participation in narrative-construction as well as for access to society's resources. Before the 1920s, women and workers added their alternative, supplementary, or counter-narratives, and from the 1930s, "ethnics," "visible minorities," "Indians," and Inuit did so. People, aware of their agency, wanted to count—*se voulaient rendre compte*—and wanted to account for what they had contributed and achieved or to understand why intentions had not been realized, options not taken.

Stories are complex. The story of European societies, from where the ancestors of the "founding nations" and the "other ethnics" came, was said to be one of nation-states and thus the concept of national and ethnocultural groups seemed self-evident. It is the function of hegemonic discourses, of the masters of the narrative, to construct and implant stories as "self-evident" in order to prevent questioning and critique. However, the past-oriented social sciences inform us that the European immigrants to Canada, from the early Basque fishermen to post-1945 wartime displaced men and women, came from mixed cultures with a rich heritage of diversity. Stories may be wealth, as Tagish elder Angela Sidney told Julie Cruikshank. They may be a

---

ism Canada, *Immigrants and Civic Participation: Contemporary Policy and Research Issues* (mimeographed, Montreal: Canadian Heritage, 1997), with papers by Raymond Breton, Davia Stasiulis, James S. Frideres, Michel Pagé, Denise Helly; France Gagnon and Michel Pagé, *Conceptual Framework for an Analysis of Citizenship in the Liberal Democracies* (mimeographed, Ottawa: Multiculturalism Directorate, 1999); Alan Sears, "In Search of Good Citizens: Citizenship Education and Social Studies in Canada," in Sears and Ian Wright, eds., *Challenges and Prospects for Canadian Social Studies* (Vancouver: Pacific Educational Press, 2004), 90–106.

suffocating burden if cast as narrow nationalist renderings of European and Canadian history. The discourses of the 1960s and the concomitant scholarship came out of both struggles and changed everyday practices rather than out of scholars' re-analyses. The social sciences, historiography, and the humanities—which I prefer to call the past-oriented, present-oriented, and discourse-centered Societal Sciences—are intricately linked, and the norm-providing discourses of religion, ethics, and law are integral to them. George Woodcock pointed to the relationship and Maria Tippett summarized: "the cultural artifact, like the historical 'event,' is shaped both by circumstance and the intention of its creator, and . . . is received, interpreted, and made functional in a society at a given point in time in ways largely determined by the political, economic, social, and institutional framework of that society." Cultural artifacts are as much the creation of the respective authors/artists as of the readers at a certain point in time.

Historians, social scientists, poets, painters, novelists, and other cultural producers such as dramatists, choreographers, and filmmakers afford insights into hidden dreams and urges, aspirations and potential directions of a society and of individual women and men as well as young and old. Since the 1960s, scholars in the data- and discourse-based sciences, with input from British neo-Marxist, American empiricist, and French *Annales* approaches as well as from discourse-theory, provided detailed studies as elements for a new integrative narrative. While scholars collect, accumulate, categorize, and interpret data, writers of the many literatures as well as performing and decorative artists may take any issue, historical memory, questions of human existence, hopes, dreams or strategies for life courses, and a society's future as starting point for a narrative, for reflection, for exploring options. They imagine possible—or even impossible—outcomes and thus engage in what everyman, everywoman, and everychild does: imagine what might be, what should be, re-imagine what happened.[664]

The British-Canadian narrative (or ideology) on the surface seemed strong, even over-powering. But, empirically, the group was fluid and its

664 : Cruikshank, *The Social Life of Stories* (1998), 27–46; Maria Tippett, "The Writing of English-Canadian Cultural History, 1970–85," *Canadian Historical Review* 67 (1986): 548–61, quote p. 549; George Woodcock, "The Meeting of the Muses: Recent Canadian Fiction and the Historical Viewpoint," *Canadian Historical Review* 60 (1979): 141–53; Dennis Duffy, "George Woodcock: Voyager of Liberty," *Canadian Literature* 83 (Winter 1979): 156–62; Mary Vipond, "The Nationalist Network: English-Canada's Intellectuals and Artists in the 1920s," *Canadian Review of Studies in Nationalism* 8.1 (1980): 32–52; Brown and Vibert, *Reading Beyond Words*; Paul Audley, *Canada's Cultural Industries: Broadcasting, Publishing, Records and Film* (Ottawa: Canadian Institute for Economic Policy, 1983); Kay Armatage et al., eds., *Gendering the Nation: Canadian Women's Cinema* (Toronto: UTP, 1999).

hold on the federal government negotiable. British Canadians, rather than consisting of a small group of ancestral founders, accommodated a continuous stream of newcomers from the four cultures of the North Sea isles. This heterogeneity did not fit the gatekeepers' storyline and thus it hardly ever entered public debate. Setting themselves off from the British Canadian imperialists of the early 1900s, the British-trained Ottawa men preferred compromise. Furthermore, it is symptomatic that the two statesmen who became symbols for Canada as a whole, Laurier and Trudeau, were not Ontarians but perfectly bilingual French Canadian Montrealers. The replacement of British by Canadian citizenship in 1947 and the addition of the category "Canadian" in the 1951 census provided Canadianness with an officially recognized slot in the discourse.[665] Finally, Anglo-Canada through British, U.S., Caribbean, imperial and other "Englishes," was larger than either Canada's boundaries or the concept "of British background" indicated. The common language permitted multiple discursive and cultural input, permitted mixing and hybridity. The 1960s music culture of young anglophones (and others) comprised the lower-class Beatles, Jimi Hendrix, and other Jamaican and West Indies influences among many others. Since the sixteenth-century voyages of Haklyt, each expansive step had exposed the Empire—and, from first European settlement, Canada with it—to the cultures of those encountered in the newly acquired social spaces though defined as subaltern. As post-colonial theorists noted, "the Empire was writing back." In fact, it was also striking, singing, and migrating back.[666]

While outside influences were important for "British-Canada's" deconstruction, that of "Quebec" began from the inside. Novelists introduced new discourses, some since the early decades of the twentieth century, more since the late 1940s.[667] The liberalization of thought after the end of the

---

665 : Robert Craig Brown, "Full Partnership in the Fortunes and in the Future of the Nation," *Nationalism and Ethnic Politics* (Fall 1995); William Kaplan, ed., *Belonging: The Meaning and Future of Canadian Citizenship* (Montreal: MQUP, 1993), and Kaplan, *The Evolution of Citizenship Legislation in Canada* (Ottawa: Multiculturalism and Citizenship Canada, 1991).

666 : Centre for Contemporary Cultural Studies, *The Empire Strikes Back* (London: Hutchinson, 1982); Bill Ashcroft, Gareth Griffiths, Helen Tiffin, *The Empire Writes Back: Theory and Practice in Post-Colonial Literatures* (London: Routledge, 1989).

667 : See Chapter 9. Roger Lemelin and Manitoba-socialized Gabrielle Roy focused on urban under-classes: Lemelin's *Au pied de la pente douce* (1944, Engl. *The Town Below*) is set in Quebec City's Saint-Sauveur; Roy's *Bonheur d'occasion* (1945, Engl. *The Tin Flute*) in Montreal's poor Saint-Henri neighbourhood. Yves Thériault and André Langevin intended to expose the hypocrisy of hegemonic views. Thériault's *Les vendeurs du temple* (1951) selected parochial piety as the butt of his satire; Langevin in *Poussière sur la ville* (1953, Engl. *Dust over the City*) addressed the human and ecological damage of open-pit

Duplessis government, as well as academic expansion with the establishment of the multi-campus Université de Québec, led to a flowering of new approaches. Since the 1940s, sociologists at Laval and at the Université de Montréal had already questioned the clerics' ruralist paradigm in view of a pluralist society. Laval scholars provided a critical review of the archaic education system in the 1960s. Regarding demography, the French-speaking segment of Quebec's population had become increasingly influential due to its birth rates and to out-migration of English-speakers since the late nineteenth century.[668] The rise in numbers and political influence was not matched by income levels and economic power. Systemic low educational attainment disadvantaged French Quebecers compared to British and immigrant Quebecers. In the '60s, family decisions ended the ideologue-propounded "natalité triomphante" and reduced the province's birth rate to the national average. At the same time, cultural producers were lifting Quebec's artistic and literary output, both in quality and quantity, to above the national average.[669]

Though the new Liberal government's reform program of 1960 appeared as a "Quiet Revolution," Quebecers had quietly slipped out of Church control since the late 1940s. The period, *un âge de l'impatience*, was characterized by *un mouvement de contestation et une affirmation de la modernité*, to use the terms of the time. In fact, the Liberals' reforms seemed not to go far enough in the eyes of many. *Cité Libre* (1950–66), edited by Pierre Elliott Trudeau and Gérard Pelletier, once mindsetting for the Quiet Revolution and concerned with democratic morality, rational humanism, and internationalism, lost readers to the more radical and nationalist *Parti pris* (1963–68), which advocated nationalism in and independence for Quebec, as well as secularism and socialism. A provocative, thoughtful, and yet traditional topical

asbestos mining in Thetford Mines. Roger Duhamel, *Manuel de la littérature canadienne-française* (Montreal: Renouveau pédagogique, 1967); Guy Sylvestre, "La recherche en littérature canadienne-française," in Baudouin, *La recherche au Canada français*, 149–61; Jean-Charles Falardeau, *Imaginaire social et littérature* (Montreal: Hurtubise, 1974).

668 : Ronald Rudin, *The Forgotten Quebecers: A History of English-Speaking Quebec, 1759–1980* (Quebec: Inst. québécois de recherche sur la culture, 1985), transl. by Robert Paré: *Histoire du Québec anglophone 1759–1980* (idem: idem, 1986); Sheila McLeod Arnopoulos and Dominique Clift, *The English Fact in Quebec* (Montreal: MQUP, 1980).

669 : Marcel Rioux, *La question du Québec* (Paris: Éd. Seghers, 1969), transl. by Hames Boake as *Quebec in Question* (Toronto: Lewis & Samuel, 1971), 95; Royal Commission on Bilingualism and Biculturalism, Report, Book 3: "The Work World," 15–24; Paul-E. Gosselin, *La crise de la natalité au Québec* (Quebec: Ferland, 1968), lamented the decline of the birth rate, as British imperialist and Canadian Britishers had done before. James Marchant, *Birthrate and Empire* (London: Williams & Norgate, 1917); W.B. Hurd, "The Decline in the Canadian Birthrate," *CJEPS* 3 (Feb. 1937), 40–57.

issue, "Portrait du colonisé québécois" (Summer 1964), set the stage for a modern version of the Conquest interpretation. The worldwide movement of decolonization became a point of reference, but the *Parti pris* authors also repeated clerical traditions when arguing that French Canada was a colony of British Canada.

Sizable segments of English-speaking Canadians had indeed continued to look down on their French-speaking co-nationals. Liberal René Lévesque, a well-known radio and television commentator, bolted party discipline in 1967 to found the Mouvement souveraineté-association, which in 1968 became the Parti Québécois.[670] Quebec's federal nationalists lost out to separatist or sovereigntist nationalism under the slogan "maîtres chez nous." However, the new ideologues did not care to define the "nous"—where were Native people, "other ethnics," and English-Quebecers? Ironically, at this very juncture, the federal Liberal government under Lester Pearson had come to accept Quebec's special status and from 1963 implemented a "co-operative federalism". The Trudeau government's further compromise, bilingual services in federal institutions, alienated Canada's West, where few French-speakers lived, but did not satisfy Quebec politicians. Then, during his visit in 1967, French President Charles de Gaulle ended a public speech with a ringing "Vive Montréal! Vive Québec! Vive le Québec libre!" His intention remains unclear but, as Canadian diplomats informed their French colleagues, the equivalent would be a ringing "Vive la Bretagne libre!" by the Canadian Prime Minister in France's Brittany.[671]

Three years later, the militant Front de libération du Québec (FLQ, founded 1963) abducted James Cross, the British trade commissioner in Montreal, and Pierre Laporte, the provincial minister of labour and immigration. In the "October Crisis," the Quebec government asked the federal authorities for help and the War Measures Act was invoked against the "apprehended insurrection." In their own pursuit of decolonization, or perhaps extremist version of self-determination, separatists also turned against Frenchness. While educational reform was bringing Quebec's French dialect closer to received metropolitan French and thus to the worldwide, once Empire-created, *francophonie*, one segment of the nationalist elite labelled metropolitan French a foreign import to be replaced by a "québécois standard." This would have impeded communication in this world language. In reaction to the threats of violence, as well as to "French-first" language legislation, businesses and personnel moved to other parts of Canada, in particular to

---

670 : In the early 1960s only the Rassemblement pour l'indépendance national (RIN) had openly advocated separatism.

671 : Information to the author by John Halstead, Canadian ambassador in Germany.

Ontario and Toronto. The colonization/decolonization discourse and politicking had reached Canada, and Quebec in particular, with a vengeance.

Quebec's chauvinists turned the decolonization rhetoric into a quest for both economic enclave status and cultural hegemony over the French-language Americas. In Canada's other provinces a francophone renaissance induced Acadians to revive their culture, New Brunswick to declare itself a bilingual province in 1969, other provincial governments to re-introduce French-language schooling, and Toronto's York University to open its French-language Glendon College. In the Prairie Provinces, Euro-French and French-Métis groups, under bilingualism and multiculturalism, experienced new freedoms from Anglo impositions only to realize that Quebec gatekeepers expected them to take second rank. For these regions' younger generation, "la nature de ce qui leur est proposé en français les laisse souvent indifférents. Les jeunes affirment ne pas s'y reconnaître et évaluent ce qui leur est proposé en français comme étant soit trop ennuyeux, soit trop québécois." Young francophones preferred to tune in to English-language programs: "le français n'est pas une valeur en soi; il se rattache à un univers bilingue qui le marginalise en prétendant lui donner une place de choix.» The perennial Quebec self-commiseration as part of trans-Canadian French-language radio broadcasting alienated francophones in the West.[672]

The Anglo-Franco dichotomy and the Quebec sovereigntist movement are two of the many issues of the politics of nationhood and national identity. From the perspective of the Prairies and British Columbia, Western interests, Chinese as a second language, and Prairie and Pacific economic issues deserved equal attention. When Alberta's oil boom boosted its economy, the political elite also engaged in politics of self-elevation. Pacific commerce in British Columbia and hydroelectricity in northern Quebec's Cree lands established secondary economic centres. From Native Canadians' perspective, treaty-based land rights and the invasion of living and spiritual spaces by

---

672 : Françoise Boudreau, " La francophonie ontarienne au passé, au présent et au futur: un bilan sociologique," in Jacques Cotnam, Yves Frenette, Agnès Whitfield, ed., *La francophonie ontarienne: bilan et perspectives de recherche* (Ottawa: Éd. du Nordir, 1995), 17–51; Roger Bernard, *Le déclin d'une culture: Recherche, analyse et bibliographie: Francophonie hors Québec, 1980–89* (Ottawa: Fédération des jeunes canadiens français, 1990), and Bernard, *Un avenir incertain: Comportements linguistiques et conscience culturelle des jeunes canadiens français* (idem: idem, 1991), quote p. 238; Pierre Bélanger and Réjean Lafrance, "Culture francophone et médias canadiens: mise en perspective des usages," *Cahiers franco-canadiens de l'ouest* 62 (1994), 215–46, quote p. 216; *La Langue, la culture et la société des francophones de l'ouest*. Les actes du troisième colloque du Centre d'études franco-canadiennes de l'ouest tenu au Centre d'Études Bilingues, 1983 (Regina: Univ. of Regina, 1984). From the 1971 to the 1996 (micro) census, francophones in the West numbered roughly 175,000 by mother tongue.

hunters, miners, and engineers stood at the fore. In the Maritimes and New-foundland, technical progress resulted in economic regress since international fishing technology and investment depleted stocks. From the perspective of small-town Canada, whether Newfoundland outports, Ontario rural communities, or settlements in northern British Columbia, progress in medical care and other public amenities, because of the costs involved, resulted in centralization of service delivery and increasing non-viability of service in small —marginal, hinterland?— communities. Since such problems remained regional or specific to social groups, they did not undercut the positivist afflu-ent consumer culture discourse. For the French language, ironically, Quebec's sovereignists had to be told by the Supreme Court to use a French compre-hensible to voters when devising referenda questions. Regarding hegemonies, English-language publishing houses and other cultural production facilities remained centered in Toronto and thus access to published discourse was difficult in the Maritimes, the Prairies, and British Columbia.

The many discourses in and about Canada brought about complex inter-actions between multiple popular cultures, mass-produced radio and TV messages, and local, regional, urban, and rural audiences. Canadian mass communications practice and research differed from British and American practices. In Britain, emphasis on social class or status remained strong; in Canada, diversity was brought to the fore and emissions had to be "sensitive to issues of context and human agency." Electronic media were state-regu-lated in Canada but privately owned and capitalized in the United States. Canadian debate, policy, and research linked technological development with questions of content, while U.S. research was technology- and mar-ket-oriented. Britain and Canada, like France, pursued a policy of radio and television as "public-service institutions" while, except for the few public broadcasting stations, the United States pursued a private-profit approach. Canadian content in the broadcasting of words and images remained skewed by unequal power relationships. In Europe, no similar power in-equalities existed—a fictive comparison would have France broadcast its culture to Britain, a few local stations providing "British folk" culture, or vice versa. Governments in Europe take protection of cultural production to be legitimate, and in Canada the Federal Information Highway Advisory Council (established 1994) listed three policy goals: "creating jobs through innovation and investment in Canada, reinforcing Canadian sovereignty and cultural identity, ensuring universal access at reasonable cost." When the broadcasting system was changed to "two pillars"—public and private— the House of Commons' Standing Committee on Canadian Heritage in 1999 posited "the Canadian model of cultural affirmation. It focuses on the development of a healthy cultural marketplace, freedom of choice for consumers and the principle of access to Canadian cultural materials." Canada as a "country has struggled for its own identity and utilized an active communication policy to preserve national integrity." Its geographic size and particular layout demanded appropriate communication technologies and, in view of fast changing technologies, high potential for innovation. As a result Canada "boasts the most sophisticated transmission hardware in the world—satellites, interactive cable, teletext," the Federal Cultural Policy Review Committee noted in 1982, and still faced the popular culture cross-border impact: "Canadian viewers spend 80 percent of their viewing time watching foreign programs on television.[673] Cultural expression was always a question of numbers: ethnocultural groups, Quebec's *francophonie*, Anglo-Canada, the United States.

In such a hierarchy of quantity and power, Canada's cultural producers had to decide whether to stand together in defence or whether to remain many-faceted. The humanities, as discourse-based science, could long have addressed such issues had they cared for grounded empirical observation and a dependency theory. The Ukrainian Canadian immigrant, who in the early twentieth century had accused the gatekeeper elites of lying when they called Alberta an English rather than a Canadian province, could have inspired humanities' scholars. By the 1970s, Canadian literary and artistic production, or perhaps the literary and artistic production within a polity called Canada, was multi-vocal: a Dionne Brand and a Michael Ondaatje, a Claire Harris and a Neil Bissoondath, a Rohinton Mistry and an M. Nourbese Philip, like earlier writers with names such as Kiriak, Lysenko, Salverson, and Bruser, provided stories and visions that related different cultures to each other,

---

673 : David Crowley and David Mitchell, "Communications in Canada: Enduring Themes, Emerging Issues," in Terry Goldie, Carmen Lambert, Rowland Lorimer, eds., *Canada: Theoretical Discourse / Discours théorétiques* [proceedings of the Saint-Jovite, Quebec, conference of Sept. 1992] (Montreal: ACS, 1994),133–52, quote p. 139; Ursula Franklin, *The Real World of Technology* (Toronto: Anansi, 1999); Hans J. Kleinsteuber, "Information Highway and Canadian Content—Zur Debatte um Neue Technologien im Kanada der 90er Jahre," *Zeitschrift für Kanada-Studien* 19.2 (1999): 57–72, quote p. 63 Information Highway Advisory Council, *Connection, Community, Content: The Challenge of the Information Highway* (Ottawa, Sept. 1995), vii; Federal Cultural Policy Review Committee, *Report*, quote p. 6; James R. Taylor, "Communication Technologies, Regional Identity, and Canadian Dualism," *Canadian Issues / Thèmes Canadiens* 5 (1983): 106–115; Standing Committee on Canadian Heritage (Clifford Lincoln, Chair), *A Sense of Place—A Sense of Being: The Evolving Role of the Federal Government in the Support of Culture in Canada.* Ninth Report of the Standing Committee on Canadian Heritage (Ottawa: Public Works and Services, 1999), quote p. 9. In general see Rowland Lorimer and Jean McNulty, *Mass Communication in Canada* (2nd ed., Toronto: McClelland & Stewart, 1991).

entwined or braided them.[674] None was quintessentially Canadian and yet their productions, like those of performing and decorative artists, added up to Canadian literatures and arts that were not uncommon, but unique. They engaged in a process of creating a belonging, of embedding and being embedded. Cultural producers, whether externally or internally born, observed and changed society. Each cultural producer, regardless of cultural "origin" or "primary socialization," adds to the cultural repertoire and adapts his or her input so that it may be decoded by audiences with particular or multiple cultural decoding capabilities. A recent commentator for the Winnipeg Symphony Orchestra commented about a soloist: "He is becoming known around the world for his distinct talent of incorporating styles of music as diverse as American bluegrass and Gypsy fiddling with the standards of the classical repertoire, . . . all music is created equal."[675]

Canadian Studies as a transdisciplinary societal endeavour is different from Societal Studies in other countries. While it relocated Canada from a British-French colonized state to independent globally active middle power, Australian Studies relocated its cultural region from appendix to Europe to part of the worlds of Asia and dissolved the White master narrative.[676] In the United States, with its discourse of *e pluribus unum*—out of the many one united people—American Studies emphasized the *unum* without defining it.[677] German Studies proceeded from a nation divided after 1945 and,

---

674 : On "ethnic" writing, see Joseph Pivato, ed., *Contrasts: Comparative Essays in Italian-Canadian Writing* (Montreal: Guernica, 1985), and Michael Greenstein, *Third Solitudes: Tradition and Discontinuity in Jewish-Canadian Literature* (Kingston: MQUP, 1989). Post-colonial perspectives are provided in Veronica Strong-Boag, Sherrill Grace, Avigail Eisenberg, Joan Anderson, eds., *Painting the Maple: Essays on Race, Gender, and the Construction of Canada* (Vancouver: UBC Press, 1998), with essays by Christl Verduyn, "Reconstructing Canadian Literature: The Role of Race and Gender," 100–12, Lisa Chalykoff, "Encountering Anomalies: A Cultural Study of Chinese Migrants to Early Canada," 155–69, Gabriele Helms, Matt James, and Patricia Rodney, "Building Transdisciplinary Standpoints: An Integrative Bibliography," 267–78; Christl Verduyn, "Disjunctions: Place, Identity and Nation in 'Minority' Literatures in Canada," *Canadian Issues / Thèmes Canadiens* 20 (1998): 164–75; Clément Moisan and Renate Hildebrand, *Ces étrangers du dedans: Une histoire de l'écriture migrante au Québec 1937–1997* (Quebec: Éd. Nota Bene, 2001).

675 : Don Anderson in Program Guide, 3 Dec. 2004, 8–9, quote p. 8.

676 : V. Kay Daniels, Bruce H. Bennett, Humphrey McQueen, *Windows onto Worlds: Studying Australia at Tertiary Level* (Canberra: Govt. Publ. Service, 1987); Martyn Lyons & Penny Russell, eds., *Australia's History: Themes and Debates* (Sydney: UNSW Press, 2005).

677 : But see Gunnar Myrdal's massive study of the late 1940s and the recent essay by Arnold R. Hirsch, "E Pluribus Duo? Thoughts on 'Whiteness' and Chicago's 'New'

since 1989, from a re-unification paradigm that by the end of the 1990s was giving way to an east-west dualism hypothesis. British Studies, more complex, started from New Left perspectives of different sub-national cultures of social classes and groups, then included youth cultures and became aware of many-cultured interactiveness and of decolonizing as well as re-creative processes. Canadian Studies emerged out of a vague but incontestable recognition that the intellectual apparatus of the humanities was seriously deficient. However, it lacked the New Left background that differentiated nationhood into class, and scholars from inside the "founding nations" did not have the decoding tools to include the many cultures. For fear of losing a presumed identity in an intellectual world with shifting meanings, hidden implications, and untested assumptions, any recognition of hegemonic centering and decolonizing decentering was phrased cautiously or glossed over rhetorically. In the 1960s, "it was legitimate to study Canada," but "the Creightonian study of Canada disintegrated" under "the de-legitimization of the nation-state and the fragmentation of the academic disciplines."

Multiple approaches emerged: attempts at interdisciplinary integrative research strategies, at a kind of "domestic comparative" studies, or of international comparisons. A certain unease (not necessarily guilt) about the status of first inhabitants led to combinations of Native and (Euro-) Canadian Studies. Pacific perspectives came only later. Few or none of the pioneering scholars had been equipped by family, education, or collective historical memory with perspectives and categories that permitted new visions. Once decolonization theory and practice had been recognized as a liberating tool, the hegemony from south of the 49th parallel—powerful, threatening, and yet attractive—incessantly questioned the integrity of whatever Canada appeared to be. Thus a constant impetus to come to terms with oneself, or one's many selves, in order to remain distinct from the Other, the more powerful penetrating as well as embracing state, informed debates about Canadian Studies—a "left-national" approach as some scholars term it.

By the early 1990s, theory-informed yet pragmatic scholars attempted an integration of the disciplining aspects (Foucault 1966) of the disciplines, but obstacles were many: in each discipline rules of evidence, theorizations, options for or limits on inserting the imagination remained different and cross-disciplinary integration was perceived from inside each field as a threat to methodological and theoretical integrity. In 1992, scholars viewing Canadian Studies as an interdisciplinary future-oriented endeavour organized

---

Immigration as a Transient Third Tier," [on relations between East and South European and Southern Black immigrants] *Journal of American Ethnic History* 23.4 (Summer 2004): 7–44. A new approach is suggested in José D. Saldívar, *Border Matters: Remapping American Cultural Studies* (Berkeley: Univ. of Cal. Press, 1997).

the "Visioning Workshop on Canadian Studies" (Stoney Lake, ON) and addressed the "Theoretical Discourse in the Canadian Intellectual Community" (Saint-Jovite, QC). Dissolving borderlines provided "the potential for a more democratic and inclusive" study, "respectful" of all Canadians.[678] At the turn toward the twenty-first century, the *Journal of Canadian Studies / Revue d'études canadiennes* could point toward an increasingly positive balance sheet: Native peoples and women had been incorporated—or had fought their way in. Interdisciplinarity was well developed. Canadian Studies encompassed the East, the Centre, the Prairie West, and British Columbia, but not yet the impact of newcomers from Asia or from Latin America onto Canada as a whole or its urban cultures.[679]

Like any study of society, Canadian Studies is necessarily a comprehensive field. In an age that values specialized research, any specialist is a non-specialist in other areas of knowledge and in everyday lives outside his or her "own" experienced worlds or social slots. While reviews of recent developments in the field—or several fields—and syntheses that place specific research and artistic productions in context and make them accessible to non-specialists have appeared, such syntheses are often devalued as mere "textbooks" or "review essays." Rather, they serve to help specialists to access neighbouring specializations and constantly to adjust the categories into which the next generation sorts information. This adjustment of categories is essential to keeping options open, both within a person's professional expertise and as regards his or her life-world. Research and synthesizing may be compared to building a house: one window or a single wall provides neither shelter nor meaning. Co-operation of numerous craftsmen and -women as well as compatible parts are necessary to build a shelter, and

678 : Cameron, *Taking Stock*, quote p. 33; Rowland Lorimer, "A Report on [the] Stoney Lake [conference on interdisciplinarity], June 11-14, 1992," *ACS Newsletter* 14.4 (1992/93): 1 and 24-27; Goldie, Lambert, Lorimer, *Canada*, as selective proceedings of the ACS's conference "Theoretical Discourse in the Canadian Intellectual Community," Saint-Jovite, Quebec, 25-27 Sept. 1992, and critical evaluation by Ian Angus, *A Border Within: National Identity, Cultural Plurality, and Wilderness* (Montreal: MQUP, 1997), 209-226. John H. Wadland, "Inter-Theoretical Canadian Studies?" *ACS Newsletter* 14.1 (1992): 1 and 13-15; and mimeographed *Interdisciplinarity: Working Documents* (Montreal: ACS, 1992), with essays by Jill Vickers, "Where Is the Discipline in Interdisciplinarity," 5-41, John Wadland, "Core Courses in Interdisciplinary Canadian Studies Programs," 42-49, and James de Finney, "Canadian Studies: Looking in from the Outside," 50-61; Vickers, "Another Look at Interdisciplinarity," *ACS Newsletter* 16.1 (Spring 1994): 14-15.

679 : *Journal of Canadian Studies* 35 (2000): no. 1 "Canadian Studies at the Millennium," no. 2 "Women and Nationalisms: Canadian Experiences," no. 3 "Locating Canadian Cultures in the Twenty-First Century," esp. John H. Wadland, "Voices in Search of a Conversation: An Unfinished Project," 35.1: 52-76.

it needs aesthetic input to make living in the shelter agreeable. The premise that people's histories do not begin and end in one single state could have informed Canadian historiography, the social sciences, and the humanities from their inception in the nineteenth century.

V. PERSPECTIVES

The new 1960s approaches to the Study of Canada were part of far-reaching changes in global knowledge production. The self-views and the scholarship of the Atlantic or so-called Western World faced the critical theories of scholars in post-colonial non-White societies and came to understand the destructiveness of nation-state perspectives. Discourse-theory forced every scholar to reflect on hidden grids of meaning and frames of reference—a type of source criticism that historians, unless assuming gatekeeper positions, count among their most basic tools.

A century and a half after the "invention" of the nation-state, recognition of its deadly implications, often supported by nationalist scholarship, could no longer be avoided. A decolonizing political practice and theoretical discourse engaged the Atlantic World's intellectuals living in the mental and material ruins of World War II and of imperialism. However, one faction of scholars clung to the old: recognizing the threat of post-colonial perspectives to their interpretations and unable to engage in post-national multiple perspectives, they attempted to reduce the understanding of the world to right or wrong in the battles of the Cold War.[680] Stalinesque or McCarthyesque thought control, however, could not protect nation-state ideology when intellectuals defected in ever larger numbers from the ancien régime to join the wide-ranging societal debates hoping to build a more equitable world. Civil rights movements, including the women's movement, challenged colour and culture hierarchies. New generations absorbed knowledge in socialization processes in which cultural borders became first permeable, then fluid.[681]

---

680 : Ian Tyrrell has discussed the militarist and imperialist approach to history in "The Threat of De-Provincializing U.S. History in World War Two: Allan Nevins and the *New York Times* to the Rescue," *Amerikastudien / American Studies* 48 (2003): 41–59. A major introductory text for history students in the U.S., Allan Nevins's *The Gateway to History*, began with the following scene: "A cartridge bag is unstrapped from the sweaty horse, and a brown hand pulls out a thick volume; it is Theodore Roosevelt in East Africa about to give half an hour at the end of a day's hunting to Carlyle's *Frederick the Great*" (rev. ed. of 1938; New York: Doubleday, 1962), p. 13.

681 : Samuel Huntington's more recent theory of yet another clash of civilizations is one more attempt to prevent diversity and creativity (*The Clash of Civilizations and the Remaking of World Order*, New York: Simon & Schuster, 1997).

Chapter 14

FROM INTEREST-DRIVEN NATIONAL DISCOURSE TO TRANSCULTURAL SOCIETAL STUDIES

Transcultural scholarship since the 1990s has sometimes been reduced to jargon-laden sociological or culturalist texts with an undertone of total innovation. But, like the wheel, critical thought does not have to be reinvented; its century-long evolution has been retraced above from seventeenth-century analytical thought that challenged "natural philosophy's" postulate of a congruency between natural and social worlds. Scottish empiricism, Enlightenment thought, and the emergent natural and social sciences, as well as comparative discursive-literary perspectives on societies and cultures, recognized relativity of narratives and values, an achievement usually credited to twentieth-century cultural materialism and discourse theory in Britain and France and to post-colonial theory in the Caribbean, India, and Africa. Eighteenth-century scholars in the natural, accounting, linguistic, and social sciences, aware of the embeddedness of positions taken and of interpretations suggested, had replaced the concept of axiomatic "truth" by empirically testable "validity" or "plausibility."

The natural and the social: *Discourse in the production of knowledges and identities*

In the natural sciences, eighteenth-century empiricism and the twentieth-century indeterminacy principle emphasized the impossibility of exact findings in those fields often called "the exact sciences." The Scottish empiricist George Berkeley (1685–1753) related "position" to "knowledge" when describing the observation of the relativity of temperatures (*Treatise Concerning the Principles of Human Knowledge*, 1710): if a person moved his hand from a bowl of cold to one of warm water, it appeared as warmer; if from a bowl of hot into the same bowl of warm water it appeared as colder. In the twentieth century, Albert Einstein's "relativity theory" (1905, expanded 1916) dealt with frames of reference that move relative to one another, and Werner Heisenberg in the "principle of uncertainty" or "indeterminacy" (1927), stated that position and momentum of a particle might not be measured at the same time with more than limited precision. Nils Bohr added the "complementarity principle": experiments on one aspect of atomic systems preclude exact knowledge of other, complementary aspects of the same system at the same time. To arrive at a common reference system, scales had to be constructed and agreed upon. Such scales were relative and differed between national discourses, as indicated by those for "objectively" measurable temperatures,

Daniel G. Fahrenheit's scale of 1714, René-Antoine Réaumur's of 1730, and Anders Celsius's of 1742. Such "yardsticks" (or in other accounting discourses, "metresticks") influence perception. French writer Louis Hémon noted in 1910s Quebec how people at a slight increase of temperatures in February happily discussed the approach of spring. As the only one to own a thermometer, he noticed that it stood at 25 degrees below zero and, as a result, was no longer able to share the hopeful feelings.[682]

While counting is allegedly neutral, it involves imposition of rule. Systematic counting, as a science, was developed by agents of rulers who wanted to know the amount of the subjects' material possessions in order to assess taxes or duties to be paid. It involved a balancing of rulers' demands with people's ability to pay—accounting as a relative science. Such "cameralist" scholars compared social and economic strata within a society. Comparative perspectives also emerged from awareness of difference of lifestyles and value systems across cultural borders. Travel literature described difference and reflected upon it. Charles de Montesquieu (1689–1755) in his *Lettres persanes* (1721, revised 1754) had two Persians describe and discuss French and European societies. He used the viewpoint of the (allegedly less civilized) Other to critically reflect on the (self-defined civilized) Self. Both travel descriptions and *lettres persanes*-type criticism became literary genres for self-reflection and scholarly reconceptualizations, and were at the origin of Country Studies.[683] Wilhelm von Humboldt (1767–1835) hypothesized upon contact with peoples in Southeast Asia and South Sea islands that language, rather than reflect a particular culture's images of the universe, in fact orders them (published 1836–40).

In the context of intercultural debates, Ferdinand de Saussure, as scholar of language and communication, was the first to differentiate between the signifier and the signified, acoustic sign and concept transmitted, and the processes of encoding and decoding (published 1931). Benjamin Lee Whorf and Edward Sapir, who studied Nahuatl (Aztec), Maya, Hopi, and other languages—contrasting them to the Standard Average European—identified language as the governing factor in thought formation (Sapir-Whorf Hypothesis). As an example to illustrate the context-language-concept relation, consider desert -based or Inuit cultures. Desert-based cultures need no more than a single term signifying "bird," while forest cultures differentiate between dozens or hundreds of them. Inuit cultures have many terms for

---

682 : Louis Hémon, *Lettres à sa famille*, ed. Nicole Deschamps (Montreal: PU Montréal, 1968), 12 Feb. 1913, p. 190.

683 : Konrad Groß, "Die Entwicklung der Kanadastudien," *Gulliver* 19 (1986): 30–36. See summary in chapter 12 above.

"snow" while in temperate-zone cultures one generic term is sufficient. How are two Canadians—for example, a Southern Ontario wine grower and an Inuvik seal hunter—to discuss their respective physical environments if terminology is not congruent? Like words, material signifiers encode messages: two boards nailed together crosswise symbolize the Christian religion, and variants of this layout symbolize variants of denominations. A piece of cloth draped in a specific fashion around the head of women becomes a signifier of Islamic faith. Understanding of languages and material systems of meaning as relational has advanced through transcultural research, with Claude Lévi-Strauss (1908–2009) perhaps the most important anthropologist and Fernando Ortiz (1881–1969) perhaps the most important cultural theorist.

Such epistemological theory was "lost" or declared inapplicable when master narratives came to be constructed and hegemonies were imposed. Absolute or single-track versions of historical backgrounds and structures served particular interests; the conceptualization of social space as "the nation" served the nineteenth-century middle classes and their scholars. Under the naming approach, the political entities in which people lived were re-designated from "Windsor realm" (or other) to "nation-state" and, under the measuring method, placed on the top of both a newly constructed scale of political organization as well as a single timeline chronology of human social organization. Inventing this frame for historians'/ideologues' master narratives involved symbolic annihilation of some of the previous intellectual achievements, censoring of previous everyday practices, and appropriation and re-fashioning of existing thought and knowledges. To develop new *"cadres de la mémoire"* or "frames of remembrance" and, for the present, new *"cadres sociaux"* (Halbwachs 1997), competitors needed to be excluded from "memory space," from the power to define, and even from the right to question scales and positions.[684] First, the architects of the new frames adopted a pre-national element: dynastic states' concept of territories delimited by boundaries without reference to practiced cultures or people living there. Second, Enlightenment philosophers in theory liberated the inhabitants of such territories from the status of subjects of rulers and made them into human beings with inalienable rights. This conceptual change invested sovereignty in "the people," but linguistically could not delete the previous meaning, sovereignty as rule over a territory. The meaning of the term *people* was also ambiguous: were women, with few exceptions by common agreement endowed with fewer rights than men, part of the nation? By law, their cultural identity depended on that of their husband.

---

684 : Maurice Halbwachs, *La mémoire collective* (new rev. and augmented ed., Paris: Michel, 1997).

Furthermore, if "the people" constituted the society and the state, what about the case of many peoples in one state? The producers of knowledge came to designate the numerically largest or most powerful group as the "nation" and relegated smaller ones through application of a new term, *minority*, to lesser status. Equality of position, a qualitative scale, was replaced by a quantitative scale. The compound "nation-state" not only compounded the vagueness of both terms, it also involved a contradiction in terms: according to enlightened republican thought all persons were equal before the law, but the subsequent Romanticist corollary required that members of such people's states share a culture. Thus non-nationals were excluded from equal political and cultural participation and were marginalized economically. Toward the end of the nineteenth century, when states fortified their borders by passport systems, the personnel guarding the borders and the ideologues of boundary construction became gatekeepers in the most literal sense.[685]

This invention of borders and the construction of boundaries had far-reaching consequences for scholarly discourse as well as for cultural diversity of resident and migrant populations. The language-embedded continuity from dynastic to democratic regime obfuscated the meanings of absolutist and democratic. In dynastic ("absolutist") polities, resident groups of subjects as well as in-migrating groups could negotiate special status for their culture—religious, professional, regional, urban, or other. In late medieval and early modern European societies, urban communities, as corporations, received certain privileges, and newcomers—the Huguenots are the most-often cited example—negotiated group status.[686] This flexibility of "absolutist" dynastic regimes came to an end when the "democratic" nation precluded cultural difference and absolutized one single culture.

Under this "political economy," which liberated the middle classes from the nobilities' claims to economic and social pre-eminence in a state, the plurality of social status was lost, and under this doctrine of nationhood, the relativity of memory, thought, and conceptualization was lost. Only in

---

685 : David Held, *Democracy and the Global Order: From the Modern State to Cosmopolitan Governance* (Stanford: Stanford, 1995), 29–140; John Torpey, *The Invention of the Passport: Surveillance, Citizenship and the State* (Cambridge: Cambridge, 2000).

686 : Bernard Chevalier, "France from Charles VII to Henry IV," in Thomas A. Brady, Jr., Heiko A. Oberman, and James D. Tracy, eds., *Handbook of European History 1400–1600: Late Middle Ages, Renaissance and Reformation*, 2 vols. (Leiden: Brill, 1994), 1: 369–401, esp. 371, 385; Henry Kamen, "The Habsburg Lands: Iberia," ibid., 1:467–98: The monarchs had to reach compromise "with the nobles and with the cities, who between them constituted the political nation" (471). The religious Orders, the Church, and the non-Christian ethno-religious groups also required special consideration.

the 1960s, decades after the natural scientists, did social scientists reassert relativity and plurality. "Participant observation" as a method of gaining knowledge, discussed in the natural sciences since Berkeley and Einstein, impacts the situations and processes observed, and thus influences the data collected. Jürgen Habermas recognized the connection between *Knowledge and Human Interests* (1968; English translation 1971): Scholarly predispositions, often imbued with childhood socialization, influence which "facts" and processes are uncovered. Each of these epistemological developments permitted self-positioning and opened new vistas. However, the relativism of some aficionados of the so-called "linguistic turn" was self-interested: it saved them from time-consuming empirical research. Rather than relativism,"perspectivism" developed, as the acknowledgement that one's viewpoint matters.

The emphasis on language and meaning, on frames of reference and climates of opinion, had its own social history. To received or official language systems in societies, Mikhail Bakhtin added the concept of internal stratification (heteroglossia), thus differentiating a language both historically and normatively at the level of usage styles into functional variations by class or profession, interest or ideology—and, it might be added, gender. Using medieval popular culture as an example, he saw the carnivalesque and folk humour as subversive of hegemonic meanings, as a language of resistance.[687] Antonio Gramsci added the concept of hegemony, a language-based moral and spiritual supremacy of an ascending or ruling social group or class in a capitalist set of socio-economic relations. Distinct from revolution, revolt, or coup, positioning struggles to acquire control over meanings, symbols, and myths—in short, over received societal discourses—take place in the realm of language and aim for consent rather than destruction of those ruled. Bakhtin and Gramsci emphasized struggle for control over meanings between those with the power to define and those subverting such meanings.

On this basis, Jacques Derrida developed his deconstruction theory: language consists of ambivalences and thus thought and meaning cannot be conclusive. Words do not define positive terms, but signify differences to other such signs, which in turn, in an infinite series, refer to further signs (inter-textuality). Language and systems of thought—philosophies, ideologies, and worldviews—attempt to impose logic on differences, or sameness on otherness. Identity and unity can only result from violent imposition

---

687 : Bakhtin emphasized the liberating element of laughter and merriment, of foolery and parody. However, in twentieth-century totalitarian regimes jokes about the powerful also served the purpose of belittling the overpowering threat of rule. Such belittling *reduced* the need for resistance as action. Belittlement was survival rather than a resistance strategy since the confronting fascist regimes could be deadly.

of sameness, from elimination of difference by force. Roland Barthes considered how (literary) texts were recreated and reproduced in the act of reading, of decoding. Hegemonic discourses and specific texts were sites of production of meaning by common readers. Shifting, unstable, and interrogative dimensions of meaning and understanding provided the possibility of negotiating cultural forms. Michel Foucault (1966) proposed an archeology of "the archive" of myths and systems that governed the emergence and transformations of discourses. He searched for the "grids of meaning" employed to sort and structure the multitude of data constantly taken in by human beings. Pierre Bourdieu expanded "text" to include the whole complex of positioning, lifestyles, and all forms of expression into a group-specific habitus. Childhood socialization did not lead into society, but into a specific social segment with a specific mode of living and style of expression. Within such structures people act. Thus structures became processual, processes are structured.

Intellectual historians have usually overlooked the social history of these theorists, all of whom, voluntarily or involuntarily, had lived multicultural lives. None had been confined to a monocultural con-text, whether text or habitus. All experienced multiple reference systems and thus, through personal experience, became aware of the construction of scales, hierarchies, and meanings as well as of symbolic annihilation or rendering invisible. Berkeley had lived as a missionary in the Bermudas and Rhode Island; Humboldt had travelled to Java. Barthes had taught French to speakers of other languages in Romania and Egypt; Derrida and Bourdieu had lived in Algeria, the latter both as soldier and sociologist. Foucault was interested in sexual Otherness and worked with psychiatric patients who experienced several "realities" within their persons. Saussure taught in quadri-cultural Switzerland; Berkeley observed how English culture clashed with and subdued Irish and Scottish culture and how it imposed the English language and its frames of reference on speakers of Gaelic. Bakhtin and Gramsci experienced major breaks in reference systems in their own societies. Bakhtin, sentenced to death in Soviet Russia, taught in a small town in Kazakhstan after commutation of his sentence; Gramsci, imprisoned under Italian fascism, conceived his most important ideas while confined in prison and prevented from social action. British theoreticians came out of the oppositional New Left or, such as Stuart Hall from the Caribbean—that is, from the outside—and refused allegiance to interest-driven hegemonic versions of discourse. Like Humboldt and Sapir, they studied the meanings of language. Youth's usages varied the meaning of received language (Paul Willis) as regional and class belongings did (Raymond Williams). Childhood-socialized language usage, thus experienced as "natural," is challenged in inter-class, inter-gender, and international contacts by competing reference systems. The monocultural nation-state narrative attempted to prevent those living under it from recognizing that other positions could be taken. The ideologue-scholars who developed this world created spaces with "no bars or visible exits," to use the felicitous words of Miriam Toews.[688]

The new epistemology resulted in a sequence of theoretical approaches to the study of societies: structuralism used linguistic principles to understand the relations of different aspects of a social system toward each other. A New Historicism contextualized (literary) texts in history, but depoliticized, desocialized, and dehistoricized them by positing that history itself comes to the present as text and thus has no privileged authority. Rejecting such relativist approaches, Cultural Materialism is less concerned with cultural objects (texts or "works") than with agency, activities, and processes (cultural practices). Writing about capitalist societies at the time of mass communication through television imagery, cultural materialists have shifted emphasis from authors to consumption processes, to assess the imposition of hegemony and to reveal the emergence of oppositional, alternative, counter-, or subcultures. They studied ownership of the means of cultural production and distribution, and began by explicating culture in materialist terms from a historical perspective (Raymond Williams). Then, at the Birmingham Centre for Contemporary Cultural Studies (CCCS), scholars studied popular culture with the dual goal of empirical observation and validation. At first, their critique of capitalist ideology was cast in the Althusserian concept of ideology as a repressive system of signification, of state superstructures geared to control the lower classes. But recognizing the potential of working-class youth cultures for resistance, they shifted their interpretation to the Gramscian notion of hegemonic consensus rather than structural repression. Ethnographic studies of how subcultural audiences respond to commodified cultural products brought to the fore the issue of multiple audiences, and thus invalidated the quasi-totalitarian interpretation of the capitalist system and mass-produced consumer culture.[689]

---

688 : The literature on critical theory and discourse theory is vast and will not be repeated here. I have relied on Simona Cerutti, "Le linguistic turn en Angleterre. Notes sur un débat et ses censures," *enquête: anthropologie, histoire, sociologie* 5 (1997): 125–140, and Harvey J. Graff, "The Shock of the 'New' (Histories): Social Science Histories and Historical Literacies," *Social Science History* 25 (2001): 483–533. Miriam Toews, *A Complicated Kindness* (Toronto: Knopf Canada, 2004), 53.

689 : David Morley, *The "Nationwide" Audience* (London: British Film Institute, 1982) and *Family Television: Cultural Power and Domestic Leisure* (London: Comedia-Routledge, 1986). For a critical review of British cultural studies see Richard Johnson, "The Story So Far: And Further Transformations," in David Punter, ed., *Introduction to Contemporary Cultural Studies* (London: Longman, 1986), 277–313.

Recognition of the multi-vocal and multiple-meaning discursive forces at work in cultural systems, in view of the resistance of heteroglot linguistic diversity to hegemonic, monoglot, social uniformity-prescribing authority, permitted recognition of cultural plurality in the past. Canadian historiography, with few exceptions, had constructed single-cultured British and French Canadians; European and subsequently Atlantic historiography took the nation-state organization for granted. To do so, historians had to render invisible polities of many cultures. "The Austrian monarchy" refers to the Austrian Habsburg dynasty that established a dual Austro-Hungarian Empire of many peoples (*Vielvölkerstaat*), complete with concomitant political theory. "The bloodthirsty Turks" refers to the Ottoman political and social organization, which intentionally avoided hegemonic culture and language and provided self-administration for religio-cultural groups and distinct ethno-religious neighbourhoods within an institutional regime operated by a non-ethnic administrative elite.[690] Such many-cultured institutional regimes were hidden by catchwords, whether "Prussian" Germany, British "nation of shopkeepers," Canada as "a cold country," among others. The producers of discourses—first in dynasties, then in nation-states—excluded multicultured polities from the memory of socio-political organization in the Atlantic World. Some linguistic practices facilitated exchange or multiple perspectives, such as the multilingualism of the illiterate in pre-World War I Balkan societies or the gender-neutral Cree language. Mentally-bound scholars never listened to the Bakhtinian subversive voices or asked along with Saussure whether their texts could be decoded by all members of society or only by clones of their own systems of thinking. When those excluded began to talk back, the master narrative turned out to be an invalid compilation of partial and often unconnected data. It had been a chimera.[691]

---

690 : Dirk Hoerder, "Pluralist Founding Nations in Anglo- and Franco-Canada: Multiple Migrations, Influences, Reconceptualisations," *Journal of Multilingual and Multicultural Development* 24.6 (2003): 525–39; Halil Inalcik and Donald Quataert, eds., *An Economic and Social History of the Ottoman Empire*, 1300–1914 (Cambridge: Cambridge Univ. Press, 1994); Fikret Adanir, "Religious Communities and Ethnic Groups under Imperial Sway: Ottoman and Habsburg Lands in Comparison," and Michael John, "National Movements and Imperial Ethnic Hegemonies in Austria, 1867–1918," in Dirk Hoerder, Christiane Harzig, Adrian Shubert, eds., *Diversity in History: Transcultural Interactions from the Early Modern Mediterranean World to the 20th-Century Postcolonial World* (New York: Berghahn, 2003), 54–86, 87–105.

691 : Ann L. Stoler, "Making Empire Respectable: The Politics of Race and Sexual Morality in 20th-Century Colonial Cultures," *American Ethnologist* 16 (1989): 634–60; Frederick Cooper and Ann L. Stoler, eds., *Tensions of Empire: Colonial Cultures in a Bourgeois World* (Berkeley: Univ. of California Press, 1997); Margaret Strobel, *Gender, Sex, and Empire* (Washington, D.C.: American Historical Assoc., 1993); Nupur Chaudhuri

Theorizations from post-colonial Europe connected with those from the formerly marginalized Latin America, South Asia, and—to a lesser degree—Canada. In Latin America, a "contact zone" where each society emerged out of Indio-Euro-African ethnogenesis in processes variously called *métissage, mestizaje,* or *créolisation,* the imposition of power was emphasized. As early as 1946, Brazilian theorist Gilberto Freyre in *The Masters and the Slaves* discussed power relations and interactions that transculturated both sides. At the same time, Fernando Ortiz developed his concept of transculturation in Cuba.[692] Later, cultural-societally oriented statements came from Martín-Barbero, Sarlo, Canclini, Monsiváis, and others.[693] They reinserted the transcultural lives emerging from the indigenous and African contributions into what had formerly been viewed from (White) "Latin" or "Ibero" hegemonic perspectives. These authors emphasize mixture or *mixté.* Concepts such as *négritude* of both French-Caribbean and French-African background were transcultural in the literal sense. The cultures of the colonizer and the colonized, of oppressor and oppressed were (and are) inextricably entwined, "the worlds the slaveholders made" with "the worlds the slaves made," as Eugene Genovese put it for the United States.[694] In such contexts of hierarchical mixture or imposition of brutal power, processes

---

and Margaret Strobel, eds., *Western Women and Imperialism: Complicity and Resistance* (Bloomington: Indiana Univ. Press, 1992); Linda Bryder, "Sex, Race, and Colonialism: An Historiographic Review," *Intl. History Review* 20 (1998): 806–22; Clare Midgley, ed., *Gender and Imperialism* (Manchester: Manchester Univ. Press, 1998). See also Husselo S. Alatas, *The Myth of the Lazy Native: A Study of the Image of the Malays, Filipinos and Javanese from the 16th to the 20th Century and Its Function in the Ideology of Colonial Capitalism* (London: Cass, 1977).

692 : Mary Louise Pratt, *Imperial Eyes: Travel Writing and Transculturation* (London: Routledge, 1992); Freyre, *The Masters and the Slaves: A Study in the Development of Brazilian Civilization* (Casa-grande e senzala) transl. from the Portuguese by Samuel Putnam (4th and definitive ed., New York: Knopf, 1946, repr. 1966; rev. Engl. ed., Berkeley: Univ. of California Press, 1986); Ortiz, "Del fenómeno de la transculturación y su importancia en Cuba" (1940), repr. in *El contrapunteo cubano del azúcar y del tabaco* (La Habana: Editorial de Sciencas Sociales, 1983).

693 : Jésus Martín-Barbero, *De los medios a las mediaciones: Comunicación, cultura y hegemonia* (1st ed., 1987; repr. Mexico, DF: Ed. Gili, 1998); Néstor Garcia Canclini, *Culturas híbridas: Estrategias para entrar y salir de la modernidad* (Mexico, DF: Grijalbo, 1989); Beatriz Sarlo, *La máquina cultural: maestras, traductores y vanguardistas* (Buenos Aires: Ariel, 1998); Carlos Monsiváis, *Aires de familia: cultura y sociedad en América Latina* (Barcelona: Anagramma, 2000).

694 : Eugene D. Genovese, *The World the Slaveholders Made: Two Essays in Interpretation* (New York: Pantheon, 1969) and *Roll Jordan Roll: The World the Slaves Made* (New York: Random, 1974).

of *hibridación* or *transculturación* occurred. Though Freyre and Ortiz had published in the 1940s, their approaches began to receive attention in the North Atlantic or "Western" world only in the 1970s and, in particular, in the 1990s. They wrote from the centre-defined margins. Few "Western" scholars read Spanish or Portuguese and quasi-fascist regimes in Iberian Europe punished receptivity to critical thought into the 1970s. The Latin American work was based on solid social histories of slaves and masters, of power relations and socialization processes.

Scholars from South Asia developed Subaltern Studies and proposed that definitions and theorizations which provide scholarly support for the colonizers' master narratives as well as for elite narratives of colonial societies be reconceptualized by two strategies: "the moment(s) of change be pluralized and plotted as confrontations rather than transitions" and it be recognized that "changes are signalled or marked by a functional change in sign systems." Their work reflected the British-Indian confrontations and that of South American scholars the graded transitions in Iberian-Indio-African societies. They received earlier attention in the Atlantic World than the Latin American approaches since they wrote in the more broadly known English language, and engaged the British inventors of the colonizer master narratives in debate and had the ear of post-colonial British scholars. Coming from a rigidly hierarchized society, they could talk from elite to elite, and rather than proposing empirical social histories often contented themselves with intellectual histories of the dichotomy of colonizer-colonized discourses.[695]

Imperial power, expressed in colonizer culture, never descended on the colonized in finished form. It adapted to circumstances and dealt with challenges from the subalternized. Empires were wounded, forced to compromise, involved in struggles until they came apart, leaving post-colonial spaces. But the (self-) decolonized had imperial ideologies inscribed on them and the continuity of imperial institutions to deal with. "Survival" was the issue, as Margaret Atwood phrased it—concentrating on White Canadians. The arenas of contest have been called "third space," neither the space of the powerful nor the space of the subalternized, but spaces in which the contestants have adapted their distinct ways in order to be able to engage

---

695 : Gayatri Chakravorty Spivak, "Subaltern Studies: Deconstructing Historiography," in Ranajit Guha and Spivak, eds., *Selected Subaltern Studies* (New York: Oxford, 1988), 3-32, quotes p. 3; Bernd-Peter Lange and Mala Pandurang, "Dialectics of Empire and Complexities of Culture: British Men in India, Indian Experiences of Britain," in Hoerder, Harzig, Shubert, *The Historical Practice of Diversity, 177–200.* For empirical research and terminology see Jan C. Breman and E. Valentine Daniel, "The Making of a Coolie," *Journal of Peasant Studies* 19.3/4 (1992): 268–95.

the opponents. Such third spaces may, of course, also emerge out of more peaceful, if hierarchical, transculturation.[696]

Canadian scholars' new concepts, their research on ethnic relations and cultural fusion, also came from the margins, as defined by European and U.S. scholars, and for more than a decade the latter showed little recognition. Within Canada, the lingering feeling that the languages and reference systems of Native peoples might have validity posed a challenge to Euro-Canadian master narratives. Furthermore, in their distinct linguistic codes immigrants from continental Europe developed their other narratives. Nineteenth- and twentieth-century scales of colour were set to exclude some of them from Whiteness. Against Anglo-Saxon White, Italians were said to be "olive," East Europeans "dark," and Jews a different race altogether. 1960s newcomers from the Caribbean and South Asia as well as from China were made aware of their "visibility" under a scale that used "white" as the norm and baseline, but in the changing frames of reference, they could write and talk back.[697] To achieve hegemony, a discourse needs consent—this, the British-Canadian version never fully achieved. In Canada's school system, the data on British culture though perhaps factually correct were invalid in everyday life. In family homes, the school children were socialized into ethnocultural groups' versions of the data and of historical memory. As a result, they lived transcultural practices long before the concept entered scholarship.

Discussing the relationship between Canada's First and Second Peoples' narratives, Julie Cruikshank noted that hegemonic projects within societies, colonial projects establishing rule over others, and hemispheric or global strategies of rule devise and reinforce categories that the ideologues of the power-wielding groups designate as "objectivity" and oppose to the "subjectivity" of those to be ruled. Emma LaRocque, a Métis scholar, noted that "we" serve as "informants" to non-Native colleagues who construct distanced narratives avoiding the "parochialism" of those who speak "their

---

696 : Homi K. Bhabha, *The Location of Culture* (London: Routledge, 1994), and Bhabha, "DissemiNation: Time, Narrative, and the Margins of the Modern Nation," in Bhabha, ed., *Nation and Narration* (London: Routledge, 1990), 291–322. See also Mieke Bal, *Travelling Concepts in the Humanities: A Rough Guide* (Toronto: UTP, 2002).

697 : Danielle Juteau(-Lee) with L. Laforge, *Frontières ethniques en devenir / Emerging Ethnic Boundaries* (Ottawa: Éd. de l'Université d'Ottawa, 1979), and Juteau(-Lee), ed., "Enjeux ethniques: Production de nouveaux rapports sociaux," *Sociologie et sociétés* 15.2 (1983); Jean Burnet, Danielle Juteau, Enoch Padolsky, Anthony Rasporich, Antoine Sirois, eds., *Migration and the Transformation of Cultures. A Project of the UNESCO World Decade for Cultural Development* (Toronto: MHSO, 1992); Wsevolod W. Isajiw, *Understanding Diversity: Ethnicity and Race in the Canadian Context* (Toronto: Thompson, 1999).

own voices" and claim this distance to signify "objectivity." The intruders use concepts of space and of time "that encourage the annexation of territories and the subjugation of former inhabitants. Gradually, those at the center monopolize what comes to be considered rational discourse and marginalize those who speak different idioms." At the beginning of cultural contact, newcomers from Europe had to develop "listening skills," to reach the level of information that "Natives" or "Aboriginals" did possess. Once the newcomers reached self-sufficiency, they used tools of power—from hegemonic discourse via written accumulation of knowledge to guns—to force indigenous people to cede voice. The powerful or "the larger world essentializes indigenous voice," assuming "all people from one community [or several] to say the same thing." This simplifies listening. Difference is thus rendered invisible, is symbolically annihilated or physically eradicated, and unitary bureaucratic rule may be imposed on people compressed into a unitary category: "the Indians," "the Chinese," "the Inuit," "the workers," or "the women." Subaltern resistances—pluralized—involve social action, which by "foregrounding communication makes audiences central to performance." Traditional sign systems are reinvoked and adapted: stories, regalia, indigenous place names, vernacular songs, all signal common points of reference, of memory. "Genealogy, place, and the ceremonial objects . . . become focal points by which cultural memory resists faceless bureaucracy" and the appropriation of voice by the institutions of rule. Memory as empowerment, however, draws on a past in order to cope and negotiate the present. Tradition and actual lifeways may clash.[698]

Since Europeans' expansion over peoples across the globe, the dominance-subaltern hierarchy has involved a centralizing of Whiteness as marker of superiority. "Race" is relational and colour a question of definition. Whiteness, the Western norm against which peoples of the Atlantic World judged all other pigmentations, skin colours, and "races," had to be invented and a scale for measuring it had to be constructed—another scale with different notches over time. While such scaled gradations had no place in human rights-based legal theory since the late eighteenth century, their continuing presence in the administration of the law spawned critical legal studies in the 1970s and in an extension, critical race and gender theory. British imperialists defined the Empire as White and named Canada a "White Do-

---

698 : Cruikshank, *The Social Life of Stories* (1998), quotes pp. 155–58; Emma LaRocque, "The Colonization of a Native Woman Scholar," in Christine Miller and Patricia Chuchryk et al., eds., *Women of the First Nations: Power Wisdom, and Strength* (Winnipeg: Univ. of Manitoba Press, 1996), 11–18, esp. 12–13; Renée Hulan and Linda Warley, "Cultural Literacy, First Nations and the Future of Canadian Literary Studies," *Journal of Canadian Studies* 34.3 (1999): 59–86.

minion." When in the 1940s men and women of African-Caribbean background began to migrate, Canada's labour market demands and some background manoeuvering from the British foreign ministry (by coincidence called "Whitehall") resulted in one more diversification of Canadian society by colour and culture. The scale of Whiteness involves economic scaling. Whiteness as property guarantees higher wages and access to political office and societal resources. Espousal of Whiteness was a racial and/or racist identification *and* a quasi-religious belief in entitlement to economic privilege. When immigration and multiculturalism legislation introduced colour-neutrality it involved a class aspect. The White Canadian working classes, the social level on which many migrants of the 1960s entered, had the least resources to share property. Analysis of Whiteness, as a characteristic of hegemony and Post-Colonial Studies in its many variants, is of particular importance to the Canadian experience.[699]

Transcultural Societal Studies: An integrative approach

The concept of culture as developed in recent non-hierarchized and comprehensive approaches that combine the expressive and the material aspects of individual lives and societies has been defined in Chapter 1:

> In order to survive and to project life courses, human beings as individuals and in communities and societies must provide for their material, emotional, intellectual, and spiritual needs. These are satisfied by culture, a complex material and symbolic system that includes tools as well as productive and reproductive work; practices, values and norms; arts and beliefs. Culture involves patterns of actions as well as processes of

---

699 : David R. Roediger, *The Wages of Whiteness: Race and the Making of the American Working Class* (London: Verso, 1991); Richard Delgado and Jean Stefancic, eds., *Critical White Studies: Looking Behind the Mirror* (Philadelphia: Temple Univ. Press, 1997), xvii-xviii; Cheryl I. Harris, "Whiteness as Property," *Harvard Law Review* 106 (1993): 1707-91; Matthew Frye Jacobson, *Whiteness of a Different Color: European Immigrants and the Alchemy of Race* (Cambridge, MA: Harvard, 1998); George Lipsitz, *The Possessive Investment in Whiteness: How White People Profit from Identity Politics* (Philadelphia: Temple Univ. Press, 1998); Birgit Brander Rasmussen, Eric Klinenberg, Irene J. Nexica, Matt Wray, eds., *The Making and Unmaking of Whiteness* (Durham: Duke Univ. Press, 2001). On specific groups, see George M. Fredrickson, *The Black Image in the White Mind: The Debate on Afro-American Character and Destiny, 1817–1914* (New York: Harper & Row, 1971); Grace E. Hale, *Making Whiteness: The Culture of Segregation in the South* (New York: Pantheon, 1998); Karen Brodkin, *How Jews Became White Folks and What That Says about Race in America* (New Brunswick: Rutgers, 1998); Noel Ignatiev, *How the Irish Became White* (New York: Routledge, 1995).

creating meaning, symbols, and signifying practices, whether oral or body language or other expressions. Culture encompasses "memory," social and historical categories which coalesce as societies' narratives. Such narratives are fluid and unstable complexes of social meanings varying from one social space to another, from one stage of material life to another. They are constantly being transformed by new material products, political conflict, published and private discourses, and by everyday practices of all. Thus, created culture is a frame from within which human beings determine their concept of reality and their life projects.

Transculturalism denotes the competence to live in two or more differing cultures and, in the process, create a transcultural space. Called a "third space" by Homi Bhabha, it is not necessarily a distinct but an overlapping, interactive space. No mechanistic dialectic of thesis, antithesis, and synthesis is involved. Strategic transcultural competence involves capabilities to act and plan life projects in multiple cultures and to choose between cultures. In the process of transculturation individuals and societies change themselves through integration of diverse lifeways into a new dynamic everyday culture. Subsequent interactions will again change this new—and transitory—culture.

The traditional, often positivist "Country self-study" (*Landeswissenschaft*) has been defined as "a single comprehensive method for examining and organizing the multifold data and phenomena which describe a group of people living in a given place at a given time."[700] This approach bounded itself explicitly by accepting as its frame political borders, often laid down arbitrarily at an accidental moment in time. It is insular. The humanities- and narrative historiography-based Cultural Studies, the social sciences- and analytical historiography-based Societal Studies may be reconceptualized and integrated as Transcultural Societal Studies (TSS). TSS incorporates both the epistemological complexity and the composition of societies as many-cultured by gender, class, ethnocultural belonging, skin colour, and other characteristics. TSS is, first, inherently transnational by cultural backgrounds of a society's members and, second, intentionally transnational by scholars' transcending of boundaries. They are transcultural by emphasizing regional and local cultural differences within countries and societies (Nova Scotia as different from Manitoba, for example) as well as by emphasizing cultural macro-regions (Anglo-North American versus In-

---

700 : Robert H. Walker cited in Robert Merideth, ed., *American Studies: Essays on Theory and Method* (Columbus, OH: Merrill, 1968), vii.

dio-African-Latin American or Caribbean societies, for example). Aspects of Canadian, U.S., or other cultures neither begin in the particular country nor do they necessarily end there. References to "national" cultures are only a convention of data collection and organization as well as of interpretive generalization.

Transcultural Societal Studies integrates the study of society and its patterns and institutions ("social sciences"), all types of representations of it ("discursive sciences"), and the actual practices ("lifeway or habitus sciences") in the context of legal, religious, and ethical norms ("normative sciences"), the somatic-psychic-emotional-spiritual-intellectual characteristics of individual men and women ("life sciences") and the physical-geographic context ("environmental sciences").[701] TSS pursues an anthropological approach to a whole way of life in family networks and community relationships, embedded in hierarchically structured power relationships, and in the complex unifying institutions of many-cultured states. They study interactions as well as borderlands between specific cultures, external or internal to a society; they analyze origins and destinations of everyday lives that transcend the space of one particular society, culture, or state. Regions are more discrete geographic and social spaces than their aggregate, the cultural nation or the geographic territory of a state. Communities, whether villages, regions, metropoles, or nations, evolve from shared narratives.[702] The concept of community changes physical place into social space, and involves conventions of thinking (the past), actual ways of life (the present), and the potential to develop individual and societal strategies (the future). The historicity of TSS thus expands the traditional, "self-understood," but analytically ungrounded emphasis on the past and on the living adult or working-age generation to an intergenerational perspective that includes the young generation engaged in shaping their own life trajectories and, thus, the trajectory of their society.[703]

---

701 : Conceptual approaches vary between societies and their languages. The distinction between scholarship and sciences in English language is not reflected in French language, the humanities—but not the humanities sciences—translates into French as sciences *humaines*.

702 : Benedict Anderson, *Imagined Communities: Reflections on the Origin and Spread of Nationalism* (1983, 3rd ed., London: Verso, 1986); Eric Hobsbawm and Terence Ranger, eds., *The Invention of Tradition* (Cambridge: Cambridge, 1983); Anthony D. Smith, *National Identity* (Reno: Univ. of Nevada Press, 1991), and Smith, *Myths and Memories of the Nation* (Oxford: Oxford, 1999); Ernest Gellner, *Nations and Nationalism: New Perspectives on the Past* (Ithaca: Cornell, 1983); Miroslav Hroch, *Social Preconditions of National Revival in Europe* (Cambridge: Cambridge, 1985).

703 : The older generation, "ancestors" or "elders," have been included, sometimes with worship or particular respect accorded to them.

Transcultural Societal Studies is aware of multiple conventions about scales of time and space. History texts often divide chronological time into segments according to rulers' lives or presidential administrations. Natural time, with the sun in the zenith as base ("noon"), meant local time. Only toward the end of the nineteenth century were the many local times standardized into the system of world time zones for the convenience of accelerating long-distance communication, travel, and transportation. Like natural time, family, life cycle, and industrial time remain part of human lives. Such scales may also be questioned altogether: Hopi language makes no distinction between past and present, rather it recognizes becoming. The Western adage of "time runs" or even "time runs out" stands juxtaposed to some Native North American peoples' concept of time as immovable, like the vertical cliffs of the Great Canyon. Human beings walk through time at a self-determined pace. Similarly, space has many aspects and may be conceptualized with Lefèbvre as (1) *espace perçu*, perceived space, (2) *espace conçu*, conceived space, and (3) *espace vécu*, lived space. Perceived space refers to the potentiality of physical space to serve human needs, as regards material and social reproduction in power relations. Conceived space refers to the ways in which space is conceptualized by special groups such as farmers or railroad magnates, by planners such as architects or engineers, or through society-wide symbols and languages. Such socially produced space "speaks" about itself and can be read. Lived space is the appropriation of space in everyday life. People live spaces for their own needs, reproducing or transforming them in the process. In Canada, space has been conceptualized by First Peoples; then, under the different discourses and frames of reference, was reconceptualized by early settlers and the scholars of the Geological Survey. It was rethought again in response to improved transportation and the evolution from a dispersed agricultural and natural-resource-based society to a spatially concentrated urban one along the 49th parallel. It expanded to include spaces across the globe with each immigrant arriving and with each internationalizing economic sector.[704]

Identities or, more cautiously, identifications are socialized in three overlays of social space: the immediate family and neighbourhood (lived, experienced social space), the regional economy (framework of options and constraints), and the polity as a whole (distant constraining or opportunity-providing normative structures). Identifications develop in the stages of

---

704 : Tamara K. Hareven, *Family Time and Industrial Time: The Relationship between Family and Work in a New England Industrial Community* (Cambridge: Cambridge, 1982); Nora Räthzel, "Youth groups and the politics of time and space," *Soundings* 24 (Autumn 2003): 90–111; Henri Lefèbvre, *The Production of Space* (London: Blackwell, 1991), 33, 38, 245.

the life cycle: infancy and childhood, adolescence, and adulthood. Family and school create local identifications first and most unconsciously. Shared and unquestioned ("natural") discourses of norms and values shape lifetime identities or, to use terms less open to essentialist readings, embeddedness and belongings. Some languages make no distinction between genders and thus permit a flexible usage of the many potentialities of sex and sexuality. Identifications may be constrained by the dead weight of the past or they may offer options for individual as well as societal development. In a second step, young people acquire a regional identity when they share cultural practices and evaluate and explore labour market segments. Schoolteachers may also teach them distinctiveness from people of neighbouring regions. The top-level identity of Canadianness or other nationality is acquired last. Nineteenth-century migrants left a region: the two southern Chinese provinces with a diasporic tradition; an English shire; the Italian Mezzogiorno, which did not provide opportunities to earn a living; or a particular region of Ukraine or the Scottish highlands, when land for a new generation of peasant children became scarce. After arrival, neither immigrant nor Canadian neighbours knew about the rich variety of regional cultures and thus labelled the newcomers Chinese, English or British, Italians, Ukrainians, or Scots, or, in the present, South Asians or Somali. National or, better, polity-wide identities are ascribed, constructed, and actuated in the context of particular usages.

Immigrant men, women, and children, who Canadianized and contributed to Canadian society their pre-migration practices and norms, sometimes formed cultural enclaves and sometimes were relegated to the margins of the polity. But through communication they crossed borders, established diasporic belongings, and socialized in many-cultured communities. The quadri-cultured so-called British immigrants, that is, the English, Scots, Irish, and Welsh, kept "roots" and emphasized multiple cultural belongings to a local cultural region, to a British state or—contested—nation, perhaps to the British Empire, and to Anglo-Canada in its many variants. Transcultural lives permit negotiating between cultures, simultaneous living in more than one culture, and respect for and coming to terms with those who live other cultures ("diversity"). The combination of culture and power by quantity (majority) or by imposition (national education, police, monocultural law) results in a hierarchization of cultures.

Transcultural Societal Studies differentiates social groups rather than aggregate generic "nationals" in the frame of

- acknowledging the political economy, economic institutions, and processes such as production, work, consumption, and exchange in local, national, and global markets;

- recognizing socially variable constructs and categories such as class, „race" or skin colour, or other physical trait, gender, nationality or ethnicity, place and space, family cycles or generations, or less variable socially defined categories such as sex and age;
- codifying legal or judicial and political or administrative institutions including the distribution of power, the interests of "civil servants," "impartial" judges or legislators, and the discourses emerging from structural hierarchizations, that is, "institutio-lects" similar to socio- or dialects;
- codifying religious institutions, gatekeeper-controlled traditions, shared ethics;
- signifying systems and praxes such as oral and body languages, forms of musical expression, communication through performance and theatre, everyday practices and norms, lifestyles, values and spiritual belonging, „high" and popular cultures, mass media, and the arts.

The many competing, reinforcing, overlapping, or sometimes contradictory signifying praxes—the "discourses" of a society in a particular period of time—influence the way the economic, social, and political institutions, structures, and processes are being viewed, questioned or affirmed, challenged or supported. The economic, social, and political institutions, structures, and processes in turn circumscribe the scope, borderlines, and directions of the discourse.

- Transcultural Societal Studies emphasizes the aspect of sub-societal regional and supra-societal macro-regional identifications across local communities and other societies of the globe;
- consumption and production patterns that include material goods and foodways from many regions worldwide as well as patterns of competition between economic and institutional regimes;
- family as well as societies' political strategies toward other societies embedded in family economies and values as well as in concepts of global governance;
- the institutional and structural settings and strategies that incorporate interests of particular groups (elites, bureaucrats, planners, or other „inhabitants of institutions") or seek to achieve common wealth and shared belongings.

Thus, Transcultural Societal Studies embraces

- on the self-analytical level of societies: the social sciences including analytical history, sociology, political science, and economics, as well as jurisprudence;

- on the self-reflective and self-representational level of societies: the humanities including narrative history and the arts, and, transcending individual and communal lifespans, religious expression;
- on the level of community: the environment and the earth sciences;
- on the level of individual identity: the life sciences (that is, community) and personally experienceable relationships, psychic and physical health sciences including psychosomatic approaches to whole human beings, study of body language, family economy, life cycle, and gender approaches, and comprehension of spirituality.[705]

TSS combines the self-views and self-representations, the internal discourses of societies with analyses from the outside, by cultural "Others." They thus place institutional practices and cultural expressions in a comparative perspective. Comparative perspectives vary over time; they may encompass the northern fur-trading hemisphere as in the seventeenth and eighteenth centuries, or economics in the frame of NAFTA in the late twentieth century. They may compare, locally, two neighbouring communities, or globally, textile production in Canada and China or elsewhere. Scholars looking from the outside need to be as much aware of their particular frame of reference as scholars looking from within, a "gaze" onto the other society or, internally, on "the Other" defies analysis. To achieve such comprehensive and yet multiple perspectives, the fragmenting boundaries between scholarly disciplines—some of which survive mainly because they are institutionalized—need to be replaced by continuous transdisciplinary selection and combination of theories and methodologies based on performance ("groundedness") rather than on intra-disciplinary traditions and canons.[706]

Research strategies involve

(1) synchronic and diachronic approaches to everyday life;

(2) multi-layered analyses at the macro-level of whole societies (or states or nations), at the micro-level of individual and family action and identity formation in social networks, and at the connecting meso-level of chosen or given units, such as socio- or ethnocultural groups, segmented labour markets, communities, or regional cultures;

---

705 : Traditionally, scholarship distinguished between life and otherworldly or transcendental beliefs (religion). However, all these aspects may better be understood as related.

706 : A "canon" is a convention, the term is derived from the Egyptian word for "reed" or "measuring rod." See also Robert Lecker, ed., *Canadian Canons: Essays in Literary Value* (Toronto: UTP, 1991).

(3) comparative or contrastive analyses to point to specific aspects of particular societies and social units (without succumbing to a hierarchization of one variant over another);[707] to understand cultural and social interpenetrations or embraces as well as interactions of interregional, transnational, or worldwide scope, or across dividing narratives of class, ethnicity, gender, or generation; to examine the spread of imagery and discourses within hierarchies and thus analyze why some definitions and some discourse strategies are promoted and bought in the marketplace of culture and adopted in the arena of communication as well as why and how others are marginalized.

Thus the concepts of nation and national identity, of state and legislative practices, are disaggregated into their many constituent parts: individuals and families are connected to polity, society, economy, as well as—by schooling and societal narratives—to belief systems and overarching identities and institutions. This new comprehensive reading replaces hegemonic but partial master narratives. It recognizes that social activities and belongings do not begin or end at political borders, but merge, entwine, braid many aspects of different cultures into a transcultural whole.

Transcultural research has been part of migration research and of studies of colonization. "Contact zones" may encourage exchange, as in "meeting places" between cultures or commerce in port cities; they may enforce exchange, as in slave-labour plantation economies; they may mandate cultural exchange in borderlands. "Official" or accepted historiography has, in the past, shunned migration history because migrants between states, in fact, have questioned monocultural stories of nationhood all along. While, at the apogee of nationalism from the mid-1880s to 1914, historians gave scholarly blessing to national identities, some twenty million Europeans left for North America and, to a lesser degree, South America. They undercut the ideological base of nation-state historiography and essentialist national identities. Without their decisions to move between cultures, Canadian culture—as well as those of all other societies in the Americas, Europe, Asia, or Africa—would not have developed. Nation-state historians preferred to render migrants' lives invisible rather than accept the challenge to the concept of genetically transmitted nationhood. Historians, other social scientists, and literary writers were not even equipped to deal with plurality or diversity among residents of a country. Of the 192 states in the world, 150 accom-

---

707 : For example, exceptionalism has been claimed for U.S. as well as German history; a model character has been postulated for nation building in France and Great Britain.

modate four or more ethnocultural groups within their political borders, another 29 accommodate three cultures, and only two states worldwide represent themselves as having only one cultural group. Settled societies are transcultural, co-operative or conflictual, before migrants add their cultural, again co-operative or conflictual, input.[708]

The study of whole lives in complex societies involves intricate methodological and theoretical issues.[709] The "community studies" approach, pioneered in the United States and refined in many national and transnational scholarly discourses, has achieved notable results.[710] Social science-based studies need to incorporate aspects of language and semiotics, the humanities to include life writings, diaries, letters, and autobiographies. Databased researchers need to deal with self-representations and the imagery in literary productions and the arts. All understanding of discursive patterns and of perceptions of realities notwithstanding, the debate on what is artificial and what is act-ual is far from being answered. Received standards of particular disciplines guide validation of data, but result in partial or fragmented stories. At the same time, the humanities have to relate every literary, decorative, performing, musical, or other production to the social environment: readers or audiences, producers and markets, mainstream discourses and alternative options, counter-, sub-, or marginal cultures as well as to institutional practices of ensuring hegemony and conformity or dynamic development and change.

Standards of validation need to be discussed in terms of data and of imagination. In the social sciences and in analytical historiography, the "facts" or data have to be traceable in the sources. Since what is not in the sources cannot enter analysis, the resulting narratives of the past or the present include many empty spaces: incomplete data provide invalid stories. Also, people who die drop out of both statistics and historical writings. But their

---

708 : Isajiw, *Understanding Diversity*, 11–15. A quarter century after the critiques of nation-state historiography, the European Science Foundation in its Programme in Humanities finally funded a study on how to represent the past in categories other than nationhood (report by Stefan Berger, European Social Science History Conference, Berlin, March 2004).

709 : To convey the complexity of his topic, one anthropologist, Anthony F.C. Wallace, needed the following title: *Rockdale: The Growth of an American Village in the Early Industrial Revolution; An Account of the Coming of the Machine, the Making of a New Way of Life in the Mill Hamlets, the Triumph of Evangelical Capitalists Over Socialists and Infidels, and the Transformation of the Workers into Christian Soldiers in a Cotton-Manufacturing District in Pennsylvania in the Years Before and During the Civil War* (New York: Knopf, 1972).

710 : Recent Canadian examples are Paul Voisey, *Vulcan [Alberta]: The Making of a Prairie Community* (Toronto: UTP, 1988), and Kenneth M. Sylvester, *The Limits of Rural Capitalism: Family, Culture, and Markets in Montcalm, Manitoba, 1870–1940* (Toronto: UTP, 2001).

absence shapes the lives of survivors; their untold stories are a corrective to the narrations of the living. No literary work would find a readership if it involved as many empty spaces as databased writings. Analyses might not neglect undocumented feelings or overlook "non-facts," such as the dead, the forgotten, or those who lived but vanished from the sources. Remedial approaches including "the forgotten" were once called the "history of the inarticulate" as if such people could not articulate themselves. It was hegemonic thought and data-collection that was inarticulate, that excluded some from a place in documentation, in collective memory. Remedial approaches are sometimes called "the view from the bottom up," but people projecting their life trajectories do not necessarily subscribe to a discourse in which societal structures are the top while they are assigned to the bottom. The connection between small-scale intimate everyday lives and structural conditions as well as historical transitions, the connection between what became and what remained an option needs "the sociological or historical imagination," as C. Wright Mills and Louise Tilly noted decades ago, an "*imaginaire social*" in the words of Quebec sociologists. A critic of the many empty spaces in the databased narrative of Canada complained about "too much accurate Canadian history and too little accurate Canadian imagination."[711]

Rather than using imagination, social scientists often turn to the "normal" by adducing statistics to discuss middle-of-the road patterns of life. To understand "problems," they often use data from crisis situations: case files of social workers, police files, court records. Since such data deviate from the average, the people covered by them have frequently been labelled "deviant." When interview and oral history techniques broadened the database, some scholars have labelled these data as "soft" as contrasted to "hard" numbers. It needs re-emphasis that "hard" statistics are based on "soft" questions and on complex answers reduced to numbers within numbers—a form of expression with the connotation of accuracy. Records of municipal, provincial, or national agencies, once taken to be routinely generated data according to institutionally determined, "objective" procedures that

---

711 : C. Wright Mills, *The Sociological Imagination* (New York: Simon & Schuster, 1958); Louise Tilly in communication to Leslie P. Moch, information by L.P. Moch to author; Fernand Duval and Yves Martin, eds., *Imaginaire social et représentations collectives: Mélanges offerts à Jean-Charles Falardeau* (Quebec: Laval, 1902); William Kilbourn in Kilbourn and Henry B. Mayo, "Canadian History and Social Sciences (1920–1960)," in *Literary History of Canada: Canadian Literature in English*, eds. Carl F. Klinck et al., 4 vols. (2nd ed., Toronto: UTP 1976, 1990), 2:22–52, quote p. 22. For historical conceptualizations of space see Lawrence Buell, *The Environmental Imagination: Thoreau, Nature Writing, and the Formation of American Culture* (Cambridge, MA: Harvard, 1996).

demanded no further scrutiny, are as reflective of administrators' perspectives and moods, of institutional biases, of communication gaps between recording clerks and clients, as are literary texts such as novels or poems. They are reflections of authors' "subjective" mindsets and goals. "Records" are the inventions of data-collecting agencies whose voluntary or involuntary informants had no say in the shaping of the recorded story. "Files" are a literary genre: they involve reflection, reconstruction, and construction. Source texts, whether diaries or census forms, demand close reading of dialects, sociolects, registers, and genres' conventions if the specific act of communication is to be understood, a whole life story is to be reconstructed, or a societal "average" to be calculated.

The relationship between fiction and factuality may by understood from a comparison of literary renderings such as Vera Lysenko's Ukrainians, Laura Salverson's Icelanders, and Joy Kogawa's Japanese with "ethnics" portrayed by historians. The former lead whole lives; the "ethnics" remain prisoners of the discipline's rules of evidence. Similarly, in the representation of working-class lives and struggles, Herbert Biberman's docu-fictive film *Salt of the Earth* (USA, 1954) about a strike of miners in a small town in New Mexico is closer to lived experience than scholarly analyses of labour organization. This "motion picture," to use an apt old-fashioned term, reflects actions of men and women in households and on the job, of children and babies, of prison life and role reversal.[712] The scriptwriters did historical research and imaginatively filled the gaps in the records to recreate lives. Social scientists, once made speechless by the silence of their sources, have come up with multiple and contradictory stories: "Understanding Diversity" or "Multi-Vocality" reflect such transdisciplinary developments.[713] Scholarly and literary narratives and analyses remain close to what has been called "authentic social construction" by critical use, contextualization, and juxtaposition of empirical data with grounded theory and grounded imagination. The social sciences and the humanities, as a continuum, thus supplement each other.

TSS aims at bridging the fault lines and gaps between the disciplines, to achieve inter- or, better, transdisciplinarity. Thus anthropological economics deals with values in economic agency, with individual profit-making or

---

712 : The writer of the screenplay, the director of the film, and some of the actors were hauled before the House of Representatives Un-American Activities Committee, because the story undercut the legally enforced master narrative of U.S. capitalism's gatekeepers.

713 : Isajiw, *Understanding Diversity*; Tamara Palmer Seiler, "Multi-Vocality and National Literature: Toward a Post-Colonial and Multicultural Aesthetic," *Journal of Canadian Studies* 31.3 (Fall 1996): 148–65.

communal solidarity, with cultural restrictions on competitiveness, with concepts of public ownership for communal goods, with ethics of trade. Market behaviour and rational economic decision-making is societally embedded. Geography, sociology, economics, and historiography developed the concept of space—long current in literary expression. In view of the deteriorating quality of physical space, scholars added environmental perspectives: human beings count or measure capacity, they account for usages, and, in a future-oriented "environmental imagination" attempt to keep spaces usable for the next generations. Literary imaginations may provide potential options for the future or multiple readings of the past. Imaginative projecting of a life course or a city's spaces requires analysis and vision to select the possible from the improbable options. Planning then selects one particular option. Imaginations and outcomes are closely related.

Cultures continuously evolve on multiple interlinked levels and thus the trajectory from past to present—the outcome of the moment—and to the potentialities of the future is never adequately described as a straight chronological line. The individual and the collective memory collapse or stretch events and developments. Societies expand the memory of some aspects of the past and forget or repress others. Each piece of memory takes on significance or recedes into the background, depending on the exigencies of and interests in the present as well as on strategies for the future. Particularizing interest-driven memory excludes groups—women, "non-nationals," "coloured," children—through imposed invisibility, symbolic annihilation, or outright purges. Male hegemonic narratives are usually no more than a "5 percent version" of societies since they exclude women, the working classes, original inhabitants, immigrants and ethnics, and those of different religious, everyday, or sexual practices. Memories fuse experiences and reports. Grandparents' "good old times" are merely reported stories to their grandchildren; their golden age may simply be gilded memory. Different generations, genders, class, or ethno-racial groups experience culture in their specific local form and hear reports about other cultures of the past or in the present. For potential migrants between cultures, the reports may indicate presumably better chances in the space where they project their future.

The many cultures, individual or societal, of migrants or of residents, evolve at uneven speed, and time is a complex aspect of memory. A cultural memory may become "frozen in time," emphasizing a particular conjuncture. Many migrants, through a "mental stop," remember their culture of origin as it was when they left. They "know" the society but no longer take note of the changes that they do not experience. Transcultural developments may be practised, for example, on a trajectory from Jamaican immigrant to Caribbean identity, to Caribbean Canadian, to Canadian Caribbean, to distant Caribbean background. They may occur through ascription ("African Caribbeans") or self-imagination (remaining true to what the culture of origin is constructed to have been). Once immigrants or their children have adopted the receiving society's culture, they may still retain pride in symbols of their heritage, like non-migrating old people take pride in the culture of their youth (symbolic or flag-waving culture). At this stage, only useful vestiges of the past, variously filtered, are still validated. Adjustment to new exigencies, experienced by and expected of migrants, is often viewed ambiguously by people staying put, mentally or geographically. Grandparents or parents may remain unaccepting of generational cultural change. Worship of ancestral ways of life or respect for over-aged political or intellectual elites slows down change and processes of transculturation in the interest of some. Segregation into social slots or into frames of historic time narrows individuals' or social groups' array of choices.

Trajectories of cultural change may be multidirectional rather than unidirectional. People may continue to move back and forth between cultures, may command the signifying registers and habituses of two or more cultures, may navigate many cultural patterns, and negotiate multiple interests. Such transcultural life-worlds may also involve class through upward or downward mobility. Code switching may involve familiarity with both gender roles, with different colour codes. Interaction, crossover, *métissage*, or multiple identities permit development of coping strategies in different cultural contexts. Moving between cultures involves processes of acculturation, of observing habitus, of decoding additional signifying and normative systems, and of adapting childhood-socialized codes by communication to relate to people using different codes. The idealization of origin or *Heimat*, its essentialization even, is not merely a remnant of bloodline descent and nationhood; it also involves a life cycle aspect. The code *"Heimat"* is a memory of childhood and, since the actor is small and, ideally, protected by loving parents, background appears as large and identity providing. Similarly, historians and ideologues have described the "nation" as cradle of identity.[714] If not invented on the drawing board, cultures are constructed by intellectual and institutional gatekeepers as well as in people's everyday

---

714 : John Gillis, ed., *Commemorations: The Politics of National Identity* (Princeton: Princeton, 1994); Paul Connerton, *How Societies Remember* (Cambridge: Cambridge, 1989); Sarah M. Corse, *Nationalism and Literature: The Politics of Culture in Canada and the United States* (Cambridge: Cambridge, 1997); Werner Sollors, ed., *The Invention of Ethnicity* (New York: Oxford, 1989); Kathleen N. Conzen, David Gerber, Ewa Morawska, George E. Pozetta, Rudolph J. Vecoli, "The Invention of Ethnicity: A Perspective from the U.S.A.," *Journal of American Ethnic History* 12 (1992): 3–41. See also Pierre Nora, ed., *Les lieux de mémoire*, 2 vols. (Paris: Gallimard, 1984–92), and Halbwachs, *La mémoire collective*.

practices. Transcultural Societal Studies acts upon the present by helping to understand the complex processes.

Education: Intergenerational transfer and transcultural embeddedness

Moulding young people of many classes and cultures into national middle-class norms demands massive effort, even force and violence. In what has been called cultural rape, it involves destruction of personalities who do not fit the cast. For newcomers, in particular, education to—or unconditional assimilation into—"the one national identity" might be compared to forcing left-handed children into right-handedness. They experience punishment for acting "wrong" and have to invest an immense amount of energy into reforming themselves according to an outside norm. Such fundamentalist dogmas attempt to achieve a kind of totalitarian conformity and thus involve processes of self-alienation. After the first generation of "human" rights, sometimes called "natural" or "foundation" rights, and the second generation of the mid-twentieth century, which added the right to material security in times of personal or individual crisis, a third generation of human rights emerges, the right to cultural distinctiveness and the right of becoming. The state of political and legal equality of each citizen and the welfare state is changing itself into a multicultural frame with shared common institutions and a shared frame of human rights-based norms. Thus the construct of "national identity" is replaced by a polity and society of shared values, customary ways of life, flexible structures, and high capacity to adapt without losing cohesion.

Transcultural education and, for adults past the age of education, transcultural attitudes involve (1) recognition, acceptance, and appreciation of differences in cultures, whether of ethnicity or race, social class, gender, religion, sexual orientation, or ability/disability. This may be a distant acceptance, but more often involves the need to interact. (2) Beyond recognition and appreciation, such education develops social skills that permit interaction between human beings of different cultures as well as agency in multiple cultural contexts. (3) Transcultural education involves achieving agreement on a common frame of reference, that is, the equality of each individual regardless of background and particular characteristics, and each individual's right to material, emotional, and spiritual aid in times of need. (4) Finally, it involves developing a sense of responsibility and commitment to participate in society and share with others one's cultural and material resources. Entitlement to self-realization is based on recognition of self-contribution to a fair societal system with equal access to resources and equal opportunity to participate in democratic change.[715] "Transcultural" equality applies to all groups and individuals. Achievements of the past deserve recognition but do not justify special position. The original goals of the policy of multiculturalism—its dynamic aspect—were the emphasis on interactive cultural processes, respect for plural identities, and help in becoming a citizen in Canada.[716]

Children of many cultural backgrounds interact in classrooms. Some have friends locally, kin and friends in the social spaces where they lived previously, and relatives and neighbours in the place where they were born. In the year 2000, children in Calgary's or Toronto's schools—like those in London's,[717] Paris's, or Frankfurt's—had as many peers from cultures in Asia as children who attended school in Winnipeg or Montreal after 1900 had peers from cultures in Europe. Each one had to make his or her own norms and practices understood, had to develop transcultural codes, and strove to fit in and to avoid marginalization, to participate in peer group activities. Such diversity has created multiple concerns about fragmentation and has raised demands to define identity or belonging in ways that provide societal cohesion. Children, to some degree, remain "strangers" to their parents and other adults. Young people will explore spaces that their parents will never know because of the different contexts in time and space of their socialization and their stage in the life cycle. They engage in activities, acquire capabilities, and develop modes of expression that remain undecipherable to their elders, who live different narratives and codes.[718]

---

715 : M. Lee Manning and Leroy G. Baruth, *Multicultural Education of Children and Adolescents* (1991, 3rd ed., Boston: Allyn & Bacon, 2000); Yvonne Hébert, "Identity, Diversity, and Education: A Critical Review of the Literature," *Canadian Ethnic Studies* 33.3 (2001): 155–85.

716 : Ian Angus, in *A Border Within: National Identity, Cultural Plurality, and Wilderness* (Montreal: MQUP, 1997), attempted to find an English Canadian identity by fusing tradition and modernity, by accepting particularities and pluralities. Diversity, that is, the specific, may be reconciled through a public philosophy. In my reading, this was part of the policy of multiculturalism and is part of the educational strategy concerned with citizenship. I prefer "identification" to "identity," even Angus's postcolonial one.

717 : A study at the University of Westminster, which received considerable newspaper coverage in early 2000, found that pupils in London's schools had 307 different home languages.

718 : See among a rapidly growing literature: Phil Cohen and Pat Ainley, "In the Country of the Blind? Youth Studies and Cultural Studies in Britain," *Journal of Youth Studies* 3.1 (2000): 79–95; Phil Cohen, Michael Keith, Les Back, *Issues of Theory and Method*, Working Paper 1 (London: Centre for New Ethnicities Research, Univ. of East London, 1996); Phil Cohen, *Rethinking the Youth Question: Education, Labour and Cultural Studies* (Durham: Duke, 1999); Yvonne M. Hébert, ed., *Citizenship in Transformation in Canada*

Intergenerational transfer, education, and transcultural embeddedness have discarded national identity for, perhaps, patriotic pride in a society and state in which all citizens share human rights, access to political participation, incorporation into social security systems, the right to specific cultural ways of life, and the right to develop according to their own best self-perceived interests and life projects. In such societies, the basic charter of rights and constitution is no longer based on bounded territory and unclear sovereignty but on consent and cosmopolitan connectedness. The right to a certain standard of living includes peaceful negotiation about limited resources that have to last for the next generations. The right to be different does involve a search for and a fostering of commonalities. If this seems to be an idealistic model, we need to remind ourselves that historians have found varying "moral economies" among people of different ages, all of which combine individual interest with common values and a common wealth. Only histories of the powerful, whether of classes such as the nobility, of economic regimes such as unrestrained liberalism, or of states based on internal policing and external militarist aggression, have overlooked such values and ways that encompass both individual security and advancement and shared frames of reference. In the present, educators develop models of "citizenship education" that provide cohesion and leave room for difference. Such education addresses both each new generation of children and each generation of newcomer adults from other societies.[719]

Such concepts are not at all new. In political theory they date from Aristotle and the *res publica*, the public affairs, of the Roman Republic. Within each period's frames of reference, people with limited access to resources developed their moral economies, and political and social theorists from Thomas Morus (More) on (*De optimo reipublicae statu deque nova insula Utopia*, 1516) on conceptualized equitable societies. These are the antecedents of "good governance" concepts and citizenship debates around 2000.

> The call for an expanded [post-Westphalian, post-nation-state] model of citizenship, be it in the form of liberalism that makes room for cultural groups [Will Kymlicka] or in the form of communitarianism which puts the politics of identity

---

(Toronto: UTP, 2003); Dirk Hoerder, Irina Schmitt, Yvonne Hébert, eds., *Negotiating Transcultural Lives: Belongings and Social Capital among Youth in Comparative Perspective* (Göttingen: V&R Unipress, 2004. Canadian edition, UTP 2006.).

719 : Yvonne M. Hébert and Lori Wilkinson, "The Citizenship Debates: Conceptual, Policy, Experiential and Educational Issues," in Hébert, *Citizenship in Transformation*, 1–36. See also Robert Adamoski, Dorothy E. Chunn, and Robert Menzies, eds., *Contesting Canadian Citizenship: Historical Readings* (Peterborough, ON: Broadview, 2002).

in the forefront of internal struggles for recognition [Charles Taylor], is crucially situated upon an issue of balance."[720]

Individualism, political power, and economic dominance need to be limited; the "personality" that people live and express should not be constructed as one identity but—as in *Anne of Green Gables*—as multiple identities suitable for the respective context as well as identifications with the whole of society or state or "Canada." "A reasonable citizen proposes fair terms of co-operation with others, settles differences in mutually acceptable ways, and abides by agreed-upon terms of co-operation so long as others are prepared to do so." Citizenship practices and values involve four domains: the civil-civic of sharing responsibility, the political of democratic life, the socio-economic of solidarity and investment into children's futures, and the cultural-collective, which recognizes both the anthropological dimension of individual persons and the self-identification with collective groups.[721] Identity is a project, acted out in communication with others. It is embedded in local, regional, and statewide Canadian community; it is part of global influence.

The cultural and the political are entwined. "Citizenship is defined by the way we see the world around us, local, [regional,] national and global, and by the part we choose to play in it." Citizenship education involves a whole way of life, not "knowledge" about a political system or celebration of ceremonial occasions.[722] Migration and consumption of goods produced in distant cultures involves a compression of time and space. Both, as well as communication strategies rather than merely new communication technologies, have contributed to a de-territorialization of residence and belonging, of work and consumption, of production and reproduction, of relationships and communities. Historically, at a time when folk culture was considered the immutable root of middle-class nationhood, folk dress in fact changed when, under colonialism, Indian weavers' colourful calicos reached European villages. At the turn to the twenty-first century, much of the music that youth in North America or Europe use to signify particular styles and subcultures is African American (jazz), Argentinean (tango), Caribbean

---

720 : Hébert and Wilkinson, "The Citizenship Debates," quote p. 19; Will Kymlicka, *Liberalism, Community, and Culture* (Oxford: Oxford, 1989), and *Multicultural Citizenship: A Liberal Theory of Minority Rights* (Oxford: Oxford, 1995); Charles Taylor, *Multiculturalism and the "Politics of Recognition"* (Princeton: Princeton Univ. Press, 1992).

721 : Hébert and Wilkinson, "The Citizenship Debates," quote p. 21; Hébert and Michel Pagé, "Citizenship Education: What Research for the Future?" in Hébert, *Citizenship in Transformation*, 228–47, paraphrased from pp. 238–39.

722 : Kenneth W. Osborne, *Educating Citizens: A Democratic Socialist Agenda for Canadian Education* (Toronto: Our Schools / Our Selves Education Foundation, 1988), 118.

(reggae), or a fusion (hip-hop). Such multiple influences notwithstanding, people articulate themselves in conventions of the society, region, or class in which they have been raised or which they have chosen as their reference group. People are embedded in multiple discourse systems.

Mental maps of migrants as well as non-migrants include courses into the future and provide options. Mobile citizens may choose multi- or trans-locality. In Lloyd L. Wong's words, "The deterritorialization of social identity challenges the nation-state's claim of making exclusive citizenship a defining focus of allegiance and fidelity, in contrast to the overlapping, permeable and multiple forms of identity." As to life course projects and belongings, states have begun to take second place to urban spheres, to "a chain of cosmopolitan cities and an increasing proliferation of subnational and transnational identities" (Cohen). Most migrants choose urban ways of life, and since the mid-1990s more than half of the world's population lives in urban conglomerates. New-type polities provide a framework of commonality in which people may interact and talk to each other. They provide relational embeddedness rather than prescriptions; they provide a frame that includes effective systems of rights, options for political and civic participation, and equal and easy access to resources—education, social security, labour markets, and spiritual experience among them.[723] As Transcultural Societal Studies, Canadian Studies has to include this complexity. So has the study of any other society, and traditional Country Studies would also have needed to do so. In a three-level model, Transcultural Societal Studies provides an analytical level, transcultural education provides capabilities for the future, and transcultural lives provide everyday practices—all three are entwined.

723 : Lloyd L. Wong, Home Away from Home: Deterritorialized Identity and State Citizenship Policy, unpublished paper presented at the 15th Biennial Conference of the Canadian Studies Association, Toronto, March 2000; Aihwa Ong, "On the Edge of Empires: Flexible Citizenship among Chinese in the Diaspora," Positions 1.3 (1993): 745–78; Robin Cohen, Global Diasporas (Seattle: Univ. of Washington Press, 1997), quote p. 175.

INTERVIEWS WITH THE AUTHOR

Jean Burnet (retired sociologist, Glendon College, York University, and former research director for the Royal Commission on Bilingualism and Biculturalism), 9 November 2000.

Richard Cavell (Canadian Studies professor, University of British Columbia [UBC]), 2 April 2001.

Marie-Laure de Chantal (Program Officer, Academic Relations, Foreign Affairs and International Trade Canada [DFAIT]), 28 November 2000.

Daniel Drache (Director, Robarts Centre, Canadian Studies, York University), 31 October 2000.

Chad Gaffield (Director, Canadian Studies Centre, University of Ottawa), 27 November 2000.

Christina Isajiw (chemist and civil rights activist), 19 August 2002.

Wsevolod Isajiw (sociologist, former director of the program in Ethnic and Pluralism Studies, University of Toronto), 19 August 2002.

Danielle Juteau (sociologist, Université de Montréal), 11 May 2002.

Jean Labrie (DFAIT, Academic Relations), 28 November 2000.

Guy Leclair (International Council for Canadian Studies [ICCS]), 28 November 2000.

John Lennox (Dean of Graduate Studies, York University, and former ICCS president), 21 November 2000.

David Ley (Geography, UBC), 14 March 2001.

Brian Long (Commonwealth of Learning, Vancouver, and former DEA official), 3 April 2001.

Kenneth McRoberts (Principal, Glendon College, York University and former editor, *International Journal of Canadian Studies*), 9 November 2000.

Valerie Preston (Geography, Metropolis Project, York University), November 2000.

Ian Radforth (History and former chair, University College Canadian Studies review committee, University of Toronto), November 2000.

Richard G. Seaborn (former DEA official, Ottawa), 23 September 2003.

Tamara Palmer Seiler (English and Canadian Studies, University of Calgary), 23 March 2001.

Allan C.L. Smith (History, UBC), 19 March 2001.

Pierre Stainforth (Academic Relations, DFAIT), 28 November 2000.

Clara Thomas (retired, former chair, Department of English, York University), 24 November 2000.

Gaëtan Vallières (ICCS), 28 November 2000.

John H. Wadland (Canadian Studies, Trent University), 7 December 2000.

John Warkentin (retired, Geography, York University), 30 November 2000.

INDEX

A

Abbé Hudon, 165
Abella, Irving
    Canadian Labour Movement, 189, 320
    None Is Too Many, 152
    Working-Class History, 320
Aberhart, William, 187
Abley, Mark, 340
Acland, Charles R., 325
    American Philanthropy, 162
    A Neglected Milestone, 162
    Continentalism and Philanthropy, 164
    Harold Innis, 177, 325
    National Dreams, 238
Acoose, Janice (Misko-Kisikàwihkwé /
Red Sky Woman), 41
    Iskwewak, 41
Acton, Janice
    Women at Work, 333
Adamic, Louis, 198
Adamoski, Robert
    Contesting Canadian Citizenship, 388
Adams, Howard
    Prison of Grass, 335
Adams, Michael
    Sex in the Snow, 25
Adanir, Fikret, 307
    Religious Communities, 368
Addams, Jane, 164
Agnew, Vijay, 284
    Where I Come From, 284, 311
Ainley, Marianne G.
    D'assistantes anonymes, 127
    Despite the Odds, 116, 121, 158
    Last in the Field, 121, 127
Ainley, Pat
    Country of the Blind, 387
Aird, John, 234
Aitken, Max (Lord Beaverbrook), 234
Akerlof, George, 229
Alatas, Husselo S.
    Myth of the Lazy Native, 369

Allen, Jules and Jay, 237
Allen, Richard, 195
    Social Passion, 172
Allende, Salvador, 263
Alper, Donald K.
    New Academic Frontier, 301
Ambrose, Linda M.
    Ontario's Women's Institutes, 134
Ames, Herbert B.
    City Below the Hill, 144
Ames, Michael
    Cannibal Tours, 101
Anderson, Alan B., 191
    Ethnicity in Canada, 344
Anderson, Benedict
    Imagined Communities, 205, 375
Anderson, Don, 356
Anderson, Joan
    Painting the Maple, 356
Anderson, J.T.M.
    Education, 139-40
Anderson, Kay
    Vancouver's Chinatown, 55
Andrews, Margaret
    Canadian Women's History, 160, 332
Angelou, Maya
    I Shall Not Be Moved, 340
Angers, François-Albert
    Naissance, 175, 179, 325
Angus, H.F., 196
Angus, Ian
    A Border Within, 251, 347, 358, 387
    Missing Links, 251
Antko, Lucy, 102
Appelle, Christine
    Politics as if Women Mattered, 330
Archibald, Jessie
    The Token, 214
Aristotle, 388
Armatage, Kay
    Gendering the Nation, 349
Armstrong, E.A., 236

Arnold, Matthew, 255-56
Arnopoulos, Sheila McLeod
  The English Fact, 351
Artibise, Alan F.J., 321
  Canada as Urban Nation, 321
  Canadian City, 321
  Interdisciplinary Approaches, 103, 192, 317
Asad, Talal
  Anthropology and the Colonial Encounter, 16
Ashcroft, Bill
  The Empire Writes Back, 350
Ashley, William J., 111, 149, 175
Asselin, Olivar, 79, 213
Atwood, Margaret, 217, 254, 257, 308, 343
  Survival, 142, 217, 257, 262, 303, 370
Aubert de Gaspé, Philippe-Joseph, 67, 107
  Les anciens canadiens, 67, 107
Audley, Paul
  Canada's Cultural Industries, 349
Augustin, Jean-Pierre
  Modernité et tradition, 49, 128, 329
Avery, Donald, 320
  British-Born 'Radicals', 242
  Dangerous Foreigners, 60, 197, 199, 242, 320
  Immigration and Ethnic Studies, 192
Axworthy, Lloyd, 302

B

Back, Les
  Between Home and Belonging, 310
  Issues of Theory and Method, 310, 387
Backhouse, Constance
  Colour Coded, 117
Bacon, Francis, 95
Bade, Klaus J.
  Migration in European History, 305
Bader, Veit, 307
Bailey, Alfred G., 280
  European and Eastern Algonkian Cultures, 202, 335
  Overture to Nationhood, 262
  Retrospective Thoughts, 202
Bain, James
  Public Libraries, 134-35

Bainbridge, Joyce M.
  Canadian Children's Literature, 264
  Canadian Picture Books, 264
Baird, Irene
  Waste Heritage, 218
Bakhtin, Mikhail, 365, 366
Bal, Mieke
  Travelling Concepts, 371
Balan, Jars
  Identifications, 193
Balch, Emily Greene
  Our Slavic Fellow Citizens, 192
Baldus, Bernd
  Make Me Truthful, 141
  Ontario Schoolbooks, 141
Bancel, Nicolas
  Zoos Humains, 100
Barbeau, Charles Marius, 102, 202, 254
Barber, Marilyn, 195
  Canadianization, 139
Baron de Lahotan
  Dialogues, 26
Barr, William, 76
Barrier, Gerald
  Sikh Diaspora, 55
Barry, Francine
  Le travail de la femme, 333
Barsh, Russel L.
  Anthropologists, 100
Barthe, J.-G.
  Fragment iroquois, 101
Barthes, Roland, 316, 366
Baruth, Leroy G.
  Multicultural Education, 387
Barzun, Jacques, 279
Bassett, Isabel, 89
Baudouin, Louis
  La recherche, 162, 207, 267, 284, 318
Bautier, Robert-Henri
  Le 'Melting Pot', 43
Bax, Janet, 297
Beard, Charles A., 188
Beauchemin, Nérée, 212
Beaugrand, Honoré
  Jeanne la fileuse, 68
Beaulieu, André
  Guide d'histoire, 317
Becker, Carl, 156

Beckwith Hart, Julia Catherine
    Tonnewonte, 69
Bédard, Pierre, 67
Bégon, Élisabeth (Dame), 64, 68
Behiels, Michael D., 221
    Canadian Thinkers, 221
    Futures and Identities, 324, 337
    Quebec and Immigration, 191
    Recent Quebec Historiography, 161, 318
Belaney, Archibald Stansfeld, 81
Bélanger, Noël
    Les Travailleurs québécois, 189
Bélanger, Pierre
    Culture francophone, 353
Bell, Andrew, 106
Bender, Thomas
    LaPietra Report, 18
    Rethinking American History, 18
    Wholes and Parts, 18
Bennett, Bruce H.
    Australian Studies, 300, 356
    Windows Onto Worlds, 356
Bennett, John W.
    Settling the Canadian-American West, 71
Bennetta, Jules-Rosette
    Black Paris, 255, 256
Benson, Eugene
    *Oxford Companion to Canadian
        Literature*, 68, 104
Bercovitch, Aleksandre, 54
Bercuson, David J.
    Recent Publications, 320
    The Great Brain Robbery, 271, 312
Berdoulay, Vincent
    Modernité et tradition, 49, 128, 329
Berger, Carl
    Approaches, 178
    Contemporary Approaches, 276, 314, 316
    Donald Creighton, 185
    The West and the Nation, 331
    Writing of Canadian History, 114, 185
Berger, Justice Thomas, 336
    Northern Frontier, 336
    Report, 336
Berger, Stefan, 381
Berkeley, George, 361, 365, 366
    Treatise, 361
Berkhofer, Robert F. Jr.
    The White Man's Indian, 23, 337

Bernard, Jean-Paul, 315
    L'historiographie, 315, 316
Bernard, Roger
    Le déclin d'une culture, 353
    Un avenir incertain, 353
Bernd, Zila, 310
Bernier, Benoît
    Guide d'histoire, 317
Bernier, Hector, 213
Berque, Jacques, 261
Berry, John
    State of the Art Review, 191
Berton, Pierre, 322
    Hollywood's Canada, 237
    The Mysterious North, 76
Bessai, Diane
    Figures in a Ground, 219
Bessette, Arsène
    Le débutant, 212
Bessette, Gérard
    Le librairie, 213
    Les pédagogues, 213
Bethune, Norman, 157
Beveridge, William Henry, 172, 173
    Social Insurance, 172
Beyer, William C., 198
Bhabha, Homi K., 374
    DissemiNation, 371
    Location of Culture, 371
    Nation and Narration, 371
Bibaud, Michel, 105, 107
    Histoire du Canada, 105-6
Bibby, Reginald W., 52
    Mosaic Madness, 312
Biberman, Herbert, 383
Bickersteth, J. Burgon, 64
    Land of Open Doors, 64
Bienvenue, Rita M.
    Comparative Colonial Systems, 300
Bierstadt, Albert, 223
Bilodeau, Charles
    L'histoire nationale, 175
    Rapport du Comité, 264
Birbalsingh, Frank
    National Identity and Canadian Novel,
      250
Birkbeck, George, 132
Birnbaum, Gudrun, 198

Bishop, Billy
Winged Warfare, 210
Biss, Irene M., 151, 159
Bissell, Claude, 278
Bissoondath, Neil, 355
Selling Illusions, 312
Black, Conrad (Black of Crossharbour), 234
Black, Norman F., 194
Blain, Jean, 180
Économie et société, 107, 111, 179
Blair, Hugh, 14
Critical Dissertation, 14
Blais, Suzelle, 106
Blaise, Clark, 322
Days and Nights in Calcutta, 142, 322
Blanchard, David
Patterns, 203
Blanchard, Jim, 133
Blanchard, Raoul, 49-50, 328
Blancke, Horst Walter
Reisen ins Ungewisse, 25
Bland, Salem
New Christianity, 149
Blank, Inge
Ethnic and National Consciousness, 346
Bliss, Michael, 314
Privatizing the Mind, 312, 315
Blodgett, Edward D., 308
Five-part Invention, 261, 308
Bloomfield, Leonard, 101
Boake, Hames, 47, 137, 351
Boas, Franz, 15, 101-3, 200, 201, 290, 340
Bohr, Nils, 361
Boissevain, Jeremy
Les Italiens de Montréal, 192
Bonaparte, Napoleon, 14, 30
Booth, Charles, 164
Borduas, Paul-Émile, 225
Borel, André
Croquis du Far-West Canadien, 211
Le Robinson de la Red Deer, 211
Bortolussi, Marisa
Culture and Identity, 264
Bothwell, Robert
The Great Brain Robbery, 271, 312
Bouchard Chantal, 80
Bouchard Gérard, 317

Boucher, Pierre
L'Histoire véritable et naturelle, 118
Bouchette, Errol, 174, 209
L'Indépendance économique, 174
Bouchette, Joseph, 105
Boudreau, Françoise
La francophonie ontarienne, 353
Boulton, James T.
Selected Writings of Daniel Defoe, 44
Bourassa, Henri, 79, 87-88, 138, 166, 174
Bourassa, Napoléon, 69
Bourdieu, Pierre, 6, 242, 316, 337, 366
Bourget, Ignace, 49
Bourhis, Richard Y.
Measuring Ethnocultural Diversity, 347
Bourinot, John G., 80, 84, 108
Canada under British Rule, 108
Our Intellectual Strength, 108
Bourne, George, 69
Bourque, Gilles, 318
Classes sociales, 318, 319
Boutilier, Beverly
Creating Historical Memory, 115, 134, 185
Bowman, Isaiah, 167
The Pioneer Fringe, 167
Boyd, Monica
Measuring Ethnicity, 62, 347
Bradbury, Bettina, 170
Women's History, 320
Bradwin, Edmund W.
Bunkhouse Man, 195
Brady, Thomas A. Jr.
Handbook of European History, 364
Brand, Dionne, 355
No Burden, 53
Brant, Mary, 110
Brasseur de Bourbourg,
Charles-Étienne,
Histoire, 107
Braudel, Fernand, 318
Brazeau, Jacques, 173
Brebner, John B., 163, 182
Mingling of Canadian and American Peoples, 183
North Atlantic Triangle, 182
Breckenridge, Sophonisba, 164
Bredbenner, Candice Lewis
A Nationality of Her Own, 60

Bredow, Wilfried von, 302
  Die Außenpolitik Kanadas, 302, 327
Breman, Jan C.
  Making of a Coolie, 370
Breton, Raymond, 283, 344
  Ethnic Identity and Equality, 344
  *The Review and the Growth of Sociology
    and Anthropology,* 284
Bridle, Augustus
  Hansen, 216
Bringhurst, Robert
  A Story as Sharp as Knife, 340
Broadfoot, Barry, 312, 341
Brockliss, Laurence
  Union of Multiple Identities, 19
Brodkin, Karen
  How Jews Became White Folks, 373
Brooke, Frances, 71
Brown, Allison, 305
Brown, Jennifer S.H.
  Reading Beyond Words, 205, 339, 349
  Strangers in Blood, 338
Brown, Robert Craig
  Full Partnership in the Fortunes, 350
Brown, William G., 31
Bruchési, Jean
  Histoire du Canada pour tous, 183
Brunet, Berthelot, 68
Brunet, Michel, 183, 317
  British Conquest, 183
Brunette, Yves, 318
Brunschwig, Henri, 31
  French Colonialism, 31
Bryce, George, 110, 111, 114, 187, 195
  A Short History, 110
  Remarkable History, 111
  The Scotsman in Canada, 115
Bryce, Peter H.
  Continental Immigrant, 195
Bryder, Linda
  Sex, Race, and Colonialism, 369
Buchignani, Norman, 191
  Continuous Journey, 55
Buck, Tim
  Thirty Years, 199-200
Buell, Lawrence
  Environmental Imagination, 382

Bugnet, Georges
  La Forêt, 211
  Nipsya, 210
Bukowczyk, John J.
  *Canadian Migration in the Great Lakes
    Region,* 35
Bumsted, J.M., 108
  Historical Writing in English, 104
  Peoples of Canada, 37, 209, 226, 248,
    256-8, 261-2, 265, 312
Burnet, Jean R., xvii, 158-9, 173, 188, 199,
242, 250, 283, 328, 341
  Coming Canadians, 315
  Late Emergence of Ethnic Studies, 191
  *Migration and the Transformation of
    Culture,* 371
  Minorities I Have Belonged To, 159, 173,
    270, 282
  Next-Year Country, 159, 188
Burpee, Lawrence J., 243
Burstein, Meyer, 346
Burt, A.L., 188
Buschlen, John P.
  Canadian Bankclerk, 215
Bush, Douglas
  Is There a Canadian Literature?, 208
Bush, George W., 146
Buxton, William J., 325
  A Neglected Milestone, 162
  American Philanthropy, 162
  Continentalism and Philanthropy, 164
  Harold Innis, 177, 325
Byron, Margaret
  Post-War Caribbean Migration, 19

C

Cabot, John (Giovanni Caboto), 22
Cairns, Alan C., 282, 335, 336
  Citizens Plus, 336
  Political Science in Canada, 282, 336
Caldicott, Helen, 238
Caldwell, William, 269
  Pragmatism and Idealism, 146
Callaghan, Morley, 215-16
  Such Is My Beloved, 218
  The Loved and the Lost, 216
  They Shall Inherit the Earth, 218

Cameron, Anne
  Copper Woman, 324
Cameron, David R., 276, 284, 285, 286,
  287
  Reflections, 271, 277
  Report, 276, 281, 285, 289
  Taking Stock, 239, 271, 276, 278, 285,
    286, 287, 288, 289, 358
Cameron, Duncan
  Explorations, 160
Campbell, Duncan, 70, 78, 105
Campbell, James, 140
Campbell, Mary L.
  Origin of the Canadian People, 116
Campbell, Persia Crawford
  Chinese Coolie Emigration, 195
Campbell, R.H.
  Inquiry, 31
Campbell, W. Wilfred
  The Scotsman in Canada, 115
Campeau, Lucien, 203
Canclini, Néstor Garcia
  Culturas híbridas, 369
Cardinal, Harold
  Unjust Society, 336
Careless, J.M.S., 188, 276, 314, 321
  Brown of the Globe, 187
  Frontierism, 188, 316
  Limited Identities, 276, 314
  Limited Identities: Ten Years Later, 276,
    314
  Rise of Cities, 321
Carey, James W.
  Innis and McLuhan, 231, 232
Carmichael, Franklin, 223
Caron, Ivanhoë, 171
Carpenter, Carole Herderson
  A Bibliography of Canadian Folklore, 201
  Many Voices, 201
Carr, Emily, 70, 223, 225
Carrier, Maurice, 202
Carrothers, William A., 197
Carter, Dyson, 218
Carter, Sarah
  Capturing Women, 41
Cartier, Jacques, 20, 22
Cartosio, Bruno
  Strikes and Economics, 189

Casgrain, Henri-Raymond, 107
Casgrain, Thérèse, 81, 240, 244
Casselman, Alexander C.
  German United Empire Loyalists, 115
Cassidy, Harry, 151
Cavell, Richard, 273, 281
  Love, Hate, and Fear, 238, 256
  McLuhan in Space, 120, 231–2
  Theoretizing Canadian Space, 273
Celsius, Anders, 362
Certeau, Michel de
  Practice of Everyday Life, 339
Cerutti, Simona
  Le linguistic turn en Angleterre, 367
Césaire, Aimé
  Culture and Colonisation, 255
  Discours sur le colonialisme, 255
Chaiton, Alf
  Canadian Schools, 264
Chakrabarty, Dipesh
  Postcoloniality, 11
Chalykoff, Lisa
  Encountering Anomalies, 356
Champagne, Claude, 254
Chance, Norman
  Cree Indians of Quebec, 336
Chang, Chian Wei, 290
Chantal, Marie-Laure de, 392
Chantal, René de, 297
Chapais, J.C., 144
Chapais, Thomas, 112, 114, 144
  Cours d'histoire, 112, 113, 114, 183
Chapman, Ethel
  The Homesteaders, 216
Charbonneau, Hubert
  La Population du Québec, 183
Charlebois, Peter
  The Life of Louis Riel, 72
Charlevoix, P.F.X.
  Histoire et description générale, 105, 106,
    118
Charron, Claude-Yves
  *Canadian Studies in the People's Republic
    of China,* 290
Charron, Jocelyn
  Social Sciences in Canada, 326
Chartrand, Harry H., 294

Charyk, John C.
   Those Bittersweet Schooldays, 139
Chaudhuri, Nupur
   Western Women, 369
Chauveau, Pierre-J.-O.
   Charles Guérin, 68
Cheng, Tien-Fang, 197
Chennells, David
   Politics of Nationalism, 251
Cherwinski, W.J.C.
   Lectures, 320
   Rise and Fall, 320
Chevalier, Bernard
   France from Charles VII to Henry IV,
     364
Cheyne, J.A.
   Sex Roles, 266
Chiappelli, Fredi
   First Images, 22
Chicanot, E.K., 196
Chief Donnacona, 20
Child, Philip
   Village of Souls, 214
Chiriaeff, Ludmilla, 263
Chodos, Robert, 37
Choquette, Ernest, 68
Choquette, Robert
   Langue et religion, 97
Chovrelat, Geneviève
   Louis Hémon, 80
Chrétien, Jean, 335
Chrétien, Raymond, 146
Christensen, E.
   Lament for a Notion, 282
Christian, William
   Inquisition of Nationalism, 177
Christie, Robert
   History, 107
Chuchryk, Patricia
   Women of the First Nations, 324, 372
Chunn, Dorothy E.
   Contesting Canadian Citizenship, 388
Clairmont, Donald H.
   Africville, 54
Clark, Christopher
   Roots of Rural Capitalism, 31
Clark, Lovell
   Manitoba School Question, 139

Clark, Paraskeva, 218
Clark, Rosemary, 159
Clark, Samuel Delbert, 159, 161, 163, 169,
   185
   Changing Image of Sociology, 166
   Church and Sect, 185
   Sociology in Canada, 166
Clarke, Colin
   South Asians Overseas, 56
Clarke, Gerry
   Social Studies Curricula, 266
Clarke, Harold D.
   Public Beliefs, 326
Clarkson, Adrienne, 251
Clarkson, Stephen
   Reflections, 271, 277
Claxton, Brooke, 241
Clement, Wallace
   New Practical Guide, 325
   Regionalism, 178
Clement, W.H.P., 140
Cleverdon, Catherine
   Frances Marion Beynon, 331
   Woman Suffrage Movement in Canada,
     331
Clifford, James
   Traveling Cultures, 27
Clift, Dominique
   The English Fact, 351
Coates, Ken
   Writing First Nations into Canadian
     History, 336
Coates, Kenneth
   Being Aboriginal, 331, 337
Coats, R.H., 172
Coatsworth, Alan, 291
Cockburn, Russel R., Malley, 166
Code, Lorraine
   What Can She Know?, 157
Codignola, Luca
   La constitution d'une identité canadiste,
     289
   View from the Other Side of the Atlantic,
     300
Cogswell, Fred
   Little Magazines and Small Presses, 219
Cohen, Mark
   Censorship, 262

Cohen, Phil
   Between Home and Belonging, 310
   Country of the Blind, 387
   Issues of Theory and Method, 310, 387
   Rethinking the Youth Question, 387
Cohen, Robin, 347
   Fuzzy Frontiers of Identity, 347
   Global Diasporas, 390
Colby, Charles W., 111
Cole, Douglas, 99
   Captured Heritage, 100
   To the Charlottes, 127
Colley, Linda
   Britons, 19, 305
Collins, Joseph E., 105
Collomp, Catherine
   Amérique sans frontière, 25
Colthorpe, S.E.
   An Aerial Reconnaissance, 129
Comfort, Charles, 218, 224
Comte, Auguste, 144
Conan, Laure (pseud. Félicité
   Angers), 80
Confiant, Raphael
   Le Nègre et l'Amiral, 137
Conibear, K., and F. Husky, 214
Connerton, Paul
   How Societies Remember, 385
Connor, Ralph, *See also* Gordon,
   Charles W., 85, 86, 89, 184, 192, 236
   Black Rock, 86
   The Foreigner, 192
   The Sky Pilot, 85-86
Conrad, Margaret
   History of the Canadian Peoples, 37, 312
Constantin-Weyer, Maurice
   L'Epopée canadienne, 211
   Manitoba, 211
   Un homme, 211
Conway, Jill Ker
   The Road from Coorain, 142
Conzen, Kathleen N.
   Invention of Ethnicity: A Perspective from
   the U.S.A., 205, 385
Cook, Ramsay, 264, 276, 280, 314, 328, 331
   Canadian Centennial Celebrations, 276,
   314
   Canadian Historical Writing, 314

Frances Marion Beynon, 331
   The West and the Nation, 331
Cooke, Alan
   Exploration of Northern Canada, 127
Cooney, Robert, 105
Cooper, Courtney R.
   Go North, 25
Cooper, Frederick
   Tensions of Empire, 368
Cooper, J.I., 319
Copans, Jean
   Anthropologie et impérialisme, 16
Copp, Terry, 170
   Working People, 320
Corbière-Lavell, Jeannette, 331
Corse, Sarah M.
   Nationalism and Literature, 254, 385
Cortesão, Luiza
   L'éducation à la citoyenneté, 267
Cotnam, Jacques
   La francophonie ontarienne, 353
Courville, Serge, 317
Couture, Claude
   La captation, 168, 319
Couture, Ernest, 265
Cowan, C.L., 85
Cowley, George A.
   Recent Growth of Interest, 296
Crabb, Peter
   Canadian Studies in Australia and New
   Zealand, 300
   Theory and Practice in Comparative
   Studies, 300
Crabtree, Charlotte
   History on Trial, 17
Craig, Gerald, 188
Craig, Terrence L.
   Racial Attitudes, 215
Creighton, Donald, 72, 161, 178, 183-5,
   190, 314
   A Life in Folklore, 201
   Canada's First Century, 314
   Commercial Empire, 183
   Dominion of the North, 184
   John A. Macdonald, 185
Creighton, Helen, 201
Crémazie, Octave, 68
Cros, Laurence
   La Représentation, 184, 303, 315

Cross, James, 352
Crowley, David
  Communications in Canada, 232, 355
Cruikshank, Julie, 339, 348, 371
  Social Life of Stories, 39, 205, 334, 339,
    349, 372
Crumaine, N. Ross
  The Power of Symbols, 339
Cruxton, J. Bradley, 109
Curnisky, Savelia, 139
Curtis, Edward S., 210
Czumer, William A.
  Recollections, 139

D

Dafoe, John W., 182, 190
  Canada, 57-58, 190
  Clifford Sifton, 57
Daniel, E. Valentine
  Making of a Coolie, 370
Daniels, V. Kay
  Windows Onto Worlds, 356
Darling, Major General
  Report on Indian Conditions, 42
Darnell, Regna, 202
Darroch, A. Gordon
  Another Look at Ethnicity, 344
Das, Rajani Kanta
  Hindustani Workers, 195
Davey, Frank, 264
David, Laurent-Olivier, 108
Davidson, John, 175
Davies, Gwendolyn
  J.D. Logan, 208
Davies, R.A.
  This Is Our Land, 199
Davin, Nicholas Flood
  The Irishman in Canada, 115
Davis, Allen F.
  Spearheads for Reform, 172
Davis, Bob
  High School History, 266
Davis, Ralph
  Rise of the Atlantic Economies, 305
Dawson, Carl A., 150, 159, 161, 163, 165-9,
  188, 283
  Pioneering, 159

Dawson, George Mercer, 126-7, 130
  Descriptive Sketch, 127
Dawson, John William, 95, 111, 126
Dawson, R. MacGregor, 186
Dawson, William Bell, 88, 126
Deacon, William Arthur, 209
de Beauvoir, Simone
  The Second Sex, 330
de Champlain, Samuel, 44, 52, 123
Dechêne, Louise
  Habitants et marchands, 44
Deffontaines, Pierre, 127
Defoe, Daniel, 44
  True Born Englishman, 43
de Gaulle, Charles, 352
Delâge, Denys
  Le pays renversé, 338
de la Roche, Mazo
  Jalna, 215
  Possession, 187
  Ringing the Changes, 221
Delgado, Richard
  Critical White Studies, 373
Dening, Greg, 99
  Death of William Gooch, 100
Denis, Claude
  La captation, 168, 319
Denison, George, 84
Dennis, Lloyd
  Living and Learning, 260
Derrida, Jacques, 365
Desaulniers, Gonzalve, 212
  Les bois qui chantent, 82
Désbiens, Jean-Paul
  Les Insolences de Frère Untel, 212
  Sous le soleil de la pitié, 212
Deschamps, Nicole, 362
  Le Mythe, 80
Deschênes, Gaston, 51
Desmarchais, Rex
  La Chesnaie, 187
  Tentatives, 187
Desmond, Jane C.
  Resituating American Studies, 18
Desrosiers, Léo-Paul, 201
  Iroquoisie, 202
Dewey, John, 143, 164

Diakiw, Jerry, 264
  Children's Literature, 205
Dick, Lyle
  A Growing Necessity, 178
Dickason, Olive P., 337
  Canada's First Nations, 335
  Myth of the Savage, 23
  Native Imprint, 103
Dickerson, James
  North to Canada, 271
Dickinson, Peter
  Queer Is Here, 334
Diefenbaker, John, 249
Dion, Gérard
  La recherche en relations industrielles, 320
Dion, Robert
  Écrire en langue étrangère, 303
Djwa, Sandra
  Giving Canada a Literary History, 262
  'Nothing by Halves', 245
  Politics of Imagination, 245
Dofny, Jacques
  Les classes sociales, 172
Dominguez, Virginia A.
  Resituating American Studies, 18
Doughty, A.G.
  Canada and Its Provinces, 112
Douglas, James, 40
Doyle, James
  Progressive Heritage, 218
Drache, Daniel, 250, 392
  Markets and Cultural Change, 244, 325
  New Practical Guide, 325
  Rediscovering Canadian Political Economy, 186, 325
  Warm Heart, Cold Country, 25
Dreisziger, N.F.
  Watson Kirkconnell, 198
Drew, Benjamin
  The Refugee, 53
Drummond, Ian M.
  Political Economy, 175-76
Dryden, Ken
  In School, 266
Drydyk, Jay
  Global Justice, 327
Dubois, Émile, 141

Ducette, Laurel
  Reclaiming the Study of Our Cultural Lives, 324
Dudek, Louis, 219
  The Making of Canadian Poetry, 199
Duffy, Dennis
  George Woodcock, 349
  Upper Canadian Loyalism, 47
Dugré, Adélard
  La compagne canadienne, 212
Duguid, A.F.
  Official History, 185
Duhamel, Roger
  Manuel de la littérature canadienne-française, 351
Dumont Fernand, 317
  Genèse, 44, 67, 108, 133, 140
Dumont Micheline
  L'histoire des femmes au Québec, 333
Dunbar, Moira
  Arctic Canada from the Air, 129
Duncan, Alma, 54
Duncan, Davison, 249
Duncan, Sara Jeanette
  A Social Departure, 80
  Cousin Cinderella, 80
  The Imperialist, 80
Duncanson, Robert, 223
Dunham, B. Mabel
  The Trail of the Conestoga, 216
Dunlop, William (pseud. Backwoodsman)
  Two and Twenty Years Ago, 71
Dupâquier, Jacques
  Histoire de la population française, 43
Duplessis, Maurice, 214
Duplessis, Regnard, 66
Durkheim, Émile, 144
Durkin, Douglas
  The Magpie, 215
Durocher, René
  Histoire du Québec contemporain, 37, 79, 107, 137, 168, 212, 268, 319
Dusenbery, Verne A.
  Sikh Diaspora, 55
Dussault, René
  Final Report, 336

Duval, Fernand,
   Imaginaire Social et représentations
    collectives, 328, 382
Dyck, Harvey L.
   Empires and Nations, 241

E

Eagleton, Terry, 163
Eastwood, David
   Union of Multiple Identities, 19
Eaton, Timothy, 75
Eccles, Harold, 103
Eccles, William J.
   A Belated Review, 106
   Frontenac, 106
   La société canadien, 106
Eggleston, Magdalena
   Mountain Shadows, 216
Eggleston, Wilfried
   The High Plains, 216
Egnal, Marc
   Divergent Paths, 301
Egoff, Sheila
   New Republic of Childhood, 264
Einarsson, Magnus
   Everyman's Heritage, 201
Einstein, Albert, 361, 365
Eisenberg, Avigail
   Painting the Maple, 356
Elliot, R.S.
   Marketing of Fresh Fruits and Vegetables,
    197
Ellis, David
   Canadian Broadcasting System, 235, 257
England, Robert, 196
   Central European Immigrant, 139, 195,
    196
Engler, Bernd
   Historiographic Metafiction, 37
Epp, Marlene
   Sisters or Strangers, 325
Erasmus, George
   Final Report, 336
Erixson, Sigurd, 200
Evans, Hubert
   Mist on the River, 210
Evenden, Leonard, 279, 328

Evenden, Mathew
   Harold Innis, 269

F

Fahrenheit, Daniel G., 362
Faires, Nora
   Poor Women, 35
Fairley, Margaret
   Spirit of Canadian Democracy, 218
Falardeau, Jean-Charles, 161, 171, 172,
206, 213, 327, 382
   Imaginaire social et littérature, 351
   La sociologie au Canada, 328
   Vie intellectuelle, 171, 263
Falconer, Robert A.
   Scottish Influence, 95
Falk, John Howard Toynbee, 145, 147
Fanon, Franz
   Wretched of the Earth, 256
Faribault, E.R., 127
Faribault, Georges Barthélemi
   Catalogue raisonné d'ouvrages, 207
Faris, Ronald L.
   Adult Education, 243
Fassmann, Heinz
   European Migration in the Late
    Twentieth Century, 305
Faucher, Albert
   L'Enseignement des sciences sociales, 171
   Social Sciences in Canada, 328
Fauteux, Joseph-Noël
   Essai sur l'industrie au Canada, 180
Fellman, Anita Clair
   Rethinking Canada, 89, 185

Ferguson, Barry G.
   Remaking Liberalism, 147
   Social Scientists, 147
Fergusson, Bruce
   Mechanics' Institutes, 133
Ferland, Jacques
   Labour Studies, 320
Ferland, Jean-Baptiste-Antoine, 107
   Cours d'histoire, 107
Fiamengo, Janice
   Legacy of Ambivalence, 89
Filion, Maurice
   Homage, 87

Fink, Leon
  Losing the Hearts and Minds, 287
Finkel, Alvin
  History of the Canadian Peoples, 37, 312
Finney, James de
  Canadian Studies, 289-90, 358
  *Canadian Studies: Looking in from the
    Outside*, 358
Fischer, Holger
  Hochschulalltag im "Dritten Reich", 11
Fischer, Linda
  Sex Roles, 266
Fischer, Michael M.J.
  Anthropology as Cultural Critique, 102
Fisher, Donald
  A Matter of Trust, 163
  Development, 163-64
  Fundamental Development, 16, 164
  Social Sciences, 163-64
Fisher, Peter, 105
Fisher, Robin
  Maps to Metaphors, 27
Fitzpatrick, Alfred, 139-40
  University in Overalls, 140
Fitzpatrick, Charles, 138
Flaherty, Robert, 210
Flanagan, Thomas
  Riel, 72
Fleming, Sandford, 85
Fohlen, Claude, 107, 317
  Canada et Etats-Unis, 106, 303, 317
  Problématique, 106, 107, 303, 317, 318
Forbes, E.R., 316
Forsey, Eugen, 151
  Canadian Labour Movement, 189
Forsythe, Dennis
  Let the Niggers Burn, 261
Foster, Kate A.
  Our Canadian Mosaic, 193
Foucault, Michel, 232, 316, 366
  The Order of Things, 11
Fournier, Jules, 79
Fowke, Edith F., 201
  A Bibliography, 201
  Folklore of Canada, 201
  Folktales and Folk Songs, 102, 201
Fox, Paul
  *Report of the Committee on Canadian
    Content*, 283

Francis, R. Douglas
  Destinies, 138
  Frank H. Underhill, 190
Frank, David
  Progressive Tradition, 218
Franklin, Ursula
  The Real World of Technology, 355
Fraser, John A., 222
Fréchette, Louis-Honoré
  Fleurs boréales, 68
  La Légende d'un peuple, 68
Fredrickson, George M.
  Black Image in White Mind, 373
Freeman, Donald, 202
Frégault, Guy
  La guerre de la conquête, 207
Frenette, Yves
  La francophonie ontarienne, 353
Frey, Marc, 17
Freyre, Gilberto
  Masters and Slaves, 369
Frideres, James S., 250, 280, 348
  Ethnicity in Canada, 344
Friedan, Betty
  The Feminine Mystique, 330
Friesen, Gerald, 276, 316, 341, 342
  Citizens and Nation, 37, 312, 342, 344
  The West, 72
Frye, Northrop, 208, 220-1, 313
  Conclusion, 208, 221
Fryer, Peter
  Staying Power, 19
Fuller, Buckminster, 263

G

Gabaccia, Donna
  The 'Yellow Peril', 57
Gaffield, Chad, 134, 139
  Canadian Distinctiveness, 301
  New Regional History, 49, 329
Gagnon, France
  Conceptual Framework, 348
Gagnon, François-Marc, 337
  Ces Hommes dit Sauvages, 324, 337
Gagnon, Jean-Louis
  Le Journalisme, 213
Gagnon, Nicole
  Histoire du catholicisme québécois, 171

Gagnon, Serge, 316
Quebec and Its Historians, 318
Galarneau, Claude, 47
Galbraith, John Kenneth
Culture of Contentment, 327
Galichan, Gilles
François-Xavier Garneau, 106
Gallagher, Paul
Teaching Canada, 285
Galloway, Christian F.J.
Call of the West, 56, 64
Galt, John, 69
Gardner, John W.
Are We Doing Our Homework, 16
Garkovich, Lorraine
Landscapes, 329
Garneau, François-Xavier, 44, 48, 68,
106-8
Histoire du Canada, 105-6, 183
Le dernier Huron, 101
Garneau, Hector, 106
Garner, Hugh, 218
Garreau, Joel
Nine Nations of North America, 25
Gaultier, Juliette, 70
Gauvreau, Claude, 225
Geertz, Clifford, 6
Interpretation of Cultures, 6
Gellner, Ernest
Nations and Nationalism, 375
Gendron, Lionel
Qu'est-ce qu'une femme, 331
Genovese, Eugene D.
Roll Jordan Roll, 369
The World the Slaveholders Made, 369
Gerber, David
*Invention of Ethnicity: A Perspective from
the U.S.A.,* 205, 385
Gérin, Léon, 168
Gérin-Lajoie, Antoine, 107
Jean Rivard, 68, 107
Un canadien errant, 68
Gérin-Lajoie, Marie, 81
Gérin-Lajoie, Paul, 268
Gerson, Carole, 157
Paddling Her Own Canoe, 118
Gesner, Abraham
Geology and Mineralogy, 121

Getty, Ian A.L.
As Long as the Sun Shines, 103
Gibbon, John Murray, 254
Canadian Mosaic, 198
New Canadian Loyalists, 199
Giddens, Anthony
Social Theory and Modern Society, 30
Gieben, Bram
Formations of Modernity, 19
Giles, Paul
Reconstructing American Studies, 18
Gillett, Margaret
We Walked Very Warily, 88
Gillis, John
Commemorations, 385
Gillmor, Don, 37
Girard, Rodolphe
Marie Calumet, 212
Giraud, Marcel
Le Métis canadien, 41
Giroux, N.J., 127
Glauser, Alfred
Le vent se lève, 211
Gleason, Mona, 186
Rethinking Canada, 60
Glynn-Ward, Hilda (pseud. Hilda G.
Howard)
Writing on the Wall, 196
Gnarowski, Michael
Making of Canadian Poetry, 199, 219
Goldie, Terry
Canada: Theoretical Discourse, 168, 232,
273, 319, 355, 358
Goldlust, John
A Multivariate Model, 327
Factors Associated with Commitment,
327
Goldsmith, Penny
Women at Work, 333
Goldstein, Kenneth S.
Canadian Folklore Perspectives, 201
Gordon, Charles W.,
To Him That Hath, 148
Gordon, Charles W. (pseud. Connor,
Ralph), 85-86
Gosselin, Paul-E.
La crise de la natalité, 351

Gould, Karen L.
    Canadian Distinctiveness, 301
    Northern Exposures, 301
Goumois, Maurice de Francois Duvalet, 211
Gourlay, Robert, 105
Gouzenko, Igor, 238
Goyette, Julien
    Lioel Groulx, 87
Grace, Sherrill E., 25
    Canada and the Idea of North, 25, 26
    Painting the Maple, 25
Graff, Harvey J.
    The Shock of the 'New' (Histories), 367
Graham, Angus
    Napoleon Tremblay, 216
Graham, John W.
    Recent Growth of Interest, 296
Graham, Roger
    Arthur Meighen, 187
Grainger, Martin A.
    Woodsmen, 56
Gramsci, Antonio, 365, 366
Granatstein, J.L., 151, 153, 316
    A Reader's Guide, 317
    The Great Brain Robbery, 271, 312
    The Ottawa Men, 152
    Who Killed Canadian History?, 312
Grandbois, Alain
    Né à Québec, 207
Grandpré, Pierre de
    Histoire de la littérature française, 27, 40, 48, 64, 66, 67, 81, 84, 86, 101, 104, 106, 110, 157, 171, 212, 213, 262, 263
Grant, Agnes
    No End of Grief, 152
Grant, George Munro, 84, 85, 96, 111, 144
Grant, George Parkin
    Lament for a Nation, 52, 312
Grant, John W.
    Moon of Wintertime, 338
Grant, William Lawson, 85
Gras, Norman S.B., 186
Graubard, Stephen R.
    In Search, 321
Greathed, E.D.
    Antecedents and Origins, 241
Greaves, Ida, 196

Greenaway, Keith R.
    An Aerial Reconnaissance, 129
    Arctic Canada from the Air, 129
Greenhill, Pauline
    Critiques from the Margin, 324
    Undisciplined Women, 102, 201, 324
Greenstein, Michael
    Third Solitudes, 356
Greer, Allan, 317
    Patriots and the People, 318
Greider, Thomas
    Landscapes, 329
Gretzschel, Matthias
    Hagenbeck, 101
Grierson, John, 238
Griffiths, Gareth
    The Empire Writes Back, 350
Grignon, Claude-Henri, 68, 212
    Un homme et son péché, 212, 213, 216
Grimson, Sybil, 134
    Mechanics' Institutes, 133
Groß, Konrad
    25 Years Gesellschaft für Kanada-Studien, 291, 303
    Entwicklung der Kanadastudien, 291, 362
    North of Canada, 25
Grossberg, Lawrence
    Cultural Studies, 18, 27
Groulx, Lionel, 85-9, 112, 113, 161, 183, 184
    Histoire, 87, 183
    La Naissance d'une race, 112
    L'Appel de la race, 87
    Nos luttes constitutionnelles, 112
    Revue d'histoire, 87
Grove, Frederick P. (Felix Paul Greve), 215, 216
    In Search of Myself, 215
    Over Prairie Trails, 215
    Settlers of the Marsh, 215
Grünsteudel, Günter
    Canadiana-Bibliographie, 299
Grzonka, Sabine A.
    Gedächtnisorte, 51
Guard, Julie
    Canadian Citizens or Dangerous Foreign Women?, 325
Guettard, Jean-Etienne, 125
Guèvremont, Germaine
    Le Survenant, 212

Guha, Ranajit
  Selected Subaltern Studies, 11, 370
Guinsburg, Thomas N.
  Perspectives on the Social Sciences, 326, 328
Gunew, Sneja, 310
Gutman, Herbert, 319
Gwyn, Richard J.
  Nationalism Without Walls, 312

H

Haase, Wolfgang
  Classical Tradition, 22
Habermas, Jürgen
  Knowledge and Human Interests, 30, 365
Hagenbeck, Carl, 100
Hahamovitch, Cindy
  Jamaicans Jump Jim Crow, 142
Haklyt, Richard, 350
Halbwachs, Maurice
  La mémoire collective, 156, 363, 385
Hale, Grace E.
  Making Whiteness, 373
Haliburton, Thomas C., 105
  The Clockmaker, 69
Hall, Catherine
  Cultures of Empire, 19
Hall, Emmett M.
  Living and Learning, 260
Hall, John, 54
Hall, Stuart, 366
  Culture, Media, Language, 19
  Formations of Modernity, 19
Hallam, John, 135
Hallman, Dianne M.
  Cultivating a Love, 186
Halpert, Herbert, 201-2
Halpert, Violetta, 201
Halpin, Marjorie M.
  The Power of Symbols, 339
Halstead, John, 352
Halstead, John G.H.
  Labor of Love, 292
Hamelin, Jean, 50, 317
  Guide d'histoire, 171
  Histoire du catholicisme québécois, 171
  Les Travailleurs québécois, 189

Hamelin, Louis-Edmond
  Nordicité Canadienne, 76
Hamilton, Earl J.
  What the New World Gave, 22
Hamilton, William, 95
Hanke, Lewis
  All Mankind Is One, 22
Hann, Russel G., 319
  Primary Sources, 320
Hannay, James, 105
Hansen, Marcus Lee
  The Mingling of Canadian and American Peoples, 183
Hare, John
  Les Canadiens français, 66
Harel, Simon, 310
Hareven, Tamara K.
  Family Time and Industrial Time, 376
Harley, J.B.
  Cartography, 122
Harney, Robert, 344-45
Harper, J. Russell
  Painting, 223, 262
Harper, Kenn, 100
  Give me my Father's Body, 100
Harper, Marjory
  Myth, 86
Harris, Cheryl I.
  Whiteness as Property, 42, 373
Harris, Claire, 355
Harris, Lawren S., 223, 225, 254
Harris, Marvin
  The Rise of Anthropological Theory, 16
Harris, R. Cole, 328
  Canada Before Confederation, 124, 328
  Historical Atlas of Canada, 129
Harris, Robert, 223-24
Harris, Robin S.
  A History of Higher Education, 94
Harrison, Charles Y.
  Generals Die in Bed, 215
Harrison, Dick
  Unnamed Country, 197
Harrison, Julia, 202
Harrison, Susie Frances (pseud. Gilbert King)
  Crowded Out, 81

Hartley, John
  Tele-ology, 177
Harvey, Fernand
  Le Mouvement ouvrier au Québec, 189, 320
  Pour une histoire culturelle, 272
Harvey, Jean-Charles, 212
  Les Demi-civilisés, 213
Harzig, Christiane, 275
  Diversity in History, 368
  Einwanderung und Politik, 275
  Historical Practice of Diversity, 12,
    306-7, 370
  Immigrant Labor Press in North
    America, 305
  MacNamara's DP Domestics, 258
  Movement of 100 Girls, 54, 153, 258
  Negotiating Nations, 258, 306
  Social Construction of Diversity, 306-7
Hawthorn, Harry B., 335
  A Survey of the Contemporary Indians of
    Canada, 336
Hayden, Michael
  So Much to Do, So Little Time, 186
Healy, William J.
  Women of the Red River, 116
Heaman, Elsbeth A.
  Inglorious Arts of Peace, 222
Hearn, Alison
  Outside the Lines, 279
Hébert, Adrien, 224
Hébert, Yvonne
  Citizenship Debates, 388
  Citizenship Education, 389
  Citizenship in Transformation, 267, 387,
    388
  Identity, Diversity, and Education, 267,
    387
  Negotiating Transcultural Lives, 310
Hedley, Alan
  The Role of National Courses, 282
Heffer, Jean
  Canada et Etats-Unis, 106, 303, 317
Heffernan, Jean D., 201, 324
Hegel, Georg W.F., 29, 32
Heidenreich, Conrad
  Huronia, 124
Heinz, Walter R.
  Restructuring Work, 333

Heisenberg, Werner, 155, 361
Helbich, Wolfgang
  News from the Land of Freedom, 217, 228
Held, David
  Democracy and the Global Order, 30, 364
Hellige, Hans Dieter
  Weltbibliothek, 227
Helly, Denise, 348
Helms, Gabriele
  Building Transdisciplinary Standpoints,
    356
Hemming, Doris, 120
Hemming, H.E., 120
Hémon, Louis, 362
  Lettres à sa famille, 362
  Maria Chapdelaine, 80
  Nouvelles Londoniennes, 80
Hendrix, Jimi, 350
Henretta, James
  Social History as Lived and Written, 17
Henry, Frances
  Forgotten Canadians, 54
Herder, Johann Gottfried, 13, 14, 32, 201
  Die Stimmen der Völker, 14
  Ideen zur Philosophie der Geschichte der
    Menschheit, 14
Heriot, George
  History of Canada, 105
Heron, Craig
  Canadian Labour Movement, 189, 320
Héroux, Raymonde
  Le Mythe, 80
Hetzer, Armin
  Linguistic Fragmentation, 305
Hewitt, Steve
  'Information Believed True', 269
Hildebrand, Renate
  Ces étrangers du dedans, 356
Hill, Christopher, 19
Hime, Humphrey, 126
Hind, Ella Cora
  A Story of Wheat, 233
  Seeing for Myself, 233
Hirsch, Arnold R.
  E Pluribus Duo, 356
Hirsch, Eric D.
  Cultural Literacy, 266
Hobsbawm, Eric J., 19, 319

The Invention of Tradition, 205, 375
Hobson, Dorothy, 18
  Culture, Media, Language, 19
Hodgetts, A.B., 265, 284
  Teaching Canada, 284-85
  What Culture?, 265-66, 284
Hoecker-Drysdale, Susan
  Women Sociologists in Canada, 158
Hoerder, Dirk,
  *25 Years Gesellschaft für Kanada-
    Studien,* 291, 303
  *American Labor and Immigration
    History,* 189
  Creating Societies, 26, 36-37, 40, 41, 58,
    71, 75, 130, 142, 179, 181, 228, 243, 262,
    312, 340
  Cultures in Contact, 227
  Diversity in History, 368
  Ethnic and National Consciousness, 14,
    346
  Ethnic Studies in Canada, 191, 341
  European Migrants, 3, 195, 305, 346
  German-Speaking Immigrants, 58, 345
  Historical Practice of Diversity, 12, 306,
    370
  *Immigrant Labor Press in North
    America,* 305
  Internationalizing U.S. History, 18
  *Labor Migration in the Atlantic
    Economies,* 305
  Labour Markets, 73, 279, 305, 346, 390
  Linguistic Fragmentation, 305
  Migrants to Ethnics, 305
  Migration in the Atlantic Economies, 195,
    305
  Negotiating Nations, 258, 306
  Negotiating Transcultural Lives, 310, 388
  Pluralist Founding Nations, 69, 204, 368
  Reconstructing Life Courses, 333
  Roots of the Transplanted, 14, 346
  Segmented Macrosystems, 306
Hoffman, Abe, 271
Hoggart, Richard
  The Uses of Literacy, 18
Holgate, Edwin, 70
Holland, Andrew and George, 235
Holland, Clive
  Exploration of Northern Canada, 127

Holmes, Colin
  John Bull's Island, 19, 305
Hood, Robert A., 214
Hopkins, J. Castell
  Canada: An Encyclopedia, 109, 134
Horn, Michiel
  Academic Freedom, 269
Houle, Ghislaine
  La femme au Québec, 333
Housser, Bess, 242
Housser, Fred
  A Canadian Art Movement, 242
Howard, Michael C.
  Contemporary Cultural Anthropology,
    324
Howard, Richard, 22
Howell, Colin
  Diversity, 285, 287
Hroch, Miroslav
  Social Preconditions of National Revival,
    375
Hubbard, Mina Benson, 127
Huber, Ludwig
  Hochschulalltag im "Dritten Reich", 11
Huel, Raymond J.A., 139
Hughes, Andrew S.
  Social Studies Curricula, 266
Hughes, Everett C., 159, 161, 168, 170, 172
  French Canada in Transition, 158
  Study of Ethnic Relations, 192
Hughes, Helen MacGill, 158, 169, 170, 172
  Maid of All Work, 158
  On Becoming a Sociologist, 159
Hugo, Victor
  Christmas in French Canada, 68
Hulan, Renée, 25
  Cultural Literacy, 2, 70, 372
  Northern Experience, 26
Hull, W.H.N.
  1971 Survey of the Profession, 283
Humboldt, Wilhelm von, 362, 366
Hunt, George, 102
Hunt, George T.
  Wars of the Iroquois, 201
Hunt, Lynn
  The New Cultural History, 17
Huntington, Samuel
  Clash of Civilizations, 360

Hurd, W. Burton
   Decline in the Canadian Birthrate, 196
Hurley, Michael
   Ralph Connor, 86
Hutcheon, Linda
   As Canadian as ... Possible, 276
Huxley, Aldous
   Texts and Pretexts, 205

I

Iacovetta, Franca
   Sexual Politics of Moral Citizenship, 258
   Sisters or Strangers, 325
Ignatiev, Noel
   How the Irish Became White, 373
Inalcik, Halil
   *Economic and Social History of the
      Ottoman Empire,* 368
Indra, Doreen M.
   Continuous Journey, 55
Innis, Harold, 4, 103, 151, 153, 161, 163,
   165, 174-7, 183, 185, 201, 229-31, 324-5,
   332
   Bias of Communication, 176, 231
   Changing Concepts of Time, 176
   Empire and Communication, 176, 231
   Political Economy, 176
   The Fur Trade in Canada, 176
Innis, Mary Quayle, 160, 218, 242
   An Economic History, 160
   Clear Spirit, 160, 332
Irwin, Robert
   Breaking the Shackles, 314
Isajiw, Christina, 250, 345, 392
Isajiw, Wsevolod W., 250, 344, 345
   Ethnic Identity and Equality, 344
   Identities, 191, 327, 345
   Multiculturalism, 306, 344, 346
   Understanding Diversity, 58, 344, 371,
      381, 383
Israel, Wilfried E., 196
Ito, Katsumi
   Issues of Canadian Studies, 300

J

Jackel, David
   Figures in a Ground, 219

Jackson, A.Y., 223
Jacobi, Otto, 223
Jacobson, Matthew Frye
   Whiteness of a Different Color, 373
Jacques et Marie, 69
Jaenen, Cornelius, 139, 337, 344
   Amerindian Views, 116
   Education and Ethnicity, 139
   Ethnic Studies, 344-45
   Friend and Foe, 337
   History of the Canadian Peoples, 37, 312
Jain, Geneviève (*See also* Laloux-Jain),
   141, 266
   Canadian History Textbooks, 141, 266
Jaine, Linda
   Residential Schools, 152
James, Matt
   Building Transdisciplinary Standpoints,
      356
Jamieson, Stuart, 335
Jean, Marcel
   Le cinéma québécois, 237
Jean, Michèle
   L'histoire des femmes au Québec, 333
Jenness, Diamond, 130
Jennings, Francis
   Invasion of America, 338
Jennyson, Mary, 172
Jenson, Jane
   From Silence to Communication, 177, 332
Jewitt, Pauline, 279
Jockel, Joseph T.
   Northern Exposures, 292, 301
Joe, Philip
   How the Squamish Remember, 28
Joe, Rita, 340
Joerg, W.L.G., 169
   Pioneer Settlement, 167
John, Michael, 307
   National Movements, 368
Johnson (Tekahionwake), E.
   Pauline, 117-18
Johnson, Richard
   The Story So Far, 367
Johnston, Franz, 223
Johnston, Hugh
   Maps to Metaphors, 27
   Voyage of the 'Komagata Maru', 55

Johnstone, John C.
    Young People's Images, 266
Jolicoeur, Catherine, 201
Jolicoeur, L.P.
    Les Mechanics' Institutes, 133
Joliet, Louis, 207
Jones, Frank E.
    La sociologie au Canada, 328
Jones, Linda M., 309
Jones, Richard
    Destinies, 138
Juneau, Pierre, 239
Juneja, Om P.
    Canadian Studies in India, 290
Jurkovic, Joseph, 297
Juteau(-Lee), Danielle, 344, 345
    Enjeux ethniques, 371
    Ethnicity and Femininity, 159
    Frontières ethniques en devenir, 345, 371
    Migration and the Transformation of
        Cultures, 371
    Social Construction of Diversity, 306, 307
    Sociology of Ethnic Relations, 191, 328
    Un métier et une vocation, 240, 318

K

Kalbach, Madelaine, 344
    Intergenerational Transfer of Ethnic
        Identity, 347
Kalbach, Warren E.
    Ethnic Identity and Equality, 344
Kallen, Evelyn
    Ethnicity and Human Rights, 341
Kallmann, Helmut
    History of Music in Canada, 223, 262
Kamen, Henry
    Habsburg Lands, 364
Kamphoefner, Walter D.
    News from the Land of Freedom, 217
Kandinsky, Wassily, 262
Kane, Paul, 222
Kant, Immanuel, 29
Kaplan, William
    Belonging, 350
    Evolution of Citizenship Legislation, 350
Karni, Michael G.
    The Finnish Diaspora, 242
Kassam, Meenaz

    Make Me Truthful, 141
    Ontario Schoolbooks, 141
Kealey, Gregory S., 319
    Australia and Canada, 300
    Canada Investigates Industrialism, 50,
        172, 298
    Canadian Studies, 289
    Essays, 320
    Labour Studies, 320
    Lectures, 320
    RCMP Security Bulletins, 74
    Stanley Ryerson, 319
    Structures, 320
    Writing About Labour, 320
    Writing of Social History, 316
Kealey, Linda, 240
    A Not Unreasonable Claim, 151, 240, 333
    Beyond the Vote, 151, 240
    Enlisting Women, 151, 240, 320
Keith, Michael
    Between Home and Belonging, 310
    Issues of Theory and Method, 310, 387
Keitner, Wendy
    Glimpses of Canadian Literature, 299,
        309
Kellogg, Paul V., 172
Kempf, Udo
    Quebec: Wirtschaft-Gesellschaft-Politik,
        298
Kennedy, Howard A.
    New Canada, 193-94
Kennedy, Leo, 218
Kennedy, Paul, 31
    Rise and Fall of the Great Powers, 31
Kennedy, Robert, 263
Kennedy, William P.M., 182
    Constitution of Canada, 181
Kerber, Linda K.
    Diversity, 17
Kerr, Donald
    Sir Edmund Head, 187
Keyfitz, Nathan, 344
Keywan, Zonia
    Ethnicity and Femininity, 142
Kilbourn, William
    Canadian History and Social Sciences,
        114, 182, 184, 185, 187, 382
    Firebrand, 187

Killam, Dorothy B., 254
Killam, Izaak W., 254
King, Martin Luther, 263
King, William Lyon Mackenzie, 173, 189,
    233, 244, 258, 342
    Industry and Humanity, 149, 189
Kingsford, William, 108
    History, 108-9
Kipling, Rudyard, 195
Kiriak, Illia (cf. Kyriak), 355
Kirk, Heather
    No Home, 264
Kirkconnell, Watson, 197-9, 280
    A Slice of Canada, 197
    Canadian Overtones, 199
    Canadians All, 199, 200
    European Elegies, 198
    The Humanities in Canada, 164
    Ukrainian Canadians and the War, 199
Klein, A.M., 74, 218
    Complete Poems, 74
Kleinsteuber, Hans J.
    Information Highway and Canadian
        Content, 355
Klinck, Carl F. (ed.)
    Giving Canada a Literary History, 262
    Literary History, 27, 82, 109, 113, 114, 157,
        182, 208, 262, 382
Klinenberg, Eric
    The Making and Unmaking of Whiteness,
        373
Klooss, Wolfgang
    From Colonial Madness, 37
    Geschichte und Mythos, 309
Kluckhohn, Clyde
    Culture, 8
Knight, Rolf, 312, 341
Knister, Raymond
    Canadian Short Stories, 218
Knowles, Norman
    Inventing the Loyalists, 47
Kogawa, Joy, 383
Kohl, Karl-Heinz
    Mythen der Neuen Welt, 22
Kohl, Seena B.
    Settling the Canadian-American West, 71
Kolboom, Ingo, 303
    Gedächtnisorte, 51

L'invention, 51
Kongas-Maranda, Elli-Kaija, 323
Korinek, Valerie
    Roughing It in the Suburbs, 248
Kostash, Myrna, 200
    All of Baba's Children, 199
Kovacs, Martin L.
    Ethnic Canadians, 139, 198
Krause, Eckhart
    Hochschulalltag im "Dritten Reich", 11
Krech, Stephen, 203
Kreisel, Henry, 280
    The Rich Man, 216
Krieghoff, Cornelius, 26, 27, 62, 108, 222
Kroeber, Alfred L.
    Culture, 8
Kroetsch, Robert
    Disunity as Unity, 276
    Gaining Ground, 308
    The Lovely Treachery of Words, 276
Krosby, H. Peter
    Empires and Nations, 241
Krueger, Helga
    Restructuring Work, 333
Kurlansky, Mark
    Cod, 23
Kymlicka, Will, 388
    Liberalism, Community, and Culture,
        327, 389
    Multicultural Citizenship, 327, 389
Kyriak, Illia (cf. Kiriak)
    Syny zemli, 217

L

Labelle, Ronald, 201
Laberge, Albert, 68
    La Scouine, 212
Labrie, Jean, 392
Lacasse, Danielle
    The National Archives, 240
Lacombe, Patrice
    La terre paternelle, 67
Lacourcière, Luc, 202
Lady Dalhousie, 121
Lafitau, Joseph-François
    Moeurs des Sauvages américains, 23
Laflamme, J.C.K., 127
Laflèche, Louis-François, 49, 83, 86

Laforcade, Geoffroy de, 43
Laforge, L.
  Frontières ethniques en devenir, 371
Lafrance, Réjean
  Culture francophone, 353
Lai, Wang Tai
  Canadian Studies in the People's Republic of China, 290
Lajeunesse, Marcel
  Les Bibliothèques publiques á Montréal, 135
L'Allier, Jean-Paul, (*See also* Jain Geneviève), 141
  Pour l'évolution de la politique culturelle, 272
Laloux-Jain, Geneviève
  Les Manuels, 141, 266
Lambert, Carmen
  Canada: Theoretical Discourse, 168, 232, 273, 319, 355, 358
Lamontagne, Blanche, 80
Lamoreaux, Naomi R.
  Economic History, 150
Lampman, Archibald, 70, 78
Lanctot, Gustave
  Faussaires et faussetés, 183
  Filles de joie, 183
  François-Xavier Garneau, 183
  Histoire du Canada, 183
  L'Administration de la Nouvelle-France, 107
  Une Nouvelle-France inconnue, 183
Landon, Fred, 319
Landry, Kenneth
  François-Xavier Garneau, 106
Lange, Bernd-Peter
  Dialectics of Empire, 12, 370
Langevin, André
  Poussière sur la ville, 350
Langley, Lester D.
  The Americas in the Age of Revolution, 28
Langlois, Georges
  Histoire, 180
Langton, H.H.
  Chronicles of Canada, 112
Laponce, Jean
  Using Footnotes, 326
Laporte, Pierre, 352

LaRocque, Emma
  Colonization of a Native Woman Scholar, 324, 372
Laurence, Margaret, 308
Laurendeau, André, 171, 249
Laurier, Wilfrid, 88, 127, 182, 284, 350
Laurin, Nicole
  Un métier et une vocation, 240, 318
Laut, Agnes C.
  Heralds of Empire, 105
  Lords of the North, 105
Lauzière, Arsène, 106
  François-Xavier Garneau, 48
Laval, François de, 95
Lavallée, Calixa
  O Canada, 249
Lavigne, Marie
  Les femmes dans la société québécoise, 333
  L'histoire des femmes au Québec, 333
LaViolette, Forrest E., 196, 199
Lavoie, Yolande
  Les mouvements migratoires, 183
Laychuck, Louis T., 139
Leacock, Stephen, 84-5, 88, 149, 175, 214
  Canada and the Immigration Problem, 194
  Sunshine Sketches, 78
  Unsolved Riddle, 149
Leavelle, Tracy N., 28
Lebel, Marc
  Aspects de l'Enseignement, 96
Lechasseur, Antonio
  The National Archives, 240
Lecker, Robert
  Canadian Canons, 379
Leclair, Guy, 392
Leduc, Ozias, 225
Lefèbvre, Henri, 232, 328, 376
  The Production of Space, 328, 376
Légaré, Joseph, 222
Leland, Marine
  Quebec Literature, 48, 209, 214
Lemelin, Roger
  Au pied de la pente douce, 350
Lemieux, Germain, 202
Lemire, Maurice
  Dictionnaire des oeuvres littéraires, 27

Lennox, John, 250, 281, 285
  Canadian Studies, 289
Lenoir, Joseph
  Chant de mort, 101
Lenz, Karl, 280
Leonard, Karen I.
  Making Ethnic Choices, 55
Leo XIII, 160
LePlay, Frédéric, 166
Leprohon, Rosanna E., 71
Lequin, Yves
  La mosaïque France, 305
Lerda, Valeria G.
  From Melting Pot to Multiculturalism,
    191
Lesage, Jean, 260
LeSueur, William D., 111
Létourneau, Jocelyn
  L'Avenir du Canada, 251
Lever, Yves
  Histoire Générale du cinéma, 237
Lévesque, Albert, 209
Lévesque, Georges-Henri, 161, 168, 171,
  251
  Continuité et rupture, 328
Lévesque, René, 352
Lévi-Strauss, Claude, 363
Levitt, Joseph
  Henri Bourassa, 88
Ley, David
  Immigration and Poverty, 344
Li, Peter S., 307
  Chinese in Canada, 55
  Race and Ethnic Relations, 55
Light, Beth, 266
  True Daughters, 25, 333
  Women in the Teaching and Writing of
    Canadian History, 266, 334
Lincoln, Clifford, 355
Lindstrom-Best, Varpu
  Defiant Sisters, 242
Linteau, Paul-André, 285, 293, 318
  Histoire du Québec contemporain, 37,
    50-1, 79, 80, 88, 90, 107, 137, 168, 175,
    212, 225, 234, 242, 268, 319
Lipset, Seymour M., 307
Lipsitz, George
  Possessive Investment in Whiteness, 373

Lismer, Arthur, 223
Litt, Paul
  Muses, 254, 256
Litvak, Isaiah A.
  Cultural Sovereignty, 234
Livesay, Dorothy, 218
Lloyd, George Exton
  Immigration and Nation Building, 194
Lockner, Bradley
  To the Charlottes, 127
Loewen, Harry
  Canadian-Mennonite Literature, 216
Logan, J.D., 208
Logan, William Edmond, 125
  Geology of Canada, 125
Long, Brian, 289, 296-97, 392
Long, Douglas
  Northrop Frye, 221
Longfellow, Henri W.
  Evangeline, 69
  Songs of Hiawatha, 70
Loosley, Elisabeth W.
  Crestwood Heights, 260
Lord Baltimore, 24
Lord Byng, 145
Lord Dufferin, 222
Lord Durham, 48, 88, 106, 182
Lorimer, Rowland
  A Report, 358
  Mass Communication, 355
  The Nation in the Schools, 266
  Canada: Theoretical Discourse, 168, 232,
    273, 319, 355, 358
Loubser, Jan J.
  Canadianization of the Social Sciences,
    282
Lovejoy, Paul E., 307
Lovell, John, 140
Low, A.P., 130
Lowe, Andrew
  Culture, Media, Language, 18-9
Lower, Arthur R.M.
  Canadians in the Making, 185
  Colony to Nation, 186, 314
  Great Britain's Woodyard, 176
  The North American Assault, 176
Lucas, Alec
  Missing, 267, 281

Lucas, Louise, 240

Lucassen, Jan
> *Migrations, Migration History, History*, 57, 306
> *Newcomers*, 57, 305

Lucassen, Leo
> *Migrations, Migration History, History*, 57, 306

Luchkovich, Michael
> *A Ukrainian Canadian in Parliament*, 240

Lumière, Louis, 235

Lumsden, Ian
> *Close to the 49th Parallel*, 270-71

Lunn, Elizabeth Jean
> *Economic Development in New France*, 180

Lunn, Kenneth
> *Hosts, Immigrants and Minorities*, 19

Lüsebrink, Hans-Jürgen
> *Écrire en langue étrangère*, 303

Lussier, Antoine S.
> *As Long as the Sun Shines*, 103

Lutz, Hartmut
> *Receptions of Indigenous Canadian Literature in Germany*, 303

Lyman, John, 225

Lymburner, Adam, 87

Lynch, Gerald
> *The Canadian Essay*, 276

Lysenko, Vera, 199, 200, 216, 355, 383
> *Men in Sheepskin Coats*, 192
> *Westerly Wild*, 139, 216
> *Yellow Boots*, 216

Lysyk, Kenneth, 335

M

MacConmara, D.R., 69

MacDonald, J.E.H., 223

Macdonald, John A., 185

Macdonald, J.W.G., 262

MacDonald, Martha
> *Diversity*, 285, 287

MacDowell, Laurel Sefton
> *Canadian Working Class History*, 320

MacEachen, Allan, 294

MacGill, Elsie G., 158

MacGill, Helen Gregory, 158

MacGregor, Mary Esther (pseud. Mar-

ian Keith)
> *The Silver Maple*, 194

MacInnis, Grace, 195

MacIver, R.M., 149
> *Modern State*, 150

Mackay, Ira, 166

Mackay, Isabel Ecclestone
> *House of Windows*, 215

Mackay, R.A., 244

Mackenzie, Ethel, 201

Mackenzie, William Roy, 201

Mackintosh, W.A., 167-68, 175
> *Economic Factors in Canadian History*, 174, 178

MacLennan, Hugh
> *Two Solitudes*, 37, 208

MacLeod, Pegi Nicol, 224

Macmillan, Ernest, 254

MacNutt, W.S., 185
> *Days of Lorne*, 187

Macphail, Agnes, 116, 143, 240

Macphail, Andrew, 84, 213
> *The Master's Wife*, 118

Macpherson, C.B.
> *After Strange Gods*, 326

Macpherson, James
> *Fragments of Ancient Poetry / The Works of Ossian*, 14

Magill, Dennis W.
> *Africville*, 54

Mahant, Edelgard
> *Invisible and Inaudible*, 292

Maheux, Arthur
> *Pourquoi sommes-nous divisés*, 183

Malcomson, J.
> *Lament for a Notion*, 282

Mandelbaum, David G.
> *Selected Writings of Edward Sapir*, 102

Mandrou, Robert, 318

Manning, M. Lee
> *Multicultural Education*, 387

Marcel, Jean
> *La Critique et l'essai*, 213

Marchak, Patricia
> *A Contribution to the Class and Region Debate*, 178

Marchant, James
> *Birthrate and Empire*, 351

Marcus, George E.
  Anthropology as Cultural Critique, 102
Marcuse, Gary
  Cold War Canada, 238
Marie de l'Incarnation, 66, 118, 278
Marlyn, John
  Under the Ribs of Death, 216
Marryat, Frederick, 69
Marsh, James H.
  Mechanics' Institutes, 134
Marsh, Leonard, 163, 169, 175, 252, 283
  Canadians In and Out of Work, 170
  Report, 172, 252
Marshall, Victor W.
  Restructuring Work, 333
Martens, Klaus
  Felix Paul Greves Karriere, 216
Martin, Calvin, 203
Martin, Chester, 182
  Empire and Commonwealth, 181
  Foundations of Canadian Nationhood,
    182
Martin, Yves
  French Canadian Society, 172
  Imaginaire Social et représentations
    collectives, 328, 382
  La société canadienne-française, 149
Martín-Barbero, Jésus
  De los medios a las mediaciones, 369
Marx, Karl, 30
Mason, Peter
  Classical Ethnography, 22
  Deconstructing America, 22
Massey, Alice, 151, 153, 240
Massey, Hart A., 254
Massey, Vincent, 85, 237, 251, 254
  On Being Canadian, 253
  Report, 251-55
Massicotte, Guy
  Les études régionales, 34
Massolin, Philip A.
  Canadian Intellectuals, 251
Masters, D.C.
  Winnipeg General Strike, 199
Mathews, Robin, 270
  Struggle for Canadian Universities, 270
Maude, Aylmer
  A Peculiar People, 115

Maule, Christopher J.
  Cultural Sovereignty, 234
Mavor, James, 149, 175
May, Karl, 302
Mayer, Louis B., 237
Mayhew, Henry, 164
Mayo, Henry B.
  Canadian History and Social Sciences,
    114, 182, 184, 185, 187, 382
McAndrew, Marie, 307
McCarroll, James, 105
McClung, Nellie, 80, 88, 89, 118, 184
  In Times Like These, 89
  Painted Fires, 216
McCrae, John
  In Flanders Fields, 210
McDonald, Neil
  Canadian Schools, 264
McDougall, R.L., 278
McDowell, Franklin D.
  Champlain Road, 214
McGee, Thomas D'Arcy, 208
McIllwraith, Thomas F., 201
McIlwraith, T.M.
  Bella Coola Indians, 42
McInnis, Edgar
  Canada, 186-87
McKay, Ian
  Quest of Folk, 201
McKelvie, Bruce
  Huldowget, 214
McKenzie, Roderick D., 165, 169, 188
McKillop, A.B.
  Arrival of Women, 156-7
  Canadian Encyclopedia, 109, 178
  Disciplined Intelligence, 98, 114
  Historiography, 109
  Matters of Mind, 114, 157
McKim, Patrick C.
  Contemporary Cultural Anthropology,
    324
McLean, Ross, 238
McLuhan, Marshall, 119, 176, 231, 232,
  235, 260, 313
  Gutenberg Galaxy, 232
  Mechanical Bride, 232
  Understanding Media, 232, 260
McManus, Sheila, 70

McMullen, John M.,
  History, 107
McMullin, Stanley E.
  The Waterloo Experience, 278
McNally, Peter
  Canadian Library History, 133, 135, 136,
    162
McNaught, Kenneth, 195
  A Prophet in Politics, 190
  E. P. Thompson vs. Harold Logan, 320
McNaughton, Janet
  John Murray Gibbon, 198
McNeill, W.H., 203
McNulty, Jean
  Mass Communication, 355
McPherson, C.B., 283
McQueen, Humphrey
  Windows Onto Worlds, 356
McRoberts, Kenneth, 250, 293, 392
McTavish, Simon, 184
McWilliams, Margaret Stovel
  Manitoba Milestones, 41, 197
Mead, Margaret, 15
Mealing, Stuart
  Concept of Social Class, 190, 319
Meinig, D.W.
  Shaping of America, 24
Menéndez, Mario
  Amérique sans frontière, 25
Menzies, Robert
  Contesting Canadian Citizenship, 388
Merideth, Robert
  American Studies, 374
Metcalfe, William
  Modified Rapture, 292
  Northern Exposures, 292, 301
  Understanding Canada, 49, 292
Meyer, Reinhold
  Classical Tradition, 22
Michaelsen, Scott
  Limits of Multiculturalism, 102
Michelet, Magali
  Comme jadis, 211
Midgley, Clare
  Gender and Imperialism, 369
Miles, H.H.
  School History of Canada, 141
  The Child's History of Canada, 141

Mill, John Stuart, 330
Miller, Christine
  Women of the First Nations, 324, 372
Miller, J.R.
  Skyscrapers Hide the Heavens, 335
Mills, C. Wright
  Sociological Imagination, 382
Milne, David, 224
Miner, Horace, 212
  St. Denis, 181
Minik, 100
Miranda, Louis
  How the Squamish Remember, 28
Miska, John P.
  Ethnic and Native Canadian Literature,
    193
Mistry, Rohatan, 355
Mitchell, David
  Communications in Canada, 232, 355
Mitchinson, Wendy, 134
Moallem, Minoo, 307
Moch, Leslie P.
  European Migrants, 3, 195, 305, 346
Modic, John L., 198
Modood, Tariq, 307
Moisan, Clément
  Ces étrangers du dedans, 356
Molho, Anthony
  Imagined Histories, 150
Moltmann, Günther
  Die 'Übersee- und Kolonialkunde', 11
Monahan, Robert L.
  New Academic Frontier, 301
Mongia, Padmini
  Contemporary Postcolonial Theory, 11
Monnet, Jean, 125
Monsiváis, Carlos
  Aires de familia, 369
Monteiro, Delia, 301
Montesquieu, Charles de
  Lettres Persanes, 362
Montgomery, Lucy Maud
  Anne of Green Gables, 78
Montigny, Benjamin-Antoine Testard
  de, 50
Montpetit, Édouard, 145-46, 149-50, 161,
171, 175, 179, 245, 324
  L'économie politique, 325

Montreuil, Gaétane de, 213

Moodie, Susanna, 69, 208, 278

Moogk, Peter
Nouvelle France, 47

Moore, W.H.
Polly Masson, 215

Morawska, Ewa
Invention of Ethnicity: A Perspective from the U.S.A., 205, 385

Morelli, Anne
Histoire des étrangers et de l'immigration en Belgique, 305

Morgan, Cecilia
History, Nation, and Empire, 111, 186

Morgan, Edmund S.
The Labor Problem at Jamestown, 39

Morgan, Henry J.
Bibliotheca Canadansis, 207

Morice, Adrien-Gabriel, 50

Morin, Marie, 66

Morin, Rosaire
L'immigration au Canada, 192

Morley, David
Nationwide Audience, 367

Morrice, James Wilson, 224

Morris, Edmund, 210

Morris, Peter
Embattled Shadows, 236, 237

Morton, Desmond
Working People, 320

Morton, William L., 72, 161, 177-9, 185, 187, 188, 279, 280
Canadian Identity, 161, 258, 314
Clio in Canada, 161
Kingdom of Canada, 161
Manitoba, 161
Progressive Party, 161, 199
The North, 161

Morus, Thomas
De optimo rei publicae statu, 388

Moss, Laura
Is Canada Postcolonial?, 250

Mount, Graeme S.
Invisible and Inaudible, 292

Mowat, Oliver, 42

Muhlstock, Louis, 224

Mukherjee, Bharati
Days and Nights in Calcutta, 142, 322

Müller, Kurt
Historiographic Metafiction, 37

Munro, Alice, 308

Münz, Rainer
European Migration in the Late Twentieth Century, 305

Murdoch, Beamish, 105

Murphy, Emily Ferguson, 88, 89, 118, 133
Janey Canuck, 80, 89
Open Trails, 89

Murray, Jean, 185

Myrdal, Gunnar, 356
An American Dilemma, 163

Myrvold, Barbara
The First Hundred Years, 135

N

Narasimhaiah, C.D.
Glimpses of Canadian Literature, 299

Nash, Gary B.
History on Trial, 17

Neatby, Hilda M.
National History, 185
So Little for the Mind, 185

Nelles, H.V.
The Art of Nation-Building, 117

Nelligan, Émile, 79

Nelson, Cary
Cultural Studies, 18, 27

Nelson, Robert, 88

Nevers, Edmond de, 78
L'avenir du peuple canadienfrançais, 47

Nevins, Allan
Gateway to History, 360

New, Chester, 182

New, W.H., 157, 254
Dictionary of Literary Biography, 86-87, 198
History of Canadian Literature, 24, 27, 38, 71, 80, 81, 87, 88, 116, 157, 254

Newbigin, Marion
Great River, Land and Men, 161

Newton, Lilias Torrance, 224

Newton, William
Twenty Years, 77

Nexica, Irene J.
The Making and Unmaking of Whiteness, 373

Nischik, Reingard M.
  Gaining Ground, 308
Niven, Frederick John
  Canada West, 216
  The Transplanted, 216
Noble, David W.
  The Eternal Adam, 180
Noiriel, Gérard
  The French Melting Pot, 43
Nora, Pierre
  Les Lieux de Mémoire, 385
Notman, William, 126
Novek, R., 193
Nowak, Elke
  Gehet hin, 101
Nowry, Laurence
  Marius Barbeau, 102
Nureyev, Rudolf, 263

O

Oberman, Heiko A.
  Handbook of European History, 364
O'Brien, Mary, 332
  Politics of Reproduction, 333
Odets, Clifford
  Waiting for Lefty, 218
O'Grady, Jean
  The Poetic Frye, 221
Okulevich, G.
  Russkie v Kanade, 193
Oliver, Michael, 341
Ondaatje, Michael, 257, 343, 355
Ong, Aihwa
  On the Edge of Empires, 390
Ormsby, Margaret, 185
Ortiz, Fernando, 363, 370
  Del fenómeno de la transculturación, 369
Osborne, Kenneth W.
  An Early Example, 143
  Educating Citizens, 389
  Hard-working, Temperate and Peaceable,
    140, 189, 266
  In Defence of History, 266
Ostenso, Martha, 216
  Wild Geese, 216
Osterhout, S.S.
  Orientals in Canada, 196
Ouellet, Fernand, 317, 318

  La recherche historique, 318
  L'éducation à la citoyenneté, 267
  Socialization of Quebec Historiography,
    319
Ouellet, R.
  Exploration and Travel Literature, 26
Ouimet, Ernest, 236-37
Overton, Grant, 86
Owram, Douglas
  Canadian History, 316
  Government Generation, 97, 143-5,
    147-52, 243, 244
  Narrow Circles, 315
  Social Scientists, 152

P

Pacey, Desmond
  Study of Canadian Literature, 209
Pache, Walter, 298
Padolsky, Enoch, 279
  Migration and the Transformation of
    Cultures, 371
Pagden, Anthony
  European Encounters, 22
  The Fall of Natural Man, 22
Page, James E., 293-94
  Reflections, 277, 285
  Some Questions of Balance, 116, 270, 277
Pagé, Michel, 389
  Citizenship Education, 348
  Conceptual Framework, 348
  L'éducation à la citoyenneté, 267
Painchaud, Robert
  Un rêve français, 50
Paizs, Ödön
  Magyarok Kanadában, 193
Palmer, Bryan D., 319
  Labour Studies, 320
  Working-Class Canada, 320
  Working-Class Experience, 320
Palmer, Howard, 58, 280, 315,
  Black Experience, 54
  Canadian Immigration, 191
  Coming Canadians, 315
  Immigration and the Rise of
    Multiculturalism, 90, 345
  Patterns of Prejudice, 215
  Peoples of Alberta, 54
  Reluctant Hosts, 192

Palmer Seiler, Tamara, 58, 280, 289, 383
  Black Experience, 54
  Canadian Studies, 289
  Ethnic Character, 197
  Ethnic Response, 193
  Multi-Vocality, 345, 383
  Peoples of Alberta, 54
Pandurang, Mala
  Dialectics of Empire, 12, 370
Panitch, Leo
  The Canadian State, 271
Panneton, Philippe (pseud. Ringuet)
  Appel de la crasse, 87
  Trente Arpents, 87
Papin-Archambault, R.P., 165
Papineau, Louis-Joseph, 133
Paquet, Gilles
  International Circumstances, 318
  Patronage, 82, 319
Pâquet, Louis-Adolphe
  Bréviaire du patriote canadien-français,
    79
Paré, Robert
  Histoire du Québec anglophone, 351
Parent, Alphonse-Marie
  Rapport Parent, 268
Parent, Etienne, 168
Parizeau, Jacques
  La recherche en science économique, 325
Park, Robert, 165, 169
Parker, Gilbert, 85
Parkin, George Robert, 84
Parkin, Maude, 85
Parkman, Francis
  The Old Regime, 106
Patmore, Greg
  Australia and Canada, 300
Patterson, Graeme
  History and Communications, 231
Paul, Daniel N., 338
  We Were Not the Savages, 23, 116, 339
Payment, Diane P.
  Les gens libres, 72
Peach, Ceri
  South Asians Overseas, 56
Pearce, Roy H.
  Significance of the Captivity Narrative,
    23

Pearson, Lester B., 60, 152, 153, 248, 302,
    352
Peary, Robert, 100
Pedley, Charles, 105
Pelc, Ortwin
  Hagenbeck, 101
Pelletier, Georges, 213
Pelletier, Gérard, 351
Penn, William, 24
Penninx, Rinus
  Newcomers, 305
Pentland, Harry Clare, 283, 319
  Labour and Capital, 190
  Labour and Industrial Capitalism, 190
  The Lachine Strike, 190
Penz, Peter
  Global Justice, 327
Perin, Roberto, 300
  Clio as an Ethnic, 191
Perkin, J.R.C.
  The Undoing of Babel, 197
Perry, Adele
  On the Edge of Empire, 111, 338
  Rethinking Canada, 60, 185-6
Persons, Stow
  Ethnic Studies at Chicago, 164
Peter, Christine St.
  Feminist Afterwords, 324
Petrone, Penny
  Breaking the Mold, 142
Philips, M. Nourbese, 355
Phillips, Donna, 218
  Voices of Discord, 160, 218
Pianos, Tamara
  Geografikationen, 71
Pickford, Mary, 237
Pierce, Lorne, 209
Pierson, Ruth, 266
  Women in the Teaching and Writing of
    Canadian History, 266, 334
Pilkington, Edward
  Beyond the Mother Country, 142
Pinard, Yolande
  Les femmes dans la société québécoise, 333
Pinkham, Joan, 255
Pitt, William, 253
Pius IX, 49
Pius XI, 170

Piva, Michael J., 321
Pivato, Joseph
  Contrasts, 193, 356
Plaunt, Alan, 234
Pletsch, Alfred, 280
Pollock, Zailig, 74
Pontiac (Obwandiyag), 70
Porter, John, 283, 319, 344
  Vertical Mosaic, 173, 320, 344
Portes, Jacques
  La Coopération universitaire, 272
Potrebenko, Helen, 142, 200
  Ethnicity and Femininity, 142
Potter, Harold H., 196
Potvin, Damase, 68
  Le Français, 211
Pozetta, George E.
  Invention of Ethnicity: A Perspective from the U.S.A., 205, 385
Pratt, Larry
  Western Separatism, 76
Pratt, Mary Louise
  Imperial Eyes, 369
Prentice, Alison
  Creating Historical Memory, 115, 134, 185
  Neglected Majority, 333
  Writing Women into History, 332
Preston, Valerie, 392
Price, John A.
  Native Studies, 103, 203
Priest, Gordon E.
  Ethnicity in the Canadian Census, 347
Prince of Wales, 117, 248-9
Prowse, J.D., 105
Punter, David
  Introduction to Contemporary Cultural Studies, 367
Purdy, Al
  New Romans, 261
Pusch, Luise, 2
Putnam, Samuel, 369

Q

Qisuk, 100
Quataert, Donald
  Economic and Social History of the Ottoman Empire, 368
Queen Victoria, 117, 318

R

Radforth, Ian, 287, 392
  Canadian Working Class History, 320
  Royal Spectacle, 117, 249
Radisson, Pierre Esprit, 45
Rae, John, 121
Rameau de Saint-Père, François-Edmé
  La France aux colonies, 107
Ramirez, Bruno
  Crossing the 49th Parallel, 35
  Immigration and Ethnic Studies, 192
Rampton, David
  The Canadian Essay, 276
Ranachan, Andrew
  Warm Heart, Cold Country, 25
Ranger, Terence
  The Invention of Tradition, 205, 375
Rankin, Pauline
  Politics as if Women Mattered, 330
Rasmussen, Birgit Brander
  The Making and Unmaking of Whiteness, 373
Rasporich, Anthony, 280
  Migration and the Transformation of Cultures, 371
Rasporich, Beverly
  A Passion for Identity, 246
  Retelling Vera Lysenko, 197
Ratcliffe, Donald J., 28
Räthzel, Nora
  Youth groups and the politics of time and space, 376
Rattray, William Jordan
  The Scot in British North America, 115
Ray, Arthur, 202
  I Have Lived Here Since the World Began, 335
Réaumur, René-Antoine, 362
Reclus, Elisée
  Nouvelle Géographie Universelle, 127
Reclus, Onésine, 127
Rees, Tim, 307
Regan, J.P., 74
Rehrmann, Norbert, 307
Reid, Allana
  Development and Importance of the Town of Quebec, 180

Reid, Dennis
  Concise History, 223, 262
  Nationale Bestrebungen, 223
Reid, George, 223
Reid, Helen Richmond Young, 197
Reid, Thomas, 95
Reinicke, Helmut
  Wilde Kälten 1492, 22
Reitz, Jeffrey G.
  Ethnic Identity and Equality, 344
Remie, Cornelius, 306
Renaud, Marc
  Social Sciences in Canada, 326

Renaud, Paul-Emile
  Les origines économiques, 180
Rendall, Stephen, 339
Rennée, Georgina, 67
Rens, Jean-Guy
  L'Empire invisible, 228
Rérolle, Raphaelle, 292
Reuber, Grant L.
  Perspectives on the Social Sciences, 326,
    328
Rex, Kay
  No Daughter of Mine, 233
Reynolds, Lloyd G.
  The British Immigrant, 51
Reynolds, Melvina
  Little Boxes, 259
Rhinewine, Abraham
  Der Yid in Kanada, 192
Ricard, François
  Histoire du Québec contemporain, 37, 51,
    79, 107, 137, 168, 212, 268, 319
Rich, Edwin E., 202
Richardson, John
  Écaté, 69
Richardson, Theresa
  Development of the Social Sciences, 163
Richler, Mordecai
  Son of a Smaller Hero, 216
Richmond, Anthony H.
  A Multivariate Model, 271
  Employment, 271
  Employment of Foreign Academics, 271
  Factors Associated with Commitment, 271
  Global Apartheid, 271

Riedel, Walter E.
  The Old World and the New, 216
Riel, Louis, 41, 72
Riesz, János
  Écrire en langue étrangère, 303
Riis, Jacob, 164
Ringuet (pseud. Phillipe Panneton)
  Trente Arpents, 87
Riopelle, Jean-Paul, 225
Rioux, Marcel
  French Canadian Society, 172
  La Folklorisation, 67
  La Question du Québec, 47, 137, 351
  La sociéte canadienne-française, 149
  Les classes sociales, 172
Rivard, Adjutor
  Chez Nous, 212
Roberge, Guz, 239
Robert, Jean-Claude
  Histoire du Québec contemporain, 37, 51,
    79, 107, 137, 168, 212, 268, 319
Roberts, Barbara
  Ethnicity and Femininity, 159, 270, 282,
    338
Roberts, Charles G.D., 70
  A History of Canada, 140
  Canadians of Old, 67
Roberts, Joseph K.
  In the Shadow of Empire, 293
Robertson, Heather
  The Man Who Invented Canada, 184
Robertson, Sarah, 224
Robins, Nora
  The Montreal Mechanics' Institute, 133
Robinson, Lewis
  Concepts and Themes in the Regional
    Geography, 329
Roblin, Rodmond, 89
Roby, Yves, 50
Rocher, Guy, 327
Rochester, Maxine K.
  Bringing Librarianship to Rural Canada,
    136
Rodgers, Daniel T.
  Atlantic Crossings, 28
Rodney, Patricia
  Building Transdisciplinary Standpoints,
    356

Rodriguez, Raul Rodriguez, 301
Roe, Frank G.
  Getting the Know-How, 74
Roediger, David R.
  Wages of Whiteness, 373
Romero, Lora
  Nationalism and Internationalism, 18
Ronald, William, 262
Ronda, James P.
  'We Are Well As We Are', 117
Roosevelt, Eleanor, 173, 244
Roosevelt, Franklin D., 173
Roosevelt, Theodore, 360
Roquebrune, Robert de (pseud. Robert Laroque), 211
Rosenberg, Leah, 141
Rosenthal, Joe, 236
Ross, Aileen Dansken, 158
  Sociology at McGill, 158
Ross, Alex
  Brigadier-General, 109
Ross, Alexander, 76, 105
Ross, G.W., 141
Ross, Sinclair, 218
Rotstein, Abraham, 202
Rouillard, Jacques
  Ah Les États, 320
  Les travailleurs du coton, 320
Rousseau, Jacques
  L'Hérédité et l'homme, 202
Routhier, Adolphe-Basile
  O Canada, 249
Rowan, John J.
  Emigrant and Sportsman, 75
Roy, Antoine, 180
Roy, Camille, 87, 113
  La nationalisation, 79
Roy, Gabrielle, 211, 308
  Bonheur d'occasion, 350
  Ces enfants de ma vie, 139
  La petite poule d'eau, 211
  Rue Deschambault, 211
Roy, Jacqueline
  Guide du chercheur, 317
Roy, Joseph-Edmond, 108, 114, 168
  Histoire de la seigneurie de Lauzon, 111
Roy, Patricia
  White Canada Forever, 215

Roy, Paul-Eugène, 165
Roy, Pierre-Georges, 180
Roy, William, 170
Rubin, Jerry, 271
Rudin, Ronald
  Making History, 316
  Revisionism, 316
  The Forgotten Quebecers, 351
Rumilly, Robert, 179
  Histoire de la province de Québec, 183
  Histoire de l'École des hautes études commerciales, 96
Rush, G.B.
  Lament for a Notion, 282
Rutherford, Ernest, 155
Ruzsa, Jenö
  A Kanadai Magyarság Története, 193
Ryan, Oscar
  Eight Men Speak, 218
Ryerson, Egerton, 88, 134, 137, 185
Ryerson, Stanley, 319

S

Sack, Benjamin Gutelius
  Geshikhte fun Yidn in Kanade, 193
Sadlier, Mary Anne, 69
Safdie, Moshe, 263
Sagard, Gabriel
  Dictionnaire, 101
Saïd, Edward, 94
  Orientalism, 12
Saint-Jacques, Denis
  François-Xavier Garneau, 106
Saldívar, José D.,
  Border Matters, 357
Salinger, Marian C.
  Portrayal, 292
Salisbury, Richard
  A Homeland for the Cree, 336
Salone, Émile
  La colonisation, 107, 161
Salter, Liora
  Outside the Lines, 279
Saltman, Judith
  New Republic of Childhood, 264
Salverson, Laura Goodman, 82, 199, 216, 218, 355, 383
  Viking Heart, 216

Sandiford, Peter, 143
Sangster, Joan
    Beyond the Vote, 151, 240
Santink, Joy L.
    Eaton, Timothy, 75
Santos, Gilberto Lacerda, 301
Sapir, Edward, 38, 102, 128, 130, 200, 362
    Indians of Canada, 130
    Language, 38
Sarlo, Beatriz
    La máquina cultural, 369
Satzewich, Vic
    Racism and the Incorporation of Foreign
      Labour, 344
Sauer, Jonathan D.
    Changing Perception, 22
Saul, John Ralston
    The Unconscious Civilization, 327
Saunders, Charles, 129
Saussure, Ferdinand de, 362, 366, 368
Savard, Félix-Antoine, 102, 211
    Menaud, maître-draveur, 212
Savard, Pierre, 110, 293
    Aspects de l'Enseignement, 96
    Exploration and Travel Literature, 26
    Jules-Paul Tardivel, 49
    Le Canada sous la loupe des savants
      étrangers, 292
Scardellato, Gabriele, 300
Scargill, M.H.
    Growth of Canadian English, 113
    Modern Canadian English Usage, 281
Schaefer, Carl, 224
Schafer, Paul D.
    Canada's International Cultural
      Relations, 289
Schmitt, Irina
    Negotiating Transcultural Lives, 310, 388
    Social Construction of Diversity, 306
Schoolcraft, Henry Rowe, 101
Schott, Carl, 280
Schultz, John
    Writing About Canada, 60, 320
Scott, Frank R., 151, 219, 261
    Canada Today, 245
    Canadian Constitution, 245
    Essays, 219, 244-45
Scott, Joan

Women, Work and Family, 333
Seaborn, Richard G., 296, 393
Seager, Allen
    Alternative Frontiers, 280, 301
Sealy, Nanciellen C., 139
Sears, Alan
    Challenges & Prospects, 348
    In Search of Good Citizens, 348
    Social Studies Curricula, 266
    What Research Tells Us about Citizenship
      Education, 266
Seeley, John R.
    Crestwood Heights, 260
Segal, Y.Y.
    Vun Mein Velt, 217
Séguin, Maurice, 317
Séguin, Normand, 317
Séguin, Robert-Lionel, 202
Selman, G.R.
    Mechanics' Institutes in British
      Columbia, 133
Selwyn, A.R.C.
    Descriptive Sketch, 127
Senese, Phyllis M.
    Lionel Groulx, 87
Sermet, J.
    Acclimatation, 22
Sero, Eliza, 117
Service, Robert, 76, 105
Seton, Ernest Thompson, 81
Shapiro, Jeremy J., 11, 30
Shea, Albert A.
    Culture in Canada, 253
Shepard, Bonnie
    Women at Work, 333
Shepard, R. Bruce
    Deemed Unsuitable, 54
Sherk, A.B.
    Pennsylvania Germans, 115
Shield, Lois de
    No Burden, 53
Shore, Marlene G., 205
    Science of Social Redemption, 98, 145,
      147, 165-7, 169, 170, 173, 206, 270
Shortt, Adam, 111, 114, 149, 175
    Canada and Its Provinces, 112
Shotwell, James T., 163
Shubert, Adrian

Diversity in History, 368
Historical Practice of Diversity, 12, 306, 307, 370
Negotiating Nations, 258, 306
Sidney, Angela, 348
Siegfried, André
Canada, les deux races, 119
Sifton, Clifford, 57, 138, 191
The Immigrants Canada Wants, 90
Sim, R. Alexander
Crestwood Heights, 260
Simard, Sylvain
La Coopération universitaire, 272
Sime, Georgina
Our Little Life, 216
Simpson, Christopher
Universities and Empire, 16
Sirois, Antoine
Migration and the Transformation of Cultures, 371
Reflections, 271, 277
Sisson, C.D.
Life and Letters of Ryerson, Egerton, 185
Sissons, C.B.
Bi-Lingual Schools, 139
Skelton, O.D., 111, 114, 146, 149, 182, 248
Language Issue, 139
Skinner, A.S.
Inquiry, 31
Slater, Patrick (=John Mitchell)
The Yellow Briar, 216
Small, Albion, 165
Smart, Patricia, 279
Les femmes du Refus Global, 225
Smiley, Donald
Must Canadian Political Science Be a Miniature Replica?, 283
Smith, Adam, 30, 32, 229, 324
Glasgow Edition, 31
The Wealth of Nations, 30-31
Smith, Allan C.L., 281, 393
Smith, Anthony D.
Myths and Memories, 375
National Identity, 62, 375
Smith, Arthur J.M.
Book of Canadian Poetry, 218
Smith, David R.
Canadian Migration in the Great Lakes Region, 35
Smith, Denis
What Are We Teaching?, 283
Smith, Donald A. (Lord Strathcona), 236
Smith, Donald B.
Destinies, 138
Smith, Elizabeth, 149
Smith, Goldwin, 84, 111, 187
Smith, Harlan I., 128, 202
Smith, Heather
Immigration and Poverty, 344
Smith, Peter J.
Observations, 186
Smith, William, 105
Political Leaders, 182
Smith, William Jr., 105
Smitmans, Maria Teresa Aya, 302
Socrates, 207
Sollors, Werner
Invention of Ethnicity, 205, 385
Sommer, Ulrike
News from the Land of Freedom, 217
Spence, Michael, 229
Spencer, Herbert
The Social Organism, 165
Spicer, Keith, 287
Spivak, Gayatri Chakravorty
Selected Subaltern Studies, 370
Subaltern Studies: Deconstructing Historiography, 370
Spock, Benjamin, 259, 265
Child Care, 265
Spry, Graham, 151, 152, 160, 234, 241, 243
Srinath, C.N.
Glimpses of Canadian Literature, 299, 309
Srivastiva, Ram
Continuous Journey, 55
Stacey, C.P.
Canada and the British Army, 185
Staines, David
Canada Observed, 208, 209
Canadian Imagination, 48, 208, 209
Stainforth, Pierre, 393
Stamps, Judith
Unthinking Modernity, 231
Stanley, G.F.S.
The Birth of Western Canada, 178

Starowicz, Mark, 37
Stasiulis, Davia, 348
Stead, Robert J.C., 214
   Grain, 215
Steele, James, 270
   Struggle for Canadian Universities, 270,
     271, 278
Stefancic, Jean
   Critical White Studies, 373
Steinem, Gloria
   Outrageous Acts and Everyday
     Rebellions, 330
Stelter, Gilbert A.
   A Sense of Time and Place, 321
   Canadian City, 321
   Urban History, 321
Stephansson, Stephan G., 242
   Andvökur, 217
Stephenson, Marylee
   Women in Canada, 52, 60, 257, 332
Stephenson, William, 233
Stevens, Paul
   A Reader's Guide, 317
Stevenson, Garth
   Western Separatism, 76
Stewart, Basil
   Handbook, 119
   Land of the Maple Leaf, 56, 84, 119, 249
Stewart, John, 105
Stewart, Marianne C.
   Public Beliefs, 326
Stiglitz, Joseph, 229
Stoddard, Jennifer
   L'histoire des femmes au Québec, 333
Stoler, Ann Laura
   Making Empire Respectable, 18
   Tense and Tender Ties, 18
   Tensions of Empire, 18
Story, Norah, 214
   Oxford Companion, 104, 157
Stowe, Emily, 80
Strachan, John, 137
Stratford, Philip, 206
   Bibliography, 155
   Canada's Two [Major] Literatures, 206,
     208
Strobel, Margaret
   European Women, 111

   Gender, Sex, and Empire, 368
   Western Women, 369
Strong-Boag, Veronica, 256, 331
   Cousin Cinderella, 52, 80, 256, 332, 333,
     334
   'Ever a Crusader', 89
   "Introduction" to Nellie L. McClung, 89
   Paddling Her Own Canoe, 118
   Painting the Maple, 356
   Rethinking Canada, 60
   True Daughters, 333
   Writing About Women, 60
Stuart, Alice, 85
Stubbs, George, 27
Sukhorev, V.A.
   Istoriya Dukhobotsev, 193
Sullivan, Alan, 214, 215
   The Rapids, 215
   Three Came to Ville Marie, 214
Sulte, Benjamin
   Histoire des Canadiens français, 108
   Les Forges Saint-Maurice, 180
Sutherland, John
   Other Canadians, 218
Sutherland, Ronald, 206
Swyripa, Frances
   Sisters or Strangers, 325
Sylvester, Kenneth M.
   Limits of Rural Capitalism, 381
Sylvestre, Guy
   La recherche en littérature canadienne-
     française, 207, 267, 351
Symons, Thomas H.B., 254, 276, 278,
   279, 293
   Report, 116, 270, 277, 289
   Some Questions of Balance, 116, 270, 277
   To Know Ourselves, 270, 277, 289
Szabo, Franz A.J.
   Austrian Immigration, 58

T

Taché, Eugène, 51
Taché, Joseph-Charles
   Esquisse sur le Canada, 125
   Forestiers et voyageurs, 68
Talon, Jean, 24, 44, 185
   Mémoire, 24
Tanner, Adrian, 203

Tanner, Helen H.
  Settling of North America, 38
Taras, David
  A Passion for Identity, 246
Tardivel, Jules-Paul, 49
Taschereau, Louis-Alexandre, 165
Taschereau, Sylvie
  L'histoire de l'immigration, 191, 193
Taylor, Charles
  Multiculturalism, 327, 389
Taylor, Elizabeth, 127
Taylor, James R.
  Communication Technologies, 355
Taylor, J.H., 304
  Canada's Foreign Policy, 304
Taylor, M. Brook
  Canadian History, 316
  Promoters, Patriots, and Partisans, 104
Teeple, Gary
  Capitalism and the National Question, 271
Teit, James, 101-2
Tessier, Albert
  Les Forges du Saint-Maurice, 180
Theall, Donald F.
  The Virtual McLuhan, 231, 232
Thelen, David
  Of Audiences, Borderlands, and Comparisons, 18
Thériault, Yves, 350
  Agaguk, 210
  Ashini, 210
  Les vendeurs du temple, 350
Thibault, Charles, 107
Thierry, Augustin, 106
Thomas, Clara, 267, 281, 393
  Canadian Social Mythologies, 80
Thomas, William I.
  The Polish Peasant, 305
Thompson, E.P., 19, 319-20
Thompson, Tom, 223
Thomson, Colin A.
  Blacks in Deep Snow, 54
Thomson, Roy (Baron Thomson of Fleet), 234
Thwaites, Reuben Gold
  Jesuit Relations, 13
Tiffin, Helen
  The Empire Writes Back, 350

Tilly, Louise, 382
  Women, 333-34
  Women Work and Family, 333
Timlin, Mabel F.
  Social Sciences in Canada, 328
Tinker, Hugh
  Indians in Southeast Asia, 56
Tippett, Maria, 240, 349
  Making Culture, 70, 82, 220, 240, 254
  Writing, 349
Tobias, John L.
  Canada's Subjugation of the Plains Cree, 338
Tocqueville, Alexis de
  L'Ancien Régime et la Révolution, 331
Todd, Alpheus
  On the Establishment of Free Public Libraries, 134
Todd, W.B.
  Inquiry, 31
Todorov, Tzvetan
  Conquest of America, 22
Toews, Miriam
  A Complicated Kindness, 367
Tolmie Adam J.
  Roughing It on the Rails, 215
Torpey, John
  Invention of the Passport, 364
Tovell, Freeman M.
  Recent Growth of Interest, 296
Toye, William
  Oxford Companion, 68, 104
Toynbee, Arnold, 164
Tracy, James D.
  Handbook of European History, 364
Traill, Catherine Parr, 69-70
Treichler, Paula
  Cultural Studies, 18, 27
Trémaudan, Auguste-Henri de
  Histoire de la nation métisse, 41
Tremblay, Arthur, 284
  La recherche pédagogique, 162, 284
Tremblay, Marc-Adélard, 335
Tremblay, Maurice
  L'Enseignement des sciences sociales, 171
Trigger, Bruce G.
  Children of Aataentsic, 203
  Natives and Newcomers, 338
  The Historians' Indian, 103, 203, 338

Trofimenkoff, Susan Mann, 43
  Dream of a Nation, 49, 88, 137
  Neglected Majority, 333
Troper, Harold
  None Is Too Many, 152
Trotter, Reginald, 182
Trudeau, Pierre Elliott, 244, 263, 350, 351
  La Grève de l'amiante, 263
Trudel, Marcel, 317
  Canadian History Textbooks, 141, 266
Truesdell, Leon E.
  The Canadian-Born in the United States, 183
Turcotte, Louis-Philippe, 108
Turgeon, Pierre, 37
Turner, Frederick Jackson, 188
Turner, Graeme
  British Cultural Studies, 19
Turpel, Mary Ellen
  Patriarchy and Paternalism, 118
Tuttle, Charles R.
  An Illustrated History, 109
Two Axe Earley, Mary
  Ethnicity and Femininity, 142, 338
Tye, Diane
  Critiques from the Margin, 324
  Lessons, 324
  Undisciplined Women, 102, 201, 324
Tylor, E.B, 17
Tyrrell, Ian
  The Threat of De-Provincializing U.S. History, 360

U

Underhill, Frank H., 52, 119, 151, 152, 188, 190, 195
  Canadian Political Parties, 191
  In Search of Canadian Liberalism, 191
Upton, Leslie F.S.
  Micmacs and Colonists, 338

V

Vachon, Georges-André, 65
Vallières, Gaëtan, 393
Vallières, Pierre
  Nègres blancs d'Amérique, 261

Vance, Michael E.
  Myth, 86
Vancouver, George, 27-28
Vangelisti, Guglielmo
  Gli Italiani in Canada, 193
Van Kirk, Sylvia
  Many Tender Ties, 338
  Toward a Feminist Perspective in Native History, 338
Van Kleeck, Mary, 167
Varley, Frederick, 223
Vecoli, Rudolph J.
  Invention of Ethnicity: A Perspective from the U.S.A., 205, 385
Verduyn, Christl
  Disjunctions, 356
  Reconstructing Canadian Literature, 356
Verma, Anil
  Restructuring Work, 333
Verne, Jules
  Le Tour du monde, 228
Vertovec, Steven
  South Asians Overseas, 56
Vézina, François, 179
Vézina, Raymond
  Aspects de l'Enseignement, 96
Viatte, Auguste
  Histoire littéraire, 261
Vibert, Elizabeth
  Reading Beyond Words, 205, 339, 349
Vickers, Jill, 278, 279
  Another Look at Interdisciplinarity, 278, 358
  Politics as if Women Mattered, 330, 333
  Thirty-Five Years on the Beaver Patrol, 279
  Where Is the Discipline in Interdisciplinarity, 288, 358
Viger, Jacques, 106, 113
  Néologie canadienne, 106
Villeneuve, Normand
  Le Mythe, 80
Vipond, Mary, 240
  The Nationalist Network, 240, 241, 243, 349
Vogel, Susan Carter, 217
Voisey, Paul, 381
  Vulcan (Alberta), 381
Voltaire, 108

W

Wadland, John H., 279, 281, 393
Core Courses, 358
Inter-Theoretical Canadian Studies, 358
Voices in Search of a Conversation, 358
Walaszek, Adam, 307
Walden, Keith
The Great March, 74
Walker, James W.St.G., 103
Racial Discrimination, 53
The Indian, 103
Walker, Robert H., 374
Wall, Sharon, 70
Wallace, Anthony F.C.
Rockdale, 381
Wallace, Elizabeth, 187
Wallot, Jean-Pierre, 318, 319
International Circumstances, 319
Le Canada français, 320
Patronage, 319
Un Québec qui bougeait, 319
Walsum, Sarah van, 307
Warburton, T. Rennie
The Role of National Courses, 282
Ward, W. Peter
Japanese in Canada, 196
White Canada Forever, 196
Warkentin, John, 279, 280, 328, 393
A Regional Geography of Canada, 129,
280, 328
Canada Before Confederation, 124, 328
Canada: A Geographical Interpretation,
129, 280
Canada: A Regional Geography, 129, 280
Warley, Linda
Cultural Literacy, 2, 70, 372
Warner, Jack, 237
Warrian, Peter
Essays, 320
Watkins, Mel, 325
Innis at 100, 244, 325
Watson, James Wreford, 280, 294
Weaver, Kent R.
Solitudes, 326
Weber, Max, 160
Weil, François
Canada et Etats-Unis, 106, 303, 317

Weir, R. Stanley, 249
Wells, H.G., 143
Westfall, William
Perspectives, 34, 178-79
Whalley, George
Writing in Canada, 261
Whitaker, Reg
Cold War Canada, 238
R.C.M.P. Security Bulletins, 74
Whitaker, Reginald
Liberal Corporatist Ideas, 189
White, Richard
Is there a North American History?, 122
Roots of Dependency, 338
Whitfield, Agnès
La francophonie ontarienne, 353
Whitton, Charlotte, 151, 153
Whorf, Benjamin Lee, 362
Wiggin, Pamela
Social Sciences in Canada, 326
Wilkinson, Lori
Citizenship Debates, 388
William III, 43
Williams, Raymond, 366-67
Culture and Society, 18-19
Keywords, 19
Willis, Paul, 366
Culture, Media, Language, 19
Profane Culture, 18
Wilson, Alan, 279
Canadian Studies, 279
Wilson, Cairine, 116, 240
Wilson, Donald C.
Portrayal, 292
Wilson, Douglas, 109
Wilson, Woodrow, 149
Windsor, Kenneth N.
Historical Writing, 109, 111, 112
Winks, Robin W.
Blacks in Canada, 53
Winter, Harry, 236
Wiseman, Adele
The Sacrifice, 216
Withrow, W.H., 140
Wolf, Eric
Europe and the People Without History,
338
Wolf, Hubert, 98

Wolfe, Tom, 232
Wolodko, Brenda
  Canadian Picture Books, 264
Wonders, William C.
  Canadian Regions, 34
Wong, Lloyd L.
  Home Away from Home, 390
Wood, Gordon S.
  Imagined Histories, 150
Wood, Joanna, 80
Wood, Samuel T., 148
Wood, Wyn, 54
Woodcock, George, 261, 349
  Meeting of the Muses, 349
Woodhouse, A.S.P.
  The Humanities in Canada, 164
Woods, John
  Reflections, 271, 277
Woodsworth, James S., 73, 190, 195
  My Neighbour, 195
  Strangers Within Our Gates, 82, 192,
    193, 195
Woodward, David
  Cartography, 122
Wray, Matt
  The Making and Unmaking of Whiteness,
    373
Wright, Donald
  Canadian Historical Association, 112
  Gender and the Professionalization of
    History, 110, 160, 186
Wright, Ian
  Challenges & Prospects, 348
Wright, J.F.C.
  The Lucas, Louise Story, 240
Wrong, George M., 111-2, 114, 168
  Chronicles of Canada, 111

Y

Young, Brian
  George-Etienne Cartier, 312
Young, Charles H., 197
Young, Kathryn A.
  '... sauf les perils et fortunes de la mer',
    318-19
Younge, Eva R., 159
Yuzyk, Paul, 200

Z

Zaslow, Morris, 185
  Opening of the Canadian North, 76
  Reading the Rocks, 125-30
Zeller, Suzanne
  Land of Promise, 188
Zetterstedt, Johan Wilhelm, 125
  Resa genom Umeå Lappmarker i
    Vesterbottens Län, 125
Ziegler, Olive, 195
Zitelmann, Thomas
  'Area Studies' in den USA, 16, 167
Znaniecki, Florian
  The Polish Peasant, 305
Zubrzycki, B.J.
  Polacy w Kanadzie, 193